ADVENTURES
IN
AMERICAN DIPLOMACY
1896-1906

REPRINTS IN GOVERNMENT AND POLITICAL SCIENCE

Editor-in-Chief: Richard H. Leach
DUKE UNIVERSITY

ADVENTURES
IN
AMERICAN DIPLOMACY
1896-1906
(From Unpublished Documents)

BY

ALFRED L. P. DENNIS

PROFESSOR OF MODERN HISTORY AT CLARK UNIVERSITY
AUTHOR OF "FOREIGN POLICIES OF SOVIET RUSSIA," ETC.

E. P. DUTTON & COMPANY
681 FIFTH AVENUE   NEW YORK

JOHNSON REPRINT CORPORATION   JOHNSON REPRINT COMPANY LTD.
111 Fifth Avenue, New York, N. Y. 10003   Berkeley Square House, London, W. 1X6BA

Adventures in American Diplomacy
Copyright, 1928, by E. P. Dutton & Company
All Rights Reserved : : Printed in U.S.A.

First reprinting, 1969, Johnson Reprint Corporation
Printed in the United States of America

TO

HAROLD W. V. TEMPERLEY

OF CAMBRIDGE UNIVERSITY

THIS FRIENDLY TRIBUTE TO HIS SCHOLARSHIP

PREFACE

THIS book is based largely on unpublished material. The Olney Papers and, for consultation, the Roosevelt Papers at the Congressional Library have been open to me; and I wish to thank Mrs. Roosevelt for her gracious courtesy and Dr. Charles Moore of the Manuscripts Division for his assistance to me. Mrs. Wadsworth with rare generosity has given me free access to her father's papers and in the unpublished papers of John Hay I am sure that the reader will find much to interest him. The Department of State has given me access to its archives and permission to use the documents which appear in the following pages; I wish to thank the officials of the Department for their unfailing assistance and courtesy.

I am indebted to the authorities of Clark University for their kind assistance; indeed it is unfortunate that I cannot acknowledge in rotation the great services of the many friends who have shown interest in this book. I wish particularly to thank my colleagues, Professor Blakeslee and Professor Langer, and British friends, including Dr. I. F. D. Morrow, who have patiently read the manuscript. My wife has typed the entire book and has given me the benefit of her literary criticism. To the many typists who have helped me in the copying of material I am also much indebted.

I have tried to make this book impartial though it is hard in a time of such crowded adventure. The United States was unexpectedly called to take a larger part in international affairs than she had hitherto filled and before the decade,

1896–1906, was ended we found ourselves one of the few great powers of the world. This rapid rise to high position involving, as it did, the increase of our navy and the assumption of new responsibilities, found the nation unprepared. Such measure of success as we achieved was due in large part to the high example set by the directors of our diplomacy at Washington. The story of their endeavors I have tried to give with the thought that it would interest the general reader and that, at all events, this book might serve as a guide to other students of the subject.

A. L. P. D.

October 1st, 1927.
The Cosmos Club,
Washington, D. C.

TABLE OF CONTENTS

	PAGE
Preface	vii
Table of Abbreviations	xi
Chapter I America and the World Outside	3
Chapter II The Venezuelan Boundary Dispute	17
Notes to Chapter II	47
Appendices to Chapter II	51
Chapter III The Spanish-American War	63
Notes to Chapter III	88
Appendices to Chapter III	93
Chapter IV Hawaii and Samoa	101
Notes to Chapter IV	111
Appendices to Chapter IV	113
Chapter V Anglo-American Relations	117
Notes to Chapter V	130
Appendices to Chapter V	132
Chapter VI The Alaskan Boundary	134
Notes to Chapter VI	146
Appendices to Chapter VI	149
Chapter VII The Canal Treaties	156
Notes to Chapter VII	166
Appendices to Chapter VII	168
Chapter VIII The Open Door in China	170
Notes to Chapter VIII	196
Appendices to Chapter VIII	202
Chapter IX The Boxer Movement	215
Notes to Chapter IX	248
Appendices to Chapter IX	254

	PAGE
Chapter X Cuba and the Caribbean	259
Notes to Chapter X	279
Chapter XI The European Powers and Venezuela	282
Notes to Chapter XI	301
Appendices to Chapter XI	304
Chapter XII The Panama Canal	309
Notes to Chapter XII	336
Appendices to Chapter XII	342
Chapter XIII The Far East, 1901–1904	346
Notes to Chapter XIII	368
Appendices to Chapter XIII	373
Chapter XIV The Portsmouth Treaty	389
Notes to Chapter XIV	420
Appendices to Chapter XIV	425
Chapter XV Jews in Rumania and Russia	430
Notes to Chapter XV	436
Chapter XVI African Questions	437
Notes to Chapter XVI	445
Chapter XVII Americans in Turkey	447
Notes to Chapter XVII	466
Appendices to Chapter XVII	469
Chapter XVIII Arbitration and the Hague Conferences	472
Notes to Chapter XVIII	484
Chapter XIX The Algeciras Conference	485
Notes to Chapter XIX	509
Appendices to Chapter XIX	513
Chapter XX Patronage and Persons	518
Notes to Chapter XX	530
Index	531

LIST OF ABBREVIATIONS

D. S. Archives of the State Department.

F R. Papers relating to the Foreign Relations of the United States. Washington (in progress).

G. P. Die grosse Politik der europäischen Kabinette, 1871–1914. Berlin, 1922–27.

H. P. Hay Papers, in the possession of Mrs. J. W. Wadsworth, Jr., Washington.

O. C. Olney Collection at the Manuscripts Division of the Library of Congress, Washington.

R. P. Roosevelt Papers at the Manuscripts Division of the Library of Congress, Washington.

ADVENTURES
IN
AMERICAN DIPLOMACY
1896-1906

ADVENTURES IN AMERICAN DIPLOMACY

CHAPTER I

AMERICA AND THE WORLD OUTSIDE

IN March, 1926, when I wrote a brief sketch of John Hay for the series, *The Secretaries of State and Their Diplomacy,* the material open to me was so large that it was suggested that I might write a book dealing with certain features of the diplomacy of the decade, 1896–1906. This was a time when the United States ventured forth on seas that were unknown to the vast majority of Americans. Maps and charts were often lacking; sailing directions were sometimes misunderstood; and the companions on the voyage were unfamiliar. Yet partly by luck, partly by commonsense, and partly by power the United States came through to a partnership in the world's affairs which was strange to most Americans and remarkable in the eyes of mankind.

In 1896 the United States was not "isolated." The earliest European settlements in America had given birth to the world politics of the sixteenth and seventeenth centuries. The war which won American independence was in one sense part of the great European international struggle which reached a stage at Waterloo. Indeed America was born amid the clash of foreign policies, and as we look back it is easy to see that Napoleon Bonaparte was the great figure in history whose shadow stretched across the Atlantic. The nineteenth century laid on the United States the great task of the development of her domain, yet foreign affairs were on her doorstep. Already America had played a part in the international affairs of the century. Small wonder that she played a larger part at the turning point of the century. Nevertheless, when England and Germany and France and Russia were playing for great stakes the astonishing thing is that the United States did not join them.

Fortunately, the conviction remained that America was set apart, aloof from other nations, to work out in her own way the rôle that she was to play. We were indeed sharers in the affairs of the world, yet we did not appreciate it. America was often unaware of the effect of her opinion and ultimate power. Ignorant of American history, entangled in the politics of the village pump, the United States was chiefly concerned in the development of the Mississippi Valley and beyond. So America was often unconscious of European politics. Certainly she was indifferent to diplomatic questions. Too often she was apt to thank God for the Atlantic Ocean, which she imagined was a barrier against the old world and its troubles. Yet that ocean was not a barrier but a highway. Soon the Pacific Ocean also was to become a second passage way along which American ships and goods made their way to Asia.

Furthermore, there had come to America from foreign countries an increasing number of immigrants who were soon to become American citizens. These had brought with them in their packs and bundles some of the prejudices and national feelings of the lands of their birth. There was much talk in the presidential elections of 1896, 1900, and 1904 of the Irish vote, of the German vote; and soon there were to be other groups as well. All of these factors exerted at times a certain amount of vociferous influence on American affairs. Their power, however, has been much exaggerated by the local politicians for, after all, American policies were, in the last analysis, determined and led by Americans who had the English-speaking sense for truth. The notion that American policy was not directed by American minds falls by the board as we see that President Cleveland and President Roosevelt were successively at the helm.

There is a chance that before I plunge into the real subject of this introductory chapter I may be able to convey the impression which I have of the Americans of importance who exerted a directing influence on our foreign policy. This must be in brief fashion, for the tug of policies which are larger than men is always at my pen. As the years go by we come to a better understanding of President Cleveland. He stands first as staunch American, as honest as can be, determined that American interests and ideals should not suffer. His lieutenant, Secretary Olney, was an able lawyer but not a diplomat. His bold interpretation of the Monroe doctrine was matched by his love for international accord. President McKinley was always genial and eager to protect and to promote what he thought were the best interests and obligations of the country. The decisions made in his day have exerted a decisive influence on our national history. Secretary Day was a tenant of brief stay, yet his devotion to duty in a period of great difficulty—that of the Spanish-American War—should win for him a larger place than has ordinarily been given. The services of Professor John Bassett Moore also are welcome proof of the fact that the Department of State could depend on the best advice as to international law.

Then comes Secretary Hay, whose reputation for long years has stood so high. He was under President McKinley the real director of our foreign policies. He had the great ability to make use of what came to his hand and to judge of the proper time and occasion for their employment. An aristocrat, a poet, an author, he brought to his task the traditions of an even greater period of American history, that of Lincoln and the Civil War. His experience abroad had ripened him; but it had not quenched his passion for righteousness and his indignation at wrong done to others. His charm and his ability were marked; his friendship conferred distinction on any man.

That friendship he gave in unstinted ways to President Roosevelt. As we shall see again in the last chapter of this book, the personal qualities and characteristics of all of these men played an important part in our history. In the case of President Roosevelt this was clear. His robust energy and the vital elements in his mind and body were factors which no one could ignore. His apparent impulsiveness and the impetuous way in which he would deal with matters have, I think, obscured in some ways the essentially conservative quality of his statesmanship. As we see the various decisions which he made during this period, the vigor of his judgment becomes apparent. He made his mistakes, as all men must, but they were not mistakes of the heart. He brought to our diplomatic policy courage, when it was needed, and yet withal a caution and a vision which are remarkable. As the years passed and as Secretary Hay's health began to give way, President Roosevelt naturally became more and more his own Secretary of State. Even with the appointment of Secretary Root his hand was still on the wheel. The admirable qualities of Secretary Root, indeed, scarcely come into our survey for most of his successes lie beyond the period to which this book is strictly limited.

Such brief notice of these men helps to explain why so much use is made of quotation. It seemed as though the actual language of the participants in the great events might help to bring out their personal qualities and to enliven the realization of what they were doing. In the appendices to various chapters are further extracts from documents, for the most part unpublished, which may serve, especially for the student, to bring life to momentous policies.

It is a matter of regret that more of these quotations and more of the policies which they illustrate do not touch on the economic aspects of our foreign policy. Within a decade this was to change. As soon as Secretary Root and his successor, Secretary Knox, came to office they recognized strongly that the trade interests of America demanded a policy which should bring out more clearly our commercial relations with the rest of the world. If we except the attention paid to the idea of the open door, and to the development of the Panama Canal, there does not seem to have been so much interest in the economics of diplomacy. This is unfortunate, for it was primarily through the development of our commercial and financial interests that people began to appreciate the significance of our foreign policy. Yet the beginnings of this may be seen even in the period prior to 1906.

As we shall see later, the lack of a real diplomatic service was a serious handicap to the United States during this decade. We had a few distinguished and capable diplomats abroad, but they were notable chiefly because they were able men, not because of their training. Indeed the haphazard methods of appointment give pause as we consider them. Fortunately, at home in the Department of State we had in Mr. Adee, a permanent official, who served his country unselfishly and with rare distinction. His was the unrecognized and often unknown task of guiding new men along unfamiliar trails. On him fell the burden of the day when his superiors were ill or out of sorts. To his ability and patience, to his whimsical humor, and to his knowledge more than a generation of our representatives abroad are much indebted. When "Adee, acting" was signed to a despatch men knew that affairs were in the hands of a man full of knowledge as well as steeped in diplomatic practice.

It is perhaps fortunate that almost any chapter in this book can be read independently. Each section of this review of our diplomatic adventures stands quite separate; at all events, every two or three chapters furnishes a view of our given policy for the period. Yet, throughout, I have tried to bring out the interdependence of affairs, the close relationship of our foreign programs till, as I hope, the book will be regarded as a compact and united review of our diplomacy for the period. This does not, of course, mean that the various topics have been treated exhaustively. There is an immense amount still to be done, and one of the chief reasons why this book has been written is that it may serve in some fashion as a signpost to materials which should be open to every American student equipped to study them. Furthermore, there is one large body of material which I have intentionally neglected.

This is current opinion as expressed in the press and in periodicals of the time. Rarely have I referred to a newspaper, for I have preferred to quote from biographies or from letters which might define the attitude of men of the day. Yet such a study of public opinion is most important. Even if that opinion is incorrect or at fault, it undoubtedly exercised a great influence and often it was used to further major policies. The truth is that the limits of space imposed a check on such an excursion. The material used in this book is for the most part official or it was written by people in official life. If I can furnish a guide to some of this material, one of my purposes will have been secured. The omission, therefore, of a review of the press of the period is not because I consider it unimportant, but because I recognize that it is so important that it could not be included in this volume.

If we turn the pages of "Life" or "Punch" of more than thirty years ago we can discover at once what changes have affected our clothes and personal appearance. The fashions of the "nineties" have all gone by. So in international relations as viewed by the American of 1895 and in any view of foreign policies as seen in 1907, 1917, or 1927 there are great differences. In 1895 we cared very little for diplomatic questions; we regarded them as of small importance compared with the great political struggle of the day—that over free silver. Our carelessness was matched by our general ignorance of foreign affairs. Yet we were proudly patriotic and we at once caught fire when the dispute regarding the boundary between Venezuela and British Guiana threatened to flame into a controversy between the United States and Great Britain. The story of that quarrel sounds rather dull to our ears today as it is told in Chapter II. It was in truth a lawyer's and surveyor's dispute; but it was the vehicle which for a time drove full tilt against the decorous belief that the days of war between England and America had forever gone by. The statement of the Monroe doctrine, which the slowness of Great Britain forced from Secretary Olney, now stands generally accepted by many Americans and known to the rest of the world. It is, however, one of the ironies of the situation that out of that dispute there came a time of better understanding between the United States and Great Britain.

So we turn now to the meat of the matter. Unless we come to close grasp with the topics which are ahead of us, there is sheer bewilderment. Indeed that bewilderment confronts me at once, for I do not know whether I can make plain to the reader what I have in mind. There were four main fields in which the United States was concerned. These were the maintenance of the Monroe doctrine, the Panama Canal policy, American relations with Europe and our conceptions of Europe at this time, and American policy as to the Far East. If we take them in turn we may be able to get some sort of map, for there is no hero in this book—no person to whom we can reverently turn as the savior of American ideals. Not even President Roosevelt or Secretary Hay stands out as the dominant man. Rather, we find that there were many people who played a part in shaping the policies of the United States. Those of us who have watched the composition of a diplomatic despatch know full well the value of the comment or suggestion made by some one of the many minor people through whose hands the paper has passed. I wish to record my belief in the unknown, unrecognized but invaluable aid which the lesser officials gave to America at this period. So we come to the four main subjects.

I. *The Monroe Doctrine.* This doctrine has become the shibboleth of American foreign policy. The interpretation given to it by Secretary Olney will last in the minds of

Americans for a long time. Yet the twentieth century with its new nationalism will probably see the change which new conditions will inevitably bring about. Senator Bingham of Connecticut once wrote a tiny volume on this subject. I am sorry that he repudiated it in the heat of later opinion. America was so far separated from European opinion when the doctrine was laid down that I think we are apt to forget its true significance. The United States said in 1823 that no more land in America should be acquired by European powers and that the land in this hemisphere was already occupied. It was a signpost that no "squatters" were allowed. As such a notice to the world the Monroe doctrine has remained. Recently the Department of State has said in effect that this is an American doctrine and that no co-operation by other states is desired. I think that is a mistake. I believe in the doctrine of co-operation, and it appears that the sooner the United States recognizes the value and importance of co-operation with the stable and established nations of Latin America the sooner we may come into accord as to our mutual interests.

There is a certain right which the French call *le droit de voisinage,* which gives any state whose orderly life is menaced by the turbulent condition of its neighbor the right to interfere to stop such revolutionary activity. That right exists always; but it is not the Monroe doctrine. Important though that doctrine is, it is not a doctrine of intervention. Indeed the many sins which have been laid at the door of the Monroe doctrine are such as to fill a student of history with regret. The true and correct application of the Monroe doctrine was in 1902. Then the United States had reason to believe that Germany might occupy Venezuelan territory. President Roosevelt said that such occupation would be contrary to the Monroe doctrine. Therein he was right, so the possible danger of a new European establishment in America was averted.

At the same time, President Roosevelt was by no means averse to the establishment in Latin America of a new national state with German approval. He thought that if such a national state should be set up it would, by its orderly processes of government and by its economic prosperity, set a valuable example to Latin America. That state never came into existence, but its establishment might not have involved any invasion of the Monroe doctrine for it would not have involved any European political intervention. In short, Americans have to remember that the Monroe doctrine is not a view of our relations with Latin American states which gives them the right to disregard nationalism. It is really a recognition of nationalism, and it should persuade America to a policy of co-operation to maintain that nationalism.

II. *The Panama Canal policy.* The building of a canal between the Atlantic and Pacific Oceans was of supreme interest to the United States. To that end American foreign policy was bent. It was during this decade, 1896–1906, the principal aim that we had in mind. Through the long negotiations under President McKinley which produced the two successive Hay-Pauncefote canal treaties, the one thought was that a canal should be dug which should be under American direction for the use of the world. As time went on, and as America came to understand the importance of protecting the approaches to the canal, her whole conception of policy shifted. The construction of the canal was chiefly responsible for the American demand that orderly government should prevail in the Caribbean. To this end, American army officers were sent on missions to study out the geography of the neighboring states, and American engineers were employed to survey various routes. Until the economic advantages of the Panama route were determined other ways were carefully studied. It became evident that whichever route was decided on the essential fact was that the approaches to the canal must be safeguarded. Recently the United States has been involved in Nicaragua because of the belief that sooner or later additional accommodation for the increasing tonnage which yearly passes through the Panama Canal must be provided. Whether that may be through the locks in Panama or whether it may be through Nicaragua is still to be seen. The main fact remains that the United States was determined to maintain a route across the isthmus.

To that end there came the long negotiations with Colombia. It appears that President Roosevelt exceeded his authority at the time of the revolution in Panama. Others who differ with me are, however, united with me in supporting the view that Panama was justified in rebellion. As the result, the Republic of Panama was restored to its independent condition and promptly gave to the United States the right to the Canal Zone. Later the United States wisely recognized the interests of Colombia and generously paid to her $25,000,000. From the point of view of economic and political interest, the American policy of maintaining a dominant interest as to the canal seems to me justified for the Panama Canal policy is first of all a policy of national defense.

III. *American Policy as to Europe.* Here certainly is fine confusion. America was established chiefly as a protest against Europe. Most Americans had in 1896 come to feel that there was an antipathy, a dislike between the United States and Europe. Many Americans had left Europe because of oppression and intolerable religious and economic conditions in the lands of their birth. It was only natural that this feeling should exist, for Europe had meant to them a tyranny of which Americans were glad to be rid in a new country of opportunity. As England was the closest European neighbor, America gave to her the most of that antipathy. Yet back of this feeling there was the latent power of a common historical heritage of language, literature, culture, and religion, a conception of law and politics that really bound the United States closer to England than to any other country. There was a habit of English-speaking honesty and fairness that gave to the United States and to Great Britain a common basis for life. From such diverse elements and feelings there naturally came confusion and often misunderstanding.

Fortunately, agreement and accord finally came out of the various disputes in which the two countries were involved. In the Venezuelan boundary dispute, in the negotiations regarding the Panama Canal, in the settlement of the Alaskan boundary, and with respect to China, a common policy was finally secured. In 1906 the United States and Great Britain had made great progress during the decade toward a friendliness which was well founded.

As regards France, American traditions were always more cordial. As America did not have so many points of difference with respect to France, there was far less opportunity for friction. Finally, in 1905 and 1906, the United States, through President Roosevelt, was able to be of real service in promoting a peaceful settlement of the Algeciras Conference.

In the case of Germany, the situation was different. Many Americans had originally come from Germany; they made a most admirable element of the population. The tremendous economic advance which the United States and Germany had both made was, however, a source of danger. The industrial competition of the time produced friction as to tariffs and eager rivalry for fresh markets. Germany was on the hunt for new colonies and settlements. Her navy was soon to develop into a major factor in international affairs. Furthermore, the military traditions of the Empire were in direct opposition to the peaceful ambitions of the great majority of Germans. For such military ideals the United States also had small sympathy. Consequently, with the Spanish-American War there came a feeling of restlessness and of uncertainty as to German intentions for the future.

The character of the German Emperor likewise gave pause. He seemed to be an unstable element in the international situation. As President Roosevelt said, he was too "jumpy," too uncertain. In 1902 the United States had to give a warning to Germany as to the Monroe doctrine. Thereafter American relations with Germany had improved for a time. President Roosevelt and the Kaiser became quite cordial in their feelings. Yet the German desire that the United States should be drawn into European affairs was resisted. At the end of this period the United States had refused to take more than a merely casual part in maintaining general peace in Europe. In fact, Germany found that the United States could not be used to promote German interests at the Algeciras Conference.

In the case of Russia, the situation was again different. There was much talk of the history of the friendly relations between the United States and Russia. Yet the cordial feeling between the two countries was largely due to the fact that America really knew little of Tsarist Russia. As the United States came to find how far apart were the ideals and standards of conduct of the two states, there was inevitable friction. In the Far East a situation developed which might have led to serious trouble. At Washington President Roosevelt and Secretary Hay both found that small reliance could be placed on Russia's word. Yet the United States was eager to assist the re-establishment of peace between Japan and Russia. The Treaty of Portsmouth was, therefore, a sign of the essential peacefulness of American policy. Soon, however, the United States was to find the situation in the Far East was still full of difficulties. These difficulties do not fall within the period 1896–1906, so we can call a halt for the time.

IV. *American Policy with Regard to the Far East.* The United States has for many years favored the establishment and maintenance of stable, strong national states in the Far East. To that end she has supported the ideal of the entity of China, the maintenance of her integrity, and the policy of the open door. As American trade and interests in the

Far East have developed, the idea has grown that those interests could be best promoted through the existence of orderly government in China. To this end American foreign policy has been exerted, and in the period of this book some of the notable illustrations of this policy have been apparent.

However, the United States has followed this policy not by intervention but by diplomacy. It is doubtful whether public opinion in America would have justified war during this decade for the maintenance of this policy. Only in the case of the siege of the legations at Peking was the employment of force regarded as right. What the future may hold forth is, of course, doubtful. Yet even today the general policy of most nations toward China is that of the United States.

In 1898 the partition of China seemed almost inevitable; but because of European rivalries and thanks also to American patience and persuasion China was maintained. Such a diplomacy was difficult to follow at times. The importance of the open door policy has been somewhat exaggerated; there was often a lack of decision in respect to American policy as to the Far East. Yet America was very fortunate on the whole. The protection of American nationals and property in China was, of course, a difficult task; but of America's generous policy there can be no question.

As regards Japan, the friendly relations existing between her and the United States during this period are marked. In the Philippines and concerning Korea the two countries came to a real understanding. It is possible that the United States did not quite appreciate the full meaning and bearing of Japanese foreign policy during this decade; but America was really satisfied with the Anglo-Japanese Alliance in 1905. She wished Japan God-speed on her new career.

Such a brief summary of American foreign policy leaves one almost breathless: from belligerency toward Great Britain in 1896 to a hearty co-operation with her in 1906; from a traditional and indiscriminating friendship with Tsarist Russia prior to 1899 to distrust and dislike of Russian policies in 1905; from aroused anger against German ventures in 1898 and in 1902 to cordial relations with the Kaiser in 1905. Thus the United States had travelled in a fashion that amazed Americans. The Panama Canal was begun; the Monroe doctrine was maintained; territory was acquired in the West Indies, in the Pacific and in the Philippines. The navy became a greater factor in the development of national policies; American troops had fought at Santiago in Cuba, at Manila and in China. The policies of the United States were world-wide in 1906. She was now a full partner in the great game of international affairs. Such diplomatic adventures had brought to Americans a keener sense of responsibility and gave them a feeling of power. The future was of course uncertain but nothing could dim the fact that the United States with all her interests and ideals must now play her own part.

CHAPTER II

THE VENEZUELAN BOUNDARY DISPUTE

THE Emperor William II was probably the *deus ex machina* who, unwittingly, acted to relieve the tension between the United States and Great Britain at the start òf 1896. This tension arose from the intervention of the United States in the old boundary dispute between Great Britain and Venezuela. On December 17, 1895, President Cleveland had declared in a message to Congress that it was the duty of the United States to inquire as to the correct frontier to be drawn between Venezuela and British Guiana and to defend its findings. In view of the fact that Great Britain had already refused the friendly mediation of the United States and her suggestions as to arbitration, such a message was pregnant with the possibilities of war. It came as a shock to both countries. As public opinion on both sides of the Atlantic became inflamed, an event in South Africa served to distract British attention from the dispute with America.

This was the Jameson Raid on the territory of the Transvaal. The failure of this foolish and ill-timed scheme was the signal for the German Foreign Office to send an open telegram to President Kruger congratulating him on his success in frustrating Jameson's flagrant attempt. Such untoward action awakened British public opinion to the possibility of trouble with Germany. A flying squadron was at once mobilized defiantly to patrol the Channel as an answer to this provocative attempt by the Kaiser to interfere in South African affairs. Thus opportunity was given in England for reflection during January, 1896, and by early February the danger of actual war between the United States and Great

Britain had disappeared. Meanwhile the discomforted Kaiser mourned the fact that he had not a navy to match that of Great Britain and that he was unable to send German troops to the Transvaal. Thus both feeling and sober reason had shown the essential friendship which existed between America and England.

The dispute as to the proper frontier between Venezuela and British Guiana had lasted for more than half a century. It arose from the increasing claims of Great Britain to territory which was extravagantly claimed by Venezuela. Only in the "eighties" had the appeals of Venezuela to the United States for the use of her good offices to secure the settlement of this boundary question led to any action by the Department of State at Washington. In 1884 and in 1886 somewhat vague instructions had been sent to the American Legation in London which indicated that the United States was interested in the matter. Then early in 1887, Mr. E. J. Phelps, the American Minister in London, was directed to offer arbitration by the United States in case "such arbitration prove acceptable to both parties."[1] To this offer the British Government replied that the attitude which Venezuela had assumed precluded for the present any resort to arbitration.[2] A year later Secretary Bayard again made a more direct offer based on the extension of British claims in the previous year. This offer of arbitration was, however, never presented by Mr. Phelps. The note was printed in our *Foreign Relations* for 1888; Secretary Olney later referred to this despatch; and President Cleveland depended on it in his review of the dispute. But Mr. James in his life of Richard Olney points out that this instruction was not presented to the British Foreign Office. The reasons given for this by Mr. Phelps are to be found in an unpublished document in the appendix to this chapter. Mr. Phelps chose to assert his own judgment as against that of the Secretary of State.[3]

Later in the same year in reply to a question in the House of Commons the Government said that the publication of a map by the Venezuelan authorities did "not confer any title to the territory" in dispute.[4] In 1889 the attempt was made by Venezuela to restore diplomatic relations with Great Britain. The result was the reception of a confidential agent who was presented at the Foreign Office by Mr. Lincoln, the new American Minister in London. Such steps and the conversation of Lord Salisbury in 1890 with Mr. Lincoln all pointed to the amicable settlement as to the disputed territory. Indeed Lord Salisbury impressed Mr. Lincoln with the idea that "if the matter had been entirely new, dissociated from its previous history I [Lincoln] should have felt from his tone that the idea of arbitration in some form to put an end to the boundary dispute was quite agreeable to him."[5]

In the meantime the Venezuelan government had impressed on the United States that "disastrous and fatal consequences would ensue for the independence of South America if, under the pretext of a question of boundaries, Great Britain should succeed in consummating the usurpation of a third part of our territory and therewith a river so important as the Orinoco." Indeed the endeavors of Venezuela to involve the United States in the dispute were constant. On the other hand the British were skeptical as to the stability of the existing Venezuelan government and were ready to discuss the boundary dispute only with respect to territory which lay east of a line drawn fifty years before by a British surveyor, Sir Robert Schomburgk. This line Venezuela did not accept and so nothing resulted from these exchanges.[6]

Thus matters drifted till Secretary Gresham, on July 13, 1894, wrote to Mr. Bayard, who had now become American Ambassador in London, reviewing the problem, and saying: "I commit the matter to your hands, leaving it to you to avail yourself of any convenient opportunity to advance the adjustment of the dispute in question."[7] President Cleveland in his annual message on December 3 said: "I shall renew the efforts heretofore made to bring about a restoration of diplomatic relations between the disputants and to induce a reference to arbitration, a resort which Great Britain so conspicuously favored in principle and respects in practice and which is earnestly sought by her weaker adversary." Congress soon passed a joint resolution favoring the arbitration of the dispute between Great Britain and Venezuela. In transmitting this resolution to Mr. Bayard, Secretary Gresham said that England was "aware of the interest which the Government and people of the United States feel in matters affecting the peace and welfare of the independent States of this hemisphere. While we do not assume to dictate to those States, or to exercise an undue influence over them, as to what their relations with other powers shall be, yet their fortunes have always been an object of solicitude, and we cannot view without anxiety the continuance of disputes in which their peace and happiness are deeply involved." [8]

Lord Kimberley, who had succeeded Lord Rosebery, in March, 1894, as Foreign Secretary, had failed to appreciate the significance of the gradual hardening of official opinion at Washington regarding the boundary dispute. He was not encouraging as to the renewal of negotiations with a view to arbitration and "he said plainly Great Britain would not arbitrate anything that did not assume the Schomburg [sic] line, which gave Great Britain territory at the mouth of the River Orinoco." Later, on February 20, 1895, he said that Great Britain would decline to submit to arbitration the question "of the right to territory long settled and governed as a part of a British Colony" nor was she ready to depart from the Schomburgk or provisional boundary line which had been proclaimed in 1886. Territory to the westward of this line could be submitted to arbitration.[9]

Mr. Bayard in sending this information to Secretary Gresham went out of his way to point out the danger that the impartial offers of the United States would be exposed to in case American citizens should acquire concessions from Venezuela within the disputed area. He added:

The geographical and political relations of the United States to the other States of the Western Hemisphere, give rise to special and strong interests, such as no European Power can be expected to possess on the Western shores of the Atlantic—and the influence of our Government will always be exerted in a friendly manner towards our neighbouring Republics—but if we are to assist them, by the aid and comfort of our moral forces, our disinterestedness must not be open to question in any case where our good offices to effect an amicable and reasonable adjustment of controversies by arbitration are tendered to *both* parties.[10]

At this juncture Secretary Gresham suddenly died on May 28, 1895. His uncouth manners and his earlier Republican politics had not made him popular in Washington, but he was a hard worker and he had spent much time in studying the documents in the Venezuelan case. He was succeeded at the Department of State by the Attorney General, Richard Olney, who was favorably known to the public by his courageous handling of labor disputes and who was also known to be an excellent lawyer. He had regarded himself as counsel for the administration and had already spent some time in study of the Venezuelan tangle. Yet until he came to Washington he was accustomed to move in a narrow Bostonian, professional circle. He was at times lacking in tact and certainly his initial handling of the Venezuelan case did not redound to his permanent credit as a diplomat.

Secretary Olney spent the month of June studying the Venezuelan dispute and in early July he left with President Cleveland the draft of a despatch to Mr. Bayard. This was accepted by the President who wrote on July 7 to Secretary Olney:

I read your deliverance on Venezuelan affairs the day you left it with me. It's the best thing of the kind I have ever read and it leads to a conclusion that one cannot escape if he tries—that is if there is anything in the Monroe Doctrine at all. You show there is a great deal of that and place it I think on better and more defensible ground than any of your predecessors *or mine.*

Of course I have some suggestions to make. I always have. Some of them are not of much account and some of them propose a little softened verbiage here and there.

What day after Wednesday of this week can you come and spend a few hours with me so that we can go over it together? [11]

It should be clear that the decision of the administration vigorously to press the issue on Great Britain was not dependent in any real way on the despatch of 1888 on which Mr. Phelps had refused to act, nor was it due to the advent of Secretary Olney at the Department of State. The decision was that of President Cleveland who showed himself to be blunt, vigorous, and sincere; he had made up his mind that here was a question which should be *settled*. As President Woodrow Wilson later said of the famous message of December, 1895: "There spoke a man as desirous and capable of peace as any in the nation, but accustomed when he spoke at all, to speak his whole mind without reserve, and willing to speak to Europe, if she must hear, as freely as he would speak to his own people." [12]

President Cleveland and his Cabinet were also inclined to suspect the "imperialism" of the greater powers and to sympathize with smaller nations. He believed so strongly in arbitration as a means of settlement of international disputes, that the very term became in his mind a shibboleth of peace. He also felt strongly that the Monroe doctrine was clearly involved by the assertions and practice of the British Foreign Office. Added to this was his impatience of delay and the irritation which naturally arose at the language of the British notes.[13] The fact that Mr. Phelps and Mr. Bayard, two Democratic representatives of the United States in England, had not had that thorough sympathy with the American point of view which would have commended them to his judgment may have had influence. Later Mr. Phelps was to say: "No advocate of the President's proclamation has undertaken to point out how it can affect us, whether the line through the jungle of bushes and water which makes up most of the territory really in dispute, is drawn a few miles one way or the other." Mr. Bayard had already in May, 1895, written: "There is no question now open between the United States and Great Britain that needs any but frank, amicable and just treatment." [14] Certainly Secretary Olney's despatch of July 20, 1895, and President Cleveland's message in December were scarcely "amicable." In other ways as well Mr. Bayard lost the confidence of the administration at Washington. Thus the whole question of responsibility for decision as to American policy in the matter rested with President Cleveland. His lieutenant in that policy was a too earnest Secretary of State who was not accustomed to draft diplomatic notes of importance. That success crowned their efforts was due to good fortune rather than to their methods.

The draft of the note of July 20, 1895, from the pen of Secretary Olney, was revised at a conference at which were present the President and Secretaries Olney, Carlisle, Lamont, Harmon, and Herbert. As McElroy says, "the 'verbiage' had been somewhat softened; but it was still far from soft. Indeed so strong were its terse paragraphs that Mr. Cleveland later christened it 'Olney's twenty-inch gun.' " [15] The facts were those which had been collected by Secretary Gresham; but the argument and method were different. Mrs. Gresham herself said "there was to be no ultimatum as my husband had prepared it." It is possible that Secretary Olney may have regretted some of the phrases of his note, for later he referred to its "bumptious" qualities. Certainly he used expressions and made *obiter dicta* and declarations which no student of history or of the political facts could accept. His statements regarding the Monroe doctrine have been severely criticized by more than one American student chiefly because he sought to give to the Monroe doctrine a place in American public law and a meaning far beyond that warranted by the language of Secretary Adams and President Monroe in 1823 or later by Secretary Webster. The Cleveland-Olney doctrine was a "loose-construction" interpretation of the Monroe doctrine. It was the "doctrine of permanent interest"; it implied the growth and development of a natural American policy. The British interpretation, on the other hand, was a "close-construction" interpretation of the

Monroe doctrine. Those who see in the American formulation of that policy "a wide umbrella" will naturally defend the Cleveland-Olney interpretation. Those who are more historically minded, but who do not necessarily deny the right of the United States to declare such policies as it may see fit, will nevertheless question the validity of the American argument in the summer of 1895.

Secretary Olney in his well-known note reviewed the history of the boundary dispute and declared that the Monroe doctrine was involved in the British assertion as to the frontier. He went on to assert that "today the United States is practically sovereign on this continent, and its fiat is law upon the subjects to which it confines its interposition." He suggested that British Guiana be left without support by Great Britain "to settle the matter with Venezuela." The United States is within its rights in demanding that "the truth shall be ascertained. Being entitled to resent and resist any sequestration of Venezuelan soil by Great Britain, it is necessarily entitled to know whether such sequestration has occurred or is now going on." He continued: "Upon what principle—except her feebleness as a nation—is she [Venezuela] to be denied the right of having the claim heard and passed upon by an impartial tribunal? No reason or shadow of reason appears in all the voluminous literature of the subject. 'It is to be because I will it to be so' seems to be the only justification Great Britain offers." Great Britain "says to Venezuela in substance: 'You can get none of the debatable land by force, because you are not strong enough; you can get none by treaty because I will not agree; and you can take your chance of getting a portion by arbitration only if you first agree to abandon to me such other portion as I may designate.'" Such an attitude is in defiance of that "love of justice and fair play so eminently characteristic of the English race." Then follows the threat that unless Great Britain consents to submit the entire matter to impartial arbitration "the transaction will be regarded as injurious to the interests of the people of the United

States as well as oppressive in itself. . . ." The "honor and welfare of this country are closely identified" with the Monroe doctrine which Great Britain proposes to "ignore." It rests with Congress to determine what should be done in such an issue. But the President wishes to have a reply before Congress next meets. This note was to be left with Lord Salisbury by Mr. Bayard. Then followed a delay of about four months in the British reply.[15]

Mr. Bayard presented the note and reported Lord Salisbury as saying that "it was his desire that Great Britain should be perfectly just in the matter, but that arbitration should only apply to cases where there was a real basis of justice and right—and was not demandable for *any* claim that could be set up—for otherwise a nation might be called upon to arbitrate its very existence."[16] In the meantime Venezuela had raised difficulties about the American suggestion that full diplomatic relations should be re-established with Great Britain. As Mr. Adee, who was Second Assistant Secretary of State, wrote: "We offered to help open the way to an eventual settlement. Venezuela accepted our offer, provided the settlement be virtually settled in advance."[17]

As the months dragged on the press began to take up the matter. Foolish and inaccurate stories were published, particularly in American newspapers. The basis of some of these was, however, correct. What was perilously close to an ultimatum had been presented to Great Britain and no reply had as yet been made. The *Morning Post* on October 11, 1895, said: "Unfortunately there is too much reason to believe that Venezuela is seeking to show that we are not so much concerned with the question of boundary as with that of extending our territorial possessions in South America. Any movement of that kind would naturally be regarded by the United States as an infringement of the Monroe Doctrine. . . ." The *Spectator* of October 26 argued that there was "no such thing known to international law as the Monroe Doctrine. We should like to see a treaty between us and them (The United States) which would guarantee the Monroe Doctrine." Mr. Bayard, meanwhile, was much annoyed by the persistence and imagination of American correspondents in London.[18] He also reported a long conversation with the French Ambassador. France as well had a boundary dispute with Brazil. In the course of their talk both Ambassadors agreed that the "consensus of international opinion should be brought to bear upon Great Britain and Venezuela for the settlement, by peaceful arbitration, of the questions in dispute between them." [19]

As November wore on Secretary Olney became impatient and cabled twice to Mr. Bayard for information. Congress was to meet on December 3 and special request had been made that the British reply should be in time for the President to comment on it. Lord Salisbury, who was much engrossed in the Eastern question at the time, made a mistake as to the date of meeting of Congress and consequently the British reply did not reach Washington in time.[20] President Cleveland, therefore, said to Congress on December 2, 1895, that the conclusions of the despatch of last July to Great Britain

are in substance that the traditional and established policy of this Government is firmly opposed to a forcible increase by any European power of its territorial possessions on this Continent . . . ; that as a consequence the United States is bound to protest against the enlargement of the area of British Guiana in derogation of the rights and against the will of Venezuela; that considering the disparity in strength of Great Britain and Venezuela, the territorial dispute between them can be reasonably settled only by friendly and impartial arbitration." He added: "the despatch in question called upon Great Britain for a definite answer to the question, whether it would or would not submit the territorial controversy . . . in its entirety to impartial arbitration.[21]

On December 4, Mr. Bayard had written to the President regarding Lord Salisbury's two notes of November 26:

The replies of Lord Salisbury to your Venezuelan instructions are in good temper and moderate in tone. Our difficulty lies in the wholly unreliable character of the Venezuelan Rulers and people,—and results in an almost undefinable, and therefore dangerous responsibility for the conduct by them of their own affairs—

I believe, however, that your interposition in this boundary dispute will check efficiently the tendency to 'land grabbing' in South America—which is rather an Anglo-Saxon disposition everywhere.

Arbitration is a most wise and honorable resort—but it must be contracted and executed in a wise and honorable spirit. . . .[22]

This view neither the President nor Mr. Olney shared. In fact the more they studied Lord Salisbury's despatches the more annoyed they apparently became; though it should be said that the President did not study the replies with the same care that Secretary Olney did. President Cleveland prepared his message within less than twenty-four hours after his return to Washington from an outing trip and after an all-night session at its composition. In the main he followed closely his Secretary's recommendations though not his actual composition. He replied by his famous message of December 17, 1895.[23] Secretary Olney had prepared a draft message, portions of which are to be found in the Appendix to this chapter.[24] The concluding paragraphs of the message follow very closely the Olney draft; but President Cleveland said to a friend some time afterwards: "As I watched the sun rise that December morning just as I finished my message I could not have told you which sentences were mine and which were Olney's." The essential passages in the message are as follows:

If a European Power, by the extension of its boundaries, takes possession of the territory of one of our neighboring Republics against its will and in derogation of its rights, it is difficult to see why to that extent such European Power does not thereby attempt to extend its system of government to that portion of this continent which is thus taken. This is the precise action which President Monroe declared to be "dangerous to our peace and safety," and it can make no difference whether the European system is extended by an advance of frontier or otherwise. . . .

The course to be pursued by this Government in view of the present condition does not appear to admit of serious doubt. Having labored faithfully for many years to induce Great Britain to submit this dispute to impartial arbitration, and having been now finally apprized of her refusal to do so, nothing remains but to accept the situation, to recognize its plain requirements and deal with it accordingly. Great Britain's present proposition has never thus far been regarded as admissible by Venezuela, though any adjustment of the boundary which that country may deem for her advantage and may enter into of her own free will cannot of course be objected to by the United States.

Assuming, however, that the attitude of Venezuela will remain unchanged, the dispute has reached such a stage as to make it now incumbent upon the United States to take measures to determine with sufficient certainty for its justification what is the true divisional line between the Republic of Venezuela and British Guiana. The inquiry to that end should of course be conducted carefully and judicially and due weight should be given to all available evidence, records, and facts in support of the claims of both parties.

In order that such an examination should be prosecuted in a thorough and satisfactory manner I suggest that the Congress make an adequate appropriation for the expenses of a Commission, to be appointed by the Executive, who shall make the necessary investigation and report upon the matter with the least possible delay. When such report is made and accepted it will, in my opinion, be the duty of the United States to resist by every means in its power as a willful aggression upon its rights and interests, the appropriation by Great Britain of any lands or the exercise of governmental jurisdiction over any territory which, after investigation, we have determined of right belongs to Venezuela.

In making these recommendations I am fully alive to the responsibility incurred, and keenly realize all the consequences that may follow.

I am nevertheless firm in my conviction that while it is a grievous thing to contemplate the two great English-speaking peoples of the world as being otherwise than friendly competitors in the onward march of civilization, and strenuous and worthy rivals in all the arts of peace, there is no calamity which a great nation can invite which equals that which follows a supine submission to wrong and injustice and the consequent loss of national self-respect and honor beneath which are shielded and defended a people's safety and greatness.[25]

We must now examine the main contentions of Lord Salisbury. He denied in the first place that the Monroe doctrine was applicable to the present dispute and questioned Secretary Olney's interpretation of that doctrine. Secretary Olney by his rash assumptions and by his arguments which had included several points not germane to the Venezuelan boundary dispute had exposed himself to Lord Salisbury's incisive "close-construction" methods of argumentation.

Thus the language and circumstances of President Monroe's message were analyzed and it was stated that the "disputed frontier of Venezuela has nothing to do with any of the questions dealt with by President Monroe." The claim made by the United States that "when a European Power has a frontier difference with a South American community, the European Power shall consent to refer that controversy to arbitration" was a "novel prerogative." The United States did not assert nor claim any responsibility for the action of any of these Latin-American communities nor "can it undertake to protect them from the consequences attaching to any misconduct of which they may be guilty toward other nations."

Lord Salisbury continued:

I will not now enter into a discussion of the merits of this method of terminating international differences. It has proved itself valuable in many cases; but it is not free from defects, which often operate as a serious drawback on its value. It is not always easy to find an arbitrator who is competent, and who, at the same time, is wholly free from bias; and the task of assuring compliance with the Award when it is made is not exempt from difficulty. It is a mode of settlement of which the value varies much according to the nature of the controversy to which it is applied, and the character of the litigants who appeal to it. Whether, in any particular case, it is a suitable method of procedure is generally a delicate and difficult question. The only parties who are competent to decide that question are the two parties whose rival contentions are in issue. The claim of a third nation, which is unaffected by the controversy, to impose this particular procedure on either of the two others, cannot be reasonably justified, and has no foundation in the law of nations.

In the remarks which I have made, I have argued on the theory that the Monroe Doctrine in itself is sound. I must not, however, be understood as expressing any acceptance of it on the part of Her Majesty's Government. It must always be mentioned with respect, on account of the distinguished statesman to whom it is due, and the great nation who have generally adopted it. But international law is founded on the general consent of nations; and no statesman, however eminent, and no nation, however powerful, are competent to insert into the code of international law a novel principle which was never recognized before, and which has not since been accepted by the Government of any other country. The United States have a right, like any other nation, to interpose in any controversy by which their own interests are affected; and they are the judge whether those interests are touched, and in what measure they should be sustained. But their rights are in no way strengthened or extended by the fact that the controversy affects some territory which is called America.

Secretary Olney had referred to the three thousand miles of ocean as a physical fact which makes "any permanent political union between a European and American State unnatural and inexpedient. . . . Thus far we have been spared the burdens and evils of immense standing armies and all the other accessories of huge warlike establishments; and the exemption has highly contributed to our national greatness and wealth as well as to the happiness of every citizen. But with the Powers of Europe permanently encamped on American soil, the ideal conditions we have thus far enjoyed cannot be expected to continue." Lord Salisbury replied:

The necessary meaning of these words is that the union between Great Britain and Canada; between Great Britain and Jamaica and Trinidad; between Great Britain and British Honduras or British Guiana are "inexpedient and unnatural." President Monroe disclaims any such inference from his doctrine; but in this as in other respects Mr. Olney develops it. He lays down that the inexpedient and unnatural character of the union between a European and American State is so obvious that it "will hardly be denied." Her Majesty's Government are prepared emphatically to deny it on behalf of both the British and American people who are subject to her crown. They maintain that the union between Great Britain and her territories in the Western Hemisphere is both natural and expedient. They fully concur with the views which President Monroe apparently entertained, that any disturbance of the existing territorial distribution in that hemisphere by any fresh acquisitions on the part of any European State would be a highly inexpedient change. But they are not prepared to admit that the recognition of that expediency is clothed with the sanction which belongs to a doctrine of international law. They are not prepared to admit that the interests of the United States are necessarily concerned in every frontier dispute which may arise between any two of the States who possess dominion in the Western Hemisphere; and still less can they accept the doctrine that the United States are entitled to claim that the process of arbitration shall be applied to any demand for the surrender of territory which one of these States may make against another. . . .

The second Salisbury note reviewed again the history of the Venezuelan boundary dispute but with less accuracy and with a certain lack of appreciation of the essential questions involved. He concluded:

> They [Great Britain] have, on the contrary, repeatedly expressed their readiness to submit to arbitration the conflicting claims of Great Britain and Venezuela to large tracts of territory which from their auriferous nature are known to be of almost untold value. But they cannot consent to entertain, or to submit to the arbitration of another Power or of foreign jurists, however eminent, claims based on the extravagant pretensions of Spanish officials in the last century, and involving the transfer of large numbers of British subjects, who have for many years enjoyed the settled rule of a British colony, to a nation of different race and language, whose political system is subject to frequent disturbance, and whose institutions as yet too often afford very inadequate protection to life and property. No issue of this description has ever been involved in the questions which Great Britain and the United States have consented to submit to arbitration, and Her Majesty's Government are convinced that in similar circumstances the Government of the United States would be equally firm in declining to entertain proposals of such a nature. . . .[25]

Complaint was later made by President Andrew D. White of Cornell that the Salisbury despatches were written in Salisbury's "cynical, 'Saturday-Review,' high-tory way."[26] Such criticism seems unwarranted. Lord Salisbury's style was cool and incisive; but his language gave the same impression as had Lord Kimberley's in 1894. That ancient squire at the Foreign Office was imbued with Palmerstonian traditions yet was wont to "embark on an account of the ravages wrought among trees by a great gale in Norfolk" while business waited.[27] Lord Salisbury was not less leisurely; but his state papers were on the whole closely argued statements of what he sincerely believed. That his despatches were "intensely disappointing" to President Cleveland can well be believed; but that the President, a few days later, should write to Mr. Bayard as he did is puzzling. His message had been pregnant with war. It was so interpreted by Wall Street and a large part of the American people. It had created intense excitement. Yet President Cleveland wrote:

> Great Britain says she has a flawless case. Our interest in the question led us to ask her to exhibit that case in a tribunal above all others recognized as a proper one for that purpose; and this was done to avoid a wrong procedure on our part in a matter we could not pass by.
>
> Great Britain refused our request. What is to be done? We certainly ought not, we certainly can not abandon the case because she says she is right, nor because she refuses arbitration. We do not threaten nor incite war because she refuses—far from it. We do not propose to proceed to extremities, leaving open any chance that can be guarded against, of making a mistake on our part as to the facts. So instead of threatening war for not arbitrating, we simply say that inasmuch as Great Britain will not aid us in fixing the facts, we will not go to war but do the best we can to discover the true state of facts for ourselves, with all the facilities at our command. When with all this, we become as certain as we can be, in default of Great Britain's co-operation, that she has seized territory and superseded the jurisdiction of Venezuela—that is a different matter. . . .[28]

There was "sturdy Americanism in every line" of the message. The critics, however, may well point out as does Mr. James Ford Rhodes that as "an assertion and exposition of the Monroe Doctrine it has to my mind the fatal defect of applying that doctrine to a mere boundary dispute between a European and an American power. A careful reading of Monroe's statement and Webster's exposition of it convinces me that it did not apply to the controversy in regard to the Venezuelan boundary." [29] Whether this be true or not the panic which now affected the business world was real and intense. The President's message was, perhaps, only the excuse for such a financial crisis rather than its sole cause but the message acted like a "bomb-shell." Mr. Depew has recorded the impression in Wall Street:

> I dined on Saturday night with a lot of financiers, among them Morgan, Lanier, and Sturgis, President of the Stock Exchange, and they all believed on Monday that the frightened English investor and European holders of our securities would be tumbling them across the Atlantic at a rate which would take out all the gold from the Treasury to pay for them; that they would find no market here capable of buying them, and so they would sell for nothing; that they would cramp the banks; that the loans would all be called in and no new

ones made; that everybody owing money would fail in business, and that we were on the eve of a financial cataclysm the like of which had never been witnessed. . . .[30]

We must also remember that within a few months American politics were to be convulsed with the battle of silver versus gold and that Wall Street was to be held up to ridicule by the adherents of Mr. Bryan. In "Coin's Financial School," that popular pamphlet of the time, the possibility of war with England was hailed with light-heartedness. It declared: "A war with England would be the most popular war ever waged on the face of the earth. If it be true that she can dictate the money of the world and thereby create world-wide misery it would be the most just war ever waged by man."[31] Such support was not, however, welcome to the administration; it revealed the ignorance of the public as to international affairs and was typical of "America the unready." The real facts as to the relative preparedness of the United States and Great Britain on January 1, 1896, are more eloquent. The American army consisted of 25,000 men and 2,160 officers. The regular army of England consisted of 147,959 and 7,496 officers. The United States had 6 battleships (of which only one was really first-class), 7 first-class cruisers, and 3 torpedo craft with a total personnel for the entire navy of 12,656 men. Great Britain had on the other hand 44 battleships, 41 first-class cruisers, and 136 torpedo craft, and the entire navy was manned by 83,400 men. What chance did the United States have in the event of war?

From another American source, from a loyal supporter of President Cleveland, Professor John Bassett Moore, the most distinguished international lawyer of the time, there had come warning. Professor Moore had written about December 10:

> I am apprehensive that, unless great judgment is exercised, the President's announcement will prove to have started us on a course that involves not only the abandonment of all our traditions, but also our participation in numberless quarrels.
> The statement that the question can be reasonably settled only

by such arbitration as Venezuela proposes, certainly was not based on any examination of the merits of the subject.

The whole system of arbitration pre-supposes that nations will be reasonable in their claims. The claim of Venezuela to all territory west of the Essequibo is not a scrupulous claim. . . . Instead of asserting that arbitration is the only reasonable way of settling the question, I should say that it would be a very unsatisfactory way of attempting it; and in so saying I do not forget that Lord Granville once consented to lump boundary and all other questions in a general arbitration.

We have arbitrated boundary disputes, and so has Great Britain, but never, so far as I am informed, where a line had not previously been agreed upon by direct negotiation. Governments are not in the habit of resigning their functions so completely into the hands of arbitrators as to say, "we have no boundaries; make some for us. . . ." It would be at least unusual to leave it to arbitrators to make a boundary.

. . . Boundaries in South America have almost universally been settled on the basis of the *uti possidetis* the only practicable basis of peaceful adjustment. . . .

For twenty years, Venezuela, instead of settling her boundary dispute, has in various ways, some of them obviously dishonest, been trying to drag the United States into the dispute, and the United States has progressed good-naturedly step by step, without examining the merits of the case, till at length with a sudden impulse it leaps over the precipice blindly. And what is the position we now hold? It is substantially this: "When a weak American republic asserts a claim to territory in America as against a strong European occupant, and offers to submit its claim to arbitration, the European power, if it refuses the offer, is to be considered as holding the territory by force, and as infringing the Monroe Doctrine." This is the sum and substance of our position. . . .

We now address Venezuela substantially thus: "You are an American Republic, and in your claims against European powers we back you. True you settled your southern boundary directly, on the basis of the *uti possidetis,* but this principle, though applicable everywhere else in South America, is inapplicable to your eastern boundary. Even the great doctrine of prescription, recognized by every publicist from the time of Grotius, and the very foundation of the peace of nations, is not applicable to that boundary. Claim what you will, and propose arbitration of it, and I will step in and say that it shall be settled in no other way. I know nothing of the merits of the controversy. I am simply backing you. This is according to the Monroe Doctrine." Of course the President never intended to say any such thing, but when we examine the facts, we find that is precisely what he said.

[In concluding his letter, Mr. Moore expressed the belief that President Cleveland would] "not be willing to launch his country on a career as mad and as fatal as that on which France was started by Louis XVI." [32]

Mr. Bayard, from London, also wrote an "anxious letter" to the President on December 18. He said, in part:

In my correspondence while I was Secretary of State—also with Judge Gresham since I came here—and personally with you—my opinions have been genuinely stated—and as the Venezuelan transactions and history are unfolded I am not able to shake off a grave sense of apprehension in allowing the interests and welfare of our Country to be imperilled or complicated by such a government and people as those of Venezuela.

It is not needful that I should repeat these views—and I now wish to study carefully and deliberately the situation as it exhibits itself under the light suddenly cast upon this profoundly important question —which includes in its principles and treatment every European claim of ownership and control of soil in the western hemisphere.[33]

The London *Times* recognized "the gravity of the situation. Indeed it rather increases our sense of the peril to which international interests are subjected by a combination of sentiment and ignorance. . . . It is unfortunately true, however, that when kinsmen fall out they can quarrel very bitterly." The President is "supported not only by a majority in both Houses of Congress, but by a great body of public opinion throughout the country. There is ground for believing that this is due to defective information and misguided public spirit. Whatever its origin and its character may be, we have to lay our account with it. As we cannot yield to the demands of Mr. Olney, whether they are supported by the people of the United States or not, without surrendering our title to almost the whole of our Empire, we must hold ourselves prepared to defend our rights in any quarter where they may be threatened." [34]

Such language did not provide a way out from the deadlock in which the two governments now found themselves involved. Sir Michael Hicks-Beach, as British spokesman, might essay to pour oil by predicting that when "the case of Great Britain . . . was laid before the people, either on this side the Atlantic or the other, the result would be happy, peaceful, and honorable to both parties." [35] Meanwhile the people raged and the heathen imagined a vain thing.

Then in early January, 1896, came the Kaiser's telegram to President Kruger of the Transvaal.[36] Immediately the direction of British belligerency was transferred eastward. The Channel was patrolled by a flying squadron. The atmosphere was tense; and the appointment of an American Commission to ascertain the facts in the case regarding the Venezuelan boundary dispute passed, if not unnoticed yet generally disregarded in England. The American press continued to fulminate; but diplomacy, whose business was to avoid war and to find a way out from the *impasse,* was given a chance. First, however, the British put forward an unofficial representative in London, an amateur diplomat, whose services have been somewhat exaggerated. This was Lord Playfair.

At this time Mr. Chamberlain, the Colonial Secretary, was in the hey-dey of his popularity in Great Britain. His wife was an American, the daughter of Mr. Endicott of Boston, former Secretary of War in Cleveland's first administration. Mr. Chamberlain sought in Lord Playfair, who was a chemist by profession and a warm friend of Mr. Bayard, a go-between. This Liberal peer had served in Parliament and had experience in public affairs, though not in diplomacy. Lord Playfair was commissioned on January 12, 1896, by Lord Salisbury and Mr. Chamberlain to give Mr. Bayard a memorandum on the situation. In view of the fact that the United States had not replied to Lord Salisbury's despatches of the previous November, the way was now perhaps open for private negotiations which might clear the way for formal exchanges between the two governments. The memorandum proposed among other things that:

(1) The Monroe doctrine, which was not accepted internationally, should be submitted to a conference of European states having interests in America. These with the United States would then accept the Monroe doctrine.

(2) The Venezuelan dispute might be submitted to such a conference.

(3) As there was an intermediate territory where there were no British and no Venezuelan settlements there might be arbitration of this territory.[37]

A version of this memorandum was cabled by Mr. Bayard to Secretary Olney; and he wrote Lord Playfair that he believed "the candid and friendly acceptance by this country (England) of the Monroe Doctrine, and non-extensions of European holdings in the Americas, will be promotive of a better feeling, by dispelling an indefinite apprehension of European intervention and control in transatlantic local Governments which has been fostered by a party of foes to the international peace." [38]

Secretary Olney replied January 14 that the suggestion through Lord Playfair was "highly appreciated." The United States rejected the idea of a conference regarding the Monroe doctrine for she was "content with the existing status of Monroe Doctrine which, as well as its application to said controversy, it regards as completely and satisfactorily accepted by the people of the Western Continents." The solution he suggested was as follows:

> Let appropriate clause be added to Behring Sea Convention, or, if deemed wisest, let there be an independent Convention which shall provide for settlement by arbitration of all controversies between the two countries including Venezuelan boundary, and which, as to that controversy, shall explicitly provide that long continued occupation of territory by Venezuelans or by British subjects shall with all the attending circumstances, be considered by tribunal of arbitration and be given all the weight belonging to it in reason and justice or by the principles of international law. Tribunal to consist of two [from] present American Commission, of two persons chosen by Great Britain and of a fifth agreed upon by the two Governments or, in case of failure to agree, nominated by. . . .[39]

The negotiations through Lord Playfair continued till the end of February.[40] Meanwhile Secretary Olney had set up another channel of communication with Great Britain. This was through Mr. Smalley, the American correspondent of the London *Times* in Washington. Secretary Olney felt that he could absolutely trust him; and through Mr. Smalley, Mr. Buckle, the editor of the *Times,* could be reached and thus the British Foreign Office. A channel for the exchange of views was thus provided which was at once private and public. The files of the *Times* from January 22 to February 21, therefore, contain a public record, and in part the negotiations between the two governments.[41]

Mr. Chamberlain, nevertheless, kept up his negotiations with Mr. Bayard through Lord Playfair and on January 20 Mr. Bayard telegraphed to Secretary Olney that England was anxious to remove from the public mind in America any idea that she was seeking more land in America. They proposed as a principle that no occupied territory should be submitted to arbitration and that a definition of such settlements should be secured later.[42] This was followed by a confidential despatch which is given in the appendix to this chapter.[43] Thus matters seemed to progress. On January 25 Mr. Chamberlain in a speech in Birmingham said:

We do not covet one single inch of American territory. War between the two nations, England and the United States, would be an absurdity as well as a crime....
The two nations are allied, and more closely allied in sentiment and in interests than any other nations on the face of the earth. While I should look with horror upon anything in the nature of a fratricidal strife, I should look forward with pleasure to the possibility of the Stars and Stripes and the Union Jack floating together in defence of a common cause sanctioned by humanity and justice.[44]

Mr. Bayard also wrote home that "there is a unanimity here in favor of an amicable settlement on grounds consistent with the self-respect and honor alike of the United States and Great Britain—and I believe they are quite ready to meet us half way—and I think we can make up the other half." [45] On the same day Mr. Bayard also wrote that public addresses by political leaders in England left "but little to be desired as expressions of unqualified approval and acceptance of the 'Monroe doctrine,' as it is commonly understood in the United States." [46]

Yet behind all these pleasant words there still lurked the unsettled question of what were the "British settlements" which Mr. Chamberlain insisted should be excluded from arbitration.[47] Secretary Olney cabled on January 22 that:

> With sincerest purpose to do so, am unable to comprehend the justice or pertinency of the proposition that mere occupation shall be decisive of title. The time, character, and all circumstances attending such occupation must necessarily be considered and must be interpreted and construed according to the principles of private and public law applicable thereto. Nor does the definition of settlements by agreement in advance seem to be feasible. Every one of the numerous elements involved in such definition would be subject of debate and of probable disagreement, while, as Venezuela must be consulted at every step, the inevitable delays would be interminable. As Great Britain desires the controversy should not drift, in which desire the United States heartily concurs, a resort to some form of arbitration which shall cover the real questions involved seems indispensable, since the moment it is agreed upon and the tribunal constituted, the controversy as far as these two countries is concerned, is at an end.[48]

Here was the "crux of the matter" and a liberal solution was essential. As Mr. Bayard wrote: "An effective occupation, by actual settlers, continuously maintained in such a region without protection of laws, with no attempt at definition of boundary or jurisdiction—creates possession—certainly entitled to favor—the favor of civilization, albeit an imperfect civilization."[49] The British had first mentioned "five years" as a test of settlement; in the end of January the *Times* sent a private message to Secretary Olney saying:

> Ultimate binding arbitration will be accepted provided that districts which have been *bona-fide* settled for ten years by either English or Venezuelans were excluded. Note that we make two great concessions, first, practical admission of your right to intervene, second, abandonment of Schomburgk line. No official proposal been received here.[50]

Later a final definition was secured which provided for fifty years occupation. But in the meantime Mr. Bayard sent home despatch after despatch breathing amity, reason and justice but failing to return any definite answers to inquiries from Washington as to what was to be done regarding the "settlements." On February 21, Secretary Olney cabled:

Times editorials presumably semi-official are in line with suggestions of my telegram of January 28—failure to respond to which is not understood. Fear importance of time is not appreciated. Most unfortunate to have matter made party issue in approaching Presidential campaign. Venezuela legislature now in session will adjourn in about sixty days. *Times* suggest that negotiations should be transferred to Washington as Venezuela is represented here and not in London must obviously be done when basis of settlement is agreed upon but which until then there is no object in doing.[51]

This was followed by the interchange of several messages which led to the end of Playfair's mission. Even Mr. Chamberlain's political finesse could not break through Secretary Olney's request for a definition of settlements. Consequently the negotiations were transferred to Washington.

Secretary Olney also became impatient that Mr. Bayard had not at once denied Mr. Chamberlain's statement of February 25 to Lord Playfair that the United States apparently now ignored the principle of the exclusion of "British Settlements" from arbitration, a principle which Mr. Chamberlain and Lord Playfair had assumed as acceptable to the United States. The result was that Mr. Bayard, a month later, finally reported that the Secretary's instructions had been carried out. Some of the documents are in the Appendix to this chapter.[52] Such misunderstandings and bickerings should not, however, disguise the fact that in both countries a new spirit of friendliness was at work. This was seen in the debates at the opening of Parliament in February, 1896.

Lord Rosebery, former Premier and Foreign Secretary, welcomed the declaration in the Queen's speech that the United States had "expressed a wish to co-operate in terminating differences" regarding the Venezuelan boundary. He said that American intervention "introduces into this controversy the important element of a solid and substantial government, which, in effect, offers a guarantee for the permanence and the reception of any settlement that may be arrived at." The leaders of the two countries had got into an *impasse;* it was now the duty of all to extricate these leaders from their position of extreme difficulty."[53] In similar and more effective fashion Sir William Harcourt, leader of the Opposition in the House of Commons, spoke at length. He said: "We ought all to endeavor to remove any matter which tends to ruffle the feelings between England and the United States." The Monroe doctrine was "a principle of natural policy" which declared that "any invasion of the territorial or political rights of American States in controversy with European Powers is a matter of special importance to the United States." The British Government had welcomed the appointment of an American Commission to ascertain the facts in the case. "Diplomacy has had this matter in hand for half a century and a mighty bad hand it has made of it." Arbitration was the proper way to settle the matter.[54] Back of this speech was the sincere and impartial effort of Sir William Harcourt to effect a settlement. The reader now knows through the publication of Gardiner's *Life of Harcourt* the effective fashion in which Sir William labored to this end.[55]

Mr. Balfour then spoke for the Government saying that there had never been "the slightest intention on the part of this country [England] to violate what is the substance and essence of the Monroe Doctrine."[56] It remained for Lord Salisbury as Prime Minister to declare "that from some points of view the mixture of the United States in this matter may conduce to results which will be satisfactory to us more rapidly than if the United States had not interfered. I do think the bringing in of the Monroe Doctrine was, controversially, quite unnecessary for the United States. Considering the position of Venezuela in the Carribbean Sea, it is no more unnatural that the United States should take an interest in it than that we should feel an interest in Holland and Belgium." He fully believed that a "middle term" as to arbitration would be found after negotiations, which would "effectually diminish the chance of conflict or difference of opinion between" Great Britain and the United States.[57]

Thus the weather signals were set fair though many

months were to pass before these long negotiations were to mature into a real agreement; and Great Britain and the United States had not, as Mowat states, "already found a way out" by February, 1896. In Congress the debates were for the most part extreme and futile in their character. One thing, however, was clear for, in early March, Lord Salisbury proposed that steps should be considered in order to draw up a treaty of arbitration between England and America.[58] This meant that the storm cloud had passed. The details of such proposals will be discussed in a later chapter. Here we must bring our account of the Venezuelan situation to a conclusion.

The transfer of the negotiations to Washington which came at the end of February provided opportunity for continuous and "almost daily" conferences between Secretary Olney and Sir Julian Pauncefote. Thus as Mr. Olney wrote to ex-President Cleveland in 1901 "so much of the negotiation took place in the course of personal interviews between Sir Julian and myself, that I cannot always easily recall the order of events."[59] No record of these interviews seems to have been kept so we are left rather in the dark. There are, nevertheless, several unpublished letters exchanged between Secretary Olney and Mr. Chamberlain which cast light on the spirit and temper of these days. We should note that, throughout the period, the American Commission to investigate as to the facts concerning the boundary line received from the British Foreign Office such assistance as it was able to give but that at times this assistance was marred by the mistakes made by British subordinates in the Foreign Office.[60]

On May 22, 1896, Lord Salisbury made, through Sir Julian Pauncefote, "a definite suggestion as to the substance and form of a treaty for the adjustment of the Venezuelan boundary dispute."[61] This was not acceptable to the United States because it did not propose a final and complete settlement. But Secretary Olney inquired on July 13: "Can it be assumed that Her Majesty's Government would submit to unrestricted arbitration the whole of the territory in dispute provided it be a rule of the arbitration, embodied in the arbitral agreement, that territory which has been in the exclusive, notorious, and actual use and occupation of either party for even two generations or say for sixty years, shall be held by the arbitrators to be the territory of such party?" [62]

This suggestion was finally accepted though the term was fixed at "fifty years" instead of at sixty years as a few recent American writers have stated. During July, 1896, Mr. John Hay was in London and in a private way did all that he could to persuade Englishmen whom he met socially to settle the Venezuelan dispute as soon as possible. Mr. Hay later wrote of this to Secretary Olney and added that "the country was a unit behind you and that there would be no retreat by Mr. McKinley from the position you had assumed." The story that Mr. Hay was in any way commissioned by the Cleveland administration to represent them in England is of course incorrect.[63] Indeed Mr. Henry White was the only Republican diplomat whom Secretary Olney called in for advice and valuable assistance. This was not till after March, 1896. Later in the spring and summer Mr. White acted as an unofficial observer in England.[64]

As statesmen escaped from their tasks during the summer of 1896 the final negotiations were postponed till the autumn. In September Mr. Chamberlain came on a visit to America and saw Secretary Olney in Massachusetts. He does not seem to have accomplished much and certainly his proposals as to terms of arbitration were not acceptable as Mr. Chamberlain himself acknowledged in a private letter to Secretary Olney. To this Secretary Olney replied on September 28, 1896. Some of these letters although they touch on other matters as well are printed in the Appendix to this chapter.[65]

By November Secretary Olney and Sir Julian Pauncefote had smoothed out all the remaining difficulties and on November 12, 1896, they signed the heads of a proposed treaty between Venezuela and Great Britain. Two members of the arbitral tribunal were to be named respectively by the United States and Great Britain. These four were to choose a fifth member who was to be the president of the tribunal. They were to examine the facts and to "determine the boundary line between the colony of British Guiana and the Republic of Venezuela." The rules which were to guide the decision were as follows:

> In deciding the matters submitted the arbitrators shall ascertain all the facts which they deem necessary to a decision of the controversy and shall be governed by the following rules, which are agreed upon by the high contracting parties as rules to be taken as applicable to the case, and by such principles of international law not inconsistent therewith as the arbitrators shall determine to be applicable to the case.

Rules

> (a) Adverse holding or prescription during a period of fifty years shall make a good title. The arbitrators may deem exclusive political control of a district, as well as actual settlement thereof, sufficient to constitute adverse holding or to make title by prescription.
> (b) The arbitrators may recognize and give effect to rights and claims resting on any other ground whatever, valid according to international law, and on any principles of international law which the arbitrators may deem to be applicable to the case and which are not in contravention of the foregoing rule.
> (c) In determining the boundary line, if territory of one party be found by the tribunal to have been at the date of this treaty in the occupation of the subjects or citizens of the other party, such effect shall be given to such occupation as reason, justice, the principles of international law, and the equities of the case shall, in the opinion of the tribunal, require.[66]

On November 10 the American Commission had been warned to cease its activities. Later the material which they had collected was laid before the tribunal of arbitration in Paris.[67] On the day before in London, Lord Salisbury at the Lord Mayor's banquet had announced the general result saying:

> It is always surprising by what very obvious arrangements problems of great difficulty are solved, and in the continent which Columbus discovered the tradition of Columbus' egg must be properly revered. But, as you are aware, in the discussion we have had with

the United States on behalf of their friends, the Venezuelans, the question has been, not whether there should be arbitration, but whether the arbitration should have unrestricted application, and we have always claimed that those who, apart from historic right, had the right which attaches to established settlements—the settled districts—that they should be excluded from arbitration. Our difficulty for many months has been to find how to define the settled districts, and a solution has been found—I think it has come from the Government which his Excellency [Mr. Bayard] represents—that we should treat the colonial empire just as we treat individuals, that the same lapse of time which protects individuals in civic life from having their title questioned should also protect the English colony from having its title questioned. And beyond that, that where that lapse of time could not be claimed, though there should be an examination of title, yet all that equity demanded in consideration of such inchoate title should be granted. It is a very simple solution. . . .[68]

Thus the controversy ended with a decisive victory for the principal American contention. The decision of the arbitral tribunal, however, followed in the main the British line. Two exceptions to this gave to Venezuela territory within the Schomburgk line. This decision was not reached till October 3, 1899, when popular interest had largely waned. In November, 1899, Secretary Olney wrote to a correspondent a review of the controversy which emphasizes certain points. He said:

You are quite right, in my judgment, in ascribing the present Anglo-American *entente* to the year 1895 and the administration's course as respects Venezuela.

It is not uncommon to have Mr. Bayard and his course as American Ambassador assigned as the real cause.

As you know, nothing could be farther from the truth. You cannot bring two nations into relations of regard and friendship if, while greatly gratifying the *amour propre* of the one, you greatly wound and offend that of the other. Mr. Bayard's sentimental speeches lauding everything English, comparing things English with things American always to the disadvantages of the latter and even attacking the domestic policy of his own Government, made his countrymen, as you know, without distinction of party excessively angry. You will remember the resolutions of censure presented in the House of Representatives.

The constant stream of taffy played by Mr. Bayard upon the English people tickled them as a matter of course—perhaps to some extent sickened them. However that may be, it gave the impression that the Americans were pining for British friendship and affection. And you will readily agree that the deeper and more wide-spread such an impression, the less the respect John Bull really entertained for us.

This state of things—this attitude of the British mind—was effectually even if rudely dispelled by the Venezuelan policy of the Government as manifested by the correspondence of the State Department and the President's message to Congress. As it had behind it the support of Congress and the entire country, Englishmen at once began to conceive that respect for us which is the foundation and essential prerequisite of all real regard.

It goes without saying that the administration's Venezuelan policy did not meet Mr. Bayard's approval. The letter of the State Department initiating it was, I have always been told, openly characterized by him as intemperate and uncalled for—while, notwithstanding the President's message on the subject, he did not hesitate to declare that the policy was not Mr. Cleveland's but one into which he had been seduced by his Secretary of State.

Under the circumstances you will understand that Mr. Bayard could be of no assistance in bringing the matter to a successful issue, although, until the negotiations were transferred to Washington and carried on between Sir Julian Pauncefote and myself, all formal communications to the British Government had to go through the American Embassy. In the interim I could not afford to be without authentic information of the state of things in England—of the views and purposes of public men in and out of office. Being deprived of the natural sources and channels of information, I was obliged to resort to others and did so with entire success. At the same time, without violence of the confidence reposed in me and without ignoring the relations which subsist between gentlemen, I could not, at this time, give any clue either as to persons or as to the means by which I possessed myself of the material facts.[69]

The net result of the entire matter, dangerous though it was at times, was the more general acceptance of the "loose-construction" theory of the Monroe doctrine. Out of the experience Anglo-American relations had decidedly improved, as was evidenced by the signature of a treaty of arbitration on January 11, 1897. More important still was the real public awakening of American opinion as to our place in the world. The mind of the people had been stimulated by this adventure in diplomacy. Soon it was to awaken to fresh opportunities and responsibilities.

NOTES TO CHAPTER II

1. *Department of State* (Hereafter to be cited as *D. S.*), From London. Vol. 155, enclosure to No. 436, Feb. 8, 1887, Phelps to Salisbury.
2. *D. S.,* From London. Vol. 155, No. 447, Feb. 24, 1887, Phelps to Bayard; Vol. 156, No. 605, Oct. 29, 1887, Phelps to Bayard—"I would further suggest that since the mediation of the United States has been declined by Great Britain, I can hardly hope that any further friendly intervention will be of any avail."
3. *Papers relating to the Foreign Relations of the United States . . . 1888.* Washington, 1889. (Hereafter to be cited as *F. R.*) Part I, pp. 698 *et seq.* Feb. 17, 1888. Bayard to Phelps. Cf. James, *Richard Olney and his Public Service.* Boston, 1923, pp. 221-222; and Appendix A to this chapter.
4. *Times,* May 2, June 5, 1888.
5. *D. S.,* From London, Vol. 163, No. 143, Dec. 27, 1889, White to Blaine (telegram). *F. R.,* 1890, p. 322, Dec. 30, 1887, Blaine to White; *Ibid.,* pp. 337-341, 776-788; *D. S.,* From London, Vol. 164, No. 165, Feb. 3, 1890, Lincoln to Blaine; Vol. 165, No. 261, June 18, 1890, same to same; Vol. 165, enclosure to No. 267, June 20, 1890, Blaine to Lincoln.
6. Many of the despatches are in *F. R.* 1894, pp. 803-846.
7. *F. R.,* 1894, p. 250-252.
8. *D. S.,* To London, Vol. 31, No. 657, April 9, 1895, Gresham to Bayard. Cf. also Nos. 574 and 580, and the Venezuelan correspondence in *F. R.* 1895, Part II, pp. 1480-1488.
9. *D. S.,* From London, Vol. 179, Enclosures to No. 404 (confidential), Jan. 23, and Feb. 20, 1895. Cf. *Times,* June 19, 1895.
10. *D. S.,* From London, Vol. 179. Unnumbered (confidential), April 5, 1895, Bayard to Gresham.
11. McElroy, *Grover Cleveland, the Statesman and the Man,* New York, 1923. 2 Vols, II, pp. 180-181.
12. Quoted in Rhodes, *History of the United States, 1877-1896,* New York, 1919, pp. 455-456.
13. McElroy, II, pp. 177-179.
14. Quoted in Rhodes, pp. 453-454.
15. The Olney Note has been frequently reprinted. It is in *F. R.* 1895, Part I, pp. 545-562.
16. *D. S.,* From London, Vol. 180, No. 492, Aug. 9, 1895, Bayard to Olney.
17. *Olney Collection* in the Manuscript Division of the Library of Congress. Hereafter to be cited as *O. C.*
18. *D. S.,* To London, Vol. 31, No. 863, Oct. 8, 1895, Olney to Bayard. From London, Vol. 181, No. 522, Oct. 18, 1895, Bayard to Olney and No. 523, Oct. 23, 1895, same to same. *O. C.* Oct. 21, 1895, same to same (personal).
19. *D. S.,* From London, Vol. 181, No. 527, Oct. 25, 1895, Bayard to Olney.
20. *O. C.,* where there are a number of telegrams and letters which indicate an increasing sense of irritation on the part of Secretary Olney. *D. S.,* From London, Vol. 181, No. 547 (confidential), Dec. 3, 1895, Bayard to Olney, expresses British regret for the delay.
21. *F. R.,* 1895, Part I, pp. xxviii-xxix.
22. *O. C.*
23. *F. R.,* 1895, Part I, pp. 542-545. Cf. McElroy II, pp. 186-189.
24. Cf. Appendix B to this chapter.
25. The two notes of Nov. 26, 1895, to Sir Julian Pauncefote, who was British Ambassador at Washington, have been frequently reprinted. They are in *F. R.,* 1895, Part I, pp. 563-576.

26. *Autobiography of Andrew D. White*, New York, 1905, 2 Vols. II, p. 123.
27. Grey, *Twenty-Five Years*, New York, 1925, 2 Vols., I, p. 17.
28. Quoted in McElroy, II, pp. 192-196.
29. Rhodes, pp. 446, 448.
30. Cortissoz, *The Life of Whitelaw Reid*, New York, 1921, 2 Vols., II, pp. 201-202.
31. Rhodes, *The McKinley and Roosevelt Administrations, 1897-1909*, New York, 1922, p. 23.
32. McElroy, II, pp. 183-186.
33. *Ibid.*, II, pp. 188-189.
34. *Times*, Dec. 20, 1895. D. S., From London, Vol. 181, No. 560, Dec. 24, 1895, Bayard to Olney. "The feeling here has been most grave since the President's Message and the resultant action of Congress—casting all other questions into comparative unimportance." On Jan. 3 and 11, 1896, Mr. Bayard was a bit more cheerful. O. C., Jan. 3 (confidential), Bayard to Olney and D. S., From London, Vol. 182, No. 567, Jan. 11, Bayard to Olney.
35. Quoted in McElroy, II, p. 196.
36. *Die grosse Politik der europäischen Kabinette*, Berlin, 1922-27, XI, No. 2610 and notes p. 32. D. S., From London, Vol. 182, No. 563, Jan. 3, 1896, Bayard to Olney and No. 566, Jan. 7, 1896; Thimme, *Die Krüger Depesche in europäische Gespräche*, May-June, 1924, pp. 201-244; Sontag, *The Cowes Interview and the Kruger Despatch in Pol. Sci. Quart.*, XL, pp. 217 et seq.
37. Reid, *Memoirs and Correspondence of Lyon Playfair, first Lord Playfair of St. Andrews*, London, 1899, pp. 416-417. James, *Olney*, pp. 227-228.
38. Reid, p. 418.
39. James, p. 229.
40. James, p. 250. An important and lengthy despatch from Bayard to Olney, Jan. 15, 1896 is also printed, pp. 229-232. Telegrams of Jan. 15-17, 1896, are in O. C. Cf. also D. S., From London, Vol. 182, No. 577, Jan. 18, 1896, Bayard to Olney.
41. James, pp. 127-129; Smalley, *Anglo-American Memories*, First Series, London, 1911, pp. 66-69.
42. James, p. 232. Cf. Reid, pp. 419-420.
43. Appendix C to this chapter.
44. Quoted in Rhodes, *History of United States*, 1877-1896, pp. 450-451.
45. O. C. (personal), Jan. 29, 1896, Bayard to Olney.
46. D. S., From London, Vol. 182, No. 588, Jan. 29, 1896, Bayard to Olney.
47. Reid, p. 420.
48. James, pp. 232-234.
49. D. S., From London, Vol. 183, No. 596 (confidential), Feb. 5, 1896, Bayard to Olney. Secretary Olney also had cabled on January 28 proposing an Anglo-American fact finding commission which, in case it failed to secure an agreement, should report to an arbitral tribunal which in turn should declare a boundary line which should be accepted by all parties, Venezuela included, James, p. 234.
50. James, pp. 234-235.
51. O. C.; D. S., From London, Vol. 183 (telegram), Feb. 25, 1896, Bayard to Olney; Feb. 25, 1896, Playfair to Bayard (telegram); Feb. 27, 1896, Bayard to Olney; F. R., 1896, pp. 421-426; Reid, pp. 421-426.
52. D. S., From London, Vol. 183, No. 605 (confidential), Feb. 15, 1896, Bayard to Olney; No. 607 (confidential), Feb. 19, 1896, same to same; No. 610, Feb. 21, 1896, same to same; No. 613, Feb. 26, 1896, same to same; No. 614 (confidential), Feb. 29, same to same; No. 619 (confidential), March

4, 1896, same to same; No. 640 (confidential), March 27, 1896, same to same; O. C., also contains several letters and telegrams for this period; and see Appendix D to this chapter for further unpublished documents where the personal qualities of the two correspondents become more evident.

53. Hansard, 4th Series, XXXVII, cc. 52-53.

54. *Ibid.*, cc. 83-90.

55. Gardiner, *Life of Sir William Harcourt,* London, 1923, 2 Vols., II, pp. 395-404. Here are several letters from Harcourt which shed light. For example: "January 18, 1896.

. . . I returned yesterday from a visit to Chatsworth where I preached "conciliation of America" I think with good effect to the host and to A. Balfour. The former and as I gather the majority of the Cabinet are strongly for accommodation. Balfour rather non-committal, but admitting that he knew little of the subject. I thought the Manchester speech on the whole good.

I tried to impress on both (1) the great danger of the situation; (2) that no other proposal but arbitration could or would have any good result.

I pointed out a plan by which I thought we could get at arbitration without discredit.

The man whose obstinacy I most fear is Joe [Chamberlain].

Throughout the spring and summer Harcourt was busy on this matter and when Sir Julian Pauncefote came to see him "saying, 'I have come to see you Sir William, about Venezuela,' W. V. H. interrupted him saying, 'Do you think that is wise? My attitude on the subject is well known, and if you come to see me it may embarrass you in your communications with the Prime Minister' [Lord Salisbury], Pauncefote replied, 'Sir William, I come to you with Lord Salisbury's knowledge and at his suggestion in order that you shall suggest the terms in which the decision shall be announced to refer the Venezuelan difficulty to arbitration.'

W. V. H. said to his son, who was present, 'sit down and write this,' and proceeded to dictate a form of words which, after some slight corrections, was taken away by Pauncefote to Lord Salisbury at the Foreign Office."

Sir Charles Dilke refers to these services of Harcourt and Pauncefote in Hansard, 4th Series, LVIII, cc. 1333-1334.

56. Hansard, 4th Series, XXXVII, c. 109.

57. *Ibid.*, cc. 52-53. McElroy, II, p. 200 curiously makes a mistake in quoting Salisbury's speech letting him say: "I do *not* think that the invoking of the Monroe Doctrine was" etc. This is exactly the reverse of what he actually did say. I must also add that Mowat, *Diplomatic Relations of Great Britain and the United States,* London, 1925, pp. 271-272 is at fault as to the date of settlement of the dispute, the importance of the Playfair episode, and the value of Chamberlain's visit to the United States in Sept., 1896.

58. F. R., 1896, pp. 222-240.

59. James, p. 249.

60. *Autobiography of Andrew D. White,* II, p. 121; F. R., 1896, pp. 242-247; D. S., From London, Vol. 184, No. 688, May 16, 1896, Bayard to Olney; No. 694, June 2, 1896, same to same; June 2, 1896, Bayard to Prof. G. L. Burr.

61. James, p. 250; F. R., 1896, pp. 247-252.

62. F. R., 1896, pp. 253-254; O. C., July 11, 1896, Olney to Cleveland. The printed documents regarding the entire dispute are for the most part also to be found in *Parliamentary Papers,* 1896, XCVII.

63. *Hay Papers;* James, pp. 247-248; Hay, *Letters and Extracts from Diary,* Washington, 1908, 3 Vols. (printed but not published), III, p. 65; O. C., where there are several letters of interest dealing with an article by Sir Maurice Low in *McClure's Magazine,* July, 1900, which erroneously represents Hay as acting for Secretary Olney.

64. James, pp. 131-132, 240-247.
65. *O. C.*, Sept. 9, 1896, Chamberlain to Olney, and documents printed in Appendix E to this chapter.
66. *F. R.*, 1896, pp. 254-255. The treaty as finally signed Feb. 2, 1897, provided for two British members, one American (all chosen by the highest judicial authorities in each country) and one member nominated by the President of Venezuela. *British Foreign and State Papers*, Vol. 89, p. 57.
67. *O. C.*, Nov. 10, 1896, Olney to Brewer (strictly confidential).
68. *Times*, Nov. 10, 1896.
69. *O. C.*, Nov. 20, 1899, Olney to Low.

APPENDICES TO CHAPTER II

A

D. S. From London, Vol. 157, No. 706, March 28, 1888, Phelps to Bayard.

I have the honour to transmit herewith copies of a recent correspondence between Mr. Guzman Blanco and myself, relative to the question pending between Great Britain and the Republic of Venezuela.

It will be in your recollection that in February, 1887, under instructions from you, I tendered to Her Majesty's Government the mediation of the Government of the United States in respect to these questions, which was declined.

It seems obvious therefore, that no further interference with that subject by our Government would be either useful or consistent with its character, unless it is prepared to espouse and maintain the cause of Venezuela as against Great Britain. This is doubtless far from your intention, however friendly the feeling that happily exists between the Republic of Venezuela and the United States. You will probably perceive no reason why our Government should enlist in a dispute between other nations in which it has no concern, and in contravention of the uniform policy of its foreign relations.

Mr. Guzman Blanco is engaged in an effort to negotiate a treaty with Great Britain while himself resident and remaining in France. And [he] appears to expect the United States Minister to sustain and assist him in accomplishing that result. It does not seem to me consistent with the dignity of the United States to engage in such a transaction as agent for another nation. And it is certain that intervention in that capacity would not be favorably received by Her Majesty's Government, and could not be useful to Venezuela.

Quite concurring in the propriety of your instruction on this subject, No. 791, of February 17, 1888, and fully intending to follow it whenever the opportunity is offered, I do not understand it to go beyond the expression to the Secretary of Foreign affairs, of the gratification an amicable settlement, by arbitration or otherwise, between Great Britain and Venezuela, would afford the United States Government, and its readiness to do anything in its power to assist in that end.

But as Mr. Guzman Blanco has apparently formed a very different expectation in respect to the proposed course of our Government, I transmit this correspondence, that you may take such steps in regard to it as you may deem to be called for.

B

Olney Collection. December 17, 1895, concerning Venezuela—being copy of draft (of a message to Congress) made at Boston, December 13, 1895 (by Secretary Olney).

To the Congress,

In the message which I had the honour to address to the Congress on the third of the present month, I called its attention to the pending boundary controversy between Great Britain and the Republic of Venezuela, and stated the substance of the request which had been made of Her Britannic Majesty's government. The answer of that government, which was then shortly expected, has since been received and with the despatch to which it is a reply, is appended to this communication.

It is embodied in two notes of the British Prime Minister to the British Ambassador at this capital and their contents have received my most careful attention. One of them is devoted exclusively to observations upon the Monroe doctrine and is apparently intended to show that that doctrine is now receiving a new and strange development at the hands of the United States. But the considerations advanced upon that point are in my judgment utterly insufficient to establish any such result. It is not impossible, of course, that the position of this government may not be correctly apprehended. Otherwise, and except on that theory, it is quite inexplicable that a serious argument should now be addressed to the United States to show, either that the identical political conditions which existed at the birth of the Monroe doctrine do not now exist or that the Monroe doctrine declares or enjoins the duty of international arbitration. This government has not fallen into any such palpable errors nor given cause to suppose that it has. Its true position has, it believes, been most explicitly stated. The long standing boundary dispute between Great Britain and Venezuela threatening to end in violent collision to the necessary discomfiture of the weaker party without regard to the merits, this government has invoked the Monroe doctrine as embodying not merely a special rule for the special state of facts existing at the time of its origin but a living and lasting principle justly applicable to the analogous state of facts presented by the territorial controversy in question. Having thus established its interest, an interest it is bound to protect and defend, this government has thereupon proceeded to inquire, as a basis for further action, whether the controversy would be referred to arbitration, and has suggested arbitration, not by virtue of anything in the Monroe doctrine, but because of the great disparity in strength between the two parties primarily concerned and because of the inherent propriety and reasonableness of such an arbitral adjustment. These are the cardinal propositions upon which this government has taken its stand, and which, if not altogether ignored, are certainly not successfully impeached by anything contained in Lord Salisbury's reply. They are supported by considerations of a conclusive character which are fully set forth in the despatch of the Secretary of State and which therefore need not be here repeated.

The note remaining to be considered contains the real answer to the inquiry made by the United States. It is there definitely declared that Great Britain will not arbitrate the whole of the contested territory, that while she will arbitrate the territory to the west of the Schomburgk line, she will arbitrate nothing to the east of it. It is at once evident that the steps already taken have not been without valuable results. In the first place, Great Britain's claim of right is distinctly formulated and indeed is asserted to have been publicly proclaimed in October 1886. In the second place, the principle of arbitration as to territory is conceded, though its application is restricted to a portion of the disputed area. It still remains to consider, however, whether this answer can be accepted as satisfactory. It may be, as Great Britain contends, that the true legal boundary between Venezuela and British Guiana is the Schomburgk line. But there is not the present question. The true question is, is the Schomburgk line the true line so clearly and incontrovertibly that any opposite conclusion cannot be reasonably arrived at, that it ought not to be the subject of debate, and that therefore Venezuela cannot be justly permitted to be heard in impeachment of it?

This government cannot answer that question in the affirmative without shutting its eyes to the most significant as well as the most palpable and indisputable facts of the situation. In the first place, if the Schomburgk line is the true one and has always been so regarded by Great Britain, it is most remarkable that the first assertion of it should have been delayed for nearly fifty years from the time when it was first drawn. In the second place, there never has been a time since its original exploitation when it was not contested by Venezuela, who broke off diplomatic relations in 1887 because of Great Britain's action respecting it. In the third place, if Great Britain has always regarded it to be the true line, it is quite unaccountable that, upon the demand of Venezuela, Great Britain should have removed the Schomburgk marks near the mouth of the Orinoco which assigned to Great Britain what in the eyes of both parties was at that time the really valuable subject matter in controversy. In the fourth place, if the Schomburgk line has always been the indisputably true line, it is equally unaccountable that in 1844 Lord Aberdeen, more familiar with the real merits of the Schomburgk line than any of his successors could possibly be, should have offered to Venezuela the line of the Moroco, a line far to the eastward of the Schomburgk line, and giving to Venezuela the exclusive possession of the Orinoco. In the fifth place, on the same hypothesis, it is most extraordinary that from 1850 until 1886, at least, the territory bounded by the line of the Essequibo river on the one side, and of the Moroco on the other, should have been dealt with as territory in dispute which each party undertook not to encroach upon. In the sixth place, the line of Schomburgk is only the line of a British agent, who by the nature of his employment, was bound to draw it so as to comprise every foot of land which by any chance or any possibility his clients could claim, and who clearly made no distinction between legal boundaries and what he deemed to be convenient natural geographical boundaries. Thus, he reported that Her Majesty's government might justly claim the whole basin of the Cuyuni and the Yuruari "on the ground that the *natural* boundary of the colony included any territory through which flow rivers which fall into the Essequibo"—and there could be no better illustration of the British view of some peculiar sanctity attaching to British pretensions than that the non-adoption of this unique mode of delimiting a frontier should now be solemnly held up to the world as a striking example of British moderation and British magnanimity. Finally, that the Schomburgk line was deemed either by Schomburgk himself or by the British government to be the true legal boundary, or to be otherwise than purely tentative, or to be anything more than a mere suggestion or proposition for use as a starting point of negotiations, is conclusively refuted by . . . a British note of 1840. . . .

It is impossible to give assent, therefore, to the proposition of the British government that no case for arbitration with Venezuela exists except as to territory west of the Schomburgk line. It is supported neither by any self-proving and incontestible qualities appertaining to its claim of title, nor by anything done or omitted on the part of Venezuela, nor by anything that may have taken place in the way of actual occupation of the soil.

The course to be pursued by this government in these circumstances does not seem to me to admit of serious doubt. It is deeply disappointing that an appeal, actuated by the friendliest feelings to both the nations concerned and addressed to the sense of justice and to the magnanimity of one of the great powers of the world in its relations to one comparatively weak and small, should have produced no more decisive results. But, having labored in season and out of season during many years, to induce Great Britain to submit her claims to impartial arbitration, and being now finally apprized that she will not, nothing remains but to accept the situation, to recognize its plain requirements, and to deal with it accordingly. Great Britain's present proposition has never been regarded as admissible by Venezuela, and there is no reason to suppose that it will be so regarded now, though any adjustment of the dispute which Venezuela may deem for her advantage and may enter into of her own free will will not of course be objected to by the United States. Assuming the attitude of Venezuela to be unchanged, however, it is now incumbent upon the United States to immediately proceed to determine for itself with sufficient certainty for its justification, what is the true divisional line between the Republic of Venezuela and British Guiana. It should conduct such inquiry judicially, of course, giving due weight to all legitimate considerations bearing upon the claims of either party, and to enable the examination to be thorough and satisfactory, it is suggested that Congress make an adequate appropriation for the expenses of a commission to be appointed by the Executive and to report upon the matter with the least possible delay. When such report is made and accepted, it will then be the duty of this government to communicate to Great Britain the boundary line thus ascertained, and to give notice that any appropriation of territory or exercise of jurisdiction by Great Britain beyond that line (except with the consent of Venezuela) will be regarded by this government as a wilful aggression upon rights and interests of the United States which this government cannot suffer to go undefended.

In making these recommendations, I do not act without a keen sense of responsibility nor without a vivid realization of all possible consequences. It pains me inexpressibly even to imagine that the two great English speaking peoples of the world can ever be other than friendly competitors in the onward march of a progressive civilization, or ever be other than strenuous and worthy rivals in all the arts of peace. I am nevertheless firm in the faith—in which I doubt not to have the hearty concurrence of all the American people—that of all the calamities to which a great nation can subject itself, none are more to be deprecated or more to be shunned, than those which follow from a supine submission to wrong and injustice and the consequent loss of national honor and self respect. That our request to Great Britain calls upon her for nothing more than justice and equity in her dealings with a weaker state, and that our honor and self-respect as well as our material interests, are deeply concerned in her action upon such request, are matters which are fully set forth elsewhere and need not be here again discussed. I therefore invoke the earnest cooperation of Congress in support of the policy initiated by the Executive, both through the specific measures as the wisdom and patriotism of Congress may dictate. Nothing will be wanting to the success of that policy, if Congress but rightly leads the way. In behalf of a cause which appeals to their sense of right, no loss and no sacrifice that may be exacted will be denied or begrudged by the American people.

C

D. S. From London, Vol. 182, No. 581 (confidential), January 22, 1896, Bayard to Olney.

. . . The mischievous and reckless sensationalism of the Press in continuing to give currency to rumours calculated to increase irritation in the relations of the two countries is, I suppose, not to be escaped from. The resources of contradiction appear to be inadequate, for the lie proverbially outruns the truth, but happily does not outlast it.

I am glad to re-affirm the statement contained in my late telegram that Her Majesty's Government are exceedingly desirous of disabusing the public mind in America of any impression that may exist, of any intention or desire whatsoever on their part, to enlarge their present possessions and jurisdiction in South America.

If I comprehend aright the meaning of your Instruction of July last, communicated by me to Lord Salisbury, and also of the President's Special Message of December 17th to the Congress, your insistence upon a submission to arbitration of the line of demarkation between the territories of British Guiana, and of Venezuela, was caused by your arrival at the opinion that the safety and interests of the United States were endangered by an apparently undefined, unexplained, and ever-progressive extension of British jurisdiction over the region lying eastwardly and northerly of the valley of the River Orinoco.

It may now be assumed that an absolute arrestation of any such expansion is expressly and positively avowed by Her Majesty's Government, coupled with an abandoment, *eo nomine,* of the Schomburgk or any other "line," as a rigid condition, precedent, and a willingness to submit the general question of rightful possession and boundary to the arbitrament of an impartial tribunal, coupled with the practical recognition, exclusive from the arbitration of actual and undisturbed enjoyment and long usage of settled points of occupation, by citizens or subjects of both the parties claimant.

In such a state of facts, the difficulties of a practical and satisfactory solution would seem almost to disappear. . . .

D

D. S. From London, Vol. 183, Telegram, February 27 (6 A.M.), 1896, Olney to Bayard.

Have your cable of 25th. I assume you have acted upon my letter of the 8th instant, but get no answer showing what Foreign Office means by settlements. Is the present situation then that Foreign Office takes two positions—first, that settlements must be reserved from arbitration; second, that it refuses to say what it means by settlements [?]. If so, there would seem to be no occasion for or utility in negotiations. Plain that informal negotiations only retard and confuse; plain also that negotiations should be conducted here, and the British Ambassador instructed accordingly. But it is an error that any negotiations are in progress, except respecting Yuruan incident, as to which alone have British Ambassador and Venezuelan Minister any authority. Please communicate above to Foreign Office immediately and cable any suggestions in reply.

Olney Collection. Olney to Bayard, Washington, March 6, 1896.

I note with surprise and regret the error into which Mr. Chamberlain has been misled and am quite at a loss to understand how it has happened. Nothing emanating from this side of the water has given the slightest countenance to the idea that this Government would consider for a moment the adoption of what Mr. Chamberlain calls the principle of exclusion—which being interpreted simply means that what Great Britain has already seized, or what her subjects have already squatted upon, she and they shall be allowed to retain without regard to length of occupation, notice actual or constructive of Venezuela's rights, conditions of the grant or license or material facts under which such occupation or jurisdiction began and has continued, and all the other circumstances qualifying and characterizing it either as a just and equitable basis of title and jurisdiction on the one hand, or as of no consequence and significance as regards such title and jurisdiction on the other. Mr. Chamberlain's misconception of our position ought to be removed without delay. While it will of course tend to somewhat prejudice and retard the successful issue of the negotiations about to be initiated here, it ought not to render them wholly abortive; while it is obvious that the quicker the correction is made the less mischief the misunderstanding is likely to do. I venture to suggest, therefore, that as soon as practicable after receiving this, you take occasion to point out to Mr. Chamberlain the error into which he has fallen, to state the true position of the United States which I am sure you apprehend, and to add that the position is one from which it is altogether improbable that this Government can be induced to depart.

D. S. From London, Vol. 183, Telegram, March 25, 1896, Olney to Bayard.

Have yours of the twenty-fourth instant. Colonial Secretary in letter to Playfair of twenty-fifth of February charges directly, and more than once, that this Government has withdrawn from position originally accepted by it through you in the informal Playfair negotiations. That charge should be emphatically refuted, and is not refuted by your letter of February twenty-third, which ante-dates the Colonial Secretary's charge, and was before him when he made the charge. The charge, not explicitly denied since it was made, has already prejudiced, and will continue to prejudice, negotiations here. It is not perceived why the channel through which the Chamberlain letter of twenty-fifth came cannot be used for a reply. If it cannot be, then please communicate unofficially with Lord Salisbury, furnishing him copy of my letter of the sixth instant, and asking either that he cause same to be transmitted to the Colonial Secretary, or assent to its transmission by you.

D. S. From London, Vol. 183, Telegram, March 26, 1896, Bayard to Olney.

Lord Salisbury leaving town. I had informal interview with the Secretary for Colonies, and made known to him your dissent from principle of exclusion of settlements from arbitration. I also explicitly denied that there had ever been any acceptance or withdrawal from such principle by me in discussion with Playfair.

E

Olney Collection. Chamberlain to Olney, Sept. 19, 1896.

I am very much obliged to you for your letter of the 17th inst., while I regret that I have not been more successful in suggesting an acceptable solution of all present difficulties, I most cordially recognize the fair spirit in which you have met my advances, and I rejoice to think that both Governments are sincerely desirous to come to an amicable settlement.

I have decided for personal reasons to prolong my stay for a few days and shall of course be at your service if anything should turn up which makes you desirous of seeing me again.

Meanwhile, I venture to ask whether you would care to express a confidential opinion as to the reception which would be given by the American Government to any proposition from our side tending to co-operation in regard to Turkey?

If you do not care to say anything, please do not bother to acknowledge this note.

Olney to Chamberlain, Sept. 28, 1896.

Your letter of the 19th came duly to hand and the contents have received my careful attention. It would have been acknowledged earlier if the question put toward the close of it had not been of such interest to the country at large, as well as to myself personally, as to make me wholly unwilling to give an answer which might by possibility be ill-considered or misleading.

The feeling universally manifested in this country at the time of the President's Venezuelan message—and which, though now latent, still prevails in all its original intensity—was then and still is much misunderstood. The college presidents, pseudo-diplomats, disgruntled office seekers, and cranks of all sorts, who, having first assumed a deep seated and chronic hostility towards England on the part of the American people, then proceeded to make labored explanations of that hostility, have all been quite wide of the mark. Their explanations are the merest rubbish because of the entire absence of their supposed subject matter. There is no such general and rooted hatred by Americans of the English people. On the contrary, if there is anything the Americans are proud of, it is their right to describe themselves as of the English race—if there is anything they are attached to, it is to ideas and principles and institutions which are distinctively English in their origin and development. For that reason and because nothing could be more un-English or more contemned of Englishmen than an appearance of fawning or toadyism, the career of an official representative which is nothing but one continued gush in laudation of men and things abroad, and in disparagement, express or implied, of men and things at home, while your countrymen view it with amusement and hardly suppressed derision, is a source of deep mortification and humiliation to mine. For the same reason, and because an injury from a friend has the intensified sting of a poisoned arrow, the seeming if not intentional contumely with which the statement of our position on the Venezuelan boundary question was received by the British Foreign Office, stirred the American heart as it has not been since the Civil War. It was thus stirred because the British position seemed to be explicable only on the theory that we had no policy such as we claimed to have, or, if we had, that we had no right to it, or, if we had, that we had neither the spirit nor the ability to stand up and defend it. And, for the like reasons and because of our inborn and instinctive English sympathies, proclivities, modes of thought, and standards of right and wrong, nothing would more gratify the mass of the American people than to stand side by side and shoulder to shoulder with England in support of a great cause—in a necessary struggle for the defence of human rights and the advancement of Christian civilization.

That a great cause of this sort is now presented by unhappy Armenia I cannot doubt—not more can I doubt that the English people and the American people are as one in their sentiments in regard to it. I am nevertheless constrained to say that even so righteous a cause, to be championed jointly with so great and prized an ally, would not, and probably ought not to, work any change in the traditional and settled policy of this country. What that is, together with the reasons upon which it rests, is something with which you are entirely familiar and need not be enlarged upon. It is enough to say that, while it enjoins certain duties upon the United States as regards the States of the Western Hemisphere, it forbids any interference in the political affairs of European States or any alliance with European States looking to such interference.

There is one feature of the situation, however, through which there might come to England some indirect aid and support on the part of the United States in any decided measures she might elect to take for the relief of Armenia. The protection owed to citizens of the United States by its government, is constantly assuming more and more the shape of a practical obligation which must be discharged at all hazards and by the use of all the necessary means. To this more than to any other cause is to be attributed the comparatively recent increase of our navy—an increase which is likely to go on somewhat indefinitely with the assent of all political parties and the general acclaim of our whole people. Now, American interests in Turkey are not pecuniarily enormous, but are nevertheless most warmly regarded and highly valued by the American people. That the enterprises in which American citizens are there engaged are almost entirely philanthropical, that they are undertaken by devoted women as well as men, and that they develop those qualities of courage, heroism and self-sacrifice which always enlist the sympathy and admiration of mankind, these circumstances give them a place in the regard and affections of the American people which no amount of monied interest could command. If, therefore, England should now seriously set about putting the Armenian charnel-house in order, there can be little doubt that the United States would consider the moment opportune for vigorous exertion on behalf of American citizens and interests in Turkey. It would feel itself entitled to demand full indemnity for past injuries to them as well as adequate security against the like injuries in the future. It would support such demands by all the physical force at its disposal—with the necessary result, I think, that its attitude would both morally and materially strengthen the hands of England. How valuable such incidental assistance might prove it is not, of course, easy to predict, but that it would be real and appreciable cannot, I think, fairly be doubted.

I shall not take it amiss if you are somewhat dismayed, as I am myself, at the length and discursiveness of this answer your innocent looking inquiry has provoked. I nevertheless conclude to leave it unchanged in the hope that, even if not precisely germane to the exact point under consideration, it may yet contribute, however slightly, to a better understanding of the true relations between the two countries we have the honor to represent.

I know you will treat the foregoing as intended exclusively for your own eye, and again wishing Mrs. Chamberlain and yourself a prosperous voyage and safe return to England, I am, etc.

Chamberlain to Olney, Sept. 28, 1896.

I am greatly obliged by your frank letter of 28th inst. We leave early tomorrow, but before I go I desire most earnestly to assure you that you have misunderstood the feeling which has actuated the British Foreign Office and the British Government in the communications which have passed on the Venezuelan question.

It is probably true that we have been equally mistaken in the interpretation we have placed on your despatches and on the President's message.

I hope that the private interchange of opinion which has taken place between us has sufficed to remove all previous misinterpretations on either side, and I can assure you with the most absolute sincerity that at the present time in Great Britain, there is no one from the highest in the land to the poorest workman who does not desire the cordial friendship and respect of the United States more than the good will of any other nation in the world, and who does not regard with horror the idea of a fratricidal conflict between the two branches of the Anglo-Saxon race.

If, as I now believe, you share our feelings I cannot doubt that all differences between us, paltry in themselves and only important as they touch the national honour, will be amicably adjusted. Neither party can desire a solution which would be humiliating to the other and it must be possible to find an arrangement free from this objection.

I will only add that I am deeply sensible of the importance of such moral and incidental co-operation in the cause of humanity as is pointed at in your letter and that I believe that it would profoundly affect the relations between the two countries and would evoke the sympathy which, even if latent, must and ought to exist between peoples with common origin, common literature, common laws and common standards of right and wrong.

CHAPTER III

THE SPANISH-AMERICAN WAR

HENRY ADAMS once wrote: "In the end far more than half the territory of the United States was the spoil of Spanish empire, rarely acquired with perfect propriety. To sum up the story in a single word, Spain had immense influence over the United States; but it was the influence of the whale over its captors,—the charm of a huge, helpless, and profitable victim." [1] This historical view of our relations with Spain extending over more than a century lends itself to closer examination as we take up the diplomatic story of our war with Spain in 1898. A study of the documents drives home the conviction that the war with Spain was, from the point of view of technical diplomacy, an unnecessary war. A careful study will show that Spain had, by April 10, 1898, yielded so much to the requests of the United States as to the direction of affairs in Cuba, that, given time and patience, the practical independence of Cuba could have been secured without recourse to war.

On the other hand it is difficult to see how the war could have been prevented. The diplomats might have arrived at a peaceful solution of the Cuban question; but the turgid currents of domestic politics, the enthusiasm of an awakened national consciousness, and the stirrings of humanitarian sympathy were eager for armed intervention. These were fed as well by the fact that large American property interests had suffered severely by the continued disorders in Cuba. The newspaper press of the time inflamed popular passion till almost any lie received currency. And at the head of the nation was a President, of whom Theodore Roosevelt once impetuously wrote, "McKinley has no more backbone than a chocolate éclair."

From a broad point of view the results attained from the war were immense. The dire menace of yellow fever, whose germs had been endemic in Cuba for generations and which had almost continuously threatened the southern ports of the United States, was practically ended as the result of the American health services. In the Far East the interest of the United States was much quickened and the vigor of our national life was enlivened and broadened. The importance of the navy was readily seen and the demand for the digging of an inter-oceanic canal between the Atlantic and Pacific was strengthened. In foreign relations also we now had better opportunity to judge of our friends and enemies. The responsibilities of rule and of administration both in the West and East Indies and in Pacific Islands though they found us unready and inexperienced, nevertheless stimulated our senses to a notion of the obligations of America to less advanced or backward races. Besides the general results were, at least for a time, undoubtedly beneficial to the populations of former Spanish dependencies. Thus, though the idea that America had been isolated these many years was of course false, the fact stood out more clearly that the United States was in reality a world power. The Venezuelan boundary dispute had stirred our patriotism; the Spanish-American War put it to the test.

The revolt against Spanish rule in Cuba had in part resulted from the failure of the Spanish government to keep its promises as to fiscal reform and political autonomy for Cuba. These promises were made at the end of the Ten Years' War, 1868–1878; now in 1895–1896 the situation was again desperate. The fact that a large amount of American capital was invested in Cuba, the devastation of the island, the harsh and violent methods employed both by the insurgents and by Spanish military governors, and the difficulty of preventing the despatch of munitions from American ports to assist the rebels, all combined to make the

Cuban struggle a matter of urgent concern to the United States. Yet, during the Cleveland administration, in spite of the natural desire of the American people to see the end of this barbarous civil war, the government had maintained a policy of entire neutrality.[2]

During the closing months of the Cleveland administration Secretary Olney was convinced that Cuba might be "in the market, for sale to the highest bidder." The President warned the world that "the United States is not a country to which peace is necessary." Yet, when a group of members of Congress came to tell the President "we have about decided to declare war against Spain over the Cuban question. Conditions are intolerable," Mr. Cleveland said that though Congress could declare war there would be no war, for as Commander-in-Chief, "I will not mobilize the army." He then referred to the possibility of buying Cuba from Spain for $100,000,000 and ended by saying: "It would be an outrage to declare war." [3]

Thus, though the Democratic executive could easily have provoked war, when March 4, 1897, came and the Republicans entered office, the Cuban situation remained unchanged. "With forebodings of impending conflict Mr. Cleveland was compelled to hand over this great responsibility to the new administration, to be by it handled in the interests of peace and ultimately disposed of by the grim methods of war." [4] But President Cleveland and Secretary Olney had commanded the respect even of Spanish diplomats and they had manfully tried to prevent an armed conflict between the United States and Spain.

In order to find a place for Mark Hanna, the Republican campaign director, Senator John Sherman of Ohio was persuaded to resign in order to become Secretary of State. Hanna became United States Senator from Ohio while Senator Sherman, who was already in his dotage, was given a place of prime importance. As Henry Adams said: "One might have shrugged one's shoulders had the President named Mr. Hanna his Secretary of State, for Mr. Hanna was a man of force if not of experience, and selections much worse than this had often turned out well enough; but John Sherman must inevitably and tragically break down." [5] The direction of affairs was gradually given to Mr. Day, the first Assistant Secretary of State, who later became Secretary when in April, 1898, Mr. Sherman was practically invited to resign. As he later wrote: "The result was that I lost the position both of Senator and Secretary. . . . They deprived me of the high office of Senator by the temporary appointment as Secretary of State." [6] From this situation it seemed as though little good could come, yet John Hay was appointed to be Ambassador to Great Britain and General Stewart L. Woodford was finally selected to be Minister to Spain.[7]

The United States notified the Spanish Government on June 26, 1897 that it was profoundly disgusted with the situation in Cuba, saying:

> the President is bound by the higher obligations of his representative office to protest against the uncivilized and inhuman conduct of the campaign in the island of Cuba. He conceives that he has a right to demand that a war, conducted almost within sight of our shores and grievously affecting American citizens and their interest throughout the length and breadth of the land, shall at least be conducted according to the military codes of civilization. . . . If the friendly attitude of this government is to bear fruit, it can only be when supplemented by Spain's own conduct of the war in a manner responsive to the precepts of ordinary humanity and calculated to invite as well the expectant forbearance of this government as the confidence of the Cuban people in the beneficence of Spanish Control.[8]

Likewise the instructions to General Woodford declared "it may not be reasonably asked or expected that a policy of mere inaction [by the United States] can be safely prolonged." There was the question of the recognition of the belligerency of the Cuban insurgents and the problem of possible American intervention to terminate a disastrous condition of affairs. The methods of warfare employed by Spain had "received very general condemnation." Consequently,

> At this juncture our Government must seriously inquire whether

the time has not arrived when Spain, of her own volition, moved by her own interests and by every paramount sentiment of humanity, will put a stop to this destructive war and make proposals of settlement honorable to herself and just to her Cuban colony and to mankind. The United States stands ready to assist her and tender good offices to that end.[9]

The reply of the Spanish government was a defence of their methods, citing the practices of General Sherman during the Civil War, and urging the co-operation of the United States with Spain "by putting an end to the existence of the public and organized direction which it [the revolt] receives and without which the rebellion would long ago have been entirely subdued by arms." Such an answer, justified though it might be under international law and American precedent, did not advance towards a settlement.[10] The Liberal party in Spain might issue a manifesto on the situation,[11] and the two governments might exchange lengthy diplomatic documents dealing with the condition of Cuba [12] and with alleged violations of neutrality;[13] but the glaring fact was that American public opinion was rapidly becoming more and more heated regarding the state of affairs in Cuba.

Meanwhile General Woodford, on his way to Madrid, conferred with the American Ambassadors to Great Britain, France, and Germany. He reported that the British favored autonomy for Cuba such as Canada enjoyed and continued:

I do not think that recognition of Cuban belligerency by the United States would be followed by any protest or unfriendly action on the part of either the French or German Governments.

I believe that most Englishmen, Frenchmen and Germans regard Cuba as within the legitimate zone of American influence and would not be disposed to resent any action by the United States that would be just, humane and in line with the progressive purposes of modern civilization. All thoughtful people in Europe realize that the United States have large interests in Cuba and that the war, which has existed in that Island during nearly half of the last thirty years, is destroying the resources of the Island; weakening its productive power; and hindering commerce. They naturally expect that we will do whatever shall be necessary to protect our great interests in Cuba so long as we do not contravene the law of nations.[14]

At Madrid in September, 1897, General Woodford explained the American attitude in a number of private interviews;[15] and it is possible that his frank but friendly attitude assisted in the overthrow of the Conservative Cabinet and the establishment of a new and Liberal ministry under Sagasta. This Cabinet decided to put into effect more liberal measures for Cuba though military pressure would continue.[16] At last at the end of November decrees were signed at Madrid which gave great satisfaction to the American Minister. At least they showed that American ideas were making progress. General Weyler, the cruel Governor-General of Cuba, had been recalled and now by these decrees a moderate degree of autonomy was granted to Cuba. All rights enjoyed by Spaniards at home were now granted in the Antilles.[17] This news reached America in time for the President to refer to it in his annual message. In this he continued to make the same mistakes that the Department of State had made in its note of June 26, 1897, respecting the laws of war which he claimed the Spaniards had been violating; but he welcomed the release of those Americans who had been held as prisoners by Spain and said: "It is honestly due to Spain and to our friendly relations to Spain that she should be given a reasonable chance to realize her expectations and to prove the asserted efficacy of the new order of things to which she stands irrevocably committed." He concluded by stating:

If it shall hereafter appear to be a duty imposed by our obligations to ourselves, to civilization and humanity to intervene with force, it shall be without fault on our part and only because the necessity for such action will be so clear as to command the support and approval of the civilized world.[18]

The United States also sent a note on December 20, 1897, repeating the sense of this message and declaring that she was maintaining her neutrality. The recognition of belligerent rights for the insurgents was further argued at length.[19] In January, riots broke out in Havana by way of

Cuban protest against Sagasta's liberal decree of autonomy
and it was decided to despatch the battleship *Maine* to
Cuban waters in order to give moral and material support
to the American Consul-General and to afford protection
to American residents. This visit, however, was of a friendly
nature and was so recognized by the Spanish authorities.
The situation, however, alarmed the government in Madrid
so that on February 1, 1898, they sent another note protesting against the continued existence in America of "revolutionary organizations which are laboring freely" for "an
absurd, unattainable separation" of Cuba from Spain. These
attempts "ought to cease entirely and without loss of time." [20]
This note Minister Woodford thought was a mistake and
he told the Spanish officials that he had advised the United
States to delay as long as possible any reply to it. As a matter of fact no reply was ever sent, for war soon intervened.
The situation, as General Woodford saw it at the end of
February, was that the Spanish ministry wanted "peace if
they can keep peace and save the dynasty. They prefer the
chances of war with the certain loss of Cuba, to the overthrow of the dynasty." [21]

Meanwhile Dupuy de Lome, the Spanish Minister at
Washington, lost his place because of the publication in the
press of a foolish private letter of his to a friend in which
he criticized the President and American policy. This incident was, however, quickly closed.[22] Infinitely more serious
was the destruction of the battleship *Maine* by an external
explosion in the harbor of Havana on the night of February
15 with heavy loss of life. Naturally the Spanish officials
were prompt in the expression of their sorrow and sympathy;
and fortunately, thanks to the admirable attitude of officials
at Washington, American public opinion was restrained and
dignified. But a tremendous impression had been created.[23]

Aside from these two events, the month of February saw
a gradual hardening of official opinion in Washington. Autonomy for Cuba did not seem to work out successfully; the
condition of the island grew worse; measures for the relief

of the population were ineffective; and in general the outlook was discouraging.²⁴ From Madrid the Minister wrote a series of important despatches to the President which reveal the admirable way in which General Woodford was fulfilling his mission, but which also make clear the increasing pessimism with which he viewed the situation. As these despatches have all been printed it is not necessary to examine them in detail.²⁵ There can be no question of the sincere desire of the President and of the American Minister to find a way out without recourse to war, of their dread of annexation on the one hand, and on the other, their belief that a radical change in Cuba must speedily take place. The rainy season would begin by May 1 and would last until about October 1. During this period the Spanish military forces in Cuba would be at a disadvantage.

Public opinion in America had been much impressed by the speech of Senator Proctor, who was a man of judgment. The new Spanish Minister in Washington telegraphed to Madrid that Senator Proctor's speech had "produced great effect because of his temperate stand. He set forth in black colors the situation of the *reconcentrados*, who were interned declaring that the country [Cuba] was opposed to autonomy and favorable to independence." ²⁶

As April 1 grew nearer the situation became more critical. On March 26 Secretary Day telegraphed to Madrid:

> The President has evidenced in every way his desire to preserve and continue friendly relations with Spain. He has kept every international obligation with fidelity. He wants an honorable peace. He has repeatedly urged the Government of Spain to secure such a peace. She still has the opportunity to do it, and the President appeals to her from every consideration of justice and humanity to do it. Will she? Peace is the desired end.²⁷

On March 27 Secretary Day again telegraphed to the American Minister to try to secure an armistice until October 1 and the revocation of the *reconcentrado* order. He proposed that in case peace were not secured by October 1 the President should act as final arbitrator between Spain and the insurgents. In the meantime negotiations were to proceed through American friendly offices and relief supplies for Cuba were to be provided by the United States. The previous day a demand for Cuban independence with a reasonable indemnity had also been made. An answer to these proposals which practically amounted to an ultimatum was necessary by Thursday, March 31.[28]

On that day the Spanish Government announced the proposal to arbitrate questions arising from the sinking of the *Maine,* the repeal of the *reconcentrado* decree for the western provinces of Cuba, relief measures, plans for the pacification of the island in conjunction with the insular parliament, which was not to meet till May 4, and an immediate suspension of hostilities if the Cuban insurgent leaders should request it. The duration and conditions of the suspension were to be determined by the Spanish General-in-Chief. General Woodford reported these terms in sorrow. They meant "the continuation of this destructive, cruel, and now needless war" for the real power in Spain now rested with the army leaders. If the ministry yielded more a revolution by the army might result.[29]

Later, on April 5, the repeal of the *reconcentrado* order was made for the entire island but the armistice was left as an event to be demonstrated by the submission of the insurgents and as such was not an offer from Spain. Papal intervention supported by the diplomacy of the great powers in Europe, now took a hand, and it was proposed that Spain should offer immediately an unconditional armistice till October 5. Of this General Woodford was strongly hopeful. Finally on April 9 this armistice was granted and on April 10 he telegraphed the President:

> In view of action of Spanish Government, as cabled Saturday, April 9, I hope that you can obtain full authority from Congress to do whatever you shall deem necessary to secure immediate and permanent peace in Cuba by negotiations, including the full power to employ the army and navy, according to your own judgment, to aid and enforce your action. If this be secured I believe you will get final settlement before August 1 on one of the following bases: either such

autonomy as the insurgents may agree to accept, or recognition by Spain of the independence of the island, or cession of the island to the United States.

I hope that nothing will now be done to humiliate Spain, as I am satisfied that the present Government is going, and is loyally ready to go, as fast and as far as it can. With your power of action sufficiently free you will win the fight on your own lines.[30]

The pressure for peace on the part of European influences had been strong. Already in September, 1897, German diplomats had debated the question of a joint intervention in behalf of the principle of monarchy. This, however, was counter-balanced by the large economic interests which some of these powers had in America and by the fact that France, who had heavy investments in Spain, could not be moved to intervene in behalf of monarchy.[31] France was, however, very anxious to prevent war and was ready to offer her good offices.[32] Public opinion on the continent was strongly pro-Spanish and the press was filled with bitter anti-American comments and hostile cartoons in which Americans were quite usually portrayed as swine. Only in England was public opinion led by the aristocracy, the politicians, and by financial interests to support the United States. As Ambassador Hay reported: "There is now (April 1) an almost universal hope that the United States will take such measures as may be necessary to bring peace to Cuba."[33] Indeed, if ever the United States had a good chance to measure the value of friendships, these days were to afford it. In spite of memories of the Venezuelan boundary dispute, the cordial support of Great Britain was manifest. Mr. Balfour told Mr. Hay on April 6 that "neither here nor in Washington did the British Government propose to take any steps which would not be acceptable to the Government of the United States."[34] In view of this attitude the Spanish appeal for the immediate exercise of the good offices of the Powers "to effect the preservation of peace and the reasonable protection of our rights" received at first only a perfunctory reply.[35] On April 6 the representatives of the Powers at Washington presented a plea for peace saying that they earnestly hoped "that further negotiations will lead to an agreement which, while securing the maintenance of peace, will afford all necessary guarantees for the re-establishment of order in Cuba." [36]

There was a second attempt at intervention by the Powers through the recommendations of their representatives at Washington. This was on April 14, 1898, and took the form of a despatch addressed by each Ambassador to his own Foreign Office proposing that an identic note should be addressed to the Department of State. The Austrian Ambassador put forward the suggestion, and a meeting was held at the Austrian Embassy of the European representatives with the exception of the British Ambassador. He, as *doyen* of the diplomatic corps, had been notified and had called a meeting; shortly the five Ambassadors crossed Connecticut Avenue from the Austrian Embassy to the British Embassy where a lengthy conference took place. As *doyen* Sir Julian Pauncefote naturally drafted a note in which there was not a word to which any American could object. There was some discussion and amendments were suggested. Finally M. Cambon, the French Ambassador, suggested that he redraft the proposed note. He wrote in French and made verbal changes, among them the phrase was inserted that American intervention in Cuba "ne sera pas justifiée." The German translation was that such intervention was not *gerechtfertig*. Such language changed the note from a friendly plea for peace to a remonstrance based on a denial of the correctness of possible American action. Unfortunately this version of the draft was permitted to stand for this phrase did not attract Sir Julian's attention. The note was despatched to Europe. In London the Austrian Ambassador called on Lord Salisbury to propose joint action along these lines. He was coldly received. In Berlin also the note which was reported by Dr. von Holleben, the German Ambassador at Washington, met with opposition; and the Kaiser made some notes on the margin of the despatch which showed his unwillingness to follow this French and Austrian lead. Nothing more was heard of the proposal at the time.

But in 1902 the German Foreign Office with singular ineptitude resurrected these documents and twice gave them to the press. This German version portrayed the British Ambassador as the author of the note and Germany as the power that out of friendship for America had blocked European intervention at the time.[37] It was an unskillful attempt to discredit Great Britain. Indeed as Secretary Hay wrote to President Roosevelt:

> Holleben has sent me an official memorandum as to the April 14 incident in which the German Government says that England "wishes to impair the friendly relations between Germany and the U. S. which relations arouse the jealousy of England (welche die Eifersucht Englands erregen).
> Is this the speech of great nations or the shrieks of angry housemaids pulling caps over the policeman?[38]

Thus ended a diplomatic squabble which aroused much hostility at the time. Secretary Hay instructed Dr. White, American Ambassador at Berlin, on February 17, 1902, to transmit to the German Foreign Office "without comment" a copy of a "letter found among the insurrectionists' papers in the Philippines, signed by G. Keocks, who describes himself as the Secretary of the Consulate of the German Empire in Manila." This letter showed conclusively that Germany was intriguing against America. No reply was ever received from the German Foreign Office.[39]

President McKinley had twice postponed his message to Congress. Finally he gave it on April 11.[40] The pressure which had been exerted on him had been great. The report on the destruction of the *Maine* had been before Congress since March 28; and public opinion as reflected in Congress was now at white heat. Hitherto there had been no encroachment on the powers of the Executive regarding diplomatic matters. To report the situation in such way as to place the issue of peace and war before Congress was tantamount to a declaration of war. To do this was to confess that diplomacy had failed and appeal was to be made to Congress whose only power in the matter related to war. Congress had early in March voted $50,000,000 as a special credit to assist in placing the country in a state of defence. If now a message should come before it leaving the matter of war to the judgment of Congress it would mean that all other resources had failed and that war was to come.

President McKinley was told that unless he took such action the Republican party might break up. He was advised that he would ruin himself and the party by opposing the will of the people. In spite of his strong personal opposition to the war and in spite of General Woodford's last message regarding the happy prospect of a peaceful solution the President gave way.[41] Following the message, Congress debated for a week and on April 19, 1898, passed four resolutions. These recognized the independence of Cuba, demanded that Spain withdraw from Cuba, directed the President to employ the entire forces of the nation to accomplish this and declared,

That the United States hereby disclaims any disposition or intention to exercise sovereignty, jurisdiction or control over said Island except for the pacification thereof and asserts its determination, when that is accomplished, to leave the government and control of the Island to its people.[42]

This fourth resolution gave the war the appearance of altruism and was undoubtedly sincerely approved by the great majority of Americans. Thus we were plunged into a war of vast import to the United States, in defiance of the best diplomatic advice, yet with the hearty support of the newspaper press of the country. Unfortunately newspapers did not make up for our unpreparedness. The rupture of diplomatic relations took place on April 20–21, and we were at war from April 21, 1898.[43] Within a few weeks Admiral Dewey had captured or destroyed the Spanish fleet at Manila and the first step had been taken toward the territorial establishment of American interests in the Far East. These indeed attracted greater attention in Europe than did our final successes on land and sea in the West Indies, in early July. The dominance of the United States in the west was to a certain extent taken for granted; but the acquisition of power in the east gave men pause.

In early May there were inquiries as to American intentions, and suggestions were made which led Ambassador Hay to suppose that England would urge upon Spain the evacuation of Cuba, should the United States so desire.[44] At the same time a discussion in another spirit and with distinctly selfish ends in view was taking place in Germany. Before it was finished good relations between the United States and Germany were threatened. On May 3, 1898, Ambassador Hay telgraphed that an "excellent authority in German matters suggests prompt action in annexation Hawaii before war closes as otherwise Germany might seek to complicate the question with Samoa or Philippine Islands." [44a]

Immediately after the American victory at Manila on May 1, the German Emperor had stated that Germany would observe the strictest neutrality during the contest and would seek to prevent, as far as possible, injury to German trade and commerce. At the same time German despatches from Manila made it evident that "Spanish dominion in the Philippines was untenable" and instructions were asked as to a proposal that a German prince should assume control and a German protectorate should be set up. The Philippine insurgents wished to be independent and not merely to exchange Spanish for American sovereignty. This gave rise to a lengthy memorandum to the Kaiser which discussed three possible solutions. These were (1) a protectorate, possibly under Germany; (2) the division of the island group between European powers, in which case Germany would naturally acquire her share; or (3) the neutralization of the Philippines under the guarantee of the powers as was the case of Belgium and Luxemburg in Europe. The decision was made to sound England with respect to a possible neutralization of the islands as such a solution would have the advantage since "the future is open to all and it leaves each one of the protectors the quiet hope that in the long run of time a suitable moment for seizure" of the islands will be found, especially when Germany would be stronger at sea.⁴⁵

The despatch of Admiral von Diedrichs to Manila in command of a squadron which was unreasonably large, soon gave rise to considerable friction between him and Admiral Dewey. The Germans seemed to be unduly aggressive and were particularly lacking in "sea manners." ⁴⁶ A telegram was also sent to von Holleben in Washington stating that the Kaiser "considers it one of the main tasks òf German policy not to allow any opportunity to slip by for the acquisition of maritime footholds in Eastern Asia. . . . It would, therefore, be of practical use for America in case she considers territorial expansion to assure herself of the friendly attitude of Germany by the practical application of the principle of 'live and let live.' " ⁴⁷ There were also despatches from Berlin declaring that England was seeking an alliance with the United States, but insisting that it would be more advantageous for the United States to come to an understanding with Germany regarding bases in the Pacific.⁴⁸ The nightmare of the German Foreign Office was a possible alliance of England, Japan, and the United States, which, however, the German Ambassador in London rejected as an impossibility. He advised that,

since the fate of the Philippines may be quickly decided, we should smooth the road for an understanding with America and thereby assure ourselves if not of considerable territorial advantages, at least of several footholds and coaling stations; for this purpose it is obviously necessary to explain to the Americans, who are only slightly acquainted with European politics, that the English reports of Germany's unfriendly intentions rest upon invention, that our claims are more modest than those of other powers, and that America has nothing to fear from the latter as soon as a settlement has been made with us. The correct way to gain this seems to me to be first of all the American Ambassador in Berlin, whose personality and influence at home does not count for so much at present, if he will only report correctly the information given him. The American representative here, who is said to stand in intimate relationship with President McKinley, has obviously English sympathies, and is besides a very silent man who, to my knowledge, has not sought political conferences with any of his colleagues. Even Lord Salisbury complains of his reticence.⁴⁹

This reticence Count Hatzfeldt sought to break down in a conversation which he had with Ambassador Hay. The report of this is given in the Appendix to this chapter.[50] In Berlin as well, von Richthofen, the acting Foreign Secretary, had a talk with Dr. White, the American Ambassador, in which he made the same points. To his delight he found that Dr. White was against annexations by the United States and that his opinions were "entirely favorable" to German desires. Dr. White reported this conversation, to Washington, saying that "close relations and co-operation of United States and Great Britain will certainly result in a continental coalition against United States. . . . I believe this represents the controlling feeling in the Government of His Imperial Majesty at present and that assurances, as far as our Government can see its way to give them, may save United States later troublesome complications."[51] In response to this, Washington telegraphed to Ambassador White:

> Nothing in the relations of the United States and Great Britain need give any ground for apprehension on the part of the Continental Powers. The United States can deal with the matters suggested in your telegram and with the whole situation in the end much better and upon broader terms, if not pressed for assurances for which no occasion has arisen.[52]

The situation became more embarrassing when the Department of State felt obliged to criticize Dr. White for his conversations with German officials. This is to be seen in the Appendix to this chapter. Meanwhile German attempts to interest Great Britain in a plan for the neutralization of the Philippines failed completely. The attempt to draw in France was abandoned and consequently Germany turned to Spain and sought to purchase from her the Spanish Carolines. Under the circumstances, the continued presence of Admiral von Diedrichs at Manila was no longer necessary and the greater part of the German squadron was withdrawn.[53] The situation was summarized by Ambassador Hay in a letter to Senator Lodge, which perhaps is colored by the views of Mr. Cecil Spring-Rice of the British Foreign Office. It is to be found in the Appendix to this chapter.⁵⁴ To Henry Adams, who viewed the situation in London with a certain proprietary feeling, for in times past he, his father, grandfather, and great-grandfather had been behind the curtains in various diplomatic crises, Anglo-American relations now entered on a new and blessed stage. As he wrote:

> After two hundred years of stupid and greedy blundering, which no argument and no violence affected, the people of England learned their lesson just at the moment when Hay would otherwise have faced a flood of the old anxieties. Hay himself scarcely knew how grateful he should be, for to him the change came almost of course. He saw only the necessary stages that had led to it, and to him they seemed natural; but to Adams, still living in the atmosphere of Palmerston and John Russell, the sudden appearance of Germany as the grizzly terror which, in twenty years effected what Adamses had tried for two hundred in vain—frightened England into America's arms—seemed as melodramatic as any plot of Napoleon the Great. He could feel only the sense of satisfaction at seeing the diplomatic triumph of all his family, since the breed existed, at last realized under his own eyes for the advantage of his oldest and closest ally (Hay). This was history, not education, yet it taught something exceedingly serious, if not ultimate, could one trust the lesson. For the first time in his life, he felt a sense of possible purpose working itself out in history.⁵⁵

Thus Lord Salisbury refused to take possession of Manila at the request of Spain, and advised the Austrian Foreign Office that Spain should "take advantage of the President's liberal disposition while it is yet possible." The United States, however, was opposed to any step which might look as though it were in any way looking for peace.⁵⁶ During June and July the French also were anxious to promote peace and thus save French holders of Spanish bonds from further losses. Various conversations to this end were held by Hanotaux, the French Foreign Secretary, with General Porter, American Ambassador at Paris. The Americans refused to name the terms of peace which they might consider, until finally the Spanish authorized the French officially to inquire as to the terms and to arrange for the suspension of hostilities.⁵⁷

These preliminaries to peace were concluded on August

12, with the signature of a protocol bringing the war practically to an end, though on August 13 the city of Manila was seized by the American force in ignorance of the agreement signed at Washington.[58]

Meanwhile the administration in Washington was trying to make up its mind as to what should be done regarding the Spanish islands both in the West Indies and East Indies. The first attempt to formulate terms was in early June when Secretary Day telegraphed to Mr. Hay that "at the present juncture" the President favored the surrender of Cuba to the United States until a stable government could be established, the cession of Porto Rico in lieu of any money indemnity from Spain, the acquisition of a port in the Philippines, the rest of the archipelago remaining under Spain, and the cession of an island in the Ladrones as a coaling station. It was pointed out, however, that the "prolongation of war may change this materially." Indeed on June 14 the situation with respect to the Philippine insurgents had so changed that the Secretary telegraphed again saying, "It is most difficult without fuller knowledge, to determine as to disposition of Philippine Islands." Finally, on July 27, the Ambassador was asked by the Department whether his previous approval of the President's terms of June 3 still stood. To this Mr. Hay replied, July 28, that he had not changed his mind, but suggested that a guarantee should be secured of fair treatment by Spain of the natives in the Philippines and a pledge that no lease or alienation of any portion of the islands should take place without American approval. These telegrams are given in the Appendix.[59]

The protocol of August 12, declared that Spain should cede to the United States Porto Rico and an island in the Ladrones in lieu of a money indemnity, that Spain should give up all claim of sovereignty in Cuba, and that as regards the Philippines "the United States will occupy and hold the city, bay and harbor of Manila, pending the conclusion of a treaty of peace which shall determine the control, disposition, and government of the Philippines." Later the use of the word "control" gave rise to differences, for the French word *"contrôle"* did not convey the same sense of domination as did the use of the English term. Five commissioners, each for the United States and for Spain, were to meet at Paris by October 1 to negotiate and conclude a treaty of peace. This left the question as to what should be done regarding the Philippines in much the same uncertain condition as was the mind of the American public in respect to such matters. The Cabinet was divided, the President was perplexed, and the debate in the press waxed hot and furious for the balance of the summer.[60]

There is good reason to believe that in early September, 1898, Japan cautiously suggested that in case the United States did not wish to assume responsibility alone for the Philippines, a joint protectorate, or a tri-partite protectorate, in conjunction with another Power having identical interests might be arranged. Japan and the United States would endeavor to form, subject to proper conditions, a suitable government for the Philippines. This suggestion was kept strictly confidential. It revealed to Washington, however, that the islands were now practically derelict and that in case the United States did not assume entire sovereignty and control over the whole archipelago other states, whether Japan, Germany, France, or Russia, would probably engage in a scramble for the territory. If the United States continued its occupation of Manila alone such inevitable developments would undoubtedly affect her interests and position. Great Britain had already urged the United States to occupy the Philippines. Thus matters stood when Secretary Day drew the instructions for the American peace commission on September 11, 1898.[61]

These instructions were to Secretary Day, himself, Senators Davis, Frye and Gray and Mr. Whitelaw Reid. Of these Davis, Frye and Reid were "avowed imperialists." They favored the acquisition of all or of a portion of the Philippines. Their instructions dealt with the acquisition of the island of Luzon alone, though of course an island in the

Ladrones and Porto Rico were to be ceded to the United States. Cuba was to be under American military occupation but no money claims on the part of Spain were to be recognized. With respect to the Philippines as a whole the instructions vaguely read as follows:

> The Philippines stand upon a different basis. It is none the less true, however, that, without any original thought of complete or even partial acquisition, the presence and success of our arms at Manila imposes upon us obligations which we can not disregard. The march of events rules and overrules human action. Avowing unreservedly the purpose which has animated all our effort, and still solicitous to adhere to it, we can not be unmindful that, without any desire or design on our part, the war has brought us new duties and responsibilities which we must meet and discharge as becomes a great nation on whose growth and career from the beginning the Ruler of Nations has plainly written the high command and pledge of civilization.
> Incidental to our tenure in the Philippines is the commercial opportunity to which American statesmanship can not be indifferent. It is just to use every legitimate means for the enlargement of American trade; but we seek no advantages in the Orient which are not common to all. Asking only the open door for ourselves, we are ready to accord the open door to others. The commercial opportunity which is naturally and inevitably associated with this new opening depends less on large territorial possession than upon an adequate commercial basis and upon broad and equal privileges.[62]

A change took place at this time in the Secretary of State for, with the proposed departure of Mr. Day for Paris, the President had offered the place to Ambassador Hay in London. He had hesitated, drafted a telegram declining the honor on grounds of health, and then finally accepted the place. Henry Adams, a warm friend of Hay, writes of this decision:

> He needed no office in order to wield influence. For him, influence lay about the streets, waiting for him to stoop to it; he enjoyed more than enough power without office; no one of his position, wealth, and political experience, living at the center of politics in contact with the active party managers, could escape influence. His only ambition was to escape annoyance, and no one knew better than he that, at sixty years of age, sensitive to physical strain, still more sensitive to brutality, vindictiveness, or betrayal, he took office at cost of life.[63]

So Mr. Hay "shouldered his pack and started for home." He became Secretary of State on September 30, 1898. His immediate concern was naturally the course of the negotiations at Paris. The story of the peace conference has been told many times; and as most of the documents relating to matters before the negotiators have been published it will be necessary only to outline the course of events and to point out certain definite stages. At Paris the American peace commissioners had private hearings in which testimony was given by American officers, experts, and a variety of others. A collection of extracts from articles published regarding the Philippines problem was also made. The burden of this was well expressed in a memorandum drawn on August 27, 1898, by General F. V. Greene:

> If the United States evacuate these islands, anarchy and civil war will immediately ensue and lead to foreign intervention. The insurgents were furnished arms and the moral support of the Navy prior to our arrival, and we cannot ignore obligations, either to insurgents or to foreign nations, which our own acts have imposed upon us. The Spanish Government is completely demoralized and Spanish power is dead beyond possibility of resurrection. Spain would be unable to govern these islands if we surrendered them. . . . On the other hand, the Filipinos cannot govern the country without the support of some strong nation.[64]

The commissioners promptly rejected the Spanish request for the *status quo* in the Philippines, as they also did Spanish attempts to delay evacuation and to turn the burden of the Cuban debt to the United States. Arbitration of such matters was also rejected.[65] As time went on the differences of opinion among the American commissioners became clearer. Finally, on October 25, a memorandum written by Mr. Reid and also signed by Senators Davis and Frye was drawn up favoring the acquisition of all of the Philippines. Secretary Day and Judge Gray each drew up separate memoranda taking the opposite point of view.[66] In response to these Secretary Hay telegraphed on October 26 as follows:

> The information which has come to the President since your departure convinces him that the acceptance of the cession of Luzon

alone, leaving the rest of the islands subject to the Spanish rule, or to be the subject of future contention, cannot be justified on political, commercial or humanitarian grounds. The cession must be of the whole archipelago or none. The latter is wholly inadmissible and the former must therefore be required. The President reaches this conclusion after most thorough consideration of the whole subject, and is deeply sensible of the grave responsibilities it will impose, believing that this course will entail less trouble than any other, and besides will best subserve the interests of the people involved, for whose welfare we cannot escape responsibility.[67]

Two days later Secretary Hay again telegraphed in behalf of the President:

The sentiment in the United States is almost universal that the people of the Philippines, whatever else is done, must be liberated from Spanish domination. In this sentiment the President fully concurs. Nor can we permit Spain to transfer any of the islands to another power. Nor can we invite another power or powers to join the United States in sovereignty over them. We must either hold them or turn them back to Spain.

Consequently, grave as are the responsibilities and unforeseen as are the difficulties which are before us, the President can see but one plain path of duty—the acceptance of the archipelago. Greater difficulties and more serious complications, administrative and international, would follow any other course. The President has given to the views of the Commissioners the fullest consideration, and in reaching the conclusion above announced, in the light of information communicated to the Commission and to the President since your departure, he has been influenced by the single consideration of duty and humanity.[68]

Thus it was that in November $20,000,000 were offered to Spain. The Philippines were to be ceded to the United States; but Spanish debts were not recognized. It is probable that after October 1 President McKinley was in favor of retaining the islands. He built up for himself a psychological and spiritual defence which justified him in his own eyes and in the eyes of the majority of the Americans. So the die was cast. The treaty was signed December 10, 1898, and proclaimed, after approval by the Senate in February, on April 11, 1899.[69]

Before long American officials were almost overwhelmed with suggestions as to what they should or should not do in the Philippines. It seemed as though everyone who had been in Asia, and many who had not, were anxious to advise us. The British, with their long experience in Asia, were full of practical, kindly unofficial hints and inquiries. The question of the "open door" in the Philippines was of special interest and Secretary Hay telegraphed personally to Mr. Henry White, Chargé d'Affaires in London, that the "open door does not mean free trade but admission of other nations to Philippine trade on equal footing with ourselves. President favors it, but ultimate decision must rest with Congress." [70] Publicly the British Prime Minister had already spoken sympathetically of the "introduction of the mighty force of the American Republic among the nations whose dominion is expanding" and declared that our "appearance among the factors of Asiatic and possibly of European diplomacy is a grave, and serious event." [71] Yet privately Lord Salisbury was skeptical concerning American friendship for England. Secretary Hay had been more of an optimist for he had written, "the dull hostility between us and England which existed a year ago has been changed into a firm friendship. . . . If we give up the Philippines it will be a considerable disappointment to our English friends. . . . I have no doubt that Germany has been intriguing both with Aguinaldo and with Spain. They are most anxious to get a foothold there; but if they do there will be danger of grave complications with other European powers." [72]

As regards Germany, Secretary Hay was right. A cable message from Mr. Henry White confirmed it. This read:

> Personal and very confidential. I have best reasons for believing German position *re* Philippine islands to be as follows: no *locus standi* under present circumstances as long as we retain control and sincere wish to avoid difficulties with us by appearing to have any desire to oppose our remaining, but every intention to establish footing there if possible in any other event.[73]

The German government was uneasy regarding American attempts to acquire new islands in the Pacific and when the commission at Paris offered a million dollars to Spain for the cession of Kusaie the Germans promptly advanced their claims. The United States did not include the cession of Kusaie as part of the ultimatum which finally forced peace from Spain; and Germany again pressed forward, this time with regard to a grant of a coaling station in the Sulu Islands. As a matter of fact on September 10 Spain had already made a tentative agreement to sell Kusaie, Ponape, and Yap in the Carolines to Germany.[74] This was to be kept secret for the time and was dependent on the terms of the peace treaty between Spain and the United States. The American proposal to acquire Kusaie was due to the supposition that it was needed as a cable station. Later, Germany offered one of her own islands in the Marshall group in return for which the United States might offer to Germany a coaling station in the Sulu Islands. This coaling station according to German ideas was to be a fairly sizable island, Palawan, Jolo, and Tawi-Tawi were mentioned. Germany was in a hurry; but the German Ambassador counseled delay and secrecy. In the end the United States found that it did not need Kusaie and, although both the President and Secretary Hay were originally not opposed to the lease of one of the Sulu Islands as a German coaling station, this step was never taken. In any case Germany soon purchased the entire Caroline group from Spain. The lesson of these negotiations is that at this time Germany was anxious not to see the Philippines pass to America "without Germany's receiving an equivalent compensation." [75]

As the situation in the Philippines became worse, owing to the outbreak of hostilities between the Americans and the local insurgents, an offer was made unofficially by a member of a former Japanese Cabinet to visit the Philippines in the endeavor to induce the natives to submit peacefully. However nothing came of this proposal.[76] The United States was, nevertheless thoroughly aware of the value of using such influences as it could to prevent the extension of the revolt in the Islands and on March 8, 1899, Secretary Hay wrote personally and confidentially to Mr. Straus, the American

Minister at Constantinople, to suggest to the Sultan of Turkey that as Khalif of the Muhammadan world he might send a message to the Sultan of the Sulu Islands counseling the development of "peaceful and harmonious relations between the Sultan and our (American) officials in that region." This was successfully done.[77]

It seemed at first as though matters could be satisfactorily settled between the insurgents and the Americans. But the personality of General Otis made strongly against a peaceable solution; and the defeat of resolutions in Congress looking for a recognition of the rights of the insurgents tended to discourage attempts at accommodation. Indeed there were many in Washington who shared the opinion of Mr. Adee, the Second Assistant Secretary of State, who wrote to Secretary Hay: "I strongly favor immediate coercive action against Aguinaldo [the insurgent leader] as a disturber of *our* peace." [78] Later, just before the outbreak of hostilities in February the appointment of a Philippine Commission gave promise of a settlement; but in the long run the suppression of disorder proved to be an arduous and lengthy task.[79]

Thus as we close this chapter in our diplomatic relations we see what an unknown future lay ahead of us. Not only was the problem of the government and administration of these recently acquired islands to perplex us for years to come, but by the extension of our influence in the West Indies, our diplomatic relations with Latin America were to be vitally affected. In the Far East, as we shall soon see, the position and condition of China were pregnant with trouble. The European powers were greedy but perplexed; Japan was preparing for her contest with Russia; and the whole development of our Asiatic trade and interests attracted the increasing attention of thinking men. At a stroke people understood that the United States must now be recognized as a world power. As Roosevelt said: "We have not the choice as to whether or not this country will play a great part in the world. All we can decide is whether we will play it well or ill." So we embarked on our voyage in world politics with high hopes and a clear eye but poorly equipped and without accurate charts.

NOTES TO CHAPTER III

1. Adams, *History of the United States of America;* New York, 1903, 9 Vols., I, p. 340. Cf. Chadwick, *The Relations of the United States and Spain. Diplomacy,* New York, 1909, pp. 432-433, 488-489.
2. O. C., Sept. 25, 1895, Olney to Cleveland and July 18, 1896, same to same (semi-official book); *Documentos presentados á las Cortes en la Legislatura de 1898 por el Ministro de Estado,* Madrid, 1898, pp. 1, 28; F. R., 1896, pp. xxxiii-xxxv, 582-846; *op. cit.,* 1897, pp. 483-548; James, ch. XIII and Appendix VI. Cf. McElroy, II, pp. 245-246, 248-249; Chadwick, ch. XXII; Rhodes, *McKinley and Roosevelt Administrations,* pp. 44-45.
3. McElroy, II, pp. 249-250.
4. *Ibid.,* II, p. 252. Cf. Cortissoz, *Reid,* II, p. 214.
5. *The Education of Henry Adams,* Boston, 1918, p. 356.
6. Rhodes, pp. 31-32.
7. *Ibid.,* p. 42; D. S., to London, Vol. 32, No. 112, June 30, 1897, Sherman to Hay.
8. *Documentos presentados,* etc., pp. 30-31, June 26, 1897, Sherman to Dupuy de Lome. Cf. Chadwick, p. 497.
9. F. R., 1898, pp. 558-561.
10. *Documentos,* etc., pp. 34 *et seq.* Cf. Chadwick, pp. 502-503. Cf. *D. S.,* Inst. Spain, Vol. 22, p. 420.
11. F. R., 1898, p. 592.
12. F. R., 1897, pp. 507-514.
13. *Ibid.,* pp. 529-540.
14. D. S., From Spain, Vol. 131, Nov. 10, Aug. 30, 1897, Woodford to Sherman.
15. F. R., 1898, pp. 562, 565-573, 576, 580. Cf. D. S., From Austria, Vol. 42, No. 17, Oct. 5, 1897, Tower to Sherman denying that Austria and Germany were establishing an understanding hostile to the United States in the event of her intervention in Cuba.
16. D. S., From Spain, Vol. 132, unnumbered (unofficial), Oct. 6, 1897, Woodford to Sherman; October 16, 1897 (personal and confidential), same to same; Numerical file, Vol. 515, Oct. 26, 1897, same to same; F. R., 1898, pp. 581, 582-589, 590, 596, 600-603, 647, *et seq.* Cf. Chadwick, p. 524; *Documentos,* etc., pp. 51-61.
17. F. R., 1898, p. 616-644. *Documentos,* etc., pp. 66-68. Cf. Chadwick, pp. 524-525.
18. F. R., 1897, pp. xx-xxi.
19. F. R., 1898, pp. 647-654.
20. *Ibid.,* pp. 658-664. *Documentos,* etc., pp. 108-116. Cf. Chadwick, pp. 533-537; Rhodes, pp. 47-48. "While the President feared that the scheme of autonomy had come to nothing, he nevertheless exhibited his continued friendship for Spain. At the diplomatic dinner of January 27, 1898, he showed marked attention to the Spanish Minister and congratulated him on the fact that 'we have only good news.'"
21. F. R., 1898, p. 665.
22. *Ibid.,* pp. 1007-1022. Cf. Rhodes, pp. 48-49; Chadwick, p. 539; even the *Daily Telegraph* of London (Feb. 11, 1898) commented on this episode; "No one must be allowed to go about with a lighted candle in a powder

magazine, and, if the Minister himself was careless enough to forget the highly explosive conditions under which he was carrying on his responsible duties, it is just as well that he should find it necessary to deprive himself of the chances of doing any further mischief."

23. *F. R.*, 1898, p. 1029. Cf. Rhodes, pp. 50-51.
24. *F. R.*, 1898, pp. 666, *et seq.* March 1, 1898, Sherman to Woodford.
25. *Ibid.*, pp. 673, 681, 685, 688, 692-698, 701, 703. These despatches run from March 2-26. Cf. Cortissoz, II, pp. 220-221; Chadwick, pp. 549-551; Rhodes, pp. 53-57.
26. *Documentos*, etc., p. 138. Cf. Rhodes, pp. 52-53.
27. *F. R.*, 1898, p. 704.
28. *Ibid.*, pp. 711-713, 718-724.
29. *Ibid.*, pp. 726-728, 730-731.
30. *Ibid.*, pp. 732-733, 735, 737, 741, 743-750; *Documentos*, etc., pp. 156-159, 162-172; Cf. Rhodes, pp. 61-64; Chadwick, pp. 566-569.
31. *G. P.*, XV, pp. 3 *et seq*, Nos. 4124, 4125.
32. *D. S.*, From France, Vol. 115, No. 199, March 31, 1898, Porter to Sherman. Cf. Rhodes, pp. 76-77.
33. *Times*, April 1, 1898; *D. S.*, From London, Vol. 191, No. 341, April 1, 1898, Hay to Sherman.
34. *D. S.*, From London, Vol. 191, No. 345, April 6, 1898, Hay to Sherman. Arrangements were made that in case of war the British Ambassador in Madrid was to take charge of the American Legation. Cf. also Thayer, *Life and Letters of John Hay*, Boston, 1915, 2 Vols., II, pp. 165-167.
35. *Documentos*, etc., pp. 158-159.
36. *F. R.*, 1898, p. 740; *G. P.*, No. 4138.
37. For this entire episode cf. Hansard, 4th. Series, Vol. CI, c. 311; *G. P.*, XV, No. 4140, 4141, 4142, 4143, 4144; Hashagen, *Zur Geschichte der Amerikanisch-Deutschen Beziehungen 1897-1907*, in *Zeitschrift für Politik*, XVI, No. 2, pp. 122-129; *D. S.*, From Germany, Vol. 75, Nos. 1850, 1852, Feb. 12 and 14, 1902, White to Hay; Reuter, *Anglo-American Relations during the Spanish-American War*, New York, 1924, pp. 80-81; *Daily Telegraph*, Jan. 22, 1902; *Times*, Feb. 12, 1902; Smalley, *Anglo-American Memories*, 2nd Series, pp. 179-182, and private conversations.
38. *R. P.*, Feb. 15, 1902, Hay to Roosevelt.
39. *D. S.*, To Germany, Vol. 21, No. 1301, Feb. 17, 1902, Hay to White.
40. *F. R.*, 1898, pp. 750-760.
41. Rhodes, pp. 59-61, and 64 (note).
42. *F. R.*, 1898, pp. 761-763. Cf. Rhodes, pp. 65-67. Whitelaw Reid deeply regretted the fourth resolution for he said: "We are making ourselves morally responsible for decent government in Cuba, and we can't wash our hands of it after turning Spain out, by merely telling them to set up for themselves." Cortissoz, II, pp. 222-223. Olcott, *Life of William McKinley*, Boston, 1916, 2 Vols., II, ch. XXIV naturally takes an optimistic view and does not mention Woodford's last despatch.
43. *F. R.*, 1898, pp. 764-769. A mournful letter from Cleveland to Olney, April 26, 1898, in *O. C.*, reads in part: "I cannot avoid a feeling of shame and humiliation. It seems to me to be the old story of good intentions and motives sacrificed to false considerations of complaisance and party harmony. McKinley is not a victim of ignorance, but of amiable weakness not unmixed with political ambition. He knew or ought to have known the cussedness of the Senate and he was abundantly warned against Lee. . . . In the meantime, we, who have undertaken war in the interest of humanity and civilization, will find ourselves in alliance and co-operation with Cuban insurgents—the most inhuman and barbarous cut-throats in the world. . . ."

44. *H. P.,* May 8, 1898, Hay to Day; May 10, same to same; *D. S.,* From London, Vol. 192, No. 386, May 10, same to same; No. 391, May 12, same to same.
44a. *D. S.,* From London, Vol. 192, telegram May 3rd, 1898. Hay to Day.
45. *G. P.,* XV, Nos. 4145, 4146
46. *Autobiography of George Dewey,* New York, 1913, ch. XVII; Private conversations; Diedrichs' reply to Dewey in *Marina Rundschau,* March, 1914, pp. 253, *et seq.* I have heard on good authority that the chapter in Dewey was toned down from the original version. Eckardstein, *Ten Years at the Court of St. James,* New York, 1922, pp. 100-101; Rhodes, pp. 79-80; Keim, *Forty Years of German-American Political Relations,* Philadelphia, 1919, pp. 220 *et seq.* Gooch and Temperley, *British Documents on the Origins of the War, 1898-1914,* London, 1927, 11 vols. I., pp. 105-106.
47. *G. P.,* XV, No. 4151; von Holleben asked for positive instructions, No. 4152. *D. S.,* From Germany, Vol. 66, Nos. 416, 460, May 5, and June 18, 1898, White to Day, show how strongly pro-German were the feelings of the American Ambassador at Berlin.
48. *G. P.,* XV, No. 4154.
49. *Ibid.,* No. 4155.
50. *Ibid.,* 4159; Appendix A to this chapter.
51. *G. P.,* XV, Nos. 4156, 4157, 4160; *D. S.,* From Germany, Vol. 66, telegram, July 12, 1898, White to Day.
52. *D. S.,* To Germany, Vol. 20, telegram, p. 655, July 13, 1898, Day to White. The same day a telegram was also sent to White expressing the displeasure of the President that such a conversation should have taken place and on July 22 (p. 656) White was directed to find out the plans regarding the German fleet then at Manila. To this White replied by saying: "I tried constantly to show that German interests in those regions will be best served by as little demonstration of force as possible and avoiding every interference likely to provoke ill feeling in our people and embarrassment to our Government. Minister seemed fully to agree to this, but it should be borne in mind that the German Government clearly regards the emergency in the East as one from which she must gain something or lose prestige with Europe, and even with her own people." From Germany, Vol. 66, telegram, July 25, 1898; Cf. Eckardstein, p. 100; *G. P.,* XV, Nos. 4163; *D. S.,* From Germany, Vol. 66, No. 506, July 30, 1898, White to Day. The truth was that White was that curious combination, an immense admirer of imperial Germany but an '"anti-imperialist" as far as American policies were concerned. Further evidence of German plans is to be found in Appendix B to this chapter.
53. *G. P.,* XV, Nos. 4166-4169.
54. Appendix C to this chapter.
55. *Education of Henry Adams,* pp. 362-363.
56. *D. S.,* From London, Vol. 192, telegram, June 5, 1898, Hay to Day; No. 425 (strictly confidential), June 8, same to same; No. 434, June 17, same to same; To London, Vol. 32, telegram, p. 681, June 7, Day to Hay; No. 689, June 11, Day to Hay; From Russia, Vol. 52 unnumbered, June 16, Hitchcock to Day.
57. *D. S.,* From France, Vol. 116, unnumbered, June 7, 1898, Porter to Day; No. 272, June 10, same to same; No. 278, June 20, same to same; No. 279, June 21, same to same; No. 298, July 13, same to same; To France, Vol. 24, telegram, p. 381, June 17, Day to Porter; *Documentos,* etc., No. 2, pp. 91 *et seq.,* 135 *et seq.; F. R.,* 1898, pp. 819 *et seq.*
58. *F. R.,* 1898, pp. 824-830; Dewey, pp. 280-282.
59. Appendix D to this chapter.
60. Cf. Rhodes, pp. 97-101; Cortissoz, II, pp. 224-225.

61. *D. S.,* From Japan, Vol. 71, No. 182, Aug. 13, 1898, Buck to Day; *F. R.,* 1898, pp. 904 *et seq.*
62. *Ibid.*
63. Adams, p. 365; *Hay Papers; D. S.,* Inst. to London, Vol. 32, telegram, p. 635, Aug. 26, 1898, Day to Hay; No. 854, Sept. 16, Day to White. For much that is more personal in the career of Secretary Hay I must refer the reader to my sketch of John Hay, written in March, 1926, for the series, on the *Secretaries of State,* to be published by Knopf. Owing to delays inevitable to a co-operative work of this sort, I cannot give precise cross references to this for I have not at the time of writing this book received any proof.
64. *U. S. Senate Document No. 62, Part I, 55th Cong. 3rd session,* Washington, 1899, p. 374.
65. *F. R.,* 1898, pp. 916, 918 *et seq.;* 930 *et seq.;* Reid, II, pp. 235-237, 242-243.
66. *F. R.,* 1898, pp. 932 *et seq.;* Reid, II, pp. 246-248.
67. *F. R.,* 1898, p. 935.
68. *Ibid.,* pp. 937-938.
69. *Ibid.,* pp. 939-961; Olcott, II, pp. 109-111; Spanish despatches relating to the Peace negotiations are in *Documentos á las Cortes en la Legislatura de 1898 por el Ministro de Estado* (No. 3), Madrid, 1899. I have not thought it necessary to give specific references to these documents.
70. *H. P.,* Nov. 23, 1898, Hay to White. Cf. *D. S.,* From London, Vol. 194. telegram, Nov. 23, 1898, White to Hay; No. 589, Nov. 26, same to same (relating to navigation laws); Vol. 195, No. 645, Jan. 13, 1899, same to same (a chartered company for the Philippines); telegram, Jan. 21, same to same; *H. P.,* April 3, 1899, Whitridge to Hay (the Indian native states as models).
71. *Times,* Nov. 10, 1898.
72. Quoted in Rhodes, p. 110; Cf. also the friendly comment of the *Times,* Dec. 6, 1898, on the cordial terms used by the President in his annual message.
73. *D. S.,* From London, Vol. 194, telegram, Oct. 28, 1898, White to Hay. Count Munster, German Ambassador in Paris, was, however, frank in his personal estimate for, in talking with Mr. Reid, who had said he could not understand why Germany wanted islands in the Far East, he said: "No more can I. I agree with you precisely; and I tell you these Colonial Department people are all alike—all savages, who can't eat without gorging—not civilized sufficiently to know when they have had enough, and unable to resist the sight of raw meat. They are tiresome, these colonials." Cortissoz, II, p. 245.
74. *G. P.,* XV, pp. 76-77. On the entire question of German policy for this period cf. Shippee, *Germany and the Spanish-American War* in *Am. Hist. Rev.,* XXX (July, 1925), pp. 754-777.
75. *G. P.,* XV, Nos. 4181, 4193, 4194; *D. S.,* Numerical File, Vol. 547, memorandum, Jan. 14, 1899.
76. *D. S.,* From Japan, Vol. 72, telegram, Feb. 12, 1899, Buck to Hay.
77. *H. P.,* March 8, 1899, Hay to Straus. Prior to this the Sultan of Sulu had asked for American protection, for Germans were "trying hard to put their foot in Sooloo." *D. S.,* From London, Vol. 194, enclosure to No. 547, Oct. 8, 1898, White to Hay; Vol. 195, enclosure to No. 620, Dec. 30, 1898, same to same.
78. *H. P.,* Dec. 30, 1898, Adee to Hay; *D. S.,* From London, Vol. 195, telegram, Dec. 20, 1898, White to Hay. Cf. for this whole subject Dennett, *Americans in Eastern Asia,* New York, 1922. Ch. xxxi. There are in the Hay papers two memoranda, unsigned and undated, which portray an envoy of the insurgents as being very anxious to come to terms. The statement is made: "Nothing would be so unfortunate for the Philippines as a conflict with

the United States. Hasty or inconsiderate action now would only delay the realization of our hopes for generations. You should know that nothing can be done for us until the sovereignty of the United States is realized. I am firmly convinced that the United States have no motive but our good, and want to be our friends and not our enemies."

79. *D. S.*, Special Agents, Vol. 3, telegram, April 4, 1899, Schuman to Hay; *H. P.*, telegram, May 23, 1899, same to same; *D. S.*, To London, Vol. 33, No. 489, Nov. 9, 1900, Hay to Choate.

APPENDICES TO CHAPTER III
A

D. S. From London, Vol. 192, No. 454 (strictly confidential), July 14, 1898, Hay to Day.

I received yesterday, by special appointment, a long visit from the German Ambassador at this Court, Count Hatzfeldt. He begged me to regard it as altogether confidential, and I will be glad if you will so treat it.

He began by referring to the false and unfounded rumors which have been disseminated by the British and American Press, as to the unfriendly attitude of Germany in the existing war. He said there was absolutely no foundation for them; that the action of Germany had been perfectly correct and loyal from the beginning and would so continue to the end. He mentioned two incidents in illustration of this. He said that at the very beginning of the war the German Consul General had refused to take charge of American interests in Havana; and on reporting his refusal to his Government he had been severely reprimanded, the German authorities having reminded him of the conduct of the American Embassy in Paris taking charge of German interests during the war of 1870. He said further that since the present war began, the Spanish Government had offered to make over the Philippine Islands to Germany, "in deposit," but that the German Ministry had promptly refused to accept them. "The Emperor," he said, "and his Ministers as well, have no disposition to interfere with, or deprive us, of our rights of conquest in any direction. It is out of the question that Germany should entertain any such intentions; Germany stands between two groups of powers, independent of each. On one side is England, on the other Russia and France in alliance. It is impossible that Germany should go far abroad seeking adventures; she needs all her power at home."

He then went on to say what Germany desired; it appeared to him "very little." They wanted a "few coaling stations," and hoped that in the final disposition of the Philippines, it might be arranged. He spoke also of the claim of Germany to the Caroline group; that they had been unjustly treated by the Pope in the arbitration submitted to him. He finally referred to the annexation of Hawaii; that Germany had no objection to that arrangement—but that there was some sensitiveness in regard to Samoa; that German interests were so greatly in evidence there, that it would seem just that German influence should also predominate.

Thus far I had allowed him to talk with little interruption, but at this point I told him that the question of Hawaii had no connection with any phase of European politics; that the people of Hawaii had constituted a government and offered us annexation six years ago, and that no observations in regard to that matter had been made, or would be considered, from any other power; that we considered our interests in Samoa sufficiently important to have taken a good deal of trouble about them, and that I could not encourage him to hope that my Government would agree to any change.

As to the general subject he had discussed I assured him that the Government of the United States appreciated at its just value the friendship of Germany, and trusted that it might never be interrupted; that I could give him no indication of what would be the final disposition of the Philippines as a result of the war. I said the inclination of the President was to a liberal and even generous treatment of Spain, when peace comes to be arranged; but that of course such treatment became more and more difficult with every additional day of war.

He asked me why there seemed so decided an opposition in America to any suggestions from Europe in the interests of peace. I told him that the President had received the Ambassadors in Washington with perfect courtesy, and no doubt would continue to listen to any proper suggestions from any of them; but that all our traditions were opposed to the entertaining of any collective representations of European powers, and that in this case I thought it improbable that we could admit the competence of others to assist in the settlement of matters concerning the United States and Spain.

Throughout this conversation I was struck with the confirmation it afforded of the information I have from time to time sent you, of the attitude of the German Government in relation to the war.

I may add, as this despatch is confidential, that I have had a brief conversation with the British Ambassador to Germany, now on leave in London. He assures me that whatever appearances may indicate, the German Government will take no practical steps which would bring them into any serious disagreement with us.

B

D. S. From Germany, Vol. 66, No. 507, July 30, 1898, White to Day.

Referring to my despatch No. 506 of July 30, 1898, I called at the Foreign Office this morning and, my other matters having been disposed of, Acting-Minister Baron von Richthofen took up my hint made at our last meeting that the German ships at Manila might perhaps be moved about somewhat to avoid the appearance of a studied observation of our doings there. He stated that he did not think it best to bring my remark to the attention of the Emperor, that it might provoke some feeling which had been happily absent thus far.

I replied that I thought he had somewhat misunderstood me, that what I said was given to him not at all as a proposal to be conveyed to His Majesty, but informally as a hint to be remembered by himself whenever the general question is discussed.

I then called his attention to a statement which has appeared widely in journals throughout Europe, which led the Japanese Chargé to visit me yesterday for the purpose of making enquiries, a statement to the effect that the continental European powers are discussing the advisability of making joint representations to the United States with reference to our occupation of the Philippines.

He assured me that he knew nothing of any such discussion or of any communications looking toward it, and that Germany had no wish to interfere in the slightest degree with our operations in those regions.

I replied that I was very glad to receive this assurance for that, of all things, interference by European powers in this matter was most likely to provoke a profound and wide-spread American feeling in favor of the permanent occupation of those islands.

He acquiesced in the naturalness of this feeling, and then said that he thought it might be well to have before long some comparison of views between the United States and Germany regarding eventual arrangements as to the disposition of territorial privileges in the East, and in his remarks generally on this subject he seemed to me to indicate a very strong wish that Germany should be able to secure something in a territorial way at the final settlement.

I asked him where such a conference could, in his opinion, be best held. He said that as the press seemed to get hold very quickly of every meeting of leading personages at Washington, he thought it might be better to have such a comparison of views made here where it would attract no observation and give rise to no rumors.

I then stated to him, as my own personal view, that, under ordinary conditions, the United States would be helped rather than hurt by any extension of such a civilizing power as that of Germany in eastern regions now undeveloped, and that the United States could not be injured by Germany's obtaining a station and centre of influence in any territory in those regions which would not embarrass us now or interfere with what we might deem it best to retain hereafter, but that the time had clearly not arrived for any full comparison of views on the subject, that everything in the matter was yet unsettled, but that I would communicate to my Government the views he had presented in the hope that at the earliest moment permitted by our proper interests I should be authorized to talk with him more fully, directly and definitely.

I reiterated the opinion here that not only in regard to the questions between the United States and Spain, but in relation to all questions arising now or hereafter between the United States and Germany, if any concession in the matter above referred to is possible it would reduce greatly present and future friction between the two nations to have such concession presented at the earliest day consistent with our interests.

D. S. To Germany, Vol. 20, No. 556, Aug. 15, 1898, Day to White.

I have received your despatches, Nos. 506 and 507, both dated the 30th ultimo, in which you report two conversations had by you with the Acting Minister for Foreign Affairs, Baron von Richthofen, in regard to the present and prospective situation in the Philippine Islands.

In your several conferences with the Acting Minister, while governing yourself in the main by the instructions conveyed in my two confidential telegrams of July 14 and 23, you appear to have endeavored to sound Baron von Richtofen as to the feelings and possible aspirations of Germany in that quarter.

Having in mind my telegraphed instructions of the 13th, I was not prepared for the turn given by you to your conversation with the acting Minister as reported in your No. 507, when you called his attention to the current newspaper rumors that the Continental European Powers are discussing the advisability of making joint representations to the United States with reference to our occupation of the Philippines. While your introduction of this aspect of the question elicited the Minister's statement that "Germany had no wish to interfere in the slightest degree with our operations in those regions" and to that extent had a reassuring result, the conversation seems to have drifted considerably beyond that point, and embraced embarrassing intimations that Germany might seek to "secure something in a territorial way at the final settlement," that "it might be well to have before long some careful comparison of views between the United States and Germany regarding eventual arrangements as to the disposition of territorial privileges in the East," and that, "there were some very moderate proposals which she [Germany] might be prepared to make." The conversation on this delicate point seems to have gone so far as to discuss the most convenient place for holding such a comparison of views, with the expression of preference for Berlin as its scene, and to have drawn from you your personal view that in certain contingencies "the United States would be helped rather than hurt by any extension of such a civilizing power as that of Germany in eastern regions now undeveloped, and that the United States could not be injured by Germany's obtaining a station and center of influence in any territory in those regions which would not embarrass us now or interfere with what we might deem it best to retain hereafter, but that the time had clearly not arrived for any full comparison of views on the subject, that everything in the matter was yet unsettled." You added that you would communicate to your Government the views Baron Richthofen had presented, in the hope that at the earliest possible moment permitted by our proper interests you would be "authorized to talk with him more fully, directly and definitely."

I naturally gather from your report, thus summarized, that you have in fact discussed with His Excellency the prospect of Germany's obtaining a share in the Philippines; expressed your views that this would not hurt but rather help the United States, and offered to obtain from your Government at as early a day as possible some definite assurance in this regard.

If this be so, you have gone distinctly beyond the attitude of absolute reserve inculcated by my telegram of the 13th July, which informed you of the President's surprise that assurance should be requested as to matters wholly in the future and uncertain; that the United States was not in possession of the Philippines, and had not determined its future relations to them while so much was dependent on the duration of the war and the events intervening a final settlement; and that we could deal with the whole situation in the end much better and upon broader terms if not pressed for assurances for which no occasion had arisen.

The terms of the protocol establishing the preliminaries of peace between the United States and Spain, which was signed on the 13th instant and of which you have been duly advised by cable, abundantly show the necessity and wisdom of the strict reserve I aimed to impress upon you in regard to the eventualities of the situation in the Philippines. By the engagement the United States will occupy and hold the city, bay, and harbor of Manila, pending the conclusion of a treaty of peace which shall determine the control, disposition and government of the Philippines. The negotiations to this end lie exclusively between the United States and Spain as the parties to the war, and it pertains only to them to determine the conditions upon which peace between them shall rest. It is obvious that the United States could not, in justice either to ourselves or to Spain, enter upon the peace negotiation constrained by assurances given in advance to any third Power not a party to the differences to be settled. Indeed, the United States has been careful in dealing with Spain itself, to formulate no conditions and announce no national policy with respect to the future of the Philippine Islands. Under these circumstances, the suggestion contained in your despatch that we foreshadow any such conditions or policy in part or by indirection through assurances given in advance to a neutral power cannot fail to be untimely and embarrassing.

C

Hay Papers, Hay to Lodge, American Embassy, London, July 27, 1898.

I am most grateful to you for your letters. I appreciate the sacrifice so busy a man makes in writing; and coming, as they do, from the very centre of news, they are most interesting and valuable.

I can send you little that is interesting in return. The daily telegrams in the papers make everything stale a few hours after it happens. There are a few things, it is true, under the surface, but the people you know tell you everything. I have been under great obligations the last few months to Spring-Rice, who knows Germany as few men do and has kept me wonderfully *au courant* of facts and opinions there. *Voilà l'ennemi* in the present crisis. The jealousy and animosity felt towards us in Germany is something which can hardly be exaggerated—*pace* Dr. White. They hate us in France, but French hate is as straw fire compared to Germany. And France has nothing to fear from us while the Vaterland is all on fire with greed, and terror of us. They want the Philippines, the Carolines, and Samoa—they want to get into our markets and keep us out of theirs. They have been flirting and intriguing with Spain ever since the war began and now they are trying to put the Devil into the head of Aguinaldo. I do not think they want to fight. In fact they frankly tell us they can't. Hatzfeldt said the other day, "We cannot remove our fleet from German waters." But they want, by pressure, by threats, and by sulking and wheedling in turn to get something out of us and Spain. There is to the German mind, something monstrous in the thought that a war should take place anywhere and they not profit by it.

This is awfully indiscreet, but I get sick of discretion once in a while. Don't file me.

I see nothing of Adams. He and Don Cameron are living the ideal life of the old Tory squire in Surrenden Manor. They never come to town and I am too busy to visit them. But now with peace in sight I may have a little leisure and we shall move down on them soon.

How splendidly things have moved our way! I do not see a ghost of a chance for Bryan in the next few years.

D

Hay Papers, Day to Hay, Washington, June 3, 1898, Telegram.

Strictly confidential.—The President, speaking for himself, would be inclined to grant terms of peace on the following basis.

First. The evacuation of Cuba, and delivery of title and possession of the Island to the United States, to restore and establish order and hold until a stable Government established; United States to protect Spanish subjects, their lives and property, while in possession.
Second. United States not demanding any money indemnity for the war, Spain to cede Porto Rico to the United States in lieu thereof, the United States to take care of the just and lawful claims of citizens of the United States arising from the Cuban insurrection and the present war.
Third. Philippine Islands to be allowed to remain with Spain, except a port and necessary appurtenances, to be selected by the United States, shall be ceded to the United States.
Fourth. Granting to the United States an Island in the Ladrones, with harbour for a coaling station.

These terms will be acceptable to the President at the present juncture, saving further sacrifice and loss of life. Prolongation of war may change this materially.

Hay Papers, Day to Hay, June 14, 1898, Telegram.

Since my telegram to you third instant conditions have changed that paragraph three (as to Philippine Islands) will probably have to be modified. The insurgents there have become an important factor in the situation and must have just consideration in any terms of settlement. It is most difficult without fuller knowledge to determine as to disposition of Philippine Islands.

Hay Papers, Day to Hay, June 23, 1898.

I have received and read with much gratification, your "strictly confidential" despatch, No. 425 of the 8th inst., in regard to the possible terms of peace, should overtures to that end be made by Spain, or the timeliness thereof be spontaneously suggested to Spain by any of the Powers. Your tact and discretion in dealing with this most delicate matter have my most cordial commendation.

Hay Papers, Day to Hay, July 26 or 27, 1898, Telegram.

Have you any reason for revising your views about the terms of peace which were submitted to you in my telegram of June 3rd, and of which in a letter to the President you expressed approval. The President will probably make answer to Spain's general proposal the last of this week.
Telegraph fully.

Hay Papers, Hay to Day, July 28, 1898, Rec'd 3.45 p. m.

Personal and confidential.—I still think terms of June 3rd equally generous and wise. Can suggest no modification in first and second clauses. Cuba and Porto Rico should be ceded to us unencumbered and without conditions. To the third clause I have to suggest the addition of strong guarantee of fair treatment of natives of prohibition of lease or alienation of any portion of the islands without our approval. To fourth clause add coaling station in Carolines, if thought desirable. According to modern usage we are entitled to indemnity; but it might be better to yield that point in consideration of advantage gained by voluntary evacuation of Cuba. I may add that British Government prefer to have us retain Philippine Islands, or failing that, insist on option in case of future sale.

CHAPTER IV

HAWAII AND SAMOA

IN connection with the Spanish-American War there came to the front our relations with the Republic of Hawaii, which till recently had been known as the Kingdom of Hawaii, or Sandwich Islands. In 1893 a Committee of Public Safety largely composed of Americans, and having the support of the American Minister, Mr. Stevens, seized control of the government in Honolulu. Angered by the intolerable native administration they resented the recent overthrow of the constitution. Supported by American naval forces this Committee issued a proclamation declaring monarchy to be at an end and organized a provisional government. Later, on July 4, 1894, a republic was proclaimed. In the meantime the United States had received a delegation from the provisional government; and a treaty providing for the annexation of the island was quickly drawn and sent to the Senate on February 15, 1893. President Harrison, whose term of office expired on March 4, asked the immediate approval of the Senate. Such untoward haste led, however to delay and the Senate let the treaty lie over till after Mr. Cleveland's inauguration. The first international problem which the new administration faced was, therefore, the question as to what should be done regarding Hawaii.

The new Secretary of State, Judge Walter Q. Gresham, was a politician with the training of a lawyer. His view of the situation was legalistic. Neither he nor the President had had any diplomatic experience; and they were aroused by the moral issue which was apparently thus presented to them. A revolution had been promoted on the territory of a friendly state, which was ruled by a woman, by Americans who now wished annexation to the United States. President Cleveland's honesty was assailed by the crudity of such an attempt to involve the United States in a proceeding which he regarded as contrary to right and justice. Under the circumstances he withdrew the treaty from the Senate and despatched Mr. Blount, the chairman of the Committee on Foreign Relations in the House of Representatives, to Hawaii to investigate and report. There was of course a partisan aspect to this and Democratic feeling ran high. A little later a new Minister, Mr. Willis, was sent to Hawaii, who was instructed to see the former Queen Liliuokalani and to express to her the regrets of the President for the "reprehensible conduct" of Minister Stevens, who had connived at her temporary expulsion from the throne, and to assure her that she might "rely on the justice of this American Government to undo the flagrant wrong." The Queen was also told that the President expected her to be "magnanimous" in her treatment of those responsible for her dethronement. To this expectation the ex-Queen replied that "My decision would be, as the law directs that such persons should be beheaded and their property confiscated." Such a reply showed President Cleveland that the use of force to restore the Queen would only lead to bloodshed. The provisional government, composed for the most part of people of American blood, furthermore refused to accept the mediation of the United States. Thus this situation, which would have seemed merely absurd had it not involved the lives and property of men of repute and honor, led to an *impasse*.

Under the circumstances it seemed that the best President Cleveland could do was to refer the situation to Congress, which alone had the power to declare war. Thus the bewildered President dismissed the question and for the time abdicated the executive control over diplomacy in favor of the legislature. The Senate, in January, 1895, passed a resolution favoring a policy of non-intervention in Hawaii and thus showed its inclination to let matters drift. The entire incident reveals President Cleveland's honesty, the hasty "imperialism" of the American settler in Hawaii, and the bewilderment of an inept diplomacy.[1]

Such was the condition of affairs when President McKinley came into office. With the Spanish-American war in the offing and extravagant tales of Japanese designs on Hawaii current in the press, the matter now took a new turn. The new government in Hawaii had, furthermore, shown its efficiency and adequacy. Consequently a movement for annexation to the United States was favorably received; and in June, 1897, a treaty providing for annexation was signed and referred to the Senate. There it faced an opposition which made it very doubtful whether it could command the necessary two-thirds majority. Consequently the annexation was accomplished by a joint resolution passed by a majority in both Houses of Congress. To this President McKinley willingly assented on July 8, 1898. This annexation thus took place as a war measure; it was a step in the protection of our coasts; and it was designed to prevent the chance that Japan might sooner or later attempt to occupy the islands. Furthermore, Hawaii was essential as a naval base if we were to retain the Philippines.[2]

In 1893–1894 the Japanese had apparently acquiesced in the proposal for annexation. Now in 1897 they demurred to the plan. There had, moreover, been friction between Japan and the Republic of Hawaii regarding the problem of Japanese immigration to Hawaii.[3] After some diplomatic correspondence on the subject the Japanese government made formal protest against the proposed annexation of the island.

The Japanese Government took the ground (1) That the maintenance of the *status quo* in Hawaii was essential to the good understanding of the Powers having interests in the Pacific; and (2) that the absorption of the islands by the United States would tend to endanger certain rights of Japanese subjects in the group, under its treaties, constitution and laws, and might result in the postponing of the settlement of claims and liabilities existing in favor of Japan under treaty stipulations. At the same time the Japanese Government took occasion to deny "the mischievous suggestion or report" that it entertained designs against the territorial integrity of the islands.[4]

To such views the United States replied that she did "not intend or admit that annexation will disturb any general interests under the *status quo*" and went on to deny that any vested alien rights in Hawaii would be disturbed by annexation. The despatch concluded by saying that,

> Mischievous reports of Japan's supposed designs upon Hawaii were not credited here and needed no denial. The Government of the United States has perfect confidence in the frank and friendly disposition of Japan, and nothing has occurred to alter the situation in the Pacific since Japan acquiesced in the annexation four years ago.[5]

The Japanese, although they acknowledged the predominant influence of the United States in the Hawaiian Islands, questioned the need of altering in any way the existing conditions by annexation, for they feared lest it would be the signal for further expansion by foreign states in the Pacific Ocean.

Such views, when coupled with quotations from previous American notes to Germany regarding the rights of American citizens in newly acquired territory in the Pacific, presented a view of the situation that enlarged the question.[6] The American reply though largely technical in its criticisms brought out very clearly the historical aspects of the problem. The note stated:

> I regret to note that your Government, notwithstanding the candid statements made in my note of June 25th, continues to insist that the maintenance of what it terms the *status quo* of Hawaii is essential to the good understanding of the Powers which have interests in the Pacific. I pointed out that the proposed annexation was nothing more than the culmination of an avowed policy, announced and furthered by successive monarchical and republican governments of the Hawaiian Islands and pursued on the part of the United States through a long series of years. The fact cited of "The augmentation that has taken place . . . in the interests of Japan in the Pacific," cannot properly be advanced as a reason, why the policy so long declared and pursued should be abandoned just on the eve of its realization. This augmentation of Japanese interests had taken place in the knowledge of certain well known historical facts, among which the following may be enumerated. More than half a century ago, the Government of the United States announced to the world that its interest in the Hawaiian

Islands was predominant, and that it could not regard with indifference any attempt to interfere with that interest—a position which has been constantly and continuously maintained. This was soon followed by a declination on its part to unite with England and France in a guarantee of the independence and autonomy of the Islands. Not long thereafter one of the native Kings authorized the negotiation of a treaty of annexation to the United States, which was not at that time consummated because of his untimely death. After repeated solicitation on the part of Hawaiian sovereigns, a treaty of commercial reciprocity was negotiated by one of them with the United States more than twenty years ago, which not only made the Islands for commercial purposes practically a part of the United States, but contained clauses of territorial rights exclusively enjoyed by the United States as against all other nations. The purpose and effect of this treaty was understood in the United States to be to prepare the way for a complete political union at the proper time. When the present Government of Hawaii was established it declared its intention to bring about annexation to the United States at the earliest possible moment, and it inserted a clause to that effect in its constitution. Under these conditions Japanese immigration to, and commerce with the Islands began and have been augmented to their present proportions. It may be added, that a very large proportion of the immigration has taken place and the commerce grown up since the present Hawaiian Government was established. The Japanese Government permitted and encouraged the immigration of its subjects and the growth of its commerce under these conditions, and with a full knowledge of the policy of the United States as to these matters. It can have, therefore, no well founded cause of complaint if only the usual and legitimate results flow from the proposed annexation. . . .

I trust that if the foregoing statement has not entirely satisfied the wishes of Count Okuma, under whose instruction your note, to which this is a reply, was written, it will at least convince him that, in the annexation of the Hawaiian Islands to the United States, the Government of the latter is not inspired by any feeling of hostility to Japan, or by any desire to restrict the legitimate sphere of its influence in the Pacific; that its subjects in those Islands will be accorded all the rights and protection to which they are entitled under international law, and which they have reason to expect from the past friendly conduct of the United States; and that every proper effort will be made to encourage and enlarge the commercial relations of the two countries, destined to nearer and more intimate intercourse with each other in the future.[7]

By December, 1898, the Japanese had withdrawn their opposition to annexation but they still advocated the rights of Japanese citizens in Hawaii in case annexation should take place and pressed financial claims which they had asserted as against the existing Government in Hawaii. Such matters were naturally postponed till after the annexation took place.[8] Then a lump sum of $130,000 was paid to settle the claims. The extension of federal immigration laws, involving the treaty of 1894 between the United States and Japan, resulted in a vigorous but unavailing protest by the Japanese authorities. So ended a controversy which leads the student to wonder whether Japan had had in mind the possibility of skillful penetration by immigration and the development of economic interests until the opportunity should arise whereby the Japanese flag might float over Honolulu.

At all events the time had now come for this formal extension of American interest. In 1893 Mr. Stevens said: "The Hawaiian pear is now fully ripe, and this is the golden hour for the United States to pluck it." In 1898 President McKinley said: "We need Hawaii just as much and a good deal more than we did California. It is manifest destiny." Later he added: "Annexation is not a change; it is a consummation." And as a consummation of the long years of adventure on the part of missionary, trader, and sailor Hawaii became American. We turn now from peaceful Hawaii to the stormy politics of lovely Samoa.

As we look back over Samoan affairs we must not despise the "day of small things" for in the remote vastness of the Pacific, out of petty, even ridiculous squabbles on these tiny islands, there was to develop a situation of great importance in international relations. Soon the United States, Great Britain and Germany were to be involved in settling the affairs of this Liliputian domain. There for nearly seventy years English missionaries had labored. Roman Catholics followed them. There came adventurers of all sorts, traders and sailors who sought to establish a foothold. A great German firm was set up to exploit the tropical produce of the island. The natives developed a habit of hymn singing and nearly all became Christians of a sort. Then politics made its intrusion as the United States in the early "seventies" attempted to secure the right to the only valuable harbor, Pagopago, on the island of Tutuila. Later in 1878 a treaty was signed which led to the transfer of the harbor and its shores to the United States. This treaty also provided that America was to offer her good offices in case of any differences developing between Samoa and a foreign state. To this treaty the Germans objected as it seemed to contain the germ of a protectorate. But soon Great Britain as well as Germany had concluded treaties which gave them rights in Samoa. These two, together with the United States, soon approved a new form of government for the municipality of Apia, on the island of Upolu. Then there began a curious contest. New Zealand was very anxious to annex the islands; the islanders themselves were apparently in favor of such a step; but Lord Granville, British Foreign Secretary, had already given an assurance to Germany that the British had no intention of annexing the islands. In the meantime the Germans had assisted in the reorganization of the native government of Samoa and the native ruler, Malietoa, was expelled. A new government, nominally under Tamassese, a German protégé, was set up; but he was soon beaten by a rival, Mataafa. During these days the presence of American, British, and German men-of-war revealed the danger of armed conflict; for the United States was now ready to offer its good offices, proposed to occupy Pagopago, and objected to the bullying policy which Germany seemed intent on pursuing.

At this moment, when personal as well as national jealousies were well aroused, a terrific storm overwhelmed six of the seven ships of war at anchor in the harbor of Apia. The British *Calliope* alone was able to escape to open sea; three American and three German men-of-war were wrecked with heavy loss of life. This act of God dispelled for the time the animosities which had threatened war. This tempest of Nature blew away the human tempest in a tea-pot. Soon an international meeting was held at Berlin; this recognized Samoa as an independent neutral state, recalled Malietoa from exile, and provided for the choice of several Europeans to assist the native government. Malietoa was again recognized as King and it seemed as though the situation was well in hand.

The next decade, 1889–1899, was, however, disastrous chiefly because of the bankruptcy of the state and the friction which developed between the European officials. The King died and civil war broke out between two candidates for the succession. The British and American consuls seemed to support one of these and the Germans the other. The situation was reported as very grave and the breakdown in government seemed to be imminent.

The Germans were also full of complaints regarding the behavior of the Chief Justice of Samoa, Mr. Chambers, an American. They frankly confessed that the system of joint supervision by the three powers over Samoan affairs had broken down and favored a final partition of the islands between Germany, the United States and Great Britain.[9] At the same time the Germans were inclined to lay most of the blame for the situation in the island on the British Consul, who it was said:

influences the Chief Justice and the American Consul General in so unfavorable a manner that, in spite of all efforts from the part of Rose [the German Consul General], an understanding between him and these two officials is confronted with serious obstacles.[10]

Whoever may have been at fault, such friction was not lessened when the American and British naval forces, under the command of Admiral Kautz on the U. S. S. *Philadelphia*, bombarded on March 10, 1899, the forces of Mataafa, who was the German candidate for the throne. Desultory fighting continued during the month and on April 1, Easter Sunday, a combined American and British landing force was ambushed by Mataafan forces and several officers and seamen of both nationalities were killed.

Feeling ran high in each of the three countries at the news of fighting in Samoa, and the respective Foreign Offices were much annoyed at these developments; but each was determined to avoid war which would be only ridiculous if the direct issues were to be considered. Consequently, when the German government promptly proposed that a joint commission should be despatched to Samoa with full powers to settle the affairs of the island group, it was eagerly agreed to by both the United States and Great Britain.[11] The instructions to the commissioners, who were to be Mr. Tripp for the United States, Baron Speck von Sternburg for Germany, and Mr. Elliott for Great Britain, were largely shaped by Secretary Hay. He stated that the objects of the commission were to be: "1. To establish peace and order in Samoa. 2. To investigate the causes of the recent troubles. 3. And to propose means of guarding against them in the future. To this end it seems advisable that the Commissioners shall be paramount authority in the Island during their stay." [12]

The general views of the Department of State were also expressed in a memorandum to be found in the Appendix to this chapter.[13] This made it clear that the United States regarded German officials at Samoa as chiefly at fault for the recent events. However, in accordance with German suggestions, two German officials and the British Consul were withdrawn and finally the indiscreet Chief Justice Chambers was relieved from his duties.[14] This enabled the Commission to proceed rapidly with their work. As Mr. Tripp reported on June 16, 1899:

> Everything is now peaceable and quiet in the islands. The chiefs and warriors have returned to their homes. The smoke is now seen ascending from the native cabins and plantations in every portion of the islands. The war song is discontinued, the war camp abandoned, and the happy, joyous nature of this unrevengeful people manifests itself in the ready forgiveness of their enemies and their glad welcome of returning peace.[15]

The report of the Commission which was made in July proposed the establishment of a new form of government and abolished the office of King; but the Commission expressed the opinion that tripartite administration of the islands was undesirable and that "the only natural and normal form of government for these islands" was government by a single power.[16]

As it developed, this solution was finally agreed to by the three countries and consequently a partition of the islands took place. In the meantime the Kaiser had indulged in a furious attack on Lord Salisbury, which he made in a personal letter to his grandmother, Queen Victoria. For this he was roundly rebuked by the Queen.[17] Such incidents as well as the increasing interest shown by Germany in the situation in South Africa, do not concern us here. However, they serve to show the squally weather through which the proposals for the partition of the islands had to navigate to a peaceful settlement.

The German government in a note to the United States, which is given in the Appendix to this chapter, proposed that for the sake of general accord a partition should take place which would give to the United States the island of Tutuila, with the American harbor of Pagopago, leaving the islands of Upolu and Savaii to be divided between Germany and Great Britain.[18] The question of claims of private citizens for damages incurred during the recent troubles at Samoa was to be submitted to arbitration.[19]

The German Foreign Office was very anxious to have the entire matter settled before the visit of the Kaiser to England in November, 1899, and they were frequently annoyed by the dilatory tactics of the British. However, as late as the third week of October the Germans were still violently quarrelling among themselves as to whether they really wanted to insist on retaining their claims in Samoa. The disasters which now overtook the British in the Transvaal at the outbreak of the Boer War also slowed up the settlement. With these matters, however, we have nothing to do.[20]

When, finally, the agreement was signed between Great Britain and Germany on November 14, 1899, it was found that Great Britain had withdrawn entirely from the Samoan Islands and in compensation had received a number of minor islands in the Soloman group, Tonga Island, and concessions as to territories in Africa. Germany, therefore, acquired the two Samoan islands of Upolu and Savaii.[21] This was followed on December 2, 1899, by the signature of a convention giving the United States Tutuila and Manua. Thus the adjustment was secured.[22] The question of claims still occasionally appeared in the diplomatic correspondence but they were soon settled. The British abandonment of Samoa was of course a source of complaint by New Zealand. Indeed Samoa became a sort of island *irredenta* in New Zealand opinion. The seizure of German Samoa by New Zealand forces on the outbreak of the World War in 1914 was, therefore, deeply gratifying to that Dominion. On the whole the acquisition of German Samoa flattered German sentimental aspirations and, as will be seen in a document in the Appendix, furnished an additional argument for the increase of the German navy.[23] The United States was awarded the harbor that she wished and was now free from the dangerous entanglements which so nearly involved her in war with Germany. Thus everyone was satisfied; and the Samoan treaty as we shall soon see, was to play an important rôle in the initial stages of the diplomatic history of the Boer War.

NOTES TO CHAPTER IV

1. For this matter of McElroy, II; *Life of Gresham,* II; James, ch. IX and Appendix III; *Foreign Relations,* 1894; Appendix II, *Affairs in Hawaii;* Rhodes, pp. 112-114; Dennett, ch. XXXI; Olcott, I, ch. XXII.
2. Dennett, pp. 609-615, 624-626; McElroy II, pp. 71-73; *O. C.,* June 19, 1897, Cleveland to Olney. Cleveland wrote: "Did you ever see such a preposterous thing as the Hawaiian business? The papers I read are most strongly opposed to it and there ought to be soberness and decency enough in the Senate to save us from launching upon the dangerous policy which is foreshadowed by the pending treaty; but I am prepared for almost anything."
3. D. S., From Japan, Vol. 70, No. 477, April 12, 1897, Dun to Sherman.
4. Moore, *Digest of International Law,* Washington, 1906, 8 Vols. I, p. 504.
5. D. S., To Japan, Vol. 4, telegram, p. 426, June 25, 1897, Sherman to Dun; Moore, I, pp. 504-509.
6. Cf. Dennett, pp. 624 et seq.
7. D. S., To Japanese Legation, Vol. I, No. 50, Aug. 14, 1897, Sherman to Toru Hoshi; Moore, I, pp. 505-507.
8. Moore, I, pp. 507-509.
9. D. S., From Germany, Vol. 66, No. 714, Jan. 25, 1899, White to Hay; Vol. 68, No. 757, Feb. 20, same to same.

10. *D. S.,* From German Embassy, Vol. 28, March 11, 1899. Memorandum.
11. *F. R.,* 1899, p. 614; *D. S.,* From Germany, Vol. 69, No. 813, April 4, 1899, White to Hay; telegram, April 6, same to same; *G. P.,* XIV, part 2, No. 4053.
12. *D. S.,* To German Embassy, Vol. 12, 369, memorandum, April 8, 1899.
13. Appendix A to this chapter. In passing I may remark that the policies shown at Berlin during the discussion of the Samoan question exhibit the German Foregin Office at its worst. This was due primarily to the influence exercised by Holstein in the course of negotiations, to divided counsels of German leaders, especially the powerful opposition of von Tirpitz to the German Foreign Office, and to the constant desire of Germany to mingle other matters which had nothing to do with the settlement of Samoan affairs in such fashion that the discussion of African affairs were frequently brought in. *G. P.,* XIV, Part I, pp. 567 *et seq.;* Eckardstein, ch. VI, which, however, contains several minor errors.
14. *H. P.,* June 26, 1899. Hay to McKinley; *D. S.,* From German Embassy, Vol. 28, memorandum, May 18, 1899.
15. *F. R.,* 1899, p. 626.
16. *Ibid.,* pp. 636 *et seq.*
17. *G. P.,* XIV, Part 2, Nos. 4074, 4076.
18. Appendix B to this chapter.
19. *D. S.,* Numerical File, Vol. 547, memorandum, Aug. 31, 1899; To London, Vol. 33, No. 214, Sept. 27, 1899, Hill to Choate; unnumbered despatch, p. 250, Sept. 27, same to same; *H. P.,* Sept. 25, 1899, Hay to Adee; Oct. 14, Choate to Hay. Mr. Choate who had become American Ambassador in London had apparently confused the partition of the islands with the settlement of claims by arbitration. *F. R.,* 1899, pp. 664-665, 669-673.
20. *D. S.,* From Germany, Vol 70, No. 1054, Oct. 24, 1899, White to Hay; From London. Vol. 198, No. 188, Oct. 25, Choate to Hay; *H. P.,* Nov. 1 and 3, Choate to Hay (private and unofficial); Nov. 16, Mumm to Hay; *D. S.,* From Germany, Vol. 70, No. 1070, Nov. 9, Jackson to Hay, giving German consent to addition of Manua and its islets as the American share in Samoa; *G. P.,* XIV, Part I, Nos. 4087, 4092, 4095, 4100, 4102, 4105, 4106, 4107-4117.
21. *F. R.,* 1899, pp. 665-666.
22. *Ibid.,* pp. 667-669.
23. Appendix C to this chapter.

APPENDICES TO CHAPTER IV

A

D. S. To German Embassy, Vol. 12, p. 368, Memorandum, April 13, 1899.

In view of the favorable prospect of a settlement of the troubles in the Samoan Islands by the dispatch thither of Commissioners of the Three Treaty Powers, it is not considered expedient at this moment to enter into a detailed examination and discussion of the various memoranda which the German Embassy has presented at the Department of State. It would seem proper, however, for the purpose of avoiding any inferences which might be drawn from entire silence on the subject, that this Department should briefly state the view entertained by the Government of the United States upon a few points in question.

It is held that the whole case of the disputed election of a King was properly and regularly, in accordance with the provisions of the Act of Berlin, before Chief Justice Chambers for decision.

That his decision when given was binding upon all parties since neither government has the power under the Berlin General Act to reverse or annul it. As will be perceived by section 6 of article 3, the signatory powers have distinctly agreed to accept it.

That in the scenes of riot and violence which followed his decision, the Mataafa party was apparently countenanced and abetted by Mr. Raffel and Mr. Rose.

That Admiral Kautz found, on arrival there, a state of anarchy and disregard for all legal process that called urgently for immediate action.

That he took the proper and evident course of immediately inviting all the Consuls to a full discussion of the situation, and that, finding a unanimity of view among them impossible, his proclamation was, under all the circumstances, in the interest of peace and good order in the Islands, and was not a misstatement of fact.

That the counter proclamation of Mr. Rose accusing Admiral Kautz of falsehood, and circulated in the Samoan language, was a direct incitement to violence and disorder and resulted in the deplorable occurrences which have ensued.

Department of State, Washington, April 13, 1899.

B

D. S. Numerical File, Vol. 547 (undated, following Memorandum of August 31, 1899).

The U. S. Government will fail no less than the Imperial German Government to perceive, that neither permanent tranquillity in the Pacific Ocean nor real concord between England, America and Germany will ever be secured as long as the Samoan question will rest unsolved. Notwithstanding the good will shown herein by America in a most gratifying way neither the decisions of the Samoan Commission will be able to change this almost insupportable state of everlasting uneasiness. This the Commission itself acknowledge frankly in concluding its report with the statement, that no lasting peace could be thought of in Samoa under the rule of three Powers.

Small as may be the importance of the Samoan question in itself to the three Powers, still it is just weighty enough to be able to cause among them daily misunderstandings of the most serious character and to restrain the Powers also in the future from the necessary and urgent improvement of their possessions in the Pacific. The Governments therefore can no longer shut their eyes to the necessity of solving the Samoan question now definitively through partition or in any other way acceptable to all parties beyond the provisions of the Samoan Acts and beyond the decisions of the Commission.

America may hereby rest assured in advance, that Germany, likewise as she never has grudged America the large acquisition of the former Spanish possessions in the South Sea and in the West Indies and likewise as Germany wishes with all sincerity for a peaceful improvement of the same in the interests of America, so likewise she will readily agree to the ceding of Tutuila to America in the case of a partition of the Samoan Islands.

The partition of the remaining Samoan Islands, Upolu and Savaii between Germany and England, would consequently be the only remaining question to be settled in view of putting aside once for all a point of controversy, which—far exceeding its real importance—has already since too long a time kept in restlessness and excitement three Powers whose natural aim should have been mutual friendship.

According to the interests of Germany and England now prevailing in Samoa, Upolu would justly fall to the lot of Germany and Savaii to England. America would act in her own interests and would render Germany a real service, if America would prevail with its whole powerful influence on England for the realization of such a just partition of the Samoan Islands.

The Imperial Government would recognize herein a valuable pledge for the further advancement of its friendly relations to America, such as they exist at the time being in a most gratifying way and America may be sure in return of Germany's good services at other occasions.

C

D. S. From Germany, Vol. 70, No. 1072, November 10, 1899, Jackson to Hay.

That the German Emperor desires to preserve the peace of Europe is an indisputable fact; that he desires to increase the prestige of the German Empire, to add to its territory and to earn the title "Mehrer des Reichs" appears to be almost equally so. It is therefore to be expected that no opportunity to acquire territory will be lost, and in this connection the proposals made in an indirect way to Ambassador White, during our war with Spain, may be recalled with advantage. The situation in Germany now is very similar to that prevailing about eighteen months ago. Then as now the Imperial Government desired to preserve its absolute neutrality, while now the German Public is just as certainly on the side of the Boers as it then was on that of Spain. Under the circumstances there are many who think that the conclusion of the agreement in regard to Samoa (which is understood to have been awaiting Lord Salisbury's signature for some little time), on the very day of the Czar's visit to Potsdam, is more than a mere coincidence. . . .

German feeling in regard to Samoa is somewhat of a sentimental nature, Samoa having been one of the first points to which German colonial enterprise was directed, and their sentimentalism has been carefully cultivated by the Government papers and those interested in the increase of the navy. (But little enthusiasm was shown, however, at the meeting of the local branch of the German Colonial Society which I attended by invitation last night, in regard to the recent agreement, as it is hardly realized as yet what Germany is giving up in order to acquire possession of the Samoan Islands.) In connection with the increase in German colonial possessions (Carolines, Samoa, etc.,) the increase in the navy becomes more and more a subject of consideration, and it is now almost certain that a bill appropriating money to this end will be submitted to the Reichstag early in the winter.

Much has been said (the Emperor's speech at Hamburg about a month ago) and written (semi-official articles in the North German Gazette and Berliner Correspondenz) in regard to this of late, and great efforts are being made to arouse enthusiasm in regard to it. It is claimed that the political and colonial situation has so changed within a year or so that the increase in the navy provided for in the bill the provisions of which are now being carried out, is wholly inadequate, and that a much larger increase is necessary to enable Germany to take and hold her proper position as a "World Power." . . .

CHAPTER V

ANGLO-AMERICAN RELATIONS

To quote once more from Henry Adams:

Himself a marvellous manager of men, McKinley found several manipulators to help him, almost as remarkable as himself, one of whom was Hay; but unfortunately Hay's strength was weakest and his task was hardest. At home, interests could easily be combined by simply paying their price; but abroad whatever helped on one side, hurt him on another. Hay thought England must be brought first into the combine; but at that time Germany, Russia, and France were all combining against England, and the Boer War helped them. For the moment Hay had no ally, abroad or at home, except Pauncefote, and Adams always maintained that Pauncefote alone pulled him through.[1]

THIS comment might be blind did we not have the facts of the Venezuelan boundary dispute, and the questions relating to American expansion so recently in our mind. A solidarity of interest with England was to the front in Hay's mind whether as Ambassador or as Secretary of State. He had come to Great Britain shortly after an outbreak in America of that "chronic, though slumbering, animosity towards the mother country" which had been caused by President Cleveland's Venezuelan message. It was his mission to assist in dispelling the fog of misunderstanding and surly bad temper that had been developed. Indeed, personally Hay undoubtedly would have wished for an alliance between the United States and Great Britain. This he recognized "must remain, in the present state of things, an unobtainable dream."[2] Even a treaty on almost any subject would have had a hard road through the Senate and as Secretary Hay wrote to Mr. Choate in August, 1899:

The Democratic press evidently thinks there is some political capital to be made by denouncing every arrangement with England, and they, in common with a large number of German newspapers, are ready to attack any treaty with England, no matter how advantageous it is to us, as a hostile act towards Ireland and Germany.[3]

Such letters should clearly, and once and for all dispel, the persistent rumor that, whether as Ambassador or Secretary, Mr. Hay had had a part in arranging any secret treaty or even an understanding between the United States and Great Britain. A most careful search through the *Hay Papers* has failed to produce a scrap of evidence in support of this story, whose most recent convert is the ex-Kaiser. The thing simply is not so, *pace* Professor Usher of St. Louis. As Secretary Hay said, in 1899: "I simply refute the Democratic platform's charge that we have made 'a secret alliance with England.' ... The fact is a treaty of alliance is impossible." [4]

Yet a sympathy of understanding and an appreciation of Britain's services to America during the Spanish-American war there undoubtedly was, for Secretary Hay wrote privately to Mr. Henry White in London: "As long as I stay here in Washington no action shall be taken contrary to my conviction that the one indispensable feature of our foreign policy should be a friendly understanding with England." [5] To that resolution Secretary Hay clung in the face of bitter attacks on him as an Anglophile and distressing opposition in the Senate to many of his projects. Such an introduction to this topic now leaves us ready to follow briefly the various fields in which Anglo-American relations developed for a few years.

First there comes the excursion toward bimetallism which President McKinley advocated for political reasons. He had said during the election campaign of 1896 that if he were elected he would do all in his power to bring about an international agreement upon bimetallism. As a preliminary step in that direction Ambassador Hay was directed to sound the British government and to introduce a commission of three Americans who went abroad in 1897 to discover the land.

Opinion on this financial problem of the day was much divided in Great Britain as well as in America. Even within the British Cabinet there were differences. Mr. Balfour was a bimetallist at the time and Mr. Chamberlain was a gold standard man. The Midlands were much more in favor of an international bimetallic agreement than was the City in London. The press was on the whole indifferent but editors of all sorts were almost unanimous in saying that the cooperation of Great Britain was impossible. This also was the opinion of the leaders of the Liberal Party who were in opposition. The existing prosperity of Great Britain made strongly for the maintenance of the gold standard. On the other hand there were a few enthusiasts like Mr. Moreton Frewen that "argento-maniac" as Hay called him, who declared that Mr. William Jennings Bryan was the "greatest and most beneficent personality in American life since Abraham Lincoln"; and he and his friends hoped vaguely for government action. Against such views rested the solid influence of great financial leaders like Lord Farrer. The outcome of this first "effort" of the Republican administration was therefore negative. Great Britain awaited any action by the United States but would not commit herself in any way. The French Ambassador in London was more enthusiastic; but nothing came of this venture. The European attitude was to wait and see. Under the circumstances President McKinley was probably wise in writing across one of Ambassador Hay's despatches: "I would not give it out in any form or channel." [6]

In July, 1897, President McKinley wrote to Ambassador Hay saying:

> Your last letter to me was delightful as all your letters are. I do not need to be reassured that you are using untiring energy and tact to help along two of the administration's greatest efforts—Bimetallism and Behring Sea Negotiations—but the details which you present are interesting and instructive.[7]

This second "effort" from Washington dealt with one of the most obstinate and long-drawn out disputes that had affected Anglo-American relations. In the regulation of sealing in Bering Sea, Ambassador Hay was faced by the force of British and Canadian public opinion. As he finally wrote to Mr. White: "We have got the Bering Sea business disposed of, for the time being. I have been amazed at the solid way in which the press of England has stood together around Lord Salisbury and steadily refused to print the truth." [8] The original Bering Sea arbitration in 1893 had merely settled the question of jurisdiction. The seals had been forgotten. In order to prevent their destruction and probable extermination the United States now proposed a joint agreement for their preservation. Great Britain refused to agree to this. It really was a battle between the experts of both governments and the controversy might well be described as Jordan vs. d'Arcy Thompson. At all events it filled many reams of diplomatic despatch paper. As early as May, 1897, the issue was thus defined by Hay:

> . . . I made some allusion to the matter of your instructions in reference to the preservation of the seals and expressed my regret that the British Government appeared disinclined to consider the subject of a new arrangement which seemed to us required by the circumstances of the case. Lord Salisbury said there was so clear a contradiction between the views of the experts on either side, the Americans thinking that the extermination of the seals was threatened, and the English being of the opposite opinion, that under the circumstances Her Majesty's Government were not inclined to interfere with the present arrangements.[9]

In this matter Great Britain was, of course, acting for Canada; and in a conversation with Ambassador Hay, Lord Salisbury said in general that the question was essentially a colonial one, that Great Britain was acting as a trustee rather than as a principal, and he approved of the Ambassador's suggestion that Mr. Chamberlain be approached directly.[10] This of course raised the question of reference to Canada by the British authorities; a fact which was to delay a decision and which was to complicate many other questions pending between the two states. Today, however, thanks to the appointment of a Canadian Minister at Washington, such a situation could scarcely arise. But in 1897 the case was different. As Mr. Adee wrote with regard to other affairs: "In copyright matters as in those of tariff, Our Lady of the Snows is disposed to be a daughter in her mother's house, but mistress in her own, with a wanion." [11]

What had greatly complicated the whole matter was the publication in the American press of Secretary Sherman's confidential instruction to Ambassador Hay, of May 28, 1897. This instruction was, as the *Times* said on July 16, "a manifest attempt to fasten upon this country (England) a charge of bad faith and this attempt is made in offensive language." The *Morning Post* said on July 20: "So far as it is possible for an observer on this side of the Atlantic to judge, there exists among Americans a widespread, and perhaps a deep-rooted feeling of animosity towards the British nation, which has not hitherto met with any response in kind." This incident, which was typical of the carelessness which was occasional at the Department of State in those days, led Ambassador Hay to send home a few clippings, which as he said "will give you some idea of the anger and resentment aroused" in the British press by this unfortunate publication.[12]

Nevertheless, Great Britain did agree to a conference of sealing experts to be held in Washington but limited her consent in such fashion that she refused later to attend a conference to which Russia and Japan had been invited. This construction of the matter took Ambassador Hay by surprise.[13] Great Britain also refused to adhere to the American-Russian-Japanese Convention of November 6, 1897, "on the ground of pending negotiations between United States and Canada." This was to render the negotiations between these three countries futile, for British subjects were more largely engaged in sealing than those of any other country. Thus the agreement that for a year sealing should be prohibited was dropped. During the time of these negotiations, however, various Canadian statesmen came to Washington and proposed that all outstanding questions between the two countries should be referred to a joint commission. This solution

Lord Salisbury finally accepted as will be seen in a later chapter.[14]

However, as the United States became involved in the war with Spain, the general expression of British good will became clearer. Thus Mr. Chamberlain, in a speech at Birmingham on May 13, 1898, made the somewhat surprising declaration:

> I don't know what the future has in store for us; I don't know what arrangements may be possible with us; but this I do know and feel, that the closer, the more cordial, the fuller, and the more definite these arrangements are, with the consent of both peoples, the better it will be for both and for the world—and I go even so far as to say that, terrible as a war may be, even war itself would be cheaply purchased if, in a great and noble cause, the Stars and Stripes and the Union Jack should wave together over an Anglo-Saxon alliance.[15]

This speech, though not its exact language, was perhaps due to a conversation with Ambassador Hay; there were rumors and reports current at the time that suggestions looking to a European coalition against the United States were being made. If so, the Chamberlain speech seems to have discouraged the continental enemies of America.[16] In similar fashion, at the conclusion of peace with Spain, Mr. Chamberlain made another interesting speech in which he referred to the possibility of joint action by the United States and Great Britain to maintain the "open door" in China, a prophecy which was to be fulfilled a year later. He then went on to say:

> The United States of America, if you have regard to its potential resources, is already the greatest of civilized States, with its immense population, chiefly of Anglo-Saxons, upwards of 70 millions of intelligent citizens, and if we are assured of the friendship of the Anglo-Saxon race, whether they abide under the Stars and Stripes or under the Union Jack, there is no other combination that can make us afraid.[17]

As a feeble echo of such British sentiment there also came in the *Times* review of German foreign policy in 1898. The writer said that "the possibility of co-operation by Great Britain, the United States, Germany and Japan for commercial objects in the Far East is generally regarded as no longer outside the sphere of practical politics." [18] However, it was in South Africa that the real test of German and American friendship was to be made. In October, 1899, the long expected break between Great Britain and the Transvaal came. The opening months of the struggle were disastrous for the British and the activities of her continental rivals were redoubled. Furthermore the press and public opinion generally in Europe were plainly anti-British. Under the circumstances it was natural that Great Britain should look about for signs of friendships which might relieve her of the fear of a combination of powers who might use the South African war for their own ends.

The Samoan Treaty had been signed in November and the Kaiser came to England for a visit. This was the occasion for lengthy conferences with Mr. Balfour and Mr. Chamberlain by both the Kaiser and Count von Bülow. The German records of these conversations indicate a friendly feeling for Great Britain but do not warrant the belief that Germany was anxious to make a formal alliance with England. Both the German and the British officials seem to have been quite ignorant of American political conditions.[19] Mr. Chamberlain in particular should have known better than to suppose that the United States could be drawn into an alliance with Great Britain and Germany. Yet the visit of the Kaiser to England at this time of war, coupled with the very friendly expressions of German diplomats toward the United States, naturally set the imaginations of high officials to work. The result was that at Leicester on November 30, Mr. Chamberlain made his famous speech in which he made the suggestion of a "new triple alliance" between Great Britain, Germany, and the United States. As for the proposal regarding Germany, Mr. Chamberlain said: "Every far-sighted statesman has long been anxious that we should not permanently remain isolated on the Continent of Europe and that from the moment that aspiration was formed it must have appeared to everybody that the most natural alliance is between ourselves and the German Empire." [20] The plan for this speech had been discussed between Mr. Chamberlain and German officials and it had been suggested to him that he should speak of the mutual interests which bound the United States to Germany as well as to Great Britain.[21] Mr. Chamberlain encouraged by these talks had gone much too far in his speech. His remarks were greeted with an outburst of Anglophobia in the Reichstag and in the German press.[22]

Count von Bülow also sought to justify himself by a cold deliverance in the Reichstag ignoring the Leicester speech. At the same time he let Mr. Chamberlain know that the German government "will abstain from every realignment of the Continental Powers against England, as well as from every joint action that might cause England embarrassment; of course on the assumption that the German interests will be taken due account of by Great Britain."[23] Mr. Chamberlain, however, was too deeply offended by what he felt was von Bülow's unfair treatment of him. He wrote to Baron Eckardstein saying: "I will say no more here about the way in which Bülow has treated me. But in any case I think we must drop all further negotiations in the question of the Alliance."[24] Thus he closed his letter with a mournful note. The truth was that Mr. Chamberlain was scarcely a diplomat; he had overdone what should have been done discreetly and delicately; and he was as ignorant of the internal conditions of German politics as he was of those of America. Under such circumstances although official relations were correct at the end of December, 1899, public opinion had been inflamed and the good results of the Kaiser's visit in November had been almost wiped out.[25]

Thus, after this little digression, we come to American policy regarding the Boer War. First, however, is the fact that France and Russia were also apparently eager to embarrass England at this time.[26] Their Dual Alliance had been formed a few years earlier as a combination, which from the Russian point of view at least, was directed to offset Great Britain in the Mediterranean and Near East. As I study the documents I am convinced that the Dual Alliance was aimed first of all against Great Britain. Indeed the British were much concerned over the Russian policies in Asia at this juncture. Consequently there was much secret talk regarding the possibility of a continental coalition either to propose mediation in the South African war, or to engage in armed intervention to stop it. In October, Count Muraviev, the Russian Foreign Secretary, had discussed with the French, while on a visit to Paris, the possibility of some sort of intervention. On his return to Russia *via* Berlin came the news of the Samoan treaty between Great Britain and Germany. This seems to have discouraged Russia, for Germany was essential to any anti-English coalition. Then in December came the breach in Anglo-German relations which I have just described. It is, therefore, quite possible that Russia put out feelers toward the United States regarding the American attitude toward mediation or intervention in the South African crisis.

At all events the German Ambassador in Washington, on January 2, 1900, had an interview with Secretary Hay, which he reported by telegraph to Berlin.[28] Secretary Hay expressed his concern for England after the "Black Week" of British defeat in South Africa. Dr. von Holleben then remarked that in case it should be necessary for England to strip herself of troops for the South African war she "would always undoubtedly be able to count upon the United States as a friend." To this Secretary Hay replied that England could "count on the good offices of the United States in every difficulty arising from the war, but he rejected completely the possibility of directly taking sides or of armed intervention, as running contrary to American traditions." He spoke of the coming American presidential election and continued saying: "If the existence of the British Empire should be called in question there is no knowing what constellation might then make its appearance among the powers"; but he believed that the "continued existence of the British Empire, even though somewhat humbled," would be of greater advantage to all European powers than its downfall.

Two days later on January 4, 1900, a foreign Ambassador called on Secretary Hay to suggest certain proposals to the United States. That evening Secretary Hay sent him a private note on stationery of the Department of State. A copy of this reads as follows:

My dear Ambassador
    I have conversed with the President in regard to the matter mentioned between us this morning. As I anticipated, he feels that we are precluded by all our traditions from joining in any representations such as were suggested.
    We are greatly gratified by such an evidence of His Imperial Majesty's confidence and esteem.
    I need not say the matter will not be mentioned to any of my colleagues in the Government.
Yours faithfully,
JOHN HAY.

This note which I found among the *Hay Papers* (secret and confidential file) is a puzzle, nor can the Department of State cast any light for they know nothing of the matter. There is no recourse to the papers of any of Mr. Hay's colleagues for, he expressly states that he will not make the matter known to any of them, and unfortunately President McKinley apparently did not keep a diary. If it had not been that the German Ambassador had seen Secretary Hay only two days before there might be reason to suspect him as the recipient. Two others are possible—the Austrian and the Russian Ambassadors. Of these it seems far more likely that the proposal should have come from the Russian Ambassador. The Russian government had been anxious to promote mediation in October and November. Her partner, France, was at the end of December much more inclined to accede to her suggestions and American-Russian relations were notably good at this time.[29] Furthermore, in February these Russian suggestions were to be revived in Europe. On February 2 the German Ambassador had another long interview with Secretary Hay in which the Secretary repeated much of what he had already said on January 2, though in a "very excited manner."[30] Thus we are left in a fog as regards this note of January 4 from Secretary Hay to an unidentified Ambassador. I make the suggestion that it was addressed to the Russian or possibly the German Ambassador and that it was in reply to overtures hostile to British interests. Someone else must complete the answer to this puzzle. At all events the fact was, that in this critical situation for the British Empire, the United States stood by and their navy was at the disposal of England during these difficult days.

In January and for months afterward, the American records are crowded with despatches relating to British seizures of ships carrying goods supposed to be for the Boers. Secretary Hay took prompt action to protect American neutral rights and generally found that the British were anxious to observe the rules of international law. There was no occasion, therefore, for sharp tension such as existed between Germany and England in early January, 1900, over the seizure of the *Bundesrat* and other German steamers. This dispute was relieved by the release of the vessels.

In the meantime public opinion in the United States was shifting in favor of sympathy for the Boers. The Irish and the Germans were pro-Boer because of dislike of England, and the older American stock was influenced by former anti-British feeling and by the brave struggle which these "embattled farmers" of South Africa were making. Consequently Secretary Hay had a full bag every morning. As typical of his replies to such correspondents as urged mediation or intervention by the United States, a sample is to be found in the Appendix to this chapter.[31] Generally he took the ground that Great Britain and possibly even the Boers would not listen to such outside efforts to end the war. However much American feeling might sympathize with the Boers there was, nevertheless, a very substantial element which saw clearly the general advantages to mankind of British success. These people, however, did not put themselves on record. Then in March, 1900, the Boers addressed the United States as well as European states asking for intervention with a view to the cessation of hostilities. In communicating this request to

Great Britain, Secretary Hay added: "I am directed by the President to express his earnest hope that a way to bring about peace may be found, and to say that he would be glad to aid in any friendly way to promote so happy a result." [32] News soon came that Germany had refused to intervene in the matter and from England came word that the British government "cannot accept the intervention of any other power." [33]

This reply was used again and again by Secretary Hay to check various movements in favor of intervention. Thus when a delegation of representatives of the Transvaal Republic and of the Orange Free State came to Washington in May, 1900, the fact of the British refusal was mentioned and reference was made to the provisions in the agreement signed at the first Peace Conference at The Hague. Article V of that convention stated the functions of a mediator in an international dispute "are at an end when once it is declared, either by one of the parties to the dispute or by the mediator himself, that the means of reconciliation proposed by him are not accepted." This of course had been the effect of the British declaration. Furthermore the American delegates to the Peace Conference had made a reservation stating:

> Nothing contained in this convention shall be so construed as to require the United States of America to depart from its traditional policy of not intruding upon, interfering with, or entangling itself with questions of policy or international administration of any foreign States; nor shall anything contained in the said Convention be construed to imply a relinquishment by the United States of its traditional attitude toward purely American questions.[34]

Thus there was nothing more for the United States to do than had been done. This attitude was also preserved by President Roosevelt in his pointed reply to a letter from the Boer representatives in December, 1901. He said in conclusion:

> This Government has already gone farther than that of any other foreign Power in the direction of exercising mediation in the interests of peace. The President is convinced that at the present time no other

course is open to him than that which this Government has hitherto consistently pursued.

Naturally the Boer delegates in America had been warmly welcomed by the Irish and German elements. Indeed, New York City was almost *en fête* on their arrival. Yet charges were common both in America and in Europe that the United States was in league with Great Britain.[36] Of course such was not the case; but it goes without saying that in Secretary Hay Great Britain had a very good friend. Mr. Chamberlain, in replying to a private letter of congratulation on the conclusion of peace with the Boers, wrote to Secretary Hay expressing his personal appreciation but adding:

> It has been somewhat of a discouragement to us to know that our motives were misunderstood, and our actions maligned by critics from abroad, and especially in the United States, with which it is the first object of my public life to cultivate a good and even an affectionate understanding.
>
> On the other hand, I have been strengthened by the extraordinary outpouring of loyalty and devotion from our great self-governing colonies when moral support has been even more valuable than their material aid. And in this politic vision of the Empire I see a promise for the future which is not too dearly paid for by the sacrifices of the war.
>
> I take this opportunity of congratulating you and the President on the satisfactory termination of the struggle in the Philippines, and I view with admiration the generosity of your public towards the rebels.
>
> I am primarily convinced that this extension of American rights and dimensions will make for the happiness of the native populations, while an experience in the problems of government, under such circumstances, will help the American people to understand our world-work.[37]

In addition to matters arising out of the Boer war there were various other affairs affecting Anglo-American relations during this period. The complaints of the Standard Oil Company regarding its exclusion from the development of oil properties in Burma fill many despatches. The discretionary powers of the subordinate governments in British India to regulate all exploitation of minerals in their territories was alleged by the British as reason for this exclusion. Nor was the United States able to secure any change in this ruling.[38] The assassination of President McKinley was the occasion of a most sincere demonstration of sorrow in Great Britain and the Embassy in London was almost swamped with the correspondence.[39] Generally the relations of the two countries continued, therefore, on a much more friendly basis than in years past. Three important subjects, however, deserve special and separate treatment. The development of a common policy toward China, 1899–1903, the abrogation of the Clayton-Bulwer treaty dealing with the construction of an inter-oceanic canal and the negotiation of the two Hay-Pauncefote treaties, and thirdly, the negotiations relating to the adjustment of disputes with Canada, particularly the final settlement of the Alaskan boundary, all came during these years. All of these matters were in progress at the same time as the Boer War and each was of far greater importance to the United States than the South African question. Each of them was settled to the advantage of the United States, which would have been impossible had America acted in any belligerent way in aid of the Boers. By selection I turn first to Canadian affairs, where a tangled skein awaits us.

NOTES TO CHAPTER V

1. *Education of Henry Adams,* p. 374.
2. Thayer, II, p. 221.
3. *Ibid.,* II, p. 218.
4. *Ibid.,* II, p. 221.
5. *Ibid.*
6. H. P., *Times,* April 13, 1897; D. S., From London, Vol. 188, No. 39, May 20, 1897, Hay to Sherman; No. 73, July 17, same to same; Vol. 189, No. 121, Sept. 22, same to same.
7. H. P., July 27, 1897, McKinley to Hay. In this connection the suggestion has been made in Thayer, II, p. 160, that Mr. Hay was opposed to a Special Embassy at the time of the Queen's Diamond Jubilee. A letter now in D. S., Vol. 188, unnumbered, May 25, 1897, Hay to Sherman, directly contradicts this; and President McKinley wrote appreciatively of Hay's attitude in the matter.
8. Hay, *Letters,* etc., III, p. 99.
9. D. S., From London, Vol. 188, No. 14, May 1, 1897, Hay to Sherman.
10. F. R., 1897, p. 299.
11. H. P., May 4, 1897, Adee to Hay.
12. D. S., From London, Vol. 188, No. 70, July 16, 1897, Hay to Sherman.
13. F. R., 1897, pp. 300, 304, 306.
14. D. S., From London, Vol. 189, telegram, Dec. 25, 1897, Hay to Sherman. The despatches in F. R., 1897, pp. 258-325, need only to be supplemented by several unpublished despatches to give a fairly complete story. These are: D. S., To London, Vol. 32, No. 51, May 21, Sherman to Hay; Nos. 325 and

326, Nov. 29, same to same; From London, Vol. 188, No. 45; May 28, 1897, Hay to Sherman; Vol. 190, telegram, Jan. 17, 1898, same to same.
   15. *Times,* May 14, 1898.
   16. Steed, *Through Thirty Years,* London, 1924, 2 Vols. I, p. 131; cf. Mowat, p. 281.
   17. *Times,* Dec. 9, 1898.
   18. *Times,* Jan. 6, 1899.
   19. *G. P.,* XV, No. 4398; *H. P.,* Nov. 22, 1899, Choate to Hay.
   20. *Times,* Dec. 1, 1899.
   21. Eckardstein, p. 130; *G. P.,* XV, p. 417.
   22. Eckardstein, pp. 143-144.
   23. *Ibid.,* pp. 144-146.
   24. *Ibid.,* p. 151.
   25. *G. P.,* No. 4401. Cf. Ward and Gooch, *Cambridge History of British Foreign Policy, 1783-1919,* New York, 3 Vols. III, pp. 278-279.
   26. *Germany Between England and Russia,* a manuscript paper prepared by my colleague, Prof. W. L. Langer, has been of service for this whole matter.
   27. *G. P.,* No. 4395; "Diplomaticus," *Count Mouraviev's Indiscretion* in *Fortnightly Review,* Dec. 1899; Mevil, *M. Delcassé and the Entente Cordiale* in *National Review,* July, 1908; *Deutsche Intriguen gegen England im Burenkriege, von einem Wissenden,* in *Deutsche Revue,* Sept., 1908; *Daily Telegraph,* Oct. 28, 1908; Ward and Gooch, III, p. 280 (note); Schwertfeger (Editor), *Zur europäischen Politik, 1897-1914,* Berlin, 1919, 5 Vols. I, Nos. 17 and 19 (extracts from the Belgian archives taken to Berlin during the World War).
   28. *G. P.,* XV, No. 4461.
   29. *Ibid.,* Nos. 4459, 4460.
   30. *Ibid.,* Nos. 4466, 4469; cf. Mevil, *De la Paix de Frankfort à la Conference d'Algésiras,* Paris, 1909, p. 57; Bülow, *Imperial Germany,* London, 1914, p. 30.
   31. Appendix A to this chapter; cf. also *H. P.,* Feb. 19, 1902, Hay to Lodge, referring to correspondence as to concentration camps in South Africa. Hay says: the war "will stop the instant Botha and De Wett wish it to stop; and in any case there is no reason why the Government of the United States should take upon itself to stop the War in which it has less concern than any nation in the world."
   32. *H. P.,* March 10, 1900, telegram, Hay to White.
   33. *D. S.,* From London, Vol. 199, telegram, March 13, 1900, White to Hay.
   34. *D. S.,* Numerical File, Vol. 515, May 21, 1900.
   35. *D. S.,* Credences, Vol. 7, Memorandum, Jan. 29, 1901.
   36. Appendix B to this chapter, where Mr. Wellman describes an interview with Mr. Fischer of the Boer delegation. The date is probably immediately after May 21, 1900. In *H. P.,* June 26, 1900, Cortelyou to Hay, there is an enclosure of the letter of the Boer delegates to President McKinley on the eve of their departure from America. Cf. *H. P.,* Jan. 12, 1901, Newel to Hay.
   37. *H. P.,* July 5, 1902, Chamberlain to Hay.
   38. There is considerable material on this topic. Only a few despatches are cited here; *D. S.,* To London, Vol. 34, No. 963, July 21, 1902, Hill to Choate; No. 1036, Oct. 23, Hay to Choate; Vol. 35, No. 14, June 30, 1905, Hay to Reid; No. 55, Sept. 9, Loomis to Reid; telegram, p. 262, March 5, 1906; From London, Vol. 205, No. 913, Aug. 7, 1902, Choate to Hay; Vol. 206, enclosure to No. 1011, Dec. 16, White to Hay; Vol. 214, enclosure to private letter, April 18, 1906, Reid to Root; No. 170, March 30, Reid to Root.
   39. *D. S.,* Vol. 203, No. 677, Oct. 9, 1901, Choate to Hay.

APPENDICES TO CHAPTER V

A

Hay Papers, Hay to Edward Everett Hale, Washington, January 13, 1900.

My dear Dr. Hale:
I have received your letter of the 12th of January and a great many from other friends on the same subject.

I think all these petitions and memorials leave out of view one essential fact. They generally refer to the Hague Conference and the treaty resulting from it as the basis of our action. In the first place, so long as the Senate has not ratified the treaty, it has no existence as a matter of law or fact, and, even if it were in full force and vigor, our delegates, by a formal declaration entered upon the minutes of the proceedings, expressly declared that the United States was not to be required to interfere in European quarrels, and intimated that the interference of Europe in quarrels this side of the ocean would not be welcomed by us. I do not mean that by this declaration we are precluded from tendering our good offices in any case where they would conduce to the preservation of peace or the cessation of bloodshed, but, as it at present appears, neither side wishes our intervention. The Boers are doing very well by themselves, and England is certainly not in a disposition to listen to outside propositions that she should acknowledge her defeat and retire from the field. It seems to me that any tender of our good offices in the present state of things would certainly exasperate one of the parties, and possibly both, and would lead to no good result.

I write this in perfect confidence that you will not misinterpret it.

B

Hay Papers, Wellman to Hay (undated).

My dear Mr. Secretary:
Congratulations upon your admirable handling of our friends from South Africa. It was done to perfection.

By the way, you may wish to know (if you do not already) that the leader of our friends (Mr. Fischer) told me this afternoon in a spirit of bitterness what they think of it all. To be brief.

They charge that the American government is in league with Great Britain. There is an understanding. The evidence of this is found in the manner which the government of the United States put in the good offices, secured an answer in the negative, and published that answer, so as to put up a fender against the remainder of the world. What you should have done, in the opinion of Mr. Fischer, was to ask the other governments what they were willing to do, and try to organize a joint movement.

Second, you did not treat them right in having your answer prepared before you heard their plea. "It was a bit discouraging to see our answer lying on the table as we entered and before we had had opportunity to open our mouths," etc., etc.

Moreover, the aim now is not to bring pressure to bear upon the American government—oh, dear no,—but to show Chamberlain that he was wrong when he said he had the sympathy of the whole civilized world "Our next work of a practical nature will be in Europe, where everyone thinks the U. S. ready to jump in and aid Great Britain in case of intervention. We want to be able to convince Europe that America will not do this, and therefore we make an appeal to the people of your country. If we can convince Europe that you will not aid England we may be able to secure intervention from some European government"—etc. etc.

I do not imagine this is important, but I thought it might interest you to know how our friends talk.

CHAPTER VI

THE ALASKAN BOUNDARY

HERE we shift from questions of the tropics and of South Africa to those which particularly concern Canada. The importance of the relations between the United States and Canada has often been shown; and there was an accumulation of matters which required adjustment. Furthermore as Canada was growing in political stature, the old way of letting the settlement of affairs rest entirely in British diplomatic hands would now no longer work. Canada was becoming a nation and in her relations with the United States was rapidly to develop her own national desires. Earlier in 1895, Secretary Olney was apparently somewhat shocked when Lord Pauncefote had proposed that the "regular channels" of diplomatic negotiations should be disregarded, and that Canada should arrange directly with the United States various regulations for the navigation of the Great Lakes.[1]

Indeed, the influence of Canada on British policy towards the United States was already marked. As we have seen, the Canadian point of view regarding the regulation of sealing in the Bering Sea had been adopted by Lord Salisbury in 1898. Now not only that question, but eleven others as well were to be referred to an Anglo-American joint commission, which included in its membership several Canadians. However, prior to this one of the most important outstanding matters, that relating to the boundary between Canada and Alaska, had already been the subject of negotiation between the United States and Great Britain. This dispute arose from the terms of the treaty of 1825 between Great Britain and

Russia, which declared that the boundary of southern coastal Alaska, along a shore which was indented and slashed by deep inlets, should follow the crests of the mountains in such fashion as to leave to Russia a strip of territory thirty miles wide along the coast. As Ambassador Choate said, the dispute was whether this treaty, which was inherited by the United States from Russia in 1867, gave a frontier which should run "around the shores of the inlets or cross their mouths." [2]

At the head of some of these deep inlets there were harbors and openings to passes leading to the interior. With the discovery of gold in the Klondike and the rush of a mining boom the chances of a clash between the turbulent elements of the new population had increased. The Canadians had put forward a claim that the frontier should not follow the indentations of the coast line, thus leaving the harbors and ports at the heads of these inlets in Canadian hands. To this the United States was opposed. At all events, until the dispute could be settled finally, a temporary frontier was essential as a *modus vivendi*. This temporary line was not to affect or prejudice in any way a future and permanent determination of the boundary.

The negotiations, which started in the spring of 1898, for the fixing of this temporary line were not at first successful; and the problem was referred to the Joint High Commission. Here again a deadlock ensued and the matter was not settled till on October 20, 1899, Secretary Hay and the British signed an agreement fixing this temporary frontier.[3] Time had been lost, tempers had been irritated, and in the United States a conviction had developed that the Canadians were attempting to bluff both the British and American authorities. Much of the correspondence need not detain us; but, for the service of the student, in the footnotes there are many references to unpublished documents, and extracts from these are given in the Appendix. For the present we are concerned only with an abridged and general statement of the course of negotiations.

Soon after the meeting of the Joint High Commission it became clear that the attitude of Lord Herschell, a member for Great Britain, was creating difficulties. Mr. Chamberlain caused careful inquiries to be made in Washington as to the "hitch" in the progress of the Commission which seemed to be stalled in its work. To this, Secretary Hay replied by a frank letter to Mr. Henry White saying that Lord Herschell was advocating "a ridiculous and preposterous boundary line." The Secretary, however, had high praise for Lord Pauncefote, saying:

> While always stoutly defending British interests, and working with great energy for his own country, he has been so reasonable, courteous and conciliatory that it has been a great pleasure to the Department to do business with him.[4]

In February the British suggested that if the United States would agree to arbitrate the Alaskan boundary, all other matters might be arranged. Thus the modification of the Clayton-Bulwer treaty and of the objectionable features of the treaty of 1818 would all be accomplished, and the entire Anglo-American slate would be wiped clean of all subjects of discussion.[5] As we shall see later, the Clayton-Bulwer treaty now stood in the way of the negotiation of a new Hay-Pauncefote treaty relating to the inter-oceanic canal. To this British proposal, Secretary Hay, much as he desired the new canal treaty, hesitated to agree, for he was confident of the justice of the American contentions as to the Alaskan boundary, and he did not wish to submit them to the dangers of a compromise decision at the hands of foreign umpires in an arbitral tribunal. As we can see in a letter to Mr. White, which is given in the Appendix to this chapter, he also maintained that the canal should be built by Americans alone.[6] The High Commission adjourned in February leaving nearly everything at odds and ends. Secretary Hay wrote again to Mr. White:

> My own explanation of their obstinate refusal to agree to close up matters is that they preferred to stand before the Canadian Parliament in the attitude of stout defenders of Canadian rights and inter-

ests, rather than as signers of a treaty which would not meet the views of their advanced supporters.[7]

However, the American Commissioners offered confidentially in February, 1899, the suggestion that the boundary line should be submitted to arbitration by six jurists, three on a side and a majority vote to determine the issue.[8] This was the proposal which was finally accepted in 1903. In the interval of four years the matter was to be vigorously debated by both sides. In the meantime the death of Lord Herschell, though it removed a great lawyer who had an immense knowledge of the questions at issue, also removed one of the most obstinate opponents to a settlement along lines which were acceptable to the United States. With his death the Canadians seem to have abandoned the idea that the Joint High Commission should again be called in session. Matters, therefore, were left to the regular diplomatic channels of negotiation; though in the case of the British the constant reference to Canada entailed delay and at times proved irritating.

The immediate question was of course the drawing of a temporary frontier line and, in the course of these negotiations, there was discussion as to whether the permanent line should be submitted to arbitration, and if so, what sort of a tribunal should be set up. In all of these affairs the importance of diligence and patience is clearly brought out. We get some notion of the task involved in an intimate personal letter of Secretary Hay to his friend, Henry Adams:

> The worst of my present job is that I can delegate so little of it. It is a grim grey world you have left me to, with nobody to talk to, or to walk with, to keep me in the straight path by showing me the crooked. I have a million things I should like to bore you with, but I cannot take time to write them. I have worked on this miserable Alaska question for six months. Yesterday Choate wired me a proposition agreed on between him, Pauncefote, and Salisbury, which I had spent weeks beforehand in getting everybody here to agree to. I thought I could intone my little *nunc dimittis,* when this morning comes in young Tower, and tells me Canada won't let Salisbury do it. Now the fat is in the fire and I "don't much care if I never get to Texas." I grow wanner and wanner, day by day.[9]

The regret felt by the United States at the failure of the High Commission to solve the Canadian disputes was also felt by Lord Salisbury. Particularly was this true for, if the Alaska boundary line could have been settled, all the other questions, including the very important matter of the tariff on lumber, could have been quickly disposed of.[10] The United States renewed its proposal of a tribunal of six jurists, three on a side, to deal with the boundary matter but that was rejected by Canada. In May, Sir Julian Pauncefote went home and in London he had interviews with Mr. Choate. Together they concocted a plan whereby the two American ports of Dyea and Skagway should be preserved to the United States, and the whole question of the boundary should be then submitted to an arbitral tribunal of seven members, the seventh member being chosen by the three jurists appointed by the United States and the three appointed by Great Britain.[11] This tentative plan was rejected by the Canadian authorities who were fearful of public opinion at home upon surrender of all claims to Dyea and Skagway. As a counter proposal, Canada urged that the entire matter be submitted to arbitration as in the case of the Venezuelan boundary dispute; furthermore, the Canadians suggested that Pyramid Harbor on the Lynn Canal, should be earmarked for Canada as Dyea and Skagway were to be given to the United States. Pyramid Harbor, however, was an American settlement which the United States intended in May, 1899, to garrison with American troops.[12] As Ambassador Choate wrote to Secretary Hay he was met

by this astounding and unreasonable demand from Canada, that the whole matter of the settled places should be taken out from the principles of Rule C., and that if Pyramid Harbor was found to be within the territory and jurisdiction of the United States, it should be turned over to Great Britain, without rhyme or reason. As I cabled you yesterday, I assume this to be utterly inadmissible, and that such will be your answer.[13]

The United States did indeed suspend sending troops to Pyramid Harbor; but the ultimate settlement was no nearer. Meantime, constant complaints from American officials in Alaska of continued Canadian encroachments made "some *modus vivendi* imperatively" necessary.¹⁴ In the bargaining which now began regarding the geographical and topographical details of a temporary boundary, the American Embassy at London was inadequately equipped with accurate maps and, indeed, several of the suggestions made by Secretary Hay seem to have been based on faulty geographical information. The British were also annoyed by the lack of satisfactory maps and word was sent to Canada to despatch a man to London with full information. Moreover, the attempts of Canada to exercise jurisdiction south of the River Klehini had aroused great excitement in the region of its tributary, Porcupine River.¹⁵ Secretary Hay telegraphed to Ambassador Choate:

> I do not ask you to assume tone of ultimatum but British Government should understand that we cannot recede from line of Klehini as proposed.¹⁶

However, Secretary Hay's own attempt at drawing a boundary line, which he did at the request of the British Embassy in Washington, was promptly rejected in London.¹⁷ Meantime the suggestion was made at the end of July that if the United States would lease to Canada some of the territory in dispute, the whole matter could be settled. Secretary Hay seized this straw as pointing the way to a solution. As he said: "the very act of granting a lease implies unquestioned possession." ¹⁸ Indeed the acceptance would *ipso facto* be a recognition of the sovereignty of the United States over that region. If Canada were ready to accept a lease from the United States, that in itself, would recognize the sovereignty of the United States in the region. Here, however, he ran directly into the face of an implacable one third and more of the Senate. A diagnosis showed that such a treaty could not command a two-thirds majority of the Senate. In those wretchedly hot days of early August, 1899, he wrote to Adams:

> I left Washington last Monday, being just able to crawl to the station. The heat has been so steady and uncomfortable that it has

nearly used us all up, and besides that, the State Department, always impossible, has been a little Hell upon earth for the last few months. It was bad enough before you went away; but it has grown constantly worse, and there being nobody to talk to, and call names, makes the whole thing intolerable.

You know I told you long years ago that there would never be another Treaty, of any significance, ratified by the Senate. The truth of this becomes clearer to me every hour. You may say I am contradicted by the ratification of the Treaty of Peace. But I hold that this is a most striking confirmation of my theory. A treaty of peace, in any normal state of things, ought to be ratified with unanimity in twenty-four hours. They wasted six weeks in wrangling over this one, and ratified it with one vote to spare. We have five or six matters now demanding settlement; I can settle them all, honorably, and advantageously to our own side; and I am assured by leading men in the Senate that not one of the Treaties, if negotiated, will pass the Senate. I should have a majority in every case, but a malcontent third would certainly dish every one of them. To such disastrous shape has the original mistake in the Constitution grown in the evolution of our politics. . . .

So that the real duties of the Secretary of State seem to be three: To fight claims upon us by other States; to press more or less fraudulent claims of our citizens upon other countries; to find offices for the friends of Senators when there are none.

The President has more nerve than any of them. He says to me:— "make a treaty as you think it should be made, and let the Senate do as they like." But I shrink from doing a thing which is foredoomed to failure and which may injure him. If I could be the scapegoat I would most gladly bind my batch of treaties to my horns and trot gaily off to the wilderness—say Paris, where you are.[19]

By September matters began to look a little brighter. The *modus vivendi* line was practically settled on the general lines for which Secretary Hay had been contending. In order to get rid of the inconveniences incident to shifting river beds and the other instabilities of geography, the frontier line was run along the south bank of the Klehini River to a point where it joined the Chilkat River about a mile and a half north of the village of Klukwan. On the Dyea and Skagway trails the summits of the Chilkoot and White passes were also fixed as boundary points. In particular, persons going to or coming from the Porcupine region could follow the trail down the Klehini whether it took them into Canadian territory or not. The rights and privileges of citizens of either country were mutually guaranteed under this arrangement, which gave a temporary jurisdiction. This agreement was signed in October.[20] But there still remained the fixing of the permanent boundary.

Lord Salisbury had on July 2, 1899, as a matter of record, sent a note proposing to submit the Alaskan boundary question to arbitration on the exact lines of the Venezuelan arbitration treaty. In reply, Secretary Hay sent a lengthy despatch to Ambassador Choate stating the differences between the two boundary disputes and refusing the British proposal. In early August Mr. Choate reported his communication of the contents of this despatch to Lord Salisbury. Mr. Choate wrote to Lord Salisbury in part as follows:

> This Alaskan dispute is entirely unlike the controversy with Venezuela—in that it is a new question, raised for the first time after the Joint High Commission had been agreed upon; up to which date the claim had never been put forward, either by Great Britain or Canada, which it is now asked shall be submitted to arbitration. Whereas, in the case of Venezuela, the controversy originated a century and a half ago, and had been, in its entirety, a subject of dispute and protest for sixty years.
>
> The coast line of the mainland (the *lisière* of the treaty) including the inlets, had been in the possession or under the control of Russia and the United States since the Treaty between Russia and Great Britain in 1825—and the settlements on the inlets, especially those about the head of the Lynn Canal, have been made with the authority and under the jurisdiction of the United States, without any protest or claim of territorial ownership on the part of Great Britain—whereas, in the Venezuela case, the British occupations and settlements involved were upon territory claimed by Venezuela, and against the constant protest of Venezuela; thus constituting, as Venezuela alleges, a series of advancing encroachments upon what that country claimed to be her territory.
>
> In support of the proposition that from the Treaty of 1825, to the cession to the United States in 1867, the Russian Government steadily maintained its claim to a strip of territory thirty miles in width, on the mainland of the Continent, beginning at 54° 40′ and extending northwest around all the inlets and interior waters to the 141st degree of West longitude, I called attention to the maps issued by the Russian Government, to its lease or license, contained

in the Treaty with the United States of 1824, for the citizens of the latter to frequent with their ships, for ten years, "the interior seas, gulfs, harbors and creeks upon the coast," for the purpose of fishing and trading with the natives; and to Russia's refusal, in 1835, to renew this privilege.

During the whole period of Russia's occupation of this strip of territory, Great Britain made no claim to it and entered no protest; on the contrary, there were acts on her part of express recognition of the claim of Russia. By the treaty of 1825, she took from Russia the same privilege for British subjects to frequent the same inland seas, gulfs, harbors and creeks, for ten years, as had been granted to American citizens by the treaty of 1824; and, after the expiration of the ten years' privileges, British subjects and vessels were excluded from these interior waters; and the British Government acquiesced in this without a protest. . . .

In the opinion of the President, the action of the two Governments during Russia's occupation of the strip of territory now in controversy, makes a wholly different condition of affairs from that between Great Britain and Venezuela—and this difference has been maintained and made more distinct since the cession by Russia to the United States. . . .

The towns, settlements and industries about the head of Lynn Canal and the other inlets embraced in this strip of territory, having been established under these circumstances—a wholly different situation has been created in regard to them from that in the Venezuelan case; so utterly different that the Government of the United States would feel that it was not properly guarding the rights of its citizens, if it should consent to put these settlements in peril, by applying to them the terms of the Venezuelan Treaty, which was designed for a wholly different state of affairs; nor would the President feel justified in submitting the questions involved to any arbitration, unless our settlements—made in good faith before this new claim was presented on the part of Canada—were expressly exempted from its operation.[21]

The British reply was given in October and rehearsed in part the language used by American diplomats fifteen years earlier in which the geographical difficulties of the frontier were stressed. The fact that no frontier had ever been drawn and that only an approximate line had been delineated on the maps as a conventional compromise was used as an argument that the Alaskan boundary dispute should be submitted to an arbitration which would probably result only in a compromise.[22] Ambassador Choate was delegated to make reply to the English. This he did on January 22, 1900, in a despatch which Secretary Hay termed "unanswerable." As a matter of fact no answer was ever attempted by the British. As this despatch is in print it does not seem necessary to quote from it. In any case it was chiefly an elaboration of points already familiar to us from Mr. Choate's despatch of August 9, 1899.[23]

Here the matter rested till it entered another stage. In this second and final stage a new fact is quickly apparent. President McKinkley had died in September, 1901, and now a younger and more vigorous man was at the head of the state. President Roosevelt, often impatient of delays, was determined in his policies; his viewpoint was that of a man who had traveled abroad and he was keenly interested in foreign affairs. International relations and diplomacy, therefore, appealed to him particularly and he was not likely to leave to his Secretary of State that monopoly of negotiation and decision which Mr. Hay had exercised under President McKinley. Of the personal relations of President Roosevelt and Secretary Hay more will be said in a later chapter. Now, however, youth was in the saddle, determination was the whip, yet wisdom was the bridle.

To Mr. Choate in January, 1902, President Roosevelt had said: "Let sleeping dogs lie." Nevertheless in May, 1901, Secretary Hay had informally outlined once more to Lord Pauncefote the American plan for the decision as to the Alaskan boundary; and in February, 1902, Lord Pauncefote in like manner had presented a *critique* of this plan which indicated Canadian opposition.[24] Then at the end of June, Lord Lansdowne, who had succeeded Lord Salisbury as Foreign Secretary, urged Ambassador Choate to have a talk with Sir Wilfrid Laurier, the Canadian Prime Minister, and Lord Minto, the Governor-General of Canada, both of whom were then in London. The result was a conference.[25] Following this Secretary Hay wrote to the President:

I send to you, in the hope that you may find a few moments of leisure to look it over, a letter just received from Harry White. If you have not time to read it all, begin at the part I have marked with red pencil, on the fourth page. From this it appears:

First. That Laurier is anxious to have boundary questions settled; that he has no longer any hope of getting Lynn Canal; that he wants to save his face by having the matter decided against him. Still, he pretends that he believes his cause to be just, and that in case of a decision in their favor, he would not insist on Lynn Canal, but on some compensation elsewhere.

Secondly. It is evident that Lansdowne is also anxious to have some settlement, and that our peremptory rejection of his suggestion last year has convinced him that if anything is to be done, it must be done on our own lines.[26]

On July 14, 1902, another letter from the Secretary which is given in the Appendix to this chapter, explained several matters.[27] Mr. Choate also wrote:

He [Laurier] avers and Lord Lansdowne says that his only motive for so doing [raising the question] is the apprehension that at any moment a serious conflict may arise in the disputed territory, or what they call disputed, upon the discovery of gold. But as everything in that region seems more quiet and peaceful than usual, I am inclined to think that there is something in Canadian politics, or in his own personal politics that would make a settlement just now particularly desirable. Dr. Hill's telegram direct from the President gave me the cue for my conversation with him. It seemed to me wise to leave the matter about where we found it, and not to encourage his idea of doing something at once. Still his concessions which I reported to you on the 5th did indicate to me that he would now go somewhat further than he was even inclined to go before, for a settlement. On Wednesday the 16th during my usual weekly call Lord Lansdowne opened the subject again, expressed his regret that I had thrown cold water upon Sir Wilfrid, repeated as from him the urgent desirability of a settlement to avoid possible conflict and disappointment. . . . I had not been willing to take the matter up where you and Lord Pauncefote had left it by your draft convention of May, 1901, and Lord P's memorandum of Feb'y, 1902. I told him that I had made no reference to that in talking with Sir Wilfrid, that in fact my first knowledge of it was when he sent me the print of Lord P's memorandum; that what I had intended to make clear to Sir Wilfrid was the President's disinclination to anything like a compromise, or to an arbitration in any form that would necessarily involve a compromise, and his strong conviction that the case of Canada had no real foundation.[28]

There was a further exchange of notes regarding the

matter in the latter part of 1902; but these did not present anything new.[29] Then under the stimulus given by the new British Ambassador, Sir Michael Herbert, who had been appointed following the lamented death of Lord Pauncefote, the matter took shape; and on January 23, 1903, a treaty was signed for the appointment of a tribunal to settle the Alaskan boundary. Cf. the Appendix to this chapter.[30] In February the treaty was approved by the Senate and in March Secretary Root and Senators Lodge and Turner were appointed the American members. For Great Britain Lord Alverstone, Sir L. A. Jetté, and Mr. A. B. Aylesworth were named. The terms of reference were, with minor amendments, those included in the American plan which Secretary Hay had advocated since 1899.[31]

The Canadian objections to the American members, endeavors to postpone the meeting of the tribunal, and the general dilatoriness of the British now affected the American temper and led to sharp letters from President Roosevelt. He wrote in July to Secretary Hay:

> With England, over the Alaska business I do hope she will understand that if we can't come to an agreement now nothing will be left the United States but to act in a way which will necessarily wound British pride.[32]

He had already written to Senator Lodge saying:

> I am by no means certain that I would acquiesce in deferring the matter until next summer. I do not want it hanging on during the presidential campaign. I dislike making any kind of a threat, but my present judgment is that if the British play fast and loose the thing to do is to declare the negotiations off, recite our case in the message to Congress, and ask for an appropriation to run the boundary as we deem it should be run. . . . The English behaved badly in Venezuela despite the fact that we had behaved with scrupulous care and impartiality during the Boer War. I don't intend that they shall do any shuffling now.[33]

Privately and unofficially these views had been given to the British in early August. Mr. Choate seems to have addressed a note to the Foreign Office which created "a great flutter in the dove-cote," for when it was finally agreed by the British and Canadians that they would be ready by September 3, the Ambassador added to Secretary Hay: "I can't stand their dawdling and I am very glad that we succeeded at last in stirring them up." [34]

Thus the matter went to argument. At the last there were hurried cables back and forth and there was talk of an adjustment. Finally, on October 20, 1903, thanks to minor changes, Lord Alverstone gave his vote for the American side on the main contention, that regarding the boundary line following the inlets instead of cutting across them.[35] Letters dealing with the decision are in the Appendix to this chapter.[36] There was of course bitter criticism of Lord Alverstone by the Canadians but his sturdy reply to these critics was:

> If when any kind of arbitration is set up they don't want a decision based on the law and the evidence, they must not put a British Judge on the commission.[37]

Thus the Alaskan boundary was settled. It had been a persistent, awkward question for several years. Alongside of it there were adjustments made with regard to sealing and fishery disputes; and the question of Canadian reciprocity was to remain for some years uncertain. Yet in the long run Secretary Hay was able to see his desires gratified.[38] One after the other, in spite of bad moments such as that caused by the Anglo-German blockade of Venezuela, most of these differences were settled amicably, to the advantage of the United States and without offence to Great Britain.

NOTES TO CHAPTER VI

1. D. S., To British Embassy, Vol. 23, No. 204, Sept. 27, 1895, Olney to Pauncefote.
2. Parl. Papers, 1904, CXI, p. 16, Jan. 22, 1900, Choate to Salisbury.
3. F. R., 1899, pp. 330 et seq.
4. Hay, Letters, etc., III, p. 136; D. S., From London, Vol. 195, telegram, Dec. 30, 1898, White to Hay.
5. D. S., Numerical File, Vol. 547, memorandum, Feb. 4, 1899; From London, Vol. 196, telegram, Feb. 15, 1899, White to Hay: "I obtained assurances from British Minister for Foreign Affairs that if High Commission should reach agreement British Government assent to your proposed Clayton-Bulwer Treaty would be given at once."
6. Appendix A to this chapter. Cf. Thayer, II, pp. 217-218; Hay, Letters, etc., III, pp. 141-143.

7. Hay, *Letters*, etc., III, p. 145.
8. D. S., From London, Vol. 196, enclosure to No. 699, Feb. 25, 1899, Hay to White; H. P., Feb. 21, 1899, private and personal, Hay to White:
"I am sure you will see on diligent reading of the last few pages that our Commissioners went to the very verge of concessions to induce the Canadians to make a treaty. They refused to consider any form of arbitration, except that which they themselves proposed. Even the scheme that Lord Salisbury and Lord Julian thought so well of—that is three arbitrators on a side—they entirely refused to consider, and finally they refused to consider the proposition to isolate the Alaska question and to agree upon all the rest, leaving that open for future negotiation, although such progress had been made in the discussion of the other matters that an agreement was in almost every one of them, clearly in sight.
I deeply regret the failure of the negotiations, yet I cannot but think that our Commissioners did all that could be done."
9. Hay, *Letters*, etc., III, p. 151.
10. D. S., To London, Vol. 33, No. 87, April 19, 1899, Hay to Choate; From London, Vol. 197, No. 81, May 5, 1899, Choate to Hay; Cf. *Times*, March 17, 1899.
11. H. P., May 12, 1899, private and confidential, Choate to Hay; D. S., From London, Vol. 197, 2 telegrams, May 12, Choate to Hay.
12. D. S., From London, Vol. 197, telegram, May 15, 1899, Choate to Hay; telegram, May 18, same to same; private and confidential, May 24, same to same; To British Embassy, Vol. 24, p. 527, May 18, Hay to Tower; To London, Vol. 33, No. 138, May 22, Hay to Choate.
13. D. S., From London, Vol. 197, private and confidential, May 19, 1899, Choate to Hay.
14. D. S., To London, Vol. 33, p. 183, telegram, May 27, 1899, Hay to Choate; From London, Vol. 197, No. 94, June 2, 1899, Choate to Hay.
15. D. S., From London, Vol. 197, No. 95, June 6, 1899, Choate to Hay; No. 99, June 14, same to same; unnumbered, June 16, same to same; No. 109, June 23, same to same; No. 110, July 1, same to same; No. 112, July 5, same to same; To London, Vol. 33, No. 164, June 23, 1899, Hay to Choate; p. 433, telegram, June 25, same to same.
16. H. P., Telegram, July 6, 1899, Hay to Choate.
17. D. S., To London, Vol. 33, p. 227, July 24, 1899, Hay to Choate; H. P., Aug. 4, 1899, private, Choate to Hay.
18. Appendix B to this chapter.
19. Hay, *Letters*, etc., III, pp. 155-157.
20. F. R., 1899, pp. 330 *et seq.*; Appendix C to this chapter.
21. D. S., From London, Vol. 197, enclosure to personal letter to Secretary Hay from Ambassador Choate of Aug. 9, 1899, No. 112, July 5, Choate to Hay; No. 144, Aug. 4, same to same; To London, Vol. 33, No. 183, July 20, 1899, Hay to Choate; the American case is also explained in a despatch criticizing the *Times* in D. S., To London, Vol. 33, No. 222, Oct. 2, Hay to Choate.
22. D. S., From London, Vol. 198, No. 187, Oct. 25, 1899, Choate to Hay; To London, Vol. 38, No. 241, Nov. 10, Hay to Choate; H. P., Nov. 22, private and unofficial, Choate to Hay.
23. *Parl. Papers*, 1904, CXI, pp. 16 *et seq.*; H. P., Dec. 29, 1899, private and unofficial, Choate to Hay; D. S., To London, Vol. 33, No. 277, Jan. 11, 1900, Hay to Choate; From London, Vol. 198, No. 236, Jan. 23, Choate to Hay.
24. H. P., Jan. 6, 1902, Choate to Hay; D. S., Numerical File, Vol. 515, memorandum, Feb. 28, 1902.

25. *D. S.,* To London, Vol. 34, p. 198, telegram, June 28, 1902, Hill to Choate; From London, Vol. 205, telegram, June 29, Choate to Hay; *H. P.,* July 5, private and confidential, Choate to Hay.

26. *Roosevelt Papers,* July 7, 1902, Hay to Roosevelt.

27. Appendix D to this chapter.

28. *H. P.,* July 19, 1902, Choate to Hay.

29. *H. P.,* Nov. 26, 1902, Choate to Hay; *D. S.,* Numerical File, Vol. 515, unnumbered, Dec. 18, 1902, Herbert to Hay.

30. Appendix E to this chapter.

31. *R. P.,* Feb. 11, 1903, Hay to Roosevelt; March 25, Roosevelt to Root; *F. R.,* 1903, pp. 494-541.

32. *H. P.,* July 29, 1903, Roosevelt to Hay; Cf. *H. P.,* Feb. 24, 1903, private and confidential, Laurier to Hay; March 22, private, Hay to Laurier.

33. *Selections from the Correspondence of Theodore Roosevelt and Henry Cabot Lodge, 1884-1918,* New York, 2 Vols., II, p. 37; Cf. Rhodes, pp. 257-259.

34. *H. P.,* Aug. 14, 1903, personal and confidential, Choate to Hay; *F. R.,* 1903, p. 543.

35. *Roosevelt-Lodge,* II, pp. 53-55, Sept. 5, 1903, Lodge to Roosevelt; *D. S.,* From London, Vol. 208, telegram, Oct. 15, 1903, Choate to Hay; *H. P.,* notes and copy of telegram, Oct. 16, 1903, Hay to Choate; *F. R.,* 1903, pp. 543-545.

36. Appendix F to this chapter.

37. Smalley, 1st Series, p. 238.

38. *H. P.,* Oct. 27, 1903, Choate to Hay.

APPENDICES TO CHAPTER VI

A

Hay Papers, Hay to Henry White, February 14, 1899.

The Canadian Commission have arrived at a critical period in their negotiations, and I am sorry to say I am not hopeful of the result. It is useless for me to say much to you on this point, however, as you will probably be informed by telegraph of the close of the negotiations before this reaches you. I do not wish to say anything injurious to Lord Herschell, but I cannot but think that if a less able lawyer had been sent, a man of diplomatic habit of mind, he might have been able to have come to an arrangement. The attitude of Lord Herschell in regard to the Alaska boundary has been throughout that of the keen lawyer intent on making a case against an adversary, instead of that of a man of affairs seeking to find a transaction which would be advantageous to both parties. The Alaska question seems the only critical one. On eleven other points there seems no insuperable obstacle in sight, but Lord Herschell insists on making his point on the Alaska boundary, even at the risk of all the rest. . . .

B

Hay Papers, Hay to Senator Davis, August 4, 1899.

I share your view of the utter baselessness of the Canadian claim to Alaska. No impartial court would entertain it, but where shall we find the impartial court? We are so sure of our case that we are not willing to put it in jeopardy before some chance arbitration. If it were as clear as the sun in heaven—as I think it is—the fatal tendency of an arbitrator to compromise would almost certainly give Canada more than what we are now talking of—a lease of a bit of ground, of which we should retain the fee, the flag and the sovereignty. This, I am convinced, is the best that can be done. And this, you think, is impossible.

To drop the matter here means a great deal, which you have doubtless considered as much as I have. We have twelve questions—mostly Canadian—to settle with England. None of them will be settled until this one is. The Clayton-Bulwer arrangement also goes by the board. We shall be left in a state of dull hostility, varied by commercial reprisals. The friendship between the two countries, of which nobody has spoken so wisely and eloquently as you have—will prove shortlived and derisory.

It was a great blunder in Sir Wilfrid Laurier to talk about war. Of course what he meant was that war was impossible and therefore we must have arbitration. But the word, War, should never be used except by philanthropists and soldiers. It is positively indecent in the mouth of a diplomatist.

It seems to me that in leasing them these terminal facilities for a railroad, the whole boundary question would be decided in our favor forever. The very act of granting a lease implies unquestioned possession.

Hay Papers, Hay to McKinley, August 19, 1899.

On arriving here I found two letters from Senator Fairbanks on the subject of the Alaska lease and an excellent despatch from Mr. Choate on the Arbitration question, which, he hopes is to be put aside by our adoption of the Lease proposition. It makes a curious and most embarrassing situation. You and all your Cabinet, Choate, Fairbanks, Foster and Kasson and Senator Morgan, one of the leading Democratic Senators, all agree that the proposition is reasonable and advantageous to us, far preferable to the probable result of any arbitration, in fact, the sort of solution for which we have been working for the last year. On the other hand, there is Senator Davis, who says it cannot pass the Senate; the Democrats of Iowa who, as far as they can, put their party on record as opposing any settlement of our differences with England; the German press almost unanimous in the same sense; and our friend, Whitelaw Reid, who warns us that the Tribune will probably attack any treaty we make.

In this state of things to make a final arrangement on the basis of Lord Salisbury's proposition would seem like "riding for a fall." It remains to be decided hereafter whether it would be preferable to make the settlement and let it take its chance in the Senate, or, confessing our inability to overcome the constitutional difficulty in the way, to drop the negotiations, and resume our old relations of simmering hostility with England, with all this implies in Canada, Nicaragua, China and elsewhere.

For the present I have drafted a formal instruction to Mr. Choate, asking him, by discreet inquiries, to ascertain whether our granting of the lease bring[s] with it the acceptance by England of our view of the Boundary question, and at the same time I have written him a private letter putting the whole case before him, and instructing him to keep up the discussion of the Arbitration proposal (which he is doing very well indeed) showing how we cannot accept the Venezuelan plan entire, and further, to delay any further conclusion of either matter until we are able to send him more definite instructions, our object being to get some approximate knowledge of the disposition of the minority in the Senate.

It is a painful and humiliating state of things, but I see no escape from it, since the Fathers in their wisdom chose to assume that one-third of the Senate in opposition would always be right, and the President and the majority generally wrong. It is a miracle that any treaty should ever go through. I should be only too glad, if it were possible, to "play goat" in the game, but unfortunately our constitution forbids that also, and any mistake I may make affects you and my colleagues more than it does me, which is what breaks my rest.

C

Hay Papers, Hay to Henry White, September 9, 1899.

I was not allowed to spend my vacation in the idleness which I needed and coveted. I had to go back to Washington near the end of August and endure a fortnight of intense heat and corresponding work and worry. So far as Tower and I are concerned the *modus vivendi* on the Alaskan boundary is settled. He evidently considers it arranged; but I put one or two absolutely essential saving clauses in my last note, and it is possible that they may induce another kick from Canada. If they do not, the work is done, for the present.

I shall be savagely attacked on the Pacific Coast, as a matter of course, but the fact remains we have done very well indeed. Naturally we have not yet got the line so far north as we claim we own, but on the other hand we have pushed the Canadians back fifteen miles from tide water, and by drawing the line north of Klukwan we have got them even away from Caux navigation. A few of our mines will be found outside of the line but we insist on equitable treatment for them, and they ought all to be very grateful—though they won't be.

I can see no immediate prospect of our agreeing on the permanent boundary. There is a dull, malignant feeling of opposition in the Senate to any arrangement, which I am afraid would be sure to carry one third of the votes. I am greatly disappointed in Cush. Davis's attitude. I thought he would be with us. Reid is also hostile —for reasons which will at once occur to you. I shall try to run the matter along till the President and I can see and talk with a number of the Senators. I should make the Treaty at once, and put the responsibility of rejecting it on the Senate; but the President very properly has to consider the political effect of a fight with the Senate, and while he agrees entirely with me in the whole matter and even says "go ahead and I will be with you," I cannot make up my mind to adopt a course which, however right in itself, may injure him.

I wish I could believe that Lord Salisbury would let the Clayton-Bulwer convention go through, independent of Canadian matters.

Whatever we do the Bryan party will attack us as slaves of England. All their state conventions put an anti-English plank in their platform, to curry favor with the Irish (whom they want to keep) and the Germans, whom they want to seduce. . . .

D

Roosevelt Papers, Hay to Roosevelt, July 14, 1899.

I regret to bother you with a matter which you seem to have already decided, and yet I feel I would not be justified in withholding these communications from you. It seemed in your letter returning Mr. White's letter that you did not quite understand my point of view, which is precisely the same as yours, in regard to the merits of the case. I do not think they have a leg to stand on, and I think any impartial court of jurists would so decide. At the same time, I recognize the danger of submitting such a matter to an ordinary arbitration, the besetting sin of which is to split the difference. My suggestion was a submission of the question of the interpretation of the treaty of 1825 to a tribunal of six, three on a side, a majority to decide. In this case it is impossible that we should lose, and not at all impossible that a majority should give a verdict in our favor. As to Sir Wilfrid's suggestion concerning compensation, it does not mean, as you seem to think, that compensation should be given in case the commission should decide in our favor. His suggestion is that, in the case—which seems to me impossible—of a commission deciding in *their* favor, they still would not insist on the possession of Dyea and Skagway, but would then consider the subject of some compensation for our retaining the strip. This is still more clearly brought out in Laurier's conversation with Mr. Choate.

You will observe by Choate's telegram that Lord Lansdowne now wishes to converse with him on the subject. I will be glad to get your instructions as to what I am to say to him. Shall I tell him to drop the matter at once, or talk with Lord Lansdowne and ascertain his wishes?

Hay Papers, Low to Hay, September 8, 1902.

You may be interested in hearing some of the details of the Pittsfield accident. The President behaved just as one might have expected. After he pulled himself together his first impulse was to go and lick the motorman. Gov. Crane told me he had to forcibly restrain the President from "smashing" the motorman, and at last the President agreed to refrain from physical violence, but he had to say what he thought. It was not ladylike; it was good, vigorous Saxon. . . .

At the time I sent my copy for the August National Review (a copy of which I believe I sent you) I wrote to my brother calling his attention to what I said in regard to the Alaska boundary. You may be interested in knowing what he says: "I have been spending some days with Laurier and I gather that his views are what they have always been. He is quite willing to submit to a judicial commission, without an umpire, on the *whole* case. If the United States Senate insist on deciding part of that case in their own favor, in advance, of course he knows that Canada cannot help herself. He does not expect, or desire, that we should quarrel with the U. S. over the Alaskan boundary. Canada will give way; but it will be under protest and with a sense of injustice. There might be a little soreness in this country too, but not very much, because we don't know where Alaska is and don't care. If Roosevelt really wants to make things pleasant, he should submit the whole case to arbitration. But I presume a high minded Senate would not agree to that."

E

Hay, *Letters and Diary*, III, p. 264; Hay to Mrs. Hay; January 24, 1902.

Yesterday was another memorable day in the family history. At five o'clock in the library of our house I signed with Sir Michael Herbert a treaty for the appointment of a tribunal to determine the Alaska Boundary question. It is substantially the same treaty which we proposed three years ago, and which was rejected by England and Canada, Lord Herschell and Sir Wilfrid Laurier breaking up the Joint High Commission on that issue. Lord Pauncefote thought our proposition reasonable and tried for two years to induce his government to accept it, but was never able to accomplish it; Roosevelt at first was not very keen about it, but after a while he came to agree with me, and gradually I got Lodge, Cullom and all the others of the Foreign Relations Committee to see it as I did. Then came Michael Herbert, who wanted to do something important to signalize his promotion and I took it up with him. Cullom kicked a while but finally consented and last night the work was done. It will go to the Senate Monday morning, with, I think, a fair chance of passing. . . .

F

Hay Papers, Choate to Hay, London, 20 October, 1903.

... Our main contention that the *lisière* goes round the inlets and not across them has been absolutely established. Pease and Wales Island are held to be British property, and in the actual definition of the line between the point where it touches the 56th parallel, and the 141st Meridian, considerable land within our traditional and nominal boundary as shown on the old maps has fallen to Canada. I regard the result as highly satisfactory both in the actual outcome of the decision and as establishing a precedent for the nations settling their differences without calling in the neighbours. I congratulate you most heartily on the event of the commission and only regret that Sir Michael Herbert is not here to share in the gratification which you must feel.

Our Commissioners, agent and counsel, are entitled to the highest possible praise for the manner in which they have performed their duties. They have all done their very best, and the dignity and courage of Lord Alverstone's conduct must be fully appreciated by the President. On Wednesday last, when there seemed to be a tendency to a deadlock between the Commissioners, I had an interview with Lord Lansdowne in which I pressed upon him very urgently the views of the President as expressed by him in our interview in June. . . .

The upshot of our conversation was that the Commissioners, all four of them, must agree on the drawing of the line, and that if necessary we might ourselves agree on what would be a satisfactory line, and perhaps if necessary advise the Commissioners what we thought. But in view of the result so happily attained this part of the conversation is no longer important. I left satisfied that he and Mr. Balfour would, if they had not already done so, tell Lord Alverstone what they thought as to the necessity of agreeing upon that line, and that the present chance of settling the controversy ought not to be lost.

Roosevelt Papers, Hay to Roosevelt, October 29, 1903.

I send you a few extracts from a letter received today from Harry White, typewritten to save you the trouble of deciphering his manuscript. He says:

"It has always seemed to me, as you so tersely put it in your letter of the 30th of September, that not being all fools in this country—nor even nearly all—they must see what the result of a failure to agree would be. To make quite sure that there would be no mistake on this point, however, I took occasion to visit Whittingehame on Friday, the 2nd instant—the very day the Prime Minister received the Duke of Devonshire's resignation—and I remained there until the night before poor Michael Herbert's funeral, which I came back to attend. I took occasion on the Sunday afternoon, the 4th, to have a long talk with him during which I left no doubt upon his mind as to the importance of a settlement nor as to the result of a failure to agree. He said to me that he attached far more importance to the agreement of the Tribunal than to any of the Cabinet questions and complications with which he was then bothered and that he thought it would be little short of a disaster if the Tribunal should break up without a decision. I then explained to him the rock on which I thought they might come to grief, and he said he would consider what he would do. I explained to him very fully the position of Alverstone, and intimated that I thought it would be very desirable that he should be told that the Government, without in any way wishing to influence him, was very anxious for a decision. I never heard directly whether he did anything nor if so what; but two days afterwards his Confidential Secretary, Saunders, who is a friend of mine, let me know that he had had two interviews with Lord A. Whenever things seemed to be approaching a deadlock—as they did once or twice during the past week—I only attributed it to Lord Alverstone's very natural and proper desire to do the best and make all the fight possible for the Canadians on the question of the width of the *lisière,* and I never for a moment doubted that the under currents of diplomacy, the force and quiet working of which you and I can appreciate, would bring about a decision in the end. . . ."

CHAPTER VII

THE CANAL TREATIES

THE years 1898–1901 were crowded ones. The Boer War was fought; the situation in China required a measure of Anglo-American co-operation; and the Alaskan boundary dispute dragged on. Alongside of these matters there were also the negotiations relative to the abrogation of the Clayton-Bulwer canal treaty. The British had attempted, as we have just seen, to trade decisions as to the Alaskan boundary and as to the canal treaty. This proposal had failed because American opinion as to the justness of their position regarding the boundary dispute was too strong. They refused to consider the two matters together. Yet it was almost impossible completely to separate them as it was also impossible to consider them apart from the other questions of the day. So we must keep in mind these problems as we turn to consider the two Hay-Pauncefote treaties for the construction of an interoceanic canal.

The Clayton-Bulwer treaty of 1850 was of course still in effect in 1898. Despite maunderings on the part of certain Senators and considerable nonsense in the press there could be no question about that. As Secretary Olney, writing in 1894, said in a memorandum, which was printed by the Department of State in 1900:

> Under these circumstances, upon every principle which governs the relations to each other, either of nations or of individuals, the United States is completely estopped from denying that the Clayton-Bulwer treaty is in full force and vigor.
>
> If changed conditions now make stipulations, which were once deemed advantageous, either inapplicable or injurious, the true remedy is not in ingenious attempts to deny the existence of the treaty

or to explain away its provisions, but in a direct and straightforward application to Great Britain for a reconsideration of the whole matter.[1]

This treaty in general provided that neither the United States nor Great Britain should exercise any exclusive control over a ship canal to be constructed between the Atlantic and Pacific Oceans. Both countries agreed not to colonize, exercise any dominion over, or enter into an alliance with a state in Central America; they also agreed not to fortify the canal or to acquire any exclusive rights in the use of the canal. The neutralization of the canal was provided, and both countries engaged to invite all other states to enter into a similar agreement. The supposition was that private parties would undertake the construction of the canal and the protection of both states was granted them. As a principle was hereby involved both countries agreed also to extend their protection to other practicable communications whether by canal or railway between the two oceans.[2]

Such was the treaty for which a substitute now was to be found. The lessons of the Spanish-American War were clearly before the American people; a canal was an urgent necessity both from a naval and commercial point of view. The President, therefore, referred to the matter in his annual message to Congress; and two days later Secretary Hay set the ball rolling by a courteous despatch to Mr. Henry White in London, saying:

> The President hopes he may take it for granted that the British Government not only have no wish to prevent the accomplishment of this great work, but that they feel a lively interest in it, and appreciate the fact that the benefits of its successful achievement will be to the advantage not only of England and America, but of all commercial nations.[3]

Already a canal commission under Admiral Walker was nearing the report stage and a bill then before the Senate planned American control over the construction of an interoceanic canal. The replies from London were encouraging, for Mr. White telegraphed that Lord Salisbury felt that it would be better that such a canal should be under the protection of a single power, such as the United States, provided that the canal should be open to all nations on equal terms.[4]

Negotiations, therefore, were set on foot between Secretary Hay and the British Ambassador in Washington. In London, meanwhile, the view was taken that the abrogation of the Clayton-Bulwer treaty would be chiefly beneficial to the United States which, however, had refused to give any concessions as to Canadian matters, whereas the British feeling was that they were entitled even to compensation for agreement as to the canal project.[5] Here the negotiations stuck on a dead center, for, as we have seen, Secretary Hay refused to modify his attitude as to the Alaskan boundary. Thus the year 1899 passed without any progress. Early in 1900, however, with an agreement already reached as to the *modus vivendi* frontier line with Canada, the canal question once more assumed priority. Indeed time had not been lost for during these months Secretary Hay and Lord Pauncefote had been quietly coming to an agreement. Nevertheless there was a chance that Canadian objections might interfere. Ambassador Choate wrote at the end of January, 1900, of a talk with Lord Salisbury:

> He said, however, very emphatically that he should have to bring it before the Cabinet so as to give Mr. Chamberlain a chance to be heard for Canada. I protested that Canada had nothing to do with it but he recalled their former claims and said that they were so angry at our position in regard to the Alaska boundary that they must be heard now. I reminded him of what had passed between him and me about it, and more emphatically between Mr. White and himself before I came, to which he replied that the (Boer) war and Canada's participation therein had changed the situation which must be considered as it now stands. So I think you must expect some difficulty here.[6]

Fortunately on January 23, Mr. Choate had sent in his "unanswerable note" on the Alaska boundary—a note which Lord Salisbury termed a "powerful document"—and Mr. Chamberlain did not make any objection. The result was British consent; and on February 5, 1900, the first Hay-Pauncefote treaty was signed in Washington. Really it had waited for a year till Canadian affairs should be in a more favorable condition.⁷

This treaty declared that the United States and Great Britain "being desirous to facilitate the construction of a ship canal" between the Atlantic and Pacific Oceans and "to remove any objection" which might arise from the Clayton-Bulwer treaty, to the construction of the canal under American government auspices without, however, "impairing the 'general principle' of neutralization established by the treaty of 1850, had agreed as follows": the canal should be constructed under the auspices of the United States. The rules for neutralization were substantially those embodied in the Suez Canal Convention of 1888 and provided:

1. The canal shall be free and open, in time of war as in time of peace, to the vessels of commerce and of war of all nations, on terms of entire equality, so that there shall be no discrimination against any nation or its citizens or subjects in respect of the conditions or charges of traffic, or otherwise.
2. The canal shall never be blockaded, nor shall any right of war be exercised nor any act of hostility be committed within it.
3. Vessels of war of a belligerent shall not revictual nor take any stores in the canal except so far as may be strictly necessary; and the transit of such vessels through the canal shall be effected with the least possible delay, in accordance with the regulations in force, and with only such intermission as may result from the necessities of the service.

Prizes shall be in all respects subject to the same rules as vessels of war of the belligerents.

4. No belligerent shall embark or disembark troops, munitions of war or warlike material in the canal except in case of accidental hindrance of the transit, and in such case the transit shall be resumed with all possible despatch.
5. The provisions of this article shall apply to waters adjacent to the canal, within three marine miles of either end. Vessels of war of a belligerent shall not remain in such waters longer than twenty-four hours at any one time except in case of distress, and in such case shall depart as soon as possible; but a vessel of war of one belligerent shall not depart within twenty-four hours from the departure of a vessel of war of the other belligerent.
6. The plant, establishments, buildings and all works necessary to the construction, maintenance and operation of the canal shall be

deemed to be part thereof, for the purposes of this convention, and in time of war as in time of peace shall enjoy complete immunity from attack or injury by belligerents and from acts calculated to impair their usefulness as part of the canal.

7. No fortifications shall be erected commanding the canal or the waters adjacent. The United States, however, shall be at liberty to maintain such military police along the canal as may be necessary to protect it against lawlessness and disorder.

Article III also stated that on ratification the United States and Great Britain would invite other states to adhere to it.[8]

Scarcely was the ink dry on this treaty when a chorus of criticism rose over its provisions. Roosevelt, who was then Governor of New York, wrote to Secretary Hay what was probably the best brief criticism of the treaty as it stood. This read:

I hesitated long before I said anything about the treaty through sheer dread of two moments—that in which I should receive your note, and that in which I should receive Cabot's. But I made up my mind that at least I wished to be on record; for to my mind this step is one backward, and it may be fraught with very great mischief; You have been the greatest Secretary of State I have seen in my time —Olney comes second—but at this moment I cannot, try as I may, see that you are right. Understand me, when the treaty is adopted, as I suppose it will be, I shall put the best face possible on it, and shall back the administration as heartily as ever; but oh how I wish you and the President would drop the treaty and push through a bill to build *and fortify* our own canal!

My objections are two-fold. First as to naval policy. If the proposed canal had been in existence in 1898, the *Oregon* could have come more quickly through to the Atlantic; but this fact would have been far outweighed by the fact that Cervera's fleet would have had open to it the chance of itself going through the canal, and thence sailing in to attack Dewey or to menace our stripped Pacific coast. If that canal is open to the war ships of an enemy it is a menace for us in time of war; it is an added burden, an additional strategic point to be guarded by our fleet. If fortified by us, it becomes one of the most potent sources of our possible sea strength. Unless it is fortified it strengthens against us every nation whose fleet is larger than ours. One prime reason for fortifying our great seaports is to unfetter our fleet, to release it for offensive purposes; and the proposed canal would fetter it again, for our fleet would have to watch it, and therefore do the work which a fort should do; and which it could do much better.

Secondly as to the Monroe Doctrine. If we invite foreign powers to a joint ownership, a joint guarantee, of what so vitally concerns us but a little way from our borders, how can we possibly object to similar joint action say in Southern Brazil or Argentine, where our interests are so much less evident? If Germany has the same right we have in the canal across Central America, why not in the partition of any part of Northern America? To my mind, we should consistently refuse to all European powers the right to control, in any shape, any territory in the Western Hemisphere which they do not already hold.

As for existing treaties—I do not admit the "dead hand" of the treaty making power in the past, a treaty can always be honestly abrogated—though it must never be abrogated in dishonest fashion.[9]

Essentially Roosevelt was right in his criticisms. But Secretary Hay, in letters published by Thayer, has given a picture of his own disgust and annoyance at the attacks leveled against the treaty. On March 13, 1900, he sent in his resignation to President McKinley, who, however, returned it to him with words of encouragement and solace. Additional letters from Secretary Hay are given in the Appendix to this chapter.[10]

Throughout the long summer of 1900, which was marked by the anxiety as to the safety of Americans in China, endangered by the so-called Boxer movement, Secretary Hay had little time to mourn over the fate of his canal treaty. He was, of course, subjected to violent attack during the presidential campaign of 1900 but the triumph of McKinley was encouraging to him. However, in December the Senate so amended the treaty as to arouse his anger. He wrote at length to Ambassador Choate saying that these amendments "deform and disfigure the treaty." But he faced the disappointment like a soldier and sought at once to remedy the situation by trying to persuade the British that:

the Amendments are not so fatally vicious as to justify the wrecking of the treaty. Why should not Lord Salisbury say to us "you made the treaty, and your Senate has marred it. It still answers the purpose of relieving you of a prohibition which prevented an undertaking of world-wide interest and value. *Ca pèche un peu par la forme*—but the substance is after all unchanged. Take your treaty, Brother Jonathan, and God send you better manners."

If you can persuade our friends to take this view, you will have done a great work for civilization and righteousness.[11]

The amendments to the treaty were briefly as follows: The Clayton-Bulwer treaty was superseded; a new paragraph was added which gave to the United States the right to use force to maintain public order and in its own defence; and Article III was struck out.[12]

There was for a few days a slight confusion as to the terms of the amended treaty for the press on both sides of the Atlantic assumed that the original prohibition of fortification of the canal had been struck out from the treaty. This was not the case; and the provisions for the neutrality of the canal still stood.[13] As the time drew nearer by which the treaty would expire unless the amendments were accepted by Great Britain, Secretary Hay became anxious. Finally word came through by a despatch from Lord Lansdowne to Lord Pauncefote rejecting the amendments. That was the end of the first Hay-Pauncefote treaty.[14]

Nothing daunted Secretary Hay started again to draft another treaty. On April 8, 1901, Mr. Adee gave to his chief the first sketch of the new canal agreement. Later in August Lord Lansdowne sent, by a private memorandum, his own views of what the new treaty should contain. The lesson of the previous defeat had been learned by Secretary Hay and he had taken into his confidence the leading Senators, whose support he thus sought to win at the outset. Throughout the summer and early autumn Ambassador Choate was hard at work with Lord Lansdowne and Lord Pauncefote in London slowly hammering into shape the clauses of the final agreement. It is indeed difficult to see how Secretary Hay could have dispensed with the services of Mr. Choate. As in the Alaskan boundary dispute the hard daily work was often thrown upon Mr. Choate. His official despatches sometimes do not indicate the full extent of his labors; but his very frequent private and confidential letters to Secretary Hay, which were all written in long hand by himself, reveal his interest and capacities. He was really a great Ambassador, a pillar on whom the Secretary could always lean.[15]

It is perhaps unnecessary to follow in detail the various changes in the original drafts which were debated in London. Each side had to consider the effect of the treaty on public opinion and the press; furthermore the draft still had to run the gauntlet of the British Cabinet. In America, however, Secretary Hay was still supreme as regards his executive functions as Foreign Secretary. His troubles usually began in the Senate.

Then like a flash there came the assassination of President McKinley and the accession of Vice-President Roosevelt. It was, therefore, a great relief to Secretary Hay to be able to telegraph to Mr. Choate, on September 21, 1901: "The President cordially approves draft of canal treaty and your instructions."[16] The fact that President Roosevelt at once made it plain to Secretary Hay that he wished him to remain in the Cabinet also cleared the air. Thus matters went on speedily and smoothly.[17]

On October 2, Mr. Choate wrote to Secretary Hay, saying:

> I am sure that in this whole matter, since the receipt by him of your new draft, Lord Lansdowne has been most considerate and more than generous. He has shown an earnest desire to bring to an amicable settlement, honorable alike to both parties, this long and important controversy between the two nations. In substance he abrogates the Clayton-Bulwer Treaty, gives us an American canal, ours to build as and where we like, to own, control and govern, on the sole condition of its being always neutral and free for the passage of the ships of all nations on equal terms, except that if we get into a war with any nations, we can shut its ships out and take care of ourselves.
>
> I shall be disappointed, in fact mortified, if now, after Great Britain has met us so manfully, we fail to come to a final agreement.[18]

Secretary Hay also wrote to Mr. White in London saying that Mr. Choate was coming home shortly on a visit and adding:

> I fancy I shall see Mr. Choate in a day or two. His last despatches

have been very hopeful that Milords Salisbury and Halsbury will not tear up the treaty—and that the stupid and vulgar shouts over "our triumph" in some of the papers will not induce the British Government to recede. It was very annoying to us—but it seems inevitable. If we keep negotiations secret from leading Senators, we incur their ill will and opposition. If we tell them confidentially what we are doing and thus secure their co-operation—their vanity leads them to blab everything to some newspaper, to show that they are "in it." [19]

The result was, when all this conferring and consulting was over, that Great Britain agreed to the treaty as drawn with one exception and this was to one of their own amendments which they withdrew. The treaty was, therefore, signed on November 18, 1901, and sent to the Senate. There it was quickly approved practically without a fight. This second Hay-Pauncefote treaty in its final form was thus the basis of future American policy with reference to the construction of the Panama Canal.[20]

It remains only to mention Secretary Hay's letter of explanation to the Senate Committee on Foreign Relations and the contents of the treaty. In this letter, which is really a brief history of the whole matter, the main points and stages in the negotiations are reviewed. The objections to the Clayton-Bulwer treaty and the urgent demands of the American people for the construction of the canal are noted. Reference to the action of the Senate regarding the first Hay-Pauncefote treaty is followed by a summary of the main points which were now to be included in a draft of a second treaty. The British suggestions and objections are outlined and the basis of agreement is described. It is a clear, temperate, and effective statement of the entire project.[21]

The treaty provided for a canal "by whatever route may be considered expedient," which should be constructed under the auspices of the United States, "without impairing the 'general principle' of neutralization established in Article VIII" of the Clayton-Bulwer treaty. Article I provided the supercession of that treaty by the present one. Article II gave authority to construct a canal between the Atlantic and Pacific Oceans as well as the "exclusive right of providing for the regulation and management of the canal." Article III adopted substantially the regulations for the navigation of the Suez Canal with certain changes from the earlier treaty. Rules 1 and 2 now read:

1. The canal shall be free and open to the vessels of commerce and of war of all nations observing these Rules, on terms of entire equality, so that there shall be no discrimination against any such nation, or its citizens or subjects, in respect of the conditions or charges of traffic or otherwise. Such conditions and charges of traffic shall be just and equitable.

2. The canal shall never be blockaded, nor shall any right of war be exercised nor any act of hostility be committed within it. The United States, however, shall be at liberty to maintain such military police along the canal as may be necessary to protect it against lawlessness and disorder.

Rules 3, 4, 5, and 6 stood as before in the first treaty; but Rule 7, which forbade fortification of the canal was now omitted. Article IV was a new one. It read:

It is agreed that no change of territorial sovereignty or of international relations of the country or countries traversed by the beforementioned canal shall affect the general principle of neutralization or the obligation of the High contracting parties under the present treaty.

By virtue of these provisions and in view of the silence of the treaty the United States was by implication now permitted to fortify the canal, though no precise permission was accorded. Furthermore in case of cessions, revolutions or other changes affecting the territory through which the canal was to be constructed the general principle of the treaty still held.

Thus the preliminary stage in the great project was accomplished. Now came the wearisome and tortuous negotiations with Latin-American states to secure the rights of construction. These, however, belong to a later period in this book together with the recognition by the United States of the independence of Panama. They will be taken up in their proper place. For the moment we must now turn back to consider American diplomacy in the Far East and to observe the way in which Secretary Hay successfully persuaded the leading Powers to unite in a common policy toward China.

But the importance of these canal negotiations must not be forgotten. President Roosevelt on July 1, 1902, well expressed his major concern in them when he wrote to Secretary Hay:

"The great bit of work of my administration, and from the material and constructive standpoint one of the greatest bits of work that the twentieth century will see, is the Isthmian Canal. In the negotiations to start this straight I must trust to you and Knox. I hope you will take personal direction." [22]

NOTES TO CHAPTER VII

1. *O. C.*, A memorandum prepared by Mr. Olney in June, 1894, of which a copy was sent to Secretary Hay at his request in 1898 and printed by the Department of State in 1900. Cf. also Moore, *Digest of International Law,* III, pp. 208-209.
2. *Parl. Papers,* 1900 (Cd. 30), Vol. 59, pp. 902-904.
3. *Diplomatic History of the Panama Canal,* Senate Docs. 63rd Cong. 2nd Sess., No. 474, Washington, 1914, pp. 1-2.
4. *Ibid.,* pp. 2-6.
5. *D. S.,* From London, Vol. 195, telegram, Jan. 26, 1899, White to Hay; Vol. 196, No. 694, Feb. 17, same to same.
6. *H. P.,* Jan. 27, 1900, private and confidential, Choate to Hay.
7. *H. P.,* Feb. 2, 1900, private and unofficial, Choate to Hay; *D. S.,* Vol. 199, telegram Feb. 3, same to same; *H. P.,* Feb. 8, 1900, Stewart to Hay (a letter of warm praise and congratulation from Senator Stewart); Feb. 7, Choate to Hay: "As Lord Salisbury described it to me 'Canada was very considerate and surrendered her special scruples.'

"I think you must give Canada a large credit mark for this considering the great heed paid to her wishes by the Imperial Government in these days of ardent loyalty.

"I congratulate you very much on this result, and hope that the rumors which reach us of obstructions in the Senate will not be realized."
8. *F. R.,* 1901, pp. 241-243; *Parl. Papers,* 1900 (Cd. 30), Vol. 59, pp. 901-902.
9. Thayer, II, pp. 339-341.
10. Appendix A to this chapter; Cf. Thayer, II, pp. 223-230.
11. *H. P.,* Dec. 21, 1900, Hay to Choate.
12. *Dipl. Hist.,* pp. 7-8. *Times,* Dec. 21, 1900, said:

"Their preaching is plain—whatever is for American interests must be done. Of American honour and pledged faith, of the American place in the concert of civilized Powers, no thought is taken. But those are matters of which in time the American people do take thought."
13. *D. S.,* To London, Vol. 33, telegrams, pp. 528-529, Dec. 29, 31, 1900, Hay to Choate. The temper in which Hay endured these days can be judged by a letter to Mr. Carnegie (Hay, *Letters,* etc., III, p. 205) of Jan. 12, 1901. It reads in part:

"I have had a dismal week of it:—getting well of the grippe is worse

than getting sick of anything else. And besides I am tired to the marrow of my bones, twisting the rope of sand which is American diplomacy. Nothing you can do stands against the caprice of a little group of statesmen who know nothing and care nothing for the principles for which you are working, nor for the facts which limit and determine your work.
"But this is a waste of time."

14. *Dipl. Hist.*, pp. 11-19; *H. P.* (Feb. 26, 1901), Feb. 27, March 9, 16, Choate to Hay. There was one paragraph in Lansdowne's note to which Hay took exception and it was consequently omitted.

15. *Dipl. Hist.*, pp. 19-36; *H. P.*, April 8, 1901, Adee to Hay; Aug. (?) 1901, Pauncefote to Hay; Aug. 5, Hay to Choate; Sept. 3, same to same; telegram, Sept. 20, same to same; Sept. 25, same to same; Sept. 27, same to same; Oct. 2, same to same; Oct. 9, same to same. Cf. Rhodes, pp. 262-263; Adams, pp. 423-424. *Parl. Papers,* 1901, Vol. 76, Cd. 905, pp. 1-11.

16. *D. S.,* To London, Vol. 34, telegram, p. 87, Sept. 21, 1901, Hay to Choate; later Hay wrote to White: "it is amusing to see how enthusiastic the President is in favor of the treaty"; Hay, *Letters,* etc., III, p. 240.

17. *Dipl. Hist.*, pp. 37-46; Hay, *Letters,* etc., III, p. 233; *D. S.*, From London, Vol. 203, telegram, Sept. 20, 1901, Choate to Hay; telegram, Sept. 27, same to same; telegram, Oct. 2, same to same; *R. P.,* Oct. 2, 1901, Hay to Roosevelt; Oct. 4, same to same; *H. P.,* Sept. 28, 1901, Roosevelt to Hay; Sept. 27, telegram, Hill to Hay; Sept. 28, Hay to Hill.

18. *Dipl. Hist.*, p. 48.

19. *H. P.,* Oct. 14, 1901, Hay to White.

20. *Dipl. Hist.*, pp. 48-53; *D. S.,* From London, Vol. 203, telegram, Oct. 23, 1901, White to Hay; *R. P.,* Oct. 24, 1901, Hay to Roosevelt; *F. R.,* 1901, pp. 243-246; *Parl. Papers,* 1901, Cd. 1007, Vol. 76, pp. 2-4.

21. *Dipl. Hist.*, pp. 53-68.

22. *H. P.,* July 1, 1902, Roosevelt to Hay.

APPENDIX TO CHAPTER VII
A

Hay, *Letters and Diary,* III, pp. 175–177, Hay to John J. McCook, Department of State, Washington, April 22, 1900.

... The thing which is almost intolerable is this; I see the opportunity of great advantage to be gained by timely negotiations, for which all the conditions are wonderfully favorable, advantages which have been the dream of American statesmen for generations, and I can do nothing on account of the attitude of the Senate. First there is the constitutional mistake of giving the absolute veto to one third of that body, and secondly the habit which has grown up of late years, of the introduction of trivial Amendments involving matters which have been thoroughly considered in the negotiations and rejected; then the practice of endless delay which gives the newspapers the chance to find subjects of attack, of which they avail themselves with imperfect knowledge of the matter in question, till the parties divide, and all hope of a two thirds vote is gone.

I long ago made up my mind that no treaty, on which discussion was possible, no treaty that gave room for a difference of opinion could ever pass the Senate. When I sent in the Canal Convention I felt sure that no one out of a mad house could fail to see that the advantages were all on our side. But I underrated the power of ignorance and spite, acting upon cowardice.

A few things I have been able to do without the Senate's cooperation. But the bulk of my time is taken up listening to the importunities of Senators demanding places for their friends which I cannot give them, and denying the perfectly just claims of foreign representatives because I have no authority to grant them and cannot get it from Congress. . . .

Hay, *Letters and Diary,* III, p. 177, Hay to Richard Watson Gilder, Department of State, Washington, April 24, 1900.

Many thanks for your kind letter from Berlin. I need all the help and comfort I can get from the apostles of sweetness and light, for verily I am in deep water these days. Matters have come to such a pass with the Senate that it seems absolutely impossible to do business. I do not believe that any treaty will ever pass the Senate constituted as it now is, if it relates to a subject about which there can be any discussion whatever. The fact that a treaty gives to this country a great, lasting advantage, seems to weigh nothing whatever in the minds of about half the Senators. Personal interests, personal spites, and a contingent chance of a petty political advantage are the only motives that cut any ice at present.

CHAPTER VIII

THE OPEN DOOR IN CHINA

SECRETARY HAY, while Ambassador to Great Britain, had abundant opportunity to inform himself as to British policy with regard to China. He must have heard the declaration of open door principles time and again; and he was aware in a dozen ways of the desire of Great Britain that the United States should join her in asserting that doctrine as regards China. Indeed in March, 1898, the British government confidentially invited the United States to co-operate in opposing any action by foreign powers in case they should violate the open door, either by procuring the lease of portions of the Chinese coast under conditions which would ensure preferential treatment to the power acquiring such lease, or by obtaining the actual cession of portions of the Chinese littoral. This was in reality a proposal for a joint declaration of the open door in China. To this the United States replied coldly. Secretary Sherman reported the British invitation as follows:

> British Ambassador by a confidential and unofficial memorandum eighth instant, inquired whether British Government could count on the co-operation of the United States in opposing action by foreign Powers which may tend to restrict freedom of commerce of all nations in China either by imposing preferential conditions or by obtaining actual cession of Chinese coast territory. British Ambassador has been answered in like unofficial and confidential manner and with the reservation of ultimate determination of policy by Congress saying that the President is in sympathy with the policy which shall maintain open trade in China, that all his advices up to the present time indicate no foreign occupation which interferes with that trade or aims at exclusive commercial privileges, and that he does not see any present reason for the departure of the United States from our tradi-

tional policy of respecting [sic] foreign alliances and so far as practicable avoiding interference or connection with European complications. I add for your information that recent advices from U. S. Ambassador to Russia communicate assurances of German Ambassador there that Germany does not contemplate reserving recently leased port to exclusive German commerce, and the German Ambassador here has made similar unofficial statements to me. I am without advices as to Russian policy touching recent demand upon China for similar lease of two ports.[1]

The first step in the declaration of the open door policy came, therefore, from Great Britain. President McKinley and Secretary Sherman between them dismissed it as being beyond American policy. Yet as a matter of historical fact, well known and abundantly proven, such was not the case. From the earliest days of established American trade with China the open door had been our avowed policy though we had not committed ourselves to any scheme for its enforcement with the aid of another foreign state. In the instruction to Caleb Cushing, who went as American Commissioner to China in 1843, Daniel Webster, then Secretary of State, said:

> Finally, you will signify, in decided terms and a positive manner, that the Government of the United States would find it impossible to remain on terms of friendship and regard with the [Chinese] Emperor, if greater privileges or commercial facilities should be allowed to the subjects of any other Government than should be granted to the citizens of the United States.[2]

Already the principle of the most favored nation clause was recognized in China. Commodore Kearny had maintained it for the United States in 1843; and an American consular agent at Canton had reported that the trade there had been thrown open on an equal footing to all foreigners. Thus out of the idea embodied in most favored nation treatment the doctrine of the open door developed. Furthermore, the idea and the practice were themselves consonant with American commercial policy at the time. Webster did not make the policy; he merely defined it. Thus, in the treaty of Wanghia of 1844, Cushing was able by Article II to secure its recognition:

Citizens of the United States . . . shall in no case be subject to other or higher duties than are or shall be required of the people of any nation whatever. . . . And if additional advantages or privileges, of whatever description, be conceded hereafter by China to any other nation, the United States, and the citizens thereof, shall be entitled thereupon to a complete equal and impartial participation in the same.[3]

This doctrine furthermore, "while obviously to the advantage of the Americans, was, equally clearly, the deliberate choice of the Chinese themselves." [4] Consequently as the years passed both Americans and Chinese were interested in its maintenance. Great Britain also rested the development of her commerce with China "on the principle of equal opportunity of trade" though to this there was added the policy of securing concessions as they had done in the earlier years of their trade in the Levant, in Persia, and in India.[5] As time went on, to the American commercial interests in China there were added the very important missionary interest and, to a minor extent, a political interest as well. For by 1858 it had become evident that,

The United States desired for its citizens an open door to trade, and the surest way to open this door and to keep it open, was on the one hand to persuade the sovereign states of Asia to open their doors, and then strengthen these states so that they themselves would be able to keep them open.[6]

Hitherto, despite the vigorous Far Eastern policy followed by Secretary Seward, the United States had halted betwixt and between. Foreign trade had been of less importance than the development of the Mississippi Valley and the construction of transcontinental lines of railway. The American frontier still lay within America; and consequently the essential quality of American expansion, the spirit of adventure stretching across the patient years, had not driven us to a decision with regard to the Far East. Now, however, almost against our will we were to make an important step forward. With the acquisition of the Philippines, Hawaii and a foothold in Samoa and with the recognition by both European and Asiatic countries of our actual power and potential interests in the Far East, the United States marched along as a leader in the old policy of the open door. The first proposal by Great Britain in March, 1898, had found us backward and poorly informed. Soon our own interests were to dictate a positive declaration in common with the other great powers.[7] First, however, it is important to examine the immediate background of American policy as regards the Far East and, secondly, to see how anxiously European states were watching each other in the development of their ambitions with respect to China.

The fundamental and persistent policy of the United States has been and still is to promote the development of Asiatic states, sufficiently strong and stable to stand by themselves. To stimulate trade and to introduce western education and culture have also been the objects of this policy; but alongside has remained the desire to avoid war and to avoid alliances and combinations with European states who did not share the dominant purpose of America. Thus, at the time of the war between Japan and China, the United States met frequent appeals to intervene in one way or another by declining to do anything which might seem to be taking one side or the other; or which might associate her with any of the European powers who were interested in the outcome of the struggle. This negative policy of the United States has of course exposed her to criticism. Particularly has she been charged with failing to live up to her treaty engagements with both China and Korea. In 1858 with China and in 1882 with Korea she had signed treaties promising the exercise of her good offices in case of injustice or oppression by some foreign state. This she has done and officially has kept a correct position—a fact which many writers, among them Americans, have ignored.[8] If, generally speaking, this negative policy on the part of the United States has seemed to assist Japan more than it has China it is due to the circumstances of the time and to the way in which Japan has managed her diplomacy and her military strength.

In 1894 Japan was determined to find in the situation in

Korea an opportunity to demonstrate her power and to prove that she had "arrived" in an international sense. Thus a Japanese diplomatic representative in Europe stated at the end of July, 1894:

> This at least I can tell you for certain, we neither can nor will leave Korea again until our aim has been attained in one way or another. We are fighting in Korea for our own future—I might also say for our independence. Once let Korea fall into the hands of a European power and our independence will be threatened.[9]

This definition was of course parallel to that by Count Okuma who had said a month earlier:

> By making a judicious use of the present unique opportunity, it will be possible for the Japanese Government to retrieve all past errors, and make the empire respected and feared, not only by Korea, but also by the rest of the world.[10]

The opportunity which had thus come was due to the outbreak of disorders in Korea which had led both China and Japan to send troops. Korea was nominally a dependency of China; but both Japan and the United States had recognized her independence. When Korea appealed to foreign diplomatic representatives to use their good offices to secure the withdrawal of Chinese and Japanese troops the American Minister at Seoul, the capital, had acted with other diplomats to this end. The Chinese had refused, as they said, because the Japanese troops had not withdrawn. The Japanese then seized control of the feeble Korean government and the war was on.[11]

At Washington the United States had pressed on Japan her desire that peace should be maintained in the Far East. To the Chinese Minister, Secretary Gresham said that America hoped for peace, that we could not intervene otherwise than by good offices and that the United States "could not unite with other powers in any kind of intervention."[12] In similar fashion the United States refused to join the European powers in an intervention to stop the war.[13] And when the French Ambassador inquired as to the intentions of the United States he was told that the President was willing to offer his services as a peace-maker in case both China and Japan should so request provided force should not be used against either belligerent. At the same time, on November 6, 1894, Gresham telegraphed to Tokyo saying by way of friendly warning to Japan:

> The deplorable war between Japan and China endangers no policy of the United States in Asia. Our attitude toward the belligerents is that of an impartial and friendly neutral, desiring the welfare of both. If the struggle continues without check to Japan's military operations on land and sea, it is not improbable that other powers having interests in that quarter may demand a settlement not favorable to Japan's future security and well-being. Cherishing the most friendly sentiments of regard for Japan, the President directs that you ascertain whether a tender of his good offices in the interests of peace alike honorable to both nations would be acceptable to the Government at Tokyo.[14]

To this Japan replied that China had not as yet approached Japan directly, and consequently the war must continue.[15] This was followed by the Japanese capture of Port Arthur and in February, 1895, by the practical destruction of the Chinese fleet. Under these circumstances China asked for peace and finally appointed Li Hung Chang as plenipotentiary. Thus peace was signed at Shimonoseki, on April 17, 1895; already, however, Russia, France, and Germany had prepared to object to the cession by China to Japan of the peninsula of Liaotung, including Porth Arthur. Before this European combination Japan was compelled to give way and surrendered the peninsula receiving in return an increased indemnity. Japan had overreached herself in failing to heed the friendly warning from Washington of the previous November. But Japan had shown her military and naval strength and had disposed of Chinese claims over Korea.[16] In these matters the United States remained merely an interested spectator.

Indeed, as regards Korea, the United States was to emphasize her determination to avoid entanglement in the perilous situation to which that state was now exposed. Mr. Sill, the American Minister, was severely rebuked by the Department of State because it was alleged that he was intervening in the "political concerns of Korea." Particularly, following a palace revolution in October, 1895, when the Queen of Korea was murdered and it was charged that Japanese were responsible for her death, did the position of the Minister become precarious. Again in February, 1896, when the King of Korea fled from the palace to the Russian Legation the course of events seemed to endanger American interests. This sudden and complete overthrow of Japanese predominance in Korea threatened to bring about armed intervention by Japan. The King still ruled nominally but his decrees were dictated to a great extent by the influence of Russia. Mr. Sill was reported to have assisted the Russian Minister in matters which did not concern the United States. Soon Japanese influence was thrown against the development of American interests in Korea. The major struggle, however, was between Russia and Japan. The King of Korea was a mere puppet, who agreed with one breath that Korea should be placed under the military protection of Russia and with the next breath secretly besought the Japanese to send twice as many troops to Korea as did Russia. This duplicity and the terror of the King led to his appeal to Dr. Allen, the new American Minister, for aid. Dr. Allen very promptly pointed out that "even if he [the King] should succeed in getting inside our gates, I would be unable to keep him long, and his condition after such an attempt would be worse than before." Thus matters dragged on with repeated opportunities for American intervention which were rejected by the United States. The stage was being set for the Russo-Japanese war which broke out in 1904. In view of the general trend of American policy, such as it was, it is small wonder that, even when our information as to the course of events was correct and unbiased, our point of view was domestic, and not international. We continued to view but we refused to see the facts in the case even in our observations. There was little to lead one to suppose that American influence could count for much in Korea.[17]

In the meantime in China on a larger scale similar events were taking place. The fact that the United States was charged, during the war of 1894–1895, with representing the interests of Japan in China, did not decrease the difficulty of the situation. Furthermore, in various parts of China there were anti-foreign riots, in which American mission stations were attacked, thus involving the problem of protecting American citizens in China. As the humiliation of China in the war with Japan became daily more certain, various European states now began to press on China their own separate ambitions. Talk of the "partition of China" was in the air. This gave to the entire situation a melancholy trend and made Far Eastern politics the stage where European rivalries could strut forward and play their dangerous parts. Indeed the danger of the partition of China among European states cannot be too strongly emphasized. The urgency and the importance of such a prospect were the chief concern of every European Foreign Office. The *débâcle* of China was imminent.

The Chinese government had informed Mr. Denby, the American Minister, at Peking, on August 3, 1894, that it undertook the protection of missionaries and merchants who were "at liberty to pursue their usual avocations without anxiety because of the hostilities being carried on against Japan." [18] By November, however, in spite of proclamations warning the Chinese not to molest neutral foreigners, some anxiety had developed as to the safety of these foreigners. In the end of May, 1895, serious anti-foreign riots were reported. As the summer advanced the situation became worse and Mr. Adee telegraphed to Mr. Denby:

> Consult with Minister of Great Britain and co-operate as far as conducive to security and welfare of United States citizens. Otherwise you will act independently, and carefully abstain from joining in any course or policy which however important to British interest does not concern those of the United States.[19]

Following a massacre of missionaries in Kutien in August, 1895, the *Foreign Relations* of 1895 contains pages of despatches. The question of Anglo-American co-operation at once arose, for the Chinese claimed that the British had an ulterior political motive in their investigation of the anti-foreign outbreaks. The American officials in China were, therefore, warned again only "to protect American interests of person and property." [20]

This resulted in the despatch of an American commission to investigate independently, which, though it involved loss of time, ultimately broke through Chinese obstinacy and delay and secured the punishment of guilty Chinese. This was perhaps due to the hearty co-operation of the Secretary of State, Mr. Olney, with American officials in China, especially with Mr. Denby who had already officially stated that in the interests "of civilization, missionaries ought not only to be tolerated, but ought to receive protection, to which they are entitled from officials, and encouragement from other classes of people." [21]

The Department, therefore, instructed Mr. Denby to take steps which might prevent the recurrence of anti-foreign riots by securing from China formal recognition of the residential rights of Americans in China and by requiring the Chinese authorities to hold local officials responsible in case of outbreaks.

Side by side with these questions affecting the safety of Americans there were also developing disputes regarding the protection of American economic interests. The Department of State had already urged Mr. Denby to "employ all proper methods for the extension of American commercial interests in China." Across all such moderate and legitimate endeavors there came the drastic action of Germany. Two German missionaries had recently been killed in riots; using this as an excuse Germany at a stroke now seized the little town of Kiauchau. Out of that seizure there developed the enforced lease of the territory about Kiauchau to Germany for a period of ninety-nine years and the assertion by Germany of her predominant economic influence in the entire province of Shantung. Of what service might be the urgent verbal representations of Mr. Denby alongside of such a demonstration of force? Germany at one stroke secured recompense for the death of her missionaries, a fine naval base, and incalculable economic advantage. The value of two dead missionaries stood high in the international market.

The shock of such events to the officials at Peking was great, as may be seen in unpublished despatches from Mr. Denby printed in the Appendix to this chapter.[22] Furthermore, within a few months Russia acquired a lease of Port Arthur from China; she already had the right to construct a railway across Manchuria, which she now proposed to extend and at the same time asserted her power more and more in Korea. The influence of such events was not lost upon Japan, as we may see in a despatch from Mr. Buck, the new American Minister at Tokyo, who wrote home:

> The occupation of Port Arthur and the influence in other respects that Russia seems to have acquired over China, as also the occupation of Kiao-Chow by Germany, added to the controlling influence obtained by Russia in Korea, are regarded as tending to destroy the influence of Japan, and to maintain her prestige in the East she is apparently preparing to assert herself as occasion may require.[23]

In Great Britain the outlook was regarded as most serious. Ambassador Hay, reporting a speech of Mr. Balfour, said he spoke with clearness and energy in regard to the situation created by recent events in China:

> Our interests there [he says], are not territorial; they are commercial. He calls attention to the fact that Great Britain asks no exclusive trading privileges and gives notice to the world that the British Government will do their best to see that that equality of opportunity which is all they claim—but which they do claim—shall not be destroyed.[24]

In similar fashion Sir Michael Hicks-Beach said with respect to the commercial relations of Great Britain with China that the British government did not regard China

> as a place for conquest or acquisition by any European or other Power; but as the most hopeful place of the future for the commerce of Great Britain and of the world at large and that they are absolutely determined at whatever cost, even—and he wished to speak

plainly—if necessary at the cost of war, that the door should not be shut.²⁵

Such language was fair warning that Great Britain was aroused; indeed she was eager to guarantee a loan of £16,-000,000 to China. This, however, met with strenuous opposition both from Russia and from France. For France as well had stuck her finger in the Chinese pie and had pulled out a lease for ninety-nine years of Kwang-chouwan. Promptly in June and July, 1898, Great Britain had secured the lease of part of Kowloon, on the mainland, as an addition to an earlier cession, opposite the island of Hongkong and also of Wei-hai-wei "for so long a period as Port Arthur shall remain in the occupation of Russia." Japan gained the promise from China of the non-alienation of Fukhien. There were several similar promises made to other European powers and in addition concessions were speedily made to foreign firms supported by their governments for the development of mines and for the construction of many railway lines in China. It was really an orgy of plunder that ensued. Only Italy failed in the demand for a naval base. It seemed as though a flock of vultures had gathered to feast over the carcass of China in the year 1898.²⁶

Under the circumstances what did the American representatives in the Far East report? The views of Mr. Denby were pessimistic. In a despatch to be found in the Appendix to this chapter he described the various steps by which Russia had secured Port Arthur and mourned the fact that Great Britain had done practically nothing.²⁷ He concluded: "with our moral support Great Britain might even now call Russia to give an account of her plans as to the occupation of Manchuria, and might save our treaty rights in that country." Again he wrote on March 29, 1898:

The action of Russia renders it almost certain that England will follow the example set by Germany, Russia and France, and will in turn demand the cession of territory.

I have heretofore commented on the non-action of England in taking no steps whatever to arrest the partition of China. The English statesmen do not seem to understand the situation at all. Lord Salisbury in his speech in Parliament on the address from the Throne says that an open port and a treaty port are the same thing. This is entirely incorrect. At a treaty port extra-territoriality prevails, and the citizens of all nations have exactly the same rights. An open port means simply that there are no tariff duties collected. Hongkong is an open port; but it is under exclusive English jurisdiction. Shanghai is a treaty port. It is an ideal republic. It is "squatter sovereignty" in its perfection. It is simply a settlement in which all men are equal, and there is no superior government whatever—though of course individuals are governed by the laws of their respective countries, civil and criminal.

If Germany, France and Russia proposed simply to open new ports to the trade of the world nobody would object; but they have not done so. They claim, or will claim, jurisdiction exactly as if they owned the ceded territory. They will monopolize the exploitation of the adjacent country. They will construct all the railroads, and work all the mines. There can be but little question but that the treaties so far as the favored nation clause is concerned will fall to the ground.

Public opinion may drive England to war. I regard the situation as very grave.[28]

As far as Japan was concerned affairs in Korea had not been going well. Her finances were not in a sound condition and she welcomed the increased indemnity from China on the surrender of Wei-hai-wei, especially as Great Britain promptly secured the lease of that port. Particularly did she welcome a breathing space given by a new Russian-Japanese convention of April 25, 1898, which recognized the "commercial and industrial interests existing between Japan and Korea." At this time, as we have already seen, Japan was seeking to promote good relations with the United States in respect to the Philippines. Thus Japan was marking time.[29]

As for the United States her interests were naturally chiefly absorbed in the situation in Cuba and the prospects of war with Spain. But the state of affairs in China attracted some attention. She was anxious as to future Russian and German policies with respect to trade in those regions in China which they had practically annexed by means of leases. Thus Secretary Sherman wrote to Ambassador White in Berlin:

The subject [of trade] is naturally one of interest to the United States, this Government having been among the first to bring about the opening of China to foreign commerce and the relations of the United States with the Chinese Empire having been since that time of large and growing importance. That it is not without similar interest to other commercial powers will appear by the enclosed copy of a despatch which I have received from the United States representative at St. Petersburg in which Mr. Hitchcock reports the substance of recent interviews he has had with the British and German Ambassadors, the Japanese Minister and the Russian Minister for Foreign Affairs with reference to the situation in China and the probable effects of the German lease of Kiao-Chau upon trade with that port and the district of which it is a feeder. You will observe that according to Mr. Hitchcock's report Prince Radolin, the German Ambassador to Russia, states that the harbor of Kiao-Chau will be open to vessels and commerce of all nations upon equal terms and conditions.[30]

On these matters Count von Bülow assured Mr. White that:

the intentions of the German Empire were entirely in accordance with this view; that there was no intention to close the port to foreign trade and commerce; that the rule of the Imperial Government of Germany was to "live and let live"; that, while the occupation of the territory as proposed might fairly be considered as a necessity to the German Empire, it had not entered into the plans of the Government to exclude other powers from the advantages of commerce with China or with any part of it.[31]

News also reached the United States that the leased port of Talienwan in Manchuria would "be open to foreign commerce and that vessels of all friendly nations will be received there with the utmost hospitality" by the Russian authorities. Thus the alarmists as to China received a set-back.[32] It was under these circumstances that the British note of March 8, 1898, proposing the co-operation of Great Britain and the United States to maintain the open door in China was received and answered. As we have already seen the United States rejected the suggestion. The result was that many of the despatches from Mr. Henry White in London, giving an accurate picture of British opinion regarding China, had no effect at Washington.[33] On March 1, 1898, a debate had taken place in the House of Commons which resolved "that it is of vital importance for British commerce and influence that the independence of Chinese territory should be maintained." [34] This and subsequent debates were reported at length to Washington and their influence on the mind of Mr. Hay was probably considerable. One factor, however, we must not forget, for it was at this period that Great Britain was making an effort to build up an alliance with Germany as well as with the United States. The situation in China seemed ready to her hand as a basis on which such an alliance might develop, though, of course, she was herself sincerely and objectively concerned over China as well. In any case it is important to recall that during these months, when the United States was acquiring the Philippines and thus a great territorial base in the Far East, all Europe was vitally interested in Chinese affairs.

Thus on March 1, Mr. [later Lord] Curzon said in the House of Commons:

> Our policy is, and must be, to prevent her [China's] disruption as long as we can, and to secure for her that fresh lease of life to which her immense and magnificent resources entitle her. We are, therefore, opposed to the alienation of any portion of Chinese territory or to the sacrifice of any part of Chinese independence. . . .
> Our belief is that the integrity of China, which we are asked by this motion to safeguard, is most likely to be secured by throwing open China to the interests and intercourse of the whole world, and not, so to speak, by closing her into separate water tight compartments, each bearing a separate label or appellation of its own.[35]

On April 5, Lord Charles Beresford, speaking on British policy, said:

> There is the question of the policy of the open door. Now it is all very well to talk about an open door policy, but that door, as far as Russia is concerned, will be open until Russia likes to close it. He would not believe Russian assurances "if they were twenty fathoms long." . . . Such assurances will not be worth the paper they are written upon when Russia has once established herself in China, and so far as the open door goes it is very nearly a brick wall now.[36]

Finally, on June 20, Sir Charles Dilke made a notable speech in which he referred to Mr. Chamberlain's speech of

May 13, at Birmingham advocating an alliance with America and saying: "I believe that if the policy of isolation is to be maintained, the fate of China probably will be decided in defiance of our interests." On this Sir Charles Dilke commented:

> It seems to me, therefore, that he [Chamberlain] has pledged himself against a policy of isolation because the Government have pledged themselves against the fate of China being decided in defiance of our interests. The Government have told us directly that the fate of China is not to be decided in defiance of our interests and the Chancellor of the Exchequer, who was defended by the Leader of the House, has gone so far as to say that even "at the risk of war" the fate of China must not be so decided. The Secretary of State for the Colonies said that if we were determined to pursue the object of equal opportunities of trade, we must not reject the idea of an alliance with those powers whose interests are most nearly approximate to our own, and I think he was specially speaking of the case of China.[37]

Such speeches, important as they may be from the point of view of British policy, are also particularly significant because Mr. Hay was Ambassador in London at the time and was reporting to Washington these and other debates and discussions along the same lines.[38] In August, 1898, he received his appointment to be Secretary of State and, as Mr. Smalley says with little exaggeration:

> A still greater career opened before him, and he was the first American Secretary of State to make an imaginative use of his opportunities, and a great name in Europe and Asia alike. He was the first American Secretary of State to take the lead in a world embracing policy; to unite the European powers in support of it; to extract a binding pledge even from Russia; to bring Japan, not very willingly, into this charmed circle; and to lay the foundations of American influence in China broad and deep.[39]

During the months that followed the Secretary was engrossed with the peace negotiations with Spain, with the Hay-Pauncefote canal treaty and with the meeting of the High Commission on Canadian affairs. In the meantime attacks on foreigners in China became more and more frequent as public opinion in China began to flout the central authorities at Peking and to express a patriotic but undiscerning reaction against foreign encroachments. The Italian government made its ill-starred attempt to secure the lease of a naval base on the Chinese coast. There was even talk in Vienna of plans for the establishment of an Austrian base in China. This, however, came to nothing. Still there was nothing to indicate that the United States had decided on a line of definite policy. Indeed Mr. Conger, the new American Minister at Peking, wrote to Secretary Hay on March 1, 1899, saying that though in his own opinion permanent ownership of territory in China was not desirable (barring perhaps a coaling station) he was there "to execute your commissions and whatever they may be I shall undertake them with alacrity." His full despatch is in the Appendix to this chapter.[40]

There were, however, two personal influences which were to affect the mind of Secretary Hay strongly. One was the great reception accorded to Lord Charles Beresford in his trip to China and the importance attached to his book—*The Break-Up of China*. The second and more important influence was the opinion of Mr. Rockhill, who had long been Hay's friend. Mr. Rockhill had been in the American diplomatic service, but was now in Washington as Director of the Pan-American Union. His own interest in China had let the Secretary to use Rockhill as an unofficial expert on Far Eastern matters. Lord Charles Beresford's book had influenced the critical mind of Rockhill as well, and during the summer of 1899 he and the Secretary exchanged ideas as to China.

Lord Charles Beresford was a British Admiral, a member of Parliament, with a breezy manner and a gift for talk, who in the year 1898, had gone out to China unofficially as a representative of the Associated Chambers of Commerce of Great Britain. On his trip, which had become almost a royal progress, he had preached the doctrine of the open door. In conversation with Americans in China he had favored

the "open door"—a fair field and no favor—for all those who come to China to trade. Moreover he insists upon having a well ordered house inside the open door. He wants the Chinese army retrenched and remodelled under European and American Officers. Out of the public funds now being spent on a mongrel mob of half a million he claims he could support an effective force of 200,000 men without asking for a single additional cent. He is perfectly willing that American, German and Japanese gun boats should join with England in policing the great river system of China. In fact, he bases all his hopes of keeping the door open by enlisting the sympathies of America during his trip across the continent.[41]

Similar views were expressed in a letter from Lord Charles Beresford to Secretary Hay:

> I am glad to tell you that nothing could exceed the cordiality that I have met with from every American citizen out here and the interest they take in my mission is most gratifying. They have all been in sympathy with the views I communicated to you before I left England. As America has got over 50% of the import trade into the north of China, it is imperative for American interests as well as our own, that the policy of the "open door" should be maintained. I have every hope that in the near future the suggested commercial alliance between Great Britain and America with reference to the "open door" in China, may become an absolute fact.[42]

Secretary Hay entertained the robustuous Admiral in Washington in February on his way back to England. During the course of the year Mr. Rockhill had arrived in the United States and also his friend Mr. Alfred E. Hippesley of the Chinese Customs Service. These two men set to work to influence Secretary Hay to take action regarding the presentation of the old American doctrine of the open door in China. Secretary Hay was of course fully informed regarding the whole matter and on August 24, 1899, he suggested, since both men were critical of parts of Beresford's plan, that Mr. Rockhill draft a memorandum on the subject. This he did on August 28, and sent it to the Secretary saying:

> In view of the great weight which Beresford's book seems to have with the American public I have reviewed in the Memorandum the principal points of his work. This shows—if it is necessary to show it—that the policy suggested as that best suited to our interests is not a British one—for England is as great an offender in China as Russia itself.[43]

This memorandum, a copy of which is in the *Hay Papers,* contained the formulation of the American doctrine of the open door in almost the exact words used by Secretary Hay in his notes to foreign states, which were sent out on September 6, 1899. Mr. Rockhill's memorandum, hitherto unpublished, is in the Appendix to this chapter.[44]

The notes which Secretary Hay sent to Great Britain, Germany, and Russia on September 6, 1899, are printed in *Foreign Relations* for that year. They are *mutatis mutandis* practically the same. The essential paragraphs of the note to Great Britain read as follows:

> The present moment seems a particularly opportune one for informing Her Britannic Majesty's Government of the desire of the United States to see it make a formal declaration and to lend its support in obtaining similar declarations from the various powers claiming "spheres of influence" in China, to the effect that each in its respective spheres of interest or influence—
>
> First. Will in no wise interfere with any treaty port or any vested interest within any so-called "sphere of interest" or leased territory it may have in China.
>
> Second. That the Chinese treaty tariff of the time being shall apply to all merchandise landed or shipped to all such ports as are within said "sphere of influence" (unless they be "free ports"), no matter to what nationality it may belong, and that duties so leviable shall be collected by the Chinese Government.
>
> Third. That it will levy no higher harbor dues on vessels of another nationality frequenting any port in such "sphere" than shall be levied on vessels of its own nationality, and no higher railroad charges over lines built, controlled, or operated within its "sphere" on merchandise belonging to citizens or subjects of other nationalities transported through such "sphere" than shall be levied on similar merchandise belonging to its own nationals transported over equal distances.[45]

In November, 1899, similar communications were made to France, Italy and Japan. In response to an anxious inquiry from China, which had heard alarming rumors of alleged plans for the partition of China, Secretary Hay wrote a personal note to Mr. Wu Ting Fang, the Chinese Minister at Washington, on November 11, saying:

> In reference to the subject of our conversation on Thursday last,

it gives me pleasure to say that this Government is not considering any proposition from European powers tending to the acquisition of territory in China. If we should ever in the future, which I do not now anticipate, desire to treat with your Government for any conveniences or accommodations upon the coast, we shall have pleasure in addressing ourselves directly to the Imperial Government of China, either through our Minister at Peking or through the accomplished envoy of China at this capital. As I observed to you in the conversation referred to we are desirous to be assured by the different powers having interests in China that the United States shall not be excluded from an equal and impartial participation in the Chinese trade through any arrangements already made or to be made in the future by these Governments, and I sincerely hope that in this effort of ours to secure an equitable share of the commerce of China, which I trust will be as advantageous to your country as to our own, we shall have the co-operation of the Chinese Government and that no arrangements will be entered into by the Government of the Emperor which shall be to the disadvantage of American commerce.[46]

The British informal reply was at first most cordial. Mr. Choate reported on September 22:

I was much gratified at the cordial and sympathetic manner in which he [Lord Salisbury] received your proposed arrangement. He said that the procuring by us of such declarations at the present time would be an excellent thing for commerce, and was in substantial conformity with the policy and spirit of his Government—and as I proceeded with the statement of the considerations contained in your Instruction, he said he thought they were unexceptionally stated.[47]

On second thought, however, the British suggested that "leased territory" should be omitted from the proposed declaration because Kowloon, British leased territory, was now an integral part of the colony of Hongkong. Lord Salisbury continued:

... it therefore stands on a wholly different footing from a "sphere of interest." It is practically an extension, conditioned by a term of years, of an existing Colony, and serious inconvenience would obviously arise if a Customs line were drawn across it and its fiscal administration were to be conducted on rules differing entirely from those of the actual British territory on which it abuts.[48]

Secretary Hay, as well as Mr. Choate, promptly pointed out that, while they understood that Kowloon stood on a different basis, the omission of "leased territories" might defeat the very object of the declaration.[49] Lord Salisbury agreed; so Mr. Choate suggested that all mention of Hongkong should be omitted, that the American note should stand, and that the British reply of acceptance should specify only Wei-hai-wei. This was finally done by a note dated November 30, 1899. Prior to this, however, the British had been rather skeptical as to the success of the American proposal. As Mr. Choate reported, Lord Salisbury seemed to think that:

> we are a little too sanguine in our expectation of obtaining Declarations from the other Powers, to whom application has already been made; and desires to be advised of what they are inclined to do before considering finally any Declaration to be made by Great Britain. He also suggests that Japan should be invited to join in the proposed Declaration, as she may at any time enter into new agreements with Russia. He recognizes that the general tenor and effect of the Declaration which you ask is only carrying out the established policy of Great Britain from which her Government can never recede.[50]

The British acceptance included permission to the United States to inform the other powers of that acceptance. Of course on September 6, 1899, a despatch had gone to Germany on similar lines to that sent to Great Britain. At Berlin matters travelled more slowly, chiefly because Germany was interested in the Samoan question, the Boer War, and, finally, in the negotiations with England. In early December Count von Bülow gave his verbal assent to the American proposal and on February 19, 1900, he wrote his formal acceptance of it. Later, in March, the Kaiser said to Ambassador White:

> "What I am most interested in at present is the open door policy in the East; I am in favor of it, indeed I am in favor of it everywhere." He then went on to say that in dealing with China and the East generally there should be a large and free policy, and that he hoped that this might ultimately be the rule in all parts of the world, and he repeated we ought all to stand together for the policy of the "open door." [51]

In the case of the note to Russia, which was also addressed on September 6, affairs did not prove so easy. For one thing, during the autumn of 1899, Count Mouraviev, the Russian Foreign Secretary, was intent on his plan for stirring up European states to intervene in the Boer War, and during October and part of November he was abroad, first in France and then in Germany. Furthermore the Russian habit of mind was suspicious; the very term "open door" was objectionable to the Russian Foreign Office largely because it had been so frequently used in England; and it was almost unprecedented for Russia to approve in writing a policy so sweeping and general in its terms. The negotiations were delayed also by the references back and forth between Washington and St. Petersburg while first the question of railway rates was discussed and then the prospects of tariff revision. At times it seemed as though Russia would fail to give an affirmative answer. Yet, when both Germany and France had accepted the plan, Mouraviev said that Russia would accept it also, though he was careful to stipulate that Russia's acceptance was independent of that by France. In Washington the negotiations with Count Cassini were skilfully conducted by Mr. Rockhill and dealt in the main with spheres of influence rather than with leased territory. Finally, after repeated inquiries, Count Mouraviev wrote a note on December 30, which, while not entirely satisfactory, was accepted by Secretary Hay as being sufficiently so. Perhaps in deference to Russian prejudices the term "open door" was hereafter omitted in any public documents relating to the entire plan. Thus the Russian acceptance could be checked off; but as Ambassador Tower wrote to Secretary Hay:

> The truth is that the Russian Government did not wish to answer your propositions at all. It did so finally with great reluctance, but it did so because of the desire upon its part to maintain the relations subsisting between the two countries, which it would not on any account disturb. It went a great way, as Russian diplomacy goes, when it put into writing the answer which you now have. I regretted when I sent it to you that it was not more definite and wider in the expression of what you wish to ascertain. But, when I said in my despatch of the 2nd of January that the inquiry had been received

with unusual attention and treated with a degree of consideration which it would not have met if it had come from almost any other conceivable source, I believed that scarcely any great Power in the world, except the United States, could obtain from the Russian Ministry for Foreign Affairs an acquiescence which implies so great consideration. There is probably nothing in the whole course of international relations so distasteful to the Russian Government as the necessity to bind itself by a written agreement where such a course is not absolutely unavoidable. It did so, however, in our case; but I think we must believe that we have gained all that was possible under the circumstances.[52]

Although the American Embassy in Paris was at once informed in September of the proposals for the plan of the open door in China, the French Government was not approached directly until November. In conversation with M. Delcassé, the French Foreign Secretary, Ambassador Porter learned that France was, generally speaking, in favor of the open door. He also learned from various sources that:

There is much apprehension felt by all diplomats in Europe regarding the possibilities of serious complications in China which may some day make it a storm center involving many of the great powers. There is the growing ambition of foreign nations to secure as large a share as possible of the great trade of that nation, the increasing influence of Russia, the undefined claims to "Spheres of influence," the numerous grants to foreigners of concessions for railways connecting with or interfering with each other, the foreign control of many ports, the weakness of the Central Government, the political intrigues at the Capital, etc., etc. It is feared that, perhaps not in the near future, the spheres of influence may become spheres of hostilities and that the great powers will be led either to sustain and strengthen the Chinese Government to enable it to enforce its treaties and agreements, or to bring about a partition of the Empire, which would probably result in a general scramble for territory, with the nations already there standing the best chance in such a contest.[53]

Of this situation Secretary Hay was of course aware. It made him all the more urgent in his endeavors to secure common action and to advocate a policy of co-operation, which had been foreign to American diplomacy in time past. He, therefore, kept in close touch with Paris, and on November 21 the direct proposal was made to France in terms identical with those already used to Great Britain, Germany and Russia. The result was that on November 24 M. Delcassé made a statement before the Chamber, which indicated his sympathy with the practice of the open door in China. Privately with Ambassador Porter he had pointed out the complexity of the issues involved and he seemed to shy at the inclusion of "spheres of influence" which he thought would always be loosely defined. On December 16 a personal note from M. Delcassé was received at the American Embassy in Paris accepting the general proposal but omitting any reference to "spheres of influence" as France did not have any such area in China. General Porter commented on the note: France "is evidently in favor of the open door and equal treatment, in the broadest sense, throughout China." All endeavors to make the French acceptance more precise failed; but Secretary Hay in phrasing his identical notes to the powers acknowledging their adhesion made use of the term habitually used by the French Foreign Office and referred only to "so-called 'spheres of interest.'" [54]

Italy was the last European country to which Secretary Hay's note of September 6 was sent. This was sent in somewhat abridged form on November 17. No difficulties intervened and, when on January 2, 1900, Italy was informed that the other powers consulted had all made favorable responses, Count Visconti-Venosta, the Italian Foreign Secretary, sent a note to Ambassador Draper agreeing without hesitation to the terms in the American despatch.[55]

As for Japan, the British government had already suggested that the United States should seek for her adherence. Consequently, on November 13, 1899, a note similar to that of September 6 was despatched. Before it could reach Japan that government had made inquiries regarding the American proposals to European powers. Viscount Aoki, Japanese Foreign Secretary, promptly accepted Secretary Hay's plan in a formal note to Minister Buck on December 26. In the course of the negotiations at Tokyo, Japan expressed a great desire that "American business men of capital should join with Japanese men of business in various enterprises in China and Korea." This proposal, apart from its economic advantage, may well have had back of it the idea that Russia would be less likely to object to such economic development if American interests were involved. Later it was Japan alone who inquired of the United States as to the discrepancies to be observed in the replies of Germany, Russia and France. As we have already seen, the adherence of these three powers scarcely went beyond the promise to apply most favored nation treatment in China. Secretary Hay had, however, secured enough for his immediate purposes by the notes received and wisely he had assumed a real acceptance by Russia, and had decided to "let well enough alone." [56]

Thus the famed "open door" doctrine was sent abroad. Its principles "were as old as the foreign relations of China"; and the doctrine was reformulated in 1899 "to meet a critical situation in China menacing alike to the reign of equal opportunity of trade and to the maintenance of the integrity of China." The situation in China had been well described by Minister Conger in a despatch of December 21, 1899; and within six months the Boxer movement had risen to such importance that its suppression provoked just the condition against which the promulgation of the open door policy was designed to be effective. In catalogue form Mr. Conger listed the situation as to the great powers:

> Russia is making rapid progress with her defenses at Port Arthur and with the public improvements at Talien-wan; also with their railroad building thence toward Siberia. It is now understood that the road will be practically completed across the Continent much sooner than had been expected,—probably in less than three years.
>
> Her demands for a direct line to Peking, reported in my despatch No. 204, of May 15 last, will undoubtedly be granted. The Russians are about to conclude arrangements for some new lines branching from the Peking-Hankow railroad (Belgian line) north and west into the provinces of Shansi and Shensi.
>
> Thus the grasp of Russia upon Northern China is continually extending and becoming more secure. Her influence with the Chinese Government, consequent upon her acknowledged strength, and the fact that that strength is wielded by an Imperial Monarch whose

policies can neither be questioned nor revised by Parliament or party, is most potent, and China by herself is powerless to resist any demand Russia may make.

France, though less strong is quite as ambitious in the South, and is sufficiently powerful to compel China, unaided, to respond favorably to any of her demands.

Germany is improving Kiao-chow slowly, but is carefully exploiting the interior of Shantung, without, however, beginning definite railroad building or mine developing.

So far as the Chinese Government is concerned, Germany can, whenever she wishes and is willing to increase her Kiao-chow force sufficiently, entirely control that province.

The English are doing very little at Wei-hei-wei, and I think care to do little there, for the place is so thoroughly detached from any territory where their interests lie, that it is really of not great value to them.

Great Britain has taken possession of her new possessions opposite Hongkong, and is expecting, of course, to retain her so-called sphere of influence in the Yangtze valley.

Since acquiring their recent concessions at Newchwang and Amoy, the Japanese seem to be doing nothing here, although considerably occupied with Corean and Formosan affairs.

No substantial progress appears to have been made in the Italian demands.

The sad occupation of England in South Africa is not creating much sympathy among representatives of European Governments here, and while there appears to be no evidence of any movement by them to take advantage of the withdrawal of Great Britain's attention from Chinese affairs, yet I am sure they would welcome any occurrence that would tend meanwhile to strengthen their position here.[57]

The victory of American diplomacy was of course acclaimed. Secretary Hay's part was clearly that of chief promoter. He sponsored and advocated the doctrine which was afterwards to bear his name. If he did not formulate it, he championed it and he deserved much of the great credit which came to him. As a summary of the verdict of the American press a despatch from New York to the London *Times* of January 6, 1900, is worth quoting:

The accession of Italy, announced officially today, completes the circle of assurances from the Great Powers concerned that the United States treaty rights with China shall remain secure in Chinese territory acquired, or to be acquired, by foreign nations. The pledges, which were heretofore conditional on the general assent, now become binding. What the *Times* has said—that this Government will take care that these assurances shall be carried out—is precisely what is said here. This piece of diplomacy is not academic, but is intended to be of practical effect; it is intended to keep the door open for American trade which Americans confidently believe is destined to a rapid increase.

The Press after some delay, has spoken strongly in support of this policy. Even protectionist organs are for free trade in China, where freedom is for the benefit of American manufacturers. Even anti-Imperialists welcome an Imperial policy which contemplates no conquests but those of commerce. The Tribune believes that American trade with China now exceeds that of Japan, and is therefore second, though by a vast interval, to that of England. It agrees with other important journals in regarding this as in a measure tending to preserve the integrity of China. The Sun considers that, with American commodities admitted on equal terms with their rivals, "our State Department has done everything for American exporters which it could reasonably be asked to do." Even that foremost champion of expansion desires no sphere of influence in Asia and would take no avoidable part in the dismemberment of China. The Times calls the agreement a victory for civilization. It recalls the refusal of an earlier Secretary of State of England's suggestion of common action on the amazing ground that we had no interests in the East, and says:

"It is a signal public service that Mr. Hay has performed. Handicapped as he was, he has won a diplomatic victory, and has succeeded in repairing the huge blunder of his predecessor, which seemed irreparable. He deserves the congratulations and thanks of his countrymen."

He gets them. A diplomatic success, won by purely diplomatic methods at nobody's expense yet with great beneficial results to his own country, is gradually seen to be a memorable achievement. Yellow journalism has no opportunity of saying that Europe has been "ordered" to do this or that, but serious journals in the East, West and South do recognize, in terms not unlike those above quoted, the value of Mr. Hay's success. It strengthens the bonds of this administration both in politics and diplomacy.[58]

Such a view was of course the comment of the quick observer. It is not the mere success of the doctrine that commands my admiration. Rather is it the skilful way in which the entire negotiation was conducted. We gave nothing; when we found that the powers would not exactly agree on the

American plan then by a clever turn we announced that their agreement to the general idea was "final and definitive." [59] That, I think, was Secretary Hay's own touch. It was a fortunate turn that he was in office for it is not impossible that President McKinley would have blunderingly approved the idea of a partition of China. Such a scheme would have plunged us into hot water at once. Secretary Hay had refused the suggestion from Lord Salisbury that the United States unite in a triple agreement with Great Britain and Germany with respect to China. Now the "open door" doctrine, though it was but an expedient and was later to become something of a fiction, served the United States both politically and commercially fully as well as any such combination would have done. Until 1921–1922, when the doctrine was embodied in a treaty, the idea of the open door was exposed to every wind that blew. In 1899–1900 those winds were favoring trade winds.[60]

NOTES TO CHAPTER VIII

1. *Hay Papers,* March 17, 1898, Sherman to White; Cf. *Ibid.,* March 18, White to Sherman. These and other documents were kept out of *Foreign Relations* for 1898 by Mr. Adee.
2. *Senate Docs. 28th Cong. 2nd. Sess.,* No. 138, p. 5, quoted in Dennett, *Americans in Eastern Asia,* New York, 1922, p. 141.
3. *British and Foreign State Papers,* XXXII, p. 791, quoted in Bau, *The Open Door Doctrine in Relation to China,* New York, 1923, p. 2; Dennett, pp. 108-110.
4. Dennett, pp. 110, 158.
5. Bau, p. 3; Dennett, pp. 167-170.
6. Dennett, p. 358.
7. *Ibid.,* pp. 608-609.
8. Dennett, *American "Good Offices" in Asia,* in *Am. Jour. of Intern. Law,* XVI, pp. 1 *et seq.;* Dennett, *Early American Policy in Korea,* 1883-7, in *Pol. Sci. Quart.,* XXXVIII, pp. 82 *et seq.;* Paulin, *The Opening of Korea by Commodore Shufeldt* in *Ibid.,* XXV, pp. 470 *et seq.;* Moore, *Digest of International Law,* V., p. 571.
9. *Kölnischer Zeitung,* July 25, 1894, quoted in Morse, *International Relations of the Chinese Empire,* III, p. 29.
10. Quoted in Morse, III, p. 29.
11. *F. R.,* 1894, App. I, pp. 23-26.
12. *Ibid.,* pp. 36-39.
13. *Ibid.,* pp. 70-71.
14. *Ibid.,* p. 76; *D. S.,* Numerical File, Vol. 520, memorandum, Nov. 8, 1894; cf. *Ibid.,* Nov. 15 (conversation with the Russian Minister).
15. *F. R.,* 1894, App. I, p. 79.
16. Cf. Morse, III, pp. 42-47.

17. I shall not attempt to indicate the large literature on the subject of Korea during this period. *F. R.*, 1895, part 2, pp. 971-977 contains a few despatches; the majority are, however unpublished and of these a few are as follows: *D. S.*, From Korea, Vol. 12, No. 187, Jan. 13, 1896, Sill to Olney; telegram, Feb. 11, same to same; No. 200, March 1, same to same; telegram, March 2, same to same; Vol. 13, No. 226, July 17, same to same; No. 243, Nov. 4, Allen to Olney; No. 262, March 11, 1897, Sill to Olney; telegram, May 8, Sill to Sherman; No. 271, May 15, same to same; No. 277, July 13, same to same; No. 279, Aug. 3, same to same; No. 286, Sept. 9, same to same; No. 3, Sept. 17, Allen to Sherman; No. 10, Oct. 2, same to same; No. 12, Oct. 5, same to same; No. 19, Oct. 14, same to same; No. 27, Oct. 25, same to same; No. 29, Nov. 7, same to same; Vol. 14, No. 48, Dec. 20, same to same; telegram, Dec. 26, same to same; No. 51, Dec. 27, same to same; No. 89, March 19, 1898, same to same, etc. To Korea, Vol. 1, telegram, p. 573, Feb. 27, 1896, Olney to Sill; telegram, May 6, 1897, Sherman to Sill; From Japan, Vol. 69, No. 345, Feb. 4, 1896, Dun to Olney; No. 348, Feb. 16, same to same; No. 352, March 3, same to same, etc., etc.
18. *F. R.*, 1894, p. 127.
19. *F. R.*, 1895, part 1, pp. 102-103.
20. *Ibid.*, p. 122.
21. *Ibid.*, p. 198; cf. pp. 150, 173 *et seq.*
22. *D. S.*, From China, Vol. 103, No. 2826, Nov. 19, Denby to Sherman; No. 2831, Nov. 29, same to same; Appendix A to this chapter.
23. *D. S.*, From Japan, Vol. 71, No. 90, Feb. 4, 1898, Buck to Sherman.
24. *D. S.*, From London, Vol. 190, No. 213, Jan. 11, 1898, Hay to Sherman.
25. *D. S.*, From London, Vol. 190, No. 222, Jan. 19, 1898, White to Sherman; Mr. White in reporting a similar speech by Chamberlain said:

"He corroborates as you will perceive, the statements of his colleague as to policy of this country, whose object he says is 'not the acquisition of new territory but the maintenance of free markets,' although he also intimates that if the acquisition of new territory be indispensable to the maintenance of such free markets Her Majesty's Government would not be averse thereto.

The article in the *Times* is of interest chiefly because it sets forth a feeling which has for some time been growing in this country and which the recent action of Germany and Russia in China has considerably intensified—viz., that measures of a more active character than have previously been customary, will in future be necessary on the part of Her Majesty's Government to prevent the closing by certain foreign Powers of channels of trade which have hitherto been open to the rest of the world and particularly to the trade of Great Britain.

I may add that there is good reason to believe that the opinion is general in this country, that Her Majesty's Government in adopting the course foreshadowed in the speeches of Ministers with regard to the maintenance of free markets, will have the sympathy and support of the people of the United States and not improbably of our Government also."
26. Cf. Bau, pp. 9-16; Morse, III, ch. V.
27. *D. S.*, From China, Vol. 103, No. 2889, March 19, 1898, Denby to Sherman, and Appendix B to this chapter. *D. S.*, From China, Vol. 103, No. 2882, March 8, Denby to Sherman:

"I content myself with saying that in my opinion an energetic protest from our Government against the dismemberment of China might have a good effect in strengthening the hands of nations like Japan and Great Britain who are freer to act in this contingency than we are."
28. *D. S.*, From China, Vol. 103, No. 2897, March 29, 1898, Denby to Sherman; *Ibid.*, Vol. 104, No. 2901, April 1, same to same; in which he says

England can choose between war or sharing in the partition of China, but the odds are heavy against her if she should act alone to "preserve freedom of trade in the whole of China."

29. D. S., From Japan, Vol. 71, No. 116, April 11, 1898, Buck to Sherman; No. 140, May 11, same to same; No. 178, July 28, same to same; *F. R.*, 1898, p. 473.

30. D. S., To Germany, Vol. 20, No. 347, Feb. 11, 1898, Sherman to White.

31. D. S., From Germany, Vol. 65, No. 318, Feb. 28, 1898, White to Sherman. Cf. No. 283, Feb. 11, same to same; No. 407, May 2, same to same.

32. D. S., To London, Vol. 32, No. 547, March 31, 1898, Sherman to Hay.

33. D. S., From London, Vol. 190, No. 739, Jan. 26, 1898, White to Sherman; No. 274 and 275, Feb. 23, same to same; Vol. 191, No. 287, March 2, same to same; No. 297, March 12, same to same; No. 308, March 18, same to same; No. 325, March 25, Hay to Sherman, in which the Ambassador clearly shows the endeavors of public men in England to stir up American interest as to China. Thus:

"I may add that in my conversation during the last few days with men connected with public affairs, the situation of things on the Pacific Coast is regarded with the utmost concern. They seem to think there is an understanding between Russia, France and Germany to exclude, as far as possible, the trade of England and America from the Far East, and to divide and reduce China to a system of tributary provinces."

34. Hansard, 4th. ser., LIV, c. 309.

35. *Ibid.*, cc. 332, 339; cf. also LVI, c. 239 when Sir William Harcourt specifically used the phrase "open door."

36. *Ibid.*, LVI, c. 287; cf. also c. 238 (Mr. Balfour's speech); cc. 1616-17, on April 29, Mr. Windham spoke of Germany and America as possibly uniting with Great Britain; on June 10, 1898 (LVIII, c. 882), Sir Michael Hicks-Beach spoke to the same end.

37. *Ibid.*, LVIII, cc. 1335-36.

38. Cf. D. S., From London, Vol. 193, No. 481, Aug. 3, 1898, Hay to Olney. Nor was the Secretary permitted to forget China; cf. Chamberlain's speech in *Times*, Dec. 9, 1898, and a letter from A. R. Colquhoun, the British explorer, of Jan. 12, 1899, reads in part:

"The result of my journey in the north—through Siberia to Peking—has been to strengthen the views held by me; and unless steps be taken by Britain to assert herself in the Yangtze Valley, so as to prevent it passing into the hands of some Power that will not allow the open door, she will be squeezed out in Central China, as she has been in the North.

The process of partition is in full operation, and Britain and the United States should make up their minds which of the two policies they will press for; to couple the two—'open door' and 'sphere' (as Lord Charles Beresford is doing I believe) will lead to failure.

I view with increasing apprehension the growing influence of Russia in China, and there is one aspect of the question which deserves attention; viz. that Russia has not only acquired an important coast line on the Pacific, but has now the command of first class and cheap material (men and coal) for building up her sea-port, for which she is at present dependent upon France.

I trust that the United States will give full consideration to the Chinese question, and that action will be taken while there is time."

The British were also anxious for joint action as to the extension of the French concessions at Shanghai and Pauncefote wrote, Jan. 8, 1899, as follows:

"Lord Salisbury cables that H. M. G. are protesting at Peking against the extension at Shanghai so as to include property owned by British subjects. He understands that your Govt. are making a similar protest and he requests me to ask you whether you do not think that if these protests were made conjointly their force would thereby be much increased."

The United States had already protested and Secretary Hay made it plain that Mr. Conger, the new American Minister in China, was only to act regarding American interests. Later he agreed to such French extension. *H. P.,* Jan. 8, 1899, Pauncefote to Hay; *D. S.,* To French Embassy, Vol. 10, No. 226, June 12, Hay to Cambon; From London, Vol. 195, No. 647, Jan. 19, White to Hay; *F. R.,* 1899, pp. 143-150. Thus the United States continued to act independently.

39. Smalley, *Anglo-American Memories,* 1st. Series, pp. 184-185.

40. *D. S.,* From China, Vol. 106, No. 155, March 1, 1899, Conger to Hay; cf. Appendix C to this chapter; From Austria, Vol. 44, No. 137, March 15, Herdliska to Hay. The Russians were bent on cajoling America and May 4, 1898, Cassini, the Russian Ambassador in Washington (*D. S.,* Numerical File, Vol. 547, memorandum) talking with Hay commented as to

"the paragraphs in the English and German press, intimating that the arrangement would have a tendency to shut out the United States from any influence in Chinese commerce, and said that such suggestions were destitute of common sense; that in the only port which Russia had open to commerce, Talien-Wan, the United States would always be most welcome, and he predicted a very considerable extension of our trade in that direction; that we should be as free as Russia in all privileges of commerce in the country under her sphere of influence; that, of course, it was unnecessary to say that our interests had suffered no diminution in the English sphere of influence; that, although the United States was the most formidable rival which England has in the trade and commerce of the world—a rival continually growing stronger while England is as constantly losing strength—there would be no possibility of shutting us out in the trade of the Orient.

He went on from that to say that it was an utterly incorrect idea that we had any enemies in Europe; that our strength and power were universally recognized and it was to the interest of all countries to be on the most intimate and friendly relations with the United States; that what has seemed, from time to time, like an unfriendly feeling on the part of Germany had really no basis in the national instinct nor in the purposes of the Government. He said that the Emperor had become much more reasonable and moderate in the last eight or ten years, and, although his susceptibilities were absolutely morbid, yet he was always amenable to reason, and sooner or later came to take a reasonable view even of questions in which his *amour propre* was at first strongly excited."

In similar fashion Mr. Charlemagne Tower, American Ambassador in Russia, wrote to Hay fulsomely (*D. S.,* From Russia, Vol. 54, No. 81, Aug. 23, 1899, Tower to Hay) regarding the Imperial Decree which opened Dalny in Manchuria:

"This, then, in so far as Russia is concerned, is the open door to China. It is gratifying to me to report to you this most important decree, which not only makes a great step forward in the progress of the world but opens the way also to the future development of American trade and the certain increase of American mercantile prosperity."

41. *H. P.,* Jan. 6, 1899, Wildman (American Consul General at Hongkong) to Hay; cf. Nov. 19, 1898, Beresford to Wildman; Nov. 25, Wildman to Hay; *D. S.,* From Japan, Vol. 72, No. 247, Jan. 28, 1899, Buck to Hay; From London, Vol. 195, No. 679, Feb. 9, White to Hay; *H. P.,* telegram, Feb. 18, Beresford to Hay.

42. *H. P.,* Nov. 29, 1898, Beresford to Hay; Beresford, *The Break-up of China,* London, 1899, pp. 453-454:

" . . . I cannot repeat too often the profound conviction held by every trader in China that the policy of the Open Door, or equal opportunity for the trade of all nations, is the one and only policy possible for the development of trade and commerce. . . . Neither is it any use keeping the door open without insuring that the room on the other side of the door is in order. To keep the door open the integrity of the Chinese Empire must be maintained."

43. *H. P.,* Holland House, New York, Aug. 28, 1899, Rockhill to Hay. Cf. Treat, *Japan and the United States, 1853-1921,* New York, 1921, pp. 169-170; Harris, *Europe and the East,* Boston, 1926, p. 412.

44. Appendix D to this chapter.

45. *F. R.,* 1899, pp. 132-133.

46. *H. P.,* Nov. 11, 1899, Hay to Wu Ting-Fang; *D. S.,* Numerical File, Vol. 547, Memo., Nov. 9, 1899.

47. *D. S.,* From London, Vol. 198, No. 165, Sept. 22, 1899, Choate to Hay; Cf. *Ibid.,* Vol. 198, telegram, Sept. 22, same to same; No. 169, Oct. 2, same to same; *F. R.,* 1899, p. 135.

48. *D. S.,* From London, Vol. 198, enclosure to No. 181, Oct. 21, 1899, Choate to Hay.

49. *H. P.,* Nov. 1, 1899, Choate to Hay; *D. S.,* From London, Vol. 198, No. 189, Oct. 25, 1899, Choate to Hay; To London, Vol. 33, No. 235, Nov. 2, 1899, Hay to Choate.

50. *D. S.,* From London, Vol. 198, No. 193, Nov. 3, 1899, Choate to Hay; enclosure to No. 216, Dec. 1, same to same; telegram, Dec. 1, same to same; To London, Vol. 33, No. 243, Nov. 14, Hay to Choate; *F. R.,* 1899, p. 136. The arrangement regarding the note of acceptance was not finally made until the spring of 1900, when the British note and the American acknowledgment of it were antedated to Nov. 30, 1899, and Dec. 6, respectively. *H. P.,* March 3, 1900, Choate to Hay; *D. S.,* From London, Vol. 199, telegram, March 8, same to same; enclosure to No. 299, April 7, White to Hay; enclosure to No. 314, May 5, Choate to Hay; To London, Vol. 33, telegram, p. 358, March 2, 1900, Hay to Choate; telegram, p. 362, March 9, same to same; No. 358, April 21, same to same.

51. *D. S.,* From Germany, Vol. 71, No. 1213, March 24, White to Hay; Cf. *F. R.,* 1899, pp. 129-131; *D. S.,* From Germany, Vol. 70, telegram, Nov. 22, 1899, Jackson to Hay; Vol. 71, No. 1188, Feb. 16, 1900, same to same; No. 1195, Feb. 21, White to Hay; No. 1205, March 9, same to same; To Germany, Vol. 21, No. 958, Nov. 2, 1899, Hay to White; No. 966, Nov. 17, same to same; telegram, Jan. 22, 1900, same to same; telegram, Feb. 15, same to same; telegram, Feb. 16, same to same; No. 1019, March 20, same to same; No. 1930, April 3, same to same.

52. *H. P.,* Feb. 12, 1900 (personal and confidential) Tower to Hay; *F. R.,* 1899, pp. 141-142. Cf. *H. P.,* Dec. 19, 1899 (memorandum from Rockhill); Dec. 27, Hay to White; Dec. 31, Cassini to Hay; *D. S.,* Numerical File, Vol. 547, Memo., Nov. 24 and Dec. 1, 1899 (conversation between Cassini and Rockhill); To Russia, Vol. 18, No. 103, Nov. 2, Hay to Tower; No. 107, Nov. 17, same to same; p. 246, telegram, Dec. 19, same to same; p. 246, telegram, Dec. 26, same to same; No. 120, Jan. 22, 1900, same to same; From Russia, Vol. 55, No. 104, Sept. 20, 1899, Pierce to Hay; No. 156, Nov. 23, Tower to Hay; telegram, Nov. 23, same to same; telegram, Dec. 9, same to same; No. 167, Dec. 11, same to same; telegram, Dec. 26, same to same; telegram, Dec. 28, same to same; No. 176, Jan. 2, 1900, same to same; telegram, Feb. 9, same to same.

53. *D. S.,* From France, Vol. 118, No. 559, Nov. 10, 1899, Porter to Hay.

54. *F. R.,* 1899, pp. 128-129, 142; *D. S.,* From France, Vol. 118, No. 567, Nov. 22, 1899, Porter to Hay; telegram, Dec. 14, same to same; telegram,

Dec. 18, same to same; No. 594, Dec. 21, same to same; To France, Vol. 24, No. 691, Nov. 17, Hay to Porter; telegram, Dec. 8, same to same; telegram, Dec. 12, same to same; telegram, Dec. 14, same to same; telegram, Jan. 4, 1900, same to same; No. 746, March 20, same to same.

55. *F. R.*, 1899, pp. 136-138; *D. S.*, From Italy, Vol. 34, No. 542, Dec. 11, 1899, Draper to Hay; No. 552, Dec. 27, same to same; To Italy, Vol. 3, telegram, Jan. 2, 1900, Hay to Draper.

56. *F. R.*, 1899, pp. 138-139, 142; *D. S.*, From Japan, Vol. 73, telegram, Nov. 30, 1899, Buck to Hay; No. 388, Dec. 18, same to same; No. 391, Dec. 28, same to same; No. 434, June 1, 1900, same to same; To Japan, Vol. 4, No. 295, June 30, 1900, Hay to Buck; To Japanese Legation, Vol. 2, p. 128, Adee to Takahira.

57. *D. S.*, From China, Vol. 107, No. 297, Dec. 21, 1899, Conger to Hay; Cf. Bau, pp. 24-25.

58. Cf. also *Times*, March 28, 1900. Of the many letters of congratulation that Hay received I have selected only two from the *Hay Papers* chiefly because of their genuine ring. The first is from his brother-in-law in Cleveland, Mr. Samuel Mather, who wrote Jan. 15, 1900:

"Is it indeed true that you have secured written guarantees from the Great Powers of our treaty rights with China, good even in the event of complete partition? If so this is indeed a great achievement—full of promise for our own Country, and of high value to all civilization, and I congratulate you on it most heartily.

It is a glorious Diplomatic triumph—how *did* you accomplish it, so quickly, quietly, and effectively? Great Britain had been at it for years, and apparently abandoned the attempt in despair."

The second, of January 24, is from his predecessor at the Department of State. It reads:

"My dear Mr. Secretary:

'Peace hath her victories,
No less renowned than war.'

"By moving at the right time, and in the right manner, you have secured a diplomatic triumph in the 'open door in China' of the first importance to your country, and greatly to your personal credit and renown. Permit me to extend my warm congratulations. Wishing you continued success,

"I am,
"Very truly yours,
"William R. Day."

59. *F. R.*, 1899, p. 142.
60. Hay, *Letters*, etc., III, p. 199; Dennett, ch. XXXII.

APPENDICES TO CHAPTER VIII

A

D. S. From China, Vol. 103, No. 2842, Dec. 11, 1897, Denby to Sherman.

The seizure of Chiao-chow by the Germans has precipitated the discussion of the partition of China. The position of China is even more humiliating than it was after her easy defeat by Japan. Before that war it would not have been possible for any power to have landed six hundred men and taken possession, without any warning being given, of a port, a bay, and a large strip of territory. The Chinese would have resisted. Now there is no heart left in them. Their experience during the Japanese war demonstrated that the Chinese have no patriotism. The people of one province have not the slightest fellow feeling for those of any other, and they have not the slightest attachment to their own local rulers. The system of government makes the people hostile to their rulers. Positions of importance are secured by bribery, and held by paying contributions to the Peking officials, and money for such purpose is extorted from the people. Reforms under this government are impossible. Offices have been bought and paid for and the buyers must reimburse themselves by stealing. In other countries, as in Turkey, there is a religious sentiment which tends to produce loyalty to the Throne. In China there is no religious sentiment. The better classes are Confucianists and Confucianism is simply a moral code. The people generally have no religion. Neither Buddhism nor Taoism has any hold except on the women.

It may, therefore, be said that the people of China would make no opposition to the partition of the Empire. They would rather welcome it, and would gladly transfer their allegiance to an [*sic*] European power. It is questionable, however, whether a partition would be for the benefit of the western powers. Certainly England would lose by such absorption. She now controls the bulk of the trade with China, and under prohibitive duties and a restrictive policy she would undoubtedly lose much of it.

By the occupation of China, Germany sees a scheme to increase her navy, and she may need it because if her example of seizing Chinese territory is followed it is not unlikely that war will result among the European powers. Conflicting interests, jealousies, international collisions cannot be avoided if this populous country is divided among several holders. For the interests of the world it is better that China should be ruled by one power than by any greater number. If I were forecasting the future of China in her own interest I would desire for her a government controlled by Chinese and not Manchus, and such a government would be best for foreign interests.

D. S. From China, No. 103, No. 2858, Jan. 31, 1898, Denby to Sherman.

In my despatch No. 2855, of the 17th instant I had the honor to inform you of the offers being made by Great Britain to China, and of the conditions attached thereto.

It is known to you by the public telegrams that Russia violently antagonized this proposal. The Russian Chargé d'Affaires has strongly protested against China's accepting the English loan, and has proffered a Russian loan in lieu thereof. The Chinese government is really anxious to accept the English proposal, which it recognizes is best for China, but it greatly fears Russia. China is not opposed to the opening of new ports, a scheme to which the people is [sic] everywhere favorable on account of the advantages derived from foreign trade, and she recognizes, also, that the British proposition is in the main just and equitable, because no special privileges are demanded by the English, but all the world will participate on equal terms in the advantages secured by England. China understands, too, that the example of the recent action of Germany with regard to the seizure of Kiachow is dangerous. She has great fears that England will take advantage of the precedent thus established and appeal to force. Whether England will so act, or not, is uncertain, but, I think, that she will take some energetic action in the lines of a stricter enforcement of Treaty rights. It is quite probable that she will demand in the interest of her enormous trade a revision of likin rules, and that at last we may have a reasonable settlement of the areas in which likin may be collected. It is probable, also, that if the Chinese refuse to open Talienwan to trade, England will insist on the opening of other ports in the North. It seems to me that events portend a serious conflict, and, perhaps, armed strife between England and Russia. It is certain that English public sentiment will revolt against the domination of Russia in Manchuria and Korea.

Looking at the treaties, and international law, it is impossible to see on what ground Russia should claim to control Manchuria, and exclude other nations from equal rights with her in that country. This question may come up between the United States and Russia.

Russia represents to China that she is her friend, and ally, limitrophe with her for thirty-five hundred miles, and that her interests alone must be consulted by China. China is weak, and timid and I greatly fear will yield. If she does England at least must show her teeth.

In the midst of these events it may not be improper to consider our own position regarding China. I am very thoroughly aware that since Washington's Farewell Address was uttered we have been, what may be called, innately conservative on the question of interfering in the affairs of foreign powers. He would be a bold man who in the United States would advocate political entanglement in the affairs of Europe, Asia, or Africa. That our abnegation tends to weaken our influence and to make us a quantité négligeable is undoubtedly true, but it has its compensations in the enforcement of the Monroe Doctrine.

Still, while preserving all the sanctity of the "Farewell Address," it is worth enquiring whether there is not some middle ground on which we may stand with advantage. We have fifteen hundred missionaries here. Should China be partitioned among the European powers it is quite certain that the work of these missionaries would be impeded. From any country under Russian control they would be excluded. In any country under French control they would be impeded and embarrassed. These missionaries are entitled to our protection just the same as mercantile people are.

Partition would tend to destroy our markets. The Pacific Ocean is destined to bear on its bosom a larger commerce than the Atlantic. As the countries in the Far East and Australia develop their resources the commerce of the United States with them will assume proportions greater in their directness and scope, than our commerce with Europe.

In these countries we are destined to find our best customers for manufactured, as well as natural, and agricultural products.

Here are diverse and varied sources of interest in the Far East which directly touch us.

Having such interests in China, is it our duty to remain mute should her autonomy be attacked? Is it exactly right to announce, as was lately done in Reuter's telegrams, that we take no interest in territorial questions? We have a certain moral interest in the affairs of the world, and, in my opinion, that influence should be exacted in all cases in which our interests demand its exercise. We should urge on China the reform of all evils in her government which touch American interests, and the adoption of vigorous measures in the line of material progress. This policy will to her be the surest pathway to independence and prosperity. I have persistently urged this policy. We should not hesitate, also, I think, to announce our disapproval of acts of brazen wrong, and spoliation, perpetrated by other nations towards China,—should any such occur.

In this connection it may not be improper to cite the following extract from the first Article of the Treaty of 1858 between the United States and China: "And if any other nation should act unjustly or oppressively the United States will exert their good offices on being informed of the case, to bring about an amicable arrangement of the question thus showing their friendly feelings."

B

D. S. From China, Vol. 103, No. 2889, March 19, 1898, Denby to Sherman.

The Chinese Government has apparently lost all power to control events which are now taking place, and which look to the reduction of China to complete helplessness.

The conduct of Russia has been characterized by tortuous treachery. By her secret treaty with China, called the "Cassini Convention," Russia bound herself to protect China against all enemies.

When the Germans invaded Kiaochow, China consulted Russia to know whether she ought to make armed resistance. The Russian Chargé here held up his hands in horror, and exclaimed that China should by no means resist, and protested that Russia would at the proper time protect her. He also declared that the Russian Admiral had been ordered to go to Kiaochow and drive the Germans out. After some days had passed, and nothing had been done, the Chinese Government again appealed to the Russian Chargé. They were told to wait, and that Russia had been assured that the German occupation was temporary, and that the order to the Russian Admiral to drive the Germans out was suspended. They waited until it became apparent that the Germans intended to remain permanently at Kiaochow, and again consulted the Russian Chargé d'Affaires, who informed them that their conduct in treating with the Germans had given offense to Russia and now she would not intervene.

They then on the 6th of this month signed the convention with Germany whereby they practically abandoned Shantung to its possession and control. As soon as that convention was signed Russia immediately demanded the cession of Port Arthur and Talienwan Bay on exactly the same terms as had been granted to Germany. The Chinese Government protested and the Chargé informed them that the Emperor of Russia was very indignant that China had entered into collusion with Germany, and had made the Convention mentioned with. Germany, and now Russia intended to pursue her own course regardless of China.

International intercourse does not contain an episode of greater moral baseness than this. Russia prevents by her advice China from defending herself, forces her, by non-compliance with her agreement with China to protect her, to abdicate her sovereign rights, and then, when she has done so, avails herself of this abdication in favor of one country as an excuse to demand a like abdication, and surrender of national rights in Manchuria! In all this matter the policy of China was plain. She should have said to Germany: "I am unable to fight you, I have no army or navy, but I will never consent to surrender any of my territory. If you invade my territory and appropriate it I will appeal to the civilized world with which I have treaties, to intervene to save those treaties, which are as important to the various treaty powers as they are to me."

Then the question would have been presented directly to Great Britain, Japan and the United States whether they would stand by, and see their treaty rights abrogated by virtue of pretended leases, and exclusive commercial concessions. That China did not do this was caused by her reliance on the false promise of Russia to protect her against all enemies.

In the event that she had protested as stated I should have hoped that you would have sent to Germany an energetic protest against a line of conduct which cannot but be injurious to our interests, as it tends to destroy our market in the ceded territory, and our ex[tra]territorial rights. I do not claim that we should have interfered if Germany had taken absolutely for her own the province of Shantung—as Japan took Formosa, and as England and all other nations have taken great strips of the earth. The laws and treaties of the conqueror take the place of those of the conquered country.

I do claim, however, that for one power to secure exclusively under the form of an extorted lease rights and privileges which are the subject of prior treaty grants to other powers is a violation of the treaties of which the parties thereto have the right to complain. In this connection I must say that the adulation that England has received in the American press for her supposed support of treaty rights is absolutely undeserved.

Her statesmen have made grandiloquent declarations as to what she would do, but she has done nothing whatever. All she had to do was to say to Germany at the beginning: "You shall not be permitted to take exclusive rights in Shantung. You shall not have the sole right to build railroads in that province or to operate mines. Englishmen everywhere in Shantung shall still be subject to British law."

Great Britain did not in the smallest particular interfere with Germany. From November to nearly April she has stood by and has not opened her mouth.

Germany may well claim that she now has "vested interests," and that Great Britain is estopped to make any objection to her conduct.

It is now reasonably to be expected that Great Britain will seize the Chusan islands, and, possibly the Yangtse valley. She, then, like Russia, would simply say to China that she demands the same rights which Germany has secured. It is generally believed here that France will shortly seize the island of Hainan, and, probably one or more of the southern provinces.

In all this matter I am only concerned for the place in history which my own country will fill.

With our moral support Great Britain might even now call Russia to give an account of her plans as to the occupation of Manchuria, and might save our treaty rights in that country.

C

D. S. From China, Vol. 106, No. 155, March 1, 1899, Conger to Hay.

I have the honor to confirm, on the overleaf, my telegram of this date.

I have not been able to ascertain the full details of the Italian request, but I am informed it is for a lease of the bay of San Moon, without sufficient adjacent land for commodious coaling and naval stations with conclusive control of the same, and authority to practically control all mining, railroad or manufacturing development in the province of Chekiang; with also an agreement that no like concessions shall be given to any other power along the coast of this province.

It is reported here that an Italian fleet is well on its way toward Asiatic waters, and if true, it is coming evidently for the purpose of emphasizing and possibly enforcing this request.

This action of the Italian Government is only additional evidence of the general belief that China is going to pieces and the purpose of another of the powers to make a preemption before it is too late, the title to which can be more easily perfected when the break up comes.

I do not know what the desire of the Department is upon this question nor its proposed policy; but if it shall deem it advisable ever to own or control a good coaling station on the Chinese coast, or if it wishes to be a party to the division and a sharer in the assets, then it is necessary that the place be selected and its cession or lease demanded at once; even now it may be too late.

A glance at the map will show Russia strongly intrenched in Manchuria, Germany in Shantung, Italy demanding Chekiang, Japan expecting Fukien, England at Hongkong and the French in Kwangtung and Tongking, with the English claiming an extended sphere along the Yangtse and a general and most important foreign settlement at Shanghai. There is practically nothing left for the United States but the province of Chili. This, however, with Tientsin as the entrepôt for all northern China, is destined in the future to be commercially one of the most valuable permanent possessions in the Orient.

The policy of the other powers seems to be to obtain possession of some unimportant harbor or bay, claiming as a perquisite a temporary control of developments in the adjacent province, with a prior claim, thus established, to the entire province at the proper time.

If our Government should have a like purpose, some point might be selected on the coast of Chili and the same tactics employed.

However, it is possible that Taku is the only suitable place along the coast of that province, and being at the entrance of the treaty port of Tientsin, such strenuous opposition would probably be made by the other powers as would render its cession impossible. But our Navy Department must be fully informed as to all possible harbor advantages along the entire Chinese coast and can make a selection if it is desired.

My own opinion is that a permanent ownership of territory (except for a coaling station if that is needed) in China is not desirable. But if all China is to fall into the hands of European powers, a strong foothold here by the United States, with something tangible to offer them, might compel them to keep permanently open doors for our commerce.

But I am here to execute your commissions and whatever they may be I shall undertake them with alacrity.

I have as yet made no protest against granting this lease to the Italians although it, like those to Russia and Germany, seems evidently in contravention of treaties, because no formal protest having been made against the other powers I can now see no good reason for making an exceptional case against Italy.

D

Hay Papers, Aug. 28, 1899, Rockhill to Hay.

No one has done more within the last few months to influence public opinion in the United States on the Chinese question than

APPENDICES TO CHAPTER VIII 209

Lord Charles Beresford, by his book *The Break-up of China,* and by the speeches he has made in the United States. By those means he has sought to prove the identity of interests of our two countries and the necessity of an Anglo-American policy in China. It seems desirable to preface the following remarks by examining the data supplied by Lord Charles, endeavoring to control his views and to show, if possible, the truth or fallacy of his conclusions.

For one who has devoted the better part of his life to the study of Chinese affairs, the book of Lord Beresford comes as an agreeable surprise—so far as regards foreign commercial relations with China, and is on the whole rather encouraging than dispiriting. The volume of foreign trade has steadily increased, and everywhere signs are not wanting for its further extension; the Chinese Government has not failed to fulfill any of its pecuniary obligations to foreigners, and is endeavoring, in a clumsy, uncertain way it is true,—but that is not entirely its fault, to take some further steps in the direction needed for its internal development. If, on the other hand, the Empire is in a disturbed condition, and if foreign interests suffer thereby, this is entirely due to the unseemly haste of some of the treaty powers in their scramble for commercial advantages and acquisition of territory. This they lament but do not seek to remedy.

Lord Beresford's interviews with the various foreign mercantile organizations at the treaty ports of China bring clearly before us the fact that they have not in the last twenty years had any new ground for complaint against the Chinese Government, that they are today suffering, not perhaps even quite so severely as years ago, from the existence of certain restrictions, especially those resulting from internal revenue taxes, which has been the subject of endless correspondence between the diplomatic representatives in Peking and the Chinese Government for the last quarter of a century and with which everyone interested in affairs in that Empire must by this time be pretty familiar.

The grievances of which the foreign mercantile class in China has to complain and a remedy to which lies with the Chinese Government are all proper subjects for diplomatic discussion and no one can doubt that if within the last two years steady and united pressure had been brought to bear on it by the Treaty Powers, some of them would be in a fair way to settlement at the present time.

Take for example *likin*. In the rush for concessions to foreigners in China and the necessity for that country to find funds to insure the payment of interest on the loans she has been forced to contract to carry out the more or less urgent public works recommended by them, the Treaty Powers have compelled her to increase her internal revenue taxes and have permanently fastened on the country this very tax (likin) they had for twenty five years and more been trying to have suppressed. Again take the transit pass system by which foreign goods are allowed to be carried throughout the Empire on the payment of one-half the import duty, and which system the British merchants claim is an utter failure, we know by the successful endeavors of the French Government in enforcing this right under the treaties for goods imported into southwestern China, that if failure it is in other parts of the Empire, the fault lies with the foreigners themselves.

Lord Beresford's opinion that it is primarily necessary for the development of China to make a military and naval power of that Empire, is, I think, the weakest part of his work, and his opinion is at variance with that of all who know best China and the Chinese. So far as the protection of foreign interests is concerned the Chinese Government is, and has been since the suppression of the Taiping rebellion, able to protect them whenever and wherever it has chosen to, as innumerable cases familiar to the Department show.

In the various memoranda submitted to Lord Beresford by the British merchants of China and published in his book, the need for China to increase her armament to insure their security, is nowhere hinted at, but in all of them we find the cause of the present stagnation of trade attributed, and rightly to my mind, to the vacillating policy of the home governments, frequently brought about by apathy and lack of knowledge regarding Chinese affairs, the resulting ability of the Chinese Government to escape the performance of its treaty obligations, and to the jealousies and lack of concerted action of the Powers in treating questions of general interest.

No more representative foreign body can be found in China than the China Association at Shanghai. In its memorandum to Lord Beresford we read: "It seems plain that such security (as foreign trade requires) can only be found in the entire reform of the present corrupt state of Chinese government. The undertaking of such a task, no doubt, bristles with difficulties, and entails responsibilities which will necessarily be complicated by international jealousies; it is, nevertheless, clear that unless the situation be boldly faced, still greater difficulties and still greater international trouble will have to be faced in the near future. . . . The establishment of a government at Peking, which is not only strong, but which is in sympathy with the wishes and feelings of the nation at large, is, we believe, a first necessity if China is to be saved from partition. . . . Weakness in Peking must inevitably mean disruption and partition of the Empire. . . . We say, then, that the one thing wanted for the development of trade, for the protection of capital, and for the extension of enterprise in China is security, which can only be effected through pressure from without. . . ."

That the task of strengthening the central government is a comparatively easy one, the history of China's progress in the last fifty years conclusively shows. The introduction of telegraphic lines throughout the Empire, the Maritime Customs service, the more recent organization of a system of imperial railways and their withal successful working, and a variety of other reforms are all operating in the same direction, so that Lord Beresford's statement (p. 231) "no reform . . . can possibly be brought about in a country so hopelessly corrupt as China until the first and initial step is taken of giving authority to those in power which only an effective military and police can supply," is a hasty and erroneous conclusion.

That the existence of a strong and well officered and disciplined army and navy in China might assist that country to ward off the attacks of a foreign foe, is likely; that, in the absence of such a force, and with the present aggressive policy of some of the Treaty Powers, the creation of "Spheres of interest" (or influence) easily reached by rail or by sea by the interested Power from its own territory, should be held to be the only way of insuring China against complete partition, is comprehensible; but that the United States should lend a hand to the carrying out of either of these two policies seems absolutely suicidal to our vast and growing interests in that part of the world.

British writers on Chinese questions, and especially Lord Beresford, have advocated in the strongest terms the "open door policy" or equality of treatment and opportunity for all comers, and denounce in the strongest terms the system of "Spheres of Influence" (or interest); but such spheres have now been recognized by Great Britain as well as by France, Germany and Russia, and *they must be accepted as existing facts.*

But while adopting the policy of spheres of interest, which, we will admit, political reasons may have forced it to do, Great Britain has tried to maintain also the "open door" policy, the only one which meets with the approval of its business classes, for by it alone can they be guaranteed equality of treatment in the trade of China. In this attempt to minimize the evils brought about by the necessities of her foreign policy, Great Britain has been, however, unable to secure to her people perfect equality of opportunity, for she has recognized special and exclusive rights first of Germany and then of Russia in their areas of activity, more particularly those relating to railways and mines. What these rights may eventually be claimed to include, no one can at present foretell, though it would not be surprising if the exercise of territorial jurisdiction and the imposition of discriminating taxation were demanded under them—at least by France. Should such rights be conceded, our trade interests would suffer a blow from which they could not possibly recover.

To sum up then, we find today in China that the policy of the "open door," the untrammeled exercise of the rights insured to Treaty Powers by the Treaty of Tientsin, and other treaties copied on it or under the most favored nation clause, is claimed by the mercantile classes of the United States and other powers as essential to the healthy extension of trade in China. We see, on the other hand, that the political interests and the geographical relations of Great Britain, Russia, and France to China have forced those countries to divide up China proper into areas or spheres of interest (or influence) in which they enjoy special rights and privileges, the ultimate scope of which is not yet determined, and that at the same time Great Britain, in its desire not to sacrifice entirely its mercantile interests, is also endeavoring to preserve some of the undoubted benefits of the "open door" policy, but "spheres of influence" *are an accomplished fact,* this cannot be too much insisted upon. (This policy is outlined by Mr. Balfour in his Manchester speech of January 10, 1898.)

Such being the condition of things, and in view of the probability of complications soon arising between the interested powers in China, whereby it will become difficult, if not impossible, for the United States to retain the rights guaranteed them by treaties with China, what should be our immediate policy? To this question there can, it seems, be but one answer, we should at once initiate negotiations to obtain from those Powers who have acquired zones of interest in China formal assurance that (1) they will in no way interfere within their so-called spheres of interest with any treaty port or with vested rights in it of any nature; (2) that all ports they may open in their respective spheres shall either be free ports, or that the Chinese treaty tariff at the time in force shall apply to all merchandise landed or shipped, no matter to what nationality belonging, and that the dues and duties provided for by treaty shall be collected by the Chinese Government; and (3) that they will levy no higher harbor dues on vessels of other nationalities frequenting their ports in such spheres, than shall be levied on their national vessels, and that they will also levy no higher railroad charges on merchandise belonging to or destined for subjects of other powers transported through their spheres than shall be levied on similar merchandise belonging to its own nationality.

In other words, we should insist on absolute equality of treatment in the various zones, for equality of opportunity with the citizens of the favored powers we can not hope to have, in view of the well known method now in vogue for securing privileges and concessions, though we should continually, by every proper means, seek to gain this also.

Such understandings with the various Powers, and it is confidently believed that they could be reached at present, would secure an open market throughout China for our trade on terms of equality with all other foreigners, and would further remove dangerous sources of irritation and possible conflict between the contending powers, greatly tending to re-establish confidence, and prepare the way for concerted action by the Powers to bring about the reforms in Chinese administration and the strengthening of the Imperial Government.

Great stress has been laid by British writers on the role of Russia in China which they contend is a "purely political and military conquest" and who, "though she may mean to eventually build up a commerce, only wants for the present the Chinese seaboard and ports for strategic purposes." (Colquhoun. "China in Transformation." 326.) Lord Beresford says (32) that he was told at Niuchaung by the British residents that "they regarded Manchuria as really a Russian province . . . that though the Russians might not impose a tariff on goods just at present, they were placing themselves in such a powerful military position that they would be able to do so in the near future, . . . and the merchants considered their trade threatened by such an exhibition of military power." In the face of these apprehensions of the British merchants at Niuchuang, who were but feeling in their persons the discomfort and restrictions which all foreigners may sooner or later have to experience when settled in the sphere of influence of some rival power, it is agreeable to have to record the opening of the port of Ta-lien-wan (near Port Arthur and an infinitely better port than Nieuchuang [sic] being below the line of winter and ice), to the merchant ships of all nations during the whole of the lease under which it is held by the Emperor of Russia's ukase of August 15th of this year. This I conceive will greatly help to allay fears and doubts as to Russia's attitude in China, and justifies the belief entertained that she would cooperate in bringing about such international understanding as is here outlined.

The recent statement of a Russian writer inspired by a personage enjoying for years the friendship of the Emperor of Russia, that "the independence and integrity of China is a fundamental principle of Russia's policy in Asia" (N. A. Rev. July, '99, p. 16), may or may not be absolutely correct; at all events, it may well be taken as indicating the present trend of Russia's policy, and seems to insure the friendly consideration at St. Petersburg of the arrangement here suggested. Whatever the ulterior object of Russia may be, its present one is unquestionably conciliation, for any haste might prove the spark which would cause the explosion by which the Chinese Empire would be shattered.

Nor does the assent of Germany to the proposed agreement seem very doubtful; she has declared Kiaochow a free port and allowed a Chinese custom house to be established there, in pleasing contrast, by the way, with the illiberal and short sighted policy of Great Britain which has expelled the Chinese custom house from Kowloon extension in front of Hongkong, and while she has insisted on certain exclusive mining and railroad rights in her sphere of interest, it seems highly probable that as German capital flows slower and slower into these enterprises, as it undoubtedly will as the vast requirements for long years to come of the already granted concessions are more exactly determined, she will find it greatly to her advantage to encourage and foster the enterprises of other nations.

No reference has been made to the way in which the Japanese Government would consider the propositions here suggested, because these measures are so clearly advantageous to Japan and so much in line with its own policy in China, that it must meet with its hearty approval.

It is particularly important for obvious reasons of both domestic and foreign policy that the initiative for these negotiations should be taken by the United States. Such a policy can not be construed as favorable to any power in particular, but is eminently useful and desirable for the commerce of all nations. It furthermore has the advantage of insuring to the United States the appreciation of Chinese Government, who would see in it a strong desire to arrest the disintegration of the Empire and would greatly add to our prestige and influence at Peking.

France is the only doubtful country from whom some opposition might be anticipated, it being her well known policy in China to claim all implied jurisdictional rights wherever possible, but it is little likely that in this question, as in others, she would decline to listen to Russia's advice and stand out in opposition alone.

The prospect seems bright therefore *at the present moment* of bringing to a successful conclusion the negotiations needed to attain the ends here indicated and which will, it is thought, relieve our commercial world from the just apprehension and perturbation in which recent events have thrown it, giving it equal treatment so far as commerce and navigation go, with the subjects of any other power.

CHAPTER IX

THE BOXER MOVEMENT

IN his reassertion of the open door doctrine Secretary Hay had to a certain extent departed from traditional American foreign policy. He had used co-operation instead of independent action. In 1900 it became apparent that the United States had moved in the nick of time. The policy of the open door had but just been accepted by the chief states interested in China when a patriotic but misguided and cruel outbreak of fanaticism took place. This anti-foreign demonstration was nicknamed the Boxer movement, or rebellion, because it had its origin in a Chinese secret society, whose name freely translated may be called the "Fists of Righteous Harmony." Hence the name "Boxer." The Chinese Government was inadequate and powerless before this popular outburst. Indeed many of the officials and the Empress Dowager herself secretly sympathized with the essential, national purpose of the Boxers. Soon affairs got beyond all control and in the attempt to restore order, to relieve their own nationals, and to punish the guilty among the Chinese the foreign powers were exposed to the extreme temptation of plundering China, of partitioning her domain among themselves and thus of inaugurating a cut-throat policy of special privilege and monopoly. Under the circumstances it was especially fortunate for China that the open door policy had been so recently adopted. Furthermore it was now a policy of concurrent action.

The story of the months immediately preceding the siege of the foreign legations in Peking need not long detain us. In 1898, as the foreign powers rivalled each other in extorting leases and concessions from the Chinese government, there came for a few months an attempt at the reform of Chinese institutions. This step, however, was abortive. The reformers and their decrees were swept away largely because they undertook their task too hastily and too thoroughly. In September, 1898, after three months of so-called reform, the Empress Dowager struck back and quickly disposed of the advisers who had won the ear of her nephew, the young Emperor. She was well aware of the unpopularity which now surrounded the Manchu dynasty and of the inadequacy of the governmental authorities. She sought, therefore, to shift attention from the imperial régime and to lay the blame for present misfortune on the presence of foreigners in China. In this policy she was assisted by the rise and formidable development of secret societies, whose main purpose was to drive out all foreigners. A drought threatened in the summer of 1899, economic conditions were most serious, and general discontent existed. Under these circumstances the outbreaks against foreigners became more frequent. It was increasingly difficult to deal with the numerous bandits who roamed much as they wished. The officials were lax in the protection offered to foreigners in the interior; and the Boxers began to circulate illustrated placards and proclamations declaring that all the misfortunes of China were due to "foreign devils."

Naturally these attacks bore most heavily on missionaries and on their native converts. Yet the Chinese did not have any specific hatred for foreigners. Rather their antagonism was against what the foreigner seemed to represent —a régime of special privilege. They were originally hostile to the Manchu dynasty and to the officials; these gentry, however, were ready to twist this social and patriotic movement and to direct it against the foreigners. Thus they tried to save themselves from popular wrath and for a time they were successful.

Since 1840 foreigners had been more or less tolerated in China; but such privileges as they enjoyed had been extorted. In the last analysis the foreigner in China depended on the use of potential force. Now the Boxer movement proposed to turn the hands of the clock back, to restore the isolation and self-sufficiency of China, and in so doing to tear up the treaties. In the course of events such an attempt involved bloodshed, untold cruelty, and the destruction of property.

During the first half of 1900 Mr. Conger at Peking repeatedly described in his despatches the chaotic conditions which existed. On January 2 he sent home a secret edict of the Empress Dowager, issued in November, 1899, to the provincial chief officials. This read in part:

> Our Empire is now laboring under great difficulties, which are becoming daily more serious. The various powers cast upon us looks of tiger-like voracity, hustling each other in their endeavors to be the first to seize upon our innermost territories. They think that China, having neither money nor troops, would never venture to go to war with them. They fail to understand, however, that there are certain things which this Empire can never consent to, and that, if hardly pressed upon, we have no alternative but to rely upon the justice of our cause, the knowledge of which in our breasts strengthens our resolves and steels us to present a united front against our aggressors. . . .
>
> It is our special command, therefore, that should any high official find himself so hard pressed by circumstances that nothing short of war would settle matters he is expected to set himself resolutely to work out his duty to this end. . . .
>
> Let no one think of making peace, but let each strive to preserve from destruction and spoliation his ancestral home and graves from the ruthless hands of the invader. Let these our words be made known to each and all within our domains.[1]

Such language, though patriotic in its spirit, clearly indicated that little was to be expected from the authorities in suppressing any local outbreaks against foreigners. These became more serious as the year advanced; and in March Mr. Conger clearly showed his alarm by urging a naval demonstration in North China waters unless the government agreed to issue a strong decree against these disorders. In his notes to the Chinese authorities he had followed the practice of sending an identical note with the other foreign diplomats. To this Secretary Hay apparently objected for he wrote advocating separate representations to the Chinese government, and saying:

> The position of the United States in relation to China makes it expedient that, while circumstances may sometimes require that it act on lines similar to those other treaty powers follow, it should do so singly and without the co-operation of other powers.[2]

The Department of State was over-cautious, or perhaps Mr. Adee was, and there was no one in the offices who really understood the situation. Secretary Hay was at this time engaged in his desperate but losing battle with the Senate over the first Hay-Pauncefote treaty. In any case he did not grasp many of the factors which were involved during the events of the next few months; and in the summer he was seriously ill for some time. Mr. Rockhill, therefore, came to be more and more the unofficial expert on Chinese affairs at the Department. Yet, as late as June 1, 1900, when conditions in China were worse than ever and the siege of the legations was about to begin, Mr. Rockhill sent a personal note to Secretary Hay which read:

> I return herewith the despatches from Mr. Conger which you kindly sent me to read. I cannot believe that the "Boxer" movement will be very long-lived or cause any serious complications. The day the Chinese authorities choose to put an end to it they can easily do so. I think they have now realized that they must act, and they will.[3]

Yet the world at large and the European chancelleries as well were equally ill-informed and surprised when the storm broke in June, 1900. Already Mr. Conger had reported on May 8, that:

> The Government either strongly sympathizes with the "Boxers" or it is afraid of them. It is reported and believed that there are many "boxers" and sympathizers with them in the army, and they all, both in and out of the army, claim to be patriotically in favor of the present dynasty. If, therefore, the Government should treat them too harshly, or punish too severely, a revolution might be the

result and the Government find itself without the ability of successful defense. This dynasty is not popular anywhere south of this province, and, with the existing palace troubles, finds considerable cause for anxiety.⁴

The Chinese authorities could not be depended on and the Legation guards were reinforced on May 31 by the arrival of small detachments coming from naval vessels at Taku. In response to inquiries Mr. Conger received instructions to "act independently in protection of American interests where practicable and concurrently with representatives of other powers if necessity arises." On June 10, Secretary Hay again telegraphed:

> We have no policy in China except to protect with energy American interests, and especially American citizens and the legations. There must be nothing done which would commit us to future action inconsistent with your standing instructions. There must be no alliances.⁵

On June 11 Mr. Conger wrote "we are besieged in Peking, entirely cut off from outside communications." This despatch did not reach Washington till September 25. Since the end of May the Boxers had commanded the countryside and now they were burning and butchering in Peking. The legation quarter was defended as far as possible by a small number of armed troops and by foreign civilians. On June 15 Mr. Conger wrote "there is no Tsungli Yamen [Foreign Office] and in no intelligent sense can there be said to be in existence any Chinese Government whatever." On the same day Secretary Hay telegraphed: "Do you need more force? Communicate with Admiral and report." This gives the measure of complete misapprehension with which the Department of State met the crisis. No communications were of course possible and Peking was finally relieved only in mid-August after nearly 20,000 foreign troops had been gathered for the rescue of the legations.³

For the moment common alarm for the situation of the legations brought about a common desire for action. Soon, however, mutual suspicion and jealousy were to threaten the accord of the western powers.⁷ America reverted to her historic policy of protecting only the "direct interests of the United States in China," though in certain contingencies she might act in common with the other powers. Lord Salisbury said to Ambassador Choate that the representatives of the powers ought to have withdrawn from Peking while it was still possible. This, of course, sounded like crying after the milk was spilt. Mr. Choate commented that, when the relief of the legations had been accomplished, he hoped that:

> We shall not be drawn into any of the schemes of the Continental Powers, looking to a partition of China. The general desire here is that England should not be, so far as I can discover. But I cannot forget what Lord Salisbury once said to me in defining a "sphere of influence" that it was a sort of an "ear mark" upon territory which in case of a break up England did not wish any other power to have.⁸

Under the circumstances the suggestion of Japan that she should at once send a considerable body of troops to Tientsin was welcomed by all the powers though the necessary inquiries required time.⁹ The United States had by early July ordered some 2,500 men to China; but in response to Chinese representations it was agreed that for the time at least no military or naval forces should be directed to the central and southern provinces of China where the Viceroys seemed to have matters under control.¹⁰ This enabled the powers to concentrate their attention on the relief of Peking.

On July 3, 1900, the United States also sent a circular telegram to various states, whose legations were besieged at Peking. This stated that in accordance with the policy initiated in 1857 the United States wished to remain at peace with the Chinese nation. But it proposed to hold those responsible for disorders in China to the "uttermost accountability." The purpose of the President was to protect American interests in China and to prevent the recurrence of such disasters as had now overwhelmed the government at Peking. The policy of the United States aimed

> to seek a solution which may bring about permanent safety and peace

to China, preserve Chinese territorial and administrative entity, protect all rights guaranteed to friendly Powers by treaty and international law, and safeguard for the world the principle of equal and impartial trade with all parts of the Chinese Empire.[11]

The Russian Government gave statements similar in content but objected to the idea that the Japanese had received a mandate to settle the whole Boxer rebellion. This, of course, was quite untrue for no power, not even the Japanese, had thought of their receiving any mandate at all. The matter of a unified command was also taken up and it was settled that Count Waldersee should be appointed. It was doubtful, however, whether he would arrive from Germany in time. On the whole the long period of the siege passed without any serious division of opinion among the powers, though at the outset the American naval forces refused to participate in the attack on the Taku forts. This was on instruction from Washington.[12]

In the meantime Secretary Hay tried to re-establish communication with Mr. Conger at Peking. A message through roundabout Chinese routes received on June 27 seemed to indicate that the Ministers were all right on June 18. Ten days passed and the press was full of reports of a terrible massacre of foreigners at Peking. On July 11, Secretary Hay sent a brief and unsigned message to Mr. Conger through the Chinese Legation at Washington saying: "Communicate tidings bearer." No reply was ever received. Yet the Chinese authorities, themselves, were able to send in requests to the United States. For example Li Hung Chang proposed that a guarantee of the territorial integrity of China should be secured by action of the United States. To this Secretary Hay replied by sending a copy of his note of July 3. Then on July 19, at the very time when the Department was still endeavoring to find means of communication with Mr. Conger, there came a long telegram signed by the *fainéant* Emperor of China to the President. This message Secretary Hay received as genuine; indeed his personal relations with Wu Ting-Fang at Washington were such that a message was

received indicating that Mr. Conger was still alive on July
18. This came at the time when the British were planning
a memorial service in St. Paul's Cathedral in honor of the
British who, it was supposed, had been killed at Peking. The
plan for this service was now abandoned; and Secretary Hay,
on July 21, sent a test message through Wu Ting-Fang
asking as a proof of the authenticity of the alleged message
from Mr. Conger that he telegraph the name of his sister.
The British, however, doubted the authenticity of the Emperor's message and of the telegram from Mr. Conger.
Their last word had been from Sir Claude McDonald, the
British Minister at Peking, by a letter dated July 4 and sent
to Tientsin. Count Lamsdorff, Russian Foreign Secretary,
well summed up the whole situation as follows:

> We were at present dealing with a country which was in a complete state of anarchy, and which had no government or constituted authority which it could be useful to menace, or even address, but we were in a state of war with anarchists, and not with China.[13]

The suspicion of a trap was further illustrated when on
July 24 a proposal came through to the Chinese Legation
that in view of the fact that the legations were all right on
July 18 provisions should be supplied them and a plan devised whereby the besieged could be escorted to Tientsin.
If that were done, it was further proposed that the movement by troops of the powers should stop. Mr. Adee wrote
to Secretary Hay:

> If this "incommunicacion" keeps up longer, and especially if it should last until the Tsungli Yamen announces the departure of the legationers from Peking "under escort," a grave foreboding of deceit and treachery would be only too legitimate, and the outcome only too possible.[14]

The fear lest the foreigners might be massacred *en route*
to safety did not, however, affect the reply of the President
to the Emperor of China. That weak tool in the hands of
the reactionary group at Peking had recalled the friendly
relations long subsisting between China and the United
States and had suggested that America take the initiative

to bring about the restoration of order and peace in China. The President telegraphed that if the rebels in China were responsible for the outrages there the Emperor should give assurance that the people of the legations were alive, give them freedom of communication, and co-operate with the relief expedition for the restoration of order. When these objects should be accomplished American good offices, with the assent of the other powers, would be exercised.¹⁵

To such terms the Chinese authorities could not bring themselves. In truth, as the fact of the relief expedition began to become real, the Chinese Government sought by every device to put off the certainty of dire punishment. Li Hung Chang again tried to mediate through Wu Ting-Fang who saw Secretary Hay on July 29. He planned to put the Ministers in Peking in communication with their governments or to deliver them under safe escort at Tientsin. Mr. Hay, however, told the Chinese Minister that:

> We could not consent to any such arrangement as the latter alternative, that if the Chinese Government was able to send them safely to Tientsin, it was able to put us into free communication with them, that if the Chinese Government undertook without previous arrangement to deliver them and failed by any accident, nothing would convince the foreign Governments that the Chinese had acted in good faith.
>
> He finally consented to telegraph Li again today, urging that the Ministers be put in communication with their Governments before any attempt is made to take them to Tientsin.
>
> He is greatly perturbed in spirit but seems to be acting squarely with us. He admits there are many things he cannot explain. He does not attempt to account for the silence of the legations, but believes the Ministers, except Ketteler, are alive.¹⁶

Perhaps one of the most absurd messages of the time came from the Chinese Governor of Shanghai transmitting a message from the Chinese authorities in Peking. This read:

> Foreign Ministers in Peking are all safe and well. Recently vegetables, fruit and provisions have been repeatedly supplied to them. Relations most friendly. At present consultations are going on for the protection of various Ministers going to Tientsin for temporary shelter, which will soon be concluded satisfactorily. But

as fighting is going on in Tientsin, it is inexpedient that cipher telegrams should be sent. Different Consuls have been notified so that they may inform their respective Governments. Please inform the Foreign Office.[17]

The provisions referred to were few; the legations were at that time under a furious bombardment; while both the Ministers and their respective Foreign Offices were refusing to trust this Chinese offer. The refusal to permit cipher communication was, of course, a continued impertinence.

On August 8 this was finally permitted. Word was also received from Mr. Conger that the proposed removal to Tientsin was looked on as "certain death." In peremptory fashion, therefore, the Chinese Minister was informed that the authorities at Peking should enter into co-operation with the relief expedition. This was received by him in some confusion.[18]

Now in quick succession, as the relief column advanced nearer and nearer to Peking, came repeated suggestions that the foreign troops should be halted before entering Peking. Indeed Li Hung Chang showed that he was playing a double game for, while he urged that the troops should be stopped, he privately informed the Japanese that he hoped the foreign expedition would enter Peking, cut off the retreat of the Imperial authorities, and at the conclusion of peace insist on the full reform of the Chinese government.[19] Such double dealing, while perhaps to be expected, got short shrift. The basis of a compromise was offered by the Department of State in the proposal that if hostilities should cease, a sufficient body of troops should be permitted to enter Peking and then return to Tientsin escorting the foreign population. Such arrangements were, however, quickly upset by the news of the arrival of the relief expedition at Peking. The Empress Dowager was now in full flight; and Li Hung Chang was appointed plenipotentiary to negotiate a settlement. Thus the relief of the legations was accomplished. The story of the siege does not, of course, enter into this account. We must now turn to the settlement with China.[20]

The advance of the relief forces had led to cruelty and looting; some of the punitive expeditions, which were to take place later, cannot be justified. Indeed, in many respects the white man in China did not make a good showing in the autumn of 1900. Yet we must remember the desperate strain of the long siege and the natural desire for adequate punishment, if not for revenge, which were prevalent at the time. At all events American troops were, for the most part, shown to be guiltless of the charge of inhuman conduct which was later made against the relief expedition as a whole. Now we once more approach diplomacy.

Henry Adams says that Secretary Hay "suddenly ignored European leadership, took the lead himself, rescued the legations and saved China. . . ." While this alleged feat was being performed Adams was in Europe and Secretary Hay was ill up in New Hampshire. To be sure the Secretary was in almost hourly communication with Washington and frequently was on the wire with President McKinley at Canton, Ohio. Yet the brunt of the work was borne by Mr. Adee, who until October 1, 1900, had been acting Secretary for the previous two months. Secretary Hay was foremost in recognizing Adee's admirable and unselfish work. So we can on the whole disregard this fulsome verdict of Adams and return to a more judicious use of the documents in the case. Yet we might well accept a judgment of Adams given in a previous paragraph of his autobiography when he wrote:

> The drama of the Legations interested the public much as though it were a novel of Alexandre Dumas, but the bearing of the drama on future history offered an interest vastly greater. Adams knew no more about it than though he were the best informed statesman in Europe. Like them all, he took for granted that the Legations were massacred, and that John Hay, who alone championed China's "administrative entity," would be massacred too, since he must henceforth look on, in impotence, while Russia and Germany dismembered China, and shut up America at home. Nine statesmen out of ten, in Europe, accepted this result in advance, seeing no way to prevent it. Adams saw none, and laughed at Hay for his helplessness.[21]

We have seen the close nip and tuck of the relief of the legations. The miracle indeed was not that the expedition reached Peking; but that the Chinese themselves did not vigorously attack when they could well have done so and thus successfully wipe out the beleaguered foreigners. Now in Peking, indeed in northern China, all was confusion. The foreign troops were in Peking; but what were they to do? Everyone was clamoring for retribution and settlement; but with whom could they settle? The Imperial court was in flight; many of the Boxer leaders had escaped from Peking; and punishment would now probably fall chiefly on the innocent. Fortunately there were a few, a very few, cool heads in China and in Washington. Secretary Adee had written cheerfully to Hay, who was prostrate at his country home, making his usual puns and jokes and then exclaiming as the moment of relief approached: "God! What a strain this suspense is!" [22] Then came the long burden of diplomatic adjustment and decision.

First of all was the suggestion by Russia that, since there was no one in Peking with whom to treat, the troops and legation staffs should retire to Tientsin, where war ships at Taku could readily assist in their protection. Furthermore, there was the question of the diplomatic status of Li Hung Chang. Was he empowered to negotiate for the Emperor of China and should he be free to communicate with the Imperial Court? There were many other aspects of the situation as well which faced the powers. Merely to list them would require time and might confuse us. As we are not dealing with diplomatic history at large, but chiefly with America's part in the tangled matter, it may be well to confine our general summary to the American views of the situation. In any case, as many of the essential documents are in print, it will be necessary only to bring out what is as yet unpublished. At the end of July, 1900, Mr. Rockhill had been named a special agent of the Department of State to go to China as Commissioner. On August 23 Mr. Adee telegraphed him at Yokohama:

Go to Peking at once. Send us full information of conditions there, and generally in China. Conger and Chaffee are informed of diplomatic events since you sailed. It may be important that you go soon to Shanghai and endeavor to secure full assurances of effective protection and order from Viceroys of Southern and Eastern China. Nanking Viceroys have already pledged protection in a telegram received through Chinese Minister dated twenty-first. Your views are requested as to this.[23]

Conditions were such that it was impossible for Mr. Rockhill to go to Peking "at once." Indeed when he got to Shanghai he was delayed there for some time because of lack of transportation, even to Tientsin. While in Japan Mr. Rockhill saw Viscount Aoki, Japanese Foreign Secretary, and Marquis Ito. From them he gained the impression that,

though Japan was heartily in sympathy with the American policy in China and would endeavor—with the assistance of Great Britain —to make it prevail, it might be forced by the action of the other Powers to take part in demanding a cession of territory from China. They both seemed to think that the independent position of the United States placed it in a position to take a leading part in formulating some basis for negotiations acceptable to all the Powers.[24]

From Shanghai Mr. Rockhill wrote of his interviews with Li Hung Chang and of the attitude of Baron von Mumm, who had been sent to take the place of von Ketteler, the German Minister at Peking, murdered by the Chinese. The letter reads, in part:

I have seen Li Hung Chang twice. He was very rough, so impolite in the second interview that I had to stop the conversation. Nothing of any importance was said beyond what I cabled you. He seemed very anxious that some Power should recognize him as plenipotentiary. He said he did not care when negotiations began. He expressed surprise at the fact that the Chinese Minister in Washington who had advised the D. of S. of the return of his credentials, early in July I think he said, had received no reply from you. I said the inference he must draw was that you were not ready to answer him. When he asked me of the policy of the U. S. I referred to the President's letter of July 23d. He knew the contents of your circular of July 3d. Referring to his promise he said he had asked the Russians to withdraw their force to Tientsin to negotiate from there, he asked if the U. S. would do likewise, if all the Powers also would. I told him that the U. S. were no more hostile to China than the other Powers and that we had shown our friendliness by the "open door" correspondence. With that the subject dropped.

Much apprehension is felt here as to the course the Germans will follow when the whole of this expeditionary force has arrived. Von Mumm told me Germany would not ask, if not forced to by other Powers, for further cession of territory. It would demand, however, the death of Tuan and all others guilty of promoting the hostilities and the death of Ketteler, the expenses incurred for the expedition and guarantees for its subjects, their rights, property, etc., as insured them by treaty. He is instructed not to see Li or have anything to do with him.

Peking is still practically cut off from the rest of China, no news of any kind, either from the Legations or private individuals has been received here. Goodnow has got two telegrams from Conger since August 15th. I not a word. Mumm has been telegraphing to Peking every day without eliciting a reply. With whom the fault lies is not known. I am very sorry I should have been delayed here so long, but as things go very slowly in this benighted land perhaps it does not matter much. I am packed and ready to leave at an hour's notice.[25]

The question whether Li Hung Chang should be accepted as Chinese plenipotentiary now became acute. The Admirals of the foreign naval forces at Taku had apparently taken action to limit the communication between Li Hung Chang and his government. The American Admiral Remey had, however, dissented. Under the circumstances Russia asked the United States to take steps to clear up the matter for, if Li Hung Chang were to act as plenipotentiary, it was essential that he should be in free communication with the authorities. This was accomplished as quickly as possible but nevertheless of course it took time.[26]

On the major question as to who should negotiate for China the powers were quite divided. Russia, and finally France, were in favor of accepting Li Hung Chang, as was also Japan. The Austrian and Italian Governments naturally followed the lead of Germany, whose views were given in a telegram from Mr. Jackson at the American Embassy in Berlin:

The position which is maintained by the German Government

is that there is at present no authoritative Government in China. The Viceroys are not considered as having authority to speak for China, or in the name of the existing Chinese Government, whatsoever that may be. Li Hung Chang is regarded with special suspicion, and the German authorities are not inclined to negotiate with him, as it is not known at present whose plenipotentiary he is or what powers he has.[27]

Great Britain was also doubtful and cautious. Lord Salisbury was not satisfied that Li Hung Chang was authorized to negotiate for China; but England cared little as to who should represent the Chinese government provided he were properly accredited. Germany seized on this and instructed the German Ambassador in London to induce the British Government to refuse to accept Li Hung Chang. This failed, for five days later the Germans were told that England favored and the United States "insisted on" Li Hung Chang as a negotiator. This victory for the American point of view had more behind it than appears on the surface. In early August the Department of State had recognized the importance of securing from China a *bona fide* representative and had consequently approved of the appointment of Li Hung Chang. If now the view of the United States should be upset by Germany the value of the moral leadership of America would be damaged at the outset. The notes which passed in the matter were from the pen of Mr. Adee and this initial success must have encouraged him. By successive stages, which it is not now necessary to follow, the German opposition gave way and on September 17 the United States accepted "the plenipotentiary authority of Earl Li Hung Chang and Prince Ching as *prima facie* sufficient for the preliminary negotiations" to secure the return of the Imperial Court to Peking and "toward the negotiation of a complete settlement" between the powers and China.[28]

Meantime a telegram of August 28, had come from Mr. Conger, who was still in ignorance of the general policy of his government as laid down in Secretary Hay's circular note of July 3, 1900. He cabled:

I have to suggest that a commissioner with full powers should be ready as soon as authorized representatives of Chinese Government appear. Prince Ching is expected in a few days, and Li early arrival probable first of all. The chief patrons and leaders of the Boxers must be punished. Then the best possible government should be established as quick as possible with proper foreign supervision. Important China should give sufficient guarantee for payment of indemnities and assurance of peace and order for the future. If it is not done speedily the partition of China is inevitable. It is possible that foreign claims are so large already as only can be paid by cession of territory. Military occupation by so many powers is creating irreparable devastation, and bringing terrible punishment upon innocent people; and if long continued will arouse such hatred among the people as to render the situation very difficult, and induce uprising against all foreigners in peaceable provinces. There are now here thirty thousand troops. If they remain this winter famine will ensue.[29]

At the same time the Russian Government had put forward another suggestion, viz.: that the United States should follow the Russian policy of withdrawing the legation staff and Russian troops from Peking to Tientsin. To this Mr. Adee replied in an important note, which although it has been printed, is given in the Appendix to this chapter. Mr. Adee welcomed the assurances of Russia that she did not wish to seize Chinese territory and noted that she now proposed to withdraw her troops, and wait till a later time to negotiate with China. But he suggested that the other powers might not agree to a joint withdrawal, and said it would be wiser to wait until a concurrent withdrawal could take place.[30]

Of course this Russian plan would have been very offensive to Germany; and it might well have duplicated the Russian success of 1860; for then she had secured the cession by China of the right bank of the Amur River on the plea that she had persuaded England and France to withdraw their expeditionary forces from Peking. Furthermore, it might give Russia special opportunity for private negotiations with China. Consequently the Department of State was both puzzled and disturbed. As far as Germany was concerned the appointment of General von Waldersee to command the foreign troops in China had been accompanied by an outburst of acclaim in Germany. The Kaiser had quite outdone himself in speeches and telegrams. Now if the troops were to be withdrawn from Peking even before von Waldersee could reach China where would be his army, what would be his position, and what would become of the Kaiser's instructions to his soldiers to behave like Huns in China? As Alfred Rothschild said in London at the time: *"c'est le ridicule qui tue."* The question was should the United States advise concurrent withdrawal or not?

The Department of State had really postponed a decision as to withdrawal. In the meantime the Secretary of War, Mr. Root, wrote a jovial letter to Secretary Hay, saying in part:

> How will you swap a murdered Old English alliance for a nice new clean Russian article painted yellow?
> I hope you take the frustration of your hellish designs with complacency and are recovering your appetite for New Hampshire farms.
> It appears that diplomacy as viewed from the opposition American standpoint has but two phases. If we agree with any other power on any subject there is a secret alliance; if we disagree there is a conspiracy to get up a war and foster a soldier on the back of every American laborer.[31]

The President was also drawn into the question for in Canton, Ohio, he received an impassioned letter from Senator Morgan begging him to withdraw American troops from China and to hold them in the Philippines. He said: "As we are not willing to share in Chinese government, or to accept a cession of territory, or the suzerainty that is falsely called a 'sphere of influence,' it is not our right or duty to participate in such arrangements, in combination with other powers" and much more to the same effect.[32]

The result was that the Department telegraphed to Mr. Conger asking whether in case the American troops should be withdrawn from Peking our Legation should remain there.[33] Before an answer could be received our London Embassy was informed that the Boxer movement was far from crushed and that unless severe punishment were inflicted on the guilty Chinese a renewal of the recent crisis might be expected.[34] Nevertheless, President McKinley wrote to Secretary Hay on September 14, showing how strongly Senator Morgan's letter had affected him and saying:

> The question as to when and how to get out of China is the serious one of course and I know of no way to get out but to come out. I am anxious that when we do come out we shall give the proper diplomatic notice to the powers co-operating there; but how that should be done I am not so clear. I talked with Dr. Hill about it. He had no suggestion to make. I assume that all we need to do is to say to the powers that we intend to withdraw to Tientsin our Legation and our army, leaving the time of our withdrawal from Tientsin to be determined later on. I have this general notion that we should now get out of Peking with the least possible delay. Russia is intending to withdraw and we should in accordance with our note, even if there was no other reason, and I think there are many reasons why we should come out. We want to avoid being in Peking for a long time and it must be a long time if we stay there for the diplomatic negotiations, and without our intending it, we may be drawn into currents that would be unfortunate.[35]

In face of this there came that same day two cables from Mr. Conger and General Chaffee. Mr. Conger telegraphed:

> Your telegram containing Russian declaration and your reply is received. Russia is now withdrawing larger part of her forces. This action, withdrawing Minister and landing forces New Chwang, indicate purpose to make their settlement in their own way. For the present the restoration of Chinese authority in Peking or order in this province [Chili] is impossible. Joint military occupation of Peking is absolutely essential to successful negotiations, and should continue until completed. One third of the present force will be sufficient. From my acquaintance with Prince Ching and Earl Li, I do not believe they can offer any feasible plan. Foreign powers must devise it. Hence the necessity of their early conference and agreement.[36]

Secretary Hay had telegraphed the President on September 11, saying: "we should withdraw our troops from Peking as soon as possible, though there is the danger lest the Chinese might accept this as a sign of weakness, but a firm attitude on the negotiations ought to correct that impression." Now, after reading the cables from Peking, he telegraphed again to the President on September 17, that,

> Your letter of the 14th received today. My personal inclination is entirely in accordance with your views. I am most anxious to get out at the earliest possible moment. Adee has sent me Conger's despatch of the 12th. It is difficult in the face of such a despatch [from Conger] to order immediate withdrawal. If the Emperor can be induced to return to Peking at once there ought to be a sufficient foreign guard left there to protect him and to preserve the peace. Unless Russia withdraws her entire force I do not think we are bound to withdraw ours. We are still free to act according to our own judgment and the requirements of the military situation.
>
> The immediate thing to do is for Conger and Rockhill to decide whether Li and Ching have adequate powers to treat and next to get the Emperor to come to Peking. If to accomplish this it shall seem advisable to diminish the foreign force in Peking we should use our influence to have this done.
>
> If as I fear the other powers are not yet ready to begin serious negotiations in Peking, it will be necessary to call a conference to decide upon terms to be presented to the Chinese Government. All these considerations lead me to think we are not yet ready at this moment to withdraw our troops and our Legation from Peking.[37]

By this narrow margin was the Kaiser saved from the humiliation of seeing his general deprived of a large part of his troops. As Mr. Adee wrote to Secretary Hay: "The whirligig has tumbled over on a new face today, and we are in the throes of another crisis." The President had just made up his mind to order General Chaffee to the Philippines and Mr. Conger to Shanghai when the two cables came in. This must have pleased Mr. Adee for, as his letter shows, he had always been in favor of keeping the troops at Peking. But of this we may better judge from the letter which is printed in the Appendix to this chapter.[38]

Alongside of Mr. Adee's letter there is another letter from Secretary Hay, which because of the freedom of some of his expressions, Mr. Adee thought, in 1907 "might well lie mouldering for a century or two." It is to be found in the Appendix to this chapter. A few days later, as Secretary Hay began to feel better in health and in spirits, he wrote to Mr. Whitelaw Reid:

About China, it is the devil's own mess. We cannot possibly publish all the facts without breaking off relations. We shall have to do the best we can, and take the consequences—which will be pretty serious, I do not doubt. "Give and take,"—the axiom of diplomacy to the rest of the world,—is positively forbidden to us, by both the Senate and public opinion. We must take what we can and give nothing—which greatly narrows our possibilities.

I take it, you agree with us that we are to limit as far as possible our military operations in China, to withdraw our troops at the earliest day consistent with our obligations, and in the final adjustment to do everything we can for the integrity and reform of China, and to hold on like grim death to the open door. . . .[39]

Now came the German note of September 18, 1900, which as Mr. Adee said "was a bomb in the allied camp." It proposed, as a preliminary to negotiation, that the Chinese Government should surrender to the foreign powers such persons as were "the first and real perpetrators of the crimes committed in Peking against international law, . . . for indifference toward the idea of a just expiation would be equivalent to indifference toward a repetition of the crime." Regarding this Mr. Adee promptly wrote Secretary Hay that:

The devil of the matter is that Germany's proposal to demand the surrender of the criminal leaders to the Powers for punishment by the Powers upsets much of what we are doing and endeavoring to do. No punishment can be effective toward a permanent settlement which is not decreed and carried out by the Emperor. For Waldersee to hang or shoot Tuan would make Tuan a demi-god to the Chinese. It is the Imperial degradation that tells—making the offender *anathema maranatha*.[40]

This very idea was, in diplomatic language, expressed in the American reply which stated the desire of the United States "to hold to the uttermost accountability the responsible authors of any wrongs done in China to citizens of the United States" but declared that the German proposal must be rejected. Fortunately a few days later news came of a Chinese Imperial edict of September 25 planning and proposing the severe punishment of those guilty of crimes. This sufficed to postpone the necessity of a decision as to the German proposal. But Mr. Adee summed up the general situation when he wrote on September 24:

> 1. Japan straddles, but will probably come round to our way of looking at it.
> 2. England is reflecting in the brain of Salisbury. He won't advise anything—only objects.
> 3. Austria accepts German proposition without reserve.
> 4. France has not been directly heard from, notwithstanding what the papers say about her flat refusal to listen to the Kaiser, who kindly repeats, etc. Jackson's telegram of the 22nd, which I sent you on Saturday, says France accepts unconditionally. I think it is very likely, after Delcassé's gory utterances for the past two months. You may remember that Mr. Conger, in his telegram of the 6th said "The Austrian Minister will insist on execution of Prince Tuan and others before serious negotiations begin, which is practically impossible." The cipher was boggled, and it read "The Eduadorian Minister." The change of one digit makes it read either "French" or "Austrian" so you have your choice. "French" now seems the most probable.
> 5. Italy has not yet peeped to us, but as Germany pulls the strings of the Italian monkey I think that what Jackson said in his cable of the 22nd is true and that the amiable creature dances to the tune of the German organ.
> 6. The Russian reply comes tonight, and I send it herewith. It is somewhat vague as to the German proposal, but as seen through Pierce's eyes it appears to be in complete accord with our view.
>
> So it stands: four certain for the German demand (Austria, Italy, France and Germany); two against it (Russia and the United States); one reflecting; and one straddling (Japan).[41]

In this summary I think that Mr. Adee was a bit hasty as regards England, for, as can be seen from later telegrams of Mr. Henry White in London, Great Britain was perhaps somewhat slow in her decisions, but on all of these questions she finally stood squarely with the United States. As his return to Washington approached, Secretary Hay wrote: "There is still plenty of trouble ahead in China, but it is a comfort to feel that thus far there have been no mistakes." [42] This was by way of a tribute to Mr. Adee. Both of them, therefore, faced the next problem.

This was a memorandum from France which might serve as the basis of negotiation with China. To this French plan the United States acceded with several minor reservations. It was pointed out that the Chinese had already indicated their intention to punish those responsible for disorders and it was quite possible that the representatives of the powers might add other names to the list. As long as the interdiction against the importation of arms was not made permanent the details of the negotiations might be taken up at Peking. In the case of indemnities the United States supported the Russian suggestion that any divergence of views might be referred to The Hague for arbitration. As to legation guards, Congress alone had the power to determine that; but as a temporary measure the United States had already provided for the protection of her legation. The President reserved his opinion as to the dismantling of the Chinese forts at Taku and as to the military occupation of several forts on the road from Tientsin to Peking. As the other powers agreed with the main French proposals Secretary Hay sought to use the occasion "to preserve the territorial integrity and the administrative entity of China, and to secure for the Chinese nation and for themselves the benefits of open and equal commercial intercourse between the Chinese Empire and the world at large." [43]

For the moment also attention was concentrated on the open door in China by the news of the Anglo-German agreement of October 16, 1900. This seemed to be of great importance. Throughout the summer Germany had been following a policy of *real politik*. In the choice of a German commander for foreign troops in China, in the matter of preventing the sale of arms to China, and later in the proposal to occupy the province of Chili, German interests were foremost. Furthermore, as differences of opinion developed among the powers, the German Foreign Office repeatedly strove to foment these and to profit by them; at all events it was clear that either willfully or through sheer stupidity American foreign policy was entirely misunderstood by Germany. It was difficult for Germany to believe that in the matter of the proposal to withdraw foreign troops from

China, as had been suggested by Russia, that the United States was really floundering about in search of a decision. We have but just seen by what a narrow margin Senator Morgan's views had failed of acceptance. If the United States had withdrawn her troops from China she would have played directly into the hands of Russia and would have mortally offended Germany. In reality President McKinley in his ignorance was only thinking of the effect on American opinion.

Great Britain was anxious at this time to assert her claim to a sphere of influence in the basin of the Yangtze Kiang. She was also keen to secure continental support against Russian expansion in the Far East. She was willing, therefore, to turn to Germany for assistance. Earlier, in 1898, she had sounded the United States and even Japan with regard to a general agreement as to the open door; but as we have seen nothing came of these suggestions. For purely selfish reasons, therefore, Germany was on the side of the open door during these months. To prevent Great Britain from asserting any exclusive monopoly in the Yangtze region she entered into negotiations with her. At the same time she consulted Russia and later agreed with Great Britain to the declaration of the open door in China, omitting Manchuria, which was of course the special region of Russian interests. Then Germany began to play on Anglo-American trade rivalry and insinuated to England that the United States was "aiming at monopolizing trade with China and in general at treating the Pacific Ocean as an American inland sea." To the Americans, the "open door" was merely a "transitory stage"; the real "instincts" of America were "protectionist and almost prohibitionist." [44]

Under these circumstances Lord Salisbury, who was failing rapidly in strength, was persuaded to agree to the omission of Manchuria from the agreement. Later von Reventlow wrote that the failure of Germany to join a declaration which included Manchuria was the beginning of the break between England and Germany. Whether he was right or not British public opinion was later much offended at von Bülow's categorical denial that Manchuria was in any way involved. The agreement, as signed on October 16, 1900, provided for the open door in China and pledged the two countries not to take any advantage of the present complications in that country to secure for themselves any territory. The third article of the convention, however, stated that in case another power should press China to secure "under any form whatever such territorial advantages" Germany and Great Britain reserved to themselves the right to consult with each other and to take such steps as might be necessary for the protection of their own interests. The other powers were to be invited to accept the principles of this accord.[45]

The blunt comment of the Duke of Devonshire on the agreement was borne out by its history. He said: "I do not understand how Lord Salisbury came to give way to Bülow's wish to exclude Manchuria. In consequence of this restriction the whole agreement is not worth the paper it is written on." [46] Germany did not wish to offend Russia by including Manchuria; but she wished to make sure of German trade in the Yangtze Kiang basin, for she did not think much of Secretary Hay's open door notes. The news of this Anglo-German agreement seems to have surprised the world, but Secretary Hay set to work at once to try to discover whether anything lay back of the third article. He found there was nothing; yet he seems to have been of two minds regarding the whole matter. To his wife he wrote happily enough, and, at the time, addressed Adams in the same vein:

> The Anglo-German pact was a bomb-shell here. None of the diplomats know anything about it. My British people say it is a victory for Germany and Russia. Choate can't get a word out of Salisbury. Pauncefote thinks it all right and apologizes for infringing my copyright. I quoted your *mot* about the dearest wish of your heart being to be pirated. All of the powers seem to be shy, except Japan, who plunged in boldly and said they were into the game, third clause and all—I imagine a little to the consternation of the two signatories.
>
> Our position was a matter of course. We can't make alliances,

THE BOXER MOVEMENT

but we can't object to other powers making alliances to do our chores for us.⁴⁷

His second thoughts, however, forced him strongly to the earlier conclusion of the Duke of Devonshire. So we turn once more to the situation in China. The French proposals had been referred to the diplomatic corps at Peking and during November and December they endeavored to formulate the precise demands which should be made to the Chinese government. The first question discussed was the punishment of people guilty of promoting disorders during the Boxer rebellion. Here the representatives of the powers nearly wrecked the diplomatic harmony which was so essential. The German government proposed that an ultimatum or irrevocable demand should be made to the Chinese authorities that certain persons should be put to death. The list included princes of the blood and persons of high rank and station.

The American, Japanese and Russian Foreign Offices were frankly opposed to these terms. President McKinley on October 27, 1900, wrote to Secretary Hay deprecating the idea of an "ultimatum." He said that before an ultimatum of this sort should be sent "the Chinese government should be afforded an opportunity for the punishment of the malefactors, which may be as full and complete as that required by the proposed ultimatum." ⁴⁸ The Japanese pointed out that such a step might be met simply by a *non possumus* on the part of the Chinese; and the Russians held similar views. The French and the members of the Triple Alliance on the other hand were blood-thirsty. Thus the British gradually swung round in support of the American view. So the term "ultimatum" was dropped.⁴⁹

Attempts to modify still further the terms of the demand were, however, blocked, except for the substitution of "the severest punishment" for the "penalty of death." The United States still protested against the words "irrevocable conditions" as being too nearly an "ultimatum." But by error in transmission of a cypher message Mr. Conger supposed that the American government had given way; thus unanimity was finally secured. Secretary Hay was, however, much irritated over the episode; he was also worried over the insertion of a clause which seemed to require that American troops should remain in Peking until these "irrevocable conditions" should be fulfilled. Altogether December, 1900, was an irritating month for him since it also saw the adoption of the wrecking amendments by the Senate to the first Hay-Pauncefote treaty.[50]

It had taken about two months merely to draw up the joint note presented to the Chinese authorities in the end of December, 1900.[51] This demanded that suitable steps be taken by the government of China because of the murders of the German Minister and a Japanese Counsellor of Legation and then elaborated somewhat the bases laid down in the French plan for negotiations of the previous October. The fact remained that only the preliminaries had been determined.[52]

Small wonder, therefore, that Secretary Hay chafed at the delays. Furthermore, as news came in of the excesses of the military punitive expeditions in the countryside, and as plans were discussed for further European invasions of the southern provinces which had remained quiet during the disorders in the north, the dangers of the situation became more evident.

The bellicose von Mumm at Peking and the restless German Admiral at Shanghai became real perils to the policy of the powers. Furthermore, friction was rapidly developing particularly between the Russian and British troops in China. Gradually two camps were forming—the American, the British and the Japanese drew together, as the European continental states began to forget their political animosities and find that their military traditions constituted a common bond which promoted forays for loot and blood.[53]

On January 3, 1901, therefore, Secretary Hay proposed that the question of indemnities and of amending the existing treaties should be settled either at Washington or in some

European capital. This plan was quickly vetoed by Germany and Japan and consequently failed. The British also were opposed to it. After this American failure there seemed nothing to do but to keep on negotiating at Peking.[54]

A much more serious prospect was also opened up by the desire of one or more of the powers to negotiate separately with China regarding questions of indemnity and concessions. At Peking matters had hitherto been on a common table. Now if each country were to go off into a separate room to discuss the situation with his Chinese vis-à-vis there might be little left of China at the end. Foreseeing such a tendency Secretary Hay had already telegraphed to Mr. Conger:

> We favor securing foreign rights at treaty ports by adequate foreign concessions either separate for the nations interested or as international settlement but forcible appropriation under claim of conquest conflicts with declared purpose of the powers and disturbs their harmonious action. Your protest is approved. We think the matter should be adjusted as part of general arrangement in which the right of the United States of America to impartial share should be reserved.[55]

This of course referred only to grants for settlements at treaty ports; now Mr. Conger reported a more serious development on the part of Russia and he feared lest Germany might follow suit. He wrote:

> The Russian Minister has several times said to me that, after these preliminaries are arranged, each power should settle all other questions, including indemnities, amendments to treaties, etc., by separate negotiations and in its own way; that Russia had no interest in indemnity for missionary losses, nor missionary work, etc., etc. Every step which Russia has taken since the capture of Peking leads along this line. The withdrawal of her troops, the temporary retirement of her Minister, the occupation of Newchwang, and the agreement made for the partial disarming of Manchuria and for a supervisory protectorate by Russian officials,—a copy of which I enclose—the arrangement for securing a permanent concession at Tientsin, and the presence here of Prince Ouhktomsky, conferring constantly with Li Hung Chang, together with the appointment of Mr. Yang Ju as a plenipotentiary for the proposed final treaty, confirm beyond

a doubt Russia's intention to withdraw, or at least conduct separate negotiations.⁵⁶

Mr. Rockhill was even more frank in his statement of the situation, saying:

I have spoken to both Sir Ernest Satow and Mumm about Russia's action in Manchuria; they both recognize the grave danger it presents, but do not seem to see their way to avert it. Komura, the Japanese Minister, as I telegraphed you, is at least preparing to do something, but I fear that Russia will be able to offer such satisfaction to Japan as will cause her to withdraw her protest while not interfering in the least with her plan in Manchuria. Pichon, the French Minister, tells me that he has openly expressed to his Government his strong objections to Russian policy in China, which he considers opposed to French interests, but of course nothing will come of his objections. . . .

Another letter read:

I omitted mentioning that Sir Ernest Satow told me that Li Hung Chang had suggested to him (last Friday I think) in conversation that the powers demand of China communication of the negotiations now in progress between it and Russia. China, Li added, would be delighted to communicate them and place itself in the hands of the powers for protection against Russia whose demands it could not deny, and whose constant threats terrified it. Li had probably in mind the treaty of San Stefano when he suggested this—I wish history could in this case repeat itself.⁵⁷

The question of the attitude of the United States promptly arose from an inquiry on the part of Japan as to what our policy would be in view of this violation by Russia of her public pledges and promises, since Russian domination of Manchuria was involved. Here was a real test of what the United States meant by its Chinese policy and by its support of the "entity of China." Secretary Hay was obliged to reply that "we were not at present prepared to attempt singly, or in concert with other Powers, to enforce these views [our well-known view as to the integrity of China] in the east by any demonstration which could present a character of hostility to any other Power." ⁵⁸

Thus a large part of our Far Eastern policy was shown to

be unstable. We were not prepared to fight for what we knew was right. Then and there the future history of the Far East was determined for the next quarter century. Russia and later Japan were to seek to exploit Manchuria. The economic penetration of that province went hand in hand with the development of a railway policy. Thus repeated violations of the open door policy were accompanied by discrimination as to railway rates. The United States was unable and unwilling to go to war for the protection of China. The best we could do was occasionally to turn the searchlight of a diplomatic note on the situation. Such moral pressure was at times successful. At best it was a temporary expedient and it left the open door policy exposed to the vicissitudes of time.

Thus on February 19, 1901, by the slower and less spectacular processes of diplomacy the United States was able to bring such moral pressure to bear that the proposed Russian dominance in Manchuria was for the time prevented. A note was sent to the Chinese Minister, which reviewed the circumstances of the time and expressed the dislike of the United States for private negotiations and her "sense of the impropriety, inexpediency, and even extreme danger to the interests of China of considering any private territorial or financial arrangements, at least without the full knowledge and approval of all the Powers now engaged in negotiation." This note was also sent to all the interested states. It was issued just in time, for Mr. Rockhill sent a mournful despatch to Secretary Hay in early March prophesying the break-up of China. Yet from all sides came prompt acquiescence in the principles of the note. The Russian note of April 5, 1901, deserves full quotation for the irony of its final words should not be lost. It read:

> In continuation of the conversation which he had yesterday evening with the Secretary of State, the Ambassador of Russia has the honor to confirm to him the intentions of the Government of His Majesty the Emperor, which he has orally brought to the Secretary's attention. It vies with the erroneous interpretations occasioned

by the arrangements which have been projected with the purpose of the evacuation of Manchuria by the Russian troops. The Imperial Government does not insist upon its conclusion by the Chinese Government, and renounces all further negotiations on the subject. Remaining immovably faithful to its original program, which has been so many times declared, the Imperial Government will quietly await the further march of events.[59]

This Russian note did not prevent Secretary Hay from trying to nail down the idea of American commercial rights in Manchuria. On April 20, 1901, he wrote a note to Count Cassini saying that the President would be gratified if he could be assured by the Russian Government that American citizens would not suffer in their rights in any part of China or of Manchuria which might be affected by arrangements which Russia might make with China or with other governments. In other words, while the United States accepted the Russian declaration of April 5, she wished nevertheless to be especially assured once more that American interests would be recognized whatever might happen. A favorable reply was received from Count Lamsdorff on June 9.[60]

With regard to the smaller but no less important question of the enlargement of foreign settlements in China Secretary Hay also took action. This was directly provoked by the Russian claim to a large concession at Tientsin by right of military occupation and asserted conquest. The matter had come up several times before; but on February 16, 1901, notes were sent to the various powers saying that such questions were for international agreement and not for private negotiation. Here again the replies were in the main favorable; therefore the United States was at least partially successful.[61]

As the spring approached the military situation in China also became acute. For, on February 18, von Waldersee telegraphed the Kaiser that in March he planned a campaign well beyond the borders of Chili. In Washington and also in London there was alarm at the news. The President was much concerned to see the re-establishment of peace and normal relations and the "cessation of bloodshed." [62] From all sides, save Germany, came acquiescence and gradually the danger of military restlessness was averted. In reality this restlessness was largely due to the impatience of men of action with the dilatoriness and feeble efforts of the diplomats at Peking. These were in general a group of very ordinary men; they were without a leader and yet they faced a situation almost without precedent. So it was with great relief that the United States learned at the end of May that at last von Waldersee was to be recalled, as the anti-foreign disturbances in China had been suppressed. American troops, with the exception of a small legation guard, had long since been withdrawn; and everyone heaved a sigh of satisfaction at the news that other foreign contingents were to be reduced in similar fashion. Later troops were also withdrawn from Shanghai.[63]

Of course adequate plans for the protection of the legations had been drawn and accepted. These had occupied the attention of the military experts and the diplomats during the winter months of 1901. Regulations as to traffic in arms were still being discussed; but their necessity soon disappeared. In the meantime everyone at Peking was doing sums in arithmetic. Calculating the amount of indemnity from China was the progressive diplomatic game of the day. In January, 1901, it was supposed that the total figure would not exceed $200,000,000. Secretary Hay had advocated demanding a lump sum as indemnity; but he was then thinking of a figure in the neighborhood of $150,000,000. Sir Robert Hart had thought that China's capacity to pay could not exceed about $250,000,000. In the end the powers asked for the colossal figure of $333,000,000 (gold), which might have been even larger if it had not been for the moderating efforts of the United States. Of course if such a heavy bill of damages were to be collected from China the question of tariffs and commercial treaties was at once raised. These commercial matters, however, were postponed for later consideration.

So we must now turn briefly to the indemnity problem.

The American plan of having China pay a fixed lump sum of about $200,000,000 based upon China's ability to pay was first discussed. This did not get very far. Indeed it was described by von Mumm as a hypocritical claim: for the United States had also proposed that $25,000,000 should be allotted as the American share of the indemnity. The German Minister said that America would make a handsome profit by such a claim.[64] On May 1, an elaborate report on China's ability to pay was presented to the diplomatic corps at Peking. There followed discussions as to how the total sum of $333,000,000 was to be paid. France wished to provide for a huge loan to China; Russia proposed that the indemnity should be guaranteed by the Powers and, earlier, she had also indicated her desire that the entire question of indemnity should be submitted to the Hague Tribunal. This the United States had favored; but it met with such opposition from Germany and other states that it was dropped. The United States was, however, at first opposed to the plan of guaranty by the powers. Endeavors to scale down the total also failed. Indeed in the negotiations regarding the indemnity the United States was flatly defeated. Finally it was agreed that bonds bearing four per cent interest should be issued, to be redeemed by China in thirty-nine years. The revenues assigned as security for the bonds were from the Imperial maritime customs, the native customs, and nearly the total of the salt gabelle.[65]

As to securing a larger revenue for China Secretary Hay was at first in favor of raising the effective customs from five per cent to 10 or even 15 per cent effective. As a matter of fact the duty was only nominally five per cent and in reality was merely 3.17 per cent. When Great Britain opposed this the best that could be secured was a real five per cent customs duty. Indeed when the colossal figure of the indemnity was clear Secretary Hay reversed his views and opposed an increase beyond five per cent especially as likin, or local duties were not abolished. The appointments of specialists to deal with the revision of Chinese tariffs followed these negotiations; but it is for the present unnecessary to follow such matters further.[66]

The terms as finally agreed on by the powers and accepted by China were embodied in a protocol signed at Peking on September 7, 1901. A convenient summary which I copy is given by Mr. Dennett in his *Americans in Eastern Asia*:

1. apology to Germany for the murder of Baron Ketteler, and the erection of a memorial to him at the place where he was shot;
2. punishment of Chinese officials responsible for the insurrection;
3. apology to Japan for the murder of Sugiyama, chancellor of the Japanese legation;
4. suspension of official examinations in all cities where foreigners were attacked or murdered;
5. erection of expiatory monuments in foreign cemeteries which had been desecrated;
6. China to forbid for two or more years the importation of arms, ammunition and material used in their manufacture;
7. indemnity of 450,000,000 Haekwan taels and a 5 per cent effective tariff;
8. reservation of the Legation Quarter at Peking under the exclusive control of the Legations with the right to make it defensible;
9. razing of forts at Taku between Peking and the sea;
10. the occupation by the foreigners of certain points, thirteen in number, including Tientsin, as a security of open communications to Peking;
11. publication of certain edicts tending to prevent renewal of Boxer propaganda;
12. China to agree to the amendment of commercial treaties and to the Pei-ho and Whangpu conservancy projects;
13. abolition of the Tsung-li Yamen and the creation of a Ministry of Foreign Affairs;
14. evacuation of Peking, with the exception of Legation guards on September 17, 1901.

The open door doctrine was still alive after an anxious two years. It is a question, however, whether Americans in general, and particularly people in Washington, understood that they might have to fight for the doctrine if it were to continue to flourish during the course of the next few years.

Small wonder that Japan and Germany regarded us as unreliable and unstable in our foreign policy. By luck, and thanks to the ground plan which Mr. Rockhill had redrawn in 1899 and Secretary Hay had again defined in bolder colors in July, 1900, the open door policy had survived the murky politics of 1901 as far as the Far East was concerned. People listened to the United States; and she had tried to help China. Yet as Mr. Rockhill wrote to Secretary Hay:

I do not look to the future with any great hopefulness. I greatly fear that under the present Chinese rule things will not improve; reforms will not be seriously undertaken except under strong outside pressure. Trade will improve—will certainly do so, but disintegration will go on, for there is no life, energy, or patriotism throughout the whole governing class. It looks to me very dark ahead for China.[67]

NOTES TO CHAPTER IX

1. *F. R.,* 1900, pp. 85-86.
2. *Ibid.,* p. 111.
3. *H. P.,* June 1 [1900], Rockhill to Hay.
4. *F. R.,* 1900, p. 122.
5. *Ibid.,* p. 143.
6. *Ibid.,* p. 155. The printed correspondence, pp. 77-155, deals with the period to June 15, 1900.
7. *G. P.,* XVI, Nos. 4518, 4520, 4532.
8. *H. P.,* June 20, 1900, Choate to Hay.
9. *D. S.,* From Japan, Vol. 73, No. 439, June 14, 1900, Buck to Hay; telegram, June 20, same to same; telegram, June 29, same to same; From London, Vol. 199, telegram, June 26, Choate to Hay; telegram, June 29, same to same; To London, Vol. 33, p. 424, telegram, Hay to Choate; *H. P.,* June 27, Choate to Hay, reporting Lord Salisbury:
"I think he realizes that the President's chief concern is for the rescue of the persons and property of American representatives and citizens in China from the peril in which they are now involved with the rest, and for which all must co-operate, as they are now doing under Admiral Seymour.
"I am very glad to see, however, that the President is sending a considerable force from Manila. Their presence will be most helpful as a means of supporting whatever he may advocate as a necessary security against a repetition of this outbreak of barbarism against American citizens and their important interests."
10. *D. S.,* To Japan, Vol. 4, telegram, June 8, 1900, Hay to Buck; *H. P.,* Memorandum of conversation with Chinese Minister, June 22, 1900; telegram, July 1, Hay to Goodnow (American Consul General at Shanghai); *D. S.,* To France, Vol. 24, circular telegram, p. 309, June 22; From London, Vol. 199, 248-252, 274-277.
11. *F. R.,* 1901, Appendix, p. 12.
12. *D. S.,* From Japan, Vol. 73, telegram, June 30, 1900, Buck to Hay;

Vol. 74, telegram, Aug. 14, same to same; From Russia, Vol. 56, No. 267, July 18, Pierce to Hay; From London, Vol. 200, telegram, July 17, Choate to Hay; enclosure to No. 359, July 18, same to same; From Austria, Vol. 46, No. 110, July 21, Herdliska to Hay; Numerical File, Vol. 547, July 13, conversation between Hay and Russian Chargé d'Affaires; To Russian Embassy, Vol. 8, unnumbered, July 20, Hay to de Wollant; To London, Vol. 33, p. 441, telegram, Hay to Choate; *H. P.*, July 18, 19, 29, Fava to Hay; Clements, *The Boxer Rebellion,* New York, 1915, pp. 129 *et seq.;* Dennett, pp. 654-655; Olcott, *McKinley,* II, pp. 231-241.

13. *Parl. Papers,* China, No. 3, 1900, No. 246; *D. S.,* From Chinese Legation, Vol. 4, June 27, 1900; July 18, Memo. on request of Li Hung Chang; To China, Vol. 6, p. 85, July 11, Hay to Conger; To Chinese Legation, Vol. 2, p. 78, July 19, Hay to Wu Ting-Fang; p. 78, July 21, same to same; From London, Vol. 200, telegram, July 21, Choate to Hay; telegram, July 24, same to same; enclosure to No. 361, A, July 25, same to same; *H. P.,* July 11, 1900, Tiffany to Hay; *F. R.,* 1900, pp. 155-156, 345-346.

14. *H. P.,* July 24, 1900, Adee to Hay.

15. *F. R.,* 1900, pp. 293-295; *D. S.,* To France, Vol. 24, p. 322, telegram, July 21, Hay to Porter.

16. Hay, *Letters,* etc., III, p. 181.

17. *H. P.,* Aug. 4, 1900, Viceroy at Shanghai to Wu Ting-Fang.

18. *Ibid.,* Aug. 5, 1900, Adee to Hay; Aug. 9, same to same; *D. S.,* From British Embassy, Vol. 133, unnumbered, Aug. 9, Pauncefote to Hay; *F. R.,* 1900, pp. 300-301.

19. *H. P.,* Aug. 8, 1900, Memo. from Adee.

20. *Ibid.,* Aug. 15, 1900, Adee to Hay; *D. S.,* To Chinese Legation, Vol. 2, Aug. 12, 1900, Memo. by Adee; To Japanese Embassy, Vol. 2, p. 27, Aug. 12, Memo. from Adee; To British Embassy, Vol. 25, p. 290, Aug. 14, Adee to Pauncefote; *F. R.,* 1900, pp. 301-302.

21. *Education of Henry Adams,* p. 392; Cf. *H. P.,* Aug. 31, 1900, telegram, Hay to Adee:
"The '*World*' threatens to publish a fool story that I am staying away from Washington because I do not agree with the recent action of the administration about China. I suggest you say to Hood that I have been in daily and hourly communication with the Department by mail and wire and that every step taken in Chinese matter has my full concurrence."

22. *H. P.,* Aug. 9 and 15, 1900, Adee to Hay.

23. *D. S.,* To China, Vol. 6, p. 90, telegram, Aug. 23, 1900, Adee to Bellows (American Consul at Yokohama) for Rockhill.

24. *H. P.,* Nagasaki, Aug. 26, 1900, Rockhill to Hay. Rockhill's feeling was that things were much more "muddled up" in the Far East than even in Washington.

25. *H. P.,* undated but written in early September, from Shanghai, Rockhill to Hay.

26. *F. R.,* 1901, Appendix, pp. 17-19; *D. S.,* From London, Vol. 200, telegram, Aug. 27, 1900, Choate to Hay.

27. *D. S.,* From Germany, Vol. 72, telegram, Aug. 25, 1900, Jackson to Hay.

28. *F. R.,* 1901, Appendix, pp. 14-23; *Ibid.,* 1900, pp. 305-306; *D. S.,* From London, Vol. 200, telegram, Aug. 27, Choate to Hay; to Chinese Legation, Vol. 2, p. 87, Sept. 1, Adee to Wu Ting-Fang; *G. P.,* XVI, Nos. 4620, 4625. Cf. Clements, pp. 145-148; Morse, ch. XI.

29. *D. S.,* From China, vol. 108, telegram, Aug. 28, 1900, Conger to Hay.

30. Cf. Appendix A to this chapter; *G. P.,* XVI, Nos. 4627, 4634 and *passim;* Eckardstein, pp. 173-175; *H. P.,* Sept. 16, 1900, Adee to Hay, on the

attitude of Italy, saying: "I fancy the Italian note is prompted by Germany, as a sort of compromise which Germany, so hopelessly committed to the mailed-fist-and-military-primacy position, could not well advance of her own motion"; *D. S.*, From Germany, Vol. 72, telegram, Aug. 30, 1900, Jackson to Hay; From Russia, Vol. 56, telegram, Aug. 30, Pierce to Hay; in which the Russian Foreign Secretary, Count Lamsdorff, "volunteered the statement Russia has not the least intention of taking or acquiring a particle of territory in China or Manchuria"; Vol. 57, telegram, Sept. 24, Pierce to Hay; *D. S.*, From Japan, Vol. 74, No. 492, Sept. 22, Buck to Hay; *H. P.*, undated but probably about Sept. 1, 1900, Sternburg (German Chargé d'Affaires in Washington) to Hay, says curiously as though he were unaware of the Kaiser's feeling on the matter:

"I'm glad to see things taking a more peaceful course in China, greatly owing to your policy and I hope the cry for blood and revenge will have diminished when the large forces we have sent out have arrived. My only hope is that the bringing back of the legations to Tientsin may be accomplished without further trouble, so that negotiations can be opened instead of fighting."

31. *H. P.*, Sept. 2, 1900, Root to Hay.
32. *H. P.*, Sept 7, 1900, Cortelyou to Hay, with enclosure.
33. *D. S.*, To China, Vol. 6, p. 108, telegram, Sept. 8, 1900, Hill to Conger.
34. *D. S.*, From London, Vol. 200, telegram, Sept. 10, 1900, White to Hay.
35. *H. P.*, Sept. 14, 1900, McKinley to Hay.
36. *H. P.*, Sept. 12, 1900, Conger to Hay; *Ibid.*, Sept. 12, Chaffee to Adjutant General.
37. *H. P.*, Sept. 11, and 17, 1900, telegrams, Hay to McKinley.
38. *H. P.*, Sept. 14, 1900, Adee to Hay, and Appendix B to this Chapter.
39. Hay, *Letters,* etc., III, p. 192.
40. *H. P.*, Sept. 18, 1900, Adee to Hay; *D. S.*, From Germany, Vol. 73, telegram, Sept. 25, 1900, Jackson to Hay; *F. R.*, 1901, Appendix, pp. 23-24; *G. P.*, XVI, Nos. 4633, 4649, 4652.
41. *H. P.*, Sept. 24, 1900, Adee to Hay; *F. R.*, 1901, Appendix, pp. 24-25.
42. *D. S.*, From London, Vol. 200, telegrams, Sept. 25, and Oct. 3, 1900, White to Hay; *H. P.*, Sept. 26, 1900, Hay to Adee; Secretary Hay was to return to Washington, Oct. 1, and in view of the special services of Mr. Adee during this summer I give two quotations. To Henry Adams Hay wrote (Hay, *Letters,* etc., III, p. 195):

"But Adee has done nothing I would not have done and he has more sense than the whole gang of newspaper men and politicians. I shall take pleasure in telling them so. They talk like—what they are—about our duty to boss the job in China, to force the other powers to follow our lead, when we have no army and no central government."

And to Adee he again wrote (*H. P.*, Sept. 27):

"But you waste your precious time referring such a thing to me. How often have I told you that you can't go wrong if you try. If it was not that I believe your judgment is better than mine in these things, I should not be here.

"Yours affectionately,

"JOHN HAY."

43. *F. R.*, 1901, Appendix, pp. 26-30; *D. S.*, From London, Vol. 200, telegrams, Oct. 5, and 10, 1900, Choate to Hay; To Japanese Embassy, Vol. 2, p. 43, Oct. 22, memorandum; *H. P.*, Oct. 10, Choate to Hay. The United States also stated (*F. R.*, 1900, p. 296) to the Chinese authorities that Mr. Conger would be instructed to report on the efficacy of the Chinese punitive

decrees. Mr. Conger seems to have impressed Mr. Rockhill as being "dispassionate, careful and clear-sighted." (*H. P.,* Oct. 3, Rockhill to Hay.) As the result more and more responsibility was laid on both him and Rockhill. It is worth noting that Mr. Rockhill first proposed at this time that the doctrine of the open door should be embodied in a general treaty with China and the powers. This was not done till February, 1922; *D. S.,* From China, Vol. 109, No. 24, Dec. 10, 1900, Rockhill to Hay; To China, Vol. 6, unnumbered, from Hay to Rockhill.

44. *G. P.,* XVI, Nos. 4582, 4586, 4701, 4702, 4705, 4707, 4711, 4712; *D. S.,* To German Embassy, Vol. 12, p. 495, memorandum, Oct. 10, 1900.

45. *F. R.,* 1901, Appendix, p. 31; *G. P.,* XVI, Nos. 4719, 4720, 4721, 4727, 4728, 4730, 4732, 4736, 4744; Bau, pp. 124-126; Reventlow, *Deutschlands auswärtige Politik, 1888-1914,* Berlin, 1916, pp. 167-173; Ward and Gooch, *British Foreign Policy,* III, p. 281; Gooch and Temperley, *British Documents on the Origins of the War,* II, pp. 1-31.

46. Eckardstein, p. 177.

47. Hay, *Letters,* etc., III, p. 201. Later, of course, on Nov. 21, to Adams, Hay wrote in a mournful fashion of England's mistake as to German intentions (Thayer, II, p. 248). To his wife Hay wrote his snap judgment, Oct. 29, 1900 (Hay, *Letters,* etc., III, p. 199):

"'When I got into the train I saw in the evening papers the news of the Anglo-German agreement to defend the integrity of China and the Open Door. This was the greatest triumph of all. Lord Salisbury proposed this to me, before I left England. I could not accept it, because I knew that unspeakable Senate of ours would not ratify it, and ever since I have been laboring to bring it about without any help, and succeeded as far as was possible for one power to do it. Now then, two great powers, who are not dependent upon the Senate, come together and form a compact to confirm and fortify my work, which makes the 20th of October a great day in my little life."

Cf. *D. S.,* To London, Vol. 33, p. 483, telegram, Oct. 22, 1900, Hay to Choate; From London, Vol. 200, telegram, Oct. 21, Choate to Hay; From Germany, Vol. 73, telegrams, Oct. 23 and 25, Jackson to Hay; *H. P.,* Oct. 23, Pauncefote to Hay; Oct. 29, telegram, Cortelyou to Hay; Oct. 31, Choate to Hay; *G. P.,* XVI, 4747-4748; *F. R.,* 1901, Appendix, pp. 30-31.

48. *H. P.,* Oct. 27, 1900, McKinley to Hay.

49. *H. P.,* Nov. 24, 1900, Choate to Hay; *D. S.,* From London, Vol. 200, telegram, Nov. 22, Choate to Hay; To London, Vol. 33, telegram, Nov. 21, Hay to Choate; telegram, Nov. 30, same to same; *G. P.,* XVI, Nos. 4661, 4669-467; *F. R.,* 1900, pp. 220-222, 224, 226, 231.

50. *H. P.,* Dec. 1, 1900, Choate to Hay; Dec. 5, same to same; Dec. 8, same to same; Dec. 19, Rockhill to Hay, *Letters,* etc., III, p. 202; *D.'S.,* To Germany, Vol. 21, telegram, Dec. 1, 1900, Hay to White; To China, Vol. 6, No. 305, Dec. 20, Hay to Conger; From Austria, Vol. 47, No. 159, Dec. 1, Herdliska to Hay; To London, Vol. 33, p. 580, Dec. 1, Hay to Choate; p. 521, Dec. 17, same to same; p. 522, Dec. 18, same to same; p. 523, telegram, Dec. 19, same to same; telegram Dec. 21, same to same; From London, Vol. 201, telegram, Dec. 4, Choate to Hay; telegram, Dec. 11, same to same; telegram, Dec. 18, same to same; telegram, Dec. 20, same to same; *G. P.,* XIV, Nos. 4672, 4676, 4678, 4679, 4684, 4687; *F. R.,* 1900, pp. 235-243; *Ibid.,* 1901, Appendix, pp. 54-58.

51. *F. R.,* 1900, pp. 244-245.

52. There is good reason to believe that while the diplomats were slowly hammering away at a solution of such questions a suggestion had been made which looked to the acquisition by the United States navy of a naval station

on the Chinese coast. Inquiries were made at Peking; but Mr. Conger felt that in view of the avowed American policy as to the open door such a suggestion should not be pressed. To demand any such concession would be totally opposed to our declared purposes. Furthermore in case a place on the Fukhien coast were requested Japan already had a non-alienation agreement with China. Japan also felt that the agreement would stand in the way and nothing further was done in the matter. The declared policy of the United States, therefore, remained what it had been, viz., the maintenance of the open door and of the administrative entity of China, and in opposition to the cession of Chinese territory to any foreign power.

53. *D. S.*, To Germany, Vol. 21, telegram, Nov. 28, 1900, Hay to White; *G. P.*, XVI, Nos. 4770, 4799; *F. P.*, Dec. 1, 1900, Rockhill to Hay; Nov. 20, same to same:

"I sincerely hope the final settlement of all this Chinese muddle is near, but I greatly fear that it is not. At all events it will certainly be a year before things in this part of China—I mean Tientsin and Peking—begin to assume their normal appearance. The people are only very slowly coming back, for they nowhere have any confidence in the offers of protection and freedom to pursue their avocations made them by the foreigners—the Americans and Japanese, to a certain degree excepted. It seems incredible but it is nevertheless true, that right here in Peking soldiers of the various Powers are daily committing open acts of lawlessness which for the most part remain unpunished though daily reported to the commanders. The Germans, French and Italians are the chief culprits. One is forced to believe that there is no desire to establish order—Tientsin is still in a more unsettled, disorderly condition. Several of the Consuls there, the British and our own among others, told me they did not deem it safe for anyone to venture out *in the foreign settlement,* after dark. The guards at Count Waldersee's house robbed Charlie Denby's coolie in broad daylight! The stealing, looting, raping, has been indulged in by them all. The guard at the gate of our Legation some time ago (they belonged to the 14th infantry) stole from a foreigner's servant $1500 he was carrying to his master from the bank. Between ourselves I think the Emperor did well to fly and he would be a fool to come back."

54. *D. S.*, To London, Vol. 33, telegrams, Jan. 3 and 10, 1901, Hay to Choate; To Austria, Vol. 4, telegram, Jan. 10, Hay to Harris; From Russia, Vol. 57, No. 379, Jan. 4, Tower to Hay; From Germany, Vol. 73, telegram, Jan. 9, White to Hay; From Italy, Vol. 36, telegram, Jan. 12, Iddings to Hay; *G. P.*, XVI, Nos. 4851, 4853.

55. *D. S.*, To China, Vol. 6, telegram, Nov. 16, Hay to Conger.

56. *D. S.*, From China, Vol. 110, No. 499, Jan. 12, 1901; Conger to Hay from Japanese Legation, Vol. 7, memo., Jan. 16; *H. P.*, Jan. 5 and 9, Rockhill to Hay.

57. *H. P.*, Jan. 29, 1901, Rockhill to Hay. The protests of the Japanese to these proceedings of the Russians are noted in *G. P.*, XVI, Nos. 4808, 4809, 4833.

58. *D. S.*, Numerical File, Vol. 547, memo., Feb. 1, 1901.

59. *D. S.*, From Russian Embassy, Vol. 13, memo., April 5, 1901 (filed under date of April 13); *Parl. Papers,* China No. 6, 1901, p. 169. The Private memo. of Secretary Hay adds that after the formal note (*D. S.,* Numerical File, Vol. 547, memo. April 6, 1901) Cassini the Russian Ambassador said:

"So much for the communication with which I have been charged. The Ambassador of Russia now retires and goes home and goes to bed. The individual, Cassini, says he does not approve it, and does not like it."

Ibid., From China, Vol. 111, No. 34, March 4, Rockhill to Hay; From Italy, Vol. 36, telegram, March 8, Meyer to Hay; From London, Vol. 201, telegram, March 6, Choate to Hay; From Germany, Vol. 73, No. 1554, March 2, White to Hay; No. 1558, March 4, same to same; No. 1584, March 27, same to same; Numerical File, Vol. 547, memorandum, March 16, March 20, April 6; *H. P.*, March 9, 1901, Choate to Hay; *G. P.*, XVI, Nos. 4816, 4827; *D. S.*, From Japan, Vol. 75, No. 554, April 11, 1901, Wilson to Hay:
"It is difficult to judge how far the Japanese will be satisfied in the future with this technical check of Russia, in her giving up the Manchurian Agreement,—if she continues quietly to strengthen her position in Manchuria —and how long the present tranquillity is likely to last."

60. *D. S.*, Numerical File, Vol. 547, June 9, 1901.
61. *D. S.*, To London, Vol. 33, telegrams, Feb. 16, 23 and 27, 1901, Hay to Choate; From London, Vol. 201, telegrams, Feb. 19 and 20, Choate to Hay; From China, Vol. 111, telegram, Feb. 14, Conger to Hay; From Germany, Vol. 73, Feb. 21, White to Hay; To Russia, Vol. 18, No. 225, March 16, Hay to Tower; From France, Vol. 119, No. 816, March 29, Porter to Hay (which tended to show a particularistic point of view); *H. P.*, Feb. 27, 1901, Choate to Hay; *G. P.*, XVI, No. 4804.
62. *G. P.*, XVI. No. 4867; *D. S.*, to China, Vol. 6, p. 170, telegram, Feb. 23, 1901, Hay to Conger; Vol. 201, telegram, Feb. 25, Choate to Hay; From France, Vol. 119, telegram, Feb. 21, Porter to Hay; From Russia, Vol. 57, telegram, Feb. 21, Tower to Hay; No. 396, Feb. 27, same to same; *H. P.*, Feb., 21, Cassini to Hay (an emphatic disapproval of further military action).
63. *D. S.*, To German Embassy, Vol. 12, p. 595, May 28, 1901, memorandum; To Germany, Vol. 21, No. 1233, Adee to White.
64. *G. P.*, XVI, No. 4906. Mr. Rockhill's report in *F. R.*, 1901, Appendix is of course very full on these financial questions. I have not thought it necessary to give specific references. *D. S.*, To China, Vol. 6, telegram, April 8, 1901, Hay to Rockhill; From Russia, Vol. 58, telegram, April 11, Tower to Hay; *H. P.*, Feb. 4, 13, 18, March 3, and April 18, Rockhill to Hay; April 26, Choate to Hay; *G. P.*, XVI, Nos. 4863, 4895, 4896, 4902. Clements in his book on the *Boxer Rebellion* makes use of *Parliamentary Papers* to such an extent that I have also omitted all references to that valuable collection.
65. *D. S.*, To London, Vol. 33, telegram, June 7, 1901, Hay to Choate. To Russian Embassy, Vol. 8, p. 332, June 8, Hay to Cassini; Numerical File, Vol. 547, June 17, memorandum; From London, Vol. 202, No. 588, June 8, Choate to Hay; *H. P.*, June 16, and July 24, 1901, Rockhill to Hay; Cf. Morse, ch. XII.
66. *D. S.*, To China, Vol. 6, telegrams, April 11, and June 21, 1901, Hay to Rockhill; From London, Vol. 202, No. 625, July 19, Choate to Hay; telegram, Aug. 13, same to same; telegram, Aug. 29, same to same; Vol. 203, telegram, Sept. 20, same to same; To London, Vol. 33, p. 659, telegram, Aug. 15, Hay to Choate; Dennett, pp. 660-662.
67. *H. P.*, June 16, 1901, Rockhill to Hay.

APPENDICES TO CHAPTER IX

A

Foreign Relations, 1901, Appendix, p. 20, Memorandum from Mr. Adee to the Russian Embassy, Aug. 29, 1900.

The Government of the United States receives with much satisfaction the reiterated statement that Russia has no designs of territorial acquisition in China and that equally with the other powers now operating in China, Russia has sought the safety of her Legation in Pekin and to help the Chinese Government to repress the existing troubles. The same purposes have moved and will continue to control the Government of the United States; and the frank declarations of Russia in this regard are in accord with those made to the United States by the other Powers. All the Powers, therefore, having disclaimed any purpose to acquire any part of China, and, now that adherence thereto has been renewed since relief has reached Pekin, it ought not to be difficult by concurrent action through negotiations to reach an amicable settlement with China by which the treaty rights of all the Powers will be secured for the future, the open door assured, the interests and property of foreign citizens conserved and full reparation made for wrongs and injuries suffered by them.

So far as we are advised the greater part of China is at peace and earnestly desires to protect the life and property of all foreigners, and in several of the provinces active and successful efforts to suppress the Boxers have been taken by the Viceroys, to whom we have extended encouragement through our Consuls and naval officers. This present good relation should be promoted for the peace of China.

While we agree that the immediate object for which the military forces of the Powers have been cooperating, viz., the relief of the Ministers at Pekin, has been accomplished, there still remain the other purposes which all the Powers have in common, which are referred to in the communication of the Russian Chargé and which are specifically enumerated in our note to the Powers of July third.

These are: to afford all possible protection everywhere in China to foreign life and property; to guard and protect all legitimate foreign interests; to aid in preventing the spread of the disorders to other provinces of the Empire and a recurrence of such disorders; and to seek a solution which may bring about permanent safety and peace to China, preserve Chinese territorial and administrative entity, protect all rights guaranteed by treaty and international law to friendly Powers, and safeguard for the world the principle of equal and impartial trade with all parts of the Chinese Empire.

In our opinion these purposes could best be obtained by the joint occupation of Pekin under a definite understanding between the Powers until the Chinese Government shall have been re-established and shall be in a position to enter into new treaties with adequate provisions for reparation and guaranties of future protection. With the establishment and recognition of such authority the United States would wish to withdraw its military forces from Pekin and remit to the processes of peaceful negotiation our just demands.

We consider, however, that a continued occupation of Pekin would be ineffective to produce the desired result unless all the Powers unite therein with entire harmony of purpose. Any Power which determines to withdraw its troops from Pekin will necessarily proceed thereafter to protect its interests in China by its own method, and we think that this would make a general withdrawal expedient. As to the time and manner of withdrawal, we think that in view of the imperfect knowledge of the military situation resulting from the interruptions of telegraphic communication, the several military commanders at Pekin should be instructed to confer and agree together upon the withdrawal as a concerted movement, as they agreed upon the advance.

The result of these considerations is that unless there is such a general expression by the Powers in favor of a continued occupation as to modify the views expressed by the Government of Russia and lead to a general agreement for continued occupation, we shall give instructions to the commander of the American forces in China to withdraw our troops from Pekin after due conference with the other commanders as to the time and manner of withdrawal.

The Government of the United States is much gratified by the assurance given by Russia that the occupation of New Chwang is for military purposes incidental to the military steps for the security of the Russian border provinces menaced by the Chinese, and that as soon as order shall be established Russia will retire her troops from those places if the action of the other Powers be not an obstacle thereto. No obstacle in this regard can arise through any action of the United States, whose policy is fixed and has been repeatedly proclaimed.

B

Hay Papers, Adee to Hay, September 14, 1900.

The whirligig has tumbled over on a new face today and we are in the throes of another crisis. The President has about made up his mind to telegraph Chaffee and Conger to withdraw to the seaboard, and I think, seriously contemplated sending Chaffee to Manila and Conger to Shanghai, to negotiate at long range—when, presto, these two telegrams from Conger and Chaffee arrived, and being telephoned to Canton by Mr. Griggs, changed the whole aspect of affairs. The President is much impressed by Conger's views (which I think are uttered second-hand and come from Claude MacDonald and possibly Pichon or the Italian). He says he will now wait a day or two and see what turn affairs take.

I think, and have steadily thought since August 28 when I drafted the first tentative reply to the Russian declaration, that while enough troops might be withdrawn from Peking to remove the appearance of an occupation of conquest, the legations, or a majority of them, and an adequate mixed military police guard should remain and guarantee the imperial authority on its return to the capital, which it should be the purpose and endeavor of the legations to negotiate with Ching and Li, withdrawal outside the walls to follow the restoration of Kwang Hsu to the throne of his fathers. Then the first step of punishment of Tuan and the ring-leaders could be taken, the foreign troops outside the wall standing ready to uphold the Emperor's hand in dealing out justice. Coincidently with the retirement of the main body of the allied troops to the seaboard, the powers, or some of them, should name as plenipotentiaries their respective Ministers at Peking and one or two associate negotiators to arrange terms of settlement. By doing this, the best possible proof of a disposition to deal fairly with the Emperor would be afforded, and would I think induce his speedy return to Peking, which latter might be made a condition precedent to opening formal peace negotiations. I think it not at all improbable that proposals in somewhat this sense may come in a day or two from Great Britain and perhaps Germany, with Italy and Austria tailing after. During the time which would necessarily elapse before the additional negotiators could reach Peking, the Powers could hold a conference at The Hague or Berne to consider the terms of settlement to be demanded from China. Indeed, whether peace negotiations are to be held at all would depend on the Emperor's preserving order, protecting foreigners and punishing the ring-leaders during the interval after his resumption of rule at Peking and before the convening of the peace plenipotentiaries.

I would be glad to have your views about these suggestions. Where all are groping, the first practical formulation of a plan based on common sense may bring the gropers together, all but Russia and perhaps Germany, whose real aim is grab. . . .

To turn the subject—have you remarked the delightful saying of Flavin, the new Irish member of the Commons:—"There beats as true, brave and loyal a heart under the tunic of a Dublin Fusileer as under the kilt of a Gordon Highlander."

C

Hay Papers, Hay to Adee; Newbury, N. H., Sept. 14, 1900.

I read every day the *Tribune, Times* and *Boston Herald.* The *Tribune* stands by us. The *Times* and *Boston Herald* while civil enough, tell us plainly that if we leave Peking we shall be forever infamous. They also say that if we do not take the lead and keep it, dragging the other Powers after us in chains, we are **N. G.** and McKinley will be beaten in November. It never seems to occur to them that the other Powers may not like the feel of a rope around their necks, and may even want to say something about their interests in China. It all sums up to this: we shall get no credit whatever we do; our friends will take it as a matter of course, and our critics will kick us all round the lot. Nothing was clearer than that the whole country would have risen in uproar if we had formed an alliance with England against Russia and Germany. And now that we seem to be agreeing with Russia, we shall be abused as wobbling and vacillating. So there is nothing for it, but to do as near right as we can, and leave the consequences to the newspapers.

The dilemma is clear enough. We want to get out at the earliest possible moment. We do not want to have the appearance of being forced out, or frightened out, and we must not lose our proper influence in the final arrangement. If we leave Germany and England in Peking, and retire with Russia, who has unquestionably made her bargain already with China, we not only will *seem* to have been beaten, but we run a serious risk of being *really* frozen out. Germany and England will feel resentful and will take no care of our interests, and Russia will see us out without winking. You have, it seems, grave suspicion of the attitude of Japan. There is, therefore, not a single power we can rely on, for our policy of abstention from plunder and the Open Door. If we try to deal separately with China, she will say to us, as she said last year, "We are not free agents. We are not able without the permission of the other powers, to fulfil any engagements we might make with you." When I tried to get them to agree not to grant any privileges to other powers which should not be equally granted to us, they said precisely that—"If they use force against us we cannot resist. Will you guarantee us against them?"—a question which I had no authority to answer. The inherent weakness of our position is this; we do not want to rob China ourselves, and our public opinion will not permit us to interfere, with an army, to prevent others from robbing her. Besides, we have no army. The talk of the papers about "our pre-eminent moral position giving us the authority to dictate to the world" is mere flap-doodle.

Anxious, therefore, as I am, to get away from Peking, I cannot help fearing that if we retire with Russia, it will end in these unfortunate consequences: Russia will betray us. China will fall back on her *non possumus,* if we try to make separate terms with her. England and Germany being left in Peking, Germany by superior brute selfishness will have her way, and we shall be left out in the cold.

If it were not for our domestic politics, we could, and should, join with England, whose interests are identical with ours, and make our ideas prevail. But in the present morbid state of the public mind toward England, that is not to be thought of—and we must look idly on, and see her making terms with Germany instead of with us.

It seems to me, if we can get the Chinese Government, or its clearly authorized representatives, back to Peking, we ought at least to initiate our negotiations there, even if, later on, we should transfer them to Shanghai or elsewhere. We ought to pay all possible civility to Li Hung Chang, to Prince Ching, and anybody whom we accept as negotiators. If we could send Li to Tientsin in a U. S. vessel, I should be inclined to do it. He is an unmitigated scoundrel, of course, thoroughly corrupt and treacherous. But he represents China and we must deal with him, with Liu-Kan-Yih, and with Chang-Chin-Tung, as if we trusted them.

Has the President come to any conclusion as to who shall represent us in negotiating with China? Conger, I take it for granted, will be one. Rockhill might help. If he is to send anyone from here I think very well of Low. I have thought he might like to send John Barrett. Moore would be an admirable man if he could get away.

CHAPTER X

CUBA AND THE CARIBBEAN

THE war with Spain had, in 1898, suddenly placed the United States in military occupation of Cuba. Porto Rico became American; and there were eager demands by naval officers and others for the extension of our interests in the Caribbean Sea. Economic forces as well as considerations of strategy were at work to draw us more and more closely into touch with this island world. Soon the Panama canal was to become the dominant factor in the situation. In Cuba there was to be a real test of the alleged imperialism of the United States. Were we to abide by the terms of the Teller resolution of 1898 which stated our altruistic intention "to leave the government and control of the island [of Cuba] to its people"? Were we to regard political and economic interests among the varied peoples who inhabited the general region of the Caribbean with indifference? These questions can best be answered at the conclusion of this brief chapter; and let me add that it is brief because it is understood there are one or more books based on the documents shortly to appear on this special field of American diplomacy. I merely wish to outline the subject and to bring out some material which is pertinent but which has not been printed before.

The establishment of a Military Governor of Cuba in December, 1898, was a sign that the United States undertook the administration as a result of the war. The appointment of Major-General John R. Brooks to that office and the personal instructions which he received from President McKinley were also signs that this undertaking was but temporary. The intention of the President was clear. It was to assist the people of Cuba "to form a government which shall be free and independent, thus realizing the best aspirations of the Cuban people"; but the "foundation of our authority in Cuba is the law of belligerent right over conquered territory."[1] Unfortunately mixed advice in Washington led to confusion in Cuba. The power of the United States was thrust into the foreground while her good-will and faithfulness were relegated to the background. The American expected the Cuban to be grateful while the Cuban expected the American to be grasping. It was only natural that Cubans should view us with suspicion in view of the fact that so many American officials and visitors ignored the declaration of our intended withdrawal. When the Cuban was not quite as grateful as we expected him to be, American opinion swung to the other extreme and held that the Cuban was unworthy. Such misunderstandings and misconceptions were perhaps to be expected; but they made the task of the day unusually difficult.

Nevertheless, particularly after General Leonard Wood became Military Governor on December 20, 1899, the machinery of administration and government, which had been set up, began to run more smoothly. Plans for evacuation were discussed and on December 31, 1901, the first Cuban Congress was elected. On February 24, 1902, Palma was chosen President; May 20 was fixed for American withdrawal and the formal establishment of the Cuban Republic. During the closing months of General Wood's administration there was considerable friction because of the autocratic way in which affairs were managed. But, in his report for 1902, he says by way of review:

> The work called for and accomplished was the building up of a republic, by Anglo-Saxons, in a Latin country where approximately seventy per cent of the people were illiterate; where they had lived always as a military colony; where general elections, as we understand them, were unknown— . . . in short, the establishment, in a little over three years, in a Latin military colony, . . . of a republic modelled closely upon the lines of our great Republic.[2]

Such brief statement does not of course do justice to the hard spade work done by the rank and file in the administration of Cuba nor naturally does it recognize the great merit of General Wood himself. On the whole his period of rule in Cuba, while not exactly a model one, nevertheless reflects great credit on him and his assistants. So far, Cuban affairs had been in the hands of the military. All orders went from the Secretary of War. During the closing year of American administration there also came up questions which affected the Department of State. In particular the future relations of Cuba to the United States were the subject of anxious consideration. In Washington there was consultation by the Cabinet and on January 11, 1901, Secretary Root of the War Department wrote to Secretary Hay, in part, as follows:

> I wish to bring the question of the ultimate relations of this country to Cuba to a point as soon as possible, and, that being determined, to organize the permanent Cuban Government to take the control of the island out of the hands of the present military authorities without any avoidable delay. I have directed General Wood to urge the Constitutional Convention, now in session in Havana, to bring its labors to a conclusion in time to lay them before Congress at the present session. When this is done, it is of course desirable that the policy which in a general way we have agreed upon should be made as definite as possible. Will you turn over in your mind, until our next meeting, the advisability of requiring the incorporation into the fundamental law of Cuba of provisions to the following effect: 1. That in transferring the control of Cuba to the Government established under the new Constitution the United States reserves and retains the right of intervention for the preservation of Cuban independence and the maintenance of a stable Government, adequately protecting life, property and individual liberty. 2. That no Government organized under the Constitution shall be deemed to have authority to enter into any treaty or engagement with any foreign power which may tend to impair or interfere with the independence of Cuba, or to confer upon such foreign power any special right or privilege without the consent of the United States, and that the United States shall be entitled to be a party, in the first instance, to any negotiation having in view any such provision. 3. That to facilitate the United States in the performance of such duties as may devolve upon her under the foregoing provisions and for her own defense, the United States may acquire and hold the title to land, and maintain naval stations at certain specified points.

4. That all the acts of the Military Governor, and all rights acquired thereunder, shall be valid and be maintained and protected.[3]

He also enclosed a copy of a letter to General Wood of January 9, from which I quote the concluding paragraph:

Another fact which the Cubans should consider is that in international affairs the existence of a right recognized by international law is of the utmost importance. We now have by virtue of our occupation of Cuba and the terms under which sovereignty was yielded by Spain, a right to protect her which all foreign nations recognize. It is of great importance to Cuba that that right, resting upon the treaty of Paris and derived through that treaty from the sovereignty of Spain, should never be terminated but should be continued by a reservation, with the consent of the Cuban people, at the time when the authority which we now exercise is placed in their hands. If we should simply turn the Government over to the Cuban administration, retire from the island, and then turn around to make a treaty with the new government, just as we would make treaties with Venezuela, and Brazil, and England, and France, no foreign state would recognize any longer a right on our part to interfere in any quarrel which she might have with Cuba, unless that interference were based upon an assertion of the Monroe Doctrine. But the Monroe Doctrine is not a part of international law and has never been recognized by European nations. How soon someone of these nations may feel inclined to test the willingness of the United States to make war in support of that doctrine, no one can tell. It would be quite unfortunate for Cuba if it should be tested there.[4]

To this might be added a third letter, which is also unpublished, from Mr. Adee to Secretary Hay. The whole question of American-Cuban matters was now in the throes of formulation. Senator Platt had been called in by the President and he was drawing up what was to be known in the future as the "Platt Amendment." Mr. Adee wrote on February 5, 1901:

Here is my paper, hasty and crude, but perhaps utilizable. May not this be the solution to the problem:
Let Congress resolve that the occupancy of Cuba shall not cease until we are satisfied that a stable and competent nationality is established, and until a treaty with such nation shall have been concluded defining the rights and obligations of the United States

with respect to intercourse with Cuba and the maintenance of public order in the Island,—the proclamation of such treaty to coincide with the cessation of our occupancy.

It was one of Judge Day's ideas to provide by such a treaty for the arbitration by the United States of all internal discussions in Cuba, and to squelch any revolutionary resort to arms which might be made in violation or defiance of the obligation to arbitrate.[5]

Meantime the members of the Cuban Constitutional Convention had been elected on September 15, 1900; and the Convention itself met in Havana on November 5. With its work regarding the domestic institutions of Cuba we have nothing to do. It had been instructed, however, to draw up a statement of the future relations which should subsist between Cuba and the United States. It now seemed as though the Convention would do little or nothing regarding this important matter. Consequently Secretary Root's letters of January 9 and 11, 1901, which I have just quoted, were directly to the point. These letters show that the interest of the United States could not expire with the adoption of the Cuban Constitution, the establishment of stable government, and the withdrawal of American troops. The underlying forces of geography and of economic and naval strategy compelled a right of political intervention should occasion arise. Our diplomatic history was filled with assertions such as that made by John Quincy Adams when he wrote in 1823 "it is scarcely possible to resist the conviction that the annexation of Cuba to our Federal Republic will be indispensable to the continuance and integrity of the Union itself." [6] Under the circumstances, desirous as we were in 1901 to fulfil the terms of the Teller resolution, the United States still had to consider the past and to look to the future safeguarding of proper American interests in the West Indies.

The Cuban Convention made two attempts to define the relations which should exist between the United States and Cuba. Neither of these proposals was acceptable to the United States; and in Cuba there was strong feeling on the part of the radical elements that even these definitions went too far. On the other hand, the statement of those relations was attempted by Secretary Root in a letter to General Wood of February 9, 1901. This well-known letter elaborated the points already made in Secretary Root's letter to Secretary Hay of January 11. To this the Cubans made a third set of counter proposals. Meanwhile time was passing and the President was anxious to conclude the matter before Congress should adjourn on March 4. Consequently, the Platt Amendment was introduced as a rider to the Army Appropriation Bill. This passed after a brief two hours' debate, and was signed by the President on March 2, 1901. As defined in this amendment the relations between the United States and Cuba were to be as follows:

(1) That the Government of Cuba shall never enter into any treaty or other compact with any foreign power or powers which will impair or tend to impair the independence of Cuba, nor in any manner authorize or permit any foreign power or powers to obtain by colonization or for military or naval purposes, or otherwise, lodgment in or control over any portion of said Island.

(2) That said Government shall not assume or contract any public debt, to pay the interest upon which and to make reasonable sinking-fund provision for the ultimate discharge of which, the ordinary revenues of the Island, after defraying the current expenses of government, shall be inadequate.

(3) That the Government of Cuba consents that the United States may exercise the right to intervene for the preservation of Cuban independence, the maintenance of a government adequate for the protection of life, property and individual liberty, and for discharging the obligation with respect to Cuba imposed by the Treaty of Paris on the United States, now to be assumed and undertaken by the Government of Cuba.

(4) That all acts of the United States in Cuba during its military occupation thereof are ratified and validated, and all lawful rights acquired thereunder shall be maintained and protected.

(5) That the Government of Cuba will execute, and as far as necessary extend, the plans already devised or other plans to be mutually agreed upon, for the sanitation of the cities of the Island, to the end that a recurrence of epidemic and infectious diseases may be prevented, thereby assuring protection to the people and commerce of Cuba, as well as to the commerce of the Southern ports of the United States and the people residing therein.

(6) That the Isle of Pines shall be omitted from the proposed

Constitutional boundaries of Cuba, the title thereto left to future adjustment by treaty.

(7) That to enable the United States to maintain the independence of Cuba, and to protect the people thereof, as well as for its own defence, the Government of Cuba will sell or lease to the United States lands necessary for coaling or naval stations at certain specified points, to be agreed upon with the President of the United States.

(8) That by way of further assurance the Government of Cuba will embody the foregoing provisions in a permanent treaty with the United States.[7]

There can be no question that, whatever we may think of the terms of the Platt Amendment, the methods of dealing with such an important matter were, to put it mildly, unfortunate. We showed our hasty bad manners before the Latin-American world in a way which naturally, and justly, provoked criticism. We attempted to ram down the throat of Cuba orders which should have been handled in diplomatic fashion. In the United States even ardent Republican administration newspapers were emphatic in their criticism. The administration began to get nervous as news came of the hostile opinion which had been provoked by its procedure both in Washington and in Havana. On April 3, Secretary Root sent a telegram to General Wood in an attempt to put a gloss on the third article of the Platt Amendment. This read:

You are authorized to state officially that in the view of the President the intervention described in the third clause of the Platt Amendment is not synonymous with intermeddling or interference with the affairs of the Cuban Government, but the formal action of the Government of the United States, based upon just and substantial grounds, for the preservation of Cuban independence, and the maintenance of a government adequate for the protection of life, property and individual liberty, and adequate for discharging the obligations with respect to Cuba imposed by the treaty of Paris on the United States.[8]

Even such consoling words, however, did not reconcile the Cuban opposition. They continued to regard only the letter of the Amendment rather than its spirit as interpreted by Secretary Root. On April 6, the Platt Amendment was defeated in the Convention by a vote of 24 to 2. Yet a committee of five was sent to Washington to negotiate. There they had long conferences with Secretary Root, who acted as spokesman for the President. The committee returned to Cuba apparently hopeful that, as the price of acceptance of the American demands, advantageous commercial relations would be established in the following year. There was no pledge given either directly or indirectly to that effect; but this impression was created only to be nullified in the next session of Congress. On May 28, the Convention gave way partially and, in response to renewed pressure from Washington, on June 12, 1901, the Platt Amendment was accepted by a vote of 16 to 11, as an appendix to the Cuban Constitution. Time had elapsed; the pressure of economic forces was powerful; and acquiescence was inevitable. Later the Platt Amendment was included in a treaty signed on May 22, 1903, and ratified on July 1, 1904.

The friends of Secretary Root have definitely and positively claimed for him the authorship of the Platt Amendment and I am inclined to think they are right, not so much on the basis of what they say, as on the basis of his letter of January 11; Senator Platt, however, has also declared that he was the author of it and that the original draft of it was his. This may be technically true; but back even of the original draft there was the mind that first conceived of the principles to be embodied. That mind was unquestionably Secretary Root's. On his shoulders, therefore, must also rest in part the responsibility for the sorry showing our diplomacy made at Havana and the long continued and continuing hostility to his plan which has existed in Cuba.[9]

At all events the fact to be borne in mind is that these arrangements with Cuba were concluded during the period of our military occupation, which was also the period during which the Hay-Pauncefote treaties were to the front. If, therefore, we wish to consider the principles laid down in the Platt Amendment as constituting a programme for our future policy in the Caribbean and towards the republics of Central America, we will not go far wrong. The Panama Canal was to be the touchstone of our policy and the Platt Amendment our declaration of intentions.[10]

President Roosevelt was, however, finally able to drive through Congress after a long and spectacular fight, the measure which secured reciprocity with Cuba. This did not take place till December 27, 1903. In the meantime, diplomatic representation had been established and, in the spring of 1902, Mr. Squiers, the American Minister, took up his post at Havana. From the first there was a certain amount of anxiety felt lest a movement in favor of annexation to the United States might gain headway and plunge the island into disorder. Secretary Hay had instructed the new Minister to give such a movement no countenance whatever and to let it be known that we desired nothing but the peace and prosperity of Cuba. Mr. Squiers reported that, though "all manner of disaster politically and financially" had been predicted for the new government of President Palma, things had quieted down. The Americans in Cuba were, perhaps with reason, disappointed for they had claimed that the United States would never haul down the flag and they looked for its restoration. Aside from this inconsiderable element, however, matters seemed to be settling themselves satisfactorily.[11]

The three chief matters which occupied the attention of the Department of State were the negotiation of a reciprocity treaty, the negotiation of a treaty embodying the principles of the Platt Amendment, and the determination of the coaling and naval stations to be leased to the United States. As to commercial relations the matter was complicated by the desire of the Cuban Congress to secure a higher revenue by a new tariff which would raise the duties on American goods. Mr. Squiers reported privately to Secretary Hay:

> The spirit of the legislation proposed or favorably acted upon up to this time, is, to say the least, not pro-American . . . About the only

important measures yet considered, are all unfavorable to American interests. . . . If Congress does nothing in the way of reciprocity I fear the ratification of a treaty will be no easy matter and the longer it is delayed the more difficult it will be, unless circumstances force its acceptance.[12]

The negotiation of the commercial treaty, difficult though it was, was further complicated by the general attitude of the people and by their desire to use the reciprocity treaty as *quid pro quo* for the treaty embodying the Platt Amendment. Thus Mr. Squiers reported mournfully:

These people have absolutely no gratitude or appreciation, excepting as expressed in cheap compliments and assurances of friendship. Since I came here I have in every possible way endeavored to win their confidence and friendship, sometimes "putting my pride in my pocket" in doing so, and yet I am unable to see wherein my position has been very materially strengthened.

To my mind the failure of the treaty would not be so serious on account of the loss of a better market as it would in encouraging the Government in its opposition and the foreign powers in their support of such opposition. The danger lies there. I am satisfied that the moral effect of a failure in the present negotiations will be bad and far reaching and that every future move will be attended with great difficulties. The Cubans say "if we refuse to ratify the Platt Amendment with its agreement as to coaling stations what are you going to do about it?"[13]

As the campaign for and against these treaties waxed hotter Mr. Squiers, in conversation with one of the leaders of the Nationalist party, took occasion to say:

That the great difficulty with Cuba was her suspicions as to the good faith and honesty of purpose of the United States; that this feeling was at the root of all our difficulties on the question of reciprocity, as well as the questions arising under the Platt Amendment; that Cuba apparently could not become accustomed to being honestly, fairly and justly dealt with; that her experience had taught her to suspect every act, everyone, even her friends. I told him that they appeared impressed with the idea that their only safety was to surround themselves with all manner of treaty hedges while he knew that their future lies only in the good faith and integrity of the American Government; that with or without the Platt Amendment, their geographical position made the political situation what it is and that their wisest policy is to so accept it.[14]

The reciprocity treaty was agreed to by Cuba in December, 1902, but its acceptance by the United States was delayed for a year because of the selfish fight made by the American beet sugar growers. Meanwhile the treaty regulating the relations between the two countries was the occasion of much argument and delay by the Cubans. Secretary Hay became impatient in April and early in May the President wrote to him, urging haste.[15]

The permanent treaty embodying the Platt Amendment was finally signed on May 22, 1903; and the third agreement, that relating to the coaling and naval stations, was approved of in July. This completed the major arrangements which the United States believed were necessary. For the next two years the economic development of Cuba proceeded apace. The very prosperity of Cuba was, however, to provoke trouble. There had been minor tariff disputes as to the preferred position which the United States occupied as regards the most favored nation clause; but these had been settled.[16]

No serious question, therefore, arose until August, 1906, when an insurrection broke out in Cuba. Political differences in the island had resolved themselves into a struggle between the "ins and the outs." American commercial and financial interests had greatly increased during these years of prosperity; and the annexationist movement had been suddenly strengthened. Political corruption was becoming more and more common; a presidential election was now about to take place; and charges were made that the machinery of election was being manipulated in behalf of the party then in power. Insurrection thus took place on the part of those who realized that the Palma administration was too strongly entrenched to be ousted save by force. This revolt gained ground; and on September 8, 1906, President Palma appealed for assistance to the United States. Property was being destroyed and American lives were endangered; above all the processes of stable government were in confusion.[17]

Roosevelt had been particularly proud of the American

record in Cuba. Furthermore he was alive to the importance of sentiment and of manners in international politics. Thus he struck the right note when he wrote of Secretary Root's proposed trip to Latin-American countries in 1906:

> I feel just as you do about Root's going to South America. This was the psychological moment for him to go, and though in a sense it may truthfully be described, as it has been described, as a sentimental journey, it is one of those journeys of sentiment which are of real importance.[18]

The President, therefore, disliked extremely the course of events in Cuba in 1906 which might require American intervention. He was anxious to have Secretary Root stop at Havana in mid-September, to tell the Cubans that by revolution and disturbance they were inviting the intervention and domination of the United States. We did "not want to intervene, but they will leave us no alternative if they reduce the country to a condition of revolutionary anarchy." President Palma was, however, so urgent that on September 12 men-of-war arrived in Cuban waters. On September 13, news came that President Palma intended to resign and that the situation was so serious that a small party of American marines had been landed at Havana.[19]

The next day intervention took place as was announced in a solemn letter from the President to Señor Quesada, the Cuban Minister at Washington.[20] Mr. Taft, as Secretary of War and the Assistant Secretary of State, Mr. Bacon, were sent to Havana. Mr. Taft acted as provisional Governor until he was succeeded by Mr. Magoon from Panama. In view of the presence of American troops in the island the insurgent chiefs laid down their arms. Later, an orderly election was held in Cuba and in January, 1909, American intervention ceased. The Cuban Republic then once more made a start as an independent state. As President Roosevelt said in February, 1907, "I am doing my best to persuade the Cubans that if only they will be good they will be happy; I am seeking the very minimum of interference necessary to make them good." [21] Can anyone imagine such temporary intervention a sign of American imperialism?

American interest in the West Indies was also made manifest in the renewed desire of the United States to secure the Danish West Indies. The acquisition of Porto Rico and later the occupation of a naval station at Guantanamo in Cuba did not quite satisfy the navy. Indeed there is a personal memorandum by Admiral Bradford to Secretary Hay as early as September, 28, 1898. This reads as follows:

1. I beg to call attention to the importance of purchasing the Danish West Indies.
2. Their possession as a coaling station, is not now as important as it was before the war, since we have other ports nearby that can be utilized for that purpose.
3. It is known, however, that their possession is coveted by Germany and that they are for sale.
4. They can be purchased, as I am informed by Mr. Chas. R. Flint, of New York, for $5,000,000 or less.
5. They are the only islands in the West Indies that are in the market or likely to be.
6. The proposition to purchase is made in order to prevent them from falling into the hands of Germany.
7. In accordance with the principles of the Monroe Doctrine this country would be forced to object to their acquisition by Germany.
8. It appears to be a good business proposition to buy rather than risk a war on their account.[22]

In this fashion a project which had previously been the subject of diplomatic negotiation came to the front. In 1867 a treaty had been made with Denmark for the purchase of the Danish West Indies; but it had been defeated in the Senate in 1870. Now a renewed attempt was to be made. The Republican party platform in 1896 had favored a purchase of the islands and the matter had been much discussed. Furthermore, a despatch from Mr. Swenson, the American Minister at Copenhagen, brought up the matter afresh in February, 1899.[23] Mr. Swenson thought that, instead of paying $7,500,000 as had been proposed by Secretary Seward, about a million and a half dollars would be an acceptable price to Denmark. Later in 1899 a certain Captain Christmas appeared and through his agency an interview was arranged between the Danish authorities and Mr. Henry White, of the American Embassy in London, who acted informally for the United States. The Danes said that they would be willing to sell but refused to name a price preferring that the United States should make an offer. Unofficially, however, Mr. White learned that though about $4,500,000 might be expected by Denmark the islands could probably be obtained for about $3,500,000. This he reported privately to Secretary Hay.[24]

Secretary Hay, on January 29, 1900, instructed Mr. Swenson to inquire as to whether Denmark would be prepared to sign a treaty, of which he sent a copy, ceding the islands to the United States. This treaty offered $3,500,000; the Danish authorities, however, asked $4,000,000. Furthermore there were certain minor changes which they proposed in the text of the treaty. A certain amount of patriotic feeling also showed itself; when the plan for the treaty was disclosed to the committees of the Danish Parliament. Nevertheless the King and the Council of State had approved of the general plan of cession.[25] The fall of the Danish ministry resulted in further delay. The new ministry, however, professed itself favorable and popular agitation against the cession had practically disappeared by June, 1900. The discussion of the changes desired by the Danes then ensued.[26]

These need not now detain us for they dragged along for nearly nine months. In the summer of 1901, however, Secretary Hay sent Mr. Henry White to Copenhagen again while Mr. Swenson was absent on leave in the United States. Indeed Mr. Swenson and Professor Freeman, lately of the University of Wisconsin, who was Consul at Copenhagen, had become involved in such personal differences and difficulties that Secretary Hay had referred to them as "two old incompetents." The absence of Mr. Swenson gave a fresh opportunity for negotiations. These negotiations were entangled by the requirement of the United States that the islands on their cession should be turned over in full, unencumbered sovereignty. There were certain Danish companies which claimed privileges by virtue of grants from the Danish Government and Mr. White was, therefore, unable to accomplish much.[27]

In reality the Danish ministry had become rather frightened over the opposition to the sale in court circles and over the danger of its own fall in case the Senate in Washington should fail to ratify the treaty when they had once signed it. Secretary Hay sought to bring pressure to bear and increased the offer of purchase price. Finally on January 24, 1902, the treaty was signed in Washington and on February 17 it was approved by the Senate.[28] In May the two houses of the Danish Parliament disagreed which forced a delay till the autumn session; then on October 22, 1902, the Danish upper house failed to ratify the treaty. Thus the plan for the purchase of the Danish West Indies failed.[29] Later, in 1917, we at last secured these islands for $25,000,000, five times the sum we were ready to offer in 1902.

This defeat was possibly due in part to German influences which were strongly against the sale. Indeed a bit of gossip is reported by Secretary Hay to the President in 1903 when he repeated portions of a letter that Mr. White had sent him. At a luncheon, where Mr. White sat at the same table with the King and Queen of England, the Queen, who was a Danish Princess by birth, rather chaffed Mr. White on the failure of the treaty. Mr. Hay continues:

> She said she could not help being delighted that they had been preserved to her country, and that "you Americans do not really want them." In reply to White's suggestion that we had only come into the matter at all to relieve Denmark of a burden upon the treasury, the Queen said: "That was all due to bad management; with the new management you will see how the islands will flourish and be made to pay," to which White replied that he feared she was mistaken, but hoped she might not be, as we have not the least desire to dispossess Denmark of them against her will. The Queen then added: "But I hope you will never let Germany have the islands; that is what we Danes would dread above all things," to

which White replied that her Majesty might make herself quite easy on that point, as it would be the grossest infringement of the Monroe Doctrine, which our country would spare no expense to put a stop to. Curiously enough, her brother, the Crown Prince, had asked White the very same question when he was in England for the coronation. The King, hearing the conversation between the Queen and White across the table, broke in saying: "I hope you know, my dear White, that I have always been in favor of your having the islands, and you will have them yet. It was a great mistake in Denmark to reject the treaty, and she will soon see it. . . ."

The letter goes on giving other incidents, indicating, in White's opinion, that, even if the Emperor of Germany was not actively engaged in causing the failure of the treaty, he was delighted that it had failed, and evidently trusted to the chapter of accidents to bring them into his possession sooner or later.[30]

The same question also crops up in a letter from Senator Lodge to President Roosevelt of June 10, 1905, in which the Senator is quite exercised over the story that the Hamburg-American Company is to establish a big coaling station at St. Thomas. Indeed suspicions of the Kaiser's influence are lively in this year, and there are positive evidences to this effect which it is unnecessary to cite.[31]

The German interest in coaling stations and naval bases in the Caribbean was also to be seen as early as 1898 in the proposal that Germany should acquire a base in the Dominican Republic. This would have been part of a bargain struck with the Dominican authorities; but the plan was finally vetoed by the Kaiser. The German Ambassador at Washington had advised that such a project would at once involve a dispute with the United States. For this, Germany was not prepared at the time and rather than risk a falling out with America over the Monroe Doctrine she gave up the idea.[32] Such suggestions, as we shall see in the next chapter, were to crop up again in the case of Venezuela whereupon the Germans denied that they planned to establish a base in South American waters. This may be quite true, but we must remember that the denial did not come from the German Admiralty. Indeed, if we may judge of foreign navies by our own, we can readily imagine that the idea of a German naval base in Santo Domingo would be welcomed by the German authorities. Our own navy people have frequently suggested that along African, Chinese, and South American coasts such establishments could be set up with the consent of the government concerned. Moreover, in April, 1900, a concrete plan was proposed for the Caribbean. In the private papers of Secretary Hay there is a note on the subject. The possession of Porto Rico, it was pointed out, made the establishment of a naval station, probably in Samana Bay, in Santo Domingo all the more desirable since there were at Porto Rico no good harbors for vessels of the largest draft. It was said that the need of the navy was indisputable.[33] Yet this, and similar plans, were rejected, for the needs of the navy had to give way before the more important aims of political action.

The affairs of the Dominican and Haitian Republics were to give the United States considerable trouble in the years to come; and it is worth while to mention briefly the factors which were to occupy our attention. In both republics revolution had been a habit; extravagance and corruption were endemic; and as the result foreign creditors suffered. Both because of domestic conditions on the island and in order to avoid the landing of European forces, who might collect monies due, the United States has felt called upon at times to intervene, or at least to exercise its power, to prevent a violation of the Monroe doctrine by foreign states.

If we consider the Dominican Republic first, we find that in 1899 the assassination of President Heureaux was the signal for a revolutionary disturbance. For nearly twenty years he had been the virtual dictator; his successor, President Jiminez, inaugurated a milder mode of government; but he was shortly forced out; and finally Wos y Gill became president. He was overthrown in 1903 and civil war broke out. In 1904 Morales succeeded to the presidency; but in 1906 he, in turn, was forced out and General Caceres became his successor until his assasination in 1911. This record of sudden death and revolution was further underscored by the financial difficulties of the state. Heureaux had left a large foreign and domestic debt which the subsequent civil disturbances increased till the Dominican Republic was really bankrupt. During the disturbances in 1903 American naval forces had been temporarily landed and a Dominican naval vessel had been compelled to stop bombarding the city of Santo Domingo.[34]

The financial claims of foreign interests had been recognized in agreements which pledged the incomes of various custom houses to the specific payment of some of these debts. Occasionally because of civil disturbances some of these ports would be closed. In any case the failure of payments under these protocols was an embarrassing feature of the situation. In 1904 an American financial agent was appointed to collect customs at Puerto Plata and other ports. This was as the result of the arbitration of claims by the San Domingo Improvement Company and was with the consent of the Dominican Government, though they balked at carrying out all the provisions of the award.[35]

As the financial situation still remained serious, and the clamor of other foreign interests increased, the United States warned the Dominican Republic that European intervention might take place. They suggested that America should take charge of the collection of all Dominican customs and should by "an equitable distribution of the assigned quotas among the Dominican Government and the various claimants" forestall an attempt by foreign governments to occupy ports and administer the collection of customs.[36] This arrangement was finally put in writing and accepted by the Dominican Republic on February 7, 1905. Unfortunately the United States Senate adjourned without taking action upon it.[37] As the foreign creditors became impatient after the end of March, President Roosevelt ordered that, pending action by the Senate, American agents should take charge of Dominican customs. Fifty-five per cent of the receipts should be deposited in New York for distribution to the foreign creditors after the ratification of the treaty. The foreign creditors, who included Italian, Spanish, German and American citizens, were in favor of this arrangement.[38]

President Roosevelt in taking this step at once loosed a storm of foolish criticism upon himself. He practically said that everyone who votes against this treaty invites foreign nations to violate the Monroe doctrine. The President's action was in accord with the prerogative of the executive; and later, when it became necessary to warn the Dominicans that revolutionary movements which might upset the *status quo* would not be permitted, his action was necessary and justified. He wrote to Secretary Hay, who was in Europe attempting to recover his health:

> In Santo Domingo we have taken the necessary step; but it was one of those cases where trouble was sure to come, whether from action or from inaction. I felt that much less trouble would come from action; but beyond a doubt we shall have flurries in connection with revolutionary uprisings and filibustering enterprises, as we assume the protection of the custom houses. I do not think that Santo Domingo itself will give us much trouble. . . .[39]

The success of this *modus vivendi* in restoring confidence and the vigor shown in preventing serious disturbances in 1905–1906 showed that the United States was determined to avoid the danger which we had confronted in 1902–1903 with respect to Venezuela. As we shall see in the next chapter the danger came not from our policy or exercise of power but from two other sources. Either by our failure to act, foreign states felt compelled to act by themselves, which of course made us nervous with respect to the Monroe doctrine, or, if we did intervene, we incurred the charge that we were imperialistic and were aiming at the domination of Latin-America. It was a choice of evils, of which, however, the second was the lesser evil. In any event, as regards Santo Domingo, we had already shown ourselves scrupulous in trying to preserve her sovereignty.

As regards the sister Negro republic of Haiti our action in the Lueders case in 1897 again showed our anxiety to avoid entanglement there. Lueders, a German subject, had been unjustly and harshly punished by the Haitian Government. The Germans sent men-of-war and under threat of bombardment secured damages and an apology. When Mr. Powell, our Minister to Haiti, referred in his despatches to the Monroe doctrine he was told by Secretary Sherman that this doctrine was "wholly inapplicable" to this case. Furthermore the suggestion of an American protectorate over Haiti at this time, which was proposed by that republic, was frowned on in 1898. Still a third instance was our objection to the proposal that a special independent tribunal should be set up in Haiti by foreign states to entertain suits between aliens whose decisions should be enforced by the Haitian authorities. Secretary Hay described such a suggestion by the German Minister to Haiti as "an essential interference with the sovereign rights of Hayti" and refused to have anything to do with the idea.[40]

With the revolutionary disturbances which led to the withdrawal of President Sam from Haiti, the United States was concerned only to protect American interests. The story that German interests had prevailed in securing the promise of a coaling station at Mole St. Nicolas is probably true; but it does not seem to play any part in the struggle. At all events with the disruption of President Sam's cabinet the plan was dropped. Later, of course, in 1915 it was to be revived. Throughout the summer of 1902, the continued civil war in Haiti provided many opportunities for American intervention; but of none of these did we avail ourselves.[41] Indeed during the decade, 1896–1906, American "imperialism" in the Caribbean simply did not exist.

The same is also true in our relations with Mexico and the five republics of Central America—Guatemala, Honduras, San Salvador, Nicaragua, and Costa Rica. We promoted the establishment of peace in 1906 to end one of those disastrous wars which involved several of these smaller states and in this we co-operated with Mexico.[42] The negotiations with Nicaragua and Costa Rica relating to an interoceanic canal will be discussed in a later chapter. Limits of space and time compel me to omit the somewhat uneventful record of our relations with other Latin-American States. There certainly was nothing startling or adventurous about them. Venezuela and Colombia alone provide anything of risk or importance. Yet the trip of Secretary Root, in the summer of 1906, to various countries of South America was a significant and valuable tour. We had neglected to emphasize the friendly relations which subsisted between the United States and those states. Now, as we entered on a new stage in our diplomatic relations, as American business interests began to give an economic trend to our political policies, we gave to our Latin-American diplomacy a special significance. However, all this lies beyond the bounds of this book.

One other matter of policy on which we have not touched is of significance. The Spanish-American war and its immediate results had fostered the idea that the further development of our navy was of the utmost importance. Our policies relating to Cuba and the Caribbean, to Venezuela, to the Panama Canal, and to the Pacific as well as to the Atlantic Oceans would be paralyzed did we not have an adequate navy. President Roosevelt, of course, saw this clearly. Indeed the greater part of the nation appreciated it. Our intervention had aimed to end misrule and civil strife. We were eager for arbitration and for the settlement of disputes, yet our navy was, in effect, both an instrument of policy and an agent for peace. The development of the navy was one of the major results of our experience in the Caribbean.

NOTES TO CHAPTER X

1. Olcott, *McKinley,* II, pp. 196-202.
2. Quoted in Robinson, *Cuba and Intervention,* New York, 1905, p. 189.
3. H. P., Jan. 11, 1901, Root to Hay.
4. *Ibid.,* Jan. 9, Root to Wood.
5. *Ibid.,* Feb. 5, Adee to Hay.
6. Quoted in Moore, *Digest of International Law,* VI, p. 380. In writing these pages I have had the advantage of reading the manuscript M. A. thesis (Wesleyan, 1923) of Mr. Leo J. Meyer on "Relations between the United States and Cuba."
7. *U. S. Statutes at Large,* XXXI, p. 897.
8. *Am. Journal of International Law,* VIII, p. 590.

9. *Ibid.*, VIII, pp. 585-591; Rhodes, *McKinley and Roosevelt Administrations*, pp. 180-181 (quoting a private letter from Senator Platt) Coolidge, *Orville H. Platt*, New York, 1910, ch. XXII.
10. *Am. Journal of International Law*, VIII, pp. 886-889.
11. R. P., July 25, 1902, Hay to Roosevelt; D. S., From Cuba, Vol. 1, No. 107, Aug. 7, Squiers to Hay.
12. H. P., Sept. 17, 1902, Squiers to Hay.
13. *Ibid.*, Oct. 10, 1902, Squiers to Hay. Squiers got the notion that Carden, the British Minister in Havana, was working against the United States and made complaint to Washington. Choate took it up with Lansdowne in London. There was absolute denial of the facts; but Squiers later reports that Carden was quieting down. This was the Carden who, ten or more years later, was also reputed as being strongly anti-American in Mexico. Cf. D. S., To London, Vol. 34, p. 269, Oct. 16, 1902, Hay to Choate; From London, Vol. 205, telegrams, Oct. 17, 22, 25, Choate to Hay; From Cuba, Vol. 3, No. 263, Oct. 27, Squiers to Hay; H. P., Oct. 27 and Nov. 19, 1902, Choate to Hay.
14. D. S., From Cuba, Vol. 5, No. 341, Dec. 18, 1902, Squiers to Hay.
15. R. P., May 13, 1903, Roosevelt to Hay.
16. D. S., To Cuba, Vol. 1, p. 386, March 20, 1905, Adee to Squiers; p. 408, June 6, Loomis to Squiers; p. 413, June 21, same to same; p. 496, May 2, 1906, Root to Morgan. From Cuba, Vol. 17, telegram, April 21 and 30, 1906, Morgan to Root; Vol. 18, telegram, May 31, Morgan to Root.
17. F. R., 1906, p. 473.
18. R. P., July 21, 1906, Roosevelt to White.
19. F. R., 1906, pp. 475-479.
20. *Ibid.*, 1906, pp. 480-481.
21. Quoted in Rhodes, pp. 364-366.
22. H. P., Sept. 28, 1898, Bradford to Hay.
23. D. S., From Denmark, Vol. 22, No. 83, Feb. 11, 1899, Swenson to Hay.
24. D. S., From London, Vol. 202, private letter on p. 1, Dec. 23, 1899, White to Hay.
25. D. S., To Denmark, Vol. 16, No. 86, Jan. 29, 1900, Hay to Swenson; telegram, Feb. 19, same to same; telegram, March 12, same to same; From Denmark, Vol. 22, telegram, Swenson to Hay; Feb. 22, same to same; H. P., May 25, 1900, MacArthur to Hay.
26. D. S., From Denmark, Vol. 23, No. 172, June 20, 1900, Swenson to Hay; To Denmark, Vol. 16, No. 109, Nov. 16, Hay to Swenson; telegram, Nov. 28, same to same.
27. D. S., To London, Vol. 33, telegram, p. 673, Aug. 22, 1901, Hay to White; Numerical File, Vol. 515, telegram, Sept. 5, 1901, White to Hay; private letters, Sept. 13 and Oct. 5, same to same; From Denmark, Vol. 23, No. 221, Oct. 4, Swenson to Hay; H. P., Sept. 13, White to Swenson (copy).
28. D. S., To Denmark, Vol. 16, telegram, Oct. 18, 1901, Hay to Swenson; No. 137, Feb. 19, Hay to Swenson; From Denmark, Vol. 23, No. 231, Nov. 27, 1901, Swenson to Hay; telegram, Jan. 2, 1902, same to same; No. 243, Jan. 31, same to same; H. P., Nov. 11 and Dec. 17, Swenson to Hay; Nov. 11, Clark to Hay.
29. D. S., From Denmark, Vol. 23, telegram, May 16, 1902, Swenson to Hay; Vol. 24, telegram, Oct. 22, same to same.
30. H. P., April 15, 1903, Hay to Roosevelt.
31. *Roosevelt-Lodge Correspondence*, II, pp. 135-138; D. S., From Denmark, Vol. 25, No. 15, Aug. 11, 1905, O'Brien to Root.
32. G. P., XV, Nos. 4201-4204.
33. H. P., Memorandum, April 30, 1900.

34. Schoenrich, *Santo Domingo, the Country with a Future,* New York, 1918, chs. V and VI; *F. R.,* 1903, pp. 390-396. A good short review of Dominican history to 1906 is in *F. R.,* 1905, pp. 379-389 and *Ibid.,* 1906, pp. 572-600.
35. *F. R.,* 1904, pp. 270-286.
36. *Ibid.,* 1905, pp. 298 *et seq.*
37. *Ibid.,* 1905, pp. 313 *et seq.*
38. *Ibid.,* 1905, pp. 355-356; *H. P.,* Feb. 21, 1905, McCauley to Hay; in the negotiation of the protocol and its subsequent enforcement Admiral Sigsbee played an important but discreet part.
39. *R. P.,* April 2, 1905, Roosevelt to Hay; April 12, Hay to Roosevelt; Bishop, I, pp. 431-435; *F. R.,* 1905, pp. 398-411.
40. Moore, VI, pp. 474-476; *F. R.,* 1900, pp. 706-713.
41. *F. R.,* 1902, pp. 587 *et seq.*
42. *F. R.,* 1906, pp. 884 *et seq.*

CHAPTER XI

THE EUROPEAN POWERS AND VENEZUELA

WE have already seen that the United States was suspicious of German activities in the Western Hemisphere, perhaps unduly so, and was keen to make it clear to the world that she intended to maintain the Monroe doctrine against all comers. As our naval dominance in the Caribbean was the sign of that policy, indeed as the Caribbean became more and more like an American lake or inland sea, it was only natural that on occasion there should be mystification because of the special position we had assumed. This was particularly evident in 1902–1903 when war threatened over the blockade of Venezuelan ports by European states who had righteous claims against that South American republic.

In this connection there has grown up a peculiar belief in the minds of some that during the years 1896–1906 there was a German conspiracy against the United States. Mr. Thayer, in a chapter entitled "The German Menace Looms Up," in his life of John Hay seeks to capitalize that alleged conspiracy. Secretary Hay had, it is true, from his young manhood a sharp feeling against Germany. This he showed in his letters at various times; but as for there being a "German Conspiracy" against the United States during these years—that is far fetched. I have been through the Roosevelt and Hay papers and through the archives of the Department of State. I have examined the *Grosse Politik,* that great collection of documents, and though I found much to persuade me of German stupidity and folly I did not find the evidence of any "German Conspiracy" as Mr. Thayer terms it. I looked for it patiently and carefully; but in these materials there was nothing which merited such a high sounding term. Mr. Thayer says: "it is necessary now to speak of the German Conspiracy against the United States. When the history of that plot comes to be written in detail, Hay's contacts with it will be seen in their true significance." [1] Such search as I have made convinces me that this suggestion falls flat.

Now we can turn to see what really did happen as regards Venezuela and to mark the limits of our historical information. At the outset, however, let us recall for a moment the trend of German policy during the years just prior to 1901. The growth of the Germany navy was of course of particular interest to the United States. Ambassador White was telegraphing about the growth of the German naval budget as early as 1897 and about the establishment of a South American squadron.[2] An important article by Dr. Anton of the University of Jena appeared in October of that year. This was summarized by Mr. Jackson as follows:

> The efforts to direct German emigration to South America, which are from time to time being made, when considered together with the arguments used in the matter, indicate clearly that Germany looks on that part of the world as a field for colonization. Germans who go to the United States soon become Americanized and are of no further use to the mother country, while those who go to South America retain their nationality and language, do not to any great extent intermarry with the native or Spanish population, and purchase in the German markets, and it is more or less an open secret that Germany expects to benefit in the anticipated breaking up of the United States of Brazil, if not in other quarters. Under these circumstances, it is natural that Germany is opposed to any international recognition, even impliedly, of the "Monroe Doctrine," is displeased with any reiteration of that doctrine by our government, and looks with a jealous eye upon any attempt on our part to form closer commercial or political connections with the Republics of South and Central America.[3]

In 1898 Germany proposed to Great Britain that they jointly make representations to the Argentine to check her armaments against Chili.[4] This, however, came to nothing. In 1901–1902 there was a circumstantial story of the attempt of the Kaiser to acquire from Mexico in his personal right a stretch of territory along the coast of the peninsula of Lower California which included two good harbors. This plan was also abandoned.[5] In 1901 there was a persistent story that Germany was looking for a coaling station convenient to the Caribbean Sea and was endeavoring to secure one on the island of Margarita off the Venezuelan coast. Secretary Hay wrote that such a step would be a "source of concern to" the United States in view of our well-known attitude as to the Monroe doctrine. Mr. Jackson stated that in conversation at the German Foreign Office he had been told "that there was *nothing whatever* in the story." [6] Later the German Embassy at Washington declared that "all reports that are circulated concerning German plans of conquest in South and Central America are lies and slanders of our enemies"; and on November 6, 1901, a declaration was made "on behalf of both the Foreign Office and the Emperor himself, that the German government had no purpose or intention to acquire the smallest foothold in South America or the Caribbean Sea." [7] Despite these denials I have small doubt, as was said in the last chapter, that the German navy, as distinguished from the German Foreign Office, was concerned in an attempt to secure a naval station in South American waters at this time. It would be only consonant with German policy in that region.

The economic hostility of Central Europe to the United States was another matter to which we were also alive. In December, 1897, the speeches both of the Austro-Hungarian Foreign Secretary, Count Goluchowski, and of Baron von Thielman, the Finance Minister of the German Empire, indicated a spirit of opposition to American commercial advance which interested the Department of State.[8] Anything like a combination of European nations, with Germany at its head, directed against the United States was, however, wisely declared to be impossible.[9] The time had come, nevertheless, for the discussion of a new commercial treaty with Germany. To do this was to face the opposition of the dyed-in-the-wool protectionists who were as ignorant of international relations as a babe unborn. Nevertheless, the readiness of the Department of State to negotiate a reciprocity treaty was clear. It became clearer as it was evident that Germany had been sounding other European nations with a view to establishing some sort of an anti-American economic accord. As a result, therefore, a commercial treaty was finally drawn up.[10]

We have already observed the policy of Germany as regards the Spanish-American war, our acquisition of the Philippines and Hawaii, the partition of the Samoan Islands, and the open door in China. As regards Haiti there was a brief passage with respect to German proposals; but nothing in any or in all of these fields together can be built up into anything like a conspiracy against the United States. That there were in certain circles in Germany a desire to profit by any American mistakes and a readiness to intrigue with our opponents cannot be denied; but that does not mean that there was a real plot against us.

Germany, Great Britain, and Italy each had certain claims that they had been unable to collect from Venezuela who had treated all three of these powers with contempt. This frivolous policy on the part of Venezuela was now to meet with punishment. Germany and Great Britain had proposed in the spring of 1901 that Venezuela should submit these claims to arbitration. This President Castro refused to do. Finally in December, 1901, the German government suggested to the United States that some measures of coercion might be applied. It declared, however, that "under no circumstances do we consider in our proceedings the acquisition or the permanent occupation of Venezuelan territory." If a blockade should not be sufficient "we would have to consider the temporary occupation on our part of different Venezuelan harbor places and the levying of duties in those places." To this statement Secretary Hay replied, saying that the President believed that no measures could be taken by the German authorities contrary to these statements and quoted from the President's recent message to Congress. The passages he cited were as follows:

The Monroe Doctrine is a declaration that there must be no territorial aggrandizement by any non-American power at the expense of any American power on American soil. It is in no wise intended as hostile to any nation in the Old World. The President further said: This doctrine has nothing to do with the commercial relations of any American power, save that it in truth allows each of them to form such as it desires. . . . We do not guarantee any State against punishment if it misconducts itself, provided that punishment does not take the form of the acquisition of territory by any non-American power.[11]

In January, 1902, von Bülow, reporting to the Kaiser, proposed that he sound Great Britain with a view to joint action against Venezuela. The Kaiser replied, "Only after the conclusion of Henry's visit." At this time Prince Henry of Prussia was planning his trip to America. In any case the Kaiser added: "If we can be sure that the British will not take advantage of these suggestions to cause the Americans to suspect us and thus weaken the effectiveness of My Brother's visit." To assist Prince Henry in his tour he was not given any formal instructions but was told that "should the Americans manifest concern about German ideas of acquisition or of influence as regards Central and South America, that should be disclaimed as an absurd fantasy by pointing to the pacific character of His Majesty's policy and to the many problems we have to solve elsewhere in the world, without, however, imparting the character of a solemn declaration to such a rather ironical denial." [12]

The Italian government on making similar inquiries received from the Department of State the same reply as had the German government with the caution "that it would be better that any demonstration which was made by Italy should not be simultaneous with that made by Germany, as it might create an injurious and erroneous impression upon public opinion in the United States." [13] In July, 1902, the British government brought forward its claims for the seizure and destruction of British shipping by the Venezuelan authorities. It was proposed that a naval demonstration should take place off the Venezuelan coast in November by a joint

Anglo-German blockade. This, however, was changed, in the end of October, to a plan to seize the Venezuelan gunboats and to hold them. On November 11, therefore, Great Britain sent a sharp note to Venezuela. Meanwhile Anglo-German agreement was reached as to joint action and on November 25, 1902, Secretary Hay was informed of the British plan of action. An unsatisfactory reply having been received from Venezuela the British Chargé was directed to present an ultimatum on December 7 in concert with the German Minister and to leave the capital of Venezuela, Caracas. Twenty-four hours later, failing acceptance of the principle that the British claims were just, he was to go on board a British man-of-war. The British and German governments also asked that the American Legation at Caracas should take charge of their legations when the break took place.[14]

President Castro, who seems to have acted like a blackguard, on receipt of the ultimatum ordered that British and German private citizens should be arrested. Mr. Bowen, the American Minister, therefore, had his hands full seeking to secure their release. In the meantime, the Venezuelan gunboats had been seized and later two were sunk.[15] This action led the Venezuelan government to propose on December 9, arbitration of the dispute with Germany and Great Britain and to ask that Mr. Bowen act as arbitrator for Venezuela. On December 11 the formal request for arbitration was made by Venezuela. This was at once transmitted to London and Berlin on December 12, and Secretary Hay agreed that in case of arbitration Mr. Bowen might act for Venezuela.[16] Already, in view of excitement in the United States, there were signs that Germany was weakening and on December 12 von Bülow advised the Kaiser that he should desist from further military operations in view of "this renewed attempt to revive the anti-German agitation" in the United States. He also spoke of the risk of disturbing public opinion in case Italy should now join in the demonstration against Venezuela. The Kaiser, however, discounted this and added that the more active the British were the better it would be for

Germany who could thus take a back seat.[17] At the same time the German Ambassador in London was instructed to point out to the British that the Americans had not sponsored but had merely transmitted the Venezuelan request for arbitration and that Washington was apparently inclined to keep aloof from the Venezuelan proposal.[18]

Count Metternich, German Ambassador in England, observed these instructions and on December 15 urged the British to reject the proposal of arbitration and to proceed at once to the blockade of Venezuelan ports. The United States had already taken exception to the idea of a "pacific blockade" and was informed that the British would have nothing to do with such a German plan. Lord Lansdowne also assured Mr. Henry White that the landing of troops on Venezuelan soil was not contemplated by Great Britain.[19] Mr. White, who was at that time Chargé, seems to have acted with courage and discretion for he sent a personal and confidential telegram to Secretary Hay saying:

> I am inclined to think whole Venezuelan matter, especially British acting with Germans, unpopular in this country. Sinking of ships certainly is. Consequently I am not without hope something may come of our transmission of arbitration proposal. I am expressing privately to my friends in the Government grave fears, of course as my personal opinion only, lest Great Britain will, if hostilities continue, be involved in course of [events? (word missing)] in some action which will estrange if not antagonize American public feeling. Have refused all information to press. Am remaining in London.[20]

On the afternoon of December 15 an arranged debate took place in the House of Lords which merely reviewed the circumstances but which gave vent to the anxiety of the British public as to the course of events. A similar debate took place in the House of Commons which revealed even more clearly the feeling that co-operation with Germany was unpopular.[21] The publication of the Blue Book on Venezuela also made it clear that Lord Lansdowne had written in November, that it was "only reasonable that if we [Great Britain and Germany] agreed to act together in applying coercion [to Venezuela] we should also agree that each should support the other's demands, and should not desist from doing so except by agreement." [22]

The pressure of public opinion now became greater. Count Metternich, after seeing Lord Lansdowne on December 16, advised the German Foreign Office to get out of the imbroglio quickly by agreeing to arbitrate. The same day von Holleben from Washington favored in cautious phrases that same policy, as opinion in financial circles in New York was also strongly in favor of arbitration, and he feared lest German trade interests in South America might suffer because of German action in Venezuela. In prompt reply von Bülow telegraphed to London that quick action was necessary to avoid the possibility that the United States might face Germany and Great Britain with a ready-made program. The American desire that arbitration should be accepted was also made evident. Consequently, on December 18, Germany and Great Britain agreed to the principle of arbitration.[23]

Prior to this, however, the United States had been concerned over the proposal to declare a blockade of Venezuelan harbors. Germany had at first favored a so-called pacific blockade but had deferred to British objections and had agreed to a regular blockade. This was announced on December 12 and was to go into effect on December 25. As there had been no declaration of war, and as the rights of neutral shipping were affected, considerable correspondence followed.[24] The blockade, which was the cause of much friction but which was maintained, apparently with the acquiescence of the United States, was finally lifted in the middle of February. Various other European states which had not taken part in the blockade now presented their claims against Venezuela and, in the case of France, it was asserted that she had a prior claim upon the revenues of Venezuela. All of these matters were also finally settled by judicial decision.

There remains the question of President Roosevelt's interference to persuade Germany that she should accept arbitration. For this there are only three historical documents available to me all of which are from the President's hand. Two are letters of 1906, to Mr. Reid and to Mr. Henry White; and the third is the long letter, with its reference to two other letters, which was sent to Mr. Thayer in 1916 for inclusion as an appendix to the second edition of his life of John Hay. This letter also forms the greater part of a chapter on this subject in Bishop's life of Roosevelt. The reason why there is nothing on this remarkable story in the archives of the Department of State is that the matter was handled entirely by the President himself. There is nothing bearing on the story in the *Grosse Politik,* nor does a careful examination of the Roosevelt letter books for the period show anything more of value. The best we can do, therefore, is to quote the paragraph in the letter to Mr. White and repeat in the Appendix to this chapter the President's letter to Thayer. In the catalogue of events which has just been given it is a bit difficult to fit in the dates on which the interviews with the German Ambassador took place. They were probably December 10 and 16. As we have seen, Metternich, in London, was already advising on December 16 that Germany should agree to arbitration. If this chronology is correct it would serve to explain von Bülow's haste in deciding for arbitration on December 17. It is a pity that President Roosevelt omits all dates in his two letters; but I do not see anything in his statement of the facts which conflicts in any way with other printed and manuscript letters of the period. The extract from the private letter to Mr. White reads as follows:

> At the time of the Venezuela business I saw the German Ambassador privately myself; told him to tell the Kaiser that I had put Dewey in charge of our fleet to manoeuvre in West Indian waters; that the world at large should know this merely as a manoeuvre and we should strive in every way to appear simply as co-operating with the Germans; but that I regretted to say that the popular feeling was such that I should be obliged to interfere, by force if necessary, if the Germans took any action which looked like the acquisition of territory there or elsewhere along the Caribbean; that this was not in any way intended as a threat; but as the position on the part of the Government which the American people would demand, and

that I wanted him to understand it before the two nations drifted into such a position that trouble might come. I do not know whether it was a case of *post hoc* or *propter hoc,* but immediately afterward the Kaiser made to me the proposition that I should arbitrate myself, which I finally got him to modify so that it was sent to the Hague.[25]

This demonstration of the "big stick" had not taken place without careful consideration of the alternatives. A naval memorandum of the end of November, 1902, bears this out. On the possible collection of money from Venezuela by Germany this reads as follows:

1st. There would be but little use in Germany's occupying one port only, as such action would divert trade to others. She must occupy all custom houses.

2nd. Castro is a perfectly irresponsible dictator and would violently oppose such action. He might prohibit all local trade with the ports occupied, causing a congestion of goods there and consequent stoppage of trade, and consequently of customs receipts.

3rd. Castro would probably oppose military resistance, and this action would bring about war with Germany. In this case the acquisition of belligerent rights would simplify her problem of dealing with other nations having trade interests with Venezuela. While not seeking war with Venezuela, Germany once started on her expedition, would not go out of her way to avoid it.

4th. In the event of war, Germany *must* win, to preserve her prestige. It would cost her much in men and money.

5th. After winning she would certainly demand indemnity for her expenses.

6th. Venezuela could not pay indemnity, and could offer nothing but territory, or mortgage her revenue in such a way as to place herself in complete political dependence on Germany.

7th. The United States could not allow either of these, and yet Germany's right to indemnity would be incontestable.

8th. The only courses open to the United States are the payment of the indemnity, taking such security as she can from Venezuela, or war. The first method is cheapest, the second most probable.

9th. The United States with this possibility in view must not allow Germany during its attempt on Venezuela to occupy, fit up, or fortify any port so as to allow of its being used as a base against us. No fortifications protecting entrances of harbors, or collection of materials for such fortifications can be tolerated.

10. An immediate examination should be made of the Guanta

region by one of our vessels, to ascertain the availability of its ports for use as bases by the Germans. Also Los Roques.

11. We must keep at all times a force in and about Culebra, [Porto Rico], equal or superior to the whole German force in the Caribbean. Stores and coal must be accumulated there, guns mounted, and a base established if necessary. Our aim must be at all times to be in a better state of preparation for war than Germany is, and her every move must be met by corresponding preparatory action on our part.

12th. The military force in Porto Rico should be increased as soon as Germany sends troops to the Caribbean.

13th. The probable operations seem to be very similar to those of last year's problem.[26]

Such a memorandum would seem to indicate that in the opinion of the navy we were not prepared for war in 1902. But we were most emphatically ready. At all events Admiral Dewey was at Culebra and ready to sail. These matters, however, were not of as lasting importance as the effect which this assertion of the Monroe doctrine had on the mind of Latin America. In particular, as President Roosevelt early in December, 1902, had not opposed the use of force by European states to collect their debts from a South American state, there was considerable discussion. Finally Dr. Drago, of the Argentine Republic, put forward a doctrine, since known by his name, which asserted that force should not be used in the collection of debts. This was done in a note dated December 29, 1902, which developed, in the main, ideas advocated by Calvo, the distinguished authority on international law. In a few paragraphs it was declared that the Monroe doctrine had as its corollary the Drago doctrine. I quote in part:

At the outset it is to be noted in this connection that the capitalist who lends his money to a foreign state always takes into account the resources of the country and the probability, greater or less, that the obligations contracted will be fulfilled without delay.

All governments thus enjoy different credit according to their degree of civilization and culture and their conduct in business transactions; and these conditions are measured and weighed before making any loan, the terms being made more or less onerous in accordance with the precise data concerning them which bankers always have on record.

In the first place the lender knows that he is entering into a contract with a sovereign entity, and it is an inherent qualification of all sovereignty that no proceedings for the execution of a judgment may be instituted or carried out against it, since this manner of collection would compromise its very existence and cause the independence and freedom of action of the respective government to disappear.

Among the fundamental principles of public international law which humanity has consecrated, one of the most precious is that which decrees that all states, whatever be the force at their disposal, are entitled in law, perfectly equal one to the other and mutually entitled by virtue thereof to the same consideration and respect.

The acknowledgment of the debt, the payment of it in its entirety, can and must be made by the nation without diminution of its inherent rights as a sovereign entity, but the summary and immediate collection at a given moment, by means of force, would occasion nothing less than the ruin of the weakest nations, and the absorption of their governments, together with all the functions inherent in them, by the mighty of the earth.

. . . As these are the sentiments of justice, loyalty, and honor which animate the Argentine people and have always inspired its policy, your Excellency will understand that it has felt alarmed at the knowledge that the failure of Venezuela to meet the payments of its public debt is given as one of the determining causes of the capture of its fleet, the bombardment of one of its ports, and the establishment of a rigorous blockade along its shores. If such proceedings were to be definitely adopted they would establish a precedent dangerous to the security and the peace of the nations of this part of America.

The collection of loans by military means implies territorial occupation to make them effective, and territorial occupation signifies the suppression or subordination of the governments of the countries on which it is imposed.[27]

This doctrine was discussed at the Third Pan-American Conference at Rio de Janiero in 1906 and again at the second Hague Conference in 1907 where in spite of a number of reservations the following resolutions were adopted:

The contracting powers agree not to have recourse to armed force for the recovery of contract debts claimed from the government of one country by the government of another country as being due to its nationals.

This undertaking is, however, only applicable when the debtor state refuses or neglects to reply to an offer of arbitration, or, after accepting the offer, prevents any "compromis" from being agreed on, or, after the arbitration, fails to submit to the award.[28]

Such considerations, however, must not divert us from the course of events with respect to Venezuela. Immediately arbitration was accepted, both England and Germany asked President Roosevelt to act as arbitrator, as did Venezuela as well. The President was at first inclined to accept; but he soon saw that the Hague Tribunal was the better authority as the United States also had claims against Venezuela.[29] Mr. Bowen was, therefore, appointed to negotiate at Washington on behalf of Venezuela. There an agreement was to be reached as to the claims which were to be admitted to arbitration at the Hague. Great Britain probably felt that the fact that Mr. Bowen was to act would involve a moral guarantee on part of America that the settlement arranged by him would be carried out. So the negotiations now were shifted to Washington.[30]

In the meantime complaints increased as to the peremptory behavior of the blockaders. Mr. Bowen telegraphed January 3, 1903: "Situation certainly is bad. If the powers are honest they should raise blockade and accept offer to settle at once. Delay will end in chaos here and blockaders would have good cause to land." The banks had refused to advance money to President Castro; there was lack of provisions and at Caracas lack even of bread and salt. Furthermore, on January 17, Fort San Carlos was bombarded by the Germans and there were rumors that, in spite of her agreement to arbitrate, Germany intended to create a situation in Venezuela which would warrant her landing marines. It was reported by the German Embassy that Secretary Hay had spoken bitterly of this attack and public opinion in America was much stirred. The Kaiser's plan to take a "back seat" and let England take the American criticisms was being wrecked by the energy of his naval officers in Venezuelan waters. As a matter of fact the Venezuelan fort had fired first on the German cruiser; but such details were lost sight of by the public.³¹

It soon became evident that Great Britain was also annoyed with Germany over her action and over disputes as to the methods of payment by Venezuela. The German Ambassador in London reported an unsatisfactory dinner conversation with King Edward VII in regard to Venezuela. The King said that it was much more important to end the whole matter quickly than to get money in satisfaction of the claims. To this the Kaiser added marginal notes to the despatch as was his custom: *"Serenissimus verliert Nerven! Das hatte Grossmama nie gesagt!"* and *"Das ist ja eine unmögliche Zumuthung!"* ³² Mr. White telegraphed in the same vein as to the state of British opinion. Baron von Sternburg, who had been hastily despatched from Berlin to Washington on a special mission to try to repair the damage done by Holleben's mistakes of the previous months, reported that the action of Germany and Great Britain had been to the decided advantage of the United States in its effect on Latin-American opinion, that the pro-German sympathies of the American public were now lost, and that Admiral Dewey's fleet was under secret orders to be ready.³³ Altogether things seemed to be in a jumble as regards Germany; and in England ministers of the crown were finding it heavy going to try to explain the policy of the government as regards cooperation with Germany.³⁴

Unfortunately at this moment Mr. Bowen, who was really no diplomat, but an injudicious and officious person, saw fit to publish in the press a private letter from Sir Michael Herbert, British Ambassador at Washington. This naturally annoyed the British who threatened to break off relations with Mr. Bowen as Venezuelan representative in Washington. It took much oil from Secretary Hay to calm the troubled waters.³⁵ This happened just at the time when the blockading powers were asking President Roosevelt to act as umpire to decide among themselves and among the states which had claims against Venezuela the terms of preferential treatment which they were asserting. The President of course refused to act and wisely referred this matter also to The Hague. This served to hasten the signing of the protocols which ended this stage of the proceedings. All matters were now to be adjusted by mixed claims commissions and then were to be left to the Hague Tribunal for final settlement. On February 14, 1903, the blockade was lifted from Venezuela.[36]

It has been impossible to touch on the many personal aspects of these negotiations; but I wish to quote from a despatch which Sternburg sent home on February 19, 1903:

> In the course of a long horseback ride which I took yesterday with the President he discussed certain current problems. First he expressed himself as being glad in a high degree at the result of the Venezuelan negotiations, which had made here the best imaginable impression as regards Germany. He had emphasized on my arrival here the urgent need of the speediest disposal of the Venezuelan question because public opinion had felt irritated in a high degree, as a result of the protracted blockade. The sinking of the Venezuelan ships and the bombardment of the forts during the negotiations had immediately aroused sympathy here for Venezuela and created a critical situation. The German blockade ships had regarded the fleet of Admiral Dewey as their future opponent while Dewey's men, on the other hand, had viewed Germany's ships as their next object of hostilities. It had been high time to terminate such a situation. This time they had been German ships, but in six weeks they may possibly be English ships.
>
> After the President had shifted the conversation to the South American republics, he remarked that he was inclined to see the best guarantee of an improvement of conditions down there in the expansion of German influence, which had already gained such solid ground in southern Brazil. In the establishment of an independent state by Germans in Brazil he saw the best solution of the South American problem. I felt a certain cooling off in the President's sympathies for England.
>
> In touching upon the question of Alaska, the President said that, if the impending negotiations should bring no results, they would without further ado proceed to mark out the boundary line claimed by them and insist upon its recognition.
>
> In discussing the causes which lie at the bottom of the anti-German movement in the United States, the President frankly

declared that it was due to the action of Admiral Diederichs at Manila. The American people had seen in it an insult to their national hero, Admiral Dewey.

I feel that the President does not treat with *absolute* confidence Germany's assurances regarding the respecting of the Monroe Doctrine. I took the opportunity to assure him emphatically that Germany was not thinking of territorial acquisitions in South and Central America.[37]

I judge from other sources that the German Ambassador may have been mistaken. Meanwhile civil war went on briskly in Venezuela and there was friction as to arbitrary decrees by President Castro.[38] Indeed only a year later Castro was to try to levy blackmail on American concerns and thus to involve himself in serious disputes with the United States. For the present, however, we must turn to the situation at The Hague, where the creditors of Venezuela were wrangling among themselves and where the counsel for Venezuela were enduring the ebullitions of Mr. Wayne MacVeagh.

That gentleman, as senior counsel for Venezuela, as an ex-diplomat, and as an acquaintance of the President and Secretary Hay took upon himself to complain of nearly everybody and everything. He threatened to throw up the case and made himself particularly disagreeable to the British. Altogether this meeting of the Hague Tribunal was anything but peaceful. Finally Secretary Hay wrote, on September 29, to Mr. Penfield, junior counsel for Venezuela, saying: "I hope you will be able to go through without a row which will discredit us at The Hague. I rely greatly on you to prevent this. It is not a matter of life and death to us which way the verdict goes, but our own standing in the court is very important." At the end, in November, 1903, the Court adjourned with good feeling shown on the part of everyone. This, however, does not seem to have been due to the behavior of Mr. MacVeagh. In February, 1904, the final allotments of claims were made against Venezuela.[39]

The natural characteristics of President Castro soon made themselves evident. A vain man, he governed by fear and force. Notoriously immoral, he nevertheless used the most august language; he would trick anyone who incurred his dislike; and his régime was a dictatorship without restraint. Under his rule the history of Venezuela had been wayward in the extreme; without gratitude or honesty, blackmail was his favored instrument. The details of the quarrel between President Castro and the New York and Bermudez Company we can pass by, but as a general illustration of the problem which confronted the United States, the dispute is illuminating. Further the failure of the Venezuelan government promptly to settle claims adjudicated against it, and the development of a new dispute involving France with Venezuela all go to demonstrate the difficulties of the situation. Should we add to this the unfortunate story of the charges brought by Mr. Bowen against his predecessor Mr. Loomis, who was now Assistant Secretary of State, the result would indeed be gloomy. This unsavory episode, however, does not fall within the limits of this book. We can dismiss it, as did President Roosevelt, who wrote to Senator Lodge on May 24, 1905:

> The Loomis-Bowen affair is most irritating. From all that appears, Loomis was entirely straight but he was certainly indiscreet and did things which enabled Bowen and the others to make an attack upon him. It is another case of disregarding Socrates' maxim as to the difference between a private man, who only has to do what is right, and a public man, who ought to so conduct himself that no one can have an excuse for *saying* that he has not done what is right. At the same time, unless something is shown against Loomis I can not possibly get rid of him, and Bowen will have to be turned out whether Loomis is innocent or not; for it appears clearly that having forwarded the charges to the Department and the Department not having acted upon them, he then secured their publication in the press and is responsible for the entire scandal. Many of his accusations are too preposterous for belief. They in effect include the statement that Loomis has conducted the affairs of the State Department in reference to Venezuela by himself, in defiance of the wishes of John Hay and myself. I really think the man is a little hipped.[40]

As for the Bermudez Company we find the pages of *Foreign Relations* full of despatches dealing with its affairs.

Mr. Bowen promptly championed its cause and begged for an American fleet, the seizure of the custom house at La Guayra, and most energetic action by the United States. Castro ordered an embargo on the asphalt exports of the Company, and the sequestration of its property. This powerful corporation had, it was charged, contributed money to the cause of Venezuelan revolutionists opposed to Castro's government. The United States refused to send an ultimatum to Venezuela but protested vigorously. Mr. Bowen then sent in a "confidential report regarding the violation by Venezuela of the Washington Protocols and the spoliation by her of foreigners and foreign corporations." It is needless to say that the Drago doctrine, which was very popular at this time in Venezuelan circles for payment of debts, was the last thing that President Castro thought of.[41]

From November, 1904, to February, 1905, the United States pressed for an impartial trial of the case against the Bermudez Company. On February 15 the Venezuelan court confirmed the sequestration order and on February 20 Mr. Bowen reported the charges against Mr. Loomis, which were that Mr. Loomis was paid for promising that the United States would not intervene in the case of the Bermudez Company. In the meantime the Venezuelan government had proposed that outstanding questions should be submitted to arbitration. This raised the matter of the payment by Venezuela of claims due under the Washington protocols of 1903; moreover, the unwillingness of Venezuela to let the Bermudez case go to arbitration interfered with this solution. The United States felt that Castro was merely juggling with these questions. A threat was, therefore, made on March 10, 1905, that it might be necessary to use force unless complete justice were done to American citizens and unless the various pending questions were submitted to arbitration. The reply of the Venezuelan government to the American proposal gave no satisfaction whatever. Matters were thus at a deadlock.[42] Meanwhile in Washington the airing of the Bowen-Loomis feud did great damage to the prestige of the United States in

Venezuela. A mournful despatch from the American Chargé at Caracas illustrates this:

> The prestige of the United States representatives to Venezuela is irrevocably damaged, so long as President Castro and his government continue, and foreign diplomats in general must come under the stigma of scandal, more or less. President Castro will take advantage, no doubt, of what he must consider his last crowning diplomatic victory, and a note of warning is sounded to foreign interests, and to the actual happiness of the Venezuelan people. I have noted the ill effect upon the local public mind, and the depression of the business spirit.
>
> I have obtained the ideas of prominent men here, and the talk of the clubs; everyone seems agreed that our last representative [Bowen] here lent momentum to a needless scandal at a most inopportune time, that he has lessened if not ruined the chance for a clean and full settlement of affairs with the United States and other nations, that the prestige of our legation and the other legations in Caracas is incalculably lessened. . . .
>
> If Castro backs down, it will be no diplomatic victory for us or our Minister who is coming, it seems to me. We have been held off successfully for about a year, and must we end with the world recounting Castro's success and perhaps making him more unamenable with praise?[43]

The studied slights which Castro now put on the United States had led to rumors of armed intervention by America. A despatch had therefore been sent out saying that we were "at peace with all the world" and that we were "not making a military demonstration in Venezuela or elsewhere."[44] With the summer President Roosevelt determined to send Judge Calhoun of Chicago as a special commissioner to Venezuela to investigate and report on the whole situation in that country.[45] His report, however, did not result in any immediate or real change in the situation. Negotiations hung on for months regarding the Bermudez Company despite proposals for direct settlement.[46] In the meantime the claims of the French Cable Company which had been mulcted by Castro provoked another foreign crisis. On December 15, 1905, at an interview between the President, Secretary Root, who had succeeded Secretary Hay, and Ambassador Jusserand in Washington, France declared that in case it were necessary to use force against Venezuela there would be no permanent occupation of Venezuelan territory. Later, at the rupture of diplomatic relations between France and Venezuela, the United States took charge of the French legation at Caracas.[47] Indeed in the spring President Castro retired from public life for a few weeks; but on his return he was greeted as a conquering hero. His grip on the country could not be lightly shaken. With his fall in 1909 affairs took a turn for the better. All of these disputes with foreign states were settled; and an improvement of conditions in Venezuela can be noted.

Such a record showed the long suffering patience of the United States. This was once more to be expressed in a speech by Secretary Root at Buenos Aires in 1906, when he stated that the United States accepted the principle of the Drago doctrine with respect to the collection of debts. He said to his Argentinian audience: "I am glad to be able to declare myself in hearty and unreserved sympathy with you. The United States of America has never deemed it to be suitable that she should use her army and navy for the collection of ordinary contract debts of foreign governments to her citizens." [48] At the last this view was qualified by the statement that the debtor state must have been ready to accept arbitration. In this decade, 1896–1906, which began with our defense of Venezuela against Great Britain and ended with the annoying higgling and violent bad manners of President Castro, there were few things more significant than this our declaration in favor of the principle of the Drago doctrine.

NOTES TO CHAPTER XI

1. Thayer, II, p. 275.
2. *D. S.*, From Germany, Vol. 64, telegram, Nov. 28, 1897, White to Sherman.
3. *D. S.*, From Germany, Vol. 64, No. 161, Oct. 29, 1897, Jackson to Sherman.
4. *D. S.*, From London, Vol. 193, telegram, Aug. 27, 1898, Hay to Day.
5. *H. P.*, undated, 1902, Choate to Hay.
6. *D. S.*, To Germany, Vol. 21, No. 1186, April 10, 1901, Hay to Jackson; *H. P.*, April 24, 1901, Jackson to Hay; cf. *D. S.*, To Germany, Vol. 21,

No. 1204, May 20, Hill to White; From Germany, Vol. 74, No. 1648, June 5, White to Hay.
    7. *D. S.*, From German Embassy, Vol. 30, Oct. 15, 1901, note; Numerical File, Vol. 547, memorandum, Nov. 16, 1901.
    8. *D. S.*, To Germany, Vol. 20, No. 272, Dec. 14, 1897, Sherman to White.
    9. *D. S.*, From Germany, Vol. 64, No. 251, Jan. 7, 1898, White to Sherman; Vol. 65, No. 274, Feb. 3, same to same; speaks of a strong desire in Germany to combat the protective tariff in the United States.
    10. *D. S.*, From German Embassy, Vol. 28, Oct. 23, 1899, Mumm to Hay; Vol. 29, March 20, 1900, Holleben to Hay; To Germany, Vol. 21, No. 967, Nov. 21, 1899, Hay to White; To German Embassy, Vol. 12, No. 410, April 5, 1900, Hay to Holleben; From France, Vol. 120, No. 969, Feb. 6, 1902, Porter to Hay; *H. P.*, March 30, 1899 and March 13, 1900, Robert P. Porter to Hay.
    11. *F. R.*, 1901, pp. 192-195. Cf. Rhodes, pp. 247-248.
    12. *G. P.*, XVII, No. 5106.
    13. *D. S.* Numerical File, Vol. 547, memorandum, March 6, 1902.
    14. *Parl. Papers,* Venezuela, No. 1, 1902. Cd. 1372, *passim; G. P.*, XVII, Nos. 5107, 5108, 5113, 5116; *British and Foreign State Papers,* Vol. 95, p. 1084; *R. P.*, memorandum, Nov. 29, 1902, Hill to Roosevelt; *D. S.*, From Venezuela, Vol. 55, No. 130, Oct. 4, 1902, Bowen to Hay, referring to the seizure of the island of Patos by the British. This island was really included with Trinidad but was only three miles off the Venezuela coast. Gooch and Temperley, *British Documents on the Origins of the War, 1898-1914,* II, pp. 153-173. Cf. Appendix B to this chapter.
    15. *D. S.*, From Venezuela, Vol. 55, telegrams, Dec. 9, 1902, Bowen to Hay; *F. R.*, 1903, pp. 788-791.
    16. *D. S.*, To London, Vol. 34, telegram, Dec. 12, 1902, Hay to White; *F. R.*, 1903, pp. 453, 790-792.
    17. *G. P.*, XVII, No. 5120.
    18. *Ibid.*, XVII, 5121.
    19. *Ibid.*, XVII, 5123; *D. S.*, From London, Vol. 206, telegram, Dec. 15, 1902, White to Hay.
    20. *D. S.*, From London, Vol. 206, telegram, Dec. 15, 1902, White to Hay.
    21. *Times,* Dec. 16, 1902.
    22. *Parl. Papers,* Venezuela, No. 1, 1902, No. 13.
    23. *G. P.*, XVII, Nos. 5124-27; *British and For. S. P.,* Vol. 95, p. 1124; *F. R.*, 1903, pp. 454-455; *D. S.*, From London, Vol. 206, telegrams, and No. 1001, Dec. 17, 1902, White to Hay; telegram, Dec. 18, same to same.
    24. *D. S.*, From London, Vol. 206, telegram and Nos. 1008, 1902, White to Hay; To London, Vol. 34, telegram, Dec. 16, Hay to White; To Germany, Vol. 21, telegram, Dec. 16, Hay to Tower; *F. R.*, 1903, pp. 421-425, 454-458.
    25. *R. P.*, Aug. 14, 1906, Roosevelt to White (printed in Rhodes, pp. 251-252); *R. P.*, June 27, 1906, Roosevelt to Reid: saying practically the same thing as to White. Cf. Thayer, II, 286-289, and Appendix in the second edition; Bishop, *Theodore Roosevelt and His Time,* New York, 1920, 2 vols., I, ch. XX; Appendix A to this chapter.
    26. *R. P.*, undated memorandum initialled H. C. T. (Admiral Taylor?) in file on Venezuela.
    27. *F. R.*, 1903, pp. 1-5. There is an interesting letter on the question of South American debts in *D. S.*, From Nicaragua, Central America, Vol. 71, No. 792, Jan. 17, 1903, Merry to Hay.
    28. *Am. Jour. of Int. Law,* II, p. 78 and Supplement, II, p. 82; *F. R.*, 1903, p. 248.
    29. *D. S.*, From London, Vol. 206, telegram, Dec. 19, 1902, White to Hay; To Germany, Vol. 21, telegrams, Dec. 20, 26 and 27, Hay to Tower; From

Venezuela, Vol. 55, telegram, Dec. 20, Bowen to Hay; *R. P.,* Dec. 21, Hay to Roosevelt; Dec. 22, Roosevelt to Shaffer; Dec. 26, to Clarkson, to Smith, to Shaw, to Schurz; Dec. 27, to Abbott; Dec. 29, to Hinman, and to St. Clair McKelway.

30. *F. R,,* 1903, pp. 410, 433-437, 460-469, 603-608, 799-803; *D. S.,* From London, Vol. 206, telegram, Jan. 1, 1903, White to Hay; To German Embassy, Vol. 13, p. 169, Dec. 31, 1902, Hay to Holleben; to Venezuela, Vol. 5, p. 183, Jan. 7.

31. *D. S.,* From Venezuela, Vol. 55, telegrams, Jan. 6 and 19, 1903, Bowen to Hay; telegrams, Jan. 19, 23 and Feb. 5, Russell to Hay; From London, Vol. 206, telegrams, Jan. 16 and 17, Jan. 24, White to Hay; To Germany, Vol. 21, No. 9, Jan. 3, Hay to Tower; Numerical File, Vol. 547, memorandum, Jan. 25; *G. P.,* XVII, Nos. 5132-5136.

32. *G. P.,* XVII, No. 5140; Cf. Nos. 5137, 5141-5144; *D. S.,* From London, Vol. 206, telegrams, Jan. 26 and 28, 1903, White to Hay.

33. *G. P.,* XVII, No. 5145; Cf. Nos. 5146, 5147, 5149; *D. S.,* From London, Vol. 206, telegram No. 21, Jan. 28, 1903, White to Hay:

"Strong representations have been made to the Prime Minister from influential quarter inside the Cabinet as to the necessity for immediate termination of situation by raising blockade even if severance from Germany necessary. Popular discontent and pressure increasing. Am therefore hopeful in spite of hitches reported in my telegram of today of an early settlement."

34. *Times,* Jan. 31, Feb. 2 and 14, 1903.

35. *D. S.,* From London, Vol. 206, telegrams, Feb. 7, 1903, White to Hay; *H. P.,* Feb. 7, memorandum from the White House and private telegrams, Feb. 9, Hay to White; *F. R.,* 1903, pp. 471-475.

36. *R. P.,* Venezuelan File, Feb. 6, 1903, Hay to Herbert; *H.-R.* corresp. undated, Hay to Roosevelt; *D. S.,* From London, Vol. 206, telegram, Feb. 10, White to Hay; *G. P.,* XVII, No. 5148; *Times,* Feb. 14, 1903; (Balfour's important speech on Anglo-German relations); *F. R.,* 1903, pp. 804-805.

37. *G. P.,* XVII, No. 5151.

38. *D. S.,* From Venezuela, Vol. 55, telegrams, March 12, July 29, 1903, Russell to Hay; To British Embassy, Vol. 26, March 13, Loomis to Herbert; telegram and personal letter, June 11 and June 17 respectively, Hay to Herbert.

39. *H. P.,* Sept. 11, 16, 21, 26, 1903, MacVeagh to Hay; Sept. 7, 9, 10, 11, 13, 27; Oct. 8, 10; Nov. 13, Penfield to Hay; Sept. 23, Hay to Roosevelt; Sept. 29, Hay to Penfield; *D. S.,* From Netherlands, Vol. 39, telegram, Sept. 9, 1903, Newel to Hay.

40. *Roosevelt-Lodge Correspondence,* II, p. 124.

41. *F. R.,* 1904, pp. 869-870; *Ibid.,* 1905, pp. 919-961; *D. S.,* From Venezuela, Vol. 57, telegrams, July 23, 24, Aug. 18 and 31, 1904, Bowen to Hay; Nos. 323, 344 and 358 of Sept. 16, Oct. 27 and Nov. 18, Hutchinson to Hay; *H. P.,* Memorandum and telegrams, July 23-26, 1904.

42. *F. R.,* 1905, pp. 972-1030.

43. *D. S.,* From Venezuela, Vol. 58, No. 411, May 14, 1905, Hutchinson to Hay.

44. *D. S.,* To Colombia, Vol. 19, p. 318, Feb. 4, 1905, Loomis to Russell; From Venezuela, Vol. 58, telegram, June 2, Hutchinson to Hay.

45. *R. P.,* July 8, 1905, Roosevelt to Russell.

46. *D. S.,* From Venezuela, Vol. 59, telegrams, Sept. 7, Nov. 23, Russell to Root; Vol. 60, 3 telegrams, Jan. 16, 1906, same to same; *F. R.,* 1905, pp. 1000-1003.

47. *F. R.,* 1906, pp. 1432-1438.

48. *Ibid.,* p. 29.

APPENDICES TO CHAPTER XI

A

Bishop, *Theodore Roosevelt and His Time*, II, pp. 221–226.

My dear Mr. Thayer:

There is now no reason why I should not speak of the facts connected with the disagreement between the United States and Germany over the Venezuela matter, in the early part of my administration as President, and of the final amicable settlement of the disagreement.

At that time the Venezuelan Dictator—President Castro—had committed various offenses against different European nations, including Germany and England. The English Government was then endeavoring to keep on good terms with Germany, and on this occasion acted jointly with her. Germany sent a squadron of war vessels to the Venezuelan coast, and they were accompanied by some English war vessels. There was no objection whatever to Castro's being punished, as long as the punishment did not take the form of seizure of territory and its more or less permanent occupation by some Old-World power. At this particular point, such seizure of territory would have been a direct menace to the United States, because it would have threatened or partially controlled the approach to the projected Isthmian Canal.

I speedily became convinced that Germany was the leader, and the really formidable party in the transaction; and that England was merely following Germany's lead in rather half-hearted fashion. I became convinced that England would not back Germany in the event of a clash over the matter between Germany and the United States, but would remain neutral; I did not desire that she should do more than remain neutral. I also became convinced that Germany intended to seize some Venezuelan harbor and turn it into a strongly fortified place of arms, on the model of Kiauchau, with a view to exercising some degree of control over the future Isthmian Canal, and over South American affairs generally.

For some time the usual methods of diplomatic intercourse were tried. Germany declined to agree to arbitrate the question at issue between her and Venezuela, and declined to say that she would not take possession of Venezuelan territory, merely saying that such possession would be "temporary"—which might mean anything. I finally decided that no useful purpose would be served by further delay and I took action accordingly. I assembled our battle fleet, under Admiral Dewey, near Porto Rico, for "manoeuvres," with instructions that the fleet should be kept in hand and in fighting trim, and should be ready to sail at an hour's notice. The fact that the fleet was in West India waters was of course generally known; but I believe that the Secretary of the Navy, and Admiral Dewey, and perhaps his Chief of Staff, and the Secretary of State, John Hay, were the only persons who knew about the order for the fleet to be ready to sail at an hour's notice. I told John Hay that I would now see the German Ambassador, Herr von Holleben, myself, and that I intended to bring matters to an early conclusion. Our navy was in very efficient condition, being superior to the Germany navy.

I saw the Ambassador, and explained that in view of the presence of the German squadron on the Venezuelan coast I could not permit longer delay in answering my request for an arbitration, and that I could not acquiesce in any seizure of Venezuelan territory. The Ambassador responded that his Government could not agree to arbitrate, and that there was no intention to take "permanent" possession of Venezuelan territory. I answered that Kiauchau was not a permanent possession of Germany—that I understood that it was merely held by a 99 year lease; and that I did not intend to have another Kiauchau, held by similar tenure, on the approach to the Isthmian Canal. The Ambassador repeated that his government would not agree to arbitrate. I then asked him to inform his government that if no notification for arbitration came within a certain specified number of days I should be obliged to order Dewey to take his fleet to the Venezuelan coast and see that the German forces did not take possession of any territory. He expressed very grave concern, and asked me if I realized the serious consequences that would follow such action; consequences so serious to both countries that he dreaded to give them a name. I answered that I had thoroughly counted the cost before I decided on the step, and asked him to look at the map, as a glance would show him that there was no spot in the world where Germany in the event of a conflict with the United States would be at a greater disadvantage than in the Caribbean Sea.

A few days later the Ambassador came to see me, talked pleasantly on several subjects, and rose to go. I asked him if he had any answer to make from his government to my request, and when he said no, I informed him that in such event it was useless to wait as long as I had intended, and that Dewey would be ordered to sail twenty-four hours in advance of the time I had set. He expressed deep apprehension, and said that his government would not arbitrate. However, less than twenty-four hours before the time I had appointed for cabling the order to Dewey, the Embassy notified me that His Imperial Majesty the German Emperor had directed him to request me to undertake the arbitration myself. I felt, and publicly expressed, great gratification at this outcome, and great appreciation of the course the German Government had finally agreed to take. Later I received the consent of the German Government to have the arbitration undertaken by the Hague Tribunal, and not by me.

At that time there was in New York as German Consul-General a very able and agreeable man, Dr. Buenz, a native of Holstein. He was intimate with a friend and then neighbor of mine, Mr. A. W. Callisen, whose father was born in Schleswig, and who, incidentally, was and is exactly as straight an American as I am. Mr. Callisen introduced Dr. Buenz to me; and I found the doctor an exceptionally well informed man about American matters and indeed about world affairs generally. He was at my house on several occasions, and I discussed many things with him, including the German and American navies. I had, however, no idea that he had any knowledge whatever of this phase of the Venezuelan affair until after your book appeared. Mr. Callisen happened to read it, was much interested in the part referring to Venezuela, and wrote to a friend of his, Mr. Ambrose C. Richardson, of Buffalo, a letter running in part as follows:

> A Chapter of Diplomacy, (Mr. Thayer's account) interested me greatly, all the more as I knew Dr. Holleben personally, and, what is still more to the purpose, his most intimate friend Dr. Buenz, at that time German Consul-General in New York. The story is absolutely true, and here is the sequel. The German and British Governments firmly counted on our well established jellyfish squashiness and felt sure they had a free hand. The Kaiser and Junker party especially had everything cut and dried, and counted the affair as accomplished. The first time Holleben informed his government that probably Roosevelt's attitude was a bluff; but on second thought went to his friend Buenz for advice as B. knew the American people better than any German living, and was a close friend of Roosevelt's (I introduced him) and hence a good judge of the situation. Buenz at once assured him that Roosevelt was not bluffing, and that he could count on his doing as threatened; and that in a conversation Roosevelt had shown that he had an intimate knowledge of the strength

and condition of the German fleet which was . . . (then) no match for ours.

Holleben was obliged to eat his own words and telegraph in hot haste to Berlin, where his message fell like a bomb shell. You know the rest. This resulted in Holleben's being recalled and dismissed from the diplomatic service. . . . When he sailed from Hoboken not a single member of the diplomatic corps or German official dared to see him off. Only Buenz (and I) dared to brave official disapproval, and went on board to bid him farewell. I went at Buenz's request.

A copy of this letter came into my possession and I showed it to Mr. Callisen when he was here, at my house, on May 7 last. He wrote alongside the part I have quoted: "The above is absolutely accurate. (Signed) A. W. Callisen." Mr. Callisen informed me that he had not intended the letter for publication, but that as the copy had been shown to several people I was at liberty to make whatever use of it I desired.

After your book appeared some person wrote a letter to the press stating that at the time of the Venezuela incident the American fleet was not mobilized under Admiral Dewey in the West Indies. The letter was sent to Mr. Henry A. Wise Wood, of the National Security League, who thereupon wrote to Admiral Dewey for information on the subject. Admiral Dewey answered as follows:

Office of
The Admiral of The Navy
Washington

May 23, 1916.

Mr. Henry A. Wise Wood,
25 Madison Avenue,
New York City.

My dear Mr. Wood:

I beg to acknowledge the receipt of your letter of May 22, asking me to set you right respecting certain facts regarding Colonel Roosevelt's action over Venezuela.

I was at Culebra, Porto Rico, at the time, in command of a fleet consisting of over fifty ships, including every battleship and torpedo boat that we had, with orders from Washington to hold the fleet in hand and be ready to move at a moment's notice. Fortunately, however, the whole matter was amicably adjusted, and there was no need for action.

Hoping the above statement is exactly what you want, and thanking you for the compliments you pay me, I am,

Very truly yours,
GEORGE DEWEY.

This letter was published in the press; and Mr. Wood then sent me copies of the correspondence.

                Sincerely yours,
                              THEODORE ROOSEVELT.

B

The British Foreign Office informs the writer of this book that the suggestion of joint action by Great Britain and Germany with regard to Venezuela came from the German Ambassador in London on July 23, 1902. He queried as to a pacific blockade in the autumn.

I judge that the agreement to act together was the result of an unofficial understanding for whose record we will have to wait till Lord Lansdowne's personal papers are available. In case Great Britain had refused to coöperate with Germany it might have seemed, not unnaturally, to be a slight, perhaps even an unfriendly refusal. This of course Great Brtiain did not wish to convey; consequently she was in rather short-sighted fashion drawn into the dispute which later assumed larger proportions.

CHAPTER XII

THE PANAMA CANAL

THE dominant fact, affecting the diplomacy of the United States as regards Latin America in this period, was the desire to dig an inter-oceanic canal. The protection of its approaches stimulated support of the Monroe doctrine; to prevent other nations from interfering in the domestic affairs of the Caribbean region became a cardinal principle of American policy; and the maintenance of our naval power involved an increasing element in the entire matter. To this end the United States insisted on the Platt Amendment; she sought to buy the Danish West Indies; she threatened war with Germany regarding Venezuela; she intervened in the Dominican Republic; she negotiated with Central American Republics; and she signed the Canal Treaties with Great Britain. The Panama Canal, therefore, became the absorbing interest of the government at Washington.

We can recall the situation as we left it with the conclusion of the second Hay-Pauncefote treaty in November, 1901. Negotiations had already begun with Nicaragua and Costa Rica regarding the possible construction by the United States of an inter-oceanic canal and Colombia was now to appear on the scene as the sovereign over the Isthmus of Panama where the alternative route lay. First, therefore, is a brief summary of these proposals at a time when the weight of expert judgment and of public opinion was strongly in favor of the route *via* Nicaragua.

To judge by Mr. Thayer's remark—"Such was the tangled skein of the Panama Canal affair when diplomacy took it up"—the negotiations regarding the Canal began in the spring of 1902.[1] This, of course, was not the case. Even before 1900 there are records of inquiries and of tentative proposals; and Secretary Hay wrote to President McKinley on September 22, 1900: "The subject is one which gives me great concern. I have not been neglecting it. I have devoted a good deal of time and labor to it since Congress adjourned." He continued:

> The situation is rather anomalous. We are to ask Nicaragua and Costa Rica to commit themselves to a plan to which we are not as yet able to pledge ourselves. They are a wily people—President Zelaya particularly—is what is called a "smooth citizen." But perhaps a dextrous negotiator may be able to arrange matters with them, so as to give us something substantial to go on.[2]

So we must plunge into these negotiations about January, 1900, at a time when the first Hay-Pauncefote treaty was to receive its baptism of fire. A despatch from Mr. Merry, the American Minister to the Central American Republics, assumed naturally enough that the inter-oceanic canal would be constructed between San Juan del Norte on the Atlantic and the probable Pacific terminal at San Juan del Sur. The question of coaling stations at these terminals concerned him and he wrote at length regarding them. Later he also consulted with President Yglesia of Costa Rica and President Zelaya of Nicaragua with reference to the Hepburn Canal Bill, then pending in Congress. For this he was promptly rebuked by Secretary Hay.[3] In Colombia as well steps were taken with regard to the acquisition of coaling stations near the Isthmus of Panama. The reply was that the time was inopportune; but that Colombia

> had not supposed for a moment that the Government of the United States has any designs whatever upon the Isthmus of Panama, or upon any other part of Colombian territory, but that evil disposed persons, hostile to the present Government of Colombia, had not hesitated, and would not hesitate, to invent anything that might seem to serve their purpose.[4]

Then for many months matters dragged. Various speculative concessionaires, intent on money, made their appearance in Nicaragua. In Washington the first Hay-Pauncefote treaty was beaten. Meanwhile President McKinley was besought by Senator Morgan, the high priest of the Nicaragua Canal Project, to send someone to Nicaragua to investigate the situation. To this suggestion Secretary Hay had said that he saw no objection to the United States taking all practical steps to ascertain the attitude of Nicaragua and Costa Rica. Later he also set to work to draft a new Hay-Pauncefote treaty, which was approved by the Senate in December, 1901.[5] Finally, in March, 1901, there came the direct suggestion that the United States acquire the reversion of a concession granted by Colombia to the French Panama Canal Company. The concession expired in 1904, and, though it had been extended by executive action, it was intimated that this was not legal. The Colombian government would ask in return for its complaisance the guarantee of a loan of $50,000,000 in silver.[6] Later the New Panama Canal Company, the estimated value of whose property and franchises was stated to be $109,141,500, offered to sell outright to the United States for $40,000,000.[7]

Meanwhile a convention was being attempted with Nicaragua. A draft agreement had been placed in the hands of the Nicaraguan government in the end of 1900. There it lay for a year under the ægis of Mr. Sanchez, the Minister of Foreign Affairs, "a gentleman both affectionate and tricky" as Mr. Merry described him. At last, on December 9, 1901, this protocol was signed but in a form totally inadmissible to the United States. Not only were the form and terms incorrect but amendments had been introduced which were objectionable. The result was that the year had been wasted and the negotiations had to begin all over again. Mr. Merry might continue to send interminable despatches on the advantages of the Nicaragua route over that *via* the Isthmus of Panama but the failure of his negotiations was apparent.[8]

However with the passage of the second Hay-Pauncefote treaty through the Senate matters began to improve. From this time on negotiations only with Colombia require our attention for the Hepburn Canal Bill, amended in the Senate to make it a reasonable act, became law in June, 1902. This represented the victory of those who favored the Panama route, though it provided, that in case a satisfactory settlement could not be made with the Panama Canal Company and with Colombia, the President should undertake the task *via* Nicaragua. The amendments introduced by Senator Spooner and the strong and vigorous arguments presented by Senator Hanna were instrumental in effecting this change. The Nicaragua line had been known as the "American line" for many years; now for sound business reasons the Panama route was given the preference. At all events the United States had a firm basis from which to start afresh.[9]

As Secretary Hay wrote to Senator Morgan the real difficulty with both Nicaragua and Colombia was that neither country knew much of the United States; each believed that the route through their country was the only possible one; and each thought it could compel the United States to meet any terms they wished to demand. This had been evident in the case of Nicaragua; now it was to be the same in the case of Colombia. As regards the Panama route there was an added factor. This was the treaty of 1846 between the United States and the Republic of New Granada. By Article XXXV of this treaty, which was still in effect:

> The Government of New Granada guarantees to the Government of the United States that the right of way or transit across the Isthmus of Panama upon any modes of communication that now exist, or that may be hereafter constructed, shall be open and free to the Government and citizens of the United States, and for the transportation of any articles of produce, manufactures or merchandise, of lawful commerce, belonging to the citizens of the United States; that no other tolls or charges shall be levied or collected upon the citizens of the United States, or their said merchandise thus passing over any road or canal that may be made by the Government of New Granada, or by the authority of the same, than is, under like circumstances, levied upon and collected from the Granadian citizens; that any lawful produce, manufactures or merchandise belonging to citizens of the United States, thus passing from one sea to the other, in either direction, for the purpose of

exportation to any other foreign country, shall not be liable to any import duties whatever; or, having paid such duties, they shall be entitled to drawback upon their exportation; nor shall the citizens of the United States be liable to any duties, tolls or charges of any kind, to which native citizens are not subjected for thus passing the said Isthmus. And, in order to secure to themselves the tranquil and constant enjoyment of these advantages, and as an equal compensation for the said advantages, and for the favors they have acquired by the 4th, 5th, and 6th articles of this treaty, the United States guarantee, positively and efficaciously, to New Granada, by the present stipulation, the perfect neutrality of the before mentioned Isthmus, with the view that the free transit from the one to the other sea may not be interrupted or embarrassed in any future time while this treaty exists; and, in consequence, the United States also guarantee, in the same manner the rights of sovereignty and property which New Granada has and possesses over the said territory.[10]

Through constitutional changes the Republic of New Granada had become the United States of Colombia, or the Republic of Colombia. Such internal changes did not, however, affect the validity of the treaty of 1846. During the course of some fifty-seven years there had been fifty-three riots or revolutions on the Isthmus, many of which had required the presence of American men-of-war and the landing of our troops. Panama was now a province of Colombia. It was almost continuously in disorder and was a crater of revolution and disturbance; furthermore, the civil wars and outbreaks in Colombia itself were a source of anxiety. Indeed, in 1902, a civil war was in progress against the government at Bogotá, the capital of Colombia. This, however, was ended in November, after the presence of American naval forces at Panama had shown that the United States would not permit interference with transit.

Under these circumstances the negotiations with Colombia regarding the Panama Canal were protracted. In response to informal inquiries the Colombian Foreign Secretary handed, on March 6, 1902, to the American Minister at Bogotá, Mr. Hart, a memorandum of the conditions demanded by Colombia as precedent to the construction of a canal across the Isthmus by the United States. Secretary Hay promptly telegraphed: "The terms are entirely inadmissible." These terms were in part due to an inquiry made by a Colombian Commission; and the government had assumed that the United States would accept them. Furthermore, the new Colombian Minister in Washington was privately opposed to the construction of a canal at this time and, under the guise of specious delays, prevented the consummation of an agreement. Finally, under pretence that the sovereignty of Colombia had been affronted by American naval officers on the Isthmus, he declared that his "conscience" would not permit him to sign the proposed treaty. In truth General Concha was the "subject of great nervous excitement" and, when he disobeyed the instructions of his government, he was recalled at the end of November, 1902, and "was taken aboard the ship at New York in a strait-jacket." [11]

In the negotiation of a draft treaty at Washington, which began in April, 1902, Mr. Nelson Cromwell, counsel for the New Panama Canal Company, was a party. He had been introduced by General Concha and was well known in Washington. The draft was presented by Colombia; but numerous amendments were necessary. In the meantime the French government had been approached to discover whether it had any objections to the plan of the United States to purchase the rights of the Canal Company, a French corporation. The title of the Company had also to be searched. So that October was far advanced before the counter proposals of the Colombian government could be discussed. At the same time friction developed over the action of American naval authorities who were attempting to preserve the peace on the Isthmus. On October 16 Secretary Hay, therefore, telegraphed to Mr. Hart that the United States regretted any misunderstanding and that there was "no intention to infringe sovereignty or wound dignity of Colombia." [12]

At this stage Concha took offence, whether willfully or because of his physical condition, and refused to negotiate, though he continued to visit the Department and to mention various changes which he hoped would be made in the proposed treaty. Finally, on November 22, he refused to accept the American proposals. Secretary Hay telegraphed to Mr. Hart as to the situation. The Colombian government responded quickly by placing Dr. Herran in charge of the Legation at Washington. Even then there was delay, and on December 30, 1902, Secretary Hay telegraphed again to Bogotá:

> Several weeks ago offered Herran ten millions down and one hundred thousand per annum rental. Cannot get from him either acceptance or refusal. Urge Government to send explicit instructions, and if possible, send copy of them to me. Movement impending in Congress to adopt Nicaraguan route.[13]

There were further delays due perhaps to the opposition of the "Liberals" in Colombia who feared lest if too large a proportion of the money were paid in a lump sum the money might be used to suppress them and to maintain the government and friends of President Marroquin indefinitely in power. They strove to compel the administration to give assurance that the receipts of the transaction should be "properly" applied. Colombia at the last moment demanded $600,000 annual rental. As a result Secretary Hay telegraphed: "If Colombian Government persists in present attitude it renders further negotiations impossible" and wrote on January 21, 1903, to Dr. Herran that the United States would pay $250,000 annual rental but that the "reasonable time" which had been allowed for negotiations had come to an end and would not be extended. He added: "I am not authorized to consider or discuss any other change whatever." Fortunately the Colombian government recognized that nothing more could be gained by further delay and on January 22 the Hay-Herran Treaty was signed.[14]

The treaty provided for a payment by the United States to Colombia of $10,000,000 in cash and an annual rental of $250,000. The French New Panama Canal Company was thereby authorized to transfer its properties and franchises to the United States, which was to construct and maintain a canal across the Isthmus for one hundred years with the option of continuing for successive periods. The United States was given control over a strip of territory three miles each side of the canal, but excluding the cities of Panama and Colon. Colombia had the right to transfer, free of charges through the canal, ships, troops and munitions and retained technical sovereignty over the strip. This treaty was approved by the United States Senate on March 17, 1903. It never was ratified by the Colombian Senate.

In order to complete the record, however, it is necessary to survey this final and futile endeavor to secure the rights of construction from Colombia. Then we can turn to the more dynamic elements which led to the successful revolution in Panama, the recognition of that Republic, and the negotiation of a new treaty, which was promptly approved by both parties. In January, 1903, the United States had negotiated a treaty to secure the right of way across the Isthmus; it still had to purchase the property and the concession of the New Panama Canal Company for $40,000,000; and as a condition precedent to any further action the treaty now had not only to pass through the fire of the Colombian Senate but to receive the popular approval of Colombian public opinion. From the first Mr. Beaupré, who had succeeded Mr. Hart as American Minister at Bogotá, warned the Department of State that:

> Without question public opinion is strongly against its ratification, but, of course, public opinion in Colombia is not necessarily a potent factor in controlling legislation.
> It is quite impossible to come to a definite conclusion as to the outcome until the result of the recent elections for members of Congress is known. It has been generally thought that the Government would be able to control the elections and that the members returned would be favorable to the administration's view on the canal question; but there has been serious disappointment to the governmental party in the result of some of the elections heard from. . . .
> It seems altogether probable that unless the Government is thoroughly in earnest in its desire to have the convention ratified, it will not be done; and there is a possibility that it may not go through in any event. . . .

It is apparent lately that the French Canal Company is to take a decided interest in securing the ratification of the convention, and that its influence to that end will be of much importance.[15]

Later, on April 15, 1903, Mr. Beaupré repeated much the same idea.[16] Again in May the Department was advised that the newly elected Congress would meet in June and that:

. . . the opposition to the ratification of the Canal convention is intensifying. The press is teeming with articles rancorous in enmity to the proposed treaty, while public opinion is veering into a current of extreme bitterness against the authors of the pact, especially Mr. Herran. . . .

Mr. Mancini, the representative of the French Canal Company at the capital, says that he is emphatically of the opinion that the Congress will refuse to ratify the convention, and that he has written to his company to that effect. . . . It is entirely impossible to convince these people that the Nicaragua route was ever seriously considered by the United States; that the negotiations concerning it had any other motive than the squeezing of an advantageous bargain out of Colombia; nor that any other than the Panama route will ever be selected.[17]

The treaty was in effect beaten before the Colombian Congress met. Party politicians now saw in the agitation against the treaty an opportunity to exert their influence and perhaps to overthrow the Colombian administration. Consequently the attempt was made to secure more money from the French Company, which received an official note from the Colombian government, "stating that it did not think that the convention would be ratified, because of the opinion that the compensation was insufficient, but that if the Canal Company would pay to Colombia about ten million of dollars, ratification could be secured."[18] However, it is doubtful whether this could have been done in the summer of 1903. Mr. Beaupré had reported once more that:

. . . the tremendous tide of public opinion against the canal treaty is appalling to the Government, and there is, in consequence, a diversity of opinion among its members as to the proper course to pursue. Some are in favor of forcing confirmation through Congress, while others, dreading the effect of such action in the present state of the public mind, counsel moderation and delay, and the adoption of measures to change public sentiment into a more favorable channel.

All of the enemies of the Government are united in an onslaught upon the canal convention. Many of them are sincere of course, in their opposition to the proposed treaty as such, but many more, regarding it as an administration measure and at present unpopular, are assailing it with the indirect object of undermining the Government.[19]

These despatches thoroughly alarmed the Department of State and, at the instigation of Mr. Cromwell, a peremptory telegram was communicated to the Colombian government.[20] Later interruption of cable services with Colombia also caused protest.[21] Meanwhile President Roosevelt, at Oyster Bay, was apparently much irritated over the situation.[22]

During July there was a see-saw of reports from Bogotá; some were optimistic but the majority were pessimistic. The amendments proposed in the Colombian Senate were promptly rejected by Secretary Hay, who wrote to the President that the Colombians were:

> mad to get hold of the **forty millions** of the Frenchmen, and they want to make us a party to the gouge. They think we *must* deal with them—that we must have the canal and that there is no other route. We may not be able to change their view in this respect, but they ought to be made to see that there is a limit to our concessions.[23]

Then on August 15, 1903, came word that, on August 12, the treaty had been rejected at Bogotá. Mr. Beaupré had hopes that this action was not final; but events were to prove that he was too optimistic. At all events his despatches for half a year had indicated that such a result was probable. This action by Colombia was no surprise and it was undoubtedly in accordance with the real desires of the Colombian people. Secretary Hay was away for the summer in New Hampshire; and to him the ever faithful Mr. Adee ("chipper as a mudlark") wrote on August 18, enclosing a memorandum from Mr. John Crawford, an unofficial friend, which contained the direct suggestion that Panama should secede from Colombia and offer the canal to the United States. Extracts from these letters are given in the Appendix to this chapter.[24]

Secretary Hay had in the meantime written to the President saying that for the moment there was nothing to be done, but rather suggesting that America should revert to the Nicaragua route. This solution he felt would be "simple and easy." The letter is given in the Appendix to this chapter.[25]

On August 15 there had also gone to the President through Mr. Loomis a memorandum from John Bassett Moore, which the President thought was "important." Unfortunately the Department of State has no copy of this document though it was returned to them by President Roosevelt several months later; nor did they know of its existence till recently. It is possible that a copy of this paper may still be found among the papers of Mr. Moore; but search so far has been unavailing. A paragraph from Mr. Loomis's letter is given in the Appendix to this chapter.[26]

President Roosevelt commented briefly on this Moore memorandum to Secretary Hay.[27] Mr. Adee again wrote to Secretary Hay on August 19, swinging on the whole in favor of negotiations with Nicaragua and saying: "We are very sorry but really we can't help it if Colombia doesn't want the canal on our terms." An extract from this letter is given in the Appendix to this chapter.[28] A day later, on news of the suspension of a too patriotic paper at Panama, Mr. Adee wrote: "The fathers at Bogotá are eating sour grapes and the teeth of the children at Panama are getting a fine edge to 'em." [29]

Both he and Secretary Hay were dubious as to a reported plan of General Reyes, a Colombian supporter of the treaty, to secure its ratification by a possible *coup d'état*. News that Chile was disturbed as early as July 8 by the thought that, in the event of the rejection of the treaty, Panama might be annexed by the United States, also came in to the Department. Meanwhile a committee had been appointed in the Colombian Senate to study the entire situation. The delays incident to cable communication between Washington and Bogotá were vexatious; but on August 29 a message had been sent saying that the President alone was the judge of what was meant by a "reasonable time." When that expired he would negotiate with Nicaragua.[30]

Such matters could wait, as Secretary Hay wrote to the President on August 22, saying:

> I have your letter of the 19th enclosing Moore's paper. It is, as you say, important, and would be useful in case you should decide to build the canal without Colombia's leave. The fact that our position in that case would be legal, and just, might not greatly impress the jack rabbit mind. I do not believe we could *faire valoir* our rights in that way without war—which would of course be brief and inexpensive.
>
> I will come to Oyster Bay on my way back from Washington as you suggest.
>
> I entirely agree with you that there is nothing to be done at present. The Spooner law gives you a "reasonable time" to make a treaty with Colombia. It is for you to decide what time is reasonable. . . . We are in no danger and in no hurry—we can bide an hour.[31]

In early September Mr. Moore was invited to spend the night at Oyster Bay and while visiting the President discussed the general situation. What he said in effect was that in addition to the treaty rights already acquired by the United States she needed a "license to dig." He had already quoted in his memorandum a letter of Secretary Cass, written in 1858 to Mr. Lamar, American Minister to Central America. This read:

> The progress of events has rendered the inter-oceanic route across the narrow portions of Central America vastly important to the commercial world, and especially to the United States, whose possessions extending along the Atlantic and Pacific coasts demand the speediest and easiest modes of communication. While the just rights of sovereignty of the States occupying this region should always be respected, we shall expect that these rights will be exercised in a spirit befitting the occasion, and the wants and circumstances that have arisen. Sovereignty has its duties as well as its rights, and none of these local governments, even if administered with more regard to the just demands of other nations than they have been would be permitted, in a spirit of Eastern isolation, to close these gates of intercourse on the great highways of the world, and justify the act by the pretension that these avenues of trade and travel belong to them, and that they choose to shut them, or, what is almost

equivalent, to encumber them with such unjust regulations as would prevent their general use.[32]

At the same time Secretary Hay exchanged letters with the President saying:

There is a question whether we ought—
1. To save time and to dissipate any uncertainty about our position—say to Colombia that we will not for a moment consider the proposition they are now discussing; or
2. Say nothing, and let them go on making fools of themselves until you are ready to act on some other basis. It is now perfectly clear that in the present state of Colombian politics we cannot now—nor for some time to come—make a satisfactory treaty with Colombia.

It is altogether likely that there will be an insurrection in the Isthmus against that régime of folly and graft that now rules at Bogotá.

It is for you to decide whether you will (1) await the results of that movement, or (2) take a hand in rescuing the Isthmus from anarchy, or (3) treat with Nicaragua.

Something we shall be forced to do in the case of a serious insurrectionary movement in Panama, to keep the transit clear. Our intervention should not be at haphazard nor, this time should it be to the profit, as heretofore, of Bogotá.

I venture to suggest you let your mind play a little about the subject for two or three weeks, before finally deciding. For my part, I think nothing can be lost, and something may be gained by awaiting developments for a while. In case you think anything ought to be said just now, I inclose a draft instruction to Beaupré which you might, if you approve send at once to Adee.[33]

To this President Roosevelt advised delay.[34] Meanwhile it fairly rained letters and telegrams from Mr. Cromwell who, as counsel for the Canal Company, had his irons in various fires. His Company was, of course, much disturbed over the situation; and soon he was to go to France to try to restore the wilting *morale* of men who thought they saw $40,000,000 go glimmering. Mr. Adee also reported on the eve of the collapse of the treaty, September 22, when it expired by limitation, that everyone was much agitated and was busy asking foolish questions, such as "if we had a brother would he like cheese" and other rubbish of this sort.[35] There was also a cheerful soul, a newspaper editor, who held a lottery concession in Panama, J. Gabriel Duque, by name, who now sought by frequent letters to Secretary Hay to furnish him with intelligence reports on the state of affairs in Panama. It is needless to say that the Secretary never acknowledged any of these letters, yet they invest the news of the day in Panama with a certain amount of interest. Duque wrote September 21:

> The feeling here is very intense for the independence of this Isthmus to be entitled the Panama Republic but I cannot see where a leader is to be had; neither the funds necessary to carry on a conflict should the revolutionists succeed in buying the military officers. . . .
>
> By the above you will very readily see that the troops are starving and that means that the Government owes them large sums of money for salaries. These soldiers are paid one dollar silver (35 cents gold) a day and they have to feed themselves out of it. They are paid every week and the Government owes them about 12 or 13 weeks. They are in debt for food and cannot get trusted any more. The officers are almost as bad off, as the Government owes them for the same length of time the only difference being, that as they get 2, 3, 4, and 5 dollars silver a day they can afford to wait a longer time.
>
> Now you will readily see how easy it is to buy these men over as necessity knows no law.[36]

While the news from Bogotá continued to be negative and while the newspaper world was prophesying a break in diplomatic relations rumors spread over night of this or that dire event. Mr. Adee used to sign his almost nightly letters to Secretary Hay "Fatiguedly but still chipperly yours"; and plans for the future were being studied at Oyster Bay, in New Hampshire, and at Washington. Colombia now proposed to postpone all action till a Congress could be secured in August, 1904. Mr. Merry in Central America, under date of August 30, 1903, prophesied a revolution in Panama which might affect the situation.[37] On October 10 President Roosevelt wrote to Dr. Shaw expressing his private wish that Panama were an independent state but adding: "for me to say so publicly would amount to an instigation of a revolt, and therefore I cannot say it." [38]

At Bogotá during October two bills were introduced in the Colombian Congress. One authorized the President of Colombia to make treaties for the construction of the canal on terms and conditions which would have been most favorable to Colombia. A second bill or report from a committee favored the termination of the concession to the New Panama Canal Company in 1904, ignoring the previous extension of their franchise to 1910. This would have made Colombia, rather than the Canal Company, the recipient of the $40,-000,000 proposed by the Spooner-Hepburn Act. Neither of these bills was acted on before the Congress adjourned on October 31. On October 21 Mr. Beaupré had reported that alarm existed lest the United States should take action at Panama in view of "the disaffection undoubtedly existing" there. This was calmed by the reading of Article XXXV of the treaty of 1846 which, it was said, pledged the United States to support the Colombian government in case of disorder.[39]

There is an interesting lack of correspondence in the Hay papers, in the Roosevelt letter books and in the Panama Canal file of the Roosevelt papers relating to the course of events from October 10 to November 3, and it may be impossible to fill up this gap. The Department of State has published practically every despatch with Colombia for this period so we are driven back to the account by a Frenchman, Col. Bunau-Varilla, for much of our information relating to these weeks and also to such bits of news as we can pick up from the hearings on the Rainey Resolution in 1913, which were published under the title of the *Story of Panama.* This latter record is marred by the fact that it is invaded by partisan politics and by misstatements of fact well known to any observer. Furthermore, Mr. Cromwell's memoirs have never been published. Within the limitation of this material, therefore, my account may be subject to correction by additional information which is not available to me.

Col. Bunau-Varilla was the able engineer who devoted his youthful talents to the construction of the canal at Panama. His middle years were also spent in an enthusiastic defence of the Panama route as opposed to the Nicaragua route. In 1901 he had assisted in the conversion of Senator Hanna; and the passage of the Spooner-Hepburn Bill was much assisted by his clever appeals. He was not an officer of the New Panama Canal Company; but in September, 1903, he came to America to observe the situation which had been created at Bogotá. On various occasions he had addressed vigorous and pertinent telegrams to officials and persons in responsible positions. To cite only a few of these—on March 26, 1902, he had telegraphed the *Star and Herald,* the leading newspaper at Panama, that the Panama Canal project was in danger because of the cupidity of the Colombian government. On November 23, 1902, he had telegraphed President Marroquin of the danger that, because of international events, the Panama Canal might be dug despite Colombia and not with her assistance. On June 13, 1903, he had telegraphed again to the President of Colombia from Paris that no European state could dare construct the canal and that failure to ratify the treaty with the United States would result either in America's choice of the Nicaragua route or in the secession and independence of Panama under the protection of the United States.[40]

Possibly by mere coincidence the New York *World,* at the instigation of Mr. Cromwell's press agent in Washington, published on the following day a story regarding a plan to secure that very action by Panama.[41] In this campaign in behalf of a project, in which Col. Bunau-Varilla whole-heartedly believed, he showed courage, vigor and resourcefulness. He was laughingly referred to as "the Frenchman who is like an American." No one can fail to appreciate his services, though at times he was open to criticism.

Into the subsequent disputes between Mr. Cromwell and the Canal Company it is unnecessary to enter. On all sides as the question of responsibility for events at Panama became a matter of dispute there was a natural tendency to boast. Consequently we have a variety of choices. We can make

Mr. Cromwell the arch-conspirator; we can suppose that the Gallic verve and foresight of Col. Bunau-Varilla are responsible; or we can turn to the men and women on the spot, to Dr. and Mrs. Amador and their friends at Panama. Certainly the money supplied to them by Col. Bunau-Varilla and later by Mr. Cromwell played a vital part in the establishment of the Republic of Panama. Not only did the conspirators in Panama grow wealthy over night; but Colombian officials, officers and soldiers took bribes offered by the agents of the French and Panaman interests in such fashion that the attempted revolution succeeded. There is no record, however, that any United States money was used at the time. The nearest we can come to that was when Commander Hubbard of the United States navy probably signed his name as one of the guarantors for the future payment of the Royal Mail Steam Packet Company for the transportation of Colombian troops away from Colon to Cartagena in Colombia. This, however, was after the revolution when it was desirable to get rid of these troops as quickly as possible. Their commander, Col. Torres, had received a bribe of $8000 from the funds available for that purpose—through money supplied by Col. Bunau-Varilla in New York—and only the transport of the soldiers was involved. Certainly there was nothing reprehensible in that.[42] But we must now return to survey briefly the course of events.

Col. Bunau-Varilla reached New York on September 22, 1903. He had been preceded by Dr. Amador who came from Panama as representative of a revolutionary *Junta* who favored the secession of Panama, its independence, and the construction of the canal across the Isthmus by the United States. Because of previous promises made by Captain Beers, who was man Friday to Mr. Cromwell at Panama, Dr. Amador came to Mr. Cromwell. He had found shortly, however, that no money was available and that Mr. Cromwell was no longer willing to see him. Of course, if Mr. Cromwell were in any way connected with this revolutionary plot, and if this plot should fail, it was quite possible that the Colombian government might at one stroke confiscate the property of the New Panama Canal Company and terminate its concession. Mr. Cromwell, as I have said, was the counsel and adviser of the Company in New York. Consequently Dr. Amador was in despair at this failure due to excess of caution on the part of Mr. Cromwell. He was also alarmed at the danger which he suddenly saw looming up for him and his friends in Panama.[43]

On September 23, however, Dr. Amador found Col. Bunau-Varilla in New York. The circumstances were explained; and in a few days an agreement was reached. It should be said that during August Col. Bunau-Varilla had been making an independent research into the question as to how the forces of the United States might be utilized under the treaty of 1846 with New Granada. We can recall the terms of Article XXXV of that treaty (quoted on p. 312). He had embodied his results in an article which he had published in *Le Matin* of Paris on September 2, 1903. By chance he now met John Bassett Moore, who had written a memorandum on this subject in early August and had visited President Roosevelt in the first part of September. Both of these facts were unknown to Col. Bunau-Varilla at the time. Later he found out the latter point. When he met Mr. Moore it was discovered that he was interested in this very article in *Le Matin* which Col. Bunau-Varilla had written. "What most astonished me," said Mr. Moore, "one day was to see this theory to which I never gave any publicity fully developed in a Paris paper." Later President Roosevelt also expressed his interest and astonishment at this coincidence. He said, according to Col. Bunau-Varilla:

"I have never been as astonished as I was when I read the article of September 2, where you described exactly what I was then preparing with Professor Bassett Moore at Oyster Bay."

"But, Mr. President," I answered, "it is purely a matter of logic. The same facts are bound to lead logical minds to the same conclusion, however far away from each other they may be."

"Well," said the President, "if that is so you are the greatest logician I have ever known."

As the butler announced that dinner was served, the President left me, saying with his usual spontaneous generosity: "They say that I have inspired you. It would be much more true to say that you inspired me." [44]

On October 3, therefore, Col. Bunau-Varilla wrote a letter to Mr. Moore to reinforce his theory that the treaty of 1846 gave the United States the right to coerce Colombia on the basis of eminent domain. Mr. Moore had privately said to him:

> I think that the Treaty of 1846 with New Granada gave the United States the right of carrying out the works necessary for the Canal. Its right of way or transit remains illusory, if Colombia, being incapable of making the Canal, prevents it from being constructed by us. To be sure this right is not explicit, but it is implied. It would certainly be necessary to settle the question of indemnity. But if it is not solved amicably one might resort to arbitration.[45]

It should, however, be clear that Mr. Moore never took the view that the United States had the right, without leave or license from Colombia, to proceed to dig a canal. He never discussed with anyone the question of a revolt on the Isthmus and the action to be taken in that contingency. Later he took the view that the recognition of Panama was an act of intervention which lay quite outside the limits of the rules governing recognition. Through Mr. Moore's private letters it is evident to me that in his memorandum he had argued that as Colombia could not bring herself to talk of "perpetual control" of the Canal zone by the United States she should be approached with a simpler proposal. The United States had under the treaty of 1846 a right to require Colombia to give a "license to dig," which of course should contain appropriate provisions as to expropriation, compensation and other matters. This, however, in the view of Mr. Moore required a consultation with Congress in order to secure necessary modification of the Spooner-Hepburn Act. Such consultation never took place, as the success of the revolution at Panama was to sweep away such legal views of the situation.

On October 9 Col. Bunau-Varilla saw President Roosevelt in Washington. He had now abandoned his idea of the coercion of Colombia and had adopted as an alternative the idea of a revolution at Panama which would lead to its independence. He told the President, in response to a question, that a revolution would break out in Panama. I quote the account which I have reason to believe is correct.

The features of the President manifested profound surprise. "A revolution," he repeated, mechanically. Then he turned instinctively toward Mr. Loomis, who remained standing, impassible, and he said in a low tone, as if speaking to himself: "A revolution. . . . Would it be possible? . . . But if it became a reality, what would become of the plan we had thought of?"

I had an intense desire to say to him, "Mr. President, the plan of which you had thought is coercion of Colombia, based on the treaty of 1846, as interpreted by Professor Bassett Moore. I have supported this idea in a letter to him and added to it the doctrine of the expropriation of sovereignty for reasons of international utility. The letter was directed to him, but it was for you, Mr. President, and you must have read it."

Of course I remained mute, and I concealed my joy at hearing the interrogation which had escaped from the mouth of the President. He quickly recovered himself, and asked: "What makes you think so?"

There was no interest in going further. I answered: "General and special considerations, Mr. President. As you know, the revolutionary spirit is endemic on the Isthmus. There is almost a certainty of seeing an endemic disease spread violently when the circumstances favorable to its development have reached their maximum. Colombia has decreed the ruin of the people of the Isthmus. They will not let things go any further without protesting according to their fashion. Their fashion is—revolution. I have furthermore certain special indications that corroborate these general conditions."

The conversation ended there. I had no desire to say more and the President on his side did not care to hear more.[46]

In New York it remained to arrange matters with Dr. Amador. During this entire period Mr. Cromwell did not see either of the two conspirators; and from mid-October till the latter part of November Mr. Cromwell was out of the country. Col. Bunau-Varilla was in no official way connected with the Canal Company, though he was a shareholder. What communications he had with Paris are not clear; but according to his account he borrowed $100,000 on securities held in Paris and, transferring that sum to New York, began operations.[47] His first difficulty was with Dr. Amador who had estimated that the revolution would cost $6,000,000. He soon overcame this difficulty and on October 20, Dr. Amador was despatched to Colon and thence to Panama to arrange for the outbreak.[48]

Col. Bunau-Varilla then went again to Washington and saw Secretary Hay. In these days the theory that the United States was bound to protect a revolution in Panama if one were to break out, became fixed in the mind of Col. Bunau-Varilla, as, indeed, it later did in the minds of several other people.[49] In this, however, he was wrong. Secretary Seward had written in 1861 to Mr. Adams, who was then American Minister in London, in connection with the report that Great Britain intended to recognize the independence of the southern states which were attempting secession from the federal union:

> On the other hand we insist that a nation that recognizes a revolutionary state with a view to aid its affecting its sovereignty and independence commits a great wrong against the nation whose integrity is thus invaded, and makes itself responsible for a just and ample redress. . . . To recognize the independence of a new State, and so favor, possibly determine, its admission into the family of nations, is the highest possible exercise of sovereign power, because it affects in any case the welfare of two nations, and often the peace of the world.[50]

From that view the United States had never departed, nor had the treaty of 1846 contemplated any revolution which would alter the sovereignty on the Isthmus. It merely stated that the United States guaranteed the neutrality of that region in order that transit might not be interrupted and guaranteed the sovereignty of New Granada over the territory. Later these questions were to be hotly debated. For the moment we must note that in mid-October Secretary Hay is reported to have said to Col. Bunau-Varilla that the hypothesis that a revolution would break out in Panama was probably correct. He added: "But we shall not be caught napping. Orders have been given to naval forces on the Pacific to sail towards the Isthmus." [51] There is also the story that Secretary Hay told two reliable newspaper men at that time that a revolution in Panama was about to break out.

This view was probably due to reports brought to President Roosevelt by two army officers on October 15. They reported that at Panama a revolutionary party was actively collecting arms, that people generally believed that a revolution was imminent, and that, with the failure of Colombia to ratify the treaty, revolution would immediately take place. On hearing this President Roosevelt immediately ordered naval vessels to be in the neighborhood of the Isthmus. On November 2, 1903, orders were sent to the *Nashville* and *Dixie* on the Atlantic side and to the *Boston* on the Pacific side to proceed to the Isthmus and to:

> Maintain free and uninterrupted transit. If interruption is threatened by armed force, occupy the line of railroad. Prevent landing of any armed force, either government or insurgent, at any point within fifty miles of Panama. Government force reported approaching Isthmus in vessels. Prevent their landing, if in your judgment, the landing would precipitate a conflict.[52]

Col. Bunau-Varilla, following his interview with Secretary Hay, wrote: "Notwithstanding Mr. Hay's silence I knew all." Preparations were swiftly made by Col. Bunau-Varilla and Dr. Amador in New York; a telegraph code was arranged; and dates were fixed. Incidentally the fact that November 3, the day on which the outbreak was to take place, was also election day in America was a mere coincidence.[53] It was not part of an unscrupulous plot by politicians in America. Mr. Hall of the New York *World* who made so much of this alleged fact during the Rainey hearings was simply talking nonsense. Col. Bunau-Varilla went again to Washington to reassure himself that an American man-of-war would be in Colon. On his return to New York he waited for news from Dr. Amador. In the meantime the *Junta* at Panama had fallen into a panic; but the news of the coming of the *Nashville* had restored their spirits and it was decided that at 5 P.M. on November 3, the final steps should be taken.

With the connivance of the railway officials at Colon, Colombian troops which had landed there were prevented from taking train to Panama. The general commanding, Tovar, did go, however. At Panama the Colombian General Huertas was offered a large bribe which he took; Governor Obaldia, who was staying in Dr. Amador's house, was put under friendly arrest. Huerta's soldiers also arrested General Tovar. The firemen of the town, really a revolutionary and political organization, co-operated and by six o'clock in the evening the stroke had been accomplished as far as the city of Panama was concerned.[54] Dr. Amador then sent a telegram to Secretary Hay which read: "Isthmus independence proclaimed without bloodshed. Canal treaty saved." This, of course, was twenty-four hours ahead of the steps which still had to be taken at Colon.[55]

The *Nashville,* then at Colon, landed a small body of men at noon the next day when news reached the town of the success of the outbreak at Panama. This was due to the foolish threats of Col. Torres, the local Colombian commander, who declared that unless General Tovar were released at Panama he would burn the town and kill every American in it. This of course gave reason for the landing of American sailors. An anxious afternoon passed but no shots were fired. The Colombian troops retired and the force from the *Nashville* re-embarked.[56] The next morning, November 5, both forces were again in Colon; but Col. Torres now accepted a bribe of $8000 and he and his troops left for Cartagena on the *Orinoco*. In the meantime the *Dixie* had arrived with marines who were promptly landed to patrol the town.[57] On November 6 the new Panama flag was hoisted at Colon by Major W. M. Black, an American army officer, who so far forgot his position as to participate in this final act. Both terminals of the route across the Isthmus were now in the possession of the Panaman revolutionary authorities. Naturally there was an immediate rush for money that had been promised. General, or Admiral, Varon of the Colombian gunboat *Padilla* had been promised $35,000; other officers on land had to be paid and $50 apiece in silver were to be distributed to Colombian soldiers at Panama. The Colombian gunboat *Bogotá*, which had fired a few shells at the town on the evening of November 3 and had killed a Chinaman, had now retired. A popular demonstration then took place; General Huertas was carried in triumph through the streets. As rain began to fall the leaders repaired to an hotel where bottle after bottle of champagne was poured over the head of General Huertas. This was the revolution of Panama in which about five hundred native Panamans actually took part.[59]

It had been quickly and peaceably accomplished. Throughout these days the popular belief on the Isthmus was that the support of the United States was responsible for its success. The arrival of the *Nashville* was timely; but the American forces did nothing except what they were rightly bound to do for the protection of American lives, interests and property. In spite of the fatuous and flamboyant speeches of the Panaman leaders there is not a scrap of evidence to show that the American government was in any way concerned with the proclamation of the independence of Panama. It turned out to be very convenient for the United States; but the movement was carried on by the *Junta,* supported by money from Col. Bunau-Varilla, and assisted by the local officials of the Panama Railroad Company.

Now we must return to the diplomatic history of this adventure. A letter written on November 2, 1903, by Duque, in Panama, to Secretary Hay gives a picture of the movement for independence that emphasizes its historical basis and its popularity.[60] Despite those who may disagree I am myself impressed with the fact that there was practically no pro-Colombian feeling in Panama. Whether the revolution included hundreds or thousands it seems to have been from the outset a genuinely popular step. Other Latin-American revolts have taken place which were on no higher plane than that at Panama, and the United States has recognized their results. The haste with which the government at

Washington acted was regrettable. President Roosevelt apparently could not be restrained; and this very haste was responsible in part for the criticism which soon concentrated on him. His orders to the navy to prevent Colombian troops from landing within fifty miles of the Isthmus undoubtedly was an undue exercise of power. The treaty of 1846 was violated by our action although some might maintain that the United States had implied power to construct and protect means of inter-oceanic communication.

Secretary Root tried in vain to arrange matters with Colombia in 1909; President Taft also attempted a solution; and a treaty providing for the payment of $25,000,000 to Colombia was signed in President Wilson's administration. Later, under President Harding, a modified treaty, which did not express our regret, but which provided for the money, was finally approved by the Senate of both the United States in 1921 and by Colombia in 1922. Thus the violent dispute which arose regarding American action in 1903 is no longer of more than academic interest. The canal has been dug; Colombia has received the money; and the independence of Panama has been maintained. Yet it is worth while to note briefly just what took place at the time.

On November 2, 1903, at 5.30 P.M. the *Nashville* had arrived at Colon. On November 3, Commander Hubbard received his orders to prevent the landing of Colombian troops in order to preserve free transit across the Isthmus. As the Colombian troops had already landed nothing was done; but on November 4, orders were given prohibiting the railway from transporting these troops to Panama.[61] Events took place at both Panama and Colon as already recorded. In Washington in the forenoon of November 3 a report was current that an uprising had taken place. A telegram was sent to the American Consul at Panama, who replied in the middle of the afternoon that the uprising was to take place that night. Mr. Loomis also telegraphed to Colon that the Colombian troops should not proceed to Panama. As the result the revolution took place on scheduled time. The next day the republic was proclaimed. Consul Ehrman on November 3 had telegraphed that the uprising had taken place but the situation was reported as serious. On November 4 a protest was made over the shelling of Panama by the *Bogotá*. On November 5 the Department of State received news of the declaration of independence and of the departure of the Colombian troops for Cartagena. On November 6 the appointment of Col. Bunau-Varilla as confidential agent of the new republic was received and the situation was reported as peaceful. The same day a despatch was sent by Secretary Hay directing Consul Ehrman to enter into relations with the government at Panama. On November 7 Col. Bunau-Varilla notified Secretary Hay that he had been appointed Minister of the Panama Republic at Washington. This was confirmed on November 11 by Consul Ehrman. The way was now cleared for the recognition of Panama by President Roosevelt and the reception of Col. Bunau-Varilla which took place on November 13.[62]

Thus within three days of the revolution the *Junta* at Panama had been recognized as the *de facto* government and, within ten days, as the *de jure* government of Panama. No less haste was now observed with respect to a new canal treaty which was drawn up and signed on November 18 by Secretary Hay and Col. Bunau-Varilla. This treaty was approved by the Panaman government on December 2, 1903, and by the United States Senate on February 23, 1904. It provided that Panama granted to the United States a zone of land ten miles in width. In return the independence of Panama was guaranteed by the United States, which agreed to pay Panama $10,000,000 and an annual rental of $250,000 beginning nine years later. Considerable correspondence followed in 1904 regarding the interpretation of some of the clauses. It was agreed that the United States had power and authority over the Canal Zone as though it were sovereign.

The statement of the United States regarding the relations entered into with Panama was the subject of criticism and correspondence. President Roosevelt of course was absolutely convinced that he was right in what he had done. Later, in 1911, he was to say in a public speech in California:

> I am interested in the Panama Canal because I started it. If I had followed traditional conservative methods I should have submitted a dignified state paper of probably 200 pages to the Congress and the debate would have been going on yet. But I took the Canal Zone and let Congress debate, and while the debate goes on the Canal does also.

Almost immediately the question of our relations with Colombia was to come up. Naturally there was high feeling in Bogotá over our prompt recognition of Panama. A protest was lodged at Washington and General Reyes was sent from Colombia to Washington to make a fresh offer as to a treaty with Colombia. These offers were futile and the mission of General Reyes was a failure though the opposition in the United States took care that the Colombian case should receive wide publicity. The question as to whether the United States would oppose by arms an attempt by Colombia to reassert her sovereignty over Panama also received attention. President Roosevelt was determined that the Panama Republic should be maintained; but he said that "if there should come a brush with Colombia I want to be dead sure that Colombia fires first." [65]

He was anxious that America should not take a provocative attitude and consequently refused to give orders to occupy Yavisa, a strategic position, in case of an attack by land from Colombia.[6e]

In the meantime Mr. Buchanan, our new Minister to Panama, assisted in the making of a constitution for the infant republic which was adopted in 1904 by a constitutional convention. In January, 1904, there also arose the danger that the Senate might amend the treaty with Panama. In case this should happen the door would be open for further amendments by Panama. As it was very desirable that this should not occur, strong pressure was brought to bear by

President Roosevelt and by Secretary Hay to avoid such an event.[67]

Fortunately the treaty was approved without amendments. As the new republic got on its feet, and as the Canal Zone was transferred to the United States, the natural development of party politics took place. A Liberal party was organized to oppose the Government party which was headed by Dr. Amador, the new President. It was made clear that the United States was impartial as regards domestic politics; but that at any signs of revolutionary activity intervention for "the establishment of public peace and constitutional order" would take place. Later, in December, 1904, the Panaman army was disbanded and General Huertas retired to his country home thus removing an element that threatened disorder. Apprehension lest the United States might assume an aggressive policy was diminished by the visit of Secretary Taft and later of President Roosevelt and of Secretary Root in 1906.[68]

Thus the start was made on the construction of the Panama Canal. The initial diplomatic steps were, I think, clouded by an attempt to make the action of the United States appear as justified by treaty. Later we paid a handsome and more than generous sum to Colombia, wiping the slate clean as far as she was concerned. The New Panama Canal Company received the $40,000,000 as provided by the Spooner-Hepburn Act. The title of the United States is now clear and an American Canal, built by the United States, protected by her army and navy, today stands as the achievement of American engineers and scientists. The power, the eagerness, and the vigilance of President Roosevelt stand evident.

NOTES TO CHAPTER XII

1. Thayer, II, p. 299.
2. *H. P.*, Sept. 22, 1900, Hay to McKinley.
3. *D. S.*, From Central America, Vol. 66, No. 373, Jan. 13, 1900, Merry to Hay; No. 379, Feb. 4, same to same; No. 387, Feb. 13, same to same; To Central America, Vol. 21, p. 632, telegram, Feb. 27, Hay to Merry.
4. *D. S.*, From Colombia, Vol. 56, No. 336, Feb. 24, 1900, Hart to Hay; Cf. To Colombia, Vol. 19, No. 365, Sept. 21, Hay to Hart.

5. *D. S.,* From Central America, Vol. 66, No. 462, Aug. 12, 1900, Merry to Hay; *H. P.,* Sept. 21, 1900, McKinley to Hay; Sept. 24, Oct. 5, Cortelyou (the President's secretary) to Hay; Sept. 22, Hay to McKinley.

6. *D. S.,* Numerical File, Memo., March 16, 1901; *H. P.,* Two letters are worth noting; one from Senator Money to Hay, April 3, 1901, who argued in belligerent fashion that the Clayton-Bulwer treaty should be abrogated, the Hay-Pauncefote treaty should be dropped, and that the:

"Monroe Doctrine should again be applied to this great American question. If Great Britain should be unwilling to abrogate the C-B treaty I would favor the legislation necessary to repeal this treaty as a part of the law of the land, build the canal, fortify it and open it to the commerce of the world. Then if Great Britain makes complaint we will consider it. Whatever power or company may build the canal this government in time of war, must be the beneficiary of its strategic value."

The second, from Mr. Merry, April 10, consists of a long discourse, saying that Great Britain does not want any canal.

7. *D. S.,* To Colombian Legation, Vol. 7, No. 13, Dec. 12, 1901, Hay to Silva; From France, Vol. 120, telegram, Jan. 12, 1902, Porter to Hay; From Colombia, Vol. 58, telegram, Feb. 21, Hart to Hay.

8. From the rich files of the Department of State I cite only a few of the more important documents. *D. S.,* From Central America, Vol. 67, No. 636, Oct. 22, 1901, Merry to Hay; No. 652, Nov. 29, same to same; Vol. 70, No. 654, Dec. 6, same to same; telegram, Dec. 9, same to same; No. 692, Feb. 25, 1902, same to same; telegram, June 12, same to same; Vol. 71, No. 769, Oct. 18, same to same; No. 772, Oct. 25, same to same; To Nicaragua, Vol. 22, telegram, Dec. 7, 1901, Hay to Merry; telegram, Jan. 4, 1902, same to same; telegram, Jan. 8, same to same; telegram, Jan. 10, same to same; No. 435, Jan. 10, same to same; (an essential despatch) No. 481, June 24, Hill to Merry (denying that any treaty with Nicaragua and Costa Rica had been signed); To Nicaraguan Legation, Vol. 2, unnumbered note, May 10, 1902, Hay to Corea.

9. Rhodes, p. 265, note.

10. Quoted in Moore, III, pp. 5-6.

11. *D. S.,* From Colombia, Vol. 58, telegram, March 6, 1902, Hart to Hay; No. 589, March 27, Beaupré to Hay; telegrams, Nov. 3 and 25, Hart to Hay; To Colombia, Vol. 19, telegram, March 18, Hay to Hart; *H. P.,* Dec. 30, 1902, Cromwell to Hay.

12. *Diplomatic History of the Panama Canal,* Washington, 1914, (Senate Doc. 474, 63rd Congress, 2nd sess.) pp. 551 *et seq.* This is a badly arranged book with many gaps in the correspondence. *D. S.,* To Colombian Legation, Vol. 7, No. 6, April 18, 1902, Hay to Concha; No. 7, April 23, same to same; No. 8, July 18, same to same; To France, Vol. 24, telegram, June 23, Hay to Vignaud; From France, Vol. 121, telegram, Aug. 13, Porter to Hay; To Colombia, Vol. 19, telegram, Oct. 16, Hay to Hart; *H. P.,* July 5, Cromwell to Hay; Sept. 23, Adee to Hay, enclosing a telegram from Commodore McLean. This read:

"The United States guards and guarantees traffic and the line of transit. Today I permitted the exchange of Colombian troops from Panama to Colon about 1000 each way, the troops without arms, in train guarded by American naval force in the same manner as other passengers, arms and munitions in separate train guarded also by naval force in the same manner as other freight. There is excellent prospect of bringing about an amicable settlement of the domestic strife."

13. *D. S.,* Numerical File, Vol. 547, memo. Nov. 4, 1902; To Colombia, Vol. 19, telegrams, Nov. 22, 25, Dec. 10, Hay to Hart; From Colombia, Vol.

58, telegrams, Nov. 25, Dec. 8 and 30, Hart to Hay; To Colombian Legation, Vol. 7, No. 9, Oct. 28, Hay to Concha; No. 11, Nov. 18, same to same; unnumbered, Dec. 30, Hay to Herran; *Dipl. Hist. Pan. Canal,* pp. 251 *et seq.*

14. *H. P.,* Jan. 2 and 15, 1903, Cromwell to Hay; *D. S.,* Vol. 59, telegrams, Jan. 5 and 10, Hart to Hay; To Colombia, Vol. 19, telegram, Jan. 16, Hay to Hart; To Colombian Legation, Vol. 7, p. 354, unnumbered, Jan. 16 and 21, Hay to Herran; *Dipl. Hist. Pan. Canal,* pp. 277, *et seq.* In view of the frequent reports in the press of the time and in view of the exaggerated ideas of Bunau-Varilla regarding German influence and intrigue in this matter (Bunau-Varilla, *The Great Adventure of Panama,* New York, 1920, chs. IX-XI) I can say that there is not a scrap regarding German opposition to the treaty with Colombia in the archives of the Department of State, the Roosevelt Papers or the Hay Papers. The nearest we come to the story is an inquiry from Hay which came to nothing. This month of January, 1903, was of course a time when public opinion was much vexed because of the German blockade of Venezuelan ports. Hay's telegram (*D. S.,* To Germany, Vol. 21, telegram, Jan. 12, Hay to Tower) to Berlin read as follows:

"Ascertain discreetly and informally what foundation if any for report cabled from London that a German offer of forty millions has been made for all rights of the Panama Canal Company, and that German Government offers to take Colombian Government shares of Company at par in full liquidation of all German claims against Colombia."

15. *F. R.,* 1903, pp. 133-134.
16. *Ibid.,* pp. 134-135.
17. *Ibid.,* pp. 142-143.
18. *Ibid.,* p. 150; *H. P.,* June 19, Beaupré to Hay; a curious rumor was reported (June 15, same to same):

"When orders were sent to Dr. Herran to sign the convention the Colombian Government had grave fears of the attitude of the United States on the Isthmus, on account of Dr. Concha's violent conduct concerning Admiral Casey's intervention and concerning the treaty, and thought that conciliatory measures were necessary; but that when the Government realized that the treaty of peace with General Herrera was in fact secured, and that the Isthmus was fully under its authority, a cipher telegram was sent to Dr. Herran instructing him not to sign the Convention; that Dr. Herran ignored this cipher telegram, and, acting under his previous instructions, signed the Convention, afterwards explaining that the cipher telegram did not reach him in time or was unintelligible."

Later it was shown that such a cable had been sent on Jan. 24. It arrived too late. (*Story of Panama,* Washington, 1913, p. 322.)

19. *F. R.,* 1903, p. 144.
20. *H. P.,* June 13, 1903, Cromwell to Roosevelt; June 14, 27, July 9 and 13, Cromwell to Hay; *F. R.,* 1903, pp. 146, 150-154. Mr. Cromwell wrote (*H. P.,* June 14) to Hay:

"The truth of the matter is, Mr. Secretary, that the Marroquin Government is unpopular and thoroughly distrusted; the elements lately in rebellion, restored to liberty and given a voice in Congress, are naturally hostile to the Government. *The Marroquin Government has become subdued, non-aggressive and apprehensive of dethronement.* Marroquin too, notes the rise of his rival Reyes, and is afraid to take a position which may not be sustained by Congress. Therefore, unless the Marroquin Government is forced to it, they will only submit the Treaty as the best the United States offers, but without endorsement or recommendation, as they had intended to do when the Treaty was made.

"The money element also plays a great part and the scheme of a large faction is to repudiate the last Canal extension; wait until next year and forfeit the concession; then sell to the United States direct and get the whole $40,000,000 (this being boldly and frequently stated in the public prints), or else force the United States and the Canal Company to make up a purse of $20,000,000.

"I think Marroquin must be *forced* to take a definite stand of *recommendation* in support of the Treaty which he proposed to the United States and induced it to sign and ratify. If he *does that* then all the resources of that Government will be employed to carry the Treaty, for it will then become an administrative measure and he must stand or fall by the result and he will probably then put it through.

"Further, the idea that by the repudiation of the Canal Extension for which they received five million francs, they can make the United States a party to an unholy bargain of sale based on such an iniquity, should be promptly extinguished, so that this influence against ratification will be dissipated."

21. *H. P.*, July 23, 1903, Cromwell to Loomis; July 24, Loomis to Hay.
22. *R. P.*, July 14, 1903; Roosevelt to Hay.
23. *R. P.*, Aug. 14, 1903; Hay to Roosevelt; Aug. 13, Loomis to Roosevelt; *H. P.*, Aug. 15, Loomis to Hay; *F. R.*, 1903, pp. 163-179.
24. Appendix A to this chapter.
25. Appendix B to this chapter.
26. Appendix C to this chapter.
27. *R. P.*, Aug. 19, 1903, Roosevelt to Hay. This is really the point at which the President took command of the situation. Up to this time Secretary Hay had been in consultation with him frequently but the negotiations had proceeded through diplomatic channels; now, however, the control of affairs passed quite definitely into the hands of the President.
28. Appendix D to this chapter.
29. *H. P.*, Aug. 20, 1903, Adee to Hay.
30. *F. R.*, 1903, pp. 179-192; *H. P.*, Aug. 20 (3 letters and a telegram), and 22, Adee to Hay.
31. *H. P.*, Aug. 22, 1903, Hay to Roosevelt.
32. *R. P.*, Sept. 5, 1903, Roosevelt to Moore; *Correspondence in Relation to the Proposed Interoceanic Canal*, Washington, 1885, p. 281.
33. *H. P.*, Sept. 13, 1903, Hay to Roosevelt.
34. *R. P.*, Sept. 15, 1903, Roosevelt to Hay.
35. *H. P.*, Sept. 5, 7 and 8, 1903, Cromwell to Hay; Appendix E to this chapter.
36. *H. P.*, Sept. 21, 1903, Duque to Hay. Other interesting letters from Duque are dated, Sept. 28, Oct. 5, 19, 26, Nov. 2, 9 and 16. They reflect the uncertainties of the time.
37. *D. S.*, From Central America, Vol. 71, No. 867, Aug. 30, 1903, Merry to Hay; Vol. 72, No. 875, Oct. 10, same to same; *H. P.*, Sept. 8, telegram from Bogotá; Sept. 22 and 23, Adee to Hay; Beaupré also had announced that the new Governor of Panama, Senator Obaldia, was in favor of the treaty. This had aroused great opposition in Colombia. *F. R.*, 1903, pp. 190, 193-194.
38. Bishop, I, p. 279; *R. P.*, Oct. 7, 1903, Roosevelt to Shaw.
39. *F. R.*, 1903, pp. 195-225.
40. Bunau-Varilla, *Panama, the Creation, Destruction and Resurrection*, London, 1913, pp. 221-222, 255, 267-268.
41. *Story of Panama*, pp. 344-345.
42. *Ibid.*, pp. 456-458.
43. Bunau-Varilla, pp. 288-289, 551-553. *Story of Panama*, pp. 362-365.
44. Bunau-Varilla, pp. 286-289, 295-296, 417.

45. *Ibid.*, pp. 295-297, 306-310.
46. *Ibid.*, pp. 310-312.
47. *Ibid.*, pp. 315-316. *Story of Panama,* Hearing of Feb. 19, 1903, pp. 37-39.
48. Bunau-Varilla, pp. 315-316.
49. *Ibid.*, pp. 313-314.
50. *Diplomatic Correspondence,* 1861, p. 71, quoted in Moore, I, pp. 105-106 and in *Story of Panama,* p. 84.
51. Bunau-Varilla, p. 318.
52. Bishop, I, p. 282.
53. Bunau-Varilla, pp. 319, 323.
54. *Story of Panama,* pp. 386 *et seq.*
55. *H. P.*, Nov. 3, 1903, Amador to Hay.
56. *Story of Panama,* pp. 441 *et seq.*
57. *Ibid.*, pp. 455 *et seq.*
58. *Ibid.*, pp. 444 *et seq.*
59. *Ibid.*, p. 453.
60. *H. P.*, Nov. 2, 1903, Duque to Hay.
61. *Story of Panama,* pp. 399, 440.
62. *F. R.*, 1903, pp. 231-240, 245-246, 247-259.
63. *Ibid.*, 1904, pp. 543-552, 598-630.
64. *Story of Panama,* p. 59; Appendix F to this chapter. Cf. Bishop, I, chs. XXIV-XXV.
65. *R. P.*, Dec. 21, 1903, Roosevelt to Moody.
66. *Ibid.*, Dec. 24, 1903, Roosevelt to Shaw; Dec. 25, Walker to Roosevelt. For the Reyes mission to Washington and subsequent correspondence with Colombia to 1906 cf. *F. R.*, 1903, pp. 225-230, 245-254, 279-281, 283-314; *Ibid.*, 1904, pp. 204-224; *Ibid.*, 1905, pp. 239-240; *Ibid.*, 1906, part I, pp. 412-442. *D. S.*, From Colombia, Vol. 60, No. 221, Nov. 12, 1903, Beaupré to Hay; telegram, Nov. 14, same to same; Vol. 61, No. 230, Nov. 17, same to same; telegram, Nov. 20, same to same; No. 238, Nov. 21, same to same; No. 239, Nov. 21, same to same; telegram, Nov. 22, same to same; telegram, Nov. 25, same to same; telegram, Nov. 27, same to same; memorandum, Jan. 11, 1904, from Beaupré; telegram, Jan. 18, 1904, Snyder to Hay; No. 277, Jan. 21, same to same; No. 293, Feb. 16, same to same; telegram, March 2, same to same; telegram, April 16, same to same; telegram, April 22, same to same; Vol. 62, No. 333, June 14, same to same; No. 362, August 27, same to same; No. 386, Nov. 8, same to same; Vol. 63, No. 96, Nov. 15, 1905, Snyder to Root; Vol. 64, No. 34, Jan. 25, 1906, Barrett to Root; telegram, April 5, same to same; telegram, June 6, same to same; unnumbered, June 13, Barrett to Bacon; To Colombia, Vol. 19, No. 27, July 2, 1906, Root to Barrett. With the course of time and prospect of negotiations with the United States relations with Colombia improved. Secretary Root's visit to South America was also a success.

Further material on this subject may be found in *D. S.*, From Venezuela, Vol. 56, telegram, Nov. 25, 1903, Russell to Hay; From Central America, Vol. 72, No. 893, Nov. 28, 1903, Merry to Hay; No. 911, Feb. 4, 1904, same to same; From Panama, Vol. 2, telegram, Aug. 11, 1904, Barrett to Hay; *R. P.*, Dec. 22, 1903, Roosevelt to Hay; Bishop I, pp. 309-311; *H. P.*, Nov. 10, 1903, Pepper to Hay; telegrams, Nov. 25 and 26, Bunau-Varilla to Hay; Dec. 9 and 14, Baldwin to Hay; Dec. 5, Jeffries to Crawford; Dec. 4, 19 and 22, 1903, and May 20, 1904, Bunau-Varilla to Hay; Dec. 24, Hay to Roosevelt; memorandum (about Reyes) Jan. 11, 1904; Jan. 13, Hoar to Hay; Feb. 25, and March 12, 1904, Cromwell to Hay; Oct. 18 and Nov. 12, 1904, Taft to Hay; Nov. 8, Buchanan to Hay; Oct. 6, 1904, Bacon to Hay (a curious letter to which I do not attach much importance); Hay, *Letters,* Vol. III, pp. 319-331; Root, *Addresses on International Subjects,* pp. 175 et seq.

67. *R. P.,* Jan. 20, 1904, Roosevelt to Spooner. A similar letter from Hay to Spooner is in the *Hay Papers.* This reads as follows:

"I send you a copy of a note received yesterday from Bunau-Varilla, which shows that the intentions of the two Governments were absolutely the same, and that the treaty was intended to cover the idea embodied in the amendments of which you spoke to me. I am going away today for a little while, and shall not have an opportunity to talk with you about it further, but, even if I had, I cannot flatter myself that I could hold my own with you in an argument over it. But the facts of the situation seem to me too plain for dispute. As it stands now as soon as the Senate votes we shall have a treaty in the main very satisfactory, vastly advantageous to the United States, and we must confess, with what face we can muster, not so advantageous to Panama. If we amend the treaty and send it back there some time next month, the period of enthusiastic unanimity, which, as I said to Cullom, comes only once in the life of a revolution, will have passed 'away, and they will have entered on the new field of politics and dispute. You and I know too well how many points there are in this treaty to which a Panaman patriot could object. If it is again submitted to their consideration they will attempt to amend it in many places, no man can say with what result, then they would feel that we had passed definitely upon the main subject; that the treaty was safe; that their independence was achieved, and that now it was time for them to look out for a better bargain than they were able to make at first. I would not say a word of all this, but would go to work and try to get the amendments accepted if they were vital and necessary to guard our interests on the Isthmus, but, as I understood from you, the intention of the amendments was to clarify points where I had not been sufficiently lucid, and it seems to me that when the intentions of both Governments are thus made perfectly evident in the sense of the amendments themselves, we ought not to risk the chances of a reconsideration.

I beg you not to imagine that I am ungrateful or unmindful of your inestimable services in helping us to make the treaty and in the magnificent way in which you have defended it in the Senate. Whatever may be the result I shall never cease to appreciate and admire the splendid work you have done from the beginning of the whole matter until now, and whether I come back well or on a stretcher I want you to know this."

Cf. *H. P.,* Jan. 20, 1904, Hay to Cullom; *R. P.,* Dec. 11, 1904, Root to Roosevelt; *D. S.,* From Panama, Vol. 1, telegram, Jan. 1, 1904, Buchanan to Hay; telegram, Jan. 5, same to same; No. 12, Jan. 2, same to same; telegram, Jan. 28, same to same; To Panama, Vol. 1, telegram, Jan. 21, 1904, Loomis to Buchanan; No. 24, March 11, Hay to Russell; *F. R.,* 1904, pp. 562-630.

68. *F. R.,* 1904, pp. 631-651; *Ibid.,* 1905, pp. 716-721; *Ibid.,* 1906, part 2, pp. 1194-1207; *D. S.,* From Panama, Vol. 3, telegram, Sept. 1, 1904, Barrett to Hay; No. 63, Nov. 8, Lee to Hay; telegram, Nov. 21, Barrett to Hay; No. 72, Dec. 13, Barrett to Hay; Vol. 5, No. 144, Aug. 3, 1906, Magoon to Bacon; To Panama, Vol. 1, No. 19, Dec. 4, 1905, Root to Magoon; *H. P.,* Nov. 24, 1904, Gudger to Hay.

I have not thought it necessary to refer to the large literature on this subject. My purpose has been in these footnotes only to cite the official documents which bear on the matter. I am well aware that many students will differ from me in my interpretation of the diplomatic history of the Panama Canal.

APPENDICES TO CHAPTER XII

A

Hay Papers, Adee to Hay, August 18, 1903.

... Another outcome of the present action is [sic (may be)] one which the Colombian Senate does not contemplate, and that is: a revolution of secession in the State of Panama and offer of annexation to the United States. Such a scheme could, of course, have no countenance from us—our policy before the world should stand, like Mrs. Caesar, without suspicion. Neither could we undertake to recognize and protect Panama as an independent State, like a second Texas. Such a state would have a hard time of it between Colombia on one side and Costa Rica on the other.

Since I began to write this, our persistent counselor, Mr. John Crawford, has sent into my desk a memorandum in which he speaks of the likelihood of Panama's secession. I think he makes a rather blind guess when he prophesies that Costa Rica would promptly recognize Panama. But possibly Costa Rica might try to make a merger with Panama in order to share in the canal at all events, whether it be built by the Panama or the Nicaragua route. I send you a copy of Mr. Crawford's memorandum.

By the time you come here, the 29th, I hope the situation will have become clear enough to talk about more intelligently than I am doing now. I am like a chess player, who must try to foresee every possible move of his opponent, however idiotic it may seem. It is human nature to do the idiotic thing sometimes.

B

Roosevelt Papers, Hay to Roosevelt, Newbury, New Hampshire, August 16, 1903.

Mr. Loomis wires me that the Bogotá Congress has rejected the Canal Treaty. I would come at once to Oyster Bay to get your orders, but I am sure there is nothing to be done for the moment. You will, before our Congress meets, make up your mind which of the two courses you will take, the simple and easy Nicaragua solution, or the far more difficult and multifurcate scheme, of building the Panama Canal *malgré* Bogotá.

Before you resolve on either solution you will probably want to talk with some of the leading Panama Senators, Hanna, Spooner, Aldrich, etc. If you could get a word with Root before he sails it would be valuable. I have written to Adee to get up the treaty of 1846 in all its bearings to have the case ready for me when I go to Washington the last of next week. It may be advisable to take a lesson from their fears about that treaty. Corea, who has plenipotentiary powers from Nicaragua, is in Europe—so that nothing will be lost by waiting a few weeks. If you finally conclude to close with Nicaragua, it will be quick work to get a treaty ready. But I presume you may think best to do nothing definite until our Congress meets, and then to lay the matter before them for some modification of the Spooner Act.

C

Roosevelt Papers, Loomis to Roosevelt, Department of State, Washington, August 15, 1903.

When I was at Oyster Bay some time ago, I had the honor of speaking to you for a moment with reference to the views of Professor John Bassett Moore concerning the diplomatic and international aspects of our relations to the Panama Canal Treaty and problem. It will be admitted, I think, that Professor Moore is one of the most profound and accurate students of international law in the United States, and that he has had a great deal of extremely valuable experience in the practical application of the principles of both public and private international law. I asked Professor Moore to put his views into writing in order that you might look over them if you so desire, and I herewith enclose a copy for your perusal. I think you will find some strong and well supported suggestions in this memorandum, which, in the event of the failure of the treaty at Bogotá, which now seems possible, may be of the very greatest importance.

D

Hay Papers, Adee to Hay, August 19, 1903.

If I fail to answer all the items of your letters, you must take the dill for the weed and charge my omissions to the stress of my present necessities of finding out all that Mr. Loomis has been doing for the last month, supplying memories to the Chief Clerk and the index room, and keeping several bureaux from contradicting each other in their communications to other departments. I read all the mail I sign, and it is surprising how many changes I have to make. It took me an hour and a half today to sign the mail. . . .

I enclose several papers you may care to see, pinning what the *Tribune* once called "an Ecce Jesus" on each. (Note on the margin. No. It was the *Times* which in the same paper spoke of Franklin's friend Beau Marche.)

I haven't had a chance yet to read the New Granada treaty of 1846 in the light of Beaupré's telegram of August 5th, as you enjoin in your letter of the 14th, but I hope to do so before you come on the 29th. At first blush I would be inclined to do nothing that would smack of resentment. I would prefer to stand pat on the Spooner law, by which the authority of the President is measured—which authority he has executed, thereby fulfilling the law—and in so fulfilling the law he has established the measure of the satisfactoriness of the treaty he has negotiated. He is no longer competent to negotiate on different bases and certainly cannot acquiesce in any new proposals whether in the form of Colombian amendments to the present treaty or as propositions put forward by way of inviting fresh negotiation—which may depart from the purview of the Spooner law. . . .

E

Hay Papers, Adee to Hay, Sept. 21, 1903.

Nearly the whole of this blessed sun-bright day has been devoted to pouring loving words and simple into the auditory meatus of newspaper men. They particularly wish to know what I am going to do at midnight. I say I am going to bed, but that does not quiet their anxiety. They asked whether an extension of time has been given for the ratification of the Hay-Herran treaty; whether it has been asked for; whether Colombia has proposed a new treaty; what are the terms proposed; have we accepted them; are we going to accept them; does an extension of time mean a revival of the Hay-Herran treaty or the negotiation of a new treaty on different lines; if the latter, what new lines would we consider; if we had a brother would he like cheese and all the rest of the rubbishy questions with which you are only too familiar.

For my part I don't see how Colombia is in a position to make any intelligent move us-ward until one of three things happens:

(*a*) the adjournment of the present Colombian Congress without doing anything—an event for which Marroquin and Reyes devoutly pray;

(*b*) the passage by this Congress of a cast-iron act under which Marroquin may offer to open up new negotiations to keep things going until—

(*c*) Reyes gets up a revolution.

At present Marroquin is tied up by having a Congress on his hands and can do nothing until it is out of the way, except tell Rico to make vague proposals to do something by-an-by if and when it can be done in such shape as to please the new Congress which is to meet next August. . . .

It seems to me that the Colombian cow, having kicked over the pail, says: "see here; if I kick over this pail, would you give me 'an extension of time' to see what I will do with another pailfull tomorrow?"

F

Foreign Relations, 1903, pp. 234 and 240, Hay to Beaupré and Ehrman.

The people of Panama having by an apparently unanimous movement, dissolved their political connection with the Republic of Colombia, and resumed their independence, and having adopted a government of their own, republican in form, with which the Government of the United States of America has entered into relations, the President of the United States, in accordance with the ties of friendship which have so long and so happily existed between the respective nations, most earnestly commends to the governments of Colombia and Panama the peaceful and equitable settlement of all questions at issue between them. He holds that he is bound not merely by treaty obligations, but by the interests of civilization, to see that the peaceable traffic of the world across the Isthmus of Panama shall not longer be disturbed by a constant succession of unnecessary and wasteful civil wars.

Roosevelt Papers, Roosevelt to John Bassett Moore, Nov. 7, 1903.

If you read Hay's statement today you doubtless recognize some of your own phrases and sentences. I took the liberty of handing your admirable piece to Hay. So you see it has borne good fruit.

CHAPTER XIII

EUROPE AND THE FAR EAST, 1901-1904

THE last three chapters have dealt with distinctively American policies. Now we must turn once more to Asia; but our route is not directly to the Far East. Rather it is through European channels that we must approach one of the out-standing problems of the day—the future of Manchuria and Korea. This method of diplomacy savors at first of indirectness, as though we were ignoring the larger interests of Japan and China. Yet it is the logical, historical avenue along which every successful attempt to deal with Far Eastern questions has advanced. Secretary Hay, when the open door policy was launched, made his first advances toward European governments. Only later in the day did he mention his proposals to Japan. Much the same was true of the negotiations relating to the settlement of affairs after the Boxer rebellion. It was only through Europe that America was able to carry forward her ideas and conceptions of a correct Far Eastern policy. President Roosevelt later adopted this method in the negotiations leading to the Portsmouth treaty of 1905. By the achievements of 1899–1901 Secretary Hay had pointed out to him the right way. One reason why so many books dealing with Far Eastern affairs and international politics blunder is because they attempt to deal with such matters without an adequate background of western politics and relations. It is, I think, foolish for a student to plunge into the tangle of Asiatic interests unless he has a ground plan of European affairs. At all events in this chapter it is essential that we should follow along the historical path and appreciate from the first that American diplomacy in the Far East had its orientation primarily in the relations of American diplomacy toward Europe.

Here I wish to digress for a moment to bring out, if possible, the close inter-relationships of diplomatic questions and to emphasize the importance of personalities in the great game. At Washington, Count Cassini, the Russian Ambassador, was a clever, vain, but lying diplomat. He stood for a court that had practiced deceit as an art, and at the end he was broken fully as much by the diverse elements which struggled for control at St. Petersburg as by his own failure to abide by the truth. In Germany the tendencies were, of course, to try to egg Russia on to further exploits in the Far East and to avoid a breach with the Tsar's government. Germany was between Russia and England. To breed bad blood between the two was a natural impulse of the Kaiser. At the same time to combine with Great Britain temporarily was to please those British diplomats who still hankered after a German alliance and to induce Great Britain to follow the lead of Germany. This was shown in the Anglo-German agreement to coerce Venezuela. Unfortunately Dr. von Holleben, the German Ambassador, had made a mistake in his judgment of President Roosevelt. The result was a rebuff for the Kaiser and for von Bülow. They took their revenge by promptly recalling von Holleben practically at twenty-four hours' notice. To Washington that meant that Cassini was deprived of an ally.

The death of Lord Pauncefote in May, 1902, had been a great loss to Great Britain and also to America. He was succeeded by Sir Michael Herbert with his American wife. They were promptly welcomed into that inner circle that had so much to do with American diplomacy during this interesting period. Unfortunately Sir Michael's health broke down and soon he was to die. His successor, Sir Mortimer Durand, was a nonentity as far as the White House was concerned and almost a failure as regards diplomacy. If the British had broken their diplomatic traditions at this time and had sent Mr. Cecil Spring-Rice as Ambassador to Washington they would have done well. He was an old hunting mate of the President's, a firm friend, who would at once have restored the British Embassy to the primacy which it had enjoyed under the "consulship" of Lord Pauncefote. In any case with Mr. Spring-Rice at Washington there would have been a real duel of wits. For the final choice of Germany for her vacant Ambassadorship was Baron Speck von Sternburg. He also had an American wife; he had known President Roosevelt well in time past; and he was at once admitted on terms of full friendship to the White House circle. His appointment to be Ambassador followed not long after his brief service in Washington on a special mission. He came to America to try to restore amicable relations with President Roosevelt after the smash in which Dr. von Holleben had involved German interests in connection with the Venezuelan dispute. Sternburg's appointment to Washington was, however, no stroke of genius on the part of the Kaiser, as Henry Adams seems to have imagined, but it was due to direct intervention by the President who requested Secretary Hay to write to Ambassador Tower in Berlin asking, if possible, that Baron von Sternburg should be appointed as Ambassador at Washington. This is shown in a confidential letter from Mr. Tower to Secretary Hay, saying:

> I told Count von Bülow that I had received a confidential letter from you in which you said to me that you did not wish me to make any official communication whatever upon the subject to the Foreign Office, but that if it came in my way I might say to the Minister for Foreign Affairs that Baron von Sternburg is greatly liked in Washington, that he is a personal and intimate friend of the President, and that the President himself, as well as the members of his Cabinet would be glad if it seemed proper to the Royal Imperial Government to accredit him as Ambassador. Count von Bülow expressed great gratification at this, and in thanking me, said it was of the highest value to him. He did not express directly the intention of the Imperial Government in regard to Baron Sternburg, although he gave me to understand that Sternburg will be accredited as Ambassador before long.[1]

Within a few months the appointment was made. Thus out of the confusion of the Venezuelan imbroglio in December, 1902, there came the significant relationship between the United States and Germany which was to continue till after 1906. Baron von Sternburg, who was one of the ablest diplomats I have ever met, now had a difficult rôle to fill. At Berlin there was the uneasy and unstable Kaiser and also the unscrupulous von Bülow. Germany sympathized strongly with Russia during this special period, but later she was to help the President to make the peace of Portsmouth. In these days the position of the United States was to grow till America occupied a place where she could throw her weight against the Slav court. In this sense, therefore, Germany for a time came into the "Atlantic Combine" of which Henry Adams was so fond of speaking. But it was only for a time.[2] To cap the situation there was the story, which came from Berlin, that the Kaiser was grieved over the proposed visit of an American naval squadron to Marseilles. He was anxious that the American ships should visit Kiel as well. When this letter was shown to Secretary Taft he commented: "Mr. Dooley ought to have this study of the griefs of childhood." Later President Roosevelt, who was alive to the importance attached to naval visits of courtesy, and who was anxious to have Sternburg at Washington, wrote, ordering the squadron to Kiel.[3] The squadron went to Kiel and later to English waters. Perhaps Sternburg's appointment was thus secured.

For the moment we must now turn briefly to the difficulties associated with the negotiation of a fresh commercial treaty with China. The question of a partial reduction of Boxer indemnity claims was brought up at this time; the restoration of Tientsin to China occupied attention; and the British proposals that *likin,* a tax on goods on inland transit, should be abolished aroused controversy. The delays incident to negotiation with the Chinese also plagued the commissioners. In particular the opening of new treaty ports in Manchuria led to protracted arguments. Finally Mukden and Antung were agreed on; but the Russians were then in possession of these places and they refused to admit our consuls to Manchuria. So we are brought back once more to the assertion of Russian claims in that region. Unfortunately Secretary Hay had acquiesced in the collection of customs at Newchwang by the Russians, thereby weakening the value of American protests as to the administrative entity of China. However, the commercial treaty with China was finally signed on October 8, 1903. Soon war was to affect all these matters and we can postpone judgment as to American policy till later.[4]

Ink was scarcely dry on the treaties which settled the Boxer affair before Japan was pressing on American attention the situation which she asserted was threatening in Manchuria. Further Russian demands that China grant concessions of timber and mines in Manchuria were said to be involved. At the very death-bed of Li Hung Chang in November, 1901, the Russian Minister at Pekin had appeared and had tried to extort his signature to a convention extremely advantageous to Russia.[5] We can recall that, in April, 1901, these attempts by Russia to secure special privileges in Manchuria had been blocked temporarily by Secretary Hay's circular note which resulted in a general denial on the part of the powers that they were attempting special and private negotiations with China. In November, 1901, much the same situation existed. As Mr. Conger wrote:

> In conversation with prominent Chinese officials, they say China is helpless and can do nothing but yield to Russia's demands, unless the other Powers interfere, and they ask, "will the United States help us?" I answer, "help you to do what? That can be quickly determined when you explain your difficulties and ask for help."
>
> The United States, England and Japan have at present, almost a monopoly of the foreign trade of Manchuria, and it seems to me that we might, on that account, conjointly say to Russia that she must, in no respect, jeopardize the commercial rights or interests which have grown up under treaty provisions, and as a result possibly secure some assurance as to a permanent open door, which may be effective. . . .

But as I have written in former despatches, protests made to helpless China or to the Russian Minister here at Peking are useless; the directing power is at St. Petersburg.[6]

The difficulty of the conditions surrounding the Manchurian question were made plain by Secretary Hay in conversation with the Chinese Minister at Washington for he pointed out that America had repeatedly made known her wish to preserve the open door and the territorial integrity of China; but that the very secrecy with which the Chinese authorities were negotiating with Russia prevented the United States from taking effective measures to assist China.[7] In similar fashion Secretary Hay told Count Cassini that as far as the United States knew, the proposed treaty providing for the evacuation of Manchuria by Russia did not "injure our interests and no obstacle had been put by us in the way of the signature of the treaty," but there should not be any violation of the integrity of Chinese territory; "that there should be nothing done which would injure the commercial interests of the United States, and nothing which would diminish the capacity of China to meet her international obligations." Further he said, in response to direct inquiries, that Great Britain and Japan had not approached the United States with the view to the establishment of any arrangement hostile to Russia.[8]

When, however, the definite news came that China, in connection with the signature of the evacuation treaty, was being pressed by Russia to sign a convention giving monopolistic rights in Manchuria to the Russo-Chinese Bank, the United States at once protested on February 1, 1902, to St. Petersburg. To Count Cassini, on February 8, Secretary Hay pointed out that, if this project went through and if this Russo-Chinese Bank should receive as a private grant the exclusive privilege of the commercial and industrial exploitation of Manchuria, the next step would be a demand from Japan that privileges should be granted her in Fukhien and that Germany, France, and Great Britain might soon follow with similar demands on China. The result would be that the United States "would be left in a position so painful as to be intolerable." To this protest the Russian Government returned a very stiff reply saying that such private grants did not concern other foreign states, but that Russia proposed to maintain the open door as she understood it.[9]

There now came to a head the negotiations which had been going on for more than a year between Great Britain and Japan. On January 30, 1902, the first Anglo-Japanese alliance had been signed. In passing I may note that, with the exception of Mr. Conger and Mr. Buck, all American diplomats practically ignored the significance and war-like possibilities of the Anglo-Japanese alliance. The negotiations leading to it also passed unnoticed. It is a sad reflection on the sort of intelligence Secretary Hay had to depend upon. Russia, however, was much troubled. The possibility that a quadruple alliance including not only England and Japan but Germany and the United States might be in the making was a source of alarm at St. Petersburg. Russia tried in vain to persuade Germany to make a counter declaration which would not leave Russia in such isolation as now seemed to threaten. The French joined Russia in a joint declaration relative to the new Anglo-Japanese alliance, but it was a mere form of words and did not involve France in any formal extension of the Franco-Russian alliance to the Far East. The immediate effect of the news of the alliance was that China felt encouraged to oppose Russian pressure as to Manchuria. This was despite the fact that the Alliance related primarily to Korea and to the Japanese interest in that country. Indeed, Baron Hayashi, the Japanese Minister in London, was later so rash as to say that Japan's interests in Manchuria were only indirect. The British, nevertheless, were concerned over Russian advances not only in Manchuria but in Central Asia and in the Near East.[10]

The United States expressed its gratification that the Anglo-Japanese alliance aimed to preserve the independence and integrity of China, but reserved liberty of action as to the protection of her own interests in China and Korea. The news from Germany had indicated that at Berlin there was no tendency to co-operate against Russia; and, in conversation with Count Cassini, Secretary Hay once more said that the American government was "entirely foreign" to the alliance. Nevertheless the Russian Ambassador gave as his personal opinion that war was bound to follow this alliance. Documents on these points will be found in the Appendix to this chapter.[11]

The German attempts to grant exclusive privileges to private German mining interests in Shantung at this time did not agree with their renewed protestations as to the maintenance of the open door in China. Nor was their proposal for an international guarantee of free trade in the Yangtse Valley region at all consonant with their hesitation over the evacuation of Tientsin. As Mr. Rockhill wrote: "Our only chance of seeing the open door strictly adhered to is by exercising constant vigilance."[12] Consequently Secretary Hay was soon busy inquiring as to reports that a special mining concession had been secured by Russia in the Kirin region. England and Japan also hotly protested this grant. The result was a flat denial by Russia that any monopoly had been established. Indeed Count Cassini was almost fulsome in his tribute to the skill which Secretary Hay had shown in making his inquiry yet at the same time avoiding anything like the appearance of joint action with Great Britain and Japan. The general position of the United States as regards Russia was defined in a letter from Secretary Hay to President Roosevelt of May 1, 1902. He said:

> We are not in any attitude of hostility towards Russia in Manchuria. On the contrary, we recognize her exceptional position in northern China. What we have been working for two years to accomplish, and what we have at last accomplished, if assurances are to count for anything, is that, no matter what happens eventually in northern China and Manchuria, the United States shall not be placed in any worse position than while the country was under the unquestioned domination of China.[13]

The fact that, following the American protest on February 1, and following the announcement of the Anglo-

Japanese alliance, Russia did not try to secure from China any special privileges in Manchuria was fortunate for American policies. When news came that the Russians were actually beginning to evacuate Manchuria in the end of September, 1902, Mr. Adee wrote to Secretary Hay, "Adam Zad seems to be getting a move on him." [14] Such ideas, however, were soon to be blasted as the full turpitude and mendacity of Russia became evident.

"Had the Russians lived up to the April Convention, 1902, and carried out the evacuation of Manchuria systematically there would have been no war. Not a single major power concerned would have disputed the Russian influence." [15] This view is undoubtedly correct; but in 1901 the Tsar had prophesied a war of 1904. The Russian position in Manchuria was a threat to Japan in Korea. Indeed the failure of a plan to give Japan a satisfactory boundary of influence in Korea was to be the final cause of the war. At St. Petersburg there were two parties. One headed by Witte favored a leisurely economic penetration and exploitation of Manchuria. The other, led by Bezobrazov and supported by the Grand Dukes and the military party, favored an aggressive policy. They proposed to build up a screen on the Yalu River from which they could threaten Japanese interests in Korea. They wished for the development of large timber concessions along that river; and in Manchuria they proposed to use the native brigands in such a way as to drive out the Chinese and all foreigners save themselves. Thus the Russians would be in complete control. In reality these plans of the military group were only part of Bezobrazov's program.

He, at least, had an all-embracing plan. The trouble with Russian policy, as he saw it, was that it lacked unity of purpose and of direction. The Minister of War is so engrossed in European problems that he is unwilling to devote sufficient attention to the Far East. Russia should strive to effect an understanding with Germany and thus bring together the Dual and Triple Alliances. The Continental powers would then be able to reduce expenditures for land armaments. Germany could throw greater weight on naval construction while Russia could strengthen her forces in the Far East. Together they could work in the Orient against England and prevent her from utilizing Japan as a tool to bring pressure on Russia. Japan supported only by England will be helpless and can be put off with some minor concessions, possibly the southern part of Korea, which she already possesses in an economic way. Meanwhile Russia must show energy and determination. Far from evacuating Manchuria the Russians should make it clear that this question concerns no one but Russia and China and that it cannot be made the subject of an international debate. Russia must greatly strengthen her forces in the Far East in order to silence the opposition.[16]

Witte was beaten by this plan which captured the imagination of the Tsar, Bezobrazov went to the Far East with imperial support; at Port Arthur he was in touch with Admiral Alexiev; and in the battle to control policies at St. Petersburg, in 1903, he was also successful. These are facts of history; but do we find the least hint of them in the letters and despatches of Mr. Tower or of Mr. McCormick from St. Petersburg? There is not a word. President Roosevelt used the term "cloth dolls" of their like in the diplomatic service of the day. It is a real question whether Secretary Hay ever understood the terrific struggle for power which was going on at St. Petersburg. From Mr. Eddy and Mr. Riddle, who were diplomatic secretaries at St. Petersburg during these years, he had more information than from their superiors; but even that did not touch the real facts with regard to Manchuria and Korea.[17]

In this contest of powerful Russian notabilities Count Lamsdorff, the Foreign Secretary, was a mere puppet. No wonder therefore, that Secretary Hay was fairly perplexed at the twists and turns of Russian diplomacy. But of this we shall see more as we plunge again into the story of events at Washington. On April 23, 1903, Mr. Conger telegraphed that Russia had made new demands on China before the evacuation of Manchuria would be completed. These applied to Manchuria and were listed as follows:

No new treaty ports or foreign consuls allowed; no foreigners except Russians to be employed in the public service; status of administration same as before; New Chwang customs receipts to be deposited Russian-Chinese Bank; sanitary commission dominated by Russians; privilege of attaching wires to all telegraph poles; no territory ever to be alienated to any power.[18]

Mr. Conger added that the Chinese would yield to these demands unless supported by more than moral force. At this news Secretary Hay telegraphed inquiries to St. Petersburg and said to Mr. Conger: "You will insist on our request for treaty ports and consulates in Manchuria and make our objection known to second clause excluding all foreigners but Russians from Chinese service. Other points reserved." [19] To the President Secretary Hay wrote:

> It is a delicate and difficult subject to deal with, and I think these brief despatches, taken with what I have said to the Russian Embassy here, will answer for a little while. We admit nothing and give up nothing during the process of explanation, which we are inviting from Russia. The Russian Secretary, speaking in behalf of Cassini, explained to me that the power aimed at was England and not ourselves, but the first two clauses of the convention are apparently injurious to us, and there is a certain lack of courtesy also in their opposing our demand for free ports and consulates in Manchuria without notice to us, although we had frankly announced to them our intentions more than a month ago.
>
> I am sure you will think it is out of the question that we should adopt any scheme of concerted action with England and Japan which would seem openly hostile to Russia. Public opinion in this country would not support such a course, nor do I think it would be to our permanent advantage. Russia is trying to impress us by the most fervent protestations that, whatever happens in Manchuria, our national interests shall not suffer. This is an object which I have been striving for for four years, and if worse comes to the worst I think we can gain it; but there is something due to self-respect also, and it is pretty hard to stand by and see an act of spoliation accomplished under our eyes. . . .
>
> I am hurrying these cables off today before any of the Powers approach us on the subject, so that the record may show we acted without concert.[20]

There followed a few days of uncertainty, for Russia promptly denied that any such demands had ever been made on China. The Japanese produced a new version of these demands and from other sources as well there seemed to be no question that Russia had made these demands but was not now pressing them. Secretary Hay, therefore, wrote the President, who was on the Pacific coast at the time, as follows:

> We have the positive and categorical assurance of the Russian Government that the so-called "convention of seven points" has not been proposed by Russia to China. We have this assurance from Count Cassini here, from Mr. McCormick directly from Count Lamsdorff in Petersburg, and through Sir Michael Herbert from the Russian Ambassador in London. The British Ambassador in Petersburg, having been informed of Count Lamsdorff's reply and McCormick's questions, took no steps to inform himself there. In addition to this information Russia informs us that they are not demanding from China the exclusion of our consulates in Manchuria, and are not opposing our proposition of treaty ports.
>
> Per contra, we have from Conger in Peking, from our Commissioners in Shanghai, from the Japanese Legation here and from the British Embassy, substantially identical copies of the "convention of seven points," which there is no shadow of doubt the Russians have been, and perhaps still are, forcing upon the Government of China.
>
> Dealing with a government with whom mendacity is a science is an extremely difficult and delicate matter. It will take a little time for us to ascertain which of two courses the Russian Government is pursuing. We know that they are making these demands of China, and we know they have absolutely denied making them. It is possible that, seeing the opposition which has been aroused by their course, they may repudiate the action of the Chargé d'Affaires at Peking, and may direct Lessar, who is now making his way by railroad through Siberia, to desist from pressing their demands. If this turned out to be the case we are all right. We are not charged with the cure of the Russian soul, and we may let them go to the devil at their own sweet will. If they have simply lied to gain time, a situation of a certain seriousness will soon be developed.[21]

In May, 1903, there also came stories of the part that the Yalu timber concession was playing on the borders of Manchuria and Korea. The Russians had a legal concession from Korea to cut timber on the Yalu. This they sought to extend both for economic profit and because it would give them a convenient base in northern Korea. The Japanese and also a few Americans had been cutting timber in that region by local arrangements which were not recognized at Seoul. Hence the dispute which soon arose between the Russian and Japanese interests. This could easily have been settled had it suited Bezobrazov and the Grand Dukes; and the importance of this Yalu timber concession has been much exaggerated. It was merely as a small yet profitable part of the general Russian plan of aggression that it figured at all.[22]

The confusion of authority which existed in St. Petersburg is now well shown. On instructions Cassini at Washington inquired as to what we really insisted on for American trade and commerce in Manchuria; the same week the Russian Legation at Peking renewed pressure for the acceptance by China of the seven demands of the previous April and informed Mr. Conger that it had had no instruction with respect to American rights in Manchuria. Meanwhile Count Lamsdorff said to Mr. Riddle, American Chargé at St. Petersburg, that he did not know much of the localities involved but that everything would be arranged at Peking. Small wonder that Secretary Hay said to Cassini that the situation caused him great distress, for American demands with respect to treaty ports and consuls at Manchuria were well known to everyone. It was a foolish game from pillar to post as can be seen from documents printed in the Appendix to this chapter.[23]

Finally, after all this fuss, the Russian government gave way on July 14, 1903, in a vague pro-memoria stating that it had never opposed the development of foreign commerce in Manchuria but objected to the establishment of foreign consuls at Harbin.[24] Meanwhile the Japanese Government undertook by direct negotiations to try to come to agreement with Russia respecting both Manchuria and Korea. With these negotiations we have nothing to do except in so far as they touch questions of interest to America. Russia showed for the first time some anxiety and hoped that in the event of a clash in Eastern Asia she "would find support" from Germany.[25] Japan also made inquiries as to

American policy and the President wrote to Secretary Hay, saying:

> I think the Russian business is in pretty fair shape. . . . I have not the slightest objection to the Russians knowing that I feel thoroughly aroused and irritated at their conduct in Manchuria; that I don't intend to give way and that I am year by year growing more confident that this country would back me in going to an extreme in the matter.[26]

From London came a long letter from Mr. Choate giving the substance of a conversation with Lord Lansdowne who

> . . . took the occasion to say that while he knew and appreciated the disposition of our Government not to take any joint action in such matter, yet that where our interests were identical as in the matter of trade in Manchuria, he thought our common [interests] would be promoted by keeping each other fully informed as to what we were doing, so as to keep in touch with each other. I replied that I thought your desire was manifest that each should keep the other advised in such situation. (Your cable seemed to me to indicate that) and that I thought you were disposed to have the two Governments keep step with each other in such a matter where their interests were exactly the same. He said yes, but that he would be quite content to have you a little in advance, and to follow you, which was a pleasant way of putting it.[27]

At Tokio, where Mr. Griscom had become our efficient Minister, the Japanese were concerned over a Russian demand for a railway concession from Wiju on the Yalu River to Seoul and they had formulated their proposals to Russia which were:

> First: integrity of China and Chinese sovereignty in Manchuria to be maintained; second: Russia not to administer Manchuria or keep troops therein except necessary guards near railroads; third: Japan to recognize all Russian rights in Manchuria based on treaties and conventions now published; fourth: Russia to recognize that Japan is interested in a peculiar degree politically as well as commercially and industrially in Korea, as already stated in Anglo-Japanese treaty alliance.[28]

At Peking the endless game went on of trying to secure promises from China to which the Russians objected. Mr.

Conger was frankly getting tired and Mr. Rockhill was in favor of putting more "ginger" into him. Finally an agreement was reached at the end of August that our commercial treaty should be signed on October 8. The somewhat melancholy impressions of Mr. Conger can be seen in a letter given in the Appendix to this chapter.[29] News also came that the appointment of Admiral Alexiev had been made practically without the knowledge of Count Lamsdorff at St. Petersburg. He was now to be Viceroy of the Far East, and this step quite definitely marked the victory of the Russian military group and of Bezobrazov. The result was at once seen in early September in a series of new demands by Russia on China as conditions for the evacuation of Manchuria. Several of these demands touched American interests in that region. But, acting on the advice of Mr. Adee and Mr. Rockhill, Secretary Hay did not take steps to protest. He was persuaded to wait till the commercial treaty with China should be signed. In this he disappointed Japan for she was anxious to see the United States step forward as a defender of the open door.[30]

We did not do so at the time, and Japan took that rôle. Indeed, in response to a direct appeal from China that America exercise her good offices to secure a settlement of the Manchurian question and the withdrawal of Russian troops the United States replied that she did not know enough about the problems involved and that in any case Russia had not intimated a willingness to accept her good offices. Even in December, 1903, when Russian replies to the Japanese proposals were most unsatisfactory, the United States was very cautious and avoided being drawn into the dispute. A letter from Mr. Griscom, which is printed in the Appendix to this chapter, gives a good view of the situation at Tokio.[31]

The United States thus bided her time in a way which some have described as selfish and heartless. She is accused of a cynical readiness to let Japan fight her battles while she clung to the ringside. Such a view is short-sighted and does not reckon at all with the force of public opinion. As a matter of fact American opinion was strongly sympathetic with Japan; but it was doubtful whether she could win against the Russian Colossus; and the idea that the United States should go to war in support of Japan was foreign to our thoughts. Only in the mind of President Roosevelt did such a notion have room. Furthermore the United States did not clearly see to what sort of use Japan might employ a victory in case she won. Certainly American neutrality was infinitely less selfish in 1904 than it was in 1914–1917. Furthermore the long traditions of her diplomacy had always been pro-Russian though her patience with the existing Tsarist government was running a bit short in view of Jewish massacres and reactionary administration.

The spectacle of international events must have been a moving one to President Roosevelt in January, 1904. At all events he was anxious to have the news of the day as soon as possible.[32] For this he did not depend only on the diplomatic service but on friends and on private channels of communication. With the exception of Mr. Choate, Mr. Meyer in Italy, and Mr. Griscom we had few first-class diplomats at the time though that fact was of course due in the last analysis to President Roosevelt himself. He had a curious sort of contempt for the service as we shall see in a later chapter. As Secretary Hay's health now began to fail badly, and as the President began to enjoy his own grip on international affairs, we see the foreign policy of the United States becoming a more personal one. The President began to be his own Secretary of State before Secretary Hay's fatal break-down in 1905.

In early January, 1904, affairs looked a bit brighter, for Russia had modified her position and conceded with respect to Manchuria much that Japan, and indeed America, had been contending for. This the Kaiser and von Bülow attributed, whether rightly or wrongly, to American influence. More significant than this official change was the news that Bezobrazov had recently declared that, while some arrangement with respect to Korea was possible with Japan, Russia did not intend to get out of Manchuria and "had no idea of permitting other nations to have equal commercial privileges with Russia there." [33] Such personal comment was worth much more than milder official notes from Russia. These were apparently to gain time, at least so the Japanese thought. The negotiations had been going on since the previous July and further delay would be to the military disadvantage of Japan. In particular Japan was anxious to avoid any offers of intervention or mediation and in the event of hostilities she would prefer that China should remain neutral.[34]

For the moment, Count Lamsdorff agreed that all the powers should have all the rights and privileges in Manchuria guaranteed to them by treaties. This narrowed the issue between Russia and Japan to the question of Russia's *bona fides* and to Korea. The divided counsels which were influencing Russia at this time were promptly seen in the announcement from Port Arthur that the recent ratification by the United States of the commercial treaty with China was "unfriendly and undiplomatic" and also by the story that Russia did not recognize Manchuria as being part of China. Secretary Hay said that he really did not know whether to believe Russia or not.[35] In general, American official sympathy was privately with Japan; and as this became known quietly the Germans began commenting on it. As France was drawing closer to Great Britain and as she had shown that the Dual Alliance with Russia did not extend to the Far East it seemed to the Kaiser that a new Crimean War combination was in the making of Japan, England, and France with America in support against Russia. His quick comment was "Then we [Germany] will rise in value to Russia, very much"; and he told von Bülow that "however the die may be cast in the East" Germany's "diplomatic intercourse with Russia should emerge from the crisis unimpaired." For this reason von Bülow had already thought of neutralizing the Baltic Sea. He was doubtful whether such a step would be considered at Washington as a measure of German coast defence or as a backing up of Russia. To this Sternburg promptly replied that American sympathies were with England rather than with Germany and that such a step would estrange the United States. The Kaiser did not like this comment; but the plan was given up.[36]

With the uncertainties and annoying delays of Russia we have nothing to do. At the end of January they cram the despatches of the time. Japan soon cut the knot of negotiation by striking at Russia first in early February. It was at this moment that the Kaiser decided unconsciously to assist Japan and to try to win official American opinion by proposing that the neutrality of China during the war should be pledged by the powers. This German proposal was finally taken up by Secretary Hay, under pressure from President Roosevelt, and a circular note was sent to the interested states. The status of Manchuria presented some difficulty, for it was to be the theatre of war, yet Secretary Hay used the phrase "administrative entity of China" in his note asking that the various governments should preserve the neutrality of China and co-operate in localizing the war. The proposal, however, was accepted with Hay's phrase included. President Roosevelt wrote as follows:

Yes, it was on the suggestion of "Bill the Kaiser" that we sent out the note on the neutrality of China. But the insertion of the word "entity" was ours. His suggestion originally was in untenable form; that is, he wanted us to guarantee the integrity of China south of the latitude of the Great Wall, which would have left Russia free to gobble up what she really wanted. We changed the proposal by striking out the limitation, and Germany cheerfully acceded: It is a good thing to give Germany all credit for making the suggestion. As a matter of fact, in this instance Germany behaved better than any other power, for England drove us half crazy with thick-headed inquiries and requests about our making more specific exactly what it was highly inexpedient to make specific at all.

Indeed the Japs showed themselves past masters in the practical application of David Harum's famous gloss on the "Do unto others" injunction. "They did it fust!"[37]

Of course the guarantee of the neutrality of China presupposed that China would herself remain neutral and the United States urged this on her. At the same time the obligations of neutrality forbade permission to Japan to lay a new cable to Guam. The interest of Japan in Pacific islands had been marked as early as the summer of 1902 and the United States had taken steps to preserve her rights at Midway and Wake Islands. In the midst of American enthusiasm over Japanese victories in the Far East there was, however, considerable quiet feeling that the best interests of the United States might be served by a war of exhaustion. Thus President Roosevelt is reported by Sternburg as follows:

> The President informed me yesterday that Spring-Rice, the prominent British diplomat at St. Petersburg, has written to him on the situation in the Far East, considering the likelihood of a coalition between Russia, France, and Germany, and aimed at England. I pointed out to the President, after he had asked for my opinion on this, the *absolute* neutrality of Germany towards Russia and Japan, which visibly reassured him. The President spoke of his extraordinary satisfaction at the effect of the neutrality proposal of His Majesty, the German Emperor, in the interests of world peace, and expressed himself as follows:
>
> It is to our interest that the war between Russia and Japan should drag on, so that both powers may exhaust themselves as much as possible and that their geographical areas of friction should not be eliminated after the conclusion of peace; and that, as regards the limits of their spheres of influence, they should remain opposed to each other in the same way as they were before the war. This will keep them on a war footing and reduce their appetite for other territories. Then Japan will not menace Germany in Kiaochau and us in the Philippines. Russia's attention is then diverted from her western frontier and remains concentrated upon the East.
>
> From this conversation it was clearly evident that the President is beginning to realize the menace of Japanese predominance in the Far East, which I had called to his attention at the time the war was declared.[38]

Such views agree on the whole with the President's determination that no second European power should join Russia in an attack on Japan. Quite early he had discreetly informed Germany and France "that in the event of a combination against Japan" he would side with Japan and go to "whatever length was necessary on her behalf." It is quite doubtful, however, whether any such declaration of policy was necessary. France had already made it plain that she disapproved the war on Russia's part; Germany was fishing in troubled waters but was anxious not to provoke an Anglo-American combination; and England was herself bound by her alliance with Japan. It seems to me, however interesting as such a declaration undoubtedly is, that it was a purely gratuitous statement.[39] Much more to the point was another conversation with President Roosevelt also reported by the German Ambassador.

His policy would be to keep a watchful eye on Japan, but to observe at the same time the greatest courtesy in the intercourse with Japan. The military successes of Japan had more than exceeded expectations here; it is to be hoped that the casualties in the coming military clashes will be divided as evenly as possible between both sides; he did not care to see Russia greatly weakened in the Far East. American financiers are of the opinion that Russia and Japan will be able to bear the burdens of the war for about a year.

Upon conclusion of peace an effort ought to be made to leave points of friction as they were before the war between the two powers. Korea may belong to Japan, and to this the United States would offer no objection, but merely demand that Japan should respect the concessions acquired there by the United States. A permanent establishment of Japan in China was positively undesirable; and Russia must remain in Manchuria, but surrender Port Arthur as a fortress. Whether Russia will be willing to do this is doubtful. The United States would admit Russia's leading position in Manchuria and only insist upon free commerce there. The President is of the opinion that the danger of a neutrality violation by China could become acute only if Russia should suffer particularly heavy defeat. Conger, he remarked, had given repeated assurances that Chinese promises to observe neutrality could be trusted; although, added the President, Conger was very much anti-Russian, which somewhat affected his judgment.[40]

We must omit all notice of the course of the war for there were problems of international law and of neutrality which chiefly occupied the attention of the Department of State. The fact that Russian men-of-war had taken refuge at Shanghai and that the Japanese had seized a Russian destroyer, the *Ryeshetelni,* at Chefoo presented difficult questions of neutrality. Secretary Hay was in New Hampshire in August, in a state of physical collapse, but he wrote to Mr. Adee as follows:

> The President is anxious lest we do or say something which would commit us to interfering—*or not interfering*—about Chinese neutrality. He thinks the Russian ships should either be disarmed or forced to "leave the port" (I assume he means Shanghai), or else, he adds "we cannot expect Japan to refrain from attacking them." I have assured him that there is no danger of your making any conclusive committal either way. I have told him also that the Japanese will take care of their own interests unless forcibly prevented by other powers—and that there were at present no signs of interference.
>
> We might instruct Conger and Goodnow as to our views so that they would not go wrong in any conference of the Diplomatic or Consular bodies. I do not see what more we are called on to do at present. If Russia persists in making Chinese ports her naval base, and refuses to comply with Chinese rules of neutrality she cannot complain—though she will—if Japan takes it on herself to enforce those rules.⁴¹

Mr. Choate, however, noted the danger of such a solution, saying in a letter to Secretary Hay:

> It seemed to me that the conduct of both Russia and Japan in treating any Chinese port, at the pleasure of either, as belligerent territory was destructive of the neutrality of China and I strongly hope that this prompt and concurrent action [advising the return of the Russian destroyer to China] of yourself and Lord Lansdowne, may induce Japan at least to stop it, otherwise it augurs badly for her treatment of China when she becomes the dominant power in the Far East.⁴²

Secretary Hay's "prophetic soul" was once more right as he read a despatch from Mr. Conger at the end of August, 1904. He wrote the President saying:

> I presume you have seen Conger's despatch saying the Russian Minister has informed him that "Japanese course warrants extension of hostile zone anywhere in China, and that Russia will no longer consider China neutral."

Amazing as this declaration is, I was not unprepared for it. It has seemed to me ever since the beginning of the war that Russia was itching to declare war on China—and that in spite of all her defeats, she fully expects to crush Japan, annex Manchuria and Korea, and then take as much of North China as she may think she needs. She accepted our plan for Chinese neutrality most unwillingly, and there has hardly been a week since then that Cassini has not made some complaint of China. Now in view of China's pathetic helplessness I have felt all along that the only motive of this continued complaint was the desire of the wolf to make a case against the lamb. There is no longer any doubt of this.

It is hard to see what her first move will be. Perhaps the apparent idiocy of her preparations to despatch the Baltic fleet to the East may have an explanation in this policy. She may think she can take a Chinese port and make a naval base of it. A crazy sort of scheme but they appear of late only to think with one half of their minds.

I wish you could have an hour's private talk with the Kaiser. If we could have some hint of what Germany's real relations are to Russia we could know what to do. For the moment the less we do the better, until our cue is spoken loud and clear.[43]

The episode of the destruction of the British fishing vessels off the Dogger Bank by the Baltic fleet under Admiral Rozhdestvensky in October, 1904, though it alarmed the world at the time, did not affect the course of the war or its diplomatic history. The United States sent Admiral Davis to Paris to serve on the international court of naval inquiry but that was all.

As time went on the desire that Secretary Hay had expressed regarding an interview between the President and the Kaiser became more natural for it was evident that something was up between Germany and Russia. This idea may have been stimulated by an anonymous, undated memorandum on the policy of the Kaiser which, from internal evidence, came into Secretary Hay's hands in the end of 1904. It is printed in the Appendix to this chapter.[44] Such information, however, did not supply the clue which could explain the relations between Russia and Germany nor did our despatches from Berlin clear the matter. In fact we were, so far as I may judge, completely ignorant at the time of the plan for a secret defensive alliance between Germany and Russia which was launched in October, 1904. That alliance does not, of course, touch American policy. But the failure of the plan, which became evident in December, was significant. The Tsar at the last moment wished to inform his ally, France, and was unwilling to face her with a *fait accompli.* This, however, was what the Kaiser wished and, when the plan broke down over this difference, he wrote to von Bülow, December 28, 1904, in disgust, saying that two months had been wasted in useless negotiations. "It is the first failure which I have experienced." Hence "America and Japan must now be cultivated so much the more."[45] From this disappointment, therefore, he quickly turned to try to persuade the United States that China was in danger of partition. These negotiations between President Roosevelt and the Kaiser led to plans which culminated in the treaty of Portsmouth in 1905 and American participation in the Algeciras Conference in 1906.

NOTES TO CHAPTER XIII

1. *H. P.,* May 11, 1903, Tower to Hay.
2. *Education of Henry Adams,* pp. 436-439. On page 440 Adams writes of the world as he saw it in 1903-04:
"These were the positions charted on the map of political unity by an insect in Washington in the spring of 1903; and they seemed to him fixed. Russia held Europe and America in her grasp, and Cassini held Hay in his. The Siberian railway offered checkmate to all possible opposition. Japan must make the best terms she could. England must go on receding; America and Germany would look on at the avalanche. The wall of Russian inertia that barred Europe across the Baltic, would bar America across the Pacific; and Hay's policy of the open door would infallibly fail."
3. *R. P.,* May 22, 1903, Roosevelt to Hay; *H. P.,* May 11, 1903, Tower to Hay.
4. *F. R.,* 1903, pp. 46-77, 91-119; *R. P.,* Aug. 14, 1903, Hay to Roosevelt; *H. P.,* July 14, 1903, Hay to Roosevelt; Jan. 18, April 16, May 15, 16, 1902, March 20, 1903 (enclosing a letter from Hippisley to Rockhill), May 25, June 6, and Aug. 3, 1903, Rockhill to Hay; Oct. 1, 1903, Rockhill to Adee; July 19, 1902, Conger to Hay; Aug. 7, 21, and 22, 1903, Adee to Hay; March 17, 1904, Hay to White; Aug. 11, 1902, Choate to Hay; May 13, Aug. 17, and Nov. 6, 1903, Takahira to Hay; *D. S.,* From China, Vol. 122, No. 1267, April 16, 1903, Conger to Hay; Vol. 123, telegram, June 14, same to same; telegram, June 19, same to same; Vol. 124, No. 1463, Dec. 26 (with enclosure), same to same; To Chinese Legation, Vol. 2, p. 172, Hay to Wu Ting Fang; To London, Vol. 34, No. 871, March 27, 1902, Hay to Choate; No. 884, April 7, same to same; telegram, p. 208, July 9, same to same;

telegram, p. 227, Aug. 7, Adee to Choate; From London, Vol. 204, telegram, April 15, 1902, Choate to Hay; Vol. 205, telegram, June 9, same to same; telegram, Aug. 6, same to same; To British Embassy, Vol. 26, p. 192, memorandum, July 2, 1902; To Germany, Vol. 21, telegram, July 5, 1902, Hay to White; To Russian Embassy, Vol. 8, p. 403, unnumbered, June 3, 1903, Hay to Cassini; Numerical File, Vol. 547, memorandum, May 22, 1903; memorandum, March 29, 1904.

5. *H. P.*, Sept. 29, 1901, Rockhill to Hay; *D. S.*, Numerical File, Vol. 547, memoranda of Nov. 6, and 14, 1901; From China, Vol. 115, No. 810, Nov. 9, Conger to Hay.

6. *Ibid.* (Conger to Hay).

7. *H. P.*, undated memorandum which belongs to early 1902.

8. *D. S.*, Numerical File, Vol. 547, memorandum, Jan. 16, 1902.

9. *F. R.*, 1902, pp. 926-929; *D. S.*, Numerical File, Vol. 547, memorandum, Feb. 8, 1902; *H. P.*, Jan. 31, and Feb. 1, 1902, Rockhill to Hay.

10. Cf. Dennis, *The Anglo-Japanese Alliance,* Berkeley, 1923, pp. 3-18; Langer, *Der Russisch-Japanische Krieg* in *Europäische Geschpräche,* 1926, No. VI, pp. 300-303; *D. S.*, From London, Vol. 204, telegram, Feb. 11, 1902, Choate to Hay; From China, Vol. 116, telegram, Feb. 13, Conger to Hay; Numerical File, Vol. 547, memorandum, Feb. 14 (a long conversation with Cassini regarding the Anglo-Japanese Alliance); Vol. 547, memorandum by Secretary Hay, March 1; *F. R.*, 1902, pp. 929-933; *R. P.*, March 19, 1902, Hay to Roosevelt (relative to the joint Franco-Russian declaration). Gooch and Temperley, *British Documents on the Origins of the War, 1898-1914,* II, pp. 89-137.

11. Appendix A to this chapter. *F. R.*, 1902, p. 931.

12. *H. P.*, April 1, 1902, Rockhill to Hay; Feb. 27 and 28, Holleben to Hay; *D. S.*, To German Embassy, Vol. 13, Feb. 17, memorandum; To Germany, Vol. 21, No. 1321, April 3, Hay to Jackson; *H. P.*, about April 1, Choate to Hay; *G. P.*, XVI, Nos. 4947-4948.

13. *R. P.*, May 1, 1902, Hay to Roosevelt (printed in Dennett, *Roosevelt and the Russo-Japanese War,* New York, 1925, pp. 135-136); July 12, same to same; *H. P.*, July 8, Cassini to Hay; July 29, Adee to Conger (copy).

14. *H. P.*, Sept. 28, 1902, Adee to Hay; Cf. Nov. 15, Cary to Hay. The German mind was in a state of confusion and uncertainty during the summer and autumn of 1903; Cf. *G. P.*, XVI, Nos. 4962, 4974; XIX, part 1, No. 5921, where Holstein says: "A general war would result from our opposition to England, Japan and America. No one can tell the result of such a war, but Germany could gain little, consequently Germany had better let Russia alone face Japan." The German F. O. seems to have anticipated the Russo-Japanese war.

15. Langer, p. 304.

16. *Ibid.*, pp. 307-308.

17. Yarmolinski (editor); *The Memoirs of Count Witte,* New York, 1921, pp. 119-124.

18. *F. R.*, 1903, pp. 53-54; *D. S.*, Numerical File, Vol. 547, memorandum, April 24, 1903.

19. *F. R.*, 1903, pp. 54, 709; *H. P.*, April 25, 1903, Hay to Conger.

20. *H. P.*, April 25, 1903, Hay to Roosevelt.

21. *H. P.*, May 12, 1903, Hay to Roosevelt; Thayer, II, pp. 368-369; *D. S.* Takahira to Hay; May 4, McCormick to Hay; April 28, Hay to Roosevelt (two letters); May 4, same to same; Appendix B to this chapter.

22. *D. S.*, From Korea, Vol. 20, No. 604, April 24, 1903, Allen to Hay; No. 612, May 26, same to same; No. 613, May 30, same to same.

23. Appendix C to this chapter; *R. P.*, June 22, 1903, Roosevelt to Abbott;

June 30, Hay to Roosevelt; *H. P.*, June 22, Hay to Roosevelt; *D. S.*, To Russian Embassy, Vol. 8, unnumbered (p. 408), June 6, 1903, Hay to Cassini (with enclosure); Numerical File, Vol. 547, memorandum, June 13; From Russian Embassy, Vol. 13, memorandum, June 5; *F. R.*, 1903, pp. 62-67, 710-711.

24. *F. R.*, 1903, p. 711.
25. *G. P.*, XIX, part 1, No. 5924.
26. *R. P.*, July 18, 1903, Roosevelt to Hay; *H. P.*, July 15, 1903, Takahira to Hay; *F. R.*, 1903, pp. 615-617.
27. *H. P.*, July 18, 1903, Choate to Hay (giving the Russian statement to England and the British reply).
28. *F. R.*, 1903, p. 616; *D. S.*, From Japan, Vol. 77, No. 7, July 20, 1903, Griscom to Hay.
29. Appendix D to this chapter; *H. P.*, July 22 (with enclosure), 23 (with enclosure), 28 (with enclosure), 30, Rockhill to Hay; Aug. 2, Hay to Roosevelt; *D. S.*, Numerical File, Vol. 547, memorandum, Aug. 31, 1903.
30. *H. P.*, Aug. 19, 1903, Takahira to Hay; Sept. 12, 16 (two letters with enclosures) 16 (telegram) and 19, Adee to Hay; Sept. 23, Adee to Conger; Sept. 18, 19 and 26 (with enclosures), Rockhill to Hay; *R. P.*, Sept. 12, 1903, Adee to Loeb (the President's Secretary); *D. S.*, From China, vol. 123, No. 1378, Sept. 1, 1903, Conger to Hay; telegram, Sept. 23, same to same; From Japan, Vol. 77, telegram, Sept. 16, 1903, Griscom to Hay; *F. R.*, 1903, pp. 617-618.
31. Appendix E to this chapter; *F. R.*, 1903, pp. 619-621; *D. S.*, From China, Vol. 123, telegram, Oct. 25, 1903, Conger to Hay; To Chinese Legation, Vol. 2, No. 25, Oct. 28, Hay to Chentung Liang Cheng; To China, Vol. 6, telegram, Nov. 2, Hay to Conger; *H. P.*, Oct. 31 and Dec. 16, 1903, McCormick to Hay; Dec. 21, Loomis to Hay; Langer, pp. 314-322; *Correspondence regarding the Negotiations between Japan and Russia, 1903-1904*, presented to the Imperial Diet, March, 1904, *passim*. Dennett, ch. VII.
32. *D. S.*, To London, Vol. 34, telegram, Dec. 30, 1903, Loomis to Choate.
33. *D. S.*, From London, Vol. 208, telegram, Jan. 1, 1904, Choate to Hay (Choate had no idea who Bezobrazov was but thought he was a person of some importance; cf. *H. P.*, Jan. 6, 1904, Choate to Hay); *G. P.*, XIX, part 1, No. 5933. Choate following a talk with Hayashi in London (*H. P.*, Jan. 8, 1904) wrote Hay saying:

"If war does ensue, I fear it will be a cruel and bloody one, and who knows what nations may be drawn in before it is finished—certainly not ours."

34. *D. S.*, From Japan, Vol. 78, telegram, Jan. 5, 1904, Griscom to Hay; Numerical File, Vol. 547, memorandum, Jan. 11.
35. *D. S.*, Vol. 547, memorandum, Jan. 11, 1904; To Russian Embassy, Vol. 8, No. 237, Jan. 20, Hay to Cassini; From London, Vol. 208, telegram, Jan. 13, Choate to Hay; telegram, Jan. 20, same to same; To London, Vol. 34, telegram, p. 548, Jan. 14, Hay to Choate; From France, Vol. 123, telegram, Jan. 11, Porter to Hay; unnumbered, Jan. 22, same to same; Vol. 80, telegram, Jan. 10, Tower to Hay; From Japan, Vol. 78, telegram, Jan. 14, Griscom to Hay; telegram, Jan. 19, same to same; From Russia, Vol. 60, telegram, Jan. 14, McCormick to Hay; *H. P.*, Jan. 19, and later undated note of Jan., 1904, Choate to Hay; *G. P.*, XIX, part 1, No. 5940.
36. *D. S.*, From France, Vol. 23, unnumbered, Jan. 7, 1904, Porter to Hay; To Japanese Legation, Vol. 2, unnumbered, Jan. 18, Hay to Takahira; To Japan, Vol. 5, telegram, Jan. 18, Hay to Griscom; From Japan, Vol. 78, telegram, Jan. 19, Griscom to Hay; *G. P.*, XIX, part 1, Nos. 5925, 5940-5945, 5966-5969, 5987 (it was alleged Russia had offered a province in China to Germany as compensation for closing the Baltic).

37. *R. P.*, Feb. 16, 1904, Roosevelt to Root; Feb. 9, Roosevelt to Straus; *F. R.*, 1904, pp. 2-3, 43-94, 118-127, 301-302, 307-312; 327-329; 405-406; 418-423; 722-725; Thayer, II, p. 372; *G. P.*, XIX, part 1, Nos. 5977-5981, 5984, 5986, 5988; *D. S.*, To London, Vol. 34, telegram, p. 560, Feb. 8, 1904, Hay to Choate; p. 567, Feb. 13, same to same; From London, Vol. 209, telegrams, Feb. 12, 13 and 18, Choate to Hay; To France, Vol. 24, telegram, p. 657, Feb. 12, Hay to Porter; To Italy, Vol. 3, telegram, Feb. 16, Hay to Iddings; From Japan, Vol. 78, telegram, Feb. 13, Griscom to Hay; From Russia, Vol. 60, No. 58, Feb. 14, McCormick to Hay; *H. P.*, Feb. 17, 1904, Choate to Hay; Feb. 18, Griscom to Hay; Feb. 6, Loomis to Hay; undated but of this period, Hay to Roosevelt; Feb. 12, telegram, Hay to Choate:

"Japan accepts the principle of neutrality of China provided Russia does so. I should think it most unwise to attempt a strict delimitation of the area of hostilities. We could never get the friends of the respective combatants to agree on any concurrent representation of that sort. This is the reason of the lack of definiteness in my note. It is not necessary that the neutral powers should join in an identic note. Let each in its own way present to powers the request for the neutrality of China and all practicable limitation of the field of hostilities. I venture to suggest the desirability of prompt action."

38. *G. P.*, XIX, part 1, No. 5992; cf. as to Pacific islands; *D. S.*, From Japan, Vol. 76, telegram, July 22, 1902, Buck to Hay; To Japan, Vol. 5, No. 420, Aug. 21, Adee to Buck; To Japanese Legation, Vol. 2, No. 81, Aug. 26, Adee to Takahira; *H. P.*, Aug. 18 and 19, Adee to Hay (with enclosures); on Guam, From Japan, Vol. 78, telegram, Feb. 25, 1904, Triscom to Hay; To Japanese Legation, Vol. 2, p. 136, March 5, Hay to Takahira; on Chinese neutrality, To China, Vol. 6, telegram, March 12, 1904, Hay to Conger; To Russia, Vol. 18, telegram, p. 512, Hay to McCormick; To Japanese Legation, Vol. 2, p. 137, Hay to Takahira; to Austria, Vol. 5, telegram, March 19, Hay to Storer (circular).

39. Dennett, p. 2.

40. *G. P.*, XIX, part 1, No. 5994.

41. *H. P.*, Aug. 23, 1904, Hay to Adee; Aug. 24, Roosevelt to Hay:

"I have directed Adee to tell the Navy that they must not interfere in case there is fighting between the Russians and Japanese in a Chinese neutral port. I am inclined to agree with you that the best solution for China would be for her to say that she can not keep the peace and they must fight it out themselves. In other words that her ports may be allowed to become spheres of hostility to which the Russians could no longer run if followed."

42. *H. P.*, Aug. 25, 1904, Choate to Hay; Sept. 5, Hay to Roosevelt:

"Choate writes me, most confidentially, that Lansdowne as soon as he heard you had advised Japan to return the *Reshitelni*, followed your lead, and gave the same advice, 'without prejudice.'"

"Imitation," Lansdowne writes from Ireland, "is the sincerest flattery. I am living in what is sometimes spoken of as 'the next parish to America' and this accounts no doubt for the readiness with which I have assimilated your ideas."

Cf. on these matters of neutrality *F. R.*, 1904, pp. 136-146, 332-337, 424-427, 727-777, 780-790; *D. S.*, To Japanese Legation, Vol. 2, p. 171, Aug. 16, 1904, Hay to Takahira; From Japan, Vol. 79, No. 113, Aug. 21, Griscom to Hay; *H. P.*, Aug. 20 and 22, 1904, Choate to Hay; Aug. 31, Cassini to Hay; Aug. 23, Hay to Roosevelt; Aug. 24, Hay to Adee; Aug. 29, Penfield to Hay; Hay, *Letters*, III, pp. 310-312.

43. *H. P.*, Aug. 27, 1904, Hay to Roosevelt; Aug. 27, Hay to Adee; *D. S.*, From China, Vol. 125, telegram, Aug. 25, 1904, Conger to Hay:

"Russian Minister informed me unofficially that Japanese course warrants extension of hostile zone anywhere in China, and that Russia will no longer consider Chinese Government neutral."

Cf. on the general situation in Japan *H. P.,* Oct. 12 and Nov. 23, Griscom to Hay.

44. Appendix F to this chapter.

45. *G. P.,* XIX, part 1, No. 6146; this volume contains a number of despatches dealing with the plans of a German-Russian alliance which might include France.

APPENDICES TO CHAPTER XIII

A

D. S., From Germany, Vol. 75, No. 1867, Feb. 26, 1902. White to Hay.

I have the honor to report that, at my interview yesterday with Baron von Richthofen at the Foreign Office, I took up the subject referred to in your instruction of the 3rd instant relating to possible efforts to tie up railway, mining and other enterprises in Manchuria, and presented your view of the interest of all the great nations in maintaining that territory free from any special control by any one nation outside China to the exclusion of others. To this he answered promptly and very frankly that Germany does not feel any especial interest in the Manchurian question; that he does not consider that Germany is especially concerned therein. At this I reminded him of the fact that Germany has the same interest to keep the Manchurian territory open to manufactures and to all forms of enterprise and activity which other nations have. This he seemed to regard as doubtful, and finally made one remark which struck me as somewhat significant, though its force was possibly broken by the fact that it was made in a jocular manner. He said, "It may be claimed that the *status quo* ought to be maintained in Manchuria," and on my asking what "status quo" was meant, he answered that there are those who may claim that it is the sort of *status quo* maintained by England in Egypt and by Austria in Bosnia.

After a somewhat lengthy discussion of various questions involved, I came away with the impression that the United States and the other Powers who support the open door policy for Manchuria will look in vain for the slightest support from Germany. It seems clear to me that the reasons which, even as far back as the Crimean War, led Prussia to take the side of Russia, in spite of the pressure brought to bear upon her by all the other leading European Powers and of the obloquy which, for a considerable time, was brought upon the Prussian monarchy thereby, are operative in this matter. You may remember that, in my despatch No. 816 of April 7, 1899, I gave an account of a long conversation with the Emperor. One part of that conversation was so frank and treated such burning questions so openly, that at the time, I thought it not best to include the bulk of it in my despatch, especially as it had no reference to any question in which we were, at that time, concerned; but much of it, and especially the part of it which I gave, in which His Majesty made a reference to the relations between his Empire and Russia, convinces me that, whatever may be his personal feelings toward Russia, he will never deliberately place himself in the position of antagonism to that Power in any matter which the Czar and his Government may have deeply at heart, or at least that he will not do so save in some great and desperate emergency, making it an absolute necessity. In spite of the interruption of the *entente* between Germany and Russia by the Conference of 1878, I think that the whole present tendency of things is toward a renewal of the old relation between the Prussian and Russian monarchs, and, therefore, between the Governments of the two countries. This being the case, all endeavors to array Germany with the other Powers in behalf of an open door policy in Manchuria will, in my opinion, be in vain, so long as there is earnest resistance from Russia.

D. S., Numerical File, No. 547, Memorandum, March 6, 1902.

The Russian Ambassador called this morning, and renewed the subject of his recent conversation in regard to matters in Manchuria and the extreme East, and, in connection with that, the recent treaty negotiated between Great Britain and Japan.

I told him I had sent to Mr. Tower the telegram I had spoken to him about in our last interview; that I had received from Mr. Tower a despatch in which he said:

"At a private interview on Monday with the Russian Minister for Foreign Affairs, I found him very uneasy because of reports which have reached him that pressure is being brought to induce the United States to join in the recent agreement between Great Britain and Japan, and that the United States Government is inclined to move in that direction; whilst he believes that these reports are not true, he expressed, with great earnestness, the hope that the Government of the United States will not consider such a step, which, he said, could be looked upon by Russia as only an unfriendly act. He declared that there can be no differences of interest between Russia and the United States as to Manchuria or as to the open door in China, and added that he is confident that Russia and the United States can reach a definite understanding now, which shall be satisfactory to both Governments. His solicitude was so important in this matter that I promised him to communicate his impressions to you at once."

I said to the Ambassador that it was impossible for me to understand the great solicitude of the Russian Minister of Foreign Affairs; that I had assured him, through Mr. Tower and also through Count Cassini himself, that the Government of the United States was entirely foreign to the recent agreement; that it was not even approached in regard to it; and that since its negotiation the Government of the United States has never been asked to give its adhesion to the arrangement. I recalled to him the letter I addressd to him on the 20th of April, saying how gratified this Government would be to be assured by the Government of His Majesty, the Emperor, that in any arrangements which might hereafter be entered into between the Russian and the Chinese or other Governments as to Manchuria and Northern China, citizens of the United States should suffer no diminution of their rights and privileges of access, of residence, and of commerce in any part of China or of Manchuria which may be affected by such arrangements.

Count Cassini said: "And have we not answered this letter, and given you these assurances repeatedly?"

I said he had certainly done so with great frankness and emphasis, but always verbally and never in writing; that I was willing to accept these assurances as being made in entire good faith, and had so reported them to the President, but that it was difficult for our public men, who were accustomed to written communications, to be so entirely satisfied with oral assurances as I was. But, I said, as your Government has now, in this formal and precise manner, assured us that nothing is to be done or contemplated in Manchuria or Northern China which would interfere with any of our rights and privileges—in short, as they have agreed that there shall be no violation of the principle of the open door so frequently discussed between us, I was ready to accept these assurances in the same frank spirit in which they were offered, and to announce, if they desired it, that there was perfect understanding between the two Governments on that subject.

He was gratified by this, but seemed to want, in addition, some assurance as to the future conduct of the United States in case of hostilities breaking out in the extreme East. He said, with great solemnity, "I am not now quoting my Government, but I am giving you my impression, which amounts to absolute certainty, that the present state of things cannot continue, and can end only in war."

I answered that I hoped his prophecy would not turn out to be true; that both the English and the Japanese Governments had assured us most solemnly, in making us acquainted with the terms of the treaty, that it was in the interest of peace; that it conveyed no menace and no intimation of hostility to any power whatever; but that, in any case, the Government of the United States had no views or intentions in the least different from those they had so frequently expressed to the Government of Russia; we desire that the traditional friendship and amity between the two countries shall last forever; that we had no part or lot in any arrangements which would put us in a position of hostility to Russia, and that the only interest we had there was the territorial integrity of China, the open door and the free participation of our citizens in the commercial and industrial development of the country. The future, I said, was in the lap of the gods, but I could assure him that the Russian Government had nothing but friendship to anticipate from the Government of the United States, so long as these vital interests of ours were safeguarded.

(Note) In the course of the conversation he read to me, translating from the Russian into French, a telegram from Count Lamsdorff saying: "You may explain yourself with the utmost frankness to the Secretary of State. Tell him that it is our desire that we come to a complete understanding in regard to all the principles which should guide us in the consideration of all questions which may present themselves in the extreme East."

B

Hay Papers, Hay to Roosevelt, Washington, May 12, 1903.

I have refrained during all the troubles of the last fortnight from worrying you with the [news], either by mail or telegraph, for the reason that my letters would have been indefinite enough to annoy you and not sufficiently definite to help you to a decision in regard to our Manchurian affair. Even now matters are in such a state that we shall have to wait a little while before we can take another step. . . .

The British Government appreciates fully our attitude of independent action, does not even ask us to enter into any arrangement with them, but [they] are ready to do everything in their power to support us, and to adopt any line of action which we may agree upon. The Japanese Government is in the same position, but, in addition to that, [they] are painfully anxious to know what we propose to do. They would accept the slightest hint of support, or even encouragement from us, and, if we gave them a wink would fly at the throat of Russia in a moment. But I have constantly told Takahira that the Government of the United States must pursue an independent course in these matters, and have used my utmost efforts to keep him and his Government quiet, and to prevent any violent action in Manchuria. He is not unreasonable—in fact one of the most ominous features of the situation is that he does not seem to care very much which way the matter results. He says very distinctly that if Russia should virtually annex Manchuria, Japan would be compelled to seek compensation elsewhere, from which I understand that they would at once occupy the Province of Fukien.

I have intimated to Cassini that the inevitable result of their present course of aggression would be the seizure by different powers of different provinces in China, and the accomplishment of the dismemberment of the Empire. He shouts in reply "This is already done. China is dismembered, and we are entitled to our share." To complete the story of my embarrassments I ought to say that, while Cassini delivers to me the assurances of his Government that they are loyally keeping their engagements he makes no pretence of concealing his individual views that Russia will never leave Manchuria, and that every one of the famous seven points of the convention are just and proper, and ought to be, and will be, insisted upon. When I called his attention to the discrepancy between the assurances of his Government and his own conversation, he simply said: "I am absolutely without instructions on this matter, and am expressing my own individual opinion."

I have done everything I could to clinch the Russian assurances. I have communicated them to England and to Japan, besides making them known to the press in this country. I have instructed Conger to make them known to the Chinese Government, so that they may not put forward any Russian demands contrary to the assurances we have received, as an excuse for their own supineness and cowardice. The despatches from China this morning in the Associated Press indicate that Conger has carried out his instructions, and there is also an indication that the Russian Chargé d'Affaires has desisted from his pressure.

C

D. S., Numerical File, 547, Memorandum, June 18, 1903. By Secretary Hay.

The Russian Ambassador called this morning, and we had a long conversation, lasting more than an hour. I made him acquainted with the contents of the despatch from Mr. Riddle, of the 15th of June, to the effect that:

"Count Lamsdorff requested that Mr. Conger should communicate to Mr. Lessar our demands relative to localities to be opened to trade, and that he promised that Mr. Lessar would be authorized to reply frankly to Mr. Conger and to the Chinese Government what the attitude of the Russian Government is. Count Lamsdorff said that, at this distance and without knowing what localities are meant, he cannot blindly commit himself, as he admits there are some ports whose opening Russia would not favor until the evacuation of Manchuria under satisfactory guarantees is completed. He recommended a frank exchange of views between the two Ministers at Peking."

I called to Count Cassini's attention that I could not understand what Count Lamsdorff meant by saying he "did not know what localities are meant," when the matter had been long since put clearly before his attention. I told Count Cassini that, although the character of this despatch was highly unsatisfactory, deficient by vagueness, and not in accordance with our understanding of the facts, I thought I would lose no opportunity of coming to the agreement which we so earnestly desired, and, therefore, communicated to Mr. Conger the purport of the despatch. I then told him that, to my amazement, I had received from Mr. Conger a telegram dated the 18th of June, saying that he had communicated to Mr. Lessar our demands relative to localities to be opened to trade, and that he replied that he had no instructions, except to [a]wait the discussion of the question at Washington; and that he could make no statement to the Chinese Government, nor to anyone, concerning the attitude of Russia. I told Count Cassini that this correspondence created a situation which caused me great distress, and one which I was absolutely unable to account for; that several weeks ago Count Lamsdorff and Count Cassini had assured us that there was no intention on the part of Russia to stand in the way of our making an agreement with China in regard to ports in Manchuria; and that, on the contrary, they welcomed the advent and development of American trade in that country; that, later, Count Cassini had created the impression that he had instructions from his Government, had asked for information under that understanding which was freely furnished him; and that I had given timely notice to him and to his Government that Mr. Conger would seek to open communication with Mr. Lessar as soon as he arrived at Peking; that Mr. Lessar had replied to Mr. Conger's approach by saying that, although the two Governments were agreed as to the question under discussion between us and China, he had no instructions from Petersburg, and should have to ask for them there. I, thereupon, instructed our Chargé d'Affaires at Petersburg to ask that such instructions be sent, in accordance with the assurances which Count

Lamsdorff had already given us. The result of this request was the astonishing despatch of Mr. Riddle, showing what appeared to me a complete change of attitude on the part of Count Lamsdorff. The substance of the despatch seemed to be that Russia would object to the opening of any ports which we might designate until after the evacuation of Manchuria, the date of which was left vague, and the intention to accomplish which seems more than doubtful. I told Count Cassini I could not exaggerate the gravity of the situation which was thus created, which seemed to indicate a lack of good will on the part of the Government of Russia towards that of the United States.

He protested vehemently against any such inference, saying that the promise which Count Lamsdorff had given (a word which I had not used), was made in good faith, and would be faithfully kept; that it was natural enough that the Government of Russia might have objection to some of the places which we had mentioned as those which we desired as open ports, owing to the peculiar circumstances of the case and the especial relations between Russia and China; but that he was sure there was no lack of good will, and no lack of a loyal intention to carry out all promises and engagements hitherto made.

I told him it seemed to me that Russia, while pledging herself to the open door in principle, was doing everything she could to defeat it in practice, and that what made the matter especially painful to me was that I had guaranteed the assurances of Count Lamsdorff. I had assured the President, my colleagues in the Government, and the members of the United States press, so far as I was able to influence it, that we had absolute confidence in the promises of Russia, and not the slightest doubt that they would be carried out; that we were asking nothing more in Manchuria than we had a right to; that what we were asking was to the advantage of the United States and China, as well as to the advantage of all commercial nations; that there was in it no possibility of offense or injury to any power in the world.

I said I could see no course open to me, except to lay the entire correspondence before the President, to confess my failure in coming to an amicable and honorable agreement with Russia; that I had been working for four years to arrange for our participation in the commercial life of the East by agreement with China, and with Russia, without entering into any combinations or groups for that purpose; that the more than secure friendship existing between the two countries made it my duty, as well as my pleasure, to try to arrange all matters affecting our national interests by agreement with Russia alone, without calling in the participation of other powers, and that my disappointment was all the keener because of my earnest desire that the good understanding of the two countries should suffer no detriment at my hands.

Count Cassini replied with the utmost energy, insisting that the promises and engagements made by Russia would be faithfully kept. When I asked him if he could harmonize the assurances given us recently by Count Lamsdorff with his present attitude, he said, after some hesitation, that he could not; that he was unable to explain all the details of the matter, and that he had no authority to discuss the question with me.

I then said, we seem to be at a deadlock; that his Excellency had no authority; that Mr. Lessar, in spite of what Count Lamsdorff had said to Mr. Riddle, disclaimed any authority to discuss the matter at Peking; that Count Lamsdorff said he was too far distant from China to discuss it at Petersburg.

The conversation took a very wide range. Among other things I told him that the attitude of his Government was inconceivable to me from every point of view, certainly from the point of view of Russian interests; we were asking for nothing to the disadvantage of Russia, but only for the things to which we had a right, which Russia, together with the whole world, had agreed to recognize; that if it were a question of honor or *amour propre,* in the very document about which there had been so much discussion, Russia insisted that ports should not be opened in Manchuria except after consultation and communication with Russia. Russia could certainly not deny that she had been consulted and communicated with; in fact we had all gone beyond the point that national dignity, strictly interpreted, would have permitted, in asking the assent of Russia to a matter, in our view, of undoubted right.

Count Cassini finally, after repeating the assurances of his entire conviction of the good faith of Count Lamsdorff and of his intention to fulfill all the assurances he had given us, said that he was about starting for Russia, and hoped he would be able in a personal conference to explain many matters which were, perhaps, not understood, to bring about an honorable and amicable arrangement of the present trouble.

I told him frankly I had very little hope that he would be able to accomplish it.

Roosevelt Papers, Memorandum, Hay to Cassini, June 21, 1903.

We have always recognized the exceptional position of Russia in relation to Manchuria. We have done nothing to interfere with her progress and her legitimate aspirations. We have only insisted upon that freedom of access and of opportunity for our commerce which has been guaranteed to us by the agreement of the whole civilized world including Russia, and confirmed to us repeatedly by the voluntary and unsolicited assurances of the Russian Government.

D

Hay Papers (Personal and Private), Conger to Hay, Pekin, China, July 24, 1903.

I have received your private letter of the 13th ultimo, and thank you heartily for its frank and cordial tone, and especially for the interesting and important information as to the situation there.

We shall be pleased to see Mr. Fletcher, who ought to arrive soon, and I feel sure he will make a most desirable addition to our Legation family.

The Manchurian question here is most annoying. I have come to the conclusion that the statements of neither the Russians nor Chinese in regard to it can be believed. The Chinese, of course, appear to be greatly annoyed by the Russian occupation, but there is an evident insincerity in their reference to it, and their appeals for aid in bringing about a solution are largely *pro forma*. The Russian officials privately insist with the Chinese that they are their best friends, and that Russia is the only Power that can or will, in case of trouble, stand between the Manchu Dynasty and revolting Chinese. The Chinese have been considerably impressed by this, and say that if the other Powers were really their friends they would, ere this, have given them substantial support in opposing the encroachments of Russia.

Mr. Lessar frankly says that there are only two things that the Russians can do; they must either annex Manchuria, or they must make some arrangement whereby they can withdraw and leave the Chinese their active and sympathetic friends. If they were to withdraw without such an arrangement it would take a very large army to protect their railway and other interests there, and Russia would thus, at her own expense, be policing and keeping in order an extensive and unfriendly country for the benefit of the trade and interests of the rest of the world. Hence he concluded that it was wiser, and would be vastly cheaper to annex, and police and restrain only for themselves.

I think it is quite plain to all out here that Russia does not intend to give back Manchuria. The recent conference at Port Arthur, I believe, was to consult as to the best methods of strengthening the weak places in its policy, as well as in its material defences, and it evidently has operated in bringing the opposing factions of the Russian Government into more harmonious relations.

Since the adjournment of the conference, all Russians speak of Manchuria in the sense of absolute ownership, and the minor officials continually talk of their perfect preparedness for war; even their declaration handed to you smacks of pretended proprietorship.

When we think of their vast expenditures in Manchuria, we may be sure that they will hold absolute control by actual Russian jurisdiction, or keep practical control by the presence, always and everywhere, of sufficient Russian forces to overawe and dominate all Chinese officials.

In my despatch of yesterday I set forth the absolute impossibility of China's taking any formal action on the question of opening Manchurian ports until after the withdrawal of Russia. Should Russia hand a copy of her declaration upon this question to China, it will be, I am certain, construed by both as referring to a time when the Government of Manchuria may be turned back to China. But if this never happens, then the conclusion of our treaty negotiations must wait indefinitely. If Russia ever does evacuate, then we can certainly secure the fulfillment of Prince Ching's promise. If she does not evacuate, then neither edict nor treaty opening of ports would be of value. Hence, I think with this promise, and the several provisions of our treaty, which make it incomparably better than the British, we will have done very well, and had better conclude and sign.

The only alternative would be to induce the Russian Government (which cannot be done) to inform the Chinese that they have no objections to the immediate opening of the ports, when the Chinese would forthwith open them by Imperial Edict. In either case we will not get them in the treaty.

The protests of England, Japan and the United States at various times directed to China, have been wholly ineffective in stopping the encroachments of Russia. She has moved steadily and successfully onward, gaining and holding her every point, and except as to the important declaration as to the open door secured by you from Russia, we have scored nothing. China is not grateful to us, and Russia is annoyed and sore, and will grudgingly yield even our rights in the future.

I do hope that before you leave the service you will undertake the adjustment of the Manchurian question, so far as the United States is concerned, at St. Petersburg, the only place where it can be done.

Since dictating the above a very interesting bit of information has come to me, pointing still more clearly to an understanding between the Russians and Chinese, and to the fact of their playing into each other's hands. The Japanese and Korean Ministers by direction of their Governments, requested Prince Ching to instruct the Chinese Minister in Korea to support the Japanese and English request for the opening of the Korean port "Wiju" on the Yalu river. He gave them to understand that he would, but instead he wrote to the Chinese Minister at Seoul that as China was herself opposing the opening of Manchurian ports to foreign trade, that she could not in consequence ask Korea to open ports. The British Chargé was also directed by his Government to ask the same instructions, but for some reasons had not done so, I believe because the Japanese Minister had informed him that it was not necessary. However, the Russian Minister at Seoul objected, and the port does not open. The British Government is very much incensed at Prince Ching, and the Chargé, Mr. Townley, has been instructed to emphatically threaten the Chinese Government with a change of their friendly attitude, if they persist in this course.

E

Hay Papers, Griscom to Hay, Tokio, December 8, 1903.

There is nothing in the situation out here which especially calls for a letter from me to you but it occurs to me that you might be glad to have the kind of description of the state of things which cannot be written in an official despatch. Last July there occurred a very important event; Japan made up her mind to open up a discussion of the whole Manchurian question and addressed a note to that effect to Petersburg. I got wind of this from Denison, the American adviser of the Foreign Office and at once reported it to you by cable. I may add that you were in New Hampshire and I received a pretty decided snub from the Department for reporting matters about which I had no positive information and for not giving my authority. Nothing would induce me to put Denison's name on record in the Department so I did not give my authority. Under the circumstances I have felt rather chary about reporting to you matters which I knew were going on, and yet could get no official statement thereon. The Russians received the Japanese proposals in quite a friendly spirit—that is Lord Lamsdorff did—but the appointment of Admiral Alexieff to be viceroy came as a thunderbolt to disturb the East; and brought about a long delay in the Japanese negotiations. Japan asked Russia to recognize that the former has special interests both commercial and political, in Korea, and also to give an assurance: (1) that the integrity of China would be maintained and, (2) that Russia would recognize the rights which Japan has acquired by treaty with China. When the Russian reply finally reached Tokyo (about September) it was to this effect: that Russia would acknowledge that Japan is especially interested in Korea, but declined to give the assurances which I have numbered (1) and (2) above. The negotiations were transferred by the Russians from St. Petersburg to Tokyo because Lamsdorff said that Baron Rosen, the Minister here, could take his instructions from an admiral in Port Arthur but the Minister for Foreign Affairs could not. Baron Rosen keeps a courier going between here and Port Arthur and undoubtedly deals directly with Alexieff. The Japanese resent this but have to pretend they don't see it. Upon receiving Russia's reply the Japanese made counter proposals insisting that Russia give some assurance about Manchuria; Baron Rosen then said that he would have to have more instructions before he could treat of such a question. He sent home for instructions early in November and now a month has elapsed and he has not heard from his Government. The reason given is that the Czarina is in poor health! That is the present state of affairs. We are momentarily expecting Rosen to say something. In the meanwhile the Diet will meet for business on the 10th instant and the Government finds itself in a very embarrassing position. Unless it has something definite to tell the Diet it will go hard with the Government, and there are only two more days in which to hear from Russia. The new Diet will be strongly in favor of meeting the issue with Russia boldly and it is quite possible that they will embarrass the Government so much that the Emperor will dissolve the Parliament. The feeling against Russia is running very strong and the whole country is pretty well worked up. The press is unanimous and even the merchants would like to see the matter settled. The condition of trade and finance is very bad indeed, and a war could hardly make it worse. And yet the best opinion is that a Government that would give in to Russia would fall at once. The only peaceful solution seems to lie in the possibility of Russia consenting to a compromise that would save the Japanese face. At the present writing this seems likely to happen. It is quite possible, however, that a very critical situation may develop and we should be prepared for such an emergency. It seems to me that it might become our duty, under the Hague Tribunal agreement, to remind both parties that that Tribunal exists for the sole purpose of avoiding war. If Russia were determined on war it would put the Czar in a very embarrassing position. It is difficult to think of anything more awkward than having to repudiate his own Tribunal. Even if there were no prospect of war it might be well for us to try to find some excuse for referring the Manchurian question, or the question of our treaty ports in Manchuria to The Hague.

If the situation here becomes very critical and we determine to suggest The Hague, it seems to me better to do so acting jointly with one other power, and after considering the situation it seems that the only possible power, acceptable to both parties would be France. Russia would not listen to Great Britain and the Japanese cordially detest the Germans since the latter allied itself so unnecessarily with Russia and deprived Japan of the fruits of the Chinese war.

I am very hopeful that no such necessity as this will arise, but should it do so I will telegraph you suggesting our intervention, joined with France, and you will understand what I mean. Delcasse has expressed himself pretty freely to the Japanese Minister in Paris as not approving all of Russia's designs in the Far East. The position of Great Britain here is a curious one. The British Foreign Office deprecates war but the British Minister, Sir Claude Macdonald, is urging Japan to fight. The Japanese mistrust him and to be frank with you so do I. The Alliance seems to count for very little— certainly the Japanese do not expect any assistance and consequently they do not consult the British about these negotiations. In my last interview with the Foreign Minister he told me the question would narrow down ultimately to whether Russia would permit open ports in Manchuria. He expresses regret that our fleet has been ordered to Honolulu, fearing that it might be taken as a sign that we withdrew our moral support. He hopes we will do something about our newly acquired treaty ports. I gave him no encouragement, not knowing what is intended. I am giving them no handle to draw us in.

F.

Hay Papers, Memorandum, [End of 1904 ?].

In 1900–1901 the K. [Kaiser] called at the Russian Embassy, and said that if the Czar wished to move his troops from Poland to Central Asia, he, the K. would guarantee the western frontier of Russia should be safe from attack, and that, should trouble break out, no [in] Poland or [sic] German army would be at the disposal of the Russian Government. At the time the military party in Russia had begun to move troops from Central Asia to the Caucasus, and it was generally stated in the European press that the invasion of Afghanistan was imminent. The movement was stopped by [blank occurs in original] owing to financial reasons, as the rumor had disorganized the money market, and it was impossible to obtain the loan which Russia needed for the Siberian railway. There was also a severe crisis in the newly started industrial enterprises in Russia, and a symptom of collapse of the St. Petersburg Bourse. The Czar ordered the military party to cease its activity, and the movement on Central Asia suddenly ceased. At the same time the Ameer absolutely refused to yield to the Russian invitation to enter into direct relations contrary to the agreement with England, which had the sanction of Russia, expressed in a formal diplomatic correspondence.

The Czar sent no answer relative to the K.'s offer. The K. called again at the Russian Embassy, and asked if an answer had been received, and observed: "I offered him my whole army; he does not even say 'thanks, damn you.'"

In 1901 the K. informed the British Embassy that he had absolutely refused to agree to the Russian proposal for joint action with a view to putting a stop to the Boer war. This referred to a scheme of Mouravieff for joint intervention. It thus appears that the K. encouraged to the best of his ability the Russian Government to attack India—at the outset I did not fear war—and subsequently disclaimed credit with England for refusing to join in a proposed joint action of the powers inimical to England.

Hayashi stated that, while the negotiations between England and Japan were going on, Ito was on a journey in Europe, and sounded the Russian Government in a somewhat private manner as to the possibility of a direct understanding between Japan and Russia. The Russian Government proposed an arrangement under which Korea should be placed under Japanese protection and Masampo ceded absolutely to Russia. This Ito regarded as inadmissible, and left St. Petersburg without continuing the negotiations, which, however, came to the knowledge of the Germans. The German Embassy with Eckardstein pressed the English Government to conclude their negotiations with Japan, as he said Ito was on the point of coming to a separate arrangement with Russia. This materially hastened the conclusion of the Anglo-Japanese treaty. Eckardstein called on Hayashi shortly before the war broke out and told him, on high German authority, that the Russians were making military preparations, and that the sooner war broke out the better for Japan.

The German Minister in Tokyo told the Japanese Legation that if the French showed any inclination to interfere, the German fleet would keep the French fleet back. The Japanese Government ordered their Legation in Berlin to ask whether this communication was official and could be depended upon. The Foreign Office answered that all Germany promised was strict neutrality and nothing more.

After the outbreak of the war, Witte at Nordeney, during the negotiations for a treaty of commerce, recalled a promise on behalf of the Kaiser, that Russia could safely remove her troops from Poland; Germany would guarantee the security of her western province. During the Kaiser's visit in 1898-9 to England he had conversations with Chamberlain in which he spoke of the possibility of an alliance with England. Chamberlain said he believed such an alliance would be popular, and even undertook to advocate it. Eckardstein, by the Emperor's instructions, reminded him of this promise and urged him to keep it. Chamberlain accordingly made his Leicester speech, in which he advocated an alliance between England, Germany and America for the protection of their mutual interests in the Far East. As soon as the speech was made, the German press attacked Chamberlain violently for supposing that Germany could ally herself with England against Russia, and Germany took advantage of the occasion to induce Russia to withdraw her opposition to the Bagdad railway concession.

When Loubet was on the point of visiting Rome, the K. who was in the Mediterranean, attempted to arrange a meeting with the King of Italy, which would have injuriously affected the chances of the vote for grabs [sic] with Germany passing the French Chamber. The Italian King put off the meeting with the K., who revenged himself by proceeding to Mainz, and there delivering a violent speech against France.

When the Franco-English arrangement had been made, but before it had passed the French Chambers, the Emperor invited the King of Italy to Kiel, and attempted to arrange a great naval demonstration, which the King denied having [sic] any reference to politics, and requested the English papers to treat the visit as personal and friendly but not political. The German papers, on the contrary, by command, treated the visit as a political event of the first importance.

It was universally believed at St. Petersburg that the Emperor of Germany had informed the Czar that Japanese torpedo boats had been fitted out in English ports and were waiting for the Russian fleet. This belief, which was shared by the Czar, accounted for his refusal to offer a more satisfactory expression of regret when the news of the North Sea incident arrived.

These are instances showing what appears to be a policy of exciting one nation against the other by means of personal suggestions or offers of friendly offices in case of trouble.

A curious incident occurred in China at the time of the evacuation of Shanghai by the international troops. The German Consul at Shanghai informed his Minister, who informed the French Legation, that the English had signed a secret treaty with the viceroy for the transference of an island on the Yangtse to England as a military station. The Germans proposed [that] the powers should refuse to withdraw their troops unless China should sign an agreement not to allow any power to have any exclusive military naval or commercial concessions in the Yangtse Valley. This the French refused to do, on the ground that the powers, several of them, had already commercial concessions in the Valley. The French Chargé informed the British Legation, who were able to prove that the whole story was unfounded.

The point of this demand on the part of Germany was [that] England had a railway concession in the Valley for a line which was to meet the German line starting from Kiau-chow, and the original arrangement with Germany was that Germany should control the Chang-tung line, and England the Yangtse line.

No one in England whom I have met has been able to solve the mystery of the Venezuela agreement with Germany. It took place immediately after the visit of the Kaiser to England, and was supposed to be in connection with it, but the suggestion did not come from the German Embassy. It is universally believed that he arranged it in personal conversation with someone connected with the Government, though how this was done has not been cleared up.

The Bagdad railway agreement, the result of which would have been to embroil England with Russia, was undoubtedly due to the personal intervention of the Emperor, but it was brought out through bankers and through their influence on the British F. O. and Mr. Balfour. At the present moment the K. appears to have England on the brain. All evidence tends to show that he is constantly suggesting to the Czar evil intention on the part of England, which the Czar is inclined to believe. In January last he believed, or said he believed, England intended to attack the German fleet, and cancelled all the Christmas leaves of former officers, sending a torpedo commission out to Cuxhaven to lay down mines on the coast. He summoned Metternich from England to report, and told the Chancellor to speak to the British Ambassador. A Politician closely connected with Buelow, made a speech in the same sense. At the same time overtures were made for some sort of an agreement with Germany. A self-invented mission of one Sir Thomas Barclay was quoted in the German press as an attempt on the part of England to enter into close relations with Germany. The K. had a long conversation with Boni Castellane and other Frenchmen at Bremen on the occasion of Prince Radziwill's funeral. They were considerably impressed with his language and very much under his charm. They belonged to the anti-English nationalists.

CHAPTER XIV

THE TREATY OF PORTSMOUTH

THE exercise of the good offices of the United States in establishing peace between Russia and Japan is a complicated story. Mr. Dennett has already given us in his *Roosevelt and the Russo-Japanese War* not only an interesting account but documentary material of prime importance. My purpose is to supplement this material, to give a brief version of what happened not only at Portsmouth but at Björkö and in Japan, and, briefly, to call attention to the German proposals as to Moroccan affairs. Indeed this chapter should be read especially in connection with that on the Algeciras Conference. Only then can we get the full sweep of American activities in 1905 and 1906 and see the part played in those important years by President Roosevelt. The fate of Korea and the protection of the Philippines naturally conclude this chapter, while the curtain is also rung up for the prologue to the great drama of the World War. Later we can watch the active way in which President Roosevelt interfered to restrain the Kaiser and to prevent the outbreak of that struggle in connection with the Algeciras Conference.

Already, in August, 1904, Witte had had the desire to meet Count Hayashi, the Japanese Minister in London, but had been blocked by the Tsar. Others of less degree had come forward with proposals of peace but as Dr. Dillon wrote: "They only write and talk. Nothing can be done." [1] Yet in America in early August President Roosevelt took the first definite step which was later to make him the mediator between the two belligerents. A despatch of August 11 from

Baron Speck von Sternburg, German Ambassador, reports a conversation with the President who said that:

> .... if Japan should annihilate General Kuropatkin's army if Port Arthur should fall, and it should come to a conclusion of peace, he would strive for the following settlement: Korea remains under a Japanese protectorate, which may be tantamount to control. The powers guarantee the neutralization of Manchuria, which is to be placed under the control of a Chinese Viceroy to be appointed by Germany, *not* England. Should the President be re-elected, he would like to go hand in hand with Germany in Eastern Asia. But first he would like to come to a clear understanding with Germany on all East Asiatic questions, and then he would be prepared to take the initiative to settle them. He gave me to understand that it would be desirable to him that I should personally report, as soon as the time arrives, to His Majesty the Emperor the particulars of the policy which he considers to be the proper one in the Far East.[2]

Count von Bülow commented to the Kaiser on this letter saying: "the President is a great admirer of Your Majesty and would like to rule the world hand in hand with Your Majesty, regarding himself as something in the nature of an American counterpart to Your Majesty." But he judged the proposal to be sincere and without any hostile design against Germany. Particularly was he pleased that von Sternburg's report showed the President to be suspicious of England which proved "that our repeated hints to that effect have not remained entirely without influence upon him." The Kaiser was interested but cautious. He wrote on the margin of the despatch: "One must not divide the hide of the bear before he has been shot." There was no need to hurry a decision and he thought the proposal that Germany should appoint a Chinese Viceroy for Manchuria was "simply nonsense! quite impossible!"[3]

In reply to von Sternburg von Bülow wrote on September 5, saying, that the Kaiser accepted the President's proposal but pointed out that Port Arthur had not yet fallen and that the future was still uncertain. The Ambassador was to seek to bring President Roosevelt to maintain the open door especially on the Yangtse where the Kaiser suspected England had designs to extend her control. The Japanese were also suspicious of British policy at this time and had hinted to London that they might enter into an understanding with Russia at the conclusion of the war. This, of course, is what Japan did after 1907 by a series of four successive secret treaties.[4]

Germany in the meantime rejoiced in the fact that it was to "the interest of the United States to go hand in hand with Germany in Chinese questions" for to her "we readily concede the right of precedence in affairs of the Pacific Ocean." But von Bülow added: "this we must keep secret [i.e. the fact of German initiative] not only for the present, but . . . for all time." [5] It was of course at the very moment when the Kaiser was addressing the Tsar as "Admiral of the Pacific" and signing his telegrams as "Admiral of the Atlantic." The Dogger Bank incident had just taken place; the Kaiser, as we have seen in the previous chapter, was begging the Tsar to sign a defensive treaty with Germany; and he was warning America of the danger that the war in the Far East might now spread to Europe and might involve France. In which case the President's earlier threat to join with Japan might be involved. This danger was of course much exaggerated; but the President promised that he would not approach the question of mediation between the belligerents without careful discussion of the whole matter with Germany and without a clear understanding with the Kaiser on the various steps to be taken.[6]

Such negotiations, however, received small aid from Secretary Hay who advised the President against any joint action with Germany relative to the open door in China during the continuance of war and pointed out the constitutional obstacles to an international agreement which might lead to hostilities.[7] With the arrival at Berlin of von Sternburg who came to spend Christmas and as a "speaking tube" to report President Roosevelt's views to the Kaiser, matters took more definite shape. American opposition to Russia and distrust of the Russian authorities were so marked that Germany, it was felt, would do well to lay stress on the possibility of a future Anglo-French-Russian-Japanese combination rather than on the alleged "yellow peril" resulting from a Japanese victory. The Kaiser repeated his phrase with respect to Russia saying: "We must treat the Russians with positive and absolute coolness and suspicion and keep America and Japan friendly." Yet this must not go so far as to antagonize Russia for the sake of the growing friendly relations between Germany and the United States. The Kaiser's disappointment at the failure of his plan for a defensive alliance with Russia was marked at this time and von Bülow was anxious to use the situation with America to extricate Germany from the "sulking corner" to which both Russia and England were inclined to condemn her.[8] In the meantime President Roosevelt at Washington was ready to weigh any suggestion which the Kaiser might make. He had already told von Sternburg that he did not think much of the English statesmen and that "the only man I understand and who understands me is the Kaiser." [9]

The Kaiser, therefore, communicated to the President his notion that France was to be the head of a powerful coalition which would persuade the belligerents "that peace without compensation to the neutral powers is impossible." China was to pay the bill at the cost of her integrity. The way to prevent this was to ask all the powers to agree to a self-denying declaration as regards China, whose territorial entity must thus be preserved.[10] The President acknowledged this and Secretary Hay wrote the well-known circular note of January 13, 1905, proposing that China should be preserved and the open door maintained. All of the neutral states replied promptly pledging themselves to respect the integrity of China.[11]

The President had said to von Sternburg that he was in harmony with the views expressed by the Kaiser.[12] Only a few days earlier he had sent a long letter to his friend, Mr. Cecil Spring-Rice of the British Embassy at St. Petersburg, in which among other things, he said:

I have reason to believe that the Japanese were disappointed and unfavorably impressed by the vehemence of speech and exceeding moderation of action in the Hull fishing fleet affair. Personally I appreciate to the full the difficulty of committing one's self to a course of action in reliance upon the proposed action of any free people which is not accustomed to carry out with iron will a long continued course of foreign policy. It would be well nigh impossible, even if it were not highly undesirable, for this country to engage with another country to carry out any policy save one which had become part of the inherited tradition of the country, like the Monroe Doctrine. Not merely could I, for instance, only make such an engagement for four years, but I would have to reckon with a possible overthrow in Congress, with the temper of the people, with many different conditions. In consequence, my policy must of necessity be somewhat opportunist; although as a matter of fact I have very definitely concluded what I intend to do if circumstances permit, so far as this Far Eastern question is concerned. . .[13]

Mr. Spring-Rice was soon to come to Washington at the President's request and was apparently to call a halt for the moment to the readiness with which the President was eager to accept the ideas of the Kaiser. Secretary Hay had already entered in his diary, apropos of the Kaiser's suggestion as to the integrity of China, "It is a most singular incident. . . . What the whole performance meant to the Kaiser it is difficult to see. But there is no doubt that we have scored for China."[14] Later Ambassador Tower sent the President a lengthy account of a conversation with the Kaiser in which he returned to the charge that France really had been planning a partition of China as the price of peace between Russia and Japan. It is quite possible that this is true but there is nothing to confirm it because the French government, unfortunately, continues to hold secret its despatches for this period.[15]

In the latter part of January the Russian government with its usual lack of adroitness chose to raise the matter of the alleged violation of Chinese neutrality and to declare that if this should continue Russia would view "China's neutrality from the standpoint of its own interests." Secretary Hay reported that both China and Japan had asserted that they had scrupulously observed this neutrality.[16]

The fact that Mr. Spring-Rice was in Washington and that the President was anxious to keep in touch with England as well as with Germany is seen in a letter to Mr. Meyer. He was American Ambassador to Italy and was about to leave for Russia to become our Ambassador there in succession to Mr. McCormick, whose work at St. Petersburg had proved unsatisfactory to the President.[17]

The President also wrote to Ambassador Tower that he did "not believe that England has any intention of taking part in the partition of China." Of France he was rather suspicious. He seems at this time to have heard definite rumors of the proposed German-Russian alliance; and on February 14, Mr. Meyer had reported a conversation with the King of Italy, who had said:

> Russia's diplomacy is based on misrepresentation and lies, and she cannot be trusted. In addition to her alliance with France, I feel sure that she has made some arrangement with Germany, even in writing. The fact that Russia is replacing her modern guns on the [German] frontier with obsolete ones is additional proof.[18]

The difficulties of the German Foreign Office with respect to the negotiations with the Tsar in the previous November and December also became apparent in a memorandum by Holstein, the anti-English "spider of the Wilhelmstrasse." This important memorandum is given in the Appendix to this chapter. It concludes with the statement that whatever might happen now it is quite certain that both Russia and England would compete with each other in the endeavor to destroy the confidential relations between the President and the Kaiser.[19] Mr. Dennett suggests that von Sternburg was never informed of the proposed German-Russian alliance for later he was to deny its existence. This of course is quite possible; but Europe is a whispering gallery where even the walls have ears. He had been in Berlin at Christmas time and it seems rather doubtful that he had not heard of the project. On the other hand he would have been justified in his denial to the President of such an alliance at the time that he made it, in the spring of 1905, because that period was between December, 1904, when the Tsar refused to sign, and July, 1905, when the notorious treaty of Björkö was made by the Kaiser and the Tsar. President Roosevelt in any case seems to have been fooled at the time; but we shall return to this later.[20]

Meantime the Germans had been busy cultivating better relations with Japan in which even they believed that they had been helped by the friendly attitude of the United States.[21] Encouraged by this von Sternburg acting under direct instructions from von Bülow spread the story that all talk of Anglo-German friction was nonsense. The President went so far as to repeat to the German Ambassador what he had said to the British Ambassador, namely, that he [Roosevelt] had "most positive assurances that Germany was not thinking of any attack on England; . . . now there was no longer any cause for England to continue to air her bitterness against Germany."[22]

These endeavors of the President to better relations between Great Britain and Germany may be responsible in part for the suggestion which was shortly made by the Kaiser that the President should try to act as mediator in Moroccan affairs. They may also spring from his desire to alleviate British anxiety as to German intentions, for later the President again repeated to von Sternburg that he had had another conversation with the British Ambassador who had said it was scarcely possible in view of German hostility for friendly Anglo-German relations to develop. Germany evidently was planning war against England at the first opportunity. The President then said: "I am giving you a pledge that Germany has no such intentions." Sir Mortimer Durand asked: "And what is that pledge?" Roosevelt then answered: "Sternburg's word." Later he said to von Sternburg: "It is remarkable what the British government sometimes imagines. At a certain stage in this war it suddenly asked me to despatch a part of our navy to the coasts of England as it had positive reports that Russia, Germany and France were planning to attack England."[23]

Yet President Roosevelt confessed his failure to improve

Anglo-German relations for as he said in the middle of May, 1905: "The British Government has given to understand clearly that it does not desire better relations with Germany. To the Acting Secretary of State, Taft, a gentle hint had even been given that England is able to attend to her own affairs. More, said the President, he cannot do without risking discourtesy." [24] The idea that Great Britain was now in such close relations with France and that the formation of a quadruple alliance of Great Britain, her ally Japan, France, and eventually her ally, Russia, was taking place at this time was strongly fixed in the mind of von Bülow. He wrote of this repeatedly and von Sternburg was surprised at the strong conviction of President Roosevelt that an Anglo-Russian entente was impossible. His own prejudice was so strong against Russia that he burst out at some new statement by von Sternburg with reference to the English-Russian rapprochement by saying: "Then they are not liars, they are curs." Spring-Rice had told him that in case of a social upheaval in Russia "the magnificent German army was a bulwark against internal turmoil in Europe." In short he would not believe that British policy was tending toward an understanding with Russia; yet this seemed obvious to many students of international affairs at the time and in 1907, when the Anglo-Russian entente was formally announced to the world, it did not take them by surprise. In the Appendix to this chapter is a paper relating to this.[25]

Earlier the President had been interested in a friendly letter of congratulation at the time of his inauguration in March, 1905, from King Edward VII. To King Edward the President wrote he thought Russia had made a mistake in not making peace before the Japanese captured Mukden in early March.[26] Port Arthur had already fallen on January 1, 1905. So we come again to the story that Russia and Germany were coming to a good understanding. The German Ambassador insisted that this story, coming from Mr. Spring-Rice, was circulated by the British only to keep up Japanese suspicions of German policy. The President replied that

"Spring had told him the very same stories, but that he had laughed at them." Yet once more President Roosevelt was wrong for within ten weeks an alliance was signed between Germany and Russia at Björkö.[27] We must recall that during this period the Kaiser was urging the President to persuade the powers to agree to a conference at Algeciras. Of course if the United States had had a real diplomatic service at the time in Berlin, at Paris and elsewhere such ignorance on the part of the President and the Department of State of the inner workings of European affairs would have been unlikely. Diplomacy to America was still a "pink-tea affair" for "cloth dolls."

After this brief excursion into European politics, as understood at the White House, we must turn once more to the course of events with regard to the Russo-Japanese war. In February Japan had intimated to both the United States and Germany that a surprise was pending which made them think that peace was on the horizon. Japan frankly wanted to know whether the revolutionary disturbances in Russia made the time opportune for Russia to suggest the discussion of peace terms. The Japanese, however, were extremely loath to take the first step in spite of the fact that President Roosevelt stressed to the Japanese Minister in Washington that it was "to Japan's interest to propose peace to Russia now, as this would justify Japan in the eyes of the world if Russia should reject Japan's advances." To this report the Kaiser commented: "Quite a rash and none too tactful act on the part of the President, pregnant with dangerous consequences." [28]

Indeed the Kaiser was strongly against peace at the moment for he thought that Russia had a chance to reinforce her armies in the Far East and thus further involve herself in Siberia. In short he wished the struggle to be "mired" in the Far East. He was concerned over the report that Russia might favor Paris as the place for peace negotiations which would give opportunity for the opening wedge of the creation of a powerful quadruple alliance of Russia, Japan, France and Great Britain directed against both America and

Germany. Finally, as a brilliant *riposte,* he suggested the possibility of a defensive alliance between the United States, Germany and Great Britain.[29] This notion of detaching England from her French connection and of reviving Joseph Chamberlain's old idea of a triple alliance of the Teutonic powers broke down, however, as we have already seen, before the phlegmatic British intimation that they could manage their own affairs. In any case such an alliance would have been impossible for the United States.

Secretary Hay had by this time gone to Europe in what was to be a vain attempt to recover his health and strength. On March 30 and again on April 5 the President wrote him of the course of events. Since these letters have been printed there is no need to quote them. As to the Kaiser he said: "What a jumpy person he is anyhow!"[30]

Meanwhile the Kaiser and von Bülow were pressing the President to act as regards Morocco; von Sternburg was told to point out the inner connection between the Moroccan and Chinese policies of Great Britain, and to welcome the President's opposition to a peace congress at Paris. Above all he was to impress the President with the candor, disinterestedness and sympathy of Germany, and to laud the value of American influence in restraining Great Britain.[31] The absence of the President in Colorado on a hunting trip in April and early May tended to interfere somewhat with the almost daily communications on the subject of peace proposals; but in any case everyone was now waiting for the expected naval combat between the Japanese and Russian fleets which finally took place in the end of May.

Ambassador Meyer in St. Petersburg reported that Russian public opinion was absorbed in domestic affairs and in the prospect of reform and representative government. This permitted the war party to reassert their ascendency especially as it became known that Japan would demand a large indemnity in money and the cession of territory in case of victory.[32] From Rome Ambassador White, who had been transferred from London, wrote on April 17, that the Italian

Foreign Secretary, Signor Tittoni, did not hold forth any hopes of immediate peace but said:

> The general idea seems to be here, as it was when I left England, that the Russian Government will take no overtures for peace into its consideration until the result is known of the expected naval battle upon which their hopes are now centered. It is thought that if Admiral Rozhdestvensky is successful, Russia will consider such a moment favorable for making peace with her prestige somewhat restored by a victory; and if the result of the battle should be favorable to Japan the idea seems to be that steps might perhaps be taken by friendly Powers, with some chance of success, toward inducing Russia, which would then have nothing favorable to hope for from a prolongation of the war, to bring it to an end.[33]

The President, because of the situation as regards Morocco and in order to be at hand in view of the Russo-Japanese situation, decided to cut short his hunting trip by a week and returned to Washington. On May 13, 1905, he wrote to his friend Mr. Spring-Rice a letter, which has been printed, in which he sought to remove the British fear that he was too much under the influence of the Kaiser.[34] He denied this, saying that the Kaiser was far "too jumpy, too volatile in his policies, too lacking in the power of continuous and sustained thought and action." He wished the Kaiser well but "I should never dream of counting on his friendship for this country." [35]

To Senator Lodge he also wrote regarding the Kaiser as follows:

> When I read such a speech as the last utterance of the Kaiser, in which he contrived in the same sentence deeply to wound Russia and to awaken in Japan the liveliest suspicion and hostility, I feel that democratic republics are not the only states guilty of shortcomings. Upon my word, I don't know a Congressman who could be guilty of such folly. It always amuses me to find that the English think that I am under the influence of the Kaiser. The heavy witted creatures do not understand that nothing would persuade me to follow the lead of or enter into close alliance with a man who is so jumpy, so little capable of continuity of action, and therefore, so little capable of being loyal to his friends or steadfastly hostile to an enemy. Undoubtedly with Russia weakened Germany feels

it can be fairly insolent within the borders of Europe. I intend to do my best to keep on good terms with Germany, as with all other nations, and so far as I can to keep them on good terms with one another; and I shall be friendly to the Kaiser as I am friendly to everyone. But as for his having any special influence over me, the thought is absurd.[36]

The news from abroad was mixed at the end of May. From Mr. Meyer there was a long private letter to Secretary Hay, chiefly about the internal condition of Russia, but saying:

It is interesting to follow the change of sentiment that is gradually forming between Russia and France, and to consider what may follow in consequence. Already France and England are coming closer together, and I think I can observe signs of Russia looking more leniently toward German ideas, although I am not prepared as yet to say anything definite in that respect. Yet the King of Italy told me before leaving he felt sure that there was some sort of an agreement, in case of certain eventualities, between Russia and Germany. When, however, a few weeks later, I had a talk with the German Emperor the tone of his conversation was not such as to give one the impression that he had any great confidence in Russia, and he was certainly anxious that the war should come to a conclusion, as he plainly saw the futility of Russia continuing it. I find, however, at the moment all the European countries very suspicious of each other's motives and the Emperor William especially so toward Delcassé. The last two months have demonstrated that.[37]

From Mr. Conger at Peking there was an earlier letter which dealt with the chances of China to recover Manchuria. He said:

If peace negotiations shall begin soon, the time is most opportune, and her position and influence are sufficiently potent, for the United States to take a most effective, if not the leading, part in the approaching drama; and I am sure, from many incidental remarks made in frequent confidential conferences with my colleagues, that the important European Powers are expecting this.

Had the other Powers in 1901 and 1902—as it has always seemed to me they ought to have done—demanded of Russia the fulfillment of all her promises, made nominally to China, but actually to all the Powers, Manchuria would have been handed back to the Chinese then and, probably, the terrible war averted. The public international good makes it now incumbent upon the same Great Powers to see to it that in the settlement some sort of international guarantee should be provided which will so fix the rights not only of the Japanese and Russians in Manchuria, but of all others, and, by its terms, prevent a recurrence of another like struggle in the near future.[38]

In this connection there was also a letter from Mr. Griscom of May 15, which gave a rough summary of Japanese peace terms. These were, of course, prior to the great naval victory of May 27 when the Russian fleet was practically either destroyed or captured. Mr. Griscom wrote of these terms:

First. That Japan be acknowledged to have a prepondering influence in Korea, and the management of Korean foreign relations.
Second. Japan to receive Saghalien.
Third. A mutual agreement to dismantle the forts at Port Arthur and Vladivostock.
Fourth. A mutual agreement that neither Russia nor Japan shall maintain more than a specified tonnage of warships in the Sea of Okhotsk and the Sea of Japan. (The intention of this is, under a semblance of mutual agreement, to limit the Russian naval force in the Pacific, whereas the Japanese force is to be unlimited.)
Fifth. Japan to agree to hand over Manchuria to China, exacting only such suitable guarantees as could be devised to insure as good as possible a Chinese administration and the proper protection of foreigners, and the maintenance of the principle of the open door.
Sixth. Japan to retain the Liao-tung Peninsula as leased by Russia from China.

In connection with the fifth condition I may mention that in my last interview with Baron Komura he stated to me formally that Japan would adhere strictly to the assurances given with regard to Manchuria and that if the war was terminated to Japan's satisfaction Manchuria would be handed over to China unconditionally, except that some form of guarantees, to be devised later, would be asked of the Chinese Government to insure good administration and protection of foreign interests.[39]

Two weeks later, on May 31, 1905, Japan made the first formal proposal for peace by a message to President Roosevelt asking him of his own "initiative to invite the two belligerents to come together for the purpose of direct negotiation" but stating "that the Japanese Government have no intention by the present communication to approach Russia either directly or indirectly on the subject of peace." [40] The overwhelming naval victory which Japan had won now made it clear that she had command of the sea in Asiatic waters; the bankers were loath to lend her more money; and her position on land was difficult for she must now operate at an increasing distance from her base. These last two factors were, however, not clearly known or seen at the time.

In Russia the news of the defeat had not at the first instant provoked a demand for peace. Later, by June 2, there was indignation against the bureaucracy and pressure for reform in the government. The danger to the Tsar's authority was at once seen in Germany and the Kaiser wrote Nicholas II on June 3 urging him to make peace, saying:

> I may turn your attention to the fact that undoubtedly the Japanese have the highest regard for America before all other nations, because this mighty rising Power with its tremendous fleet is next to them. If anybody in the world is able to influence the Japanese or to induce them to be reasonable in their proposals, it is President Roosevelt. Should it meet with your approval, I could easily place myself—privately—en rapport with him, as we are very intimate with each other.[41]

At the same time he sent word to President Roosevelt on June 4 of what he had done and said that he feared lest the news of the naval defeat would create at St. Petersburg "such a commotion that grave disorders, even revolution are to be expected, if not an attempt on the Tsar's life." The Kaiser looked on the continuation of the war as hopeless from the Russian side. "Peace must be made at once" he told Ambassador Tower.[42] After President Roosevelt had received these messages and was assured of the Kaiser's aid he at once ordered Ambassador Meyer to see the Tsar and to urge on him the necessity of peace. He proposed that Russia and Japan should enter into direct negotiations somewhere in the Far East and he offered to ask Japan to agree to such a meeting, without, however, indicating that Russia had consented.[43] On this very day (on June 5) the President also wrote an important letter to Senator Lodge, which has been printed, detailing much of these negotiations with his own shrewd and interesting comments.[44] At the same time he informed Ambassador Jusserand and the British Chargé d'Affaires in Washington of what he had done. It is rather curious that the President should have supposed that M. Delcassé, French Foreign Secretary, who was anathema to the Kaiser, would help at this time. Owing to an intrigue by his fellow ministers, and because of pressure from the Kaiser, Delcassé was forced to resign from the French Cabinet at this juncture. Indeed in these hectic days there was much that even well-informed Americans missed at the time. At the news of the fall of Delcassé the Kaiser in his joy hurriedly·created von Bülow a Prince. Von Bülow's wife later said: "We didn't ask for his [Delcassé's] head; they [the French] offered it to us." [45] The chief obstacle to the Algeciras Conference had fallen from power on June 6; and the Kaiser renewed his persuasion to President Roosevelt to propose such a meeting. Secretary Hay, who was returning on the *Baltic* to die within a month, wrote to his friend Adams:

> I see your friend, the Kaiser, has at last taken the scalp of Delcassé. He will be after mine next—to which he is welcome. He has evidently done it out of sheer wantonness, to let people know there is a God in Israel. Characteristic, his rushing to Bülow's house and making him a Prince on the spot to advertise his score.
>
> Spring-Rice turned up in London yesterday. He says he does not think the Kaiser means or wishes war with France. He wants merely to insult her publicly by way of notifying her that if she does not want him to do it again, she had better make friends with him.
>
> The situation is not, as it appears, satisfactory to anyone. France has been profoundly humiliated and does not care to show any resentment. England is not inclined to sympathize with her, as she seems unconscious of her injury. The Bear is licking his own wounds and does not care what happens to the Cock and the Lion. It was a good time for the Kaiser to tread the stage in the Ercles vein.
>
> I do not quite see what Theodore is doing. He is busy—that's of course.[46]

That last sentence told much for during his absence in Europe the world had been moving; soon Secretary Hay was to leave it. What steps he would have taken during these past few months if he had been well it is interesting to surmise but impossible to say. He had just come from London where Mr. Whitelaw Reid was presenting his credentials as American Ambassador. Mr. Reid was, therefore, at the post where President Roosevelt was most perplexed. Lord Lansdowne, and particularly Mr. Balfour, were inclined to go slowly. I suspect that they feared that the President might be a bull in a diplomatic china-shop, and in any case they were alarmed over his friendliness with the Kaiser. But Great Britain was emphatically in favor of peace.[47] The fact that Sir Mortimer Durand did not have the confidence of the President was unfortunate. Mr. Spring-Rice, or Lord Jersey, would have been admirable substitutes for the British Ambassador at this time. But the notion which was shortly set abroad by Mr. Melville Stone, of the Associated Press, that Great Britain had done nothing "to stay the war" was a mistake.[48] President Roosevelt later intimated that England had given no aid in securing peace.[49] But Lord Lansdowne, in early June, 1905, had told Mr. Reid that "the idea would be most abhorrent to them [the British] of doing anything that might tend to prolong bloodshed." At the same time England did not wish to bring pressure on Japan; but she did not attempt to delay the peace negotiations and she was eager for peace though she was ignorant at the time of the Japanese need to make peace.[50] Furthermore there is an undated and unsigned copy of a despatch in the *Hay Papers* for this period which reads as follows:

> The British Ambassador in Petersburg has pointed out to Count Lamsdorff the advantages which a speedy conclusion of peace would have for the interests of Russia. The Ambassador stated that Lamsdorff seemed to agree with him. Benckendorff has addressed Lamsdorff in a similar way.[51]

After this digression to give the background for the actual initiation of peace negotiations, we return to the reception of President Roosevelt's despatch to Ambassador Meyer on June 5, 1905. The story of these days has already been given with such detail and documentary material by Mr. Dennett that it is possible to abridge the account of the next few weeks adding to the record only such documents as may seem essential. Ambassador Meyer saw the Tsar on June 6 and received his personal consent and acceptance of the President's offer. Count Cassini at this juncture sent a despatch from his superiors to President Roosevelt which ignored Mr. Meyer's interview with the Tsar. Indeed Cassini was inclined to question the accuracy of Mr. Meyer's account. He also protested against the President's frequent interviews with the Japanese Minister and representatives of the neutral states, saying that he "was trying to make Russia move too quickly" and adding that the internment of Russian men-of-war at Manila was illegal. This the President rightly termed impertinent. Within a short time it was established that Mr. Meyer's report was accurate and that Cassini was uninformed. On June 8 the formal invitation to Russia and Japan was publicly announced according to the schedule and arrangement which had been suggested by the President. Both powers then gave their acceptances which had been agreed on earlier.[52]

In the course of the next few days several incidents and hitches occurred which annoyed the President but which were successfully surmounted. The Japanese raised the question of the full powers of the Russian diplomats whom they were to meet and the text of the Russian reply gave reason for certain qualms. The place at which the negotiations were to be held was also the subject of telegraphic correspondence. These matters are all touched on by Dennett and Bishop so we pass them by. Both Japan and Russia were to be represented by plenipotentiaries to make peace, and Washington was agreed on as the place of meeting.[53]

On June 16 Secretary Hay, who had just returned from Europe, wrote the President congratulating him on his success and saying:

. . . But the big news was of your success in bringing Russia and Japan into conference. It was a great stroke of that good luck which belongs to those who "know how" and are not afraid. I need not have worried about my being sick and away. I have evidently not been missed. Reid once told me when I had been running the Tribune in his absence that "the paper had been disgustingly good." That is what I find your management of the State Department during my tenancy.⁵⁴

Some notion of the President's ideas for the future may be gained from a letter to Dr. Wheeler of the University of California, saying:

> You see the significance of the world movement of which we are a part just as I do./I believe that our future history will be more determined by our position on the Pacific facing China than our position on the Atlantic facing Europe.⁵⁵

The rest of the month of June was spent in arranging the appointment of plenipotentiaries and in negotiations for an armistice which the Russians had suggested but which the Japanese refused. The final appointment of Witte and Rosen for Russia and of Komura and Takahira for Japan did not take place until a little later, the Russians being as usual uncertain and dilatory.⁵⁶ To the Kaiser, through Ambassador Tower, the President now expressed his thanks saying:

> . . . I greatly appreciate the Kaiser's action. Whether we can get the Japanese and Russians to make peace I do not know; but I hope you will personally tell the Kaiser how much I value what he has done, and that in my judgment it may be imperative to get his aid in order to make the Czar conclude peace. I hope that the Japanese will be moderate in what they ask, and I shall endeavor to make them moderate; but it must be kept clearly in mind that they are the victors; that their triumph has been complete and overwhelming, and that they are entitled to demand very substantial concessions as the price of peace. The difficulty will come with Russia, for she will find it hard to make up her mind to give what it is entirely right and proper that the Japanese should ask.⁵⁷

The anxiety of China gave some concern at this time for it was essential that she should remain quiet until after the coming peace conference. A despatch was prepared to Mr. Rockhill, who had now succeeded Mr. Conger as American Minister at Peking, saying that, though the United States had nothing to do with the peace negotiations, she would do all in her power to preserve the territorial integrity of China.[58] The state of affairs in Russia was also alarming, for a mutiny had broken out in the Black Sea fleet and attempts at revolution in Odessa and Libau.[59] It seemed at one time as though the authority of the Tsar might be invaded before the peace conference could meet.

The death of Secretary Hay on July 1, 1905, was of course a severe personal loss to the President. Of this I shall say more in the last chapter. Meantime the question of peace terms had begun to loom large. There is good reason to believe that the Japanese had already made it clear that the intrigues and corruption in Korea were such that in self-protection Japan intended to assume the complete control and direction of the destiny of Korea. As regards Port Arthur as we have already seen they proposed to succeed to the Russian lease of the Liaotung peninsula; and as regards Manchuria they planned its return to China subject to guarantees of reforms and the maintenance of the open door. The President was much concerned that the Japanese should not wreck the chances of peace by excessive terms, particularly by the demand of an indemnity which he was informed Witte had already categorically refused in advance. He was at this time quite oblivious to anything save the fact that Japan had won great victories both on land and sea and he wrote of the possibility of Japan's driving the Russians back to Lake Baikal in Siberia. As we know now the Japanese were at the time quite unable to do anything of the sort. They were faced with financial ruin unless they secured peace. This, of course, was not then apparent. The United States was impressed by the apparent duplicity and insincerity of Russia. She had not known how to secure victory; now she was blind to her defeat and did not know how to make peace.

In the case of Great Britain, as we have already seen, President Roosevelt was eager for her aid and was annoyed when he felt that he did not receive it. As for Germany, American policy seemed to travel along the same road with the Kaiser's diplomacy. Both the United States and Germany wished for peace, but that was for quite different reasons. Germany fostered the idea of peace because she wished to make an alliance with Russia and because through peace President Roosevelt might be drawn into European politics as an ally of the Kaiser. Yet the President was so strongly opposed to Russia that if the Kaiser's plans should become known inopportunely at Washington the projected American-German entente would be endangered.

So before we take up the peace negotiations we must turn briefly to consider the attitude of the Kaiser and the relations existing between him and President Roosevelt in order that we may appraise also the relations between the Kaiser and the Tsar and thus see how the President used the Kaiser to influence the Tsar during the peace conference at Portsmouth. As we have already seen the President had expressed his appreciation to the Kaiser on June 24. It was a time of serious anxiety regarding the negotiations for a conference to settle Moroccan affairs and the President's advice for an amicable settlement may well have annoyed the Kaiser somewhat. Of this we shall see more in a later chapter. There is no hint of this, however, in the communications which passed between them during July. After he had received the President's letter the Kaiser had replied by telegraph on July 8 saying that he "perfectly agreed with the President's views" but warning him once more against England. Later von Bülow added that the Kaiser expected that England and France might again attempt the partition of China. Mr. Tower was naturally a poor telephone connection but his pleasure at thus being the medium of communication in such matters of "high politics" is evident. He received for transmission to the Kaiser a letter from the President acknowledging on July 27 the previous communication and saying "I should absolutely refuse to submit to such action by any of the Powers." He expressed again his determination to support the open door and the integrity of China and "my great obligation to him [the Kaiser] for his courtesy and my pleasure at the way in which Germany and the United States are working together, and my feeling that this means well for the good of the world, for its peace and progress." [60]

If we consider that this letter was written three days after the secret treaty of Björkö was signed between the Kaiser and the Tsar, we can get some notion of how close to the wind the Kaiser was sailing. Naturally the President knew nothing of this secret defensive agreement; he had relied on von Sternburg's absolute denial of any such proposals. He did know, however, by a cable from Mr. Meyer of July 24 that the Tsar had suddenly departed for the coast of Sweden on his yacht for a conference with the Emperor William. This conference had been arranged by the two rulers themselves and not through their Foreign Offices. Consequently the European press was almost hysterical over it. The British were suspicious and the French alarmed over Morocco; but opinion was generally held that the conference related to the state of domestic affairs in Russia. Indeed it was not for months afterwards that the fact of the alliance leaked out. In the long account of this imperial tryst and in the voluble telegrams exchanged in connection with it there is much to be learned by the student of European history. For our purposes we have to note that the plan which the Kaiser failed to secure in the previous December was now successful. Furthermore, it was not England but Germany which first made terms with Tsarist Russia, with "Adam-zad—the bear that walks like a man." [61]

The Kaiser's joy over this achievement was immense; he fairly chortled as he wrote to von Bülow. He quoted from the Bible and imagined Frederick William III, Queen Louise, his Grandfather, and Nicholas I as being there in spirit when the treaty was signed. "The Alsace-Lorraine question is closed once for all, thank God!" said the Tsar. The Kaiser declared that a turning point in the history of Europe was reached on the morning of July 24 at Björkö. Now at last Germany was free from the horrible grip of the Franco-Russian alliance. In his excitement he hastily wrote a telegram to President Roosevelt of which only the first part was finally despatched. The second half was withheld by the intervention of von Bülow and Holstein. This second section of the telegram gave news of the treaty in which he as the head of the triple alliance of Germany, Austria and Italy now became a partner in the dual alliance of Russia and France, thus making it a new triple alliance. "The peace of Europe is guaranteed," he exclaimed as he now saw the complete isolation and encirclement of England. Indeed he fancied for a moment the entrance of Japan into this combination. To God he gave the credit for this masterpiece of diplomacy.[62]

The first part of the telegram, which alone was sent to the President on July 28, was harmless, reassuring and polite. It read:

> Just had an interview with Emperor Nicholas. His Majesty quite collected, firm, of peaceful disposition. Is most deeply grateful to you for your offering to bring about peace, and most touched by your letter to him. He is most satisfied with Mr. Meyer whom he trusts completely. He hopes and trusts that your powerful personality and genial statesmanship will enable you to bring too exorbitant Japanese conditions down to sensible level. This communication is strictly confidential only for you personally, and you will kindly not mention it till after conclusion of peace.[63]

From such ecstasies of the Baltic Sea we must now turn to the hard drudgery of the peace conference at Portsmouth. Later we can note what happened to the treaty of Björkö. The outlook was none too bright for President Roosevelt. He wrote more than once in early August that the negotiations would probably fail; but characteristically he summoned all his wits and power to win success in the diplomatic battle. The story of the peace conference has been told by Dennett and Bishop in such fashion that it is only necessary to note a few additional facts.

The Russian delegation headed by Witte and Rosen soon began to win favor in the American press and one of the most astonishing shifts in public opinion took place. America from a pro-Japanese country became almost overnight friendly to Russian contentions. The Japanese delegation, on the other hand, lost the favor of the public by their stiffness and taciturnity. They failed to appreciate the value of a wise "publicity." This of course did not directly affect the negotiations but it created an atmosphere which was significant. On August 10 the conference began and before the week was out two cables from Berlin had come to Washington warning the President of the alleged intrigues of England and France. Whether there was any real basis in fact for these warnings by von Bülow and Holstein I do not know, but I doubt it exceedingly. It may have been merely the German point of view which could not resist the temptation to overdo any matter.[64] As negotiations came to a deadlock on August 16 they gave reason, however, for a telegram to Germany from the President giving the text of a cable message to the Tsar and asking for the Kaiser's support.[65]

In his message to the Tsar the President urged that, since the two Japanese proposals which were offensive to Russia would probably be withdrawn—and on eight points the conference had come to agreement—the two remaining questions, that of the cession of Sakhalin and the payment of money might be compromised. He proposed that Japan restore to Russia the northern part of Sakhalin and receive from Russia a sum of money for this retrocession and for the payment of the expenses of maintenance of Russian prisoners. In conclusion he urged the Tsar to make peace on these terms as the exact amount of money involved could later be settled by negotiation. In his message to the Kaiser the President urged that he advise the Tsar to accept the principle involved.[66]

The Kaiser had already telegraphed the Tsar that it would be desirable to consult the Duma, the new consultative council which had just been established in Russia, as to peace terms. In reply the Tsar had insisted that he would not give an inch of territory or a rouble of indemnity. The Kaiser, therefore, replied to the President on August 24 that he would do what he could but that the Tsar was determined on his stand.[67] The President had already sought, through Baron Kaneko in New York, who was relaying his messages to Portsmouth, to persuade the Japanese to modify their terms. He wrote a letter on August 22 in which he warned Japan against continuing the war for the sake of an indemnity. On the next day he renewed his argument on larger and ethical grounds.[68] At the same time he denied to Witte that his proposals involved a payment to Japan by Russia of the whole of the expenses of the war. Further on August 25 he renewed all of his arguments in another long cable message for the Tsar.[69] This was of no avail for on August 28 the Tsar telegraphed Witte to end the negotiations for he would rather renew the "war than await gracious concessions from Japan." As Dr. Dillon comments: "Luckily for Russia, Witte paid no heed to this behest and ended everything satisfactorily."

In the meantime the President on the advice of Mr. Stone, of the Associated Press, arranged for a cable to the Kaiser. This proposed that a neutral arbitral commission should fix the amount to be paid Japan for the return of northern Sakhalin to Russia. There was a hitch as to this cable for it was uncertain whether the Japanese would abide by this decision. Finally they agreed to this; but it did not move the Tsar. Indeed, because of the delays there was no action by the Kaiser. The next day Witte gave his ultimatum; Russia would cede southern Sakhalin but not pay a penny. This the Japanese accepted on August 29. The treaty was signed on September 5.[70]

From all sides there came a paean of congratulation to President Roosevelt. Unfortunately we cannot stop to record this, but there was no question of the verdict of the world that he had done a great work. This was expressed in the award of the Nobel Peace Prize the next year; and the verdict of history approves it. In Japan alone were there serious riots and the picture of the President was turned to the wall in many Japanese houses. This was the expression of an opinion that had been too much stimulated by the victories of the war.[71] The President himself was much impressed by the honorable behavior of the Japanese delegation. His verdict on Witte was less favorable. His comment to Secretary Root that "Kings and such-like are fundamentally just as funny as American politicians" is matched by his earlier remark to Secretary Hay that the more he saw of the Kaiser and the Tsar the more respect he had for American Senators. Secretary Hay, however, said he was unable to make such fine distinctions. His real agreement with England, in spite of Lansdowne's slow policies, was seen in his approval of the Anglo-Japanese alliance.

This brings us, therefore, to the signature, ahead of time, of the second edition of the Anglo-Japanese alliance on August 12, 1905. This treaty, which had been foreshadowed for some months, made the alliance broader in scope and involved immediate assistance by one party to the other in case of attack. The effect of the treaty, which became publicly known on August 25, was at once seen, and it undoubtedly had a decided influence on the Japanese in leading them finally to accept the Russian peace terms. Later we may see its significance as to Korea.[72]

This leads us briefly to consider the fate of the treaty of Björkö, which had been so joyously signed on July 24 by Germany and Russia. It was really a sort of counterpart of the Anglo-Japanese alliance. There is no evidence to show that America was in any way informed of this alliance of Tsar and Kaiser and, therefore, its history does not exactly belong to a survey of American diplomatic history. But it is worthwhile noting that, following the treaty of Portsmouth and the Anglo-Japanese treaty, our relations with Great Britain were strengthened and that in 1906 we were consulting freely with Great Britain regarding the preliminaries to the Hague Conference. Witte, who had now been made a Count by the Tsar, has left a record of his astonishment at the news of the treaty of Björkö. His appointment as chief minister of Russia gave opportunity for him to oppose the conclusion and publication of that treaty. The Tsar was persuaded that a private declaration should be made showing that Russia was not bound by the treaty of Björkö in case

France and Germany went to war. The Kaiser protested in vain that the Franco-Russian alliance was only a defensive alliance and did not in any way collide with the terms of the Björkö treaty. His anger and disappointment at the Russian refusal to proceed with the matter were great. France had made difficulties over this Russo-German combination; and Count Witte and others about the Tsar had advanced the view that the Dual Alliance and the Björkö agreement were incompatible. With the end of 1905, as an Anglo-Russian understanding approached, the treaty of Björkö was slowly smothered.[73]

There remained at least two important results of the treaty of Portsmouth with which the United States was concerned. First was Korea and second was Manchuria and our Chinese policy. The Korean question had been before us for many years; as we have seen in Chapter VIII the growth of Japanese influence in Korea had been gradual. Now by the war and by the treaty of Portsmouth it was to be complete and positive. Yet it is worthwhile recalling the situation as it had developed in the last five years. American interests in Korea were represented chiefly by the work of missionaries and by commercial and industrial concerns which were fairly prosperous. The United States, as we have already seen, had from the first shown an interest in Korea and the first article of the treaty of 1882 had read:

> If other Powers deal unjustly or oppressively with either government, the other will exert their good offices, on being informed of the case, to bring about an amicable arrangement, thus showing their friendly feelings.

This exercise of good offices did not mean an alliance nor did it imply intervention though Koreans had attempted so to interpret it. Many Americans had indeed understood it to mean as much. For this there was no justification in law or practice. In 1900 Korea was anxious, in view of the growing rivalry between Japan and Russia, to secure an international guarantee of her neutrality and independence. In particular

Koreans had in 1900 approached the United States to this end and were for a time misled by the off-hand language of Mr. Buck, the American Minister at Tokyo, and by the story of alleged conversations with Secretary Hay at Washington. These, however, proved to be much exaggerated.[74] In 1902 the Russians expressed a strong desire that the United States and Japan should join with them in securing the inviolability of Korean territory. M. Isvolsky, the Russian Minister at Tokyo, feared lest the first Anglo-Japanese alliance might be a harbinger of war between Japan and Russia and urged that something should be done to protect Korea. Japan had already declined a similar Russian proposal and Mr. Buck reported privately to Secretary Hay that in a conversation with Baron Komura, Japanese Foreign Secretary, it had appeared that:

> Japan would not consent to be a party in complying with Mr. Iswolsky's suggestion respecting Korea. That if Japan should join in such a movement, Russia, continuing in, [sic] would absorb Manchuria and later, regardless of her engagement would for some pretext at some convenient time, attempt to seize upon Korea and bring on a conflict over possession of the peninsula, in which event Japan would oppose her to the limit of her power.
> The Baron said further that Japan herself had no design on Korea other than that of peaceful and free commercial intercourse; that she had large material interests and a large number of her people in Korea engaged in business enterprises and she must protect them.[75]

In 1903 disputes as to the opening of ports in Korea and fear of Russian aggression on the Yalu had brought about conversations by the Koreans with the American Chargé at Seoul, Mr. Paddock, which had shown American interest in the development of Korea. A few months later on the outbreak of war between Russia and Japan the Emperor of Korea reported that Japan proposed an alliance which would protect Korea and give to Japan control over Korean policy. He appealed to the United States for advice and assistance. Two days later, on February 23, 1904, a protocol was signed at Seoul establishing a Japanese protectorate over Korea.

Dr. Allen, the American Minister at Seoul, later reported that the Emperor was much distressed at this and that he

confidently expects that America will do something for him at the close of this war, or when opportunity offers, to retain for him as much of his independence as is possible. He is inclined to give a very free and favorable translation to Article 1 of our Treaty of Jenchuan of 1882. I trust to be able to prevent a direct invocation of this treaty however though I am obliged to assure His Majesty that the condition of Korea is borne in mind by the United States Government who will use their good offices when occasion occurs.[76]

In May, 1904, the Korean Emperor, under Japanese pressure, reluctantly annulled all treaties and agreements with Russia, including the Yalu timber concession. In August, Korea agreed to a Japanese financial adviser, promised to submit all matters relating to foreign finance to the Japanese, and authorized and accepted an American, Mr. D. W. Stevens, of the Japanese service, as adviser to the Korean Foreign Office. The cowardice of the Emperor and the corrupt Korean favorites who surrounded him would have made any intervention in his behalf impossible. In any case as the war progressed Japanese domination advanced.[77] In May, 1905, the Russian government renewed its protests at the state of affairs; but two weeks later the defeat of the Russian fleet showed that such protests were now grotesque and futile.[78]

During these months President Roosevelt had expressed the view that it was useless to intervene in behalf of the Koreans for "they could not strike one blow in their own defence." Great Britain saw the derelict condition of Korea when she recognized the interest of Japan in that region by the Anglo-Japanese alliance of August 12, 1905. Yet a fortnight earlier the United States had practically done the same for on July 29, while Secretary Taft was on a visit to Japan on his way back from a tour of the Philippines the Japanese Premier, Count Katsura, had drawn up a memorandum dealing with the status of Korea. Secretary Taft said he had no mandate from the President for this purpose but gave it as his judgment that President Roosevelt would concur in the views expressed and in this he was correct. This memorandum, which is given in the Appendix to this chapter, was first printed by Mr. Dennett.[79] Its significance will at once be seen since it contained: (1) a disclaimer by Japan of any hostile intentions as regards the Philippines, (2) a proposal for an informal understanding with the United States which would make her in certain respects a silent friend to the Anglo-Japanese alliance, and (3) the view expressed by Secretary Taft that Japanese troops might set up Japanese suzerainty in Korea in such fashion that Korean foreign affairs should be under Japanese control. I reject the phrase that the United States by this document became a "silent partner" in the Anglo-Japanese alliance for I do not think our acquiescence meant more than a friendly approval of it. There are many letters which express the views of President Roosevelt in favor of this alliance; but to say that we became a partner or unsigned member goes too far.

In October, 1905, Mr. Morgan reported from Seoul that Japan was pressing for a protocol by which she would have the complete protection of Korea. The unruly character of Japanese immigrants to Korea had provoked friction with the native Koreans and the dominating attitude of Japanese officials was a cause for regret. Nevertheless President Roosevelt approved the idea that Japan should take over the foreign relations of Korea.[80] In November the actual transfer of authority took place. Marquis Ito came from Japan on a special mission to Seoul; the Korean Cabinet was to all intentions and purposes coerced into an agreement; and the Emperor accepted the new political arrangements on November 17. Thus came to an end the formal independence of an ancient empire. The Japanese assumed control of Korean diplomatic affairs and the American legation at Seoul was withdrawn.[81]

We turn now to the state of affairs in China after the war. Generally speaking China had been quiescent during the war. The commercial treaty of 1903 had provided for the abolition of *likin,* an internal tariff on goods in transit, and had stated that when the United States was "satisfied that the state of Chinese laws, the arrangement for their administration, and other considerations warrant it in so doing" extraterritoriality should be relinquished. *Likin,* however, still flourished and the reform of the courts was still only on paper. The condition of affairs generally was bad. Anti-foreign feeling was on the increase; there had been a serious boycott on American goods; and a feeling of unrest existed which showed itself in the desire to prevent foreign developments in China. The Government denied this; but the facts were too strong for them.[82]

Particularly as regards Manchuria it soon became evident that the Japanese were slow in returning that province to China as they had promised in the summer of 1905. They had lightly referred to administrative reforms in Manchuria which were to precede its return to China. These so-called reforms now apparently were to affect the open door and American treaty rights. On February 21, 1906, the United States made its first complaint as to Japanese restrictions on the entry of American traders into Manchuria while Japanese commercial agents were permitted to enter. Soon this discrimination and the Japanese military administration became a subject of serious concern not only as regards Manchuria but in Korea as well. On March 24 Secretary Root telegraphed to Mr. Wilson, our Chargé at Tokyo saying:

We learn through our agents in China that the action of Japanese authorities in Manchuria during Japanese occupation is so generally directed towards establishing Japanese commercial interests in the principal towns, and toward acquiring property rights for Japanese in all available quarters as to leave little or no opening for other foreign trade by the time the territory is evacuated. This course painfully impresses the Government of the United States in view of Japan's earnest declarations heretofore in favor of the open door for legitimate trade and enterprises of all the world. It would be a grievous disappointment if the abortive attempt of Russia to create a national monopoly of material interests in that quarter were to be succeeded by a similarly exclusive establishment of Japanese interests there. You will make our apprehensions impressively known to the

Japanese Government, in the expectation that they shall be dispelled by frank and positive assurance to the contrary. This is our second despatch on this general subject.[83]

The Japanese government was voluble as to promises to maintain the open door in Manchuria but ineffective in accomplishment. A further telegram from Secretary Root stated the matter even more clearly:

> Obstruction due to military exigencies while perhaps explaining temporary restrictions of visiting aliens does not meet the rapidly developing situation of the absorption of a great part of the commercial and mining opportunities of Manchuria by the freely'admitted Japanese. Such opportunities are absolutely closed now to aliens, and even the establishment and recovery of rights acquired, by American citizens and others, before the late war, are so impeded as to occasion loss and injury to the interested parties. We are informed that in some quarters, as at Newchwang, the military authorities have decreed land-registration for effecting valuable transfers with a view to constraining their subsequent validation by China. If this condition continues, China will find herself—after the Japanese occupancy has ceased—the merely nominal sovereign of a territory the material advantages of which have been appropriated by the temporary occupants.[84]

Nevertheless correspondence relating to the state of affairs in Manchuria continued for months. The protocol for the withdrawal of both Russian and Japanese troops, from Manchuria had been signed on October 30, 1905, yet it was only in the following summer that steps were taken to re-establish Chinese customs houses. The opening of ports was also much delayed. A report which reached Washington in July was the subject of a despatch to General Wright, who was our new Ambassador at Tokyo, in August. This report read in part as follows:

> The Japanese are unquestionably taking advantage of their military occupation and the tardiness of the Chinese government, to introduce their goods throughout Manchuria, and they will be the more strongly entrenched the longer this province remains under their control. The Powers should, therefore, be urged, through the usual channels, to use their good offices in expediting the time when the Chinese will assume jurisdiction, and also in concluding arrange-

ments whereby the important port of Dalny, through which the Japanese, in the absence of a Chinese customs station, are now bringing in their goods not only free of import duty but free of all likin charges to any point in the interior where transportation can be effected by rail, will be placed on a basis similar to that of the port of Tsingtau, viz., open to the trade of all nations and a Chinese customs station established for the purpose of collecting the customary duties on the goods passing out of Dalny into Manchuria.[85]

Such a state of affairs, though it improved somewhat by the end of 1906, indicated that the United States now had a long fight ahead. The Russians had been beaten; now the Japanese were in their place. The Chinese government was as usual weak. The stage was therefore set for those events which were to perplex American diplomats at least until the time of the Washington Conference of 1921–1922. The fundamental difficulty was the lack of a strong, stable authority in China. That has not as yet been achieved and the duty of the United States continues to protect American interests and nationals and as far as possible to keep the peace. Thus, as we look back on the treaty of Portsmouth, we find that it did not provide a solution of the problems of Far Eastern policy. It merely defined them in a new sense and with fresh opponents.

NOTES TO CHAPTER XIV

1. *H. P.*, Aug. 11, 1904, O'Laughlin to Hay; April 5, 1905, McCormick to Hay; Dillon, *The Eclipse of Russia*, London, 1918, p. 297; *G. P.*, XIX, part 2, No. 6167. In November Witte said he was still anxious to meet Hayashi who was ready to discuss matters in case of peace pourparlers.
2. *G. P.*, XIX, part 2, No. 6264.
3. *Ibid.*
4. *Ibid.*, XIX, part 2, No. 6265. Cf. Nos. 6259, 6260, 6262, 6267; Dennis, *Anglo-Japanese Alliance*, Berkeley, 1923, pp. 28-31, 50-51; Dennis, *Foreign Policies of Soviet Russia*, New York, 1924, pp. 270-275. Reports in the press that America was on the point of offering her friendly offices to bring about peace were denied in October. (*D. S.*, From Russia, Vol. 62, telegram, Oct. 19, 1904, Eddy to Hay; To Russia, Vol. 18, telegram, p. 599, Oct. 19, Hay to Eddy.)
5. *G. P.*, XIX, part 2, Nos. 6268, 6269.
6. Bernstein, *The Willy-Nicky Correspondence*, New York, 1918, passim; *G. P.*, part 2, Nos. 6203, 6270, 6271.
7. *G. P.*, XIX, part 2, Nos. 6272, 6273.
8. *Ibid.*, Nos. 6158, 6172, 6176, 6178, 6274.
9. *Ibid.*, No. 6266.

10. *Ibid.*, No. 6276; Thayer, II, pp. 385-386; Appendix A to this chapter.
11. *F. R.*, 1905, pp. 1-4; *G. P.*, XIX, part 2, Nos. 6275, 6277-6284; *D. S.*, To London, Vol. 35, telegrams, p. 58, Jan. 13 and 19, 1905, Hay to Choate; To France, Vol. 25, telegram, p. 52, Jan. 17, Hay to Porter; To German Embassy, Vol. 13, p. 407, Jan. 19, Hay to von dem Bussche-Haddenhausen; *H. P.*, Jan. 18, 1905, Choate to Hay; Jan. 31, Hay to Roosevelt; Jan. 31, Choate to Hay (with enclosure); Thayer, II, pp. 386-388.
12. Hay and the President were impressed with the fact that the Kaiser seemed to be alarmed as regards France and England.
13. Dennett, pp. 44-45.
14. Thayer, II, pp. 387-388; *G. P.*, XIX, part 2, foot note to Nos. 6284, 6288. That Hay was anxious to counteract German influence may be seen in *R. P.*, Jan. 10, Hay to Roosevelt.
15. Dennett, pp. 78-82.
16. *F. R.*, 1905, pp. 136-138, 757-760; *G. P.*, XIX, part 2, No. 6280. As the Baltic fleet made its way toward Japan the question of coaling in neutral ports became important. In *H. P.*, Jan. 19, 1905, Griscom to Hay, there is an important letter dealing with the whole matter.
17. Howe, *George von Lengerke Meyer, his life and public services*, New York, 1920, pp. 110-111; *G. P.*, XIX, part 2, Nos. 6285, 6288 from von Sternburg to von Bülow reporting on Spring-Rice's trip to Washington, which was quite successful from the English standpoint. Yet Roosevelt was frankly critical of the British upper class.
18. Howe, pp. 122, 126; Dennett, pp. 82-83.
19. Appendix B to this chapter.
20. Dennett, pp. 72-76; *H. P.*, Feb. 3, 1905, Hay to Roosevelt; *R. P.*, Feb. 11, [1905] Hay to Roosevelt (with its important enclosure from Japan).
21. *G. P.*, XIX, part 2, Nos. 6186, 6289.
22. *Ibid.*, Nos. 6292, 6293. For the melancholy record of Sir Mortimer Durand as British Ambassador at Washington, cf. Sykes, *Sir Mortimer Durand*, London, 1926. Chaps. XX-XXIII.
23. *Ibid.*, No. 6300. This British navy scare was probably in December after the Dogger Bank incident.
24. *Ibid.*, No. 6308.
25. *Ibid.*, Nos. 6307, 6308; Appendix C to this chapter.
26. Bishop, II, pp. 261-264.
27. *G. P.*, XIX, part 2, Nos. 6308, 6309.
28. *D. S.*, Numerical File, Vol. 547, memorandum, Feb. 27, 1905; From Japan, Vol. 80, telegrams, March 9, 11, 12 and 13, Griscom to Hay; *H. P.*, March 14, 1905, telegram from Komura; March 15, Griscom to Hay; *G. P.*, XIX, part 2, Nos. 6290, 6294, 6295 reporting, according to von Sternburg, March 21, 1905, Roosevelt's views as to the reasons why he wished Japan to make peace now:

"Already since the battle of Liachiang I have been urging the necessity of early peace, to prevent the Japanese from pushing on to Kharbin and Vladivostock, so that Russia should be able to conclude peace on easy terms and without indemnities, turn all her attention to her internal reforms, and avoid a serious catastrophe. The folly of the Russians is incredible! For they have missed a favorable opportunity. From my talk with the Japanese Minister I can see that a strong party is now forming in Japan which not only demands a large indemnity, for the heavy sacrifices at Mukden, but also territory on the mainland. The longer Russia keeps waiting the harsher become the peace terms, and the more threatening to you and to us becomes the Japanese power. This is the reason why I demand with all emphasis the strengthening of our navy. Within ten years we may have to go through heavy fighting over there, and if Russia now makes peace and reorganizes her military forces, she can think of renewing the fight in ten years. Japan tells me that if she offers peace to Russia at present, Russia would interpret the step as a sign of weakness and only feel emboldened to continue the struggle. I should like to communicate my views to the Russian Ambassador, but I don't know how he is going to take that after his recent statements. I would ask you to look him up, have a talk with him and draw him out cautiously."

29. *G. P.*, XIX, part 2, Nos. 6296, 6297, 6299.
30. Bishop, I, pp. 377-379.
31. *G. P.*, XIX, part 2, Nos. 6298, 6301-6305.
32. *D. S.*, From Russia, Vol. 62, No. 11, April 17, 1905, Meyer to Hay.
33. *D. S.*, From Italy, Vol. 41, No. 5, April 28, 1905, White to Hay.
34. Dennett, pp. 88-91.
35. These were phrases which the President used in other letters as well to describe the Kaiser.
36. *Roosevelt-Lodge Correspondence*, II, p. 123.
37. *H. P.*, May 23, 1905, Meyer to Hay.
38. *D. S.*, From China, Vol. 127, No. 1845, March 31, 1905, Conger to Hay.
39. *H. P.*, May 15, 1905, Griscom to Hay.
40. Bishop, I, p. 383; Dennett, pp. 215-216.
41. *G. P.*, XIX, part 2, No. 6193; Dennett, p. 217.
42. The documents are published in Dennett, pp. 217-220; *G. P.*, XIX, part 2, Nos. 6311-6314.
43. Dennett, pp. 220-221.
44. *Roosevelt-Lodge Correspondence*, II, pp. 130-135.
45. Stuart, *French Foreign Policy*, New York, 1921, pp. 189-190.
46. Thayer, II, pp. 404-405.
47. Cortissoz, *Reid*, II, pp. 304-307.
48. *G. P.*, XIX, part 2, No. 6337.
49. Roosevelt, *Autobiography*, p. 543.
50. Cortissoz, II, p. 305; Dennett, pp. 210-214; and private conversations.
51. *H. P.* Furthermore in connection with British policy during the spring and summer of 1905 we must remember that Morocco was an ever present problem. Until British documents are published for this period we are groping in the dark. *D. S.*, From London, Vol. 212, telegrams, June 5 and 14, Reid to Hay; To London, Vol. 35, telegram, June 15, Loomis to Reid; *G. P.*, XIX, part 2, Nos. 6315, 6321, 6322, 6331, 6334. These German despatches all contradict what I have suggested in the text.
52. Dennett, pp. 191-202, 222, 226; Bishop, I, pp. 386-388; Howe, pp. 157-165; *Roosevelt-Lodge Correspondence*, II, pp. 138-144; *F. R.*, 1905, pp. 807-811; *G. P.*, XIX, part 2, Nos. 6196, 6197, 6315, 6316; *D. S.*, From Russia, Vol. 63, telegram, June 11, 1905, Meyer to Hay.
53. Dennett, pp. 226-231; Bishop, I, pp. 388-395; Howe, pp. 165-170; *Roosevelt-Lodge Correspondence*, II, pp. 145-156; *D. S.*, From Russia, Vol. 63, Nos. 65, 66, 67 and telegram, June 16, 1905, Meyer to Hay.
54. *H. P.*, June 16, 1905, Hay to Roosevelt.
55. *R. P.*, June 17, 1905, Roosevelt to Wheeler.
56. *D. S.*, From Russia, Vol. 63, telegrams, June 20, 1905, Meyer to Hay; telegrams, June 24, 25, 26 and June 30, same to same; No. 90, June 29, same to same; telegrams, July 1, Meyer to Pierce; telegrams, July 3 and 11, Meyer to Adee; To Russia, Vol. 19, telegrams, June 23 and 26, 1905, Hay to Meyer; telegram, July 10, Adee to Meyer; *F. R.*, 1905, pp. 812-820; Bishop, I, p. 400; *Roosevelt-Lodge Correspondence*, II, pp. 165-166.

57. Bishop, I, p. 398; *G. P.,* XIX, part 2, No. 6318. Roosevelt said to von Sternburg on July 5, 1905, "for the first time Russia seems prepared for straightforward and quick action. . . . Difficulties are caused by England, who refuses to counsel moderation to Japan." Whereat the Kaiser comments: "Aha! Now America sees for the first time where the real disturber of the peace of the world lies hidden!"
58. *F. R.,* 1905, pp. 816-817; *D. S.,* From China, Vol. 127, No. 22, July 1, 1905, Rockhill to Hay; From German Embassy, Vol. 34, memorandum, undated but filed under July 5, 1905.
59. Howe, pp. 173-179; *D. S.,* From Russia, Vol. 63, telegrams, June 30, 1905, Meyer to Hay.
60. Dennett, pp. 233-235; *G. P.,* XIX, part 2, Nos. 6321, 6322.
61. *D. S.,* From Russia, Vol. 63, telegram, July 24, and No. 140, July 31, 1905, Meyer to Secretary; *G. P.,* XIX, part 2, Nos. 6202-6220.
62. *G. P.,* XIX, part 2, Nos. 6220 and 6221. Cf. Nos. 6222-6235. The text of the treaty of Björkö as given in No. 6220 follows:

Leurs Majestés les Empereurs de toutes les Russies et d'Allemagne, afin d'assurer le maintien de la paix en Europe ont arrêté les Articles suivants d'un Traité d'Alliance défensif.

Article I

En cas où l'un des deux Empires serait attaqué par une Puissance Européenne son allié l'aidera en Europe de toutes ses forces de terre et de mer.

Article II

Les hautes parties contractantes s'engagent a ne conclure de paix séparée avec aucun adversaire commun.

Article III

Le présent Traité entrera en vigueur aussitôt que la paix entre la Russie et le Japon sera conclue, et restera valide tant qu'il ne sera pas dénoncé une année à l'avance.

Article IV

L'Empereur de toutes les Russies, après l'entrée en vigueur de ce traité, fera les démarches nécessaires pour initier la France à cet accord et l'engager à s'y associer comme alliée.

Wilhelm I. R.	Nicolas
von Tschirschky und Bogendorff	A. Birleff

63. *Ibid.,* No. 6319.
64. *Ibid.,* Nos. 6323, 6324.
65. Dennett, pp. 265-267. It is significant that the President at the same time sent the text of his cable to Meyer to Ambassador Jusserand and asked for French support.
66. *G. P.,* XIX, part 2, No. 6325.
67. *Ibid.,* Nos. 6200, 6201, 6326, 6328; Howe, pp. 195-202; Dennett, p. 255. At this time the Russian Foreign Office was apparently in possession of the American code book and could read any message save those sent by courier to Berlin and from there telegraphed to Washington. The President seemed indifferent to this fact.

68. Dennett, pp. 254, 256, 258-267, 274-275; Bishop, I, pp. 406-408.
69. *Memoirs of Count Witte*, pp. 154-158; Dennett, pp. 257-258, 270-274; D. S., From Russia, Vol. 64, telegrams, Aug. 23, 24 and 26, 1905, Meyer to Root; Dillon, pp. 305-309.
70. Dillon, p. 310; Dennett, pp. 259-264, 275-277; *Memoirs of Witte*, pp. 158-160; Bishop, I, pp. 409-412; Howe, pp. 203-207; D. S., From Russia, Vol. 64, telegram, Aug. 28, 1905, Meyer to Root; G. P., XIX, part 2, Nos. 6329-6332; Smalley, *Anglo-American Memories*, 2nd Series, pp. 363-365. According to Howe Mr. Meyer reported that a French banker who came from Tokyo said that the Japanese were in hard straits financially and thus the unyielding attitude of the Tsar was strengthened.
71. D. S., From Japan, Vol. 81, telegrams, Sept. 6, 8 and 10, 1905, Griscom to Root.
72. G. P., XIX, part 2, No. 6446; Dennis, *Anglo-Japanese Alliance*, pp. 22-27.
73. G. P., XIX, part 2, Nos. 6247-6258; *Memoirs of Count Witte*, pp. 425 et seq.
74. D. S., From Korea, Vol. 16, No. 278, Sept. 10, 1900, Allen to Hay; No. 286, Oct. 9, same to same.
75. D. S., From Japan, Vol. 76, No. 669 (confidential) Aug. 15, 1902, Buck to Hay; H. P., Aug. 27, 1902, same to same.
76. D. S., From Korea, Vol. 20, No. 621, Nov. 19, 1903, Paddock to Hay; No. 720, April 14, 1904, Allen to Hay.
77. D. S., From Korea, Vol. 21, telegram, May 19, 1904, Allen to Hay; No. 782, Aug. 17, same to same; No. 787, same to same; No. 793, Sept. 10, same to same; No. 799, same to same; No. 824, Nov. 18, same to same; Vol. 22, No. 859, Jan. 12, 1905, same to same; From Japan, Vol. 80, No. 233, April 14, 1905, Griscom to Hay; H. P., Dec. 24, 1904, Allen to Hay.
78. D. S., From Russian Embassy, Vol. 13, unnumbered, May 13, 1905, Cassini to Loomis; F. R., 1905, pp. 625-628.
79. Dennett, pp. 110-116; Appendix D to this chapter. The Japanese were unable to keep this striking diplomatic document secret. On October 4, 1905, the *Kokumin* (a newspaper) declared that this memorandum was in effect "a Japanese-Anglo-American alliance." This of course the United States denied and the Japanese in turn tried to make it appear that nothing like a bargain had been struck over the Philippines and Korea.
80. D. S., From Korea, Vol. 22, telegram, Oct. 14, 1905, Morgan to Root; No. 23, Oct. 19, same to same; F. R., 1905, p. 628.
81. D. S., From Korea, Vol. 22, No. 29, Nov. 10, 1905, Morgan to Root; Nos. 34 and 35, Nov. 20, same to same; No. 36, Nov. 22, same to same; To Korea, Vol. 2, telegram, Nov. 24, Root to Morgan; To Japan, Vol. 5, telegrams, Nov. 24, 1905 and March 24, 1906, Root to Wilson; From China, Vol. 128, telegram, Nov. 27, Rockhill to Root; Vol. 129, No. 171, Dec. 16, same to same; F. R., 1905, pp. 629-634.
82. F. R., 1905, pp. 125-135, 161-166, 204-233; *Ibid.*, 1906, pp. 308-315; D. S., From China, Vol. 128, No. 150, Nov. 14, 1905, Rockhill to Root; Vol. 129, telegram, Feb. 22, 1906, same to same; Vol. 130, telegrams, March 2 and 8, same to same; To China, Vol. 7, telegram, Feb. 26, Root to Rockhill.
83. D. S., To Japan, Vol. 5, telegram, p. 281, March 24, 1906, Root to Wilson; F. R., 1906, pp. 170-177.
84. D. S., To Japan, Vol. 5, telegram, p. 281, March 30, 1906, Root to Wilson; F. R., 1906, pp. 177-188.
85. D. S., To Japan, Vol. 5, No. 21, Aug. 8, 1906, Bacon to Wright; F. R., 1906, pp. 188-227.

APPENDICES TO CHAPTER XIV

A

G. P., XIX, pt. 2, No. 6276, Telegram, Bülow-Sternburg to President Roosevelt, Berlin, Jan. 4, 1905.

After explaining your views on the developments in the Far East to the Emperor, His Majesty has requested me to wire to you the following: He is highly gratified to hear that you firmly adhere to the policy of the open door and uphold the actual integrity of China, which the Emperor believes at present to be gravely menaced. Close observation of events has firmly convinced him that a powerful coalition headed by France is under formation directed against the integrity of China and the open door. The aim of this coalition is to convince the belligerents that peace without compensation to the neutral powers is impossible. The formation of this coalition, the Emperor firmly believes, can be frustrated by the following move: You should ask all Powers having interest in the Far East including the minor ones, whether they are prepared to give a pledge not to demand any compensation for themselves in the shape of territory or other compensations in China or elsewhere for any services rendered to the belligerents in the interests of peace or for any other reason. Such a request would force the Powers to show their hands and any latent designs directed against the open door or integrity of China would immediately become apparent. Without this pledge the belligerents would find it impossible to obtain any territorial advantages without simultaneously promoting selfish aims of the neutral brokers. In the opinion of the Emperor a grant of a certain portion of territory to both belligerents eventually in North China is inevitable. The open door within this territory might be maintained by treaty. Germany, of course, would be the first to pledge herself to this policy of disinterestedness. Conversations I have had here with leading men of other countries have also personally given me the impression that the danger of considerable compensations being demanded by neutrals seems serious. Any written reply addressed to the Chargé d'Affaires, German Embassy, Washington, would be safely cabled to me in English cipher.

B

G. P., XIX, pt. 1, No. 6148, Memorandum by Holstein, Feb. 2, 1905.

When the Tsar suggested an alliance to our All Gracious Lord last November there were in the discussions two view-points of importance to us.

1. Several different signs point to the view—which Herr Combes recently privately confirmed in an interview—that France is working for a friendly agreement between England and Russia with prospects of success, and that this understanding between the three powers would be made easy by a partition of Chinese territory.

2. That this distinguished grouping, disadvantageous to Germany, could hardly be checked in any other way than by Germany meeting with Russia. On this ground one could perhaps have explained a German-Russian alliance to the government at Washington in a satisfactory way since a French-English-Russian combination to which Japan would very likely have adhered on British advice, would be as undesirable to America as to Germany.

Today the situation is an entirely changed one. President Roosevelt has confided the main points of his Eastern Asiatic program to His Majesty the Kaiser and has requested his high advice. The President has shown immediate and complete comprehension of the situation, that the danger of the moment was to be seen in the partition of China, because only enormous compensations, which in such an event could be cut out of the great body of China, would make the fusion of the two dual alliances, the Russo-French and the Anglo-Japanese possible. In keeping with this trend of thought the President followed without delay the desire of His Majesty the Kaiser to challenge the neutral powers to make a declaration of disinterestedness.

The neutrals acquiesced without perceptible opposition to the American proposals and the danger of a new triple or quadruple alliance is postponed because the reason for the formation of a consortium for acquisition collapses when there is nothing to be gained. With it, however, the motive through which we could have made plausible our union with Russia also ceases. Such a step would make the American statesmen much more suspicious today than would have been the case two months ago and it would serve to bring nearer the realization of an Anglo-American unity for which England has been striving with the greatest effort and perseverance. For Roosevelt is an impulsive and powerful character who would have the inclination to react immediately if he believed a hoax had been played on him. It would be difficult to argue him out of such ideas. With his well known courage he would tell us directly "I have trusted you and have openly shared my program with the Kaiser. Part of this program is that Russia shall not retain Port Arthur. Port Arthur was, however, until now a recognized Russian possession. Your alliance with Russia even if it were only a simple defensive alliance, would bind you to procure the return of Port Arthur to Russia. How does the matter stand and how do we then stand in regard to each other?"

On the other hand a German-Russian alliance in which we would guarantee the recognized Russian possessions with the exception of Port Arthur and Liaotung could not become a practical question.

Upon one thing we can already count with certainty at this time; namely that Russia and England will compete with each other in the effort to destroy again the confidential relations which have been gradually developed between His Majesty the Kaiser and President Roosevelt and to change them into the opposite sort of relations.

C

G. P., XIX, part 2, No. 6306, Bülow to Sternburg, May 16, 1905.

Signs of a new alignment of powers—England, France, Russia, and later also Japan—are multiplying.

"We may evidently rest assured of President Roosevelt's concurrence when we regard it as an axiom that the growth of a trust of powers around a Franco-Russo-English nucleus will prove to be an event of incalculable consequences for America as well as Germany. To prevent its realization, we have only one remedy, i.e., to allow as little opportunity as possible to the future business partners for a successful functioning of the partnership. This applies to the Moroccan as well as to the East Asiatic question. . . ."

As regards the East Asiatic question von Bülow feels that "whoever brings about peace will have the temporary advantage. . . . Should peace really be brought about through the mediation of France and England, we can regard the quadruple alliance as being close at hand. It would therefore seem urgently desirable from the German point of view that the President should persuade the Japanese Government first to communicate all changes in its peace terms to him, and not to England (which forwards them to Paris). . . . At all events it is of far reaching importance to Germany that it shall not be the Franco-English group, but President Roosevelt, who shall win the prestige that goes with success."

D

Dennett, *Roosevelt and the Russo-Japanese War*, pp. 112–114.

... First, in speaking of some pro-Russians in America who would have the public believe that the victory of Japan would be a certain prelude to her aggression in the direction of the Philippine Islands, ... [the American] observed that Japan's only interest in the Philippines would be, in his opinion, to have these islands governed by a strong and friendly nation like the United States, and not to have them placed either under the misrule of the natives, yet unfit for self-government, or in the hands of some unfriendly European Power. Count Katsura confirmed in the strongest terms the correctness of his views on the point and positively stated that Japan does not harbor any aggressive designs whatever on the Philippines; adding that all the insinuations of the yellow peril type are nothing more or less than malicious and clumsy slanders calculated to do mischief to Japan.

Second, Count Katsura observed that the maintenance of general peace in the extreme East forms the fundamental principle of Japan's international policy. Such being the case, he was very anxious to exchange views with ... [the American] as to the most effective means for insuring this principle. In his own opinion the best, in fact the only, means for accomplishing the above object would be to form good understanding between the three governments of Japan, the United States, and Great Britain which have common interests in upholding the principle of eminence [sic]. The Count well understands the traditional policy of the United States in this respect and perceives fully the impossibility of their entering into a formal alliance of such nature with foreign nations, but in view of our common interests he could [not] see why some good understanding or an alliance in practice if not in name, should not be made between these three nations, in so far as respects the affairs in the Far East. With such understanding firmly formed, general peace in these regions would be easily maintained to the great benefit of all Powers concerned.

... [The American] said that it was difficult, indeed impossible, for the President of the United States of America to enter even to any understanding amounting in effect to a confidential informal agreement, without the consent of the Senate, but that he felt sure that without any agreement at all the people of the United States was [sic] so fully in accord with the people of Japan and Great Britain in the maintenance of peace in the Far East that whatever occasion arose appropriate action of the Government of the United States, in conjunction with Japan and Great Britain, for such a purpose could be counted on by them quite as confidently as if the United States were under treaty obligations to take [it].

Third, in regard to the Korean question, Count Katsura observed that Korea being the direct cause of our war with Russia, it is a matter of absolute importance to Japan that a complete solution of the peninsula question should be made as the logical consequence of the war. If left to herself after the war Korea will certainly draw back to her habit of entering into any agreements or treaties with other Powers, thus resuscitating the same international complications as existed before the war. In view of the foregoing circumstances Japan feels absolutely constrained to take some definite step with a view to precluding the possibility of Korea falling back into her former condition and of placing us again under the necessity of entering upon another foreign war.

. . . . [The American] fully admitted the justness of the Count's observations and remarked to the effect that, in his personal opinion, the establishment by Japanese troops of a suzerainty over Korea to the extent of requiring that Korea enter into no foreign treaties without the consent of Japan was the logical result of the present war and would directly contribute to permanent peace in the East. His judgment was that the President would concur in his view in this regard, although he had no authority to give assurance of this; indeed, . . . [the American] added that he felt much delicacy in advancing the views he did for he had no mandate for the purpose from the President. . . . He could not, however, in view of Count Katsura's courteous desire to discuss the question, decline to express his opinions. . . .

CHAPTER XV

JEWS IN RUMANIA AND RUSSIA

IN cases of oppression exercised by foreign states on their own citizens the United States was often called upon to protest. As the great liberal republic of the western world to whose shores had come both poor and stalwart, both radical and adventurer, America had become the home of varying strains of alien blood. She was the land of liberty and of opportunity. It was only natural, therefore, that she became, in the eyes of untold millions a rock of defence against oppression, cruelty, and massacre. The Irishman, the Jew, the Armenian, the Korean, and even the Negro of the Congo were taught to look to America as the home of plenty and the land of the free. From Ireland to Ararat people had

> Heard a whisper of a country that lies beyond the sea,
> Where rich and poor stand equal in the light of freedom's day.

Naturally much of this sentiment was mere idealism; yet there was something to be said for a country which for more than a century had sympathized with practically every attempt at revolt against oppression in Europe and South America. Indeed the westward advance of the American frontier and the successive waves of alien immigration to the United States can be traced in the names of new settlements which recall those of revolutionary leaders in foreign lands, —thus our Emmets, our Bolivars, our Kossuths and our Ypsilanti. It is true that western airs had fanned our adventurous spirit; but we still listened aghast at tales of struggles for liberty, of torture, and of broken faith as they came to us across the Atlantic. Our Secretary of State, Mr. Hay, who was a poet as well as a diplomat, had written verses from which I quote:

> Not in dumb resignation
> We lift our hands on high;
> Not like the nerveless fatalist
> Content to trust and die.
> Our faith springs like the eagle
> Who soars to meet the sun,
> And cries exulting unto Thee,
> O Lord, Thy will be done!
>
> * * * * *
>
> Wherever man oppresses man
> Beneath Thy liberal sun,
> O Lord, be there, Thine arm made bare,
> Thy righteous will be done! [1]

Small wonder that the distressful condition of the Jews in Rumania and in Russia should be brought to his attention and to President Roosevelt's. As regards Rumania this was at a time when the United States was trying to secure a naturalization treaty with that country and was encountering difficulties. It was a period when our doors were still wide open, when the restriction of immigration by adequate medical inspection and by quotas was unknown. Unfortunately it was true that oppression and restriction laid on Jews in Rumania had as their effect the practical expulsion of many of them. The United States had become the goal of these expatriated Jews, and, once in America, owing to the administration of easy naturalization laws, many of these Jews would secure American citizenship. Then armed with that as a protection, in case they returned to Rumania, they would claim the services of American consuls to avoid the restrictions laid on them as Jews by Rumanian law. The Rumanian government, therefore, objected to making a treaty which could give the Jews such an opportunity. The fact that the Rumanians themselves raised the complication of the Jewish question in Rumania as reason for refusing to make such a treaty gave renewed opportunity to the United States to bring up the entire matter.²

After consultation with leading Jews in the United States Secretary Hay and Mr. Adee agreed to send an identical instruction to American diplomats abroad for verbal communication to the governments of France, Germany, Great Britain, Russia and Turkey, who had all signed the treaty of Berlin in 1878. The note remonstrated against the treatment of Jews in Rumania as a violation of Article 44 of that treaty. This article read as follows:

> In Roumania the difference of religious creeds and confessions shall not be alleged against any person as a ground for exclusion or incapacity in matters relating to the enjoyment of civil and political rights, admission to public employments, functions and honors, or the exercise of the various professions and industries in any locality whatsoever.
> The freedom and outward exercise of all forms of worship shall be assured to all persons belonging to the Roumanian State, as well as to foreigners, and no hindrance shall be offered either to the hierarchical organizations of the different communions, or to their relations with their spiritual chiefs.
> The subjects and citizens of all the powers, traders or others, shall be treated in Roumania, without distinction of creed, on a footing of perfect equality.³

Such action by the United States was futile. No one of the powers addressed made any representations to Rumania and nothing came of the matter. No Jew could become a Rumanian citizen unless by legislative act and the charges and counter charges as to the condition of the Jews remained about as before. In Russia the fact that the remonstrance was only a *note verbale* gave Count Lamsdorff a feeble excuse for saying to the British that no such note had ever been received.⁴

The fact that Rumania, which was well aware of the American remonstrance, chose to consider the whole matter as a domestic question was also made evident at a lunch given by the King and Queen to the new American Minister, Mr. Jackson. There a spokesman for the King stated privately to Mr. Jackson that the entire Jewish question was considered as one of Rumanian national existence. The laws restricting the Jews were laws to protect Rumanians. The authorities were hurt rather than offended that the United States should have taken this action. Thus it was evident that the American protest, however satisfactory to the administration in America from the point of view of its domestic politics, was internationally useless.[5]

In 1903 there took place at Easter a massacre of Jews at Kishinev, in Russia, and the practical destruction of the Jewish quarter where rioting and looting prevailed. The failure of the local authorities to deal adequately with what was evidently a prearranged and organized attempt aroused universal indignation in the United States. Mr. McCormick, at St. Petersburg, in response to instructions, inquired whether, in view of reports of distress among the Jews at Kishinev, financial aid and supplies would be permitted to reach the survivors of the massacre. He was told that no distress existed among the Jews of that region and the offer was declined.[6] This peremptory reply naturally excited wrath among American Jews who blamed Mr. McCormick for failure to read the Russian daily press which stated that subscriptions were being taken up in Russia for the sufferers. They likened him to a messenger boy for the Tsar; and they made plans to draw up a great petition, which could be forwarded to Russia through the American Embassy there, protesting against the treatment of Jews in Russia. When news of this petition reached St. Petersburg a false rumor was circulated that Count Cassini at Washington had apologized for events at Kishinev. He was at once ordered to give to the press in America an absolute and categorical denial of the alleged apology and to state that the Russian government would not receive any petitions or representations from foreign states regarding Russian internal affairs. This outburst by Cassini irritated President Roosevelt, who ordered that a statement should be issued saying that no attention would be paid to any statement from the Russian

Embassy save a formal official one and expressing deep sympathy for the Jews who had suffered in recent outrages. The President also linked the whole matter with Russian behavior toward China and her attempted violation of the open door in Manchuria.[7]

Under the circumstances plans were made to forward the petition. Mr. Riddle, the Chargé at St. Petersburg, was instructed to inquire whether the petition would be received and transmitted to the Tsar. Count Lamsdorff, anticipating the inquiry, sent for Mr. Riddle and said that:

> he thought it would be better to notify me informally that such a petition would not be received; if I delivered it to him in person he would at once hand it back without looking at it. If I sent it accompanied by an official note he would at once place it in another envelope and return it to me unopened, unread; that the Emperor whose will is the sole law of this land had no need of information from outside sources as to what is taking place within his dominions and that even a respectful petition or prayer relating to internal matters could not be received from foreigners.[8]

With this refusal of the Russian government to receive the petition the matter dropped officially; but the President showed his willingness to use the situation, if need be, to win support for his foreign policies. He had been the driving element behind the American petition. To Secretary Hay the President had already written of the force of public opinion and of his belief that with regard to Manchuria the country would be increasingly ready to support him in case he went to "extremes" in his objection to Russian policy. In reply the Secretary said:

> Your letter of the 18th came yesterday. I am entirely of your mind on both the subjects, Kishinev and Manchuria. Poor Chamberlain never said a truer word than "when you sup with the Devil you should have a long spoon." Four years of constant conflict with them have shown me that you cannot let up a moment on them without danger to your midriff. The bear that *talks* like a man, is more to be watched than Adam Zad.
> I am more and more convinced that your statement was a good thing. The only inducement they have to do us justice in Manchuria

is the fear that we may take part with Japan in the impending quarrel. The statement of July 1, was a notice that our patience vas becoming exhausted, and, I have no doubt, it hastened their declaration of "honorable intentions" in Manchuria. Of course I do not wish to exaggerate the value of their professions. There is a lot of pressure and patience needed yet. But I felt the time had come to take them at their word, and to announce to the world their engagements and our belief in their sincerity. Every such incident makes future treachery more difficult for them. . . .

I am greatly interested in what you say about the country backing you in "extremes." I have always regarded it as a handicap to us in our negotiations that the country would *not* stand for an extreme policy in that direction. But your judgment of popular currents is better than mine, and if you are right, this would be a trump card to play, in some moment of crisis.[9]

On the question of admission to Russia of American citizens of Hebrew descent the results were also negative. The refusal of the Russian Government to recognize American passports when issued to people of such ancestry was absolute and effective.[10] As time passed public opinion in the United States and in England was affected by stories of rioting against Jews in Russia in 1906. Endeavors to persuade the Russian government to discuss the matter failed. The horror felt by Americans at events in Russia was the same sort of horror which affected them at the news of what had befallen the Armenians in Turkey.[11] Yet, as President Roosevelt wrote, "to send war-ships to take away the fugitives would strike me as a spectacular bit of folly." Indeed he became a bit annoyed by the persistence with which the friends of oppressed peoples sought his aid to do the impossible. The United States had shown its sympathy with the Jews; but she did not intend to go farther. As some one with a touch of cynical humor remarked at the time, apropos of the passport question: "I don't see why Russia does not send some Russian citizen, armed with a Russian passport, who is of distinctly Chinese blood to try to get into the United States." In view of the American stand on the exclusion of Asiatic immigrants such a step might have been interesting.

NOTES TO CHAPTER XV

1. *Harper's Magazine,* October, 1891.
2. *F. R.,* 1902, pp. 910-915; *H. P.,* July 29 and Aug. 27, 1902, Adee to Hay; Aug. 12, Hay to Adee.
3. *F. R.,* 1902, pp. 42-45.
4. *F. R.,* 1903, pp. 702-707; *H. P.,* Sept. 25, 1902, Tower to Hay.
5. *H. P.,* Aug. 1, 1903, Jackson to Hay; Aug. 13, Adee to Hay.
6. *F. R.,* 1903, p. 712.
7. *H. P.,* May 19, 1903, Schiff to Hay (with enclosures); July 1, and 3, Hay to Roosevelt; July 3, Loomis to Hay; *R. P.,* July 1, 1903, Loomis to Roosevelt.
8. *R. P.,* July 16, 1903 (telegram), Hay to Roosevelt, giving the text of a cable from Riddle. Cf. *H. P.,* July 11, 1903, Hay to Roosevelt; July 16, same to same; July 31, Riddle to Hay; *D. S.,* Numerical File, Vol. 515, telegram, July 14, 1903, Barnes (the President's Secretary) to Hay; To Russia, Vol. 18, p. 462, telegram, July 15, Hay to Riddle, giving the text of the petition; *R. P.,* July 16, Roosevelt to Hay ordering that the entire matter be made public and that Straus, Wolf and Levi of the American Jews "be told that they can now say what they choose as regards the matter."
9. *H. P.,* July 22, 1903, Hay to Roosevelt.
10. *H. P.,* Aug. 27, Sept. 9 and Sept. 30, 1904, McCormick to Hay, in which he recounts the absolute failure of his negotiations regarding passports, discounts the stories regarding the persecution of Jews, and states that no revolution is likely to be attempted in Russia. In October, 1904 and in 1905 there were, however, serious attempts at revolution.
11. *D. S.,* From London, Vol. 214, No. 213, June 21, 1906, Reid to Root; From Russia, Vol. 66, telegram, June 25, Meyer to Root; *F.R.,* 1906, pp. 1296 *et seq.* Howe, *George von Lengerke Meyer,* New York, 1920, pp. 239, 242, 297, 302, 316-319.

CHAPTER XVI

AFRICAN QUESTIONS

IF the Jews were anxious to involve us with Russia the British were scarcely less concerned to draw America into their African disputes with France. The last decade of the nineteenth century presented a picture of envenomed Anglo-French rivalry which ranged from French rights on the Newfoundland shore to the proper boundaries for Siam, from Anglo-French interests in Pacific islands to the frontiers of African dependencies. Such a contest must have ended in war or in an amicable agreement to wipe the slate clean and by settlement of all outstanding questions to promote a new *entente cordiale*. Fortunately for the world both Great Britain and France chose this latter method in 1904.

In the years before that date, however, there were repeated opportunities for friction between England and France. Especially was this true in Africa, which was really to be penetrated and partitioned during the last quarter of the nineteenth century. Such hasty grabs at territory, whose geographical features and characteristics were scarcely known, were frequently productive of frontier disputes. Often unknowingly or heedlessly the local troops of European states would violate each other's boundaries or penetrate into regions which were under the quasi-protection of their nearest and dearest rivals. When, however, such a violation of the frontier of a neighboring state took place the fact that this state had long been recognized as an independent republic, which had been established under the protection of the United States, made the step a serious one.

Liberia had been founded in 1822 as a colony to which free men of color from the United States could repair. Out of this infant settlement, which was sponsored by the American Colonization Society, the Republic of Liberia had developed. Organized in 1847, it had been recognized by several European states in 1848, and in 1862 by the United States. American relations with this feeble state had been intermittent; but as early as 1843 the United States had declared a special interest in the welfare of the infant community. In 1880 the Department of State was quite ready to recognize publicly the "peculiar relations" existing between America and Liberia; and in 1899 Secretary Hay had said that "our position in reference to the citizens of Liberia is such that we could not be justified in regarding with indifference any attempt to oppose them or deprive them of their independence."[1]

Already, in 1897, it was alleged that in the previous year the French had penetrated Liberian territory to a distance of over fifty miles. This they had done from their neighboring French Ivory Coast Colony, ignoring the integrity of Liberian territory. Such encroachments they could make with impunity as the authority of the Liberian Government often did not extend much beyond the littoral of the Atlantic; but if such violations should go unchecked the days of independent Liberia might well be numbered. The state was insolvent and the Germans as well were reported as being eager to establish financial if not political control at Monrovia, the capital. When such information came to the United States and to Great Britain, the proposal was revived of joint action by the two powers to protect the independence of Liberia. In 1892 the Secretary of State had declined to act for such a purpose pending the delimitation of the Franco-Liberian boundary which was then taking place. In 1897, however, Mr. Sherman agreed to send a note which would indicate the interest of the United States. On May 20, therefore, copies of a promemoria exchanged by the Secretary of State and the British Ambassador at Washington were sent to Mr. Hay in London and to the representatives of the two countries at Monrovia.[2]

Later the plan was again broached by the British that an Anglo-American syndicate should be organized to put in order Liberian finances in order to arrest aggression by other powers to whose citizens unpaid debts were due. Nothing came of this suggestion; but immediately after the close of the Spanish-American war the story of disputes between Germany and Liberia aroused some interest. It was now proposed by Liberia that the United States and Great Britain sign a convention jointly guaranteeing her independence and integrity. In return special concessions and privileges would be pledged to the citizens of these two countries. Such a proposal was made because of the draft secret treaty which the Governor of the German Cameroons had drawn up; by this an eventual German protectorate over Liberia was planned. Appeals from Liberian officials to Bishop Hartzell of the American Methodist Episcopal Church led to the submission of the whole matter to the Department of State. Liberia now felt that in this world of fierce international rivalries and ruthless seizures she had become a Naboth's vineyard. The Bishop argued strongly for a favorable decision by the Department and emphasized the value of the Liberian coast as a naval and coaling base, the opportunity afforded to American capital, and the moral and religious gains to the Liberian people. The American navy was also much interested in the plan. Great Britain was apparently anxious to wait for the views of the United States.[3]

As a result Secretary Hay wrote to Berlin, saying:

> You are aware of the interest which the people and Government of the United States have always taken in the welfare of the Liberian Republic. It was founded by colored men emigrating from the United States. Its territory was purchased by the Colonization societies of America, and it has always been an object of kindly care and encouragment from the American Government. For these reasons and because of its weakness and helplessness which render it unable to resist a serious aggression from any great power, the United States could not view without grave concern any procedure from any quarter which would threaten its liberty of action or the extinction of its independent existence.[4]

To this von Bülow, who had already been approached by the British Ambassador, replied that Germany had claims against Liberia which she hoped would be paid but that she had "no wish to interfere with her independent existence." [5] In similar fashion it was asserted in 1899 that Liberia was again subject to encroachment by the French; and Secretary Hay addressed a despatch to Paris, reading:

> the Government of Liberia, naturally predisposed by their helplessness to timidity in face of foreign aggression, are under some apprehension of the action of France in the direction of an effective occupation of the country back of Liberia.
>
> I would be glad if you would consult with your colleague, Her Britannic Majesty's Ambassador in Paris, and agree upon some manner of intimating, separately and independently of each other, to the French Government the concern with which your respective Governments would regard any action by any European government that might threaten the integrity or independence of Liberia.[6]

Certainly it was now clear that while the United States was unwilling to unite with Great Britain in joint action she had positive ideas as to the necessity of preserving the independence of Liberia. The years 1897–1899 were years in which, owing to French advance in Africa, relations had become strained between France and England. The Fashoda incident had all but involved the two countries in war. It was nevertheless important that America should not be drawn into that dispute; yet I think that our sympathy with Great Britain was shown in various ways.

It is interesting, however, to note that in 1900 the United States sent a note to Great Britain, France, and Germany showing that she was alive to the dangers of monopolistic concessions for she sought to prevent the granting of an exclusive privilege of mining in Liberia to an English syndicate. Such a grant would have affected the rights of Americans which were co-extensive with Liberian territory itself as it was "conveyed to the Republic by the original holders of the native grants of land," who were at the time the American Colonization Society.[7] In any case such an exclusive grant was a violation of the principle of the open door.

As time went on, and as Great Britain and France had buried the hatchet in 1904, the rumors of a joint protectorate over Liberia by these two states aroused Germany to make inquiries at Washington regarding our attitude toward such a step. Further the activities, in 1905, of Sir Harry Johnston in seeking to regulate Liberian finances and to promote the interests of his recently formed company to develop the rubber sources of Liberia aroused interest. A plan had been considered whereby the British were to grant access to certain oil fields on the borders of northern Nigeria to France; in return France was to cede a considerable tract of land to Liberia; and Liberia was to turn over to private British management the control of her finances and the collection of customs. No attempt at a protectorate was suggested, though the Germans protested against the proposed financial arrangements. This scheme was adopted in part and continued until 1911. In that year the United States undertook with British and French assistance the general direction of Liberian finance.[8] Later modifications of this system were introduced. At present British financial interests predominate, though the development of American rubber plantations is promised. Such have been our guarded relations with Liberia. The United States resisted any attempt to draw her into formal guarantee of Liberian integrity; but she made it plain that, in view of her historical and moral interest in Liberia, America would be opposed to any attack upon Liberian independence.

On the other side of Africa the United States sought to develop trade with Abyssinia and in 1903 sent Mr. Skinner to negotiate a commercial treaty which was fairly successful. The general aspect of politics in that region in 1904 can be judged by an extract from one of his letters:

> I obtained all that could be obtained, and in fact all that you really desired or expected, but the Emperor wavered at several points during the negotiations. Surrounded as he is and badgered by rival

influences, he hardly dared to do all that he wanted to do. I was told confidentially, and I repeat it to you confidentially, that the Russians were the leaders in the campaign against American influence. The Minister was personally all graciousness and hospitality. The Russians are playing a great game of politics in Ethiopia, as I read the situation. They are spending large sums of money annually maintaining free hospitals, contributing to the church, etc., etc., although their commerce in that region is nil. They are building up what they fancy to be a great influence, with the expectation that eventually the Emperor, who is a strong character, will die, and that then Italy, France and Great Britain will carve up the country. When that time comes, Russia will interpose, on the ground that it likewise has invested heavily in Ethiopian stock, and is entitled to consideration; and then, having set forth this claim, will agree to relinquish all pretensions, and to deliver the various influences under its control, on consideration of receiving, from any of the powers in a position to deliver the goods, a port upon the Red Sea. What Russia really wants, is possession of some point on the Red Sea, and France, Italy, and Great Britain, having a long coast line, can supply her with this requisite, although Italy is presumed to be the power most likely to prove complacent in this respect in the end. All the possibilities are expected to mature in the long distant future; but as we know, Russian diplomacy exists, not for today nor for tomorrow, but having in mind the probable trend of events of a century.[9]

Another aspect of African life was presented in 1903 when the treatment of the natives of the Congo Free State roused international attention. The United States had failed to approve the general act of the Berlin Conference of 1885 by which the status of the Congo was regulated; but America had always shown an interest in the welfare of the natives of Africa. Furthermore we had citizens there engaged in missionary and educational work so it was only natural that appeal should be made to us to assist in the redress of grievances. The conditions of misery and cruelty affecting the native population were serious. Mr. Casement, British Consul General, had made an elaborate report on the situation. As is usual in circumstances such as these the friends of the aborigines outdid themselves in the charges which they brought against the Belgian administrators. The result was that the very purposes for which these philanthropists labored were in part defeated. Yet the net result was to the good and conditions in the Congo Free State improved. The United States, however, did little more than call the attention of the administrators of the Congo Free State to evils of which a report had been made and refrained from pressing matters. The reform of the Congo Free State, desirable though it was, did not seem to fall within the field of action of the United States though, finally, at the close of 1906, she expressed the desire to co-operate with Great Britain in seeking reform of that administration.[10]

It was possibly due to the pressure of public opinion, for President Roosevelt had already spoken his mind on the subject in vigorous language, saying, of a petition for action on behalf of the Negroes of the Congo Free State, that such a position aimed to make the United States appear as an international "meddlesome Mattie."

Of a different sort, however, was the action of the United States when, in 1904, an alleged naturalized American citizen Perdicaris by name, was kidnapped and held for ransom in Morocco by one of the native chieftains, Raisuli. As we shall see in the next chapter, an American lady, Miss Stone, had been kidnapped by Macedonian bandits, in 1901, and held for ransom. The Department had had great difficulty in effecting her release and consequently was anxious for prompt action in the case of Mr. Perdicaris. This matter was of a totally different category from that of the Jews in Rumania and Russia or from that of the Negroes in the Congo for it involved adequate protection of the life of an American citizen. Mr. Perdicaris was a man of education, a writer for the magazines, who had been seized in his own home, three miles from Tangier, and carried off.[11] The abduction took place on May 18, 1904; and Mr. Gummeré immediately asked for an American man-of-war. He reported the situation as serious and he told the Moorish authorities that they would be held personally responsible. Daily telegrams indicated that the Department of State was aroused; the Mediterranean squadron reached Tangier; and it was shortly reinforced by the South Atlantic squadron. Mr. Varley, a British subject, and a step-son of Mr. Perdicaris, had been kidnapped at the same time so that the British authorities were also disturbed and had sent a man-of-war to Tangier. Efforts were also made to enlist the aid of France who promptly instructed her Minister to co-operate.[12]

The terms named by Raisuli were deemed preposterous; but a threat of death unless they were agreed to showed that Raisuli was determined. President Roosevelt, while anxious to secure the release of the captives, did not wish the United States to be put in the position of guaranteeing the fulfilment of terms for Morocco. Negotiations continued but without effect. It became evident that the powers concerned would have to be ready to undertake the punishment of Raisuli; for he was contemptuous of the Sultan of Morocco, whose power was very limited. President Roosevelt, therefore, wrote to Secretary Hay, saying:

Of course it would be out of the question to surrender to the demands of those Morocco brigands. We have gone just as far as we possibly can go for Perdicaris. Our position must now be to demand the death of those that harm him if he is harmed.

. . . I think it would be well to enter into negotiations with England and France, looking to the possibility of an expedition to punish the brigands, if Gummeré's statement as to the impotence of the Sultan is true.[13]

French intervention, furthermore, seemed to complicate the situation for the French were very unpopular in Morocco because of the terms of the Anglo-French entente which had recognized, since April, 1904, the dominant position of France in Morocco. So there were international complications as well. Money terms as to ransom were tentatively settled on June 17; but on June 21 Mr. Gummeré was convinced of double dealing and treachery. He telegraphed:

We have come to a point when our position has now become undignified and humiliating. I would urge that if the effort to arrange for the exchange of captives reported yesterday fail we may be empowered to present an ultimatum immediately for large indemnity for every day's further delay and that marines will be landed and customs seized. Convinced such action absolutely necessary to secure the release of captives and prevent further delay and double dealing. Rear Admiral cables to same effect.[14]

It was at this stage of affairs that Secretary Hay, following an interview with the President, sent a notable message. He demanded "Perdicaris alive or Raisuli dead"; but warned against the landing of marines. Later he entered in his diary under June 23 "My telegram to Gummeré had an uncalled for success. It is curious how a concise impropriety hits the public." At the meeting of the Republican Convention which was then in session at Chicago the assumption was, of course, that the President was the author of the terse phrase and popular enthusiasm was great.[15] On June 24 Mr. Perdicaris reached Tangier as the result of negotiations which had been conducted at the same time that Secretary Hay was writing his message in Washington. It does not appear that the message had any effect on the final stage. The expense of the ransom was borne by the Moorish court and the United States presented a bill for $4000 additional.[16] Thus ends the famous Perdicaris case. The following is Admiral Chadwick's comment on the matter:

> The presence of our fleet has been of the greatest value as a moral pressure. It has given the Moors quite another idea of our power. Everything on our part has been done to avoid injuring Moorish susceptibilities. No objection of course could be taken to the couple of marines stationed at the Consul-General's residence, at the Perdicaris's and the Belgian [British?] Legation. They have been kept inside the grounds. This whole question, however, was covered by the Sultan's letter to the British Minister, in which, while objecting to the presence of ships, he recognized the "right of countries to land men to protect their nationals." [17]

NOTES TO CHAPTER XVI

1. Moore, V, pp. 762-768.
2. D. S., To London, Vol. 32, No. 46, May 20, 1897, Sherman to Hay.
3. Personal letter of Bishop Hartzell, an American citizen, to Secretary Hay, Oct. 19, 1898, is in D. S., From Liberian Legation, Vol. I; From London, Vol. 193, telegram, Aug. 27, 1898, Hay to Day.
4. D. S., To Germany, Vol. 20, No. 641, Nov. 18, 1898, Hay to Jackson; a similar protest was made in 1900 to Germany; Cf. D. S., Vol. 21, No. 998, Jan. 22, 1900, Hay to White.
5. D. S., From Germany, Vol. 67, No. 643, Dec. 5, 1898, Jackson to Hay.
6. D. S., To France, Vol. 24, No. 640, June 28, 1899, Hay to Porter.

7. *D. S.*, To London, Vol. 33, No. 417, July 13, 1900, Hay to Choate; To Germany, Vol. 21, No. 1072, July 13, Hay to White; To France, Vol. 24, No. 810, July 13, 1900, Hay to Porter.

8. *D. S.*, To London, Vol. 35, No. 77, Nov. 8, 1905, Root to Reid; To France, Vol. 25, No. 71, Nov. 8, 1905, Root to McCormick; From London, Vol. 213, No. 83, Nov. 24, 1905, Reid to Root; No. 88, Nov. 28, same to same; Vol. 214, No. 156, Feb. 21, 1906, same to same; From Liberia, Vol. 14, No. 138, Dec. 16, 1905, Lyon to Root; Nos. 140, 141 and 142, Dec. 18, same to same; No. 147, Jan. 1, 1906, same to same; To Liberia, Vol. 2, No. 68, Feb. 6, 1906, Bacon to Lyon; *Statesman's Year Book, 1912.*

9. *H. P.*, Feb. 9, 1904, Skinner to Loomis; *F. R.*, 1904, pp. 298 *et seq.*

10. *D. S.*, To British Embassy, Vol. 26, personal, Sept. 22, 1903, Adee to Raikes; *H. P.*, Sept. 21, 1904, Hugh Reid to Hay; Gwynn and Tuckwell, *Life of the Rt. Hon. Sir Charles Dilke*, 2 Vols., New York, 1917, II, pp. 381 *et seq. Treatment of Natives in the Congo, a statement submitted to His Majesty's Government on behalf of the Aborigines Protection Society*, London, 1902; the matter was also frequently debated in Parliament and was the subject of diplomatic negotiations (*Cambridge History of British Foreign Policy*, III, pp. 366-372).

11. *H. P.*, July 9, 1904, Chadwick to Hay; writing of the episode after the release of Perdicaris this naval officer adds: "The Perdicaris business has given me a good deal of a lift in Europe, or rather it has put another support under our already lofty situation. The Government's very prompt and emphatic action was somewhat of a surprise. Perdicaris himself seemed to think somewhat that it was for P. as Perdicaris. I did not attempt to disabuse him. He is a most excellent specimen of the thorough going dilletante; his whole life spent in the atmosphere of bric-à-brac. His letter published regarding Raisuli was simply the outcome of this feeling for the picturesque side of his situation. I think he revelled in it finally. I can sympathize with him somewhat, for Morocco is the most picturesque of lands. To see old Torres (the Commissioner for Foreign Affairs) who is as fair as your little granddaughter, go up the street a mass of beautiful white wool draperies, his old calves bare, and his feet naked but for his yellow slippers and these wild fellows stoop and kiss his shoulder as he goes by, is a sight to give even a government architect an aesthetic sensation."

12. *F. R.*, 1904, pp. 307-308, 496-498.

13. *H. P.*, June 15, 1904, Roosevelt to Hay; *F. R.*, 1904, pp. 338, 498-501; *D. S.*, To London, Vol. 34, telegram, p. 632, May 28, 1904, Hay to Choate; From Morocco, telegram, June 8, Gummeré to Hay.

14. *D. S.*, From Morocco, telegrams, June 16, 17 and 21, 1904, Gummeré to Hay.

15. *F. R.*, 1904, pp. 503; Thayer, Hay, II, pp. 383-384; Bishop, I, pp. 320-322.

16. *D. S.*, From Morocco, telegrams, June 22, 24, 26, 28 and 29, 1904, Gummeré to Hay; *F. R.*, 1904, p. 504.

17. *H. P.*, June 24, 1904, Chadwick to Hay. A later letter of Dec. 17 includes the following story from Tangier which I rescue from the dusty files of the *Hay Papers:*

"Nathan at the Consulate told me a story. He had taken aboard one of our training ships Mohammed, Torres' son. It was the first time the young Torres, who by the way is a splendidly handsome specimen of the Moor, had ever been aboard a ship. Nathan tried to explain that the blacks in America were not Mohammedan, turned to the Captain for proof. The Captain said "Sam, are you a Mohammedan?" "No sah, I'se no Mohammedan, I'se a Republican."

CHAPTER XVII

AMERICANS IN TURKEY

THE economic interest of the United States in the Ottoman Empire was negligible in 1896. Only Denmark, Montenegro, Serbia, Spain, and Sweden had less commerce with Turkey than did America. Our flag was rarely seen in Turkish ports and American financial investments in Turkey were practically unheard of. Yet our citizens had been resident in Turkey for more than seventy-five years and American missions and schools had long been established there. Hence the missionary element was predominant in our relations with the Ottoman Empire. Second was the protection of naturalized American citizens who were formerly Ottoman subjects. These multiplied rapidly in number, but for the decade 1896–1906 they did not fill the difficult position which they later came to occupy. American consuls did not often at that time have to face the problem presented by returning citizens who carried their new colors in a country which did not recognize their right of expatriation or of naturalization in America. The protection of missionaries was, therefore, the main occupation of American diplomats in Turkey and the chief object of their negotiations.[1]

In 1912 President Nicholas Murray Butler addressing a conference on international arbitration said:

> Foreign missions are largely responsible for the development of whatever international mind the United States now possesses. In so far as that phrase indicates a consideration of other parts of the world and concern for their welfare we owe much sympathetic and eager outlook to our foreign missionary enterprise. Exploration, commerce, travel and politics have done much to bring to the knowledge and

the interest of this Western Hemisphere all foreign lands. They have opened up to us in many cases far off portions of the world of which otherwise we had not heard. But foreign missions also have no inconsiderable share in exploration and investigation; and what is more missions have taught us to care for these people with whom we have become acquainted.[2]

This, of course, is particularly true of missions in the Far East and in the Near East. We have already noted the rôle played by our Chinese missions and the vigorous way in which Mr. Denby and Mr. Conger supported the claims of missionaries to carry on their work. In the Near East the situation was more complicated because international politics pressed more closely and because the division of Turkish subjects into Muhammadan and Christian groups was further entangled by the nationalistic leanings of various subdivisions of the Christian element. The advent of American missionaries to Turkey, a land officially Muhammadan, was originally intended to attempt the conversion of the followers of Islam. Soon, however, the work progressed in such fashion that the major interest of American missions became educational and social, while the converts won were for the most part from native Christian churches. Scarcely a Muhammadan was converted; in Armenia and in Syria, however, considerable progress was made among the natives. As time went on and as the Turkish authorities became more and more hostile to the development of national aspirations, particularly on the part of Armenians, the general situation became more acute.

The missionaries in general paid small attention to politics yet it was inevitable that they should be unfavorable to the Ottoman officials who ruled over them. They undoubtedly sympathized with the Armenians in their desire to secure freedom from direct Turkish control. This did not mean, however, that they were even cognizant of the revolutionary plots which came to a head in the last decade of the nineteenth century. In all the propaganda which has been directed against the American missionaries in Turkey there seem to be scarcely any authentic instances in which the charge can be made that they assisted in any direct attempts against the Turkish government.

In reality the missionaries were between two fires. On the one hand they were hated by the revolutionary leaders because they did not take part in assisting their cause; and they were exposed to danger, for it was the purpose of these leaders to instigate attacks on the missionaries and on mission property and thereby to provoke foreign intervention. On the other hand the work of the missionaries was exposed to every sort of interference by the Turkish authorities because their educational and social, as well as their religious endeavors were chiefly for the benefit of the native down-trodden Christian population. Under the circumstances missionary work was much damaged from these two sides. We may add that Mr. Terrell, the American Minister in 1896, was not an effective agent for the protection of American interests though he labored under special difficulties.

In 1894 and particularly in the last two months of 1895, terrific massacres had taken place in Armenia. The land was drenched in blood. These massacres had arisen from the fear engendered in the mind of the Sultan Abdul Hamid II by plots formed by Huntchagist bands of Armenian revolutionists whose widespread organization included as centers of anti-Turkish conspiracy places as far distant as Athens, Greece, and Worcester, Massachusetts. The Armenian argument was that they were determined to be free. "Europe listened to the Bulgarian horrors and made Bulgaria free [in 1878]. She will listen to our cry when it goes up in the shrieks and blood of millions of women and children." So the Huntchagist bands, some of whom probably received Russian money, made ready and the Turks fell on the defenceless and innocent Armenian population. They put thousands to the sword; but Europe did not intervene. She was somewhat deafer than she had been in 1876–1878 at the time of the Bulgarian massacres and she was busy about other things. So the sacrifice, which was of course great was also useless. Out of such losses and out of the destruction of missionary property there developed the general situation which the United States faced in 1896.[3]

The protection given to missionaries by Turkish guards during the height of the storm of massacre and assault had undoubtedly saved many American lives but claims for damages had piled up. The loss of life among native teachers and helpers had also been great. The Turkish government refused to accept the bill for damages that was presented; and they countered by charging that missionaries had themselves instigated the Armenian plots which had led to the massacres and disorders. Further they forbade the admission to Turkey of any Armenian who had emigrated from Ottoman territory during the past twenty years. It was the custom of European Embassies at Constantinople to have small gunboats or *stationnaires* off the city; and when Mr. Terrell requested a similar privilege for the United States this was at first refused but later permission was given. In the meantime a year and more dragged on without any settlement. Mr. Joseph Chamberlain had asked Secretary Olney in September, 1896, whether the United States would join with Great Britain in any action with regard to Turkey. The reply was that:

> if England should now seriously set about putting the Armenian charnel-house in order, there can be little doubt that the United States would consider the moment opportune for vigorous exertion on behalf of American citizens and interests in Turkey. It would feel itself entitled to demand full indemnity for past injuries to them as well as adequate security against the like injuries in the future. It would support such demands by all the physical force at its disposal—with the necessary result, I think, that its attitude would both morally and materially strengthen the hands of England. How valuable such incidental assistance might prove it is not, of course, easy to predict, but that it would be real and appreciable cannot, I think, fairly be doubted.[4]

This plan Lord Salisbury finally refused. In December of 1896 President Cleveland had expressed the pious but futile hope that the "present sombre prospect in Turkey" would not long be "permitted to offend the sight of Christendom." [5] Such expressions when they were not backed up by force were of course useless. The appointment of Dr. Angell as American Minister at Constantinople led to further delays in the settlement of American claims for he was not acceptable to the Ottoman authorities. His mission to Turkey was, therefore, a failure and he returned in disgust. In September, 1898, Mr. Oscar Straus, who had been Minister to Turkey in the first Cleveland administration, left again for Constantinople on his second mission.

The record of his stay at Constantinople is a bright spot in an otherwise gloomy series. The Turkish authorities had required, since the Armenian massacres, that all foreigners should secure, in addition to their own national passport, a special local Turkish passport, or *tezkirah,* in order to travel to the interior of the Empire. This *tezkirah* the Turks would delay granting, sometimes indefinitely, in violation of treaty rights. So Mr. Straus after weeks of fruitless negotiation finally signed a permit for one of the Americans thus delayed. He also informed the authorities of what he had done and told them that he would hold them responsible in case of any mishap. This ended the passport trouble for the *tezkirah* was shortly afterward abandoned.

There was also a long series of negotiations relating to the rights of naturalized American citizens of Turkish origin. The Turkish government still held fast to its rule of refusing to recognize the right of expatriation and consequently each case, as it came up, was decided on its merits. Mr. Straus was unable to shake the Turks in their stand on this matter. Lastly there was the question of claims for damages inflicted on missionary property during the recent disorders in Turkey. The Sultan had never admitted liability and it was with great difficulty that in December, 1898, he was persuaded to agree to the claims. In February, 1899, he proposed that, in order to "save his face," and to avoid difficulties with other countries which also had claims, the amount of the indemnity should be added to the price of a cruiser which he planned to order in the United States. This method of payment was accepted and following weary delays $95,000 was paid in June, 1901, to settle these claims.⁶

Secretary Hay was divided between mirth and indignation at this proposal. As he wrote to Mr. Adee:

> There is something ludicrous about the lying of these Turks. They have never mentioned the indemnity to Cramp—although for a year they have been talking of it in Washington and Constantinople. When the new Minister comes I think the President should distinctly refer to their breach of faith, in receiving him.⁷

It happened that the U. S. S. *Kentucky* was in Turkish waters at the end of 1900 and her presence undoubtedly hastened the signing of the contract for the construction of the cruiser on Christmas morning. Mr. Griscom who was American Chargé d'Affaires wrote to Secretary Hay:

> I need not say that I never made use of the *Kentucky's* visit by threat or implication but the moral effect was considerable. I sent an open telegram to the Captain which was read by the Turks and gave them to understand that the Legation was interested in their visit. I would have liked to present a demand for the direct payment of our claims but after feeling the ground it was evident that it would not have been successful, short of a threat to bombard Smyrna or the like. The Sultan is childish about some things and feels that to admit the responsibility for the massacres and to pay the damages would prejudice him forever in the eyes of his own people. It seemed better to fall in with his suggestion. After sending me solemn assurances as to the payment, he insisted that Captain Chester should come to Constantinople to show the world that we are great friends and that whatever he does is of his own free will. His reception to Captain Chester was something remarkable and we had a love feast at the palace. He countermanded an invitation to the Greek Minister for the same night in order that it might be a purely American affair. I sat next him at dinner and his conversation was highly interesting, jumping from one childish question to the most astute pumping. He seems very friendly to everything American and there can be no doubt that Captain Chester's visit has had an admirable effect on the relations between American interests and the Ottoman Government. I think the missionary interests will profit by it for some time to come.⁸

With the resignation of Mr. Straus as Minister the appointment of Mr. Leishman followed. From this time on the question of the rights of naturalized citizens became increasingly vexatious and there are pages of despatches regarding the matter. The Turks remained obdurate and each case had to be decided by itself. It does not seem necessary to enter further into this matter. Thus we pass to the kidnapping of Miss Stone, an American missionary, by Macedonian brigands in early September, 1901. Before she was released in February, 1902, tempers were to be badly frayed.

Macedonia was at this time in a condition of unrest bordering on disorder, due primarily to the existence on the borders of Bulgaria and European Turkey of bands or *commitadjis* of rough mountaineers who were suspected of having a political purpose, viz., to unite Macedonia to Bulgaria or to provoke a Macedonian uprising which might lead to the establishment of an independent Macedonian state. To both of these ends the Turks were naturally opposed. The plan to kidnap and hold Miss Stone for ransom was part of the terroristic scheme of these brigands, who, however, were also anxious to make some money.

The demand for ransom was not immediately made; and in view of the danger to Miss Stone's life in case the brigands were pressed too hardly by Turkish troops the first endeavors of American officials were to restrain the Turkish authorities. By October the situation had changed as the real need for a large sum of money was now apparent and as the fact with respect to the political purposes of the brigands became clearer. Mr. Adee for once in his life, seems to have miscalculated the whole matter. He suspected the Turks and referred to the amateurishness of the Turks in attempting to get the money in return for the payment by them of American claims for damages in the previous June.[9]

Mr. Adee continued to flounder and to make suggestions which were impracticable until in the end of October Secretary Hay came back. The question really was whether Miss Stone was being held in Bulgaria with the connivance of the Macedonian Revolutionary Committee or whether she was being held in Turkey. In any case it was important that the brigands should not be ruthlessly pressed with capture for, to judge by previous occurrences of a similar sort, such procedure would undoubtedly lead to her murder. The sum of $66,000 was raised in America by private subscription to secure her release; and in Macedonia and Bulgaria conferences took place with agents of the brigands and American friends and officials which aimed to settle the exact amount which should be paid in advance to secure her release.[10] The impression created in the mind of the American Chargé, Mr. Eddy, of the Sultan Abdul Hamid at this time is worth preserving; it is given in the Appendix to this chapter.[11]

In December negotiations took a quicker turn. Dr. Washburn of Robert College in Constantinople had paid a visit to Sofia, where he had great influence and was hailed as the "father of Bulgaria." His report was that Miss Stone had been captured in Turkey by Bulgarian bandits acting for the Macedonian Committee and was probably still in Turkey. Terms must be made with the brigands and after Miss Stone's release attempts to seize the brigands could be made either in Turkey or Bulgaria. In early January the Department of State suggested that it might be better to stop all negotiations and wait on the turn of events. This, however, seemed to be too risky. Consequently payment of $68,200 was made in February by Dr. Peet, who was the treasurer of the American mission in Constantinople, to agents of the brigands and within two weeks Miss Stone was released.[12]

The question of responsibility for the kidnapping remained doubtful for Mr. Leishman recommended that no claim for damages should be presented against Turkey. The money had been raised by voluntary subscription in America with the widest sort of publicity. He wrote on February 6, 1902, as follows:

> ... the band is composed of Bulgarians, aided and possibly directed by leading Macedonian agitators and that while the principal object was, no doubt, to obtain money for personal use in a manner not as uncommon as one might wish, it is quite reasonable to sup-

pose that a considerable amount of the ransom may find its way into the coffers of the Macedonian Committee to be used for revolutionary purposes. As the Turkish officials are firmly of this belief, one can readily understand why they were loath to have the ransom paid on Turkish soil, to slacken their efforts to catch the criminals or to retire their troops and relax their vigilance along the frontier and although they caused me some trouble and kept me up pretty late on several occasions, on the whole they have acted very generously and rendered very valuable assistance. I have nothing but words of praise for them and although I have steadily maintained a position protecting the rights of the United States Government to file a claim for damages that may be deemed proper and right, as no moral blame could be laid at the door of the Turkish Government, I am inclined to recommend that no claim be made. I am moved to this conclusion not only by the belief that it would be a stroke of good policy which besides being highly appreciated would place the Legation on a most friendly basis that might help us in many matters, but also by the belief, that, while the Ottoman Government may be legally and technically liable for Miss Stone's capture on account of the abduction having taken place on Turkish soil, no real moral responsibility attaches for even if the generally accepted belief that the miscreants were Bulgarians should be disproved by subsequent developments, the fact would still remain that the abduction took place in a disturbed and sparsely settled section where the inhabitants are practically of the same race and imbued with the same ideas as the Bulgarians, merely divided by an imaginary line, those on the Bulgarian side having thrown off the Turkish yoke and the remaining half desiring to do the same thing. As [*sic*] they sympathize with the revolutionary ideas and plots of the "Macedonian Committee" which they look upon as a holy cause and it would not be an altogether unfounded belief that many would even applaud kidnapping a missionary, especially when done in a way that would, besides throwing discredit on the Ottoman Government, furnish funds for the Macedonian cause. One thing is almost certain, that the brigands whoever they may be, are Christians, as there is no record of any of the bands that have infested European Turkey for many years, having been composed of Moslems.[13]

The Department of State was inclined to wait until it had more information and Secretary Hay wrote to Mr. Leishman saying:

Pressure upon the Turkish Government or imputation of responsibility on its part for the capture and ransom of Miss Stone would apparently tend at this stage of the matter to further the objects of the [Revolutionary] Committee and play into its hands by raising the issue between the United States and Turkey which it may have been the purpose of the abduction to promote. Before coming to any conclusion in this regard, or even forming a plausible conjecture, it appears to be advisable to await the full testimony of the ransom committee, and especially that of Miss Stone, before forming a conclusion. It is obvious that her testimony, if she be in a situation to furnish it, would be of the first importance in fixing the international responsibility for the abduction.[14]

The Porte naturally made much of the fact that the American authorities had urged the withdrawal of Turkish troops from the pursuit of Miss Stone's abductors because of their fear lest her life might thereby be endangered. The question of the moral responsibility of the Turkish authorities was, therefore, gradually allowed to slip from view and in the end the claim was never recovered.[15] The whole record of the Stone case exhibits lack of ability on the part of American officials. The first Dragoman of the Legation, Mr. Garguilo, alone has much to his credit as have Dr. Peet and Mr. House of the mission board, supported as they were by Dr. Washburn. The hysterical excitement shown by missionary friends of Miss Stone in America and the publicity given in the American press were chiefly responsible for the large amount which had to be paid.[16]

In August of 1902 Mr. Leishman became involved in a dispute with the Grand Vizier, who was probably acting under instructions from the Sultan. At the time of his appointment Mr. Leishman was unwelcome to the Sultan and it required the diplomacy of Mr. Griscom, who was then Chargé at Constantinople, to secure his acceptance by Abdul Hamid. Now, owing to repeated failures on the part of the Grand Vizier to fulfill his promises with regard to a number of outstanding questions and finally owing to his refusal to receive Mr. Leishman, that Minister was in high dudgeon and talked of demanding his passports. Fortunately the Sultan intervened to prevent an actual break and Mr. Leishman took a short vacation. Mr. Adee thus described the situation to Secretary Hay:

Leishman's complaint was that the Vizier refused to see him. He carried his complaint to the Sultan, who promptly arranged for him to see the Vizier the next day. This Leishman politely but firmly declined to do. I fancy he wishes us to direct him to demand that the Sultan discipline the Vizier and order him to cease from overriding the agreement already reached by Leishman with the Minister for Foreign Affairs touching the emigration of families of naturalized Armenians. As the Vizier is doubtless acting under the Sultan's private orders, it is not easy to see what could be accomplished by so doing, but Mr. Leishman seems to anticipate very good results from "a firm stand."

It seems to be a pity to have a break with Turkey over a comparatively unimportant question in which there is plausible warrant for the Turkish contention under the doctrine of perpetual allegiance, which any sovereign government has a right to maintain. The Vizier's position is that the families may freely emigrate, but upon the petition of the *pater familias* and not upon the request of the Government of the United States which the Minister of State had admitted as sufficient and competent. After all, the wives and children are Ottoman subjects while within Turkish jurisdiction, for no law of ours can naturalize them outside of our jurisdiction. It is true that in international law the *wife* follows the husband's status wherever she may be, but Turkey holds that the husband remains a Turk until released from allegiance by the sovereign's consent. As every European power holds the doctrine of sovereign consent being necessary before renunciation of allegiance, our isolation in this respect makes our position initially weak.[17]

At this time the Sultan again heard of difficulties with the inhabitants of the Sulu Islands in the Philippines and he offered his aid to pacify them for they were *Sunni* Muhammadans who recognized him as their Khalif. In 1899, as we have already seen, his services in that direction had been useful; but on this occasion his offer was declined by the President.[18]

There remained several matters in which the delays and opposition of the Turkish authorities operated to interfere with the work of the missionaries. One result of the Armenian massacres had been that the care of an immense number of refugees and orphans had suddenly been thrust upon American missions. The money which philanthropists in America had subscribed to assist in this work and the money received in 1901 from the settlement of claims was now available but permission to build these new orphanages and schools was lacking. Furthermore the construction of buildings to replace those destroyed during the recent Armenian disorders was likewise held up. Other matters such as permission to take the local medical examination for students of the American Medical School at the Syrian Protestant College at Beirut were also involved. Permits for archaeological excavations by Americans were delayed and in general a distinction was made by the Turkish authorities to the detriment of American interests. The French had succeeded by threat of the use of their navy, in compelling the Turks to grant such permits as were asked for Roman Catholic institutions. The question, therefore, was whether the presence of American men-of-war on a friendly visit in Turkish waters might not assist in securing action by the Ottoman government. Mr. Eddy was frankly in favor of such a course; Mr. Leishman was more or less opposed. He blew hot and he blew cold on such a plan. Mr. Eddy's judgment is given in a despatch of November, 1902, which reads:

> Upon long reflection, and consultation with many persons who have a very thorough knowledge of the country, I have come to the conclusion that there is only one way by which we can settle all differences promptly and effectively,—and that is by having the squadron of men-of-war, now in the Mediterranean, pay a friendly visit either to the port of Smyrna, Salonika or Mytilene. If this were done it would probably have the same effect as when the *Kentucky* arrived at Smyrna in 1900, in consequence of which the indemnity was settled.
>
> It is a patent fact to anyone residing in the Ottoman Empire that American prestige here is at a very low ebb. American commerce has not the advantages and opportunities it should have. The prohibition of American pork and the troubles and annoyances to which American Insurance Companies are subjected may be taken as instances. To put it briefly, the United States, when they are considered at all, are looked upon as a power of the Second class, and, consequently, the American Consulates throughout the Turkish Empire have much more difficulty in doing their work than the Consulates of Italy or Austria, or any of the so-called Great Powers.

The American flag is almost never seen in Turkish waters, and it is only at very long intervals that an American man-of-war appears.

It is therefore my firm conviction that, were the present Mediterranean squadron to pay a friendly visit to Smyrna, and, if possible to Salonika and Mytilene as well, the result of this visit would be at once apparent.[19]

After months of delay during which the patience of all concerned was seriously tried, endeavors were made to oust Mr. Leishman and vigorous complaints against him were made in Washington. These failed and the Turkish authorities grudgingly gave way. Only the opening of new schools seemed to hang fire. Mr. Adee wrote as follows to Hay:

I send you this telegram, received last night from Leishman. I confess to having read it with little complacency. Two rival ambitions are apparently working in the same direction, ——— seeks to discredit Leishman and be sent as Ambassador to supplant him, while Leishman wishes to display such energy as to be promoted to be Ambassador and so enabled to transact business with the Porte.

Leishman has won many of the points in contention, notably the Beirut examinations and the emigration of the wives and children of Armenians. The schools question is one of routine as much as principle. The Turks asked him for a list of the American schools for which firmans were sought, and he sent a list of about two hundred, more, I fancy, than England, France and Italy combined. It would take two years to dispose of that batch, for each case will have to be examined, and the Sultan insists on doing the work in person.[20]

Meantime disorders in Macedonia had been followed by grave unrest in other portions of the Empire at Harpoot and finally in Syria. Mr. Adee, who seems to have misunderstood the Turkish character and to have failed to appreciate the value of showing the flag in foreign waters, was at last forced to give way, and this by a comedy of errors. On August 27 it was reported from Constantinople that Mr. Magelson, the American Vice-Consul at Beirut, had been assassinated. Local authorities seemed to be dilatory and in haste the European squadron was ordered to Beirut. There had been no murder; but a pistol had been fired at the Vice-Consul as he was driving home at night. A mistake in coding or decoding the telegram from Beirut had been made which should have read that an attempt at murder had failed. This was serious enough in any case especially as conditions were now notoriously unsafe in Beirut.[21]

Unfortunately almost immediately on the arrival of the American men-of-war at Beirut a riot broke out in the city which cost the lives of about twelve people. Admiral Cotton agreed to land marines in case of necessity. The excitement in Syria was considerable while at Constantinople the Turkish government was also disturbed by the presence of other men-of-war in Turkish waters. The Embassies and Legations there made preparations in case of an attack by mobs who were excited by news of revolutionary successes in Macedonia. Altogether the situation was pregnant with trouble. Secretary Hay was fortunately in Washington and saw the Turkish Minister, Chekib Bey, who protested against the presence of the American squadron at Beirut. Mr. Adee later told him that:

> while the immediate occasion of the orders given for the sailing of the fleet was the reported assassination of our Vice-Consul, it was still the opinion of the President that the conditions of trouble and excitement in the Turkish Empire were such as to justify some measures of precaution on the part of this Government for the protection of American interests, which might be seriously threatened from day to day.
>
> I then said to him that it was a matter deeply to be regretted by this Government that the Turkish Government seemed so slow or so unwilling to do justice to the claims and requests which we had been vainly urging upon them for the last six months; that the matters we were asking to have settled, while not of very great importance, were, nevertheless, of much interest to a large number of our citizens; that our requests had been extremely moderate and reasonable; that we were asking nothing to which we were not perfectly entitled by international comity and by express agreement with the Turkish Government; that promises which had been made had not, as yet, been fulfilled; that our Minister received scant and grudging consideration at the Sublime Porte, and that it was almost impossible for him to obtain an audience of the Sultan and that the kind assurances which he had from time to time received from His Majesty were not carried into effect by the Ottoman Government; that I hoped he would immediately communicate these views to his

Government, and use what influence he had, so that justice might be done to our entirely reasonable and moderate demands."²²

Mr. Adee added in a letter to Secretary Hay that he thought that he would get a decree regarding the opening of schools from the Turks within a few days and that then Admiral Cotton could sail away from Beirut with a clear conscience.²³ Secretary Hay also wrote the President saying:

> Leishman ought to be able to finish up our little chores with Turkey in a few days, and report that the fleet is no longer needed. I have had two long talks with the Turkish Minister and have told him that if he does not want our ships in Turkish waters, it is very easy to cause them to depart. The Sultan has only to keep his word with us, and settle the two or three matters which have dragged too long. Of course I was not brutal, I was very friendly and polite.²⁴

At this moment a division of opinion appeared among the President's advisers. Dr. Albert Shaw, editor of the *Review of Reviews,* and Mr. Oscar Straus were concerned lest some attempt might be made to drag us into the entanglements of the Eastern question and were urgent that the American squadron should be withdrawn. This would have, of course, defeated the very purpose of its arrival; nothing had as yet been done as to the settlement of affairs at Beirut and the departure of the fleet in response to Turkish demands, would have been regarded as a confession of weakness and neglect. Secretary Hay promptly diagnosed the situation and wrote the President:

> I have read Dr. Shaw's letter with great care, as also the letter and the telegrams which you sent me from Mr. Straus.
> I will try to see Mr. Moody before I leave, and go over the matter thoroughly with him, so that, when Cotton has given his views to the Navy Department and Leishman his to the State Department, Mr. Adee will be in a position to put the matter before you for final decision. Both sides of the question are strongly represented in letters to me and in the newspapers. Leishman thinks that the presence of the fleet there for a little while will be of great advantage to him in his negotiations. Dr. Shaw evidently thinks not. Of course I do not think it possible you will want to keep the fleet there any length of time, but it seems to me it is only fair to Leishman, now they are there, to give his judgment some weight in regard

to the business in which he is engaged. Beirut is not in the immediate sphere of disturbance, and, therefore, I pay less regard to the agitated entreaties of the Turkish Minister here, that the fleet shall be immediately ordered away. I intimated to him that it rested exclusively with the Sultan to show to the world that our relations were entirely friendly, by carrying out the promises that have hitherto been made, and the settlement of two or three matters, which while not of the first importance, have been dragging too long.[25]

To this view President Roosevelt gave his unqualified approval. As a last minute note Secretary Hay had written him on his return to New Hampshire:

I had my tickets in my pocket and my carriage was at the door, when that abject Turk wriggled and squirmed into my library and almost made me miss my train by his piteous pleading that we should recall the ships. He seemed to think their presence at Beirut encouraged the Christians of Syria to such an extent, that when a Turk tried to kill a few of them they would fight back. I told him with an energy made necessary by my hurry that he must not think they could fool with us indefinitely—that we must insist on our reasonable and moderate demands for things already promised, and that our ships would probably go or stay as the President thought our interests and dignity required; that the Sultan knew perfectly that we had no ulterior purposes, etc. I then told him I would communicate his prayer to you and ask a report from Leishman.[26]

With the news of the riot at Beirut the Turkish Minister again called on Mr. Adee who reported: "Chekib has just been in to assure me that all is lovely at Beirut. Only 11 were killed and 15 wounded, through mere misunderstanding due to inflammation of minds by erroneous rumors. I am tranquilly waiting." [27] Meanwhile the demands for the removal of the Governor of Beirut had succeeded and affairs seemed to quiet down. The Turks acceded to a variety of demands and the purpose of the visit of the squadron having been accomplished it was withdrawn in the end of October to the relief of the Turkish authorities.[28]

By January, 1904, conditions had again become bad and this time the fleet was ordered to Smyrna. On this occasion, however, the presence of the fleet was used as an excuse by the Turks to hinder negotiations. It was consequently withdrawn on February 1. Mr. Leishman had reported the situation as disappointing. He said:

> The most bitter and determined opposition has been encountered against the granting of equal privileges to American schools on the ground that they are hot-beds of sedition, and this idea has been fostered and stimulated by foreign intrigue and encouraged somewhat by the very impolitic actions of some of the missionaries.
>
> I can see no signs of an immediate settlement and have no confidence in the daily promises which are broken with as little compunction as they are lightly made, and I am continually batted like a shuttle-cock between an irresponsible Porte and an invisible Sultan.
>
> No stone has been left unturned in my efforts to secure a peaceable adjustment of the schools question, but I fear that it will be next to impossible to obtain a proper settlement without resorting to more forcible measures, as the Imperial Ottoman Government continues to act in a manner that warrants the belief that it considers itself able to commit a flagrant violation of its treaty obligations with impunity, and is resting easy under the impression that the presence of the squadron need cause no particular uneasiness, having been informed by the Turkish Minister in Washington that its real influence cannot be exerted without express authority of Congress; and as long as this impression lasts the presence of the squadron is more of a hindrance than an assistance in securing a peaceful settlement.[29]

In April he reported officially that the same condition of affairs still existed, that our treaty rights were ignored, and that other countries could secure privileges denied to Americans.[30] On the other hand the complaints of the Sultan with respect to revolutionary activities in America also began to appear. The delays of the Sultan and of the Turkish authorities finally became intolerable and the fleet was again ordered to Smyrna in early August. As the result the Turks gave way. Possibly this was to the regret of Mr. Leishman who had expected that he would depart on one of the men-of-war and then return with a grand gesture as Ambassador, which was his present chief ambition. The agreement of the Turkish authorities to treat American institutions as they did those under French protection prevented this; and Mr. Leishman was instructed to assume that the schools were now officially recognized.[31] He had transmitted the Turkish reply, which was regarded at Washington as satisfactory. This read, with the Minister's comment, as follows:

The Minister of the United States has laid before His Imperial Majesty a memorandum in which he sets forth that a discrimination in privileges granted to foreign schools is made against American schools. His Imperial Majesty has answered that there should be no distinction between American schools and those of other nationalities, and that in order to secure the recognition of schools, resort must be had to the legal procedure.

In regard to the Embassy question, the financial conditions of the Government do not at present permit of raising the Ottoman Legation at Washington to the rank of an Embassy, and His Majesty reserves to himself the matter of bringing up this question as soon as this fiscal situation will permit. . . .

If the foregoing statement concerning the schools should be unsatisfactory to the United States, the Imperial Ottoman Government is ready to submit the question to arbitration.

The reply regarding the schools is rather ambiguous and misleading, as the conversation clearly developed the fact that the Sublime Porte wished to treat all American institutions not in possession of local permits as non-existing, which would have to apply for recognition in the same manner provided in French settlement for entirely new schools. This would interfere with a great number of our institutions which have been in existence for many years on sufferance, and is contrary to my understanding of the manner in which similar institutions in the French list were treated at the time of Mytilene agreement.[32]

However disappointed Mr. Leishman may have been at his failure to secure the elevation of his position to an Ambassadorship the fact was that the school question had been somewhat advanced. Now another complaint came to the front. This related to the sale of Bibles. The colporteurs, or native agents engaged in their distribution, were frequently arrested in violation of agreements of long standing with the Turkish authorities. The protests of both American and British were, however, finally successful in persuading the Turks at least to mitigate their action in this respect.[33] In 1906 the long delays in securing the decrees necessary to permit the construction of new mission buildings was also a cause of complaint as were the discriminations against American institutions as to customs duties levied on goods imported for their use. In each of these matters the United States merely asked for the same treatment accorded to other nations.[34]

In July of this year Mr. Leishman's desire was at last granted and he was made Ambassador. Much was expected of this change for it gave him personal access to the Sultan in whose hands power had been concentrated. The Porte and the Foreign Office had become places where only minor affairs could be handled for in the closing years of the reign of Abdul Hamid he and his private secretaries were the real directors of public policy. This policy now bore more and more harshly on Turk as well as on Christian. Complaints regarding the condition of the Armenians were particularly bitter. To a petition in their behalf Secretary Root defined the rôle and status of the United States. He pointed out that the signatories of the treaty of Berlin had a special right and position in the matter and that the United States as an American state was not a party to that treaty. Arbitration did not meet the situation nor was there opportunity at The Hague unless one of the European states should introduce it as a political question. He concluded by expressing the greatest sympathy with the Armenians but declared that the United States could do nothing short of intervention. He said:

> ... in equal sincerity I am convinced that efforts on our part short of rightful and potential intervention could accomplish nothing, and, implying, as they necessarily would, unstinted reprobation of the acts and motives of another state, would do more harm than good to the unfortunate creatures whom it is aimed to benefit. As for moral persuasion being brought to bear, that implies a susceptibility to persuasive influences which is hardly to be presumed in the present instance.[35]

The situation was much as in 1904 when Secretary Hay wrote the President on a similar question saying:

> We can neither undertake to reform Turkey and Persia, nor can we enter into the reasons *why* it is impossible. To the professional philanthropist there seems no flaw in the logic of the question they always ask. "You admit that it is wrong—why will you not at least try to set it right?"[36]

The fact was that America strained her diplomacy to the utmost in taking care as best she could of the interests of the missionaries. The United States had long had a dispute with Turkey regarding a section in the general treaty which affected the rights of our citizens in judicial processes. The difference between the Turkish text of this treaty and its English translation had provoked much discussion. Now to propose that the United States should intervene in the domestic affairs of the Ottoman Empire was to suppose that her interests in Turkey were political. This, of course, was not so and consequently, however much American moral sympathy might be aroused against the Turk, we avoided political entanglements of every sort in the Eastern Question.

NOTES TO CHAPTER XVII

1. I have had the advantage of reading in connection with this chapter a Ph. D. thesis (Clark University, 1924) by L. Lucile Morse on "Relations between the United States and the Ottoman Empire."
2. Quoted by Morse, pp. 65-66.
3. *F. R.*, 1895, p. 1416.
4. *O. C.*, Sept. 28, 1896, Olney to Chamberlain; *F. R.*, 1896, pp. 848-938; *O. C.*, Nov. 20, 1895, Olney to Chamberlain; *D. S.*, from Turkey, Vol. 61, No. 770, Jan. 14, 1896, Terrell to Olney; Vol. 63, No. 1000, Sept. 28, same to same, on the danger of another massacre at Constantinople.
5. *F. R.*, 1896, p. xxix.
6. Straus, *Under Four Administrations*, Boston, 1922, pp. 139-142; *F. R.*, 1898, pp. 1097-1101; *Ibid.*, 1899, pp. 765-775; *Ibid.*, 1900, pp. 906-919, 938-946; *D. S.*, To Turkey, Vol. 7, telegram, p. 368, Aug. 15, 1899, Adee to Straus; From Turkey, Vol. 69, telegram, Oct. 7, 1899, Straus to Hay; To Turkey, Vol. 7, telegram, p. 379, Oct. 13, Adee to Straus; From Turkey, Vol. 69, unnumbered, June 25, 1900, Griscom to Hay—this contains the following passage:

". . . it is a private instruction from the Sultan to the Minister for Foreign Affairs informing the latter that it has been decided to purchase a cruiser from a private firm in America and to include the £T. 20,000 claimed as indemnity by American citizens in the purchase money and so dispose of the difficulties with the Americans.

"Of course this action of the Minister was entirely informal and confidential, but it appears to me to be the only convincing indication I have yet received that the Sultan intends to pay the indemnities. The Minister's action was absolutely spontaneous and he was unmistakably laboring under considerable excitement. He informed me that he was keeping this *Irade* in order to protect himself and he hoped to be able to use it as an authority to give the Legation an official answer."

Cf. Appendix A to this chapter; To Turkey, Vol. 7, telegram, p. 461, Aug. 17, 1900, Adee to Griscom; Numerical File, Vol. 575, Aug. 20, 1900, Cramp to Adee; *H. P.*, Sept. 7, 1900, Cramp to Hay; Aug. 14, Griscom to Hay.
7. *H. P.*, Sept. 10 [1900], Hay to Adee.

8. *H. P.,* Dec. 27, 1900, Griscom to Hay; *F. R.,* 1901, pp. 514-515.
9. *H. P.,* Oct. 7, 1901, Adee to Hay; *F. R.,* 1902, pp. 997-1011; *H. P.,* Oct. 5, telegram and letter, Adee to Hay, saying:

" . . . Judson Smith and President Capen of the A. B. C. F. M. [American Board of Commissioners for Foreign Missions] came this morning. I found their minds virgin soil on all matters of fact, law and history of brigandage. They believed the demand for ransom is a bluff. They got scared at the real state of things. They were appalled at the intricacies of the international questions involved. They seemed pretty considerably sot back by the independent appeal of the Stone family and friends, and the sot-backness increased when I told him that Klotz of the Christian Herald was going to canvass New York today. They hurried back to Boston, after a long talk with the President (in the course of which they got some rather hard knocks) surprised at all we had done and are doing and grateful for it. They are to have a meeting of the Board tomorrow to reconsider the matter. It would not at all astonish me if they should cable the whole sum to Peet on Monday, so as to head off the Boston and New York appeals for charitable contributions."

10. *D. S.,* To Turkey, Vol. 7, telegrams, Oct. 22, 1901, Hill to Eddy; Oct. 24, 25, 28, 31, Nov. 2, 5, 6, 8, 9 and 23, Hay to Eddy.
11. Appendix B to this chapter.
12. *F. R.,* 1902, pp. 1011-1023; *D. S.,* From Turkey, Vol. 70, telegram, Nov. 26, 1901, Eddy to Hay; To Turkey, Vol. 7, telegrams, Dec. 16, and 17, Hay to Eddy; telegram, Jan. 2, 1902, Hill to Leishman; No. 91, Jan. 7, Hay to Leishman.
13. *D. S.,* From Turkey, Vol. 71, No. 134, Feb. 6, 1902, Leishman to Hay; telegram, Feb. 25, same to same.
14. *D. S.,* To Turkey, Vol. 7, No. 124, March 4, 1902, Hay to Leishman.
15. *D. S.,* To Turkey, Vol. 8, No. 218, Aug. 19, 1902, Adee to Leishman; No. 246, Sept. 26, Adee to Eddy; From Turkey, Vol. 72, No. 269, Sept. 6, Leishman to Hay.
16. Private conversations and Washburn, *Fifty Years in Constantinople,* Boston, 1909, pp. 277-278. One of the elements in the situation was the fact that it was necessary to deceive the Turkish authorities as to the fact of payment and as to the occasion. It is probable that the money was used by the revolutionists in Macedonia to purchase arms with which to fight the Turks in the summer of 1902.
17. *H. P.,* Aug. 12, 1902, Adee to Hay; Aug. 15, same to same, adds the following:

" . . . I am very much afraid that Mr. Leishman is in the unfortunate condition of a man with a grievance and that perhaps the best thing we can do is to rather encourage him in going away and leaving Eddy in charge for a time, but under circumstances which will not amount to a complete rupture. From what I remember of Tewfik Pasha, I should say that he was a hard man for Leishman to get along with and from what I hear the Grand Vizier is older and more cross-grained. Eddy can probably manage somewhat better by bringing his sublime imperturbability to bear."

Cf. *F. R.,* 1902, pp. 1044-1048; *D. S.,* To Turkey, Vol. 8, telegram, p. 46, Aug. 14, 1902, Adee to Leishman.

18. *D. S.,* From Turkey, Vol. 72, telegram, Sept. 27, 1902, Eddy to Hay; To Turkey, Vol. 8, telegram, p. 63, Oct. 13, Hay to Eddy; *H. P.,* Sept. 29, Adee to Hay; Straus, pp. 143-147.
19. *D. S.,* From Turkey, Vol. 72, No. 301, Nov. 1, 1902, Eddy to Hay; Unnumbered, Nov. 6, Leishman to Hay; telegram, Nov. 15, Eddy to Hay; Vol. 73, telegram, Feb. 8, 1903, Leishman to Hay; telegram, March 26,

same to same; To Turkey, Vol. 8, No. 207, Aug. 4, 1902, Adee to Leishman; Cf. *F. R.*, 1903, pp. 735-758; *H. P.*, July 2, 1903, Coolidge to Hay; Feb. 7, telegram, Hay to Leishman, which read as follows:

"You bear a friendly message from the President to the Sultan. Its delivery should not be unnecessarily delayed. Cannot audience be arranged, without appearing to over-ride Minister for Foreign Affairs, but rather in furtherance of your negotiation with him?"

20. *H. P.*, Aug. 1, 1903, Adee to Hay; Aug. 5, Adee to Hay reads as follows:

"On receipt of your letter to Mr. Loomis I cooked up this telegram to Leishman:

"'Extreme action not deemed advisable at present. You have already accomplished much. Continue to press for settlement of remaining matters, making some one school license a test case.'

"Mr. Loomis signed and sent it.

"What a whoop the Sultan would give if Leishman should suspend relations. This would give them a breathing spell while our shop was closed, tranquilly relying on the Six Powers to see that we had no chance to pass the Dardanelles and blow him sky-high, —— and Leishman do not seem to comprehend that we are helpless to take any material action against Turkey."

21. *F. R.*, 1903, pp. 762-776; To Turkey, Vol. 8, telegrams, p. 217, Aug. 27 and 28, Loomis to Leishman.

22. *D. S.*, Numerical File, Vol. 547, memorandum, Aug. 31, 1903; From Turkey, Vol. 74, No. 547, Sept. 2, Leishman to Hay.

23. *H. P.*, Sept. 2, 1903, Adee to Hay.

24. *H. P.*, Sept. 3, 1903, Hay to Roosevelt.

25. *H. P.*, Sept. 7, 1903, Hay to Roosevelt; *R. P.*, Sept. 4, 1903, Roosevelt to Shaw.

26. *R. P.*, Sept. 10, 1903, Hay to Rocsevelt; *H. P.*, Sept. 11, 1903, Roosevelt to Hay, saying:

"Under the circumstances it was out of the question for us not to send our squadron to Beirut, and out of the question for us to withdraw it afterwards, unless we are given the satisfaction that should be given. You have done your part, and there was nothing whatever for you to do if you had remained in Washington."

27. *H. P.*, Sept. 11, 1903, Adee to Hay.

28. *F. R.*, 1903, pp. 777-787; *D. S.*, From Turkey, Vol. 74, telegrams, Sept. 5, 7, 10, 16, 1903, Leishman to Hay; *R. P.*, Sept. 8, 1903, Hay to Roosevelt; *H. P.*, Sept. 9, 10, 11, 14, 17, 18, 21 and 28, 1903 (each with an enclosure) Adee to Hay; Sept. 14, Hay to Adee.

29. *H. P.*, Dec. 31, 1903, Leishman to Hay.

30. *F. R.*, 1904, p. 819.

31. *Ibid.*, 1904, pp. 820-833; *D. S.*, From Turkey, Vol. 74, No. 592, Oct. 5, 1903, Leishman to Hay; Vol. 75, No. 652, Dec. 10, same to same; telegram, Jan. 24, 1904, same to same; telegram, April 28, same to same; *H. P.*, June 7, 1904, Leishman to Hay; Aug. 8 and 9, telegrams, same to same.

32. *D. S.*, From Turkey, Vol. 75, telegram, Aug. 12, 1904, Leishman to Hay; No. 870, Aug. 15, same to same; *H. P.*, Aug. 22, Hay to Adee; Sept. 1, 1904, Leishman to Hay.

33. *F. R.*, 1905, pp. 898-911.

34. *Ibid.*, 1906, pp. 1372-1395.

35. *Ibid.*, p. 1418.

36. *H. P.*, July 22, 1904, Hay to Roosevelt.

APPENDICES TO CHAPTER XVII

A

Hay Papers, Griscom to Hay, Constantinople, July 10, 1900.

... The situation here at present seems to require more patience than anything else. Admiral Achmet Pasha is expected here this week and his return is the Turk's present excuse for procrastination. The Palace promises that soon after he arrives the negotiations will assume a definite shape. The Porte says it cannot give me a definite answer until it has his report. Both assure me that the indemnities will be paid and that I need not worry. However I know that when he does get here there will be an indefinite discussion of the plans he brings. I am pursuing a nagging policy which wise men here tell me is sure to succeed in the end with Turks. We do not let the Palace or the Porte alone for three days running and the Sultan, his secretary, and the Foreign Minister are heartily sick of the "American question." Garguilo, whose thirty-two years of experience and high order of intelligence give his opinion weight says that he is firmly convinced that they mean to pay the claims. It is quite certain they will never officially admit any liability for the massacres. Rather than this the Sultan would prefer to have us take the money at the point of a pistol, which would not be so great a humiliation in the eyes of his subjects. There are some reasons for thinking that he would not be at all averse to this method of settling the difficulty.

I think that inside of two months we should know if the present diplomatic pressure, alone, will meet with success. After that, should matters take no more definite shape, I think they will not pay the claims short of an ultimatum and the presence of a war-ship in Turkish waters. I have watched with great attention the effect of the three severe notes already presented and on the whole it is disappointing. They do not believe we will carry matters to a serious pass and this belief is due largely to the exaggerated idea of the effect of the coming elections on the President's mind. I need not tell you who has originated this impression, but apparently it is the only word from Ferrough which they have chosen to believe. My colleagues here tell me that Russia, also, is encouraging the Sultan to resist our claims thus carrying out its general policy of keeping Turkey in a turmoil. On the other hand the German Ambassador, "persona grata," has strongly counseled the Sultan to pay us and get the question off the boards. The Foreign Minister understands the situation and takes our representations very seriously. When I presented the last note his hand trembled so that he could not hold the note. I am really sorry for him. He tells me that he has done his best to convince the Palace people that we are in earnest, but meets with little success, and yet, as he says, in the event of a crisis being reached he is the one who will suffer.

D. S., Numerical File, Vol. 515, August 23, 1900, From Adee to Cramp (Strictly Confidential).

I have your letter of the 20th and am pleased with your accurate interpretation of my phrase "an attitude of discreet receptivity" on your part in regard to the negotiations for the building of a warship for the Ottoman navy.

In all my conversations with Mr. Hay on the subject it was distinctly understood that this Government could not take any part in introducing a collateral transaction or consideration into any contract you might make in a business way with the Porte through its contracting representative.

So far as I understand, the arrangement which Mr. Griscom's telegrams indicate has never taken shape this side of the water. The Turkish Minister professes to have no instructions whatever in regard to the settlement of our indemnity claims. On the contrary, he denies all liability on the part of his Government. Admiral Ahmed appears to be tongue-tied on the subject in his negotiations with you and we, of course, have nothing to do with him. If he should speak to you and you should report anything to me in a confidential way the case would be different, but as it is I see nothing save to continue your "attitude of discreet receptivity." You certainly cannot be expected to broach the subject. Permit me to congratulate you on the success of the Variag, it is noteworthy what we Americans can do when we try,—as Dr. Johnson says, "from Peking to Peru."

B

D. S., From Turkey, Vol. 70, No. 107, November 26, 1901, Eddy to Hay.

. . . It must be borne in mind, however, that the Ottoman Government is simply the will of Abdul Hamid II. The Grand

Vizier, who formerly was a man of great power and influence, is now merely a figure which represents an older and more liberal government. The present Sultan no longer issues his wishes to the heads of the different departments of the Porte or to the important State Officials. All such communications are sent directly from His Majesty to the persons concerned. No matter seems to be too small for the Imperial notice; even the arrest and trial of unimportant persons are brought to his attention—what I have been able to gather from all sources and from my personal contact with His Majesty would tend to show that he is (contrary to the generally accepted belief), a man of temperate and moderate character; one who would be influenced to a very great extent by personal prejudices and personal affection. He has great executive ability and great power of concentration, but his views and almost his entire knowledge of the world are bounded by the four walls of Ildiz Kiosk. In his character he is a Turk of the Turks—and it seems as though in dealing with him, France should have used methods which are the reverse of coercive. More could possibly have been done, with much less trouble, by considering the personal character of the Sultan, and by treating him personally with courtesy, tact and consideration. For it can be stated as a fact that Abdul Hamid II will do more from personal motives of affection and esteem for the representative of a Great Power, than he will for the united voice of the people who are represented. It is to be regretted that this is so—but it is a certainty which must be faced and taken as an existing fact which can not for the present be altered.

CHAPTER XVIII

ARBITRATION AND THE HAGUE CONFERENCES

OUT of the dispute with Great Britain in 1895-1896 relating to the Venezuela boundary there had come a significant movement for the settling of international differences by arbitration. That movement had gained during the decade, though the Senate for purely political and local reasons had failed to approve the Anglo-American arbitration treaty which had been negotiated in 1897 by Secretary Olney and Sir Julian Pauncefote. In 1899 the Tsar had called the First Hague Peace Conference. In 1902 the United States and Mexico had submitted to arbitration their dispute as to the "Pious Fund of the Californias," and in the same year the subject of arbitration was discussed at the Second International Conference of American States held at the City of Mexico. In 1902 also the whaling and sealing claims of the United States against Russia went to arbitration at The Hague.

In 1903 the claims of several states against Venezuela had finally been referred to the Tribunal at The Hague for settlement. The initial movement, which led to the Anglo-French *entente cordiale,* grew out of the Anglo-French arbitration treaty which was signed in 1903; and in 1904 a similar agitation in favor of international arbitration began to make headway in the United States. In 1904 the United States took the initiative in proposals for a second peace conference at The Hague. Owing to the Russo-Japanese War this invitation was postponed for a time. In 1905 the general form of arbitration treaties which the United States was negotiating with various states was so amended by the Senate that both President Roosevelt and Secretary Hay abandoned their efforts to secure approval. In 1906 Russia and Holland took up the proposal for a second peace conference which was finally held in 1907. Meantime there was considerable private discussion as to the program for that meeting. Such was the record.

On the whole, therefore, the United States had little to its credit in positive advance as to arbitration owing to the attitude of the Senate; but in a more general way the cause of arbitration had been greatly promoted by American recourse to judicial settlement rather than to war and by the endeavors of the Executive to assist in such solutions of international disputes. With such a brief and general survey of the field we now turn to consider more exactly the ideas which lay at the basis of such a movement for peace. We must see why, in large part, they failed. This view, however, does not include the details of the negotiations, for that would lead us too far; rather I wish to point out a few salient features so that we can appraise the situation on the eve of the Second Hague Peace Conference in 1907.

In March, 1896, Lord Salisbury proposed that an arbitration treaty between Great Britain and the United States might be negotiated. He referred to earlier American suggestions to this end and remarked that the United States wished to go further than Great Britain in providing for arbitration of disputes which did not involve national honor or integrity. Continuing, he pointed out:

that a system of arbitration is an entirely novel arrangement, and, therefore, the conditions under which it should be adopted are not likely to be ascertained antecedently. The limits ultimately adopted must be determined by experiment. In the interests of the idea, and of the pacific results which are expected from it, it would be wise to commence with a modest beginning, and not to hazard the success of the principle by adventuring it upon doubtful ground.[1]

The two states thereupon exchanged drafts of such a treaty. In the negotiations which ensued it was made plain by Secretary Olney that the settlement of the Venezuelan boundary dispute was not to be included in this Anglo-American arbitration treaty but that the United States was eager even for such moderate arrangements as might be welcomed by Great Britain. Lord Salisbury did not propose universal arbitration but a general plan for specific sorts of cases which should be arbitrated. He planned a court of six members, three on a side, whose verdict in order to be final should be five to one. This meant that the majority of the judges, even on the losing side, must be convinced of the justice of the verdict.[2] Secretary Olney, on the other hand, argued that the presumption was in favor of arbitration and he proposed that all cases, except those involving national honor or integrity, should be submitted to arbitration unless Congress or Parliament should specifically except them. He favored arbitration which would involve "territorial rights, boundaries, sovereignty or jurisdiction" or financial claims. He insisted on a final award by a majority of the judges with opportunity, in case of a protest, for review by a tribunal which might include jurists of a country not involved in the dispute.[3]

In reply Lord Salisbury said that obligatory arbitration was as yet untested. The danger that many claims, which had hitherto not been brought forward, might now be pressed was a serious one. So looking at the matter from the point of view of the British Empire with its diverse interests and variety of territory Lord Salisbury hesitated to accept the more than generous proposals of the United States. Secretary Olney, however, was insistent that arbitration should be of itself "automatic."[4] The result was the signature of a treaty on January 11, 1897, which provided generally that "pecuniary claims" and "all other matters in difference, in respect of which either of the high contracting parties shall have rights against the other under the treaty or otherwise" should be submitted to arbitration with the special exception of territorial claims. Such claims might be submitted to arbitration; but a final award required a majority of five to one. Provision was also made that in the case of a territorial claim the mediation of a third state should be sought before recourse to war. In case any other claim should be found to involve a "principle of grave general importance" which affected "national rights" it should be treated as a territorial claim. As Mr. James says:

> Thus Olney succeeded in embodying in the treaty his idea that arbitration must be automatic and must not depend upon a special vote or agreement in each instance; and he had carried as far as he could the principle that arbitration must be final.[5]

This treaty President Cleveland and later President McKinley strongly urged upon the Senate for approval; but on May 5, 1897, it did not secure the necessary two-thirds majority and consequently failed. It was a sharp disappointment not only to the British and to Secretary Olney but to President McKinley and his friends. The American view had been throughout that of "nothing venture, nothing have." Later views regarding arbitration show that opinion was not ready at that time to go as far as Secretary Olney was anxious to go. His treaty was "a novel departure in international affairs and very broad." Its defeat was, as he said "a calamity, not merely of national but of world wide proportions."

As time went on the Spanish-American War and the Boer War did not present any opportunities for arbitration nor naturally did the Chinese troubles of 1900 or the insurrection in the Philippines. But in 1899 there came from Russia a call to a general international conference at The Hague for the promotion of peace and of plans for the limitation of armaments. The specific program for discussion laid down by the Russian Foreign Office included the following list:

> 1. An understanding stipulating the non-augmentation, for a term to be agreed upon, of the present effective armed land and sea forces, as well as the war budgets pertaining to them; preliminary study of the ways in which even a reduction of the aforesaid effectives and budgets could be realized in the future.
> 2. Interdiction of the employment in armies and fleets of new firearms of every description and of new explosives, as well as powder more powerful than the kinds used at present, both for guns and cannons.

3. Limitation of the use in field fighting of explosives of a formidable power, such as now in use, and prohibition of the discharge of any kind of projectiles or explosives from balloons or by similar means.

4. Prohibition of the use in naval battles of submarine or diving torpedo boats, or of other engines of destruction of the same nature; agreement not to construct in the future warships armed with rams.

5. Adaptation to naval war of the stipulation of the Geneva convention of 1864, on the base of the additional articles of 1868.

6. Neutralization, for the same reason, of boats or launches employed in the rescue of the shipwrecked during or after naval battles.

7. Revision of the declaration concerning the laws and customs of war elaborated in 1874 by the conference of Brussels, and not yet ratified.

8. Acceptance, in principle, of the use of good offices, mediation, and voluntary arbitration, in cases where they are available, with the purpose of preventing armed conflicts between nations; understanding in relation to their mode of application and establishment of a uniform practice in employing them.[7]

The United States in the instructions given to her delegates by Secretary Hay stated that she regarded Article I of the program as inapplicable to her; Articles II, III and IV seem to be lacking in practicability and the delegates were "enjoined not to give the weight of their influence to the promotion of projects the realization of which is so uncertain." Articles V, VI and VII should meet with the earnest support of the American representatives. Article VIII dealing with arbitration should provide a most fruitful field of endeavor. They were instructed to press for the establishment of an international court of justice and further to advocate the exemption of private property from destruction or capture on the sea as well as on land contraband of war excepted.[8]

The spirit in which many of the delegates attended this unique meeting ranged from cynical skepticism to enthusiastic devotion. Some, like Ambassador White, were really never to recover their capacity to discuss international problems without long exegesis of what the Hague Conference stood for and what it had accomplished. Others like Count Munster were doubtful from the first. Thus a letter to Mr. Whitelaw

Reid shows the German point of view as regards the Conference:

> The Emperor has appointed me to represent the German Empire at that conference, and so I am sorry to see that I do not find your name. I could not refuse and have to obey orders, although I think it a difficult and ungrateful task. Beating empty straw is always a tiresome job, which may even be dangerous if it is, like in this case, Russian straw, that may conceal an apple of contention. As to disarmament, it is out of the question and it is ridiculous to have proposed it at this moment. The only important question to discuss would be arbitration and to come to an understanding on that point is, I fear, rather hopeless. We may agree about some points of international law and some new regulation of the Red Cross. We can, in regard to Russia, not allow the conference to end with an entire fiasco and must try to cover it with a peaceful looking cloak.[9]

Speaking generally the United States contributed directly to the organization of a panel or bench of jurists from whom at any given time a court could be constituted to consider any case that might be brought before it. The "plan for the pacific settlement of international disputes" contained the germ of a possibly satisfactory system, but anything like compulsory arbitration was at once ruled out. Likewise the American plan for the exemption of private property at sea was objected to and was referred to a future conference. As regards "special mediation" an American proposal was adopted which stated that:

> The Signatory Powers are agreed in recommending the application, when circumstances allow, of special mediation in the following form:
> In case of a serious difference endangering the peace, the States at variance choose respectively a Power, to whom they entrust the mission of entering into direct communication with the Power chosen on the other side, with the object of preventing the rupture of pacific relations.
> For the period of this mandate, the term of which, unless otherwise stipulated, can not exceed thirty days, the States in conflict cease from all direct communication on the subject of the dispute, which is regarded as referred exclusively to the mediating Powers, who must use their best efforts to settle it.
> In case of a definite rupture of pacific relations, these Powers are

charged with the joint task of taking advantage of any opportunity to restore peace.[10]

The gain in the establishment of the Hague Tribunal was of course evident; and the provisions for international commissions of inquiry as well as for voluntary arbitration were good as far as they went. Indeed the great merit of this First Hague Conference was that it provoked discussion out of which public opinion might develop. As we read its preliminary *agenda* and recall the horrors of the recent World War we can well appreciate the momentous questions which were laid before it. On the whole the historical position of the United States was well maintained, for she said that she did not wish to intrude into essentially European questions; yet it was made plain that she favored a resort to the courts and to arbitration rather than a resort to arms for the settlement of justiciable disputes. After all so much of what was proposed was to be blown away by the guns of the World War that comparatively little remains of the great plans of 1899 and 1907. In their place new machinery for peace and fresh suggestions for adjustment now occupy the first place in our minds.

The outbreak of the Russo-Japanese War brought forth renewed private endeavors to promote arbitration. These, however, came to nothing as far as that war was concerned for neither party would admit even of mediation. Such discussion as took place regarding the promotion of peace turned in the main to the idea that the time had come for a second general international conference. At the time the United States proposed to negotiate with France, Great Britain, and other states a series of arbitration treaties. We took as our model the recent Anglo-French arbitration treaty. This agreement signed at London, October 14, 1903, provided that, in view of Article XIX of the Hague convention of 1899, which permitted individual states to agree to refer to arbitration by the permanent court at The Hague any disputes in which they might be involved, Great Britain and France now agreed that:

Differences which may arise of a legal nature, or relating to the interpretation of treaties existing between the two Contracting Parties, and which it may not have been possible to settle by diplomacy, shall be referred to the Permanent Court of Arbitration established at The Hague by the Convention of the 29th July, 1899, provided, nevertheless, that they do not affect the vital interests, the independence, or the honor of the two Contracting States, and do not concern the interests of third Parties.

In each individual case the High Contracting Parties, before appealing to the Permanent Court of Arbitration, shall conclude a special agreement defining clearly the matter in dispute, the scope of the powers of the Arbitrators, and the periods to be fixed for the formation of the Arbitral Tribunal and the several stages of the procedure.[11]

With the addition of a clause providing for the approval of the treaty by and with the advice and consent of the Senate this was the form adopted by the United States. By the end of December, 1904, such treaties had been signed with France, Germany, Portugal and Switzerland; treaties had been agreed to with Great Britain, Italy and Mexico; and negotiations had begun with Austria-Hungary, Russia, Japan, Belgium, the Netherlands, Spain, and Denmark. This impressive list of treaties was now imperilled by the proposal of the Senate that amendments should in each case be made to the treaty. The Senate now planned to say that in case any matter were to be admitted to arbitration under this form that a separate and additional treaty should then be negotiated and approved by the Senate before any given matter should go forward to arbitration. Such a proposal aroused the wrath of President Roosevelt who had heartily supported the negotiation of such general arbitration agreements. From a number of letters I quote from one to Senator Lodge, who was himself the proposer of the amendment and who had opposed the Olney-Pauncefote agreement in 1897. The President said:

> I think that this amendment makes the treaties shams, and my present impression is that we had better abandon the whole business rather than give the impression of trickiness and insincerity which would be produced by solemnly promulgating a sham. The amendment, in effect, is to make any one of these so-called arbitration

treaties solemnly enact that there shall be another arbitration treaty whenever the two governments decide that there shall be one. Of course it is mere nonsense to have a treaty which does nothing but say, what there is no power of enforcing, that whenever we choose there shall be another arbitration treaty. We could have these further special arbitration treaties in special cases whenever desired just exactly as well if there were no general arbitration treaty at all. Now, as far as I am concerned, I wish either to take part in something that means something or else not to have any part of it at all. During the campaign last summer I announced and Hay announced that we were negotiating these treaties with the various countries concerned. Our party speakers on the stump made a great deal of it, and I now believe that the people generally approve of what has been done. If they do not approve, and if their representatives object to providing the exceedingly small measure of arbitration which these treaties actually provide, then let them be beaten. But for Heaven's sake do not let us take part in a sham and be pretending to do something that we do not really do. If these arbitration treaties are ratified the President will be bound by the supreme law of the land not to submit to arbitration anything that is of vital concern to the honor or interest of the country. He could be impeached if he transgressed this law. The fear that he would transgress it is in my judgment utterly chimerical, and in any event has no greater warrant than the fear that he will in any other way violate the law of the land and run the risk of impeachment.

In any event, if there is this fear as to what the President will do, then the objection to all arbitration treaties is fundamental; and it is unpardonable, under such circumstances, ever to have undertaken to negotiate them or to have sanctioned such negotiation. In such case we must be relegated to making arbitration treaties on each separate subject that comes up; and if this is the fact, then a general arbitration treaty is nonsense and ought not to be gone into.[12]

The President in February, 1905, withdrew the treaties and notice was sent to all countries negotiating such agreements that the United States was not prepared to go on with them. The blow to the cause of arbitration was considerable; and this invasion by the Senate of the prerogative of the Executive was, to say the least, dangerous. Later, of course, Secretary Root agreed to the contention of the Senate and arbitration treaties were approved with a number of states.[13]

Meanwhile the President had decided to propose the meeting of a second peace conference. On October 21, 1904, a circular despatch was sent to our representatives abroad, accredited to states which had been represented at the first conference at The Hague in 1899, directing them to inquire as to how far these various governments were now prepared to join in another meeting of the same sort. This notice was prefaced by reference to the resolutions passed by the interparliamentary Union which had met at St. Louis in the previous September. These resolutions read as follows:

Whereas, enlightened public opinion and modern civilization alike demand that differences between nations should be adjudicated and settled in the same manner as disputes between individuals are adjudicated, namely, by the arbitration of courts in accordance with recognized principles of law, this conference requests the several governments of the world to send delegates to an international conference to be held at a time and place to be agreed upon by them for the purpose of considering:
1. The questions for the considerations of which the conference at The Hague expressed a wish that a future conference be called.
2. The negotiation of arbitration treaties between the nations represented at the conference to be convened.
3. The advisability of establishing an international congress to convene periodically for the discussion of international questions.
And this conference respectfully and cordially requests the President of the United States to invite all the nations to send representatives to such a congress.[14]

All the powers replied favorably with the exception of Russia who pleaded the war with Japan as an excuse. Japan agreed on condition that the conference should not take action relative to the existing war. Under the circumstances the conference was postponed till after the re-establishment of peace but the *agenda* was made the subject of private discussion.[15]

The first suggestion of Russia in 1906 was for a conference at The Hague in July of that year; but as that proved to be inconvenient it was postponed till 1907.[16] The question of limitation of armaments was foremost in the President's mind at this time. He notified Russia that the United States planned to bring up this matter at the Hague Conference and there was some correspondence with London on this subject. Sir Edward Grey promised British support in the matter. The President thereupon wrote to Mr. Andrew Carnegie, expecting that he would show the letter to Sir Edward Grey. He also wrote to Mr. Reid in London as follows:

> I enclose you a copy of a letter to Carnegie. As he speaks very freely with Grey, I think it just as well for you to see this letter and to tell Grey that you have seen it. I do not want this new Liberal Government, with which in many matters I have such hearty sympathy, to go to any maudlin extremes at the Hague Conference. It is eminently wise and proper that we should take real steps in advance toward the policy of minimizing the chances of war amongst civilized people, of multiplying the methods and chances of honorably avoiding war in the event of controversy; but we must not grow sentimental and commit some Jefferson-Bryan-like piece of idiotic folly such as would be entailed if the free people that have free governments put themselves at a hopeless disadvantage compared with military despotisms and military barbarisms. I should like to see the British navy kept at its present size but only on condition that the Continental and Japanese navies are not built up. I do not wish to see it relatively weaker to them than is now the case. As regards our own Navy, I believe in number of units it is now as large as it need be, and I should advocate merely the substitution of efficient for inefficient units. This would mean allowing for about one new battleship a year, and of course now and then for a cruiser, collier, or a few torpedo-boat destroyers.[17]

A part of the letter to Mr. Carnegie, already printed by Bishop, follows:

> In such matter as the Hague Conference business the violent extremists who favor the matter are to be dreaded almost or quite as much as the Bourbon reactionaries who are against us. This is as true of the cause of International peace as it is of the cause of economic equity between labor and capital at home. I do not know whether in the French Revolution I have most contempt and abhorrence for the Marat, Hebert, Robespierre, and Danton type of revolutionists, or for the aristocratic, bureaucratic, and despotic rulers of the old régime; for the former did no good in the Revolution,

but at the best simply nullified the good that others did and produced a reaction which re-enthroned despotism; while they made the name of liberty a word of shuddering horror for the time being.

I hope to see real progress made at the next Hague Conference. If it is possible in some way to bring about a stop, complete or partial, to the race in adding to armaments, I shall be glad; but I do not yet see my way clear as regards the details of such a plan. We must always remember that it would be a fatal thing for the great free peoples to reduce themselves to impotence and leave the despotisms and barbarians armed. It would be safe to do so if there were some system of international police; but there is now no such system.[18]

Such ideas and plans occupied much of the attention of the United States during the balance of 1906. Generally speaking the President was becoming more and more favorable to arbitration and to the peaceful settlement of international disputes; he even suggested the possibility of fixing a limit for the size of future battleships. His feeling toward Great Britain was also more friendly. The real conversion of the President to arbitration can be seen in a more marked way in a letter which he wrote to Admiral Mahan many years later:

I regard the British navy as probably the most potent instrumentality for peace in the world. I do not believe we should try to build a navy in rivalry to it but I do believe we should have the second navy in the world. Moreover I am prepared to say what fifty years ago I would not have said, I think the time has come when the United States and the British Empire can agree to a universal arbitration treaty. In other words I believe the time has come when we should say that under no circumstances shall there ever be a resort to war between the United States and the British Empire, and that no question can arise between them that cannot be settled in judicial fashion.[19]

Such progress has been made in the promotion of Anglo-American understanding on which the peace of the world now stands, that these words can, as Mr. Rhodes says, "be taken as his [Roosevelt's] legacy to his countrymen." But in 1906 the United States still had a long road to travel.

NOTES TO CHAPTER XVIII

1. *F. R.*, 1896, p. 222.
2. *Ibid.*, pp. 222-224.
3. *Ibid.*, pp. 224-228.
4. *Ibid.*, pp. 228-237.
5. James, *Olney*, p. 148; *F. R.*, 1896, pp. 238-240.
6. James, p. 150 and Appendix V; McElroy, II, pp. 242-245; Cf. Moore, VII, pp. 74-78; *Olney Papers*, Juiy 16 and 17, 1896, Olney to Cleveland; Rhodes, *McKinley and Roosevelt Administrations*, pp. 40-41.
7. *F. R.*, 1899, p. 511.
8. *Ibid.*, pp. 511-513.
9. Cortissoz, II, p. 258.
10. *F. R.*, 1899, pp. 523-524; Cf. the report of the American delegation, which consisted of Ambassador White, Dr. Seth Low, Minister Newel, Capt. Mahan, Capt. Crozier, with Mr. Hollis as Secretary, in *Ibid.*, pp. 513-547.
11. *F. R.*, 1904, p. 9.
12. *Roosevelt-Lodge Correspondence*, II, pp. 110-112.
13. *H. P.*, Feb. 14, 1905, Mead to Hay; Feb. 20, Trueblood to Hay; *D. S.*, To Austria, Vol. 5, circular, p. 126, Jan. 2, 1905. A valuable discussion of the constitutional and legal aspects of this action by the Senate is in an opinion by Mr. Magoon of the Isthmus Canal Commission and in a letter to Senator Lodge from Secretary Taft which are in the *Hay Papers*.
14. *F. R.*, 1904, pp. 10-11.
15. *D. S.*, From Russia, Vol. 62, telegrams, Nov. 16, 1904, Eddy to Hay; From Japan, Vol. 79, telegram, Dec. 8, 1904, Griscom to Hay; Numerical File, Vol. 547, memorandum, Nov. 28, 1904 (relating to the German reply); *F. R.*, 1904, pp. 13-14; Cf. *H. P.*, Dec. 3, 1904, Chirol to Hay.
16. *D. S.*, To London, Vol. 35, telegram, p. 286, April 6, 1905, Root to Reid; To France, Vol. 25, circular telegram, April 12, Root to McCormick.
17. Cortissoz, I, p. 343; *D. S.*, From London, Vol. 214, No. 231, July 26, 1906, Reid to Root; No. 232, Aug. 1, same to same.
18. Bishop, II, pp. 21-22.
19. Quoted in Rhodes, p. 260.

CHAPTER XIX

THE ALGECIRAS CONFERENCE

THIS chapter should be considered in connection with that on the Portsmouth treaty. The negotiations which led to the Algeciras Conference took place at the same time that the preliminaries of the Portsmouth meeting were occupying a prominent place. Furthermore, though the attention of the statesmen of three continents was centered on the Portsmouth negotiations, the diplomacy of Europe was also concerned in trying to find a way to peace through the international maze of the Moroccan question. We may well ask why such a topic as the Algeciras Conference, which temporarily adjusted affairs in Morocco, should find a place in American foreign policy. What new diplomatic adventure placed the United States in a position of strategic importance as regards a problem which was of significance chiefly to European affairs?

The answer will become clearer if we recall the situation which was responsible for the Moroccan problem as it presented itself to the world in 1905. Briefly the fact of the establishment of the *entente cordiale* between Great Britain and France in 1904 was the inciting element. The situation of Morocco had been unsatisfactory in time past, but it was the agreement of Great Britain and France to wipe the slate clean of their previous and varied disputes that brought Morocco to the front as a major question of world-wide importance. France now recognized the predominant interest of England in Egypt, and Great Britain in turn recognized French interests in Morocco. Thus at a stroke through the Anglo-French accord so established German policy suffered a shock.

Since the time of the British occupation of Egypt in 1882 German diplomacy had used Anglo-French rivalry as to Egypt as a tool to forward German interests. German support had been necessary to the development of British policies in Egypt, consequently German approval had to be secured by Great Britain at a price. Now with the ending of Anglo-French differences German support was no longer to be of such value to England. There had been a new deal and the trump had changed. British foreign policy which had been directed to an exaggerated degree by anxieties as to Egypt, was now to a great extent free from German influence. France in turn had taken a long preliminary step to the development of her African interests. Germany's "place in the sun" seemed to be shadowed by passing clouds and consequently the Kaiser and von Bülow looked about for support and naturally turned to the United States to try to use her in the Moroccan situation and if possible to drag her into the solution of a problem which was essentially of European origin. We shall now briefly survey this attempt; but throughout this chapter it is quite clear that we are at present concerned not with the larger problem of European diplomacy but chiefly with the American share in it.

Nevertheless it behooves us to take a bird's-eye view of German policy as to Morocco in 1904 for it will serve to explain the lines on which von Bülow developed his attempt to persuade President Roosevelt to assist German desires. German diplomacy in 1904 was in some confusion; there were cross currents which pulled and twisted till it is at times difficult to tell in which direction her policy was aimed. With this, of course, we have nothing to do in the present book. Yet it is evident that von Bülow and Holstein in Berlin were pulling strongly for a more active German policy in the Mediterranean and with respect to Morocco. They were supported by many other German diplomats. Against this the Kaiser was apparently all for caution and delay. The correspondence in *Grosse Politik* is full of this struggle. Every sort of argument was brought forward; and in the end von

Bülow won by securing the Kaiser's assent to an active German policy as to Morocco.[1]

In January, 1905, von Bülow inquired of von Kühlmann, German Chargé at Tangier, whether American economic interests in Morocco might not be affected by proposed reforms as to administration which were being urged by France at the time.[2] In February von Bülow telegraphed von Sternburg, German Ambassador in Washington, instructing him to sound President Roosevelt as to American interests in Morocco. He declared that Germany had no special ambitions in Morocco but aimed only to maintain the open door for all powers. He pointed out that it would be easy to hold France in check there if Germany and the United States acting separately should advise the Sultan that his proposed Convocation of Notables to discuss the French projects for reform was wise and likely to assure the maintenance of law and order in Morocco in which both Germany and America were much interested. This astute instruction had followed a report from von Sternburg that President Roosevelt was already apparently interested in Moroccan affairs and that for the first time he had shown distrust of France. This of course had pleased von Bülow who had replied by praising von Sternburg, saying that "the President is now convinced of the sincerity of German policy. We are in a position to justify this confidence." [3]

Baron von Sternburg had perhaps misinterpreted this interest for, shortly after this, he reported President Roosevelt as follows:

Tell his Majesty the Kaiser, that I value his communications highly. In my foreign policy, I am meeting with enormous difficulties in the Congress, for they understand foreign affairs there with difficulty. My Far Eastern policy is at last understood, and my cooperation there with Germany is approved everywhere. Two years ago this would have been absolutely inconceivable. But my policy in the Caribbean and in the southern hemisphere is still entirely incomprehensible to the people here, and the Congress is causing me the greatest difficulties in the conduct of this policy. Were I to get involved also with Morocco, a country that is entirely unknown here, I would expose myself to the most severe attacks. In the Perdicaris affair the life of an American citizen was at stake, and for this reason the intervention was not so risky. Were I to approve of the meeting of the Notables and encourage the Sultan to hopes, I would have to be prepared also for further steps. But, as a matter of principle, I never take a step in foreign policy unless I am assured that I shall be able eventually to carry out my will by force. I shall instruct my new Minister at Morocco to get into close touch with his German colleague.[4]

This conversation was in reply to a memorandum from the German Embassy which is printed in the Appendix to this chapter.[5] Immediately following these approaches von Bülow felt sufficiently assured of American support to press forward cautiously the idea of an international conference on Moroccan affairs. The coming visit of the Kaiser to Tangier was announced on March 23, 1905. This took place on March 31 and despite the contretemps of delays and of a violent "Levanter" blowing, which made the Kaiser loath to land, he did so, making his brief but significant speech to the Moroccan authorities.[6]

This speech referred to the Sultan of Morocco as an independent sovereign and expressed the hope that a free and open Morocco would continue; German interests were to be protected and the proposed reforms in Morocco should be dealt with cautiously. The intent, which was directed by the German Foreign Office, was that France should understand that she now had Germany to deal with.[7] To the Kaiser, von Bülow telegraphed that his speech at Tangier had placed the Moroccan question to the forefront and that Mr. Gummeré, American Minister at Tangier, on being informed that the Kaiser had supported the idea of the open door, was reported to have exclaimed: "That is just exactly what we also want." Further, von Bülow said that, secure of America's support, Germany should refuse separate economic concessions from the French and insist on an international conference on Morocco. He added:

... The most effective thing will be the realization on the part of the British that American diplomacy is also on the side of Germany's open door policy. The fear of Roosevelt is growing visibly in England; whether love, too, I don't know. . . .⁸

In response to urgent instructions from von Bülow, President Roosevelt also received from von Sternburg another communication on April 5. This sought to establish a connection between Morocco and the Far East. As I have already pointed out elsewhere Korea and Morocco, both weak states, were to pay the cost of imperialistic ambitions. Their sacrifice was to provide peace between Japan and Russia on the one hand and on the other to give to France a *quid pro quo* for the British position in Egypt.⁹ Of these matters, however, I cannot speak at present. Extracts from von Sternburg's message of April 5 are in the Appendix to this chapter.¹⁰

On April 13 the Kaiser again sent word through von Sternburg, reviewing the situation and urging the President to make American policy clear to Great Britain. This also is given in the Appendix.¹¹ Meanwhile in Tangier both von Kühlmann and Tattenbach, German Minister at Lisbon, had sought in various ways to make friends with Mr. Gummeré. He, however, was cautioned by the Department of State to say nothing but to listen well.¹² In Paris there had taken place the famous conversation between Delcassé and the German Ambassador who counselled that Germany should come to an understanding with France.¹³ In Colorado President Roosevelt sought to kill bears with one hand while with the other he wrote letters to von Sternburg and to Secretary Taft in Washington. It is by no means clear, however, that von Sternburg understood the definite way in which the President stated that America had practically no interests in Morocco. Particularly was the President insistent that as between France and Germany, America would not take sides.¹⁴

At all events immediately on his return to Washington President Roosevelt was again confronted with the lively mutual suspicions of Great Britain and Germany. He told von Sternburg (as reported in *Die Grosse Politik*):

I feel very indignant at the attitude of England in the Conference question, especially when there are voices to be heard in France favoring the Conference idea. It seems as if England in Morocco wants to dispose as it sees fit of the rights of others. I shall let the British Chargé [Townley] come here and tell him my opinion. My endeavors to bring about harmony between Germany and England in the Morocco question have met with but slight success. I have received on the British side the same old answer: "England cannot forget Germany's hostility during the Boer War." My reply was: "How is it that England has forgiven France, which pursued the same policy?" I have asked the recently departed British Ambassador [Durand] to emphasize it to the King and Lord Lansdowne that I emphatically wish to see an improvement in the relations between Germany and England. . . .[15]

He also received from von Sternburg another long memorandum on the Moroccan question. This was a curious jumble in which the Kaiser is portrayed as following a simple and direct policy in favor of the open door in Morocco; yet at the same time the old note is struck again of the danger to President Roosevelt's main plan to promote peace between Russia and Japan. This danger it was again asserted came from the alleged plans of England and France to partition China as the price of their intervention in the Far East. As to Morocco it was said that if America should pass the word to England that she was in favor of a settlement that did not fully meet the ideas of Delcassé the whole matter could be settled. It was, however, in this memorandum that Germany first used the word "war" in connection with Morocco.[16] On May 25 von Bülow telegraphed to von Sternburg that the entire question of an international conference on Morocco now rested with President Roosevelt. Whether this were true or not, even the alleged responsibility was a grave one, for if the conference did not take place war might well result.[17]

Then on May 31 there came a short but striking German memorandum the text of which is given in the Appendix. Here the Kaiser let President Roosevelt suppose that it was Germany's unwillingness to join the Dual Alliance, to come to terms with Russia and thus with France that was at the root of the difficulty. We know how bitterly the President felt toward Russia and we must also recall that within two months the treaty of Björkö was to be signed between Germany and Russia. The alleged choice for the Kaiser was an understanding between Germany, France and Russia, or war with France, or an international conference on Morocco. The decision as to whether or not there should be a conference rested with President Roosevelt. Thus we can get a glimpse into the minds of von Bülow and the Kaiser.[18]

It was only at this late day that the question of historical precedents came up. In 1880 there had been an international conference at Madrid relating to Morocco. In this the United States had had a small part and she had signed the convention which regulated the rights of foreigners in Morocco. This might have supplied a precedent for American action in 1905; but it does not seem to have been regarded as of enough importance. At all events the President ordered that a message should be sent to Mr. Reid in London. This read:

> The President has informed German Ambassador that he does not see how America could join in any conference regarding Morocco unless France acquiesced. The President has also told Jusserand of this but does not desire publicity given to the matter.[19]

At this moment, on June 6, 1905, Delcassé fell from power in France because of the opposition of his colleagues in the cabinet who feared lest his policy might mean war with Germany and who were otherwise unfriendly to him. The German comment was that with this event "the acute stage of the Morocco question is probably at an end."[20] But Great Britain had already opposed the idea of a conference to be called by the Sultan of Morocco. Now the matter was to come up again in different form because of a circular note from the German Government advocating the acceptance of the Moorish proposal.[21] This proposal France also considered a national humiliation at the hands of Germany.[22] Europe was not yet out of the woods.

At Washington President Roosevelt was reported by von Sternburg as being loath to accept the German view as to

American participation in a conference on Morocco. The Ambassador said on June 8:

> In a conversation concerning Morocco, the President told me he could hardly participate in a conference for the settlement of the Moroccan problem without exposing himself to the sharpest attacks both in political spheres and by public opinion. Since the Perdicaris affair people here believe that absolutely uncontrollable tribes are carrying on in the interior of Morocco, over whom the Sultan has no authority, and who will always constitute a menace to the foreign merchants. For this reason we find here some thinking people who would gladly see Morocco getting civilized by some foreign power in some such way as Egypt. I have been told that the French Ambassador here has also expressed himself in this sense. I stressed the point, in speaking to the President, that this would be a grave violation of all the rights of treaty powers, among which America likewise belongs. The treaty powers are mutually bound to see to it that the treaty is respected by everybody. To let France do as she pleases would create a dangerous precedent which would certainly react on the situation in the Far East. I left with the President a memorandum in which I gave a clear exposition of the legal aspect of the problem. He has promised me a definite answer.[23]

Three days later there came the special news and the special plea which were to influence President Roosevelt. This has been printed in Bishop so I quote only a short extract from the German instructions on which it was based. To von Sternburg von Bülow had written as follows:

> If England intends to support France in a war against Germany, it is, of course, not because of Morocco, but because of the East Asiatic question. . . . Should England and France succeed in the course of a war over Morocco in annihilating the German sea-power, England would have come much nearer to acquiring the Yangtse Basin than she is now, since an isolated America will hardly be in a position to prevent the partition of China. . . . It will be much easier for President Roosevelt to avert such a contingency either by promoting . . . a conference or, if this does not suit him, by preventing England from participating in a German-French war that may be provoked by the aggressive policies of France toward Morocco.
>
> The menace of the formation of a group opposed to the German and American interests is something we have been pointing out for some time past. A Moroccan war would hasten such an alignment.

It would also be favored by the circumstance that, under the terms of peace, Russia will hardly agree to pay an indemnity and to the cession of Sakhalin (as this is Russian territory). These two difficulties, however, might be eliminated at once if, after Germany has been crippled as a maritime power, there would be created a situation in which both Russia and Japan could be compensated at the expense of Chinese territory.[24]

The story, quoted by President Roosevelt, that England had offered an offensive and defensive alliance to France at this time is of course false. It has been repeatedly denied, yet on such a falsehood is based the main German argument to President Roosevelt that his intervention alone could save the world from war and Bishop reprints the story without even a footnote to indicate any doubt as to its authenticity.[25] Yet the German version and argument over the situation had a powerful influence over President Roosevelt, perhaps wisely so. In any case he promptly set to work to persuade Ambassador Jusserand that France should agree to a conference. This can best be told in his own words. Writing nearly a year later to Mr. Reid the President said:

I told him that as chief of state I could not let America do anything Quixotic, but that I had a real sentiment for France; that I would not advise her to do anything humiliating or disgraceful; but that it was eminently wise to avoid a war if it could be done by adopting a course which would save the Emperor's self-esteem; that for such purpose it was wise to help him save his face. I urged upon the French Government, in the first place, the great danger of war to them, and the fact that British assistance could avail them very, very little in the event of such a war, because France would be in danger of invasion by land; and in the next place I pointed out that if there were a Conference of the Powers France would have every reason to believe that the Conference would not sanction any unjust attack by Germany upon French interests, and that if all the Powers, or practically all the Powers, in the conference took an attitude favorable to France on such a point it would make it well nigh impossible for Germany to assail her. I explained that I would not accept the invitation of the Conference unless France was willing, and that if I went in I would treat both sides with absolute justice, and would, if necessary, take very strong grounds against any attitude of Germany which seemed to me unjust and unfair.[26]

The effect of the President's intervention as regards French diplomacy was immediately apparent to Germany. On June 18 von Sternburg wrote to him that his activity had been in the opinion of the Kaiser "the greatest blessing to the peace of the world" and much more to the same purpose.[27] We must also recall that these were the very days when the preliminaries of the Portsmouth conference were being settled and that all through these negotiations the President repeatedly expressed his appreciation of German support. Later in November, 1905, the Kaiser was to write through von Sternburg to the President and say:

Tell President Roosevelt that he can rest assured that from the very beginning I have not treated the Morocco question as an isolated rock, but as a portion of the extended and dangerous coral reef which we may designate as the Delcassé programme.[28]

What was this alleged program which seemed so dangerous? It represented very briefly the attempt by France through the *entente* with England, through treaties with Spain, and through an understanding with Italy to establish herself in a powerful position in northern Africa. The failure of Delcassé to provide for some form of compensation for Germany was the vital mistake that he made. His fall from office in early June left Rouvier, Prime Minister of France, to become Foreign Secretary. It was, therefore, to him that President Roosevelt's plea for agreement went through Ambassador Jusserand. The documents in this matter are printed in the long letter from President Roosevelt to Mr. Reid which is divided into two chapters of Bishop's *Life of Roosevelt*. They need not detain us here except for brief mention.

In response to the President's appeal to Jusserand which I have just mentioned the French reply was on the whole favorable. On June 25 there was a further answer and a definite acceptance by France of the plan for a conference to which she had hitherto objected.[29] Italy had also agreed to the conference "as a friend of France and with the intention of supporting French views."[30] This was despite the fact that she was a member of the Triple Alliance. So President Roosevelt's intervention was plainly a great success. It remained to deal with Germany.

At this point I wish to refer to a story which I heard in France in May, 1926. This was that there existed somewhere a letter from President Roosevelt to the Kaiser saying that it would be a crime against civilization for Germany to declare war against France. It is apparently to be traced to Thayer's *Life of Roosevelt*, written in 1919, at the time when Mr. Thayer was still subject to his anti-German feelings. I have searched in vain for a letter of this sort. There is none which makes use of such a phrase nor does Mr. Thayer give any fixed date for such a letter. I imagine, therefore, that he refers in picturesque but exaggerated language to the letter written by the President on June 26, 1905, to von Sternburg which was transmitted by telegraph to Berlin. This has since been printed, twice, in Bishop and in *Die Grosse Politik*. Portions of this letter, however, deserve quotation here as a brief statement of the case. The President wrote:

> I say with all possible emphasis that I regard this yielding by France, this concession by her which she had said she could not make and which she now has made, as representing a genuine triumph for the Emperor's diplomacy; so that if the result is now accepted it will be not merely honorable for Germany but a triumph. You know that I am not merely a sincere admirer and well-wisher of Germany, but also of His Majesty. I feel that he stands as the leader among sovereigns of today who have their faces set toward the future, and that it is not only of the utmost importance for his own people but of the utmost importance for all mankind that his power and leadership for good should be unimpaired. I feel that now, having obtained what he asks, it would be most unfortunate even to seem to raise questions about minor details, for if under such circumstances the dreadful calamity of war should happen, I fear that his high and honorable fame might be clouded. He has won a great triumph; he has obtained what his opponents in England and France said he never could obtain and what I myself did not believe he could obtain. The result is a striking tribute to him personally no less than to his nation, and I earnestly hope that he can see his way clear to accept it as the triumph it is.[31]

The final and official acceptance of the plan for the Algeciras Conference took place July 8 when France and Germany exchanged notes on the subject. The impression created in France was most favorable. As Senator Lodge reported from Paris: *"La conduite des États Unis é'tait épatante."* Indeed the real friendship which the President felt for France was to be demonstrated more than once before the whole matter was closed. There were various questions which came up from time to time in which the good offices of the United States were required. The *agenda* of the conference were as a matter of fact later adopted from a hastily pencilled memorandum which the President wrote in early July. On July 13, 1905, Great Britain agreed to the conference as did finally all the other European powers concerned. With the approach of the Portsmouth conference the President was more and more concerned over its fate and consequently there is less and less regarding the proposed conference at Algeciras in American official correspondence of the time.

As has been said the strictly European aspects of the Moroccan question do not at present concern us. Indeed President Roosevelt tried to make this plain by telegraphing on July 24 to von Sternburg, who was in Germany on leave, saying:

Will communicate with Jusserand, but am sure you will understand my great reluctance to interfere further. America has no interest in the matter and it has only been my strong feeling for the Emperor and my anxiety for peace that have enabled me hitherto to act as the Emperor has suggested.[32]

The particular stumbling block at the moment was the German belief that Delcassé's coterie in France was still in power and that they were pulling the wires with intent hostile to Germany. It was shown that this was not so and later the President telegraphed the Kaiser to that effect. In the meantime the United States formally accepted the invitation of Morocco to the international conference. Senator Lodge, who had just returned from Europe, was insistent that our delegate to the conference, whoever he might be, "must keep on the best terms with the German delegate, and yet when it comes to action support France to the extent of his power." [33]

On September 28, 1905, the formal agreement of France and Germany to submit the Moroccan question to a conference was signed. At the last it is possible that Count Witte, fresh from his success at Portsmouth, exerted some influence. He saw Radolin, the German Ambassador in Paris, and later the Kaiser in Germany and urged the acceptance of the terms proposed. Witte's own egotistical account of what happened we can scarcely accept.[34]

As the time approached for the conference, which was now definitely fixed for Algeciras, the anxiety and uncertainties of France came out more clearly. Both she and Great Britain were apprehensive of a German policy which might be too aggressive.[35] Some of these anxieties were shown to Sir Edward Grey as he took office as British Foreign Secretary on Dec. 11, 1905, at the resignation of Lord Lansdowne. The French on January 10, 1905, put a critical question to Great Britain. The French Ambassador, M. Paul Cambon, asked "whether, in the event of aggression against France by Germany Great Britain would be prepared to render to France armed assistance?" This very question serves once more to demonstrate the mistake which the Germans made six months earlier in asserting that Great Britain had offered to France an offensive and defensive alliance against Germany. If that had been true why should such a question be asked at this late day? Sir Edward Grey had no objection to military and naval conversations taking place between the two nations but he refused to pledge England to more than a benevolent neutrality in the event of war.[36]

After the general election of January, 1906, the question was repeated on January 31. In the meantime Sir Edward Grey had said to Count Metternich, the German Ambassador, that "in the event of an attack upon France by Germany arising out of our Morocco agreement, public feeling in England would be so strong that no British Government could remain neutral." It appears that British policy at this stage may be criticized, for in permitting the military and naval conversations to continue Great Britain came close to "an honorable understanding." In view of the situation would it not have been wiser either to give the undertaking asked for by France or to have refused permission to continue these unofficial yet direct conversations? [37]

The atmosphere of suspicion and of dread that filled the minds of European statesmen was not cleared. Indeed it increased. Already in early January Ambassador Meyer had telegraphed from Russia that:

French Government fears that German instructions may make rupture of the Conference inevitable. They are earnestly anxious that Czar should personally warn Emperor of Germany that Russian and French alliance is still in force, and beg as friend to friend, German Emperor not to precipitate crisis. Witte promised at once to send message to the Czar in this sense, and Count Lamsdorff this morning, January 9th, was with Russian Emperor. French Embassy quite aware that military aid of Russia cannot be depended upon. What they hope for is the creation of a moral atmosphere, making it impossible for the military part of Germany in extreme case to precipitate war. French Government fears Germany taking advantage of present condition in Russia. In the event of certain circumstances, the President of the United States of all persons, may have an opportunity to exercise moral influence with both France and Germany.[38]

In like manner Germany was intent on persuading the United States that her hands were clean and on the eve of the Conference von Sternburg once more asserted Germany's good intentions, saying:

We are not following special advantages in Morocco, but merely desire freedom and equality in our economical progress. The instructions which our delegates have received are as simple as they are clear. They are to uphold the principle of the open door and of equal treatment of all nations. They are further to try to procure absolutely equal rights in economic questions and to endeavor to prevent the establishment of a preponderating influence of any one power which would curtail the rights of another.[39]

One matter which was outside the *agenda* but which might come up in the course of discussion was the alleged desire of Germany to secure a coaling station at Mogador on the Atlantic coast of Morocco. Ambassador Reid, informed of this possibility and of the tension in the public mind in England, asked for instructions. Secretary Root wrote him that the policy of the United States remained unchanged:

Our interests are not sufficient to justify us in taking a leading part; and while, of course, we should be very glad to contribute towards keeping the peace, we do not wish to get into a position where we will be justly charged with intermeddling or to become a party to the controversy, and we have not yet considered that there was a situation in which any move by us would be practically useful.[40]

This of course was not exactly helpful as regards Mogador. It appears that Sir Edward Grey had already expressed the private opinion that possibly the whole Moroccan question might be settled or at least eased by the granting to Germany of such a port. At the time he was ignorant of the fact that in the previous year Lord Lansdowne had urged the French "on no account to concede a port in Morocco to Germany." The matter did not arise directly at Algeciras; but within a few weeks the story was put about, whether by Germans or others, that Great Britain was ready to abandon France and it was some days before the *entente* could once more be restored to an even keel. Such episodes were serious enough at the time and more than once the conference was nearly wrecked. The chief difficulty from which most of the trouble came was with respect to the policing of Casablanca.[41]

The American delegates were Mr. Henry White and Mr. Gummeré, who sent a joint message almost daily to Washington. In addition there are many confidential telegrams signed only by Mr. White. From these messages, from Washington information, and from private material it is possible to draw a fairly complete picture of the proceedings. However it is our concern only to touch on the major elements in the story and chiefly as they affected American interests. President Roosevelt soon became convinced that "Germany was aiming in effect at the partition of Morocco, which was the very reverse of what she was claiming to desire." [42] This was perhaps suggested by a memorandum submitted by the German Embassy on January 23, 1906. It dealt with the organization of police, protested against a mandate for France, and, for the policing of Morocco, favored the use of minor states such as Holland, Switzerland, Denmark, Norway or Sweden as the ones least likely to arouse jealousy.[43] In each case, however, German influence at home was to be predicated.

On January 28, as France began to give way in her original demand that all police should be under her direction, Germany became bolder and proposed that the Sultan of Morocco should select such officers as he saw fit, under international control as to funds, etc. This Germany wished the United States to advocate.[44] Mr. White, in reply to inquiries, pointed out the connection between police control and financial questions and advised delay.[45] On February 1 these financial matters came to the front and occupied the attention of the delegates for some time especially as the organization of the state bank was involved. The sessions on the bank were at times rather bitter; but neither France nor Germany wished to have the conference go on the rocks entirely on this financial issue so compromises were made and plans for the bank were accepted. American interests were not involved though American bankers were invited to subscribe.[46] Furthermore there was the minor point as to the protection of Jews in Morocco on which President Roosevelt had instructed Mr. White to take steps. Quite early it became apparent that any active intervention on behalf of the Jews by the United States would be misunderstood. So at the end of the conference Mr. White contented himself with the expression of the hope that all subjects of the Sultan of Morocco, including Jews, would be treated with justice and equity without distinction of creed.[47]

We now come to the major question of the police with respect to which President Roosevelt directed that American influence should be cast to prevent a break-up of the conference and he himself interfered to persuade the Kaiser to give way. The police question, as had been foreseen by publicists of the day, involved the real control over the chief ports of Morocco and, therefore, implied the regulation of foreign commerce and the maintenance of the open door. It is interesting to recall that Sir Edward Grey in a postscript to his chapter on these matters remembers a conversation he had with ex-President Roosevelt in 1910 regarding the Algeciras Conference and writes: "Roosevelt believed, and from what he told me had reason to believe, that the part he took influenced a peaceful solution. This should be on record and is of interest." [48]

In Algeciras, matters relating to the controversy over the police question had taken a turn for the worse. Mr. White telegraphed on February 5, 1906:

I believe France will allow the Conference to fail rather than recede from it [her position], which, I think, German colleague realizes. Upon his communicating to me the interview with Revoil and asking whether that is my opinion I replied in the affirmative. France claims that her interests with 70 million francs invested as against German's five too great to confide police to another Power; that to turn out her officers and instructors, for sometime past in Morocco, would be compromising to her national dignity, and to question good faith of guarantees she is willing to give regarding open door etc., is inadmissible imputation upon her honor.[49]

The French position was that the police should be turned over to her and to Spain. To this, Germany had objected, favoring either some of the smaller disinterested European states or desiring that the whole matter should be left to the Sultan of Morocco, who of course had come to look on the Kaiser as his one friend in Europe. This was to be seen in von Sternburg's memorandum for President Roosevelt of January 29. The dead-lock was further reflected in another despatch from Mr. White, who said:

... France asks and will accept no other principle for all the ports only and their vicinity—not the whole of Morocco as stated in German press—than police of which rank and file Moors to be paid and commanded by French and Spanish officers assisted by non-commissioned officers furnished by the native troops of two latter countries, under nominal authority of Moorish Government. ... I am, therefore, satisfied Conference is likely to fail unless Germany can be got to accept French position in principle. There are indications that realizing she cannot get Conference to support her views, Germany beginning to think better terms obtainable by direct negotiations with France. If so, she should admit it and stop Conference. It will be very undignified for us to continue several weeks more making regulations none of which will have validity without organized authority to enforce them.[50]

It was at this stage that the President interfered. He instructed Secretary Root to propose to the German Ambassador a possible compromise. This was, (1) that the organization of the police force should be left to the Sultan, (2) that the funds for its support should be supplied by the proposed international state bank, (3) that French and Spanish officers and non-commissioned men should be in charge reporting annually to the Sultan and to Italy as a third Mediterranean power, and that in the fourth place:

full assurances be given by France and Spain, and made obligatory upon all their officers who shall be appointed by the Sultan, for the open door, both as to trade, equal treatment and opportunity in competing for public works and concessions.[51]

On February 22, Germany replied accepting all points except the third. She expressed the most lively gratitude to the President for his mediation and proposed an alternative to point 3. This alternative would have left the Sultan free to choose the officers from among the states of Europe.[52] Already all over Europe there was anxiety and alarm at the turn affairs were taking at Algeciras. From Austrian, British, Russian, French, Italian, and neutral sources there came but one plea, namely that some solution should be found. At first the notion had been that the Kaiser was not properly informed; now the cry was that his *amour propre* had been offended and that he was taking too great a personal interest in the matter.[53]

So on March 7 a further letter was sent to von Sternburg by Secretary Root in which the President said to the Kaiser that he could not ask France to make any further concessions. He then reminded the Kaiser of what he had already done in the interests of peace and recalled the letter of the previous June, from the Kaiser, which stated that in case differences should threaten the proposed conference the Kaiser declared that "he, in every case, will be ready to back up the decision which you [Roosevelt] should consider to be the most fair and the most practicable." The President continued, saying that if Germany rejected the plan, proposed (by America), then:

> the general opinion of Europe and America would be unfavorable, and Germany would lose that increase of credit and moral power that the making of this arrangement would secure to her, and might be held responsible, probably far beyond the limits of reason, for all the evils that may come in the train of a disturbed condition of affairs in Europe.[54]

This was fairly plain speaking, or rather writing; but the Kaiser still hung on—this time to another alternative, which was proposed by Austria at the instigation of Germany. At first this proposal seemed to be acceptable to the delegates at Algeciras. The British representative though nominally supporting the French privately said he did not think France could continue to object to this German-Austrian plan. It was, as described by Mr. White:

> French officers to organize police under Sultan in Tangiers, Safi, Rabat, Tetuan, the Spanish in Mogador, Larache, Mazagan, and Swiss or Dutch the officer of superior rank in Casablanca, the latter to be also inspector general of police in all other ports and report results to diplomatic body at Tangiers. General opinion favorable to Austrian proposals even Russian and British Ambassadors thinking it might, with modifications of detail, be accepted by France and that she could not afford to break up Conference by rejecting it. Casablanca is port in which German interests predominate.[55]

At this point the President stepped in with vigor; and a telegram was despatched by von Sternburg retailing his views. There is of course no mention of this in Bishop. The telegram to Berlin reporting Roosevelt's views was as follows:

> This Austrian proposal in my [Roosevelt's] mind is absurd because it favors the very ideas the conference has been trying to eliminate namely partition and spheres of influence. Placing Spanish and French officers in the same ports gives according to my view a safer guarantee than placing them separately in single ports. This has distinctly the flavor of a French, a Spanish and a Dutch or Swiss sphere of influence. I also do not see how the duties of the police inspector can be made compatible with military discipline. Austria wants an officer, who performs the same duties in the port of Casablanca as his French and Spanish comrades do, to act in all ports as their superior and inspector. That would bring friction at the start. The proposal I suggested is the better and safer and the only one I can support.[56]

The same day, March 14, Secretary Root had a talk with von Sternburg and stated that the American delegates would not vote for the Austrian plan. This was followed three days later by a note to von Sternburg recapitulating the whole matter from the American point of view.[57] However, on the same day, March 17, the President had a long talk with von Sternburg in which he pointed out the great difficulties of the United States with respect to the Algeciras Conference, the complaints and criticisms which were pouring in and the undoubted fact that the American people were rapidly taking sides against Germany. To this the Ambassador also bore witness.[58] The result was a prompt reply in which von Bülow and the Kaiser gave way completely. The victory of the President was decisive as can be seen:

> Sincere regret is expressed that the attitude of Germany would have led to certain misunderstandings. The Kaiser had suggested the conference so as to find a peaceful way to solve the question of Morocco. He appreciates the fundamental idea of your proposal: co-operation of French and Spanish officers, to be about equally divided in each of the ports. He would readily join in any proposal at the conference which would contain this mixed system and an inspector general to which France has already agreed in principle. Germany

abstains from entering into details so as to prevent that [sic] these should obscure the main points. The telegram concludes in saying that the immediate removal of all misunderstandings is far more important to Germany than the whole Morocco affair.[59]

This change of front on the part of Germany is probably due to three things: (1) a real desire on the part of the Kaiser and von Bülow to avoid a European war, (2) the threat of President Roosevelt to publish all the correspondence, (3) an appreciation of the fact that public opinion in the world and particularly in America was against German contentions. At all events the President promptly expressed himself as greatly pleased at the result; and on March 20 he suggested to von Sternburg that, at a meeting of German-American veterans, praise should be given the Kaiser for this triumph of Germany diplomacy at Algeciras. This was done on April 12 in a speech by the President which previously had been carefully gone over by von Sternburg and also by Jusserand.[60]

On April 1 Mr. White telegraphed from Algeciras:

> At the meeting yesterday Russian second delegate communicated to Conference the following distribution of ports agreed upon by France and Spain: Tangiers and Casablanca, French and Spanish officers; Tetuan and Larache Spanish; four others French.
>
> The agreement reached appears to be as satisfactory to the German as to the French delegates and to every one else here. I think it may be safely predicted as a result not only that French-German relations will be better than for some time past, but those of several other powers also. The important step taken by the President and yourself is fully appreciated.[61]

Prior to this, on March 22, Secretary Root had tried to draw Great Britain to the active support of the compromise which the President had suggested to the Kaiser, saying to Sir Edward Grey that the President was satisfied that no further concessions would be made by Germany and urging British influence to prevent trifling matters from interfering with the French acceptance. In this he was only partially successful for, though the British government would not oppose anything which was acceptable to France and Spain, there was a feeling that the arrangement was not workable. As for Germany British impressions remained that her intervention in Moroccan affairs arose directly from Anglo-French relations and England consequently would stand by France though she also wished to have the best sort of relations with Germany.[62]

Perhaps the background of Anglo-American relations during these months and weeks of anxiety may be better seen in a letter which Ambassador Reid wrote to the President on June 19. In the course of this letter it is delicately suggested that perhaps the President's relations with von Sternburg had been such as to give pause to some Englishmen. Mr. Reid added:

> The truth is that the Emperor's assiduous efforts to cultivate the most intimate relations with you have attracted the attention of all the chancellories in Europe, and a common comment upon it is that the Emperor overdoes his love-making as he does his diplomacy, with a certain German confidence in the value of brute vigor in either pursuit! What I have sometimes feared was that this might affect the feeling here which might not be beneficial in Mr. Root's coming negotiations on the questions still unsettled between us. The truth seems to me that our relations with England are of far greater importance to us than those with Germany—there being more points at issue, more chances of friction and greater difficulty in almost every question that arises. . . . I cannot personally see anything to be gained from unusually good relations with Germany which would compensate us for the least jar in our relations with Great Britain, since I know of no serious questions we have to settle with Germany, while there are certainly a good many with Great Britain still unsettled. Aside from that, Germany isn't planted all along our frontier, and our negotiations with her will ordinarily therefore be on subjects less acute and ticklish.[63]

This was good advice; the future was to prove its value. Yet the President never did a more adroit thing in international affairs than in his intervention as to the Moroccan question in June, 1905, and in February and March, 1906. That most people supposed he was hand in glove with the Kaiser was perhaps not surprising. Yet his final stand was unquestionably in support of France. It was only natural that until that became very clear there should be some suspicion of his activities. As we turn to France there is prompt and unquestioned appreciation of his services. Mr. McCormick reported from Paris that the French government was eager to recognize "the signal aid rendered by President Roosevelt in arriving at a just solution of the differences between France and Germany with reference to Morocco—*Ni vainqueur ni vaincu.*" Such a view was "as profound as it is general in Europe, springing from President Roosevelt's successful intervention in the Russo-Japanese war, and now, strengthened and confirmed, it singles him out as the arbitrator to whom all can turn when dissentions threaten to bring on war in any part of the globe." [64] There is furthermore a truly fine letter from the President to Ambassador Jusserand of April 25 in which credit for the happy solution is given whole-heartedly to Jusserand.[65] This is especially significant as the lack of the physical and moral weight of Russia had been so evident during 1905-1906. The Russo-Japanese war had drawn Russia away from western Europe and her troubles both domestic and external had been a severe blow to her partner in the Dual Alliance. There can be no question, however, of the cordial relations between the United States and France as the result of the Algeciras Conference.

As regards Germany it was to be expected that following the tactical defeat of von Bülow's plans there should be a certain cooling off. The President, however, had aided Germany's strategical victory in securing the meeting of the Algeciras Conference. That was the clear fact. Germany neither by bluff nor by diplomatic persistence could have won such a victory without the aid of the United States. The Kaiser expressed himself at length to Mr. O'Brien, American Minister to Denmark, at a dinner given in Berlin by Ambassador Tower, on April 4, 1906. He seemed to be particularly pleased at the outcome of the conference at Algeciras. He pointed out in the course of a two-hour conversation that:

. . . the expansion of German commerce and the increase of its manufactured products, required that all markets should be kept free for unobstructed dealings, and that if the arrangement between France and Morocco had remained undisturbed, in a very short time Germany, and everyone else would be practically excluded, and it would then have been too late to complain.

He therefore had determined both as regards the present incident as well as possible future needs, to have established if possible, the principle of the open door. He pointed out that the interests of the United States were identical with those of Germany and that the value of the conference would be appreciated more and more by these two nations, and that the time was ripe to have the principle established when it might be done through peaceful negotiations. . . .

He said that the United States and Germany were the only countries that were making real progress at this time,—that England was at a standstill, that France was receding, and while Italy was improving in a limited way, it could never be really prosperous while the people were so burdened with taxation, and that the most of their apparent improvement was due to the American money which was spent in the country, and to the savings of workmen who went abroad for employment and returned with their earnings.

In the course of his conversation he said that while it was proper for a nation to be aggressive and keen to do business, he believed it possible at the same time to have a constant regard for the Ten Commandments, and to treat others with polite consideration.

He said that the views of Prince Bismarck were wholly different from his in this regard, and that this difference accounted for their failure to agree. He said Prince Bismarck believed that all men were at bottom scoundrels, and that all could be dealt with from that point of view. He said that he openly disagreed with the Prince, and told him that while these opinions could be tolerated in a prince and temporary office-holder, they could not be acceded to by a sovereign, and that he would not begin his career as such, holding such views of mankind.

The conversation then drifted to the possible danger in the future from too close an alliance with the Eastern peoples. He thought England had made an irreparable mistake by its treaty with Japan, and he hoped we would preserve our past policy of keeping clear of alliances in that direction. . . .[66]

There can be no question that the German attempt to make further use of the United States in European affairs finally failed; and for this we have to thank not only President Roosevelt but also the common sense of America. That such assistance as the United States did give was directed mainly to the preservation of peace is also clear. When it

12. *D. S.*, From Morocco, Vol. 1, No. 11, April 5, 1905, Gummeré to Hay; telegrams, April 7, 10, 13, 17 and 18, same to same; to Morocco, Vol. 16, telegrams, April 6 and 17, Loomis to Gummeré.
13. *G. P.*, XX, part 2, Nos. 6621, 6622.
14. Bishop, I, pp. 470-474.
15. *G. P.*, XX, part 2, No. 6852. Roosevelt wrote to Reid a year later that he had returned to Washington at the end of May, 1905. Of course that is a mere slip for this despatch of von Sternburg's is dated May 13.
16. *D. S.*, From German Embassy, Vol. 34, memorandum, May 13, 1905.
17. *G. P.*, XX, part 2, No. 6667; Bishop, I, pp. 474-475.
18. Appendix D to this chapter. The course of events in Morocco can be seen in *D. S.*, From Morocco, Vol. 1, telegram, April 29, 1905, Gummeré to Hay; No. 18, May 9, same to same; No. 22, May 19, same to same; telegram, June 1, same to same which read:
"Have received information Sultan refuses French proposals. Has ordered refusal read in mosques throughout the country, as well as the announcement that the future of Morocco will be confided to the treaty powers for their advice and assistance in reforms."
Cf. *D. S.*, From German Embassy, Vol. 34, memorandum, May 29, 1905, reading:
"The German Embassy in London reports that Mr. Balfour is anxious that France should grant Germany a sphere of interest in Morocco, so as to settle the Morocco question. The British Minister in Morocco informed the German Minister there, giving him a detailed explanation, that the whole question could be easily disposed of if Germany would accept a sphere of interest in Morocco from France. Germany has been given to understand by France (probably through British influence) that she is ready to settle the question in the aforesaid manner. The Emperor has given to understand that his position remains unchanged. He stands for the maintenance of the *status quo* and for the open door, and for equal treatment of all nations whose rights are established by treaties.
"As regards the sphere of influence in Morocco the Emperor more than a year ago clearly stated his views to the King of Spain. He declared that his policy was distinctly directed against the acquisition of any territory in Morocco or elsewhere."
19. *D. S.*, To London, Vol. 35, telegram, June 6, 1905, Loomis to Reid; Cf. *G. P.*, XX, part 2, No. 6687.
20. *Ibid.*, No. 6692.
21. *D. S.*, From London, Vol. 212, telegram, June 7, 1905, Reid to Hay; *R. P.*, undated copy of German note in Moroccan file; *F. R.*, 1905, p. 668.
22. *G. P.*, XX, part 2, No. 6700.
23. *Ibid.*, No. 6696.
24. *Ibid.*, No. 6856; Bishop, I, pp. 476-477. The text of this memorandum is in *D. S.*, From German Embassy, Vol. 34, memorandum (Morocco), June 11, 1905.
25. There are many proofs that the story is false. *Cambridge History of British Foreign Policy*, III, pp. 342-343; *G. P.*, XX, part 2, No. 6858 and note. The note leaves the despatch undisturbed and does not affect the matter.
26. Bishop, I, pp. 477-478. Cf. *G. P.*, XX, part 2, Nos. 6707, 6709, 6713, (Sternburg to German Foreign Office, June 17, 1905) saying among other things,
"As I hear, after Mr. Hay's reception in London by the King and Lord Lansdowne, there was an exchange of cable despatches between Mr. Hay and the President, by which the former attempted to win over the President for the British view on the Moroccan question. That he did not succeed in this I could see clearly today from the President's remarks. . . .

came to the approval of the Algeciras convention by the Senate it was made evident that the United States had not assumed any new responsibilities but had accepted the doctrine of the open door as applied to Morocco.[67] The Senate then made an unnecessary reservation and one that in part was incorrect declaring that the participation of the United States in the conference was due to the fact that she had signed the treaty of Madrid in 1880. This, as we have seen throughout this chapter, was not the real reason. The reservation went on to state that this American participation was "without purpose to depart from the traditional American foreign policy which forbids participation by the United States in the settlement of political questions which are entirely European in their scope." [68] It is a real question however whether the Moroccan situation, the question of peace or war in 1905–1906, was one that could be defined in such terms. The whole matter was European in origin but was it European "in scope"? I doubt it. The treaty was approved by the Senate in December, 1906. The Algeciras Conference did not of course end the Moroccan problem; it merely gave part of the prologue to a drama which was soon to have the whole world as its setting and which was to bring modern civilization almost to the breaking point in the World War.

NOTES TO CHAPTER XIX

1. The divergent German policies as to Morocco in 1904 can well be studied in the following despatches which are only samples. *G. P.*, XVII, No. 5203; XX, part 1, Nos. 6512, 6513, 6515-6523, 6527, 6536, 6538, 6542, etc.
2. *Ibid.*, No. 6547.
3. *Ibid.*, No. 6558 and footnote.
4. *Ibid.*, No. 6559. Cf. for von Bülow's reply, No. 6560.
5. Appendix A to this chapter.
6. D. S., From Morocco, Vol. 1, telegram, March 23, 1905, Gummeré to Hay; No. 7, April 1, same to same; *G. P.*, XX, part 1, No. 6573; *H. P.*, March 30, 1905, Chadwick to Hay.
7. Tardieu, *La conférence d'Algésiras*, Paris, 1907, pp. 6-9.
8. *G. P.*, XX, part 2, No. 6599.
9. Dennis, *Anglo-Japanese Alliance*, pp. 21-22.
10. Appendix B to this chapter. Instructions by von Bülow are in *G. P.* XIX, part 2, No. 6302. As I have not found in the *Roosevelt Papers* an satisfactory material for these matters and as in Bishop's *Life* there a; only one and a half pages which refer to the period prior to the end April, 1905, it seemed better to pay some attention to them.
11. Appendix C to this chapter.

THE ALGECIRAS CONFERENCE   511

"We have positively made good political capital out of Mr. Hay's absence. With respect to Eastern Asia, the conclusion of peace, and Morocco, the President has pursued a policy which has run directly counter to Hay's principles; this has been admitted even by the press. By the notable successes of the President in his own foreign policy, which has turned out to be distinctly a peace policy, and which has been praised all over the country, certain circles which had been of the opinion that the President's foreign policy would be aggressive and warlike and needed the experienced old Mr. Hay as a counterbalance, have now been completely reassured. It is to be hoped, therefore, that will give Mr. Hay occasion to think of his retirement."
There is no record at Washington of any such exchange of cable messages between Secretary Hay and the President.

27. *R. P.,* June 18, *1905,* Sternburg to Roosevelt; Bishop, I, p. 481.
28. *R. P.,* Nov. 10, 1905, Sternburg to Roosevelt.
29. Bishop, I, pp. 478-486.
30. *D. S.,* From Italy, Vol. 42, telegram, June 19, 1905, White to Hay.
31. Bishop, I, pp. 484-495; *G. P.,* XX, part 2, No. 6638; the Kaiser's concluding marginal remark on this letter was "Not yet! A little bit 'previous' this letter!!" Cf. *Ibid.,* Nos. 6739, 6740, 6742-6744; *D. S.,* From German Embassy, Vol. 34, June 26, 1905, Sternburg to the President enclosing a memorandum on Morocco; same to same June 28 and 30.
32. *D. S.,* To German Embassy, Vol. 13, telegram, July 24, 1905, Roosevelt to Sternburg, printed in *G. P.,* XX, part 2, No. 6778.
33. *D. S.,* To Morocco, Vol. 16, telegram, July 29, 1905, Adee to Gummeré; From German Embassy, Vol. 34, July 24, Sternburg to Roosevelt; *R. P.,* July 25, Roosevelt to Jusserand; July 29, Roosevelt to William II (printed in *G. P.,* XX, part 2, No. 6779); Aug. 3, Roosevelt to Reid; *Roosevelt-Lodge Correspondence,* II, pp. 170-172. Various names were discussed and the post was first offered to Mr. Choate; later when he withdrew Mr. Henry White, Ambassador to Italy, was selected as one of the American delegates to the Algeciras Conference.
34. *G. P.,* XX, part 2, Nos. 6819-6834; Witte, pp. 417-422.
35. *D. S.,* From Special Agents, Vol. 5, telegrams, Nov. 24 and Dec. 8, 1905, White to Root; From Italy, Vol. 42, telegrams, Nov. 20 and Dec. 31, 1905, White to Root; From France, Vol. 125, unnumbered, Dec. 15, 1905, McCormick to Root. Generally Mr. McCormick's despatches for this period can be disregarded by the student.
36. Grey, *Twenty-Five Years,* I, pp. 70-72.
37. *Ibid.,* I, pp. 76-91.
38. *D. S.,* From Russia, Vol. 65, telegram, Jan. 9, 1906, Meyer to Root.
39. *D. S.,* From German Embassy, Vol. 35, Jan. 8, 1906, Sternburg to Root.
40. Cortissoz, II, p. 329.
41. Grey, I, pp. 109-118.
42. Bishop, I, p. 489.
43. *D. S.,* From German Embassy, Vol. 35, Jan. 23, 1906, memorandum.
44. *Ibid.,* Vol. 35, Jan. 28, 1906, memorandum; Jan. 30, Sternburg to Root.
45. *D. S.,* From Special Agents, Vol. 5, Jan. 26 and 30, 1906, White to Root. The other White-Gummeré despatches from Jan. 16-31 are in the same volume.
46. The despatches relating to financial matters include particularly the following: *D. S.,* From Special Agents, Vol. 5, telegrams, Feb. 1, 3, 6, 11, 14, 20, 22, 24, 26, 28, March 5, 7, 8, May 2, 1906, White to Root; From German Embassy, Vol. 35, Feb. 1, 12, 13, 24, March 14, 1906, Sternburg to Root; To German Embassy, Vol. 13, Feb. 12, 1906, Root to Sternburg.
47. *D. S.,* From Special Agents, Vol. 5, telegrams, Jan. 23, Mar. 28, April 2, 1906, White to Root.

48. Grey, I p. 118.
49. *D. S.*, From Special Agents, Vol. 5, Feb. 5, 1906, White to Root.
50. *Ibid.*, Feb. 11, 1906, White to Root; telegrams of Feb. 17 and 19 indicated that the situation was getting worse but White said: "I still do not despair of a settlement."
51. *D. S.*, To German Embassy, Vol. 13, No. 333, Feb. 19, 1906, Root to Sternburg (printed in Bishop, I, pp. 489-491 and *G. P.*, XXI, part 1, No. 7019).
52. *D. S.*, From German Embassy, Vol. 35, Feb. 22, 1906, Sternburg to the President. (Printed in Bishop, I, pp. 491-493 and *G. P.*, XXI, part 1, No. 7020.)
53. Howe, pp. 262-265; Cortissoz, II, pp. 329-330; *D. S.*, From Russia, Vol. 65, No. 447, Feb. 28, 1906, Meyer to Root.
54. *D. S.*, To German Embassy, Vol. 13, No. 342, March 7, 1906, Root to Sternburg (printed in Bishop, I, pp. 493-495 and *G. P.*, XXI, part 1, No. 7074).
55. *D. S.*, From Special Agents, Vol. 5, telegram, March 8, 1906, White to Root. Cf. *Ibid.*, telegrams, March 10, 12, 16, 17, 1906, same to same; From German Embassy, Vol. 35, March 13, 1906, Sternburg to the President (printed in Bishop, I, pp. 495-497 and *G. P.*, XXI, part 1, No. 7093).
56. *G. P.*, XXI, part 1, No. 7102.
57. *D. S.*, From German Embassy, Vol. 35, March 14, 1906, memorandum; To German Embassy, Vol. 13, No. 347, March 17, 1906, Root to Sternburg (printed in Bishop, I, pp. 497-499 and *G. P.*, XXI, No. 7115).
58. *G. P.*, XXI, part 1, Nos. 7112, 7113.
59. *D. S.*, From German Embassy, Vol. 35, March 19, 1906, Sternburg to the President (printed in Bishop, I, pp. 499-500 and in *G. P.*, XXI, part 1, No. 7118).
60. *G. P.*, XXI, part 1, No. 7121, 7130; Bishop, I, pp. 500-501.
61. *D. S.*, From Special Agents, Vol. 5, telegram, April 1, 1906, White to Root; Cf. *Ibid.*, telegrams, March 19, 20, 23, 26, 27, 29, 31, same to same.
62. *D. S.*, To London, Vol. 35, telegram, p. 273, March 22, 1906, Root to Carter; From London, Vol. 214, telegram and letter, March 22, Carter to Root; to British Embassy, Vol. 27, unnumbered, March 22, Root to Durand.
63. Cortissoz, II, pp. 330-332.
64. *D. S.*, From France, Vol. 125, unnumbered, April 6, 1906, McCormick to Root.
65. *R. P.*, April 25, 1906, Roosevelt to Jusserand.
66. *D. S.*, From Denmark, Vol. 25, No. 90, April 7, 1906, O'Brien to Root.
67. *R. P.*, June 27, 1906, Roosevelt to Hale giving the treaty of Madrid of 1880 as the basis of American participation; but as we have seen this was a technical excuse.
68. *Treaties and Conventions*, II, p. 2183. I regret that I must disagree with Latané, *American Foreign Policy*, New York, 1927, pp. 571-573, in his treatment of this subject; he seems to think that President Roosevelt sought to conceal his part during the Conference because of the Senate. As can be seen every document of any real significance is in the files of the Department of State and there are practically no additional papers in the Roosevelt Collection which are of value. Consequently the Senate could have called for the documents at any time.

APPENDICES TO CHAPTER XIX

A

D. S., From German Embassy, Vol. 34, Memorandum, Undated [March 6, 1905].

Last December the Emperor expressed some apprehension with regard to the open door in Morocco. Later reports which he has received from there have convinced him that all seafaring and commercial nations are bound to suffer harm if they continue to remain any longer simple onlookers in those regions where France is pursuing her policy at present with utmost care.

France and Spain which my people think have almost to be treated now as a political unity, externally, favor a policy of prohibitive protection. Further they believe that if these two countries should divide up Morocco between themselves, her markets would be lost to the rest of the world. Should Spain occupy Tangiers and France the Hinterland, these two countries would be able to dominate the roads to the Near and to the Far East.

As regards the attitude of Great Britain toward Morocco a considerable portion of public opinion in England, as we have noticed, does not hide its discontentment with regard to the coming loss of the markets of Morocco (which recently hit at this with bloody sarcasm).

The Emperor thinks that now the progress of France in Morocco could be checked easily and without any danger if the Sultan of Morocco were informed diplomatically that the convocation of the chiefs (notables) is considered an important step towards the consolidation of the Governments and the establishment of law and order within his domains, which is the interest of all commercial nations.

Should the Sultan backed by his notables, reject the submission which under the name of reform has been demanded from him, France would scarcely risk a war with Morocco. The Emperor feels confident that a diplomatic action would strengthen the Sultan's position and intimidate France.

The German Consul at Fez has reported that the French mission has given Morocco to understand that she must not trust Germany.

Her reserved attitude so they pointed out shows that she is hoping to acquire a portion of Morocco from France.*

The Emperor feels sure that if a keen interest were shown in the maintenance of the open door in Morocco and in the improvement of her internal conditions by a power outside of France, the whole question of Morocco could be rapidly and peacefully settled.

He further is of the opinion that such a solution would be welcomed in England because it would insure the open door. He likewise believes that England would prefer not to be asked to join in a demonstration in connection with Morocco, owing to the fact that she gave France a free hand there. He does not doubt that England would gladly remain inactive if she feels sure that it is not intended to occupy any point in the neighborhood of the Straits of Gibraltar, not only any point along the Straits, but likewise no portion whatever of Morocco or Moorish territory.

*What Germany desires is the preservation of the present status encouraging the Sultan to improve the conditions in the interior of his domains.

D. S., From German Embassy, Vol. 34, March 7, 1905, Sternburg to the President.

In my statements made yesterday I omitted the following:— When the Emperor suggested a diplomatic move in Morocco he thought that the best results could be achieved if this move were made independently by America and Germany. Both countries to inform the Sultan of Morocco that they would consider a convocation of the notables as an important step towards the strengthening of his Government, and as being in the interest of law and order within his lands. This would not only be welcomed by America and Germany, but also by other commercial nations.

B

D. S., From German Embassy, Vol. 34, April 5, 1905, Sternburg to the President.

. . . The Emperor has further requested me to tell you that he has observed a close connection between France and England in the questions of the Far East and Morocco.

In Morocco Germany stands for the open door, that is for the protection of the interests of all trading nations, as opposed to the special interests of France. The semi-official French press has recently declared that France intends to place Morocco in the same relationship as Tunis. This would mean the annihilation of all non-French trade and commercial interests in Morocco.

Strange to say the larger portion of the British press, especially of that which is associated with the Government, opposes Germany in the question of Morocco and favors France and the closed door in Morocco. This attitude, which appears so unnatural, is met by a strong counter movement all over England, and this makes the Emperor believe that France has secretly assented to give England her assistance in China after England has abandoned all her political and commercial interests in Morocco.

This is the only way he is able to explain why so far the British Government has shown an attitude in the question of Morocco which is diametrically opposed not only to her economical but also to her political interests (think of Tangier!). This attitude of England seems to be absolutely without any precedent in her history.

The Emperor firmly believes that the only object which could have induced her to make such a great sacrifice is the Yangtze Valley. For the acquisition of ports in Persia and Arabia England would not need French assistance. At the time when the Anglo-French Morocco convention became perfect (April 8, 1904) Russia was already deeply engaged in the war with Japan.

The question of Morocco now is entering into a new phase. The Sultan of Morocco is on the verge to declare that the French demands shall be submitted to the ministers of the powers which are accredited to him. These are to examine if the changes demanded are in harmony with the interests of Morocco and with the general interests.

Conferences regarding the question of Morocco have already taken place. The last one met at Madrid in 1881 and the United States participated in it.

As regards Germany she seeks no gains in Morocco. She simply defends her interests and stands for equal rights for all nations there. Besides this she is bound to think of her national dignity. This made it necessary for her to point out to France that her national interests can not be disposed of without asking her for her consent and cooperation.

Since 35 years Germany has been obliged to keep on an armed defensive toward France. As soon as France discovers that Germany meekly submits to her bullying, we feel sure that she will become more aggressive in other quarters and we do not consider a demand for a revision of the Treaty of Frankfurt to be far off.

A year has passed by since the Anglo-French treaty with regard to Morocco became a reality, but the French Government never showed an intention to have an exchange of ideas with Germany with regard to its stipulations. On one occasion the German Ambassador in Paris mentioned the treaty to M. Delcassé. The answer he received was: "You will find all in the yellow book."

According to the information which the Emperor has received he feels sure that England's aid to France in the matter will not go beyond a "diplomatic support." This, he hopes, will keep France isolated, and with or without a conference he expects that the status quo in Morocco can be peacefully improved and, above all, the rights of foreigners safeguarded there. . . .

C

D. S., From German Embassy, Vol. 34, April 13, 1905, Sternburg to the President.

The Emperor has requested me to give you the following news with regard to the development of the Morocco questions:

To the President of the United States of America. The Italian Government has just stated her attitude which is:—She stands for the independence of Morocco; for the open door for all nations; she is against the granting of special favors there with regard to commerce and trade.

The Italian Government further expresses her conviction that France will only continue her aggressive policy in Morocco, aimed at all non-French interests, if she feels sure that England will stand by her and eventually show herself ready to back her up by force of arms. This communication the Emperor begs you to treat as absolutely confidential. He further states that he is convinced that it never was the intention of England to dispose of the interests of other treaty nations in Morocco. She simply left it to France to come to a direct agreement with the other interested powers in the same correct manner which England has observed in Egypt. Hence he scarcely believes that the British Government can be of the opinion that France is in her right in brushing aside all non-French interests in Morocco by altogether ignoring the rights of the other treaty powers, large and small. The Emperor feels convinced that the attitude of England with regard to the question, will entirely depend on your attitude. He thinks that it would greatly facilitate the British cabinet to come to a decision on the question if it could clearly understand your attitude before settling down on a definite policy.

The Sultan, it is expected, will within a short time, ask the treaty powers to express their opinions with regard to the French reform proposals.

The Emperor feels sure that if you should feel inclined to give England a confidential hint as to your attitude in the question it would greatly aid to a peaceful solution.

D

D. S., From German Embassy, Vol. 34, May 31, 1905.

MEMORANDUM.

The reason why the Emperor attaches so much importance to the Morocco question is the fact that he does not consider it as an isolated question. He believes that it may develop into a starting point for a new grouping of the powers. Quite recently the Russian press has been discussing the idea of an understanding between France and Germany in a sympathetic manner, because this would naturally draw Germany towards the Dual Alliance. The German Ambassador in St. Petersburg has reported in the same sense. Immediately after the conclusion of the Anglo-Japanese alliance the Russian Government inquired in Berlin if Germany would be ready to enter as a third partner into an agreement between France, and Russia with regard to the Far East. The Emperor refused, and this was probably the reason why the Far Eastern protocol, signed between France and Russia soon afterwards (March, 1902) was so colorless in character. Today the Morocco question is used for another attempt to draw Germany into the Dual Alliance. If England is successful in causing the refusal of France to join in a conference to settle the Morocco question, Germany will have to choose between war with France or between an understanding with France with regard to Morocco, which repeatedly has been sought for by France. Such an understanding, the Emperor believes, is to form the basis of a new grouping of European powers to which he is strongly opposed, especially with regard to the Far East, as clearly explained to you. Everything he thinks depends on the attitude *you* may consider fit to take towards a conference of the treaty powers to settle the Morocco question. England is the only power which opposes such a conference, though it seems sure that she will drop her objections in case you should participate in the conference.

According to information from St. Petersburg, France will be careful in avoiding trouble with Germany over Morocco, **and it seems clear that Russia has done her best to reconcile her.**

CHAPTER XX

PATRONAGE AND PERSONS

IT must be clear to us by this time that in all the difficulties of our foreign policies during the decade, 1896–1906, the United States had little to expect from her foreign representatives abroad. There was no diplomatic service in those days. Certain individuals who had enough money and who were interested in international relations occasionally stand out as capable diplomats. They had to have the money because neither by salaries nor by post allowances did the United States pay more than a small percentage of the necessary and essential expenses of her foreign representatives. A few of these were really interested in foreign affairs. Their knowledge and their observations were sometimes of value to the Department of State. The social aspects of diplomacy were of course of great importance; and the man who could give a good dinner was rightly forgiven many sins. The chances of geographical residence in the United States, a distinguished career at home, the possession of large wealth, and political and social ambition were chiefly responsible for the appointment of an uneven and uneasy group of men to diplomatic office abroad. That the nation suffered from this helter-skelter method of appointment goes without saying

From the private letters of Secretary Hay and elsewhere we may gain a better picture of the situation. This of course was involved with the state of domestic politics. Too often the vote of a Senator for a treaty, which had a perilous passage to face in the Senate, could be preserved by the appointment of a consul or higher official on his recommendation. Indeed, the indirect as well as the direct power of the Senate in our foreign relations was at times immense.

The country at large knew little of international affairs and took no pains to see that we were efficiently and adequately represented abroad. Americans care more about the visible decisions as to the approval or rejection of certain treaties; but there was as yet no forcible public opinion which could be brought to bear on matters of foreign policy. The slow processes of education and of national experience still waited on the patient years.

Secretary Hay was by no means a strong man physically when he was called from London to be Secretary of State. He was an emotional person and he had a strong prejudice against the exercise of their power by Senators with whom he disagreed. Indeed as time passed his feeling against the Senate became almost an "obsession" as he himself frankly said. His letter of August 11, 1899, reflects this opinion. He wrote to Mr. Henry White as follows:

We both doubted whether I should survive a year of the State Department; but here I am, not much the worse for wear, so far as I can see. But the other forebodings have been fully realized. It is impossible to exaggerate the petty worries and cares which added to the really important matters make the office of Secretary of State almost intolerable. The unrestricted freedom of access which members of Congress and especially senators, insist upon; the venomous greed with which they demand and quarrel over every scrap of patronage that falls in, the clamor of private claimants, and their attorneys, for pressure to be applied to poverty-stricken Latin-American states, who may or may not owe them money; all these things, which are outside of my legitimate work, would take every hour of my day, if allowed. And in addition there were never so many questions of actual weight pressing upon the department as now. No less than twelve subjects are under discussion between us and Canada, some of them capital; then there is the Clayton-Bulwer matter, and serious affairs with Italy, Austria, Germany and China—besides the usual scraps with South America.

The worst of all is the uncertainty about what the Senate may do in any given case. You may work for months over a treaty, and at last get everything satisfactorily arranged, and send it into the Senate, when it is met by every man who wants to get a political advantage or to satisfy a personal grudge, everyone who has asked for an office and not got it, everyone whose wife may think mine has not been attentive enough—and if they can muster one third of their Senate and one, your treaty is lost without any reference to its merits. That is our predicament now in our Canadian controversy. I could draw up in twenty-four hours a settlement which would·be perfectly satisfactory to Lord Salisbury and me. But the odds are two to one that Canada would not accept it or that our Senate would throw it out. It is a well nigh hopeless case. The President and the Cabinet are squarely with me. They tell me to go ahead, do what I think is right and chance the Senate. But I must feel [sure] of my ground somewhat, before risking a defeat in the Senate, which ought to involve my continuance in the Government. I would gladly go out on such an issue, if it were not to damage the President next year. So summing up my year at the head of the Cabinet I may say that while I have got on fully as well as I imagined, the annoyances have also been precisely what I expected—and there had hardly been an hour of real enjoyment in the whole year. . . .

I have never yet had the evil courage to tell him [McKinley] I shall not stay. I shall wait till after the elections. But the bore and worry of it would be intolerable, the daily contact with greedy Senators and claimants of all sorts, and worse than all, the two-thirds rule in the Senate which makes it impossible for this department to carry out any large or liberal policy.[1]

Again to Mr. Nicolay, his partner in the authorship of the life of Abraham Lincoln, he wrote in 1900, criticizing the Senate but in a different mood from that shown in the letter to Mr. White:

My work has been easy to do, and not worrying. The thing that has aged me and broken me up has been the attitude of the minority of the Senate which brings to naught all the work a State Department can do. In any proper sense of the word, Diplomacy is impossible to us. No fair arrangement between us and another power will ever be accepted by the Senate. We must get everything and give nothing,—and even then some malignant Senator or newspaper will attack the deal, and say we have surrendered everything,—and that scares our cowardly friends out of their wits.[2]

His closest friend Mr. Henry Adams commented on the situation as he saw it in 1900, saying:

Senators could seldom give a reason for obstruction. In every hundred men, a certain number obstruct by instinct, and try to invent reasons to explain it afterwards. The Senate was no worse than the board of a University; but incorporators as a rule have not made this class of men dictators on purpose to prevent action. In the Senate, a single vote commonly stopped legislation, or, in committee, stifled discussion.

Hay's policy of removing, one after another, all irritations, and closing all discussion with foreign countries, roused incessant obstruction, which could be overcome only by patience and bargaining in executive patronage, if indeed it could be overcome at all. The price actually paid was not very great except in the physical exhaustion of Hay and Pauncefote, Root and McKinley. No serious bargaining of equivalents could be attempted; Senators would not sacrifice five dollars in their own state to gain five hundred thousand in another; but whenever a foreign country was willing to surrender an advantage without an equivalent, Hay had a chance to offer the Senate a treaty. In all such cases the price paid for the treaty was paid wholly to the Senate, and amounted to nothing very serious except in waste of time and wear of strength. "Life is so gay and horrid!" laughed Hay, "the Major [McKinley] will have promised all the consulates in the service; the Senators will all come to me and refuse to believe me dis-consulate; I shall see all my treaties slaughtered one by one, by the thirty-four per cent of kickers and strikers; the only mitigation I can foresee is being sick a good part of the time; I am nearing my grand climacteric, and the great *culbute* is approaching." [3]

With the death of President McKinley it became evident that under the new President Secretary Hay would have little to say regarding patronage. Thus we find him consulting President Roosevelt regarding such a minor appointment as a consular clerkship. He wrote that he had an excellent man for the vacant position whom both of the Senators from his native state supported and he inquired whether the President had any objections to the appointment.[4] Such reference to the President on a small matter like this is enlightening as to the political methods of the day. Occasionally there is a vein of humor which joyfully intrudes. Thus Secretary Hay wrote the President regarding a consular vacancy:

> I have your letter in regard to the ——— vacancy. I suppose the Senator will require a little time to look through the Keeley cures in ——— for a fitting candidate. I admit that the comic is the salt of life, but really no man has the right to be so funny as that.[5]

In little notes of gossip and discussion as to places higher in the service there is small comment on the merits or qualifications of men. Though by rare exception Secretary Hay did say "it is a pity you have not a place for Jackson who has really earned a promotion" from Berlin. Later Mr. Jackson received a position as Minister to Greece, Rumania, and Servia. Indeed the great majority of the posts were given to men whom the President had to refer to as "cloth dolls," that is to people who could not and would not work but who had money and of whom the Senators of their native states would approve. Occasionally Secretary Hay would depart from the practice. There is for example a fine letter to the President regarding Dr. Hill, who had been serving in the Department. Later he was appointed to be Ambassador at Berlin. Of him the Secretary wrote:

> I have several times said to Dr. Hill when this subject has been mentioned, that while I had always carefully avoided the expression of any personal desires of my own in regard to diplomatic appointments, I should take pleasure in saying, if my opinion was asked, that I knew no one more competent and trustworthy than he is for high diplomatic appointment. He is thoroughly versed in international law and history; an elegant and correct writer, and morally, has all the qualities that can be wished for, truthfulness, courage, and unshakable integrity. His means are such as to render him independent of the meagre salaries we pay.
> I could not in conscience refuse to say this much in behalf of a valuable and estimable public servant—but I must add that I wish not to increase by a feather's weight your load of care and annoyance, the result of cruel pressure for place to which you are constantly subjected.[6]

On the other hand Secretary Hay could roast a man to a turn as is shown by a letter regarding the proposed appointment of a man to act as umpire in an arbitration case. He wrote:

> I meant right when I offered the unspeakable —— that umpire's place; but it has waked him up to a tempest of interviews, expressive of pleasure, gratitude, rapture, dubiety, hesitation and finally a conviction that his vast interests public and private, make it impossible

to accept. The place was offered and declined in five minutes by telephone—but he has been oozing interviews about it ever since.⁷

There had been a long question as to the fitness of a man for a South American consulship and after reams of paper had been spoiled the President broke out, saying:

> Does not the enclosed letter from Senator ―――― justify an outbreak of "large Batavian mirth" on my part? For Heaven's sake! promote ―――― to Callao; and then we will fill ――――'s place possibly with Conant if that is agreeable.⁸

Secretary Hay was always loyal to his friends and his endorsement of Mr. Rockhill was wholehearted. Later, in view of the following letter, he was sent to Peking to succeed Mr. Conger:

> I hope you will not send Rockhill away to the Philippines in case of a vacancy there. He is perfectly loyal to you, and will go where you send him without a kick. But he is so rare a product that he ought to be used where he can be most valuable. He is of great service where he is—I would miss him enormously. Of course if you saw a chance to send him to Peking nothing ought to stand in the way of that. But there are other men who would do as well as he in the Philippines, and he would rather stay where he is, and wait his chances in the diplomatic service, where he would be "one man picked out of ten thousand."⁹

To Mr. Henry White, who during these years was First Secretary at London and acted repeatedly as Chargé d'Affaires until he was promoted to be Ambassador to Italy, both the President and the Secretary were especially friendly. His appointment as Ambassador to Italy was the result of his admirable work in London and represented a promotion for the good of the service.

The view taken at the time was that if a man filled a position in the diplomatic service reasonably well he should be retained until political pressure was brought to bear to secure his place for another candidate. Men like Mr. Meyer at St. Petersburg or Mr. Griscom in Japan were promoted and sent to places where they could really work for they were anxious to make themselves useful. The idea of a diplomatic examination for entrance to the service was but just beginning. It was to serve only for the younger secretaries, whose connection with the Department of State would probably only be for three or four years. The idea that the higher grades of Minister or Ambassador should ultimately be filled by promotion from within the service was uncommon. Certainly it was the exception rather than the general practice. As regards the consular service Secretary Root made some important changes by inaugurating the idea that it was a career for young men and not a refuge for elderly party workers.

If we turn now to the relations of the Senate to our diplomacy we have a remarkable record. Only once in the decade, 1896–1906, the Senate was right in amending and so defeating a treaty. This was the first Hay-Pauncefote treaty dealing with the inter-oceanic canal. On all other occasions, when it differed with the Executive, the calm opinion of sensible men today is, I think, that the Senate was wrong. There is no time now to take up the long list of treaties which were hung up in the Senate as were Bluebeard's wives in his closet. We have already noted Secretary Hay's complaints as to this matter. President Roosevelt was at times almost as emphatic.

On economic and trade questions as well as on political issues the Senate was generally a liability and not an asset. This appears in a letter from Secretary Hay, written while he was in Europe in May, 1905. He said:

> Tower thinks the moment ripe for a treaty of Reciprocity between us and Germany. Frank Mason—who is far more intelligent as to things of commerce—not only thinks the time is propitious, but the consequences of not making a treaty very serious. Spencer Eddy came all the way from Petersburg to say how anxious the Russians were to make such a convention with us, ready to give almost anything we want. And I had to send them all away heart broken, with the reminder of the fact which they seemed to have forgotten, that we have a Senate; and that no reciprocity treaty can pass the Senate to which any constituent of any Senator can object. It is a sickening situation which nothing but the pinch of serious disaster can remedy. And when our hard times come, and we ask

for reciprocity, we shall not be able to get the terms which everybody is now eager to offer us.[10]

The long record of commercial negotiations which failed of effect because of senatorial opposition can be matched, as we have seen, by the persistent and determined stand of the Senate against the wisdom of the arbitration treaties of the period. Yet until there can be a constitutional amendment which will change the two-thirds majority now required to a simple majority of one there is no chance of a change in the situation. That I fear is for the Greek Kalends. The influence of the Senate as to appointments to office has been gradually reduced both by executive order and by legislation. Its power over treaties remains inviolate.

Still another matter which was of some concern to Secretary Hay lay in the fact that the law of presidential succession had certain flaws. Under President McKinley, after the death of Vice-President Hobart, Secretary Hay was next in line for the duties of the presidency in case of President McKinley's death. After the election of 1900 and with the assassination of the President, Vice-President Roosevelt naturally took his place. Once more, therefore, until inauguration day in March, 1905, when Roosevelt succeeded himself as President and Fairbanks became Vice-President, Secretary Hay was next in line of succession to the work of the presidency. Such a perilous possibility was naturally a source of anxiety to him. Furthermore it was not clear as to what should be done in September of 1901 when President McKinley was struck down. He lingered for a week before he died. Had this period of suspense continued longer was the Vice-President to assume his functions? Or again when President Roosevelt was twice near to death, once by a trolley collision at Pittsfield, Mass., and once by a fall from his horse while riding in Washington, would Secretary Hay have been obliged to perform his duties in case the President's injuries had incapacitated him? Fortunately none of these dire events took place yet their possibility served as good reason why Secretary Hay should have had the matter investigated. He found on reading Tucker on the *Constitution of the United States*, from the recollection of various employees of the Department of State, through a letter from Mr. Adee, and later from information given informally by Attorney-General Knox and by Mr. Charles S. Hamlin that in case he should perform the duties of the presidency it would only be by virtue of the fact that he continued to be Secretary of State. If he should resign as Secretary of State in order to perform the duties of the presidency the Secretary of the Treasury would automatically succeed to the presidential position. Furthermore there was no provision as to the determination of the inability or disability of the President. Was he to remain in office if he continued "able" in a legal sense, that is *compos mentis* regardless of his physical condition? Again the term during which the Secretary was to continue to perform the duties of the President was not even defined in the statute of 1886. He was to call an extra session of Congress within twenty days after the death or disability of the President but the earlier provision for a special election for a new President had been repealed. So a variety of matters seemed to be left to the occasion of the moment. Whether Secretary Hay wished to have these uncertainties removed is not clear. Attorney-General Knox's letter concludes as follows:

> Indeed in my opinion the moment the Secretary of State resigned his office to appoint another, the Secretary of the Treasury would first become acting President, for two reasons: First, because he then ceased to be an officer and under the constitution only an officer of the United States can act as President; Second, because the Act of Congress says when the Secretary of State resigns, after the disability of the President or Vice-President, the Secretary of the Treasury shall act.[11]

It is pleasant after such thoughts to consider in what cordial relations the President and the Secretary of State continued during this decade. If we except the brief tragedy of the collapse of Secretary Sherman we have an unbroken record of friendly co-operation. President Cleveland and Secretary Olney not only had a high mutual regard and respect for each other; but, what is rarer, they both liked the same sort of policies and were united in disliking others. Neither was, however, much concerned over international questions. Their interests lay in domestic affairs and it was an ironical luck which brought to both men the fame of staunch defenders of the Monroe doctrine. President McKinley was also a man of domestic politics. Chance and the fortune of war brought to him the opportunities of making great decisions. He had never been outside of the United States and his ultimate choice of Mr. Hay as Ambassador to Great Britain and later as Secretary of State was possibly due first of all to the respect he felt for a man who had had European experience. Secretary Day had been a faithful if not brilliant administrator. His retirement was at his own wish and he left behind him a good though brief record. With the advent of Secretary Hay and later with the rise of President Roosevelt a new situation developed. Both men had been abroad and were acquainted with the European world; both were intensely interested in international affairs. The President had, while Governor of New York, criticized the first Hay-Pauncefote canal treaty. Later he gave to the altered version his wholehearted support. For Secretary Hay's Chinese policy he also had the frankest admiration. In Alaskan matters he agreed and was inclined to rush matters somewhat at the end of that boundary dispute. Occasionally, as in the Venezuelan blockade question, the President took the lead. As to South American matters there seems to have been the fullest sort of co-operation; and in the Panama Canal problem Secretary Hay was his faithful and loyal aid in every respect. So it was in almost every step, though as Secretary Hay's health failed his leadership naturally decreased. The vigor and energy of President Roosevelt were continually manifest and throughout the Russo-Japanese war it was the President who naturally stepped to the front.

Of the personal friendship of the two men there can be no question. The President wrote to Senator Lodge on Secretary Hay's death as follows:

John Hay's death was very sudden and removes from American public life a man whose position was literally unique. The country was the better because he had lived, for it was a fine thing to have set before our young men the example of success contained in the career of a man who had held so many and such important public positions, while there was not in his nature the slightest touch of the demagogue, and who in addition to his great career in public life had also left a deep mark in literature. His "Life of Lincoln" is a monument, and of its kind "Castilian Days" is perfect. This is all very sad for Mrs. Hay. Personally his loss is very great to me because I was very fond of him, and as you know always stopped at his house after church on Sunday to have an hour's talk with him.[12]

Later, on July 18, he also wrote saying that John Hay

died within a very few years of the period when death comes to all of us as a certainty, and I should esteem any man happy who lived till 65 as John Hay has lived, who saw his children marry, his grandchildren born, who was happy in his home life, who wrote his name clearly in the record of our times, who rendered great and durable services to the nation both as statesman and writer, who held high public positions, and died in the harness in the zenith of his fame. When it comes our turn to go out into the blackness, I only hope the circumstances will be as favorable.[13]

The question of Secretary Hay's health had been a constant thought to the President. As early as 1902 we find him writing: "For Heaven's sake take a real and thorough rest. Whenever I see you and Root looking under the weather I sympathize deeply with Mr. Winkle's emotion when he besought Mr. Pickwick for his sake not to drown." [14]

Secretary Hay had an unfailing esteem and love for President Roosevelt. At Christmas of 1902 he had essayed once more to write a sonnet for him of which I quote the closing lines:

> Be yours—we pray—the dauntless heart of youth,
> The eye to see the humor of the game—
> The scorn of lies, the large Batavian mirth;
> And—past the happy fruitful years of fame,
> Of sport and work and battle for the truth—
> A home not all unlike your home on earth.[15]

Of Secretary Root there is comparatively little to be said for he came to the Department of State only in July, 1905. The President had full charge of the negotiations regarding the Portsmouth treaty and the Algeciras Conference. Yet it is as an administrator and as a lawyer as well as a politician that Secretary Root's career opened well. He brought to the Department a new conception of the functions of the consular service. He had no hesitation, no mistaken sense of dignity, which prevented him from urging the needs and desires of his division of the government upon the Senate. He bid fair to be an able successor to Secretary Hay at his prime.

We have already reviewed the course of events which raised this country to a proud and important position among the nations. Within this decade were crowded affairs of supreme effect upon our national history. Certainly as we Americans look back we can congratulate ourselves on our good fortune. As America looks to the future she must recall the fact that her diplomatic adventures within this decade, 1896–1906, bound her closely with the life of the world. As time has passed this connection has grown stronger and more complicated till it is now impossible for Americans to live alone or for the United States to lead her national life apart. Indeed as President Wilson said in 1919:

> The facts of the world have changed. It is impossible for the United States to be isolated. It is impossible for the United States to play a lone hand, because it has gone partners with all the rest of the world with regard to every great interest it is connected with. What are you going to do? Give up your foreign markets? Give up your influence in the affairs of other nations and arm yourselves to the teeth and double your taxes and be ready to spring instead of ready to co-operate? We are tied to the rest of the world by kinship, by sympathy, by interest in every great enterprise of human affairs. The United States has become the economic center of the world, the financial center. Our economic engagements run everywhere, into every part of the globe. Our assistance is essential to the establishment of normal conditions throughout the world. Our advice is constantly sought. Our standards of labor are being extended to all parts of the world just so fast as they can be extended. America is the breeding center for all the ideas that are now going to

fecundate the great future. You can no more separate yourselves from the rest of the world than you can take all the tender roots of a great tree out of the earth and expect the tree to live. All the tendrils of our life, economic and social and every other, are interlaced in a way that is inextricable with the similar tendrils of the rest of mankind.[16]

NOTES TO CHAPTER XX

1. Hay, *Letters,* etc., III, pp. 159-163. I have extended the names left blank in this edition.
2. *Ibid.,* III, p. 185.
3. *Education of Henry Adams,* pp. 393-394.
4. R. P., May 5, 1902, Hay to Roosevelt.
5. *Ibid.,* May 29, 1902, Hay to Roosevelt.
6. *Ibid.,* August 4, 1902, Hay to Roosevelt.
7. *Ibid.,* May 16, 1903, Hay to Roosevelt.
8. *Ibid.,* June 19, 1903, Roosevelt to Hay.
9. Hay, *Letters,* etc., III, p. 273.
10. H. P., May 20, 1905, Hay to Roosevelt.
11. H. P., Sept. 9, 1901, Adee to Hay (with enclosures); Sept. 3 and 4, 1902, same to same; Jan. 12, 1903, Mosher to Hay; Dec. 3, 1904, Hamlin to Hay; [undated], Knox to Hay; Sept. 3, 1902, Hay to Adee in which the Secretary, after the accident to President Roosevelt at Pittsfield said:
"I had a hideous appreciation for a moment yesterday of how I should feel if the President should be taken away. I could not help asking myself if it is right for me to stay in a place with such possibilities."
12. *Roosevelt-Lodge Correspondence,* II, p. 115.
13. Bishop, I, p. 370.
14. H. P., July 17, 1902.
15. R. P., Christmas Eve, 1902, Hay to Roosevelt.
16. *The Messages and Papers of Woodrow Wilson,* 2 vols., New York, 1924, II, pp. 1046-1047.

INDEX

(Chiefly of names and places)

Abdul Hamid II, Sultan, 87, 449, 454, 456, 457, 465, 470.
Abyssinia, 441.
Adams, Henry, 63, 79, 82, 117, 137, 139, 225, 348, 403, 520.
Adams, Secretary, 263.
Adee, 7, 25, 87, 162, 177, 218, 225, 226, 230, 233-235, 254-257, 262, 318, 319, 321, 322, 342-344, 354, 360, 366, 432, 452, 453, 456, 459-462, 470, 526.
Aguinaldo, 85, 87.
Alaskan boundary dispute, 130, 134-146, 149-154, 156.
Alexiev, Admiral, 355, 360, 383.
Algeciras Conference, 14, 368, 389, 397, 485, 496, 497, 502, 504, 505, 507, 509, 529.
Allen, Dr., 176, 416.
Alverstone, Lord, 145, 146, 154, 155.
Amador, Dr., 325, 326, 329-331, 336.
American Colonization Society, 438, 440.
Angell, Dr. (American Minister to Turkey), 451.
Anglo-American arbitration treaty (1897), 472, 473-475.
Anglo-French arbitration treaty (1903), 472, 478, 479.
Anglo-French entente (1904), 437, 472, 485.
Anglo-German agreement (1900), 236-239.
Anglo-Japanese alliance, 352, 353, 413, 416, 417.
Anglo-Russian treaty of 1825, 134-135, 141.
Anton, Dr., 283.
Aoki, Viscount, 192, 227.
Apia, 107.
Armenia, 60, 448-450, 457, 465.
Austria, 228, 235, 256, 284, 479, 503, 504.
Aylsworth, A. B., 145.

Bacon, Robert (Assistant Secretary of State), 270.
Balfour, 41, 72, 119, 155, 179.
Bayard, Ambassador, 20, 22, 26, 31, 35, 38-40, 45-46, 56-58.
Bayard, Secretary, 18, 51.
Beaupré (American Minister at Bogotá), 316-318, 323.
Beirut, 458-460, 462.
Belgium, 479.
Beresford, Lord Charles, 183, 185, 186, 209-214.
Bering Sea, 120, 134.
Berlin, Treaty of (1878), 432.
Bezobrazov, 354, 355, 358, 360, 361.
Bimetallism, 118-119.
Björkö, Treaty of, 389, 395, 409, 410, 413, 414, 491.
Blanco, Guzman, 51.
Blount, 102.
Boer War, 110, 111, 124-130.
Boston, U. S. S., 330.
Bowen, 287, 294, 295, 298-300.
Boxers, 215-219, 221, 247, 349, 350.
Bradford, Admiral, 271.
Brazil, 283, 296.
British Guiana, 17, 24, 55.
Brooks, General John R., 259.
Bryan, William J., 33, 119.
Buchanan, 335.
Buck (Minister to Japan), 179, 192, 352, 415.
Buenz, Dr., 306, 307.
Bulgaria, 453-455.
Bülow, von, 123, 124, 182, 189, 286, 287, 289, 347, 349, 361, 368, 390, 392, 396, 403, 408-410, 425, 427, 440, 486, 487-491, 505, 507.
Bunau-Varilla, Colonel, 323-332, 334.
Bundesrat (German steamer), 127.
Burma, 129.
Butler, Dr. N. M. (on missionaries), 447.

INDEX

Caceres, President, 275.
Calhoun, Judge, 300.
Callisen, A. W., 306-307.
Cambon, Paul, 73, 497.
Canada, 120, 121, 134-144.
Caribbean, 279, 282, 284, 305, 309.
Carnegie, Andrew, 482.
Caroline Islands, 78, 86, 98, 100.
Casablanca, 505.
Casement, 442.
Cass, Secretary, 320.
Cassini, Count, 347, 351, 353, 357, 358, 374-380, 405, 433.
Castro, President, 285, 287, 291, 294, 297-301, 304.
Central America, 278, 283, 284, 309.
Central Asia, 385.
Chadwick, Admiral, 445.
Chaffee, General, 232, 233.
Chamberlain, Joseph, 36-40, 42, 43, 58-59, 119, 120, 122-124, 129, 158, 450.
Chambers, Chief Justice, 108, 109, 113.
Chefoo, 366.
Chekib Bey, 460, 462.
Chester, Captain, 452.
Chili, 208, 236.
China, 14-15, 16, 130, 170-196, 202-214, 215-247, 254, 255, 257, 258, 349-368, 373-385, 392, 393, 401, 406, 417-420, 434, 490.
Ching, Prince, 230, 258, 382.
Choate, Ambassador, 117, 135, 138, 141-146, 158, 161-163, 188, 189, 220, 359, 361, 366.
Christmas, Captain, 272.
Clayton-Bulwer Treaty, 130, 136, 156, 158, 162-164.
Cleveland-Olney doctrine, 23, 46.
Cleveland, President, 5, 18, 21, 23, 26-28, 31, 46, 65, 101-103, 450, 475, 526.
Colombia, 12, 309-321, 324, 327, 328, 333, 335, 342-344.
Commitadjis, 453.
Concha, General, 314.
Conger (Minister to China), 185, 193, 207, 217-224, 229, 232-235, 239, 241, 350, 352, 355, 357, 358, 360, 365, 366, 377, 378, 381, 400.
Congo Free State, 442, 443.
Convocation of Notables in Morocco, 489.
Costa Rica, 309-311.

Cotton, Admiral, 460, 461.
Cramp, 452, 470.
Crawford, John, 318.
Cromwell, Nelson, 314, 318, 321, 323-326.
Cuba, 63, 66-73, 80, 99, 259-270.
Curzon, 183.
Cushing, Caleb, 171.

Danish West Indies, 271-274, 309.
Davis, Admiral, 367.
Davis, Senator, 81, 83, 149.
Day, Secretary, 5, 66, 70, 80-83, 93, 94, 96, 99-100, 527.
Denby, 177-180, 202-205.
Delcassé, 191, 192, 235, 403, 489-491, 494, 496.
Denmark, 271, 272, 479.
Dennett, Tyler, 247, 389, 394, 405, 410, 417, 428.
Depew, Chauncey, 32.
Devonshire, Duke of, 238.
Dewey, Admiral, 75, 290, 292, 295-297, 304-308.
Diedrichs, Admiral von, 77, 78, 297.
Dilke, Sir Charles, 183.
Dillon, Dr., 389, 412.
Dixie, U. S. S., 330, 331.
Dogger Bank, 367, 391.
Dominican Republic, 274-277, 309.
Drago Doctrine, 292-294, 299, 301.
Dual Alliance, 124, 362, 490, 507, 517.
Dupuy de Lome, 69.
Duque, J. Gabriel, 322, 332.
Durand, Sir Mortimer, 347, 395.
Dyea, 138, 140.

Eckardstein, Baron, 386.
Eddy, Spencer, 355, 454, 458, 470.
Edward VII, 295, 396.
Egypt, 485, 486, 489.
Ehrman, Consul, 334.
Elliott, 109.
Empress Dowager of China, 215-217.
England (*see* Great Britain).

Fashoda, 440.
France, 13, 72, 126, 175, 191, 192, 208, 228, 235, 239, 242, 289, 301, 351, 362, 368, 391, 394, 396, 397, 411, 437-441, 479, 486, 488-507, 513-517.
Frewen, Moreton, 119.
Frye, Senator, 81, 83.
Fukhien, 180, 208.

Garguilo, 456, 469.
German policy *re* Morocco, 485-508, 513-517.
German policy *re* Philippines and Hawaii, 76, 78, 85, 86, 93, 95-98.
German policy *re* Samoa, 106-111, 113-116.
German policy *re* Venezuela, 284, 286-295, 304-308.
Germany, 13, 16, 76, 123-125, 175, 178, 187, 189, 194, 196, 202-208, 214, 225, 228-230, 235, 239, 240-242, 256, 271, 274, 282-292, 294-297, 304-308, 309, 347, 351, 352, 358, 362-365, 373, 374, 390, 391, 394, 395-398, 407-410, 438-441, 479, 486-508, 513-517.
Gilder, 168.
Goluchowski, Count, 284.
Granville, Lord, 107.
Gray, Senator, 81, 83.
Great Britain, 9, 13, 15, 22, 24-25, 33, 41, 52, 78, 81, 106, 109, 110, 117, 118, 121-125, 129, 170-173, 180-183, 187-189, 196, 203, 206-208, 212-214, 220, 222, 229, 235, 256, 283, 285, 304, 308, 309, 347, 351-353, 362, 374, 376, 382, 385, 387, 390, 392, 394-398, 404, 407, 411, 416, 437-441, 479, 483, 486, 489, 490, 496-499, 513-517.
Greene, General F. V., 83.
Gresham, Secretary, 19, 101, 174, 175.
Grey, Sir Edward, 482, 497, 499, 501, 505.
Griscom, 359-361, 401, 452, 456, 469, 523.
Gummeré, 443-445, 488, 489, 499.

Hague Peace Conference (first), 128, 472, 475-478, 479.
Hague Peace Conference (second), 472, 473.
Hague Tribunal, 291, 294, 297, 472, 478.
Haiti, 277, 278.
Hale, Edward Everett, 132.
Hanna, Senator, 65, 312, 324.
Hanotaux, 79.
Harcourt, Sir William, 41.
Harding, President, 333.
Harpoot, 459.
Harrison, President, 101.
Hart (American Minister at Bogotá), 313, 314.

Hartzell, Bishop, 439.
Hatzfeldt, Count, 77, 93.
Havana, 68, 263, 265, 270.
Hawaii, 101-106.
Hay, John, 43.
Hay, Ambassador, 66, 72, 78, 80, 82, 93, 98-99, 119, 120-122, 170, 184.
Hay, Secretary, 5, 74, 76, 83-86, 117, 118, 125, 126, 132, 135-146, 149-154, 157-164, 166, 170, 185-196, 207, 208, 218, 219, 221-226, 229, 231-235, 238-248, 256, 257, 261, 262, 272, 273, 275, 277-278, 282, 285, 295-300, 310-315, 318-322, 330-332, 342-345, 350-363, 366, 367, 373-385, 391-393, 400, 403, 405, 407, 413, 415, 431, 432, 438, 439, 444, 445, 452, 453, 455, 459, 461, 465, 473, 518-528.
Hay-Bunau-Varilla Treaty, 334.
Hay-Herran Treaty, 314, 315.
Hay-Pauncefote Treaty (1st), 130, 136, 158-162, 310.
Hay-Pauncefote Treaty (2nd), 162-166, 311.
Hayashi, Baron, 352, 386, 389.
Henry, Prince (of Prussia), 286.
Hepburn Canal bill, 310, 312, 324.
Herbert, Sir Michael, 145, 153-156, 295, 347, 357.
Herran, Dr., 315.
Herschell, Lord, 136, 137, 149.
Heureux, President, 275.
Hicks-Beach, Sir Michael, 35, 179.
Hill, 232, 522.
Hippesley, A. E., 186.
Hobart, Vice President, 525.
Holleben, Dr. von, 73, 77, 289, 305-307, 347.
Holstein, 394, 410, 409, 426, 486.
Hongkong, 180, 188.
Hubbard, Commander, 325.
Huertes, General, 331, 332, 336.
Huntchagist, 449.

International Conference of American States (2nd), 472.
Interparliamentary Union, 481.
Islam, 448.
Isvolsky, 415.
Italy, 180, 192, 206-208, 228, 235, 256, 285, 286, 387, 394, 479, 494, 516.
Ito, Marquis, 227, 386, 417.
Ivory Coast, 438.

Jackson, 228, 283, 284, 432, 522.
Jameson Raid, 17.
Japan, 15, 81, 103-106, 121, 192, 193, 206, 208, 220, 224, 227, 228, 229, 235, 239, 247, 257, 351-368, 374-377, 382-387, 391, 392, 397-399, 401, 402, 405-407, 411-413, 479, 481, 489, 493.
Japan in Korea, 173-176, 181, 352, 354, 359, 383, 384, 386, 390, 401, 407, 414-417.
Jersey, Lord, 404.
Jetté, Sir L. A., 145.
Jews in Rumania, 431-433.
Jews in Russia, 433-435.
Jiminez, President, 275.
Johnson, Sir Harry, 441.
Joint High Commission (United States and Canada), 135-138.
Jusserand, 300, 403, 493, 494, 496, 507.

Kaiser, the (*see* William II).
Kaneko, Baron, 411.
Katsura, Count, 416, 428.
Kautz, Admiral, 108, 113.
Kearny, Commodore, 171.
Kentucky, U. S. S., 452, 458.
Keocks, G., 74.
Ketteler, Baron von, 227, 247.
Khalif, 87, 457.
Kiauchau, 178, 182, 202-205, 214, 388.
Kimberley, Lord, 20, 31.
Kishinev, 433.
Klehini River, 139, 140.
Knox, Attorney-General, 166, 526.
Komura, Baron, 401, 406.
Korea, 15, 173-176, 203, 346, 352, 355, 358, 362, 383, 413-417, 489.
Kowloon, 180, 188.
Kruger, President, 17, 36.
Kühlmann, von, 487, 489.
Kuropatkin, General, 390.
Kusaie, 86.

Ladrones, 80, 82.
Lamar, 320.
Lamsdorff, Count, 222, 244, 355, 357, 358, 362, 375, 377-380, 383, 384, 432, 434.
Lansdowne, Lord, 143, 144, 162, 288, 289, 308, 359, 404, 497, 499.
Larache, 505.

Laurier, Sir Wilfred, 143, 144, 150-152.
Leicester (speech of Mr. Chamberlain), 123-124, 387.
Leishman (American Ambassador to Turkey), 453-465.
Lessar, 378, 380, 381.
Liao-tung Peninsula, 175, 401.
Liberia, 437-441.
Li Hung Chang, 175, 221, 223, 224, 226-229, 232, 241, 258, 350.
Liliuokalani, Queen, 102.
Lincoln (American Minister at London), 19.
Lodge, Senator, 78, 145, 298, 399, 403, 479, 496, 527.
Loomis, 298, 299, 319, 333.
Lueders Case, 277.
Lynn Canal, 138, 141, 142.

McCook, 168.
McCormick, Ambassador, 355, 357, 394, 433, 507.
McDonald, Sir Claude, 222.
McKinley, President, 5, 43, 64, 74, 75, 84, 103, 106, 118, 119, 126, 129, 143, 150, 161, 163, 171, 196, 225, 231-233, 239, 259, 310, 475, 521, 525, 527.
MacVeagh, Wayne, 297.
Macedonia, 453-455, 459.
Macedonian Committee, 454.
Magelson, 459.
Magoon, 270.
Mahan, Admiral, 483.
Maine, U. S. S., 69, 71.
Malietoa, 107.
Manchuria, 179, 182, 203, 206, 208, 213, 237, 238, 241-244, 346, 349-363, 365, 373-385, 390, 400, 418-420, 434.
Manila, 75, 79, 80, 81.
Margarita, island of, 284.
Marroquin, President, 315, 324.
Mataafa, 108, 113.
Merry (American Minister to Central America), 310, 311.
Metternich, Count, 288, 289, 497.
Mexico, 479.
Meyer, George, Ambassador, 361, 394, 398, 400, 402, 405, 409, 498, 523.
Midway Island, 364.
Minto, Lord, 143.
Mogador, 499.

Mole St. Nicholas, 278.
Monroe, President, 23, 29.
Monroe Doctrine, 9-11, 16, 22, 24, 25, 29, 34, 36-38, 41, 52-54, 262, 271, 274, 275, 277, 284, 286, 292, 309, 393.
Monrovia, 438.
Moody, 461.
Moore, John Bassett, 5, 33, 319, 320, 326-328.
Morales, President, 275.
Morgan, Senator, 231, 232, 311, 312.
Morocco, 389, 398, 408, 485-492, 494, 496, 498-503, 507-509, 513-517.
Muhammedan, 448, 457.
Mumm, Baron von, 227, 228, 240, 242, 246.
Munster, Count, 476.
Muraviev, Count, 125, 190.
Mytelene, 464.

Nashville, U. S. S., 330-333.
Netherlands, the, 479.
Newchwang, 241, 350, 356.
New Granada, treaty with (1846), 312, 313, 323, 326-329, 333.
New York & Bermudez Co., 298-300.
New Zealand, 107, 111.
Nicaragua, 309-311, 319.
Nicolay, 520.

O'Brien (American Minister to Denmark), 507.
Olney, Secretary, 5, 18-24, 26-61, 65, 134, 156, 178, 472, 474, 475, 526.
Open door, 85, 170, 190, 509.
Open door in China, 122, 170-180, 185-196, 208-214, 215, 352, 353, 392, 434.
Orange Free State, 128.
Otis, General, 87.
Ouhktomsky, Prince, 241.

Paddock, 415.
Pagopago, 107, 110.
Palawan, 86.
Palma, President, 260, 267, 269, 270.
Panama, 313, 318, 324, 325, 328-336, 342-345.
Panama Canal, 11-12, 16, 164, 259, 267, 309, 324, 335.
Panama Canal Co., 311, 312, 314-317, 321, 323, 324, 326, 336.
Panama Railroad Co., 332.
Pauncefote, Sir Julian, 42, 43, 46,
73, 134, 136, 138, 143, 158, 162, 347, 472.
Peace Conference at The Hague, 472, 473, 475-478.
Peet, Dr., 454, 455.
Peking, 215, 217, 219-247, 359.
Penfield, 297.
Perdicaris, 443-445.
Phelps (American Minister at London), 18, 22, 51.
Philadelphia, U. S. S., 108.
Philippine Islands, 16, 80-87, 99.
Pious Fund of the Californias, 472.
Platt Amendment, 262, 264-269, 309.
Playfair, Lord, 36-40.
Poland, 385, 387.
Ponape, 86.
Port Arthur, 175, 179, 180, 355, 362, 381, 390, 396, 401, 407.
Porter, Ambassador, 79, 191, 192.
Porto Rico, 80, 82, 99, 259, 275, 305-307.
Portsmouth, Treaty of, 14, 349, 368, 412, 420, 529.
Portugal, 479.
Powell (American Minister to Haiti), 278.
Proctor, Senator, 70.
Puerto Plata, 276.
Pyramid Harbor, 138.

Quesada, Señor, 270.

Rainey Resolution, 323.
Raisuli, 443-445.
Reid, Whitelaw, 81, 83, 233, 290, 404, 477, 491, 493, 499, 506.
Remey, Admiral, 228.
Reyes, General, 319, 335.
Rhodes, J. F., 32.
Riddle, 355, 358, 379, 380, 434.
Rockhill, 185-187, 208, 218, 226-228, 242, 243, 248, 353, 360, 523.
Roosevelt, President, 6, 63, 74, 87, 128, 143, 145, 160, 161; 163, 166, 270, 276, 277, 289, 290, 292, 294-296, 298, 300, 318-323, 326-328, 330, 335, 336, 342, 343, 345, 346-349, 353, 356-359, 361, 363-368, 376, 390-413, 425-429, 431, 433-435, 443-445, 457, 461, 462, 465, 473, 479, 483, 486, 487, 489-496, 500-508, 521-529.
Root, Secretary, 6, 145, 231, 261, 263-

266, 270, 300, 301, 333, 336, 413, 418, 419, 465, 480, 499, 502-505, 529.
Rosebery, Lord, 40.
Rosen, Baron, 384, 406, 410.
Rouvier, 494.
Rozhdestvensky, Admiral, 367, 399.
Rumania, 431-433.
Russia, 14, 15, 121, 175, 176, 180-182, 187, 190, 193, 203-208, 213, 221, 225, 228, 230, 233, 235, 239-244, 246, 254-258, 347, 350-368, 373-388, 391-415, 433-435, 442, 479, 481, 489, 491, 493, 517.
Russo-Chinese Bank, 351, 356.
Ryeshetelni (Russian destroyer), 366.

Sagasta, 68.
Saghalin, 401, 411, 412, 493.
Salisbury, Lord, 25, 28-31, 36, 41, 43, 73, 79, 85, 120, 134, 138, 141, 157, 158, 164, 188, 189, 196, 220, 450, 473, 474.
Sam, President, 278.
Samana Bay, 275.
Samoa, 106-111, 113-116.
Sanchez, 311.
San Domingo Improvement Co., 276.
Satow, Sir Ernest, 242.
Schomburgk, Sir Robert, 19, 20, 45, 53-54, 56.
Seward, Secretary, 172, 271, 329.
Shantung, 178, 353.
Shaw, Dr. Albert, 322, 461.
Sherman, Secretary, 65, 170, 181, 202-205, 438, 526.
Shimonoseki, Treaty of, 175.
Sill (American Minister to Korea), 175.
Skagway, 138, 140.
Skinner, 441.
Smalley, 37, 184.
Smyrna, 458, 462, 463.
Spain, 63, 66, 72, 84, 86, 99, 259, 479, 494, 501.
Spooner, Senator, 312, 324.
Spring-Rice, Cecil, 78, 347, 392-394, 396, 399, 403, 404.
Squiers (American Minister to Cuba), 267, 268.
St. Thomas, 274.
Standard Oil Company, 129.
Sternburg, Speck von, 109, 295-297, 348, 349, 363-365, 390-395, 425, 427, 487, 489-492, 494, 498, 501, 504.

Stevens (American Minister to Hawaii), 101, 102, 106.
Stone, Melville, 404.
Stone, Miss, 453-456.
Straus, Oscar, 86, 451, 452, 461.
Suez Canal, 159.
Sulu Islands, 86, 457.
Swenson (American Minister at Copenhagen), 271, 272.
Switzerland, 479.
Syria, 459, 460.
Syrian Protestant College, 458.

Taft, Secretary, 270, 336, 349, 396, 416, 489.
Takahira, Baron, 376, 406.
Tamassese, 107.
Tangier, 444, 445, 488, 505.
Tattenbach, 489.
Ten Years' War (in Cuba), 64.
Terrell (American Minister to Turkey), 449, 450.
Tetuan, 505.
Tezkirah, 451.
Thayer, 161, 282, 304, 309, 495.
Thielman, Baron von, 284.
Tittoni, Signor, 399.
Torres, Col., 325, 331.
Tovar, General, 331.
Tower, Ambassador, 190, 348, 355, 374, 375, 393, 394, 402, 406, 408, 507.
Transvaal, 123, 128.
Tripp, 109.
Tuan, Prince, 234, 235.
Turkey (Turkish, Turks), 59-61, 447-466.
Turner, Senator, 145.
Tutuila, 107, 111.

Usher, 118.

Varon, General, 331.
Venezuela, 297-301, 309.
Venezuelan blockade, 146, 282, 285, 287-292, 295, 296, 304-308.
Venezuela boundary dispute, 17, 18-24, 42-44, 51-58, 64, 72, 117, 141, 142, 472.
Victoria, Queen, 110.
Visconti-Venosta, Count, 192.
Vladivostok, 401.

Wake Island, 364.
Waldersee, Count, 221, 230, 232, 244, 245.

INDEX

Wanghia, Treaty of (1844), 171.
Washburn, Dr., 454.
Webster, Secretary, 171.
Wei-hai-wei, 180, 181, 189.
Wellman, 133.
Weyler, General, 68.
Wheeler, Dr., 406.
White, A. D. (American Ambassador at Berlin), 31, 74, 78, 94, 182, 189, 283, 373, 476.
White, Henry, 43, 85, 118, 136, 149, 151, 154, 157, 158, 163, 182, 235, 272, 273, 288, 290, 295, 398, 499-501, 503, 505, 519, 523.
Wiju, 359, 383.
William II, Emperor, 17, 77, 110, 123, 189, 231, 233, 274, 284, 286, 287, 294, 295, 347, 348, 349, 361-364, 367, 368, 373, 390-393, 395, 397-400, 402, 403, 406, 408-414, 486-491, 494-498, 501-508, 513-517.
Willis, 102.

Wilson, President, 22, 333, 529.
Witte, Count, 354, 386, 389, 406, 410, 412, 413, 497.
Wood, Henry A. W., 307.
Wood, General Leonard, 260, 262, 264.
Woodford, General Stewart, 66-71, 75.
Wos y Gill, President, 275.
Wright, Ambassador, 419.
Wu Ting Fang, 187, 221-223.

Yalu River, 354, 359.
Yalu timber concession, 354, 357, 358, 416.
Yang-Ju, 241.
Yangtse Kiang, 208, 237, 238, 353, 388, 390.
Yap, 86.
Yglesia, President, 310.

Zelaya, President, 310.

Augsburg College
George Sverdrup Library
Minneapolis, Minnesota 55404